drawnandquarterly.com. First edition: May 2018; Printed in South Korea 10 9 8 7 6 5 4 3 2 1; Library and Archives Canada Cataloguing in Publication; Kominsky-Crumb, Aline, 1948–, author, illustrator; *Love that Bunch* / Aline Kominsky-Crumb. ISBN 978-1-77046-305-9 (hardcover); 1. Graphic novels. I. Title. PN6727.K66L68 2018   741.5'973   C2017-905434-1; Published in the USA by Drawn & Quarterly, a client publisher of Farrar, Straus and Giroux. Orders: 888.330.8477; Published in Canada by Drawn & Quarterly, a client publisher of Raincoast Books. Orders: 800.663.5714; Published in the United Kingdom by Drawn & Quarterly, a client publisher of Publishers Group UK. Orders: info@pguk.co.uk

Love That BUNCH

Aline Kominsky-Crumb

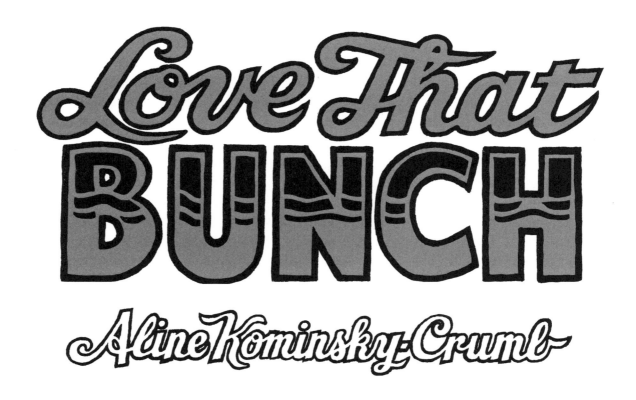

DRAWN & QUARTERLY

Foreword by Hillary Chute

In 2013, when I was co-editing a special issue of *Critical Inquiry*, Aline Kominsky-Crumb sent me a brilliant two-page comics piece called "Of What Use is an Old Bunch?" (pages 210–211—It was published in the issue alongside two separate interviews with her.) The title refers to the nickname—the Bunch—she gives to her own character in her comics. She chose it in part because it "sounded disgusting," she has explained. The title also refers to a story collected here, first published almost 35 years earlier, called "Of What Use is a Bunch?" (pages 83–85). In this famous, controversial strip, Kominsky-Crumb tries to answer that question about herself with statements accompanied by vignettes drawn in packed panels, in her signature expressive, wobbly hand.

The list includes a host of negative pronouncements above illustrated examples: "The Bunch can't draw"; "The Bunch's low self-esteem causes her to brag when loosened up"; "When sober, the Bunch is nasty and compelled to put people down!!". After thirteen such statements, Kominsky-Crumb concludes the piece with two positives: she likes to shop, and "her animalistic passion and deep-seated masochism make her the perfect sex object for some boys!". The image shows the Bunch with an open mouth, in a t-shirt and polka-dot underwear, as a man rides on her back, calls her a horsie, pulls her hair, and whacks her behind.

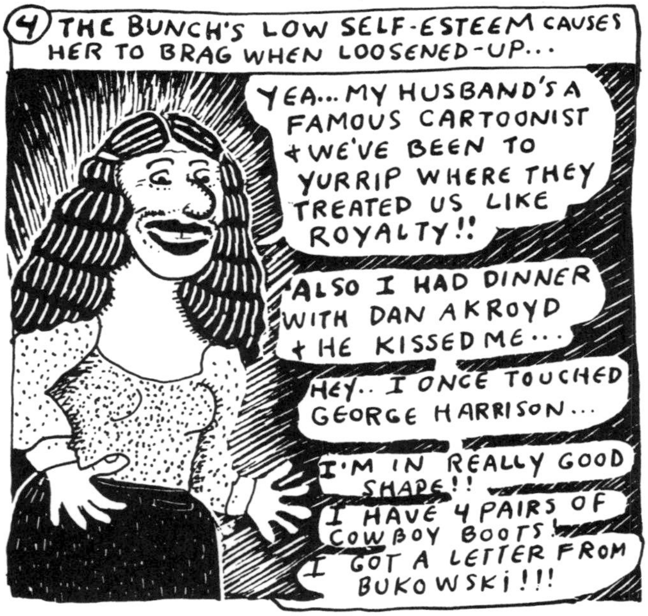
4 THE BUNCH'S LOW SELF-ESTEEM CAUSES HER TO BRAG WHEN LOOSENED-UP...
YEA... MY HUSBAND'S A FAMOUS CARTOONIST + WE'VE BEEN TO YURRIP WHERE THEY TREATED US LIKE ROYALTY!!
ALSO I HAD DINNER WITH DAN AKROYD + HE KISSED ME...
HEY.. I ONCE TOUCHED GEORGE HARRISON...
I'M IN REALLY GOOD SHAPE!!
I HAVE 4 PAIRS OF COWBOY BOOTS!
I GOT A LETTER FROM BUKOWSKI!!!

"Of What Use is A Bunch?" galled some readers for its apparent relentless self-deprecation, especially in the author-protagonist's ceding to her own sexual objectification as one of the few proffered positives. But to others—including me—this piece is riveting, classic Kominsky-Crumb: it's revealing, funny, ironic, and intimate. It also, significantly, refuses to shy away from the subject's own desire, however unconventional or "incorrect." Kominsky-Crumb claims her own objectification as her active desire; as Maggie Nelson points out throughout her recent acclaimed memoir *The Argonauts*: sexual expression is not a matter of good or bad but rather of people finding other people with whom their perversities are compatible. And Kominsky-Crumb may draw, in her approachable and scratchy hand, demonstrations of her laziness and loutishness, but she also draws a scene of sexual pleasure: "I'm so bad!", the Bunch says to the man on her back, participating with enjoyment. "Punish me good!!"

There were few stories then—in comics or anywhere else—that captured the texture and range of women's lives, demonstrating the reality of abjection *and* pleasure and everything in between. Kominsky-Crumb's comics offer a revelatory look into the complicated, contradictory lived lives of women. They changed my life and the lives of a lot of other readers, too. "Of What Use is an Old Bunch?" ends with a sweet nod to the original, in a large concluding panel that pictures Aline on all fours, with her grandson riding her back. "Is this sick??", she wonders. "I hope not… 'cause we're havin' fun!"

Aline Kominsky-Crumb is by no means old—and she has more vigor and effervescence than most young people I know—although this is an appropriate moment to consider her four-plus decades of influence as an artist, editor, and all-around tastemaker. The kind of work she pioneered, evident from

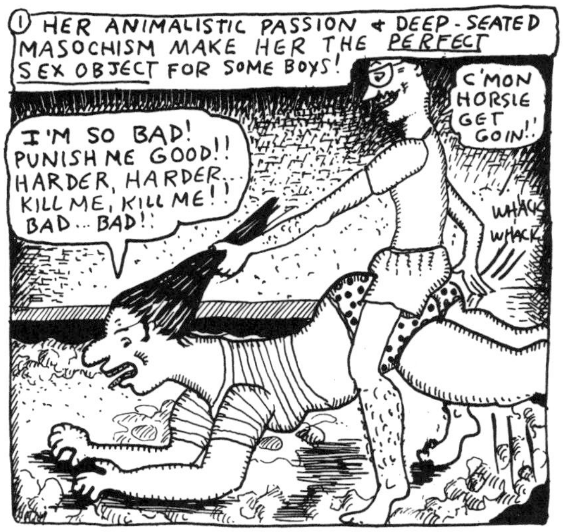

1 HER ANIMALISTIC PASSION + DEEP-SEATED MASOCHISM MAKE HER THE PERFECT SEX OBJECT FOR SOME BOYS!
C'MON HORSIE GET GOIN'!
I'M SO BAD! PUNISH ME GOOD!! HARDER, HARDER... KILL ME, KILL ME!! BAD... BAD!!
WHACK WHACK

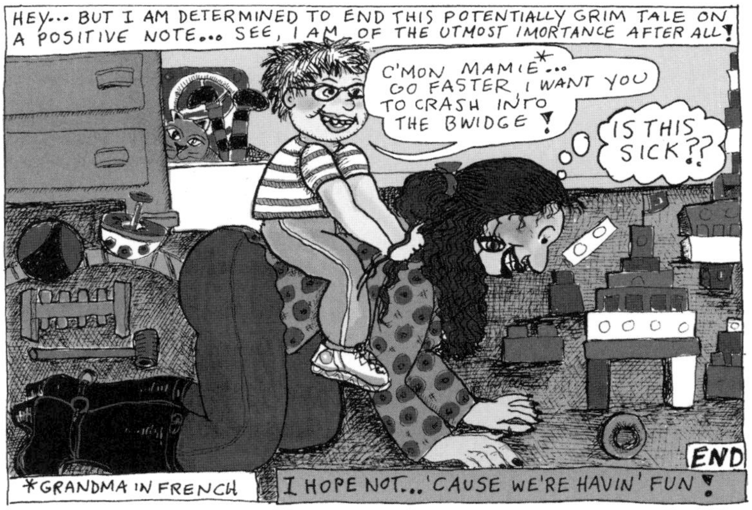

HEY... BUT I AM DETERMINED TO END THIS POTENTIALLY GRIM TALE ON A POSITIVE NOTE... SEE, I AM OF THE UTMOST IMORTANCE AFTER ALL!
C'MON MAMIE*... GO FASTER, I WANT YOU TO CRASH INTO THE BWIDGE!
IS THIS SICK??
END
*GRANDMA IN FRENCH
I HOPE NOT... 'CAUSE WE'RE HAVIN' FUN!

her very first published comics piece, "Goldie: A Neurotic Woman," (in the 1972 inaugural issue of *Wimmen's Comix)*, has finally become more accepted and mainstream. As *Huffington Post* correctly pointed out in 2017 about Kominsky-Crumb's oeuvre: "It's a breed of unapologetic, confessional humor that young women today might recognize in television shows like 'Girls,' 'Broad City,' or 'Fleabag,' shows that make space for female characters who are sloppy, complex, sexual or, as they're often described, 'difficult.'" But while today we watch stories like these on mainstream media platforms like HBO or Amazon, in the 1970s, it was rare for a woman to put herself—the good, the bad, and the ugly—at the center of stories the way Kominsky-Crumb did. It was even rare in the no-holds-barred context of underground comics, where the men and women responsible for developing the serious "graphic novel" field we have today published their comics entirely outside of mainstream production and distribution channels—and commercial strictures. What is widely credited as the first autobiographical work in comics: Justin Green's groundbreaking stand-alone comic book *Binky Brown Meets the Holy Virgin Mary*, about Catholic guilt and obsessive compulsive disorder, didn't appear until 1972. Kominsky-Crumb, inspired by Green, published her own autobiographical comics work—the first such work created by a woman—later that year.

Even within the world of underground comics, which valued smashing taboos, Kominsky-Crumb broke barriers, especially with her consistent attention to embodiment. Among other groundbreaking images, "Goldie" (the title refers to Kominsky-Crumb's maiden name, Goldsmith) pictures the bodily pain of puberty and adolescence—"I was a giant slug living in a fantasy of future happiness..."; unhappy mental images of paternal erections; sexual intercourse with many different men; and masturbation with vegetables. In one panel, Goldie stares straight ahead—engaging the reader's gaze: "I was always horny and guilty." The story ends with Goldie recognizing that she has "a lotta putencial" (misspellings are a deliberate part of the Kominsky-Crumb universe) and moving to San Francisco, the epicenter of underground comics: "I set out to live in my own style!". The rest, as we might say, is history. Kominsky-Crumb arrived in the underground comics scene and made her way, creating out of whole cloth a funny, courageous, and tonally complex aesthetic idiom and opening the floodgates for raw autobiographical stories to take shape in comics form.

Even within the feminist comics collective that produced *Wimmen's Comix*, Kominsky-Crumb's work stood out for its striking attention to the routine functions of the female body, both painful and pleasurable—and also for producing such work under the rubric of the first person. We see this attention to capturing the everyday experience of embodiment in "Bunch Plays With Herself," (pages 27–28) from 1975, a two-page piece with same-size frames throughout that reveals a day in the life of the Bunch: popping a pimple, scratching her behind and smelling her finger, eating a sandwich, masturbating, tanning outside, getting sunburned, napping. "My body is an endless source of entertainment!" the last panel reads. Pieces like this are confrontational about all functions of the body—it slows down to pay attention to the scratching, the smelling, and to deliver a detailed close-up panel of the Bunch's vagina while she "plays with herself."

Kominsky-Crumb eventually broke with the *Wimmen's Comix* collective, and founded her own title with Diane Noomin in 1976, the anthology *Twisted Sisters*. "They had images of women being glamorous or heroic," she explained in an interview with Peter Bagge. "I didn't have that background." The infamous, and un-heroic, cover of *Twisted Sisters* is a drawing of herself on the toilet, looking into a handheld mirror, grunting and worrying about calories. "I would completely deconstruct the myth or romanticism around being a woman," Kominsky-Crumb told me. "I was just vulgar and gross and everything. I enjoyed pushing it in people's faces." Her story about her formative teenage years, "The Young Bunch: An Unromantic Nonadventure Story," (pages 13–24) saw print in the first issue of *Twisted Sisters*. In this story, as everywhere, Kominsky-Crumb mixes humor and a wry levity with dark content, particularly in the depiction of sex (rape is a theme). She claims the tradition of Jewish stand-up comedians—Alan King, Jackie Mason, Milton Berle—as a big influence, what she calls "a certain kind of Jewish fatalistic humor" that threads through her work.

Kominsky-Crumb went on to also publish her autobiographical stories in underground publications including *Arcade: the Comics Revue*, founded by Art Spiegelman and Bill Griffith (1975–1976); *Power Pak*, her own solo comic book (1979–1981); and *Weirdo* (1981–1993), the acclaimed, influential anthology founded by cartoonist Robert Crumb and edited by Kominsky-Crumb for seven years. With Crumb, whom she married in 1978, she also founded the titles *Dirty Laundry* and *Self-Loathing*, which featured the couple's collaborative confessional strips; their collaborations started appearing in *The New Yorker* in 1995, and many were collected in their book *Drawn Together*.

TWISTED
SiSTERS
comics
75¢
ADULTS ONLY
FEATURING
DIDI GLITZ
I LOOK LIKE A 50 YR. OLD BUSINESSMAN!
GRUNT!!
WHAT IF SOMEONE COMES WHILE I'M MAKING??
HOW MANY CALORIES IN A CHEESE ENCHILADA?

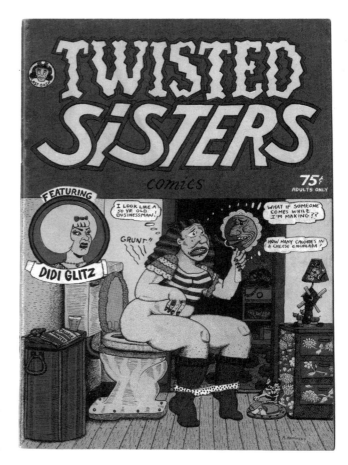

Love That Bunch, her first book, appeared in 1990, a loosely chronological grouping of twenty-nine stories that begin in her childhood and end in her forties. All of the stories engage the nexus of gender, sexuality, and subjectivity.

When I interviewed her about ten years ago, Kominsky-Crumb pointed out that her work has always been completely unsuccessful. *Twisted Sisters*, she said, had "no impact.... We had no feedback; it sold hardly any copies." She went on, referring to her comic book titles as well as to *Love That Bunch*: "I had no success ever. In any terms.... I never had any kind of feedback from the fine arts scene or the comics world." At least in part, this situation seems to be a reaction to her particular style. Kominsky-Crumb has a fine art background. She grew up in Woodmere, in the Five Towns area of Long Island, which she describes as materialistic, striving, and "horrible," but started taking art lessons and painting at age 8. As a young teenager, she became enamored with New York City's museums, and inspired by avant-garde idioms. One panel from *Love That Bunch* shows her as a teenager staring at a Cubist painting thinking, "If I can figure this out I can escape from Long Island!!" Kominsky-Crumb attended Cooper Union in New York City for a semester before moving to Tucson to earn a BFA in painting at the University of Arizona.

Despite her training with paint and canvas, it was comics that would become the medium in which Kominsky-Crumb first realized her artistic vision. She eventually fled the (often male- and Abstract Expressionist-dominated) world of art school and painting for the world of San Francisco underground comics publishing, which felt more open, porous, urgent, and truly experimental, a realm where personal stories, and women's personal stories, could find shape. But while her comics work operates in conversation with fine art idioms—she is particularly influenced by German Expressionist artists such as Otto Dix and George Grosz—the lack of mimetic realism in her drawings have coded to comics fans as unskilled rather than expressionistic; as "bad" rather than communicating emotional urgency and immediacy in the febrility of the line and distortion of perspective. Kominsky-Crumb is also influenced by painters who delved into the dark and the personal, such as Alice Neel, Frida Kahlo, and James Ensor, along with Matisse, Picasso, and Cézanne—painters known for eschewing correct perspective and academic realism in favor of expressivity and essence.

Kominsky-Crumb has a thin, wavering line, and her panels, while much of the drawing lacks realistic detail, are regularly crammed and crowded, especially in reproducing pattern and texture. When Kominsky-Crumb first started collaborating with Robert Crumb to produce comics, many fans of his work—known for its fluid crosshatching and masterful control—found Kominsky-Crumb's shaky hand, which can look so uncrafted, an insult; they wrote nasty letters.

Yet, an art critic as powerful and exacting as *The New York Times*'s Roberta Smith understands the value of Kominsky-Crumb's style. In 2007, reviewing a 33-year retrospective of Kominsky-Crumb's comics at the Adam Baumgold Gallery in New York, Smith wrote that Kominsky-Crumb "excels at the drawn-and-written confessional comic…. Her clenched, emphatic style echoes German Expressionist woodblock in its powerful contrasts of black and white, and her female faces…have a sometimes uncontainable fierceness." While Kominsky-Crumb has described her comics style variously as ugly, primitive, tortured, and scratching, for many readers, including me, its roughness, irregularity, and "imperfection" is welcoming, charming, and every bit as (if not more) compelling than "fine rendering." Her images feel vital, fluid, and direct. One way to think of her style is as importing a tradition of painting into a younger tradition: comics, built on print. (We can understand this happening in the "ratty line" aesthetic of another cartoonist starting out in the 1970s: Gary Panter, who also trained in fine art and exhibits in both comics and painting today.) For his part, Robert Crumb—who Kominsky-Crumb explained "got" her work instantly and is her best fan, realizes that "fine rendering doth not an artist make," despite being held up by his own fans as a paragon of fine rendering. In the introduction to the collected volume of *Dirty Laundry* comics, Crumb addressed his wife directly: "Fine rendering can be a trap, a web of clichés and techniques. Your work is entirely free of such comic-book banalities…. You remain amazingly impervious to the pernicious influence of all cartoon stylistic tricks…which is mainly why so many devotees of the comics medium are put off by your stuff."

But not all of them. While in comparison to other major, terrain-shifting figures in contemporary comics, Kominsky-Crumb's work has remained in the shadows, there have always been ardent admirers for whom her influence has been profound. Her comics stories and the landmark *Love That Bunch* opened up the field of comics to be more confessional—more open both stylistically and in terms of content. She has inspired countless cartoonists and readers, especially women and girls who weren't used to seeing multifaceted representations of their everyday lives on the page—or anywhere—reflected back at them with such honesty. The cartoonist Phoebe Gloeckner first discovered *Twisted Sisters* as a young teenager.

It changed her life and the kind of groundbreaking artist she in turn would also become, unflinchingly revealing sexuality, as does Kominsky-Crumb, in registers including both degradation and delight. (While both cartoonists make heavy use of anamorphism, especially when it comes to the male body, Gloeckner has a devastatingly realistic hand, in contrast to Kominsky-Crumb's messier expressive hand.)

On a panel I organized in 2012 with Kominsky-Crumb, Justin Green, Phoebe Gloeckner, and Carol Tyler, Gloeckner told Kominsky-Crumb of *Twisted Sisters*: "I memorized that comic…I read it so many times and every time I would get something more out of it." At age 15, she sent Kominsky-Crumb fan mail, and the two eventually met. When Gloeckner's book *The Diary of a Teenage Girl* (2002) was recently made into a feature film, Aline Kominsky-Crumb appeared as a fairy godmother–like character, an animated drawing interacting with actors on screen. To note just one of countless other cartoonists for whom Kominsky-Crumb led the way, Alison Bechdel, of *Dykes to Watch Out For, Fun Home*, and *Are You My Mother?*, has noted that the Crumb/Kominsky-Crumb collaborations "were very much an influence in terms of trying to be as honest as I can, especially about sexual stuff." And Kominsky-Crumb—in her hugely significant role as editor of *Weirdo* from 1986–1993, during a key time for the establishment of comics as an important contemporary form—extended her taste and legacy by nurturing the careers of artists like Gloeckner, Julie Doucet, Carol Tyler, and many others (the majority of whom would go on to be represented in the two important book volumes titled, like the comic, *Twisted Sisters*).

There has been an uptick of critical attention in the past ten or so years to the significance and ongoing appeal and relevance of Kominsky-Crumb's comics (she also has a separate life as an exhibiting artist working in a variety of media, which has also drawn important attention—where her style appears very different from what appears in her comics—which for her is a direct, confessional form). Kominsky-Crumb and I have known each other since 2005; she has even welcomed me into her home in France—and taught me yoga the one and only time I've ever done it, with an enthusiastic group of French women and her as my very rigorous teacher (I couldn't lift a shirt on or off my body without pain for days). I write about her in my books *Graphic Women: Life Narrative and Contemporary Comics*, which opens by examining her legacy, and *Why Comics? From Underground to Everywhere*—the latter in a chapter about comics as a space for picturing the illicit and uncensored, whether fantasy or reality. The title of a recent scholarly book—*"How Come Boys Get to Keep Their Noses?": Women and Jewish American Identity in Contemporary Graphic Memoirs*, by Tahneer Oksman—is a direct quote from Kominsky-Crumb's sad, hilarious 1989 story "Nose Job," (pages 105–107), about standards of beauty growing up in her Jewish enclave of Long Island. Kominsky-Crumb was also featured in *Graphic Details: Jewish Women's Confessional Comics in Essays and Interviews*.

And with more and more regularity, Kominsky-Crumb's work is being taught in the space of the classroom. One of my former students, a current college senior who wrote a final paper that examined Kominsky-Crumb's work, among others, for an art history class, wrote to me: "Her scratchy drawing style and the distorted anatomy of her characters remain unlike anything I've ever seen…. Her work uniquely marries images of lust and repulsion and brings visibility to the 'disgusting' aspects of women's bodies and desires. It's thrilling to read Kominsky-Crumb, to see her defy all censorship, and track how she inspired many fearless female artists to come." Other students have commented on the humanity in her work, with its textured, messy surfaces, and lively, uncontainable line.

Kominsky-Crumb shies away from nothing, tackling some of America's most persistent taboos. In the long story "My Very Own Dream House," printed here in complete form for the first time (pages 177–209), she reveals how she got pregnant at 18 ("But I thought LSD was a form of birth control!") and gave birth to a healthy baby boy in 1967, whom she put up for adoption. "I had wild sex and took lots of drugs right up until the minute I was ready to give birth," she writes in *Need More Love*, her 2007 graphic memoir. In these days of heightened scrutiny and huge moral judgment about women's maternal behaviors, admitting to doing "lots of drugs" during pregnancy is not a conventional fact to publicly disclose, especially because, here, it is resolutely not in the form of asking for an apology, and sidesteps shame altogether. Kominsky-Crumb has also published, in collaboration with Robert Crumb, a story about her experience having a face lift: "Saving Face," which appeared in *The New Yorker* in 2005. Another taboo: detailing your plastic surgery. Her mother, Kominsky-Crumb told me, was horrified: "How could you tell everybody that? You're supposed to hide it! No one can tell! You look gawgeous!" She explained to me, "I want to liberate people so that they can feel free to talk about it and not feel bad about stuff they decide to do…that was, to me, one of the most radical things I ever drew." And I was, even knowing them, honestly shocked and fascinated in the winter of 2017 to discover that Kominsky-Crumb and Crumb tackled the topic of their own wealth in a confessional comics story for *Harper's*. (Crumb has said that Kominsky-Crumb inspired his work to be more confessional.) Coming at the subject of money from this privileged perspective is, truly, one of America's last strong taboos, and they dove right into it. "Aline & Bob in Troubles With Money" opens with the news that original Crumb artwork has sold for 2.9 million dollars, and the story is about advice the couple gets for how to handle their influx of money. Drugs, plastic surgery, money: the sense that there is nothing Kominsky-Crumb won't share in her art—the unfettered access she gives readers—is exhilarating.

Kominsky-Crumb's comics are shot through with a brave sense of possibility, both in her sensitive and humorous approach to her subjects, and her view of the always-fluid self. In one of my favorite panels, from *Love That Bunch*'s "Up in the Air" (pages 78–82), Kominsky-Crumb draws a frame jammed with eleven different versions of herself, with various lipstick and hairstyles (one is even a man smoking a cigar), facing and insulting each other. "I can't stand myselves!" several of the selves declare in a shared speech balloon.

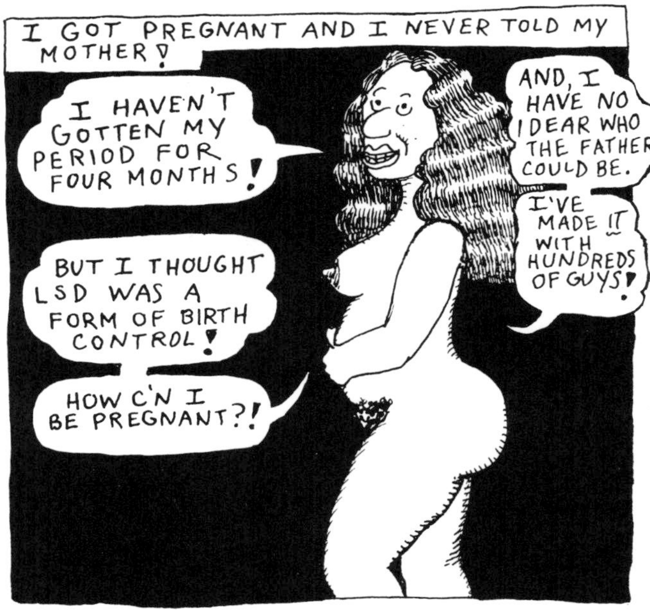
I GOT PREGNANT AND I NEVER TOLD MY MOTHER!
I HAVEN'T GOTTEN MY PERIOD FOR FOUR MONTHS!
AND, I HAVE NO IDEAR WHO THE FATHER COULD BE.
I'VE MADE IT WITH HUNDREDS OF GUYS!
BUT I THOUGHT LSD WAS A FORM OF BIRTH CONTROL!
HOW C'N I BE PREGNANT?!

"I'm so tired of my personality already." "Asshole!" one hilariously calls out to another. None of them is the one "real" self—they all are. As opposed to being depressing or self-deprecating, this non-continuous, unfixed view of self and proliferating potential, undergirds Kominsky-Crumb's work in the most positive way: it models how selves shift and change with time—embodying contradictions in order to keep on living life to the fullest.

Hillary Chute, Oct 10, 2017

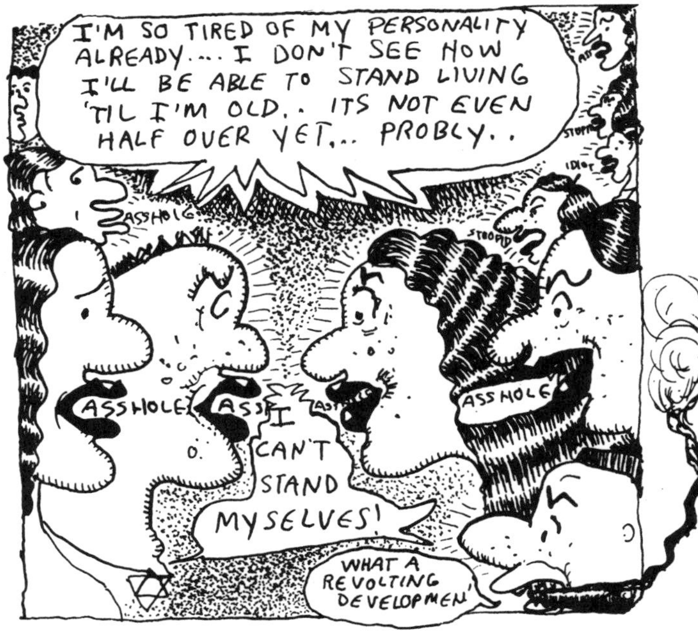
I'M SO TIRED OF MY PERSONALITY ALREADY.... I DON'T SEE HOW I'LL BE ABLE TO STAND LIVING 'TIL I'M OLD.. ITS NOT EVEN HALF OVER YET... PROBLY..
ASSHOLE
ASSHOLE
I CAN'T STAND MYSELVES!
WHAT A REVOLTING DEVELOPMEN'

SO RELAX.. DON'T GET UPSET.. DON'T GET NERVOUS!
DAHLING DEAHR DORDAH!

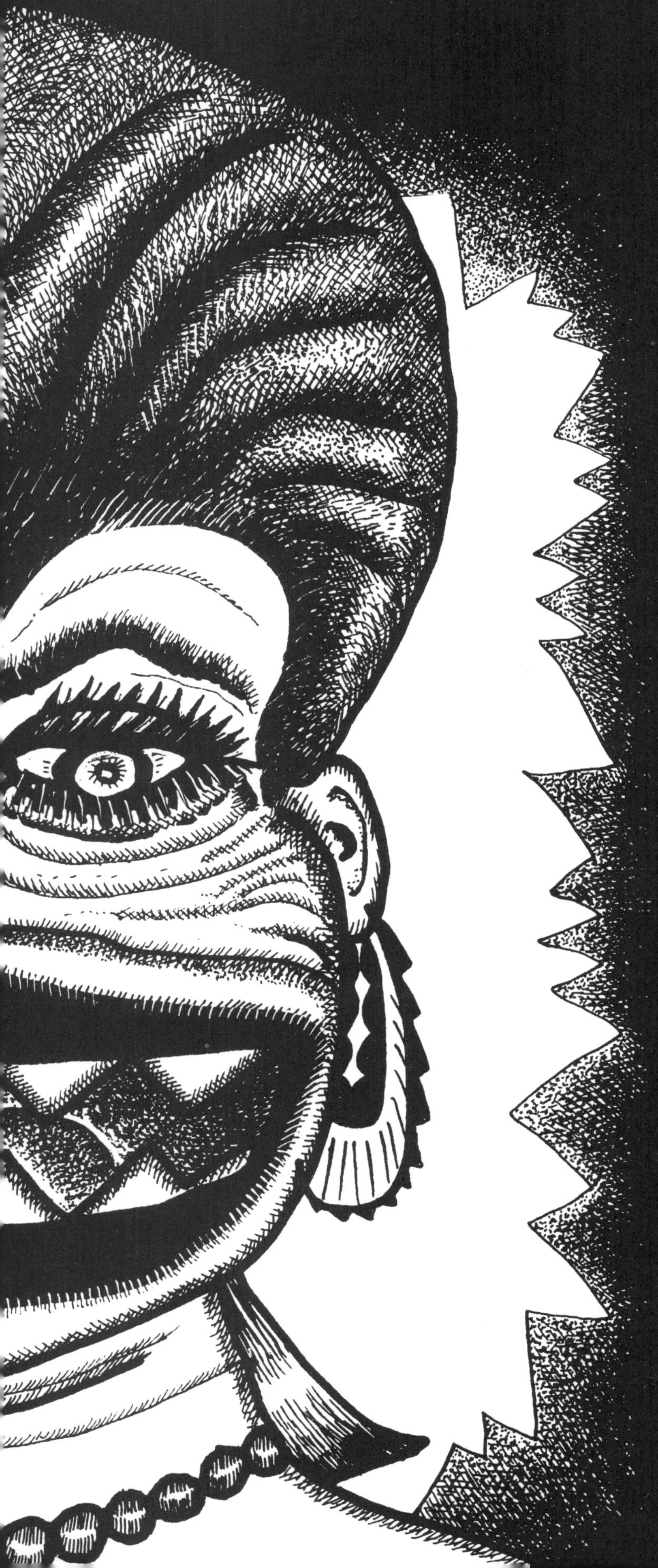

Contents

the YOUNG BUNCH
unromantic an nonadventure story

These are the formative years...fourteen, fifteen, sixteen...

WELL I HOPE I LOOK TOUGH ENOUGH.

HM, I THINK I NEED A LITTLE MORE OF THIS WHITE LIPSTICK.

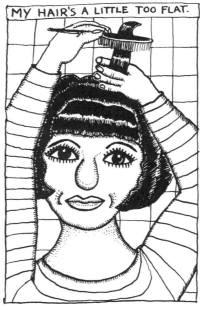

MY HAIR'S A LITTLE TOO FLAT.

ONE MORE THING..

OH DEAR GOD PLEASE MAKE HIM NOTICE ME AND FALL IN LOVE WITH ME. THANK YOU FOR LISTENING.

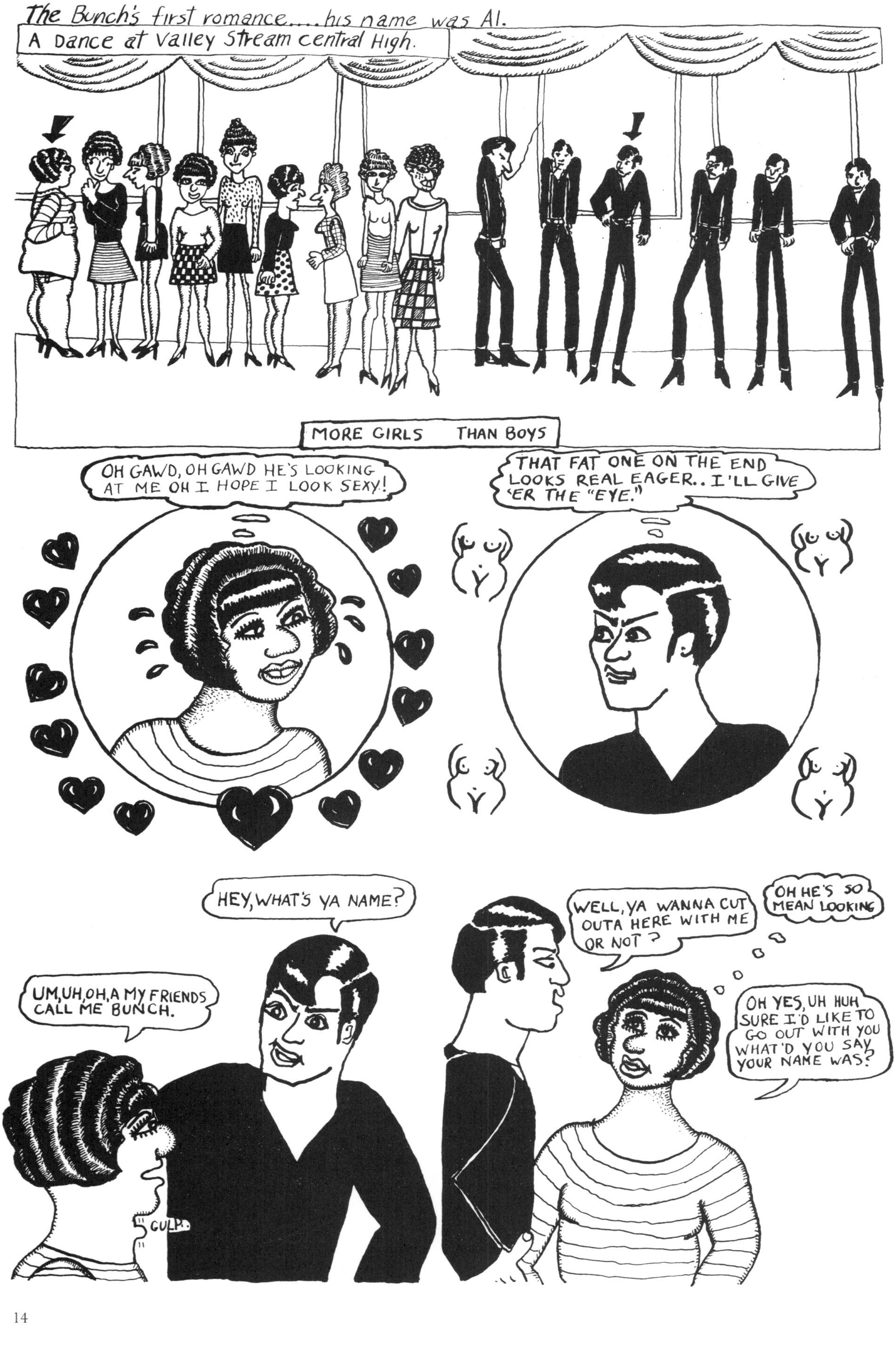

The Bunch's first romance.... his name was Al.
A Dance at Valley Stream central High.
MORE GIRLS THAN BOYS
OH GAWD, OH GAWD HE'S LOOKING AT ME OH I HOPE I LOOK SEXY!
THAT FAT ONE ON THE END LOOKS REAL EAGER.. I'LL GIVE 'ER THE "EYE."
HEY, WHAT'S YA NAME?
UM, UH, OH, A MY FRIENDS CALL ME BUNCH.
"GULP."
WELL, YA WANNA CUT OUTA HERE WITH ME OR NOT ?
OH HE'S SO MEAN LOOKING
OH YES, UH HUH SURE I'D LIKE TO GO OUT WITH YOU WHAT'D YOU SAY YOUR NAME WAS?

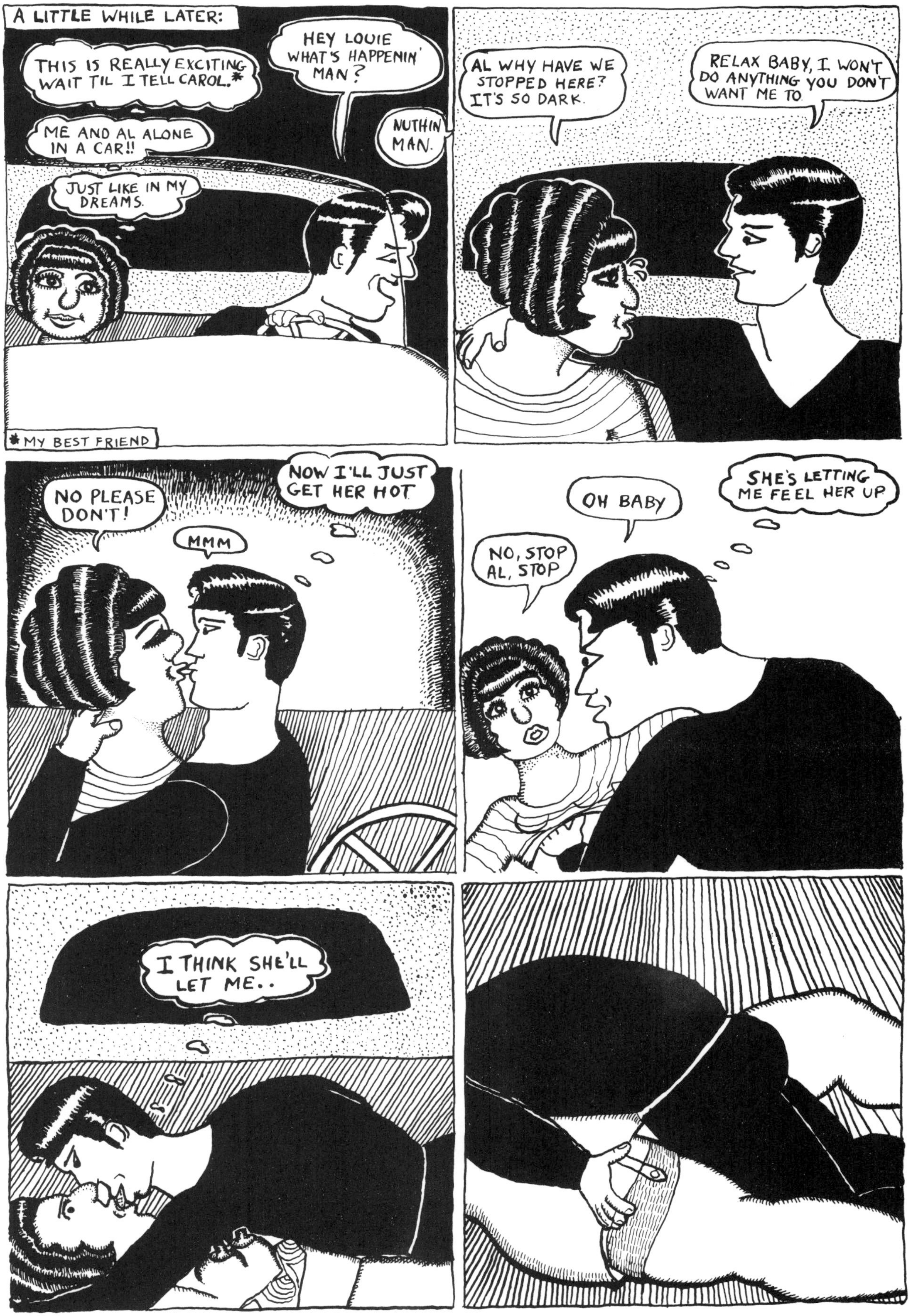
A LITTLE WHILE LATER:
THIS IS REALLY EXCITING WAIT TIL I TELL CAROL.*
HEY LOUIE WHAT'S HAPPENIN' MAN?
ME AND AL ALONE IN A CAR!!
NUTHIN MAN.
JUST LIKE IN MY DREAMS.
* MY BEST FRIEND
AL WHY HAVE WE STOPPED HERE? IT'S SO DARK.
RELAX BABY, I WON'T DO ANYTHING YOU DON'T WANT ME TO.
NO PLEASE DON'T!
NOW I'LL JUST GET HER HOT
MMM
OH BABY
SHE'S LETTING ME FEEL HER UP
NO, STOP AL, STOP
I THINK SHE'LL LET ME..

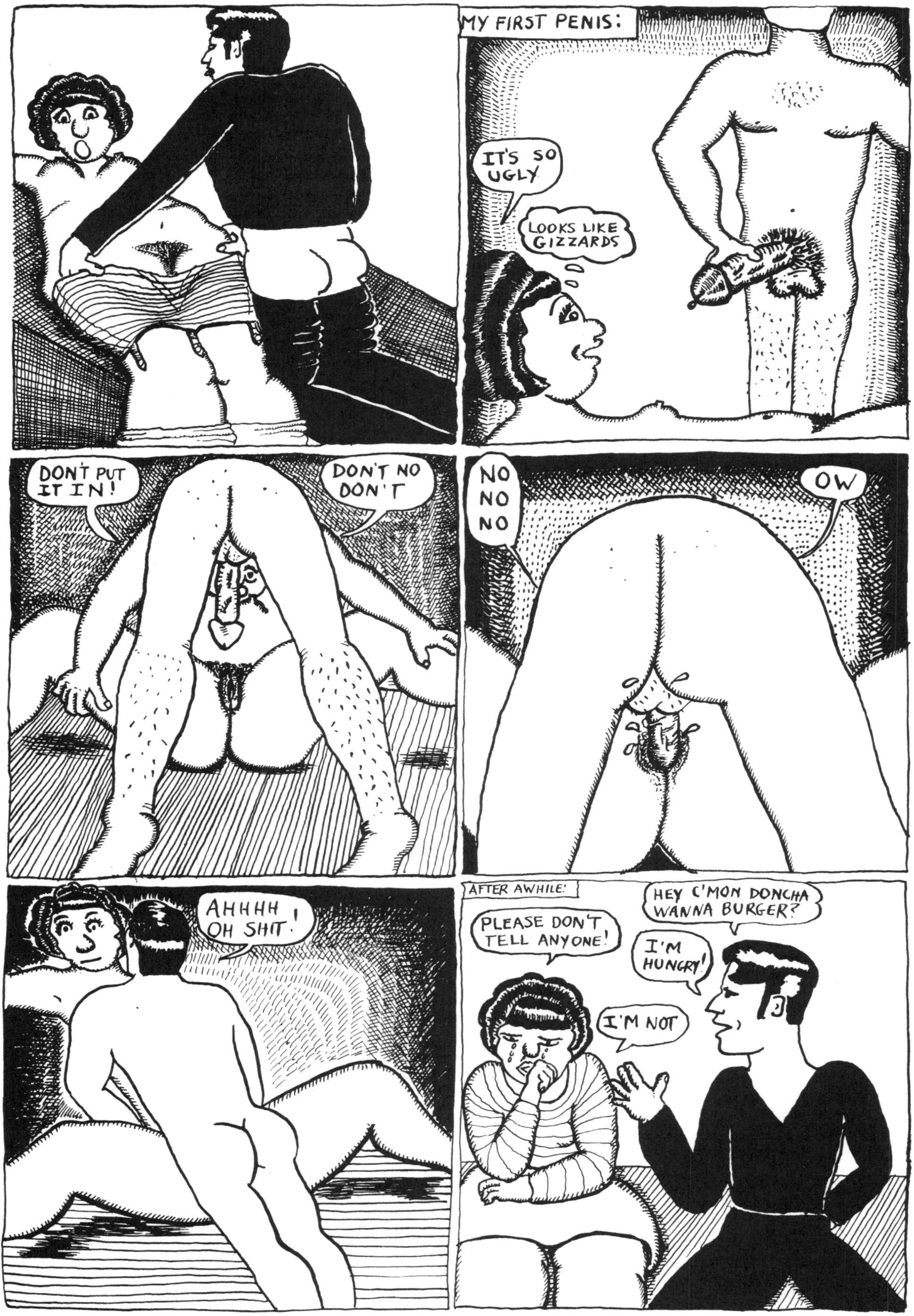
MY FIRST PENIS:
IT'S SO UGLY
LOOKS LIKE GIZZARDS
DON'T PUT IT IN!
DON'T NO DON'T
NO NO NO
OW
AHHHH OH SHIT!
AFTER AWHILE:
PLEASE DON'T TELL ANYONE!
HEY C'MON DONCHA WANNA BURGER?
I'M HUNGRY!
I'M NOT

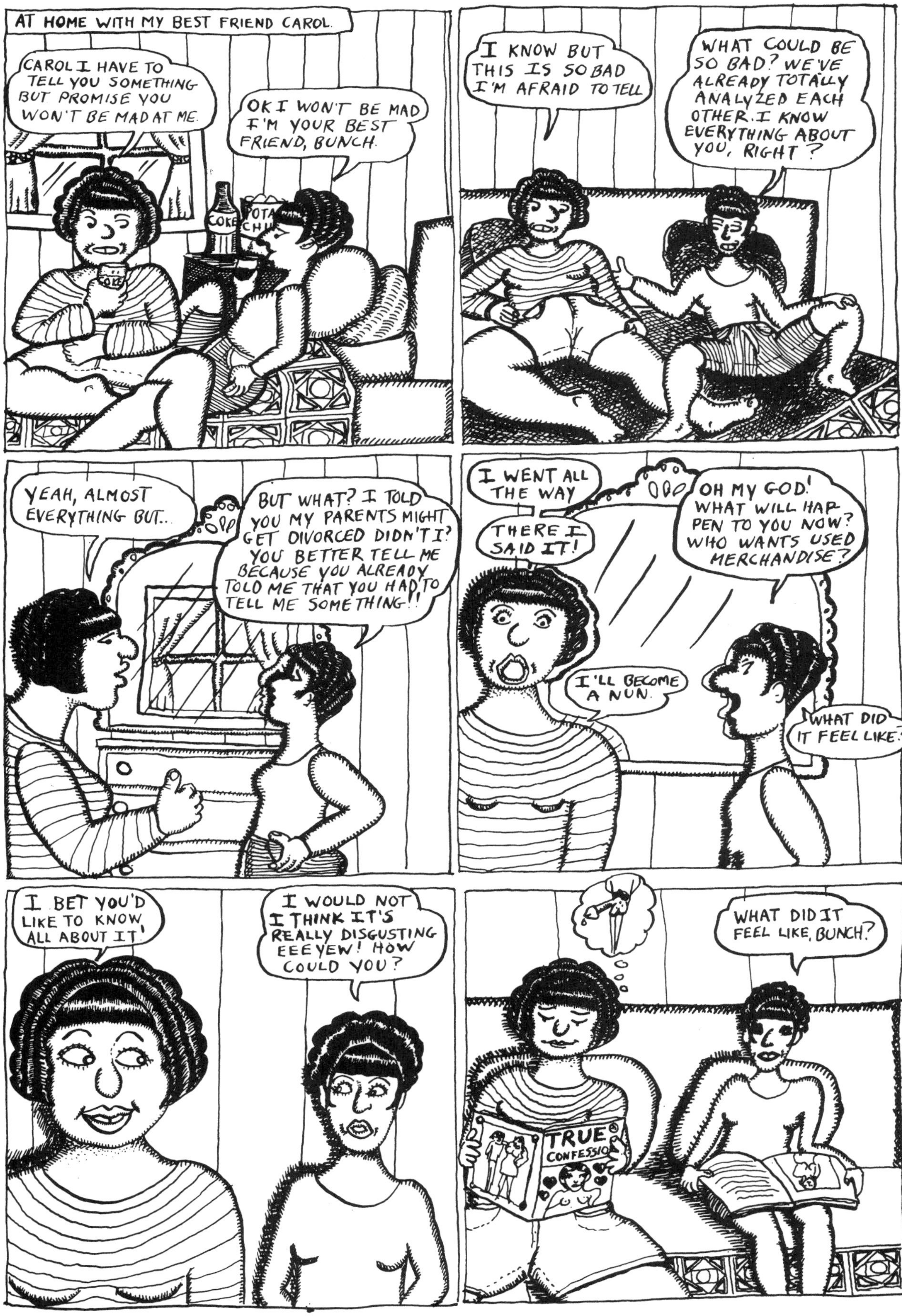
AT HOME WITH MY BEST FRIEND CAROL.
CAROL I HAVE TO TELL YOU SOMETHING BUT PROMISE YOU WON'T BE MAD AT ME.
OK I WON'T BE MAD I'M YOUR BEST FRIEND, BUNCH.
COKE
I KNOW BUT THIS IS SO BAD I'M AFRAID TO TELL
WHAT COULD BE SO BAD? WE'VE ALREADY TOTALLY ANALYZED EACH OTHER. I KNOW EVERYTHING ABOUT YOU, RIGHT?
YEAH, ALMOST EVERYTHING BUT...
BUT WHAT? I TOLD YOU MY PARENTS MIGHT GET DIVORCED DIDN'T I? YOU BETTER TELL ME BECAUSE YOU ALREADY TOLD ME THAT YOU HAD TO TELL ME SOMETHING!!
I WENT ALL THE WAY
THERE I SAID IT!
OH MY GOD! WHAT WILL HAPPEN TO YOU NOW? WHO WANTS USED MERCHANDISE?
I'LL BECOME A NUN.
WHAT DID IT FEEL LIKE?
I BET YOU'D LIKE TO KNOW ALL ABOUT IT!
I WOULD NOT I THINK IT'S REALLY DISGUSTING EEEYEW! HOW COULD YOU?
WHAT DID IT FEEL LIKE, BUNCH?
TRUE CONFESSIO

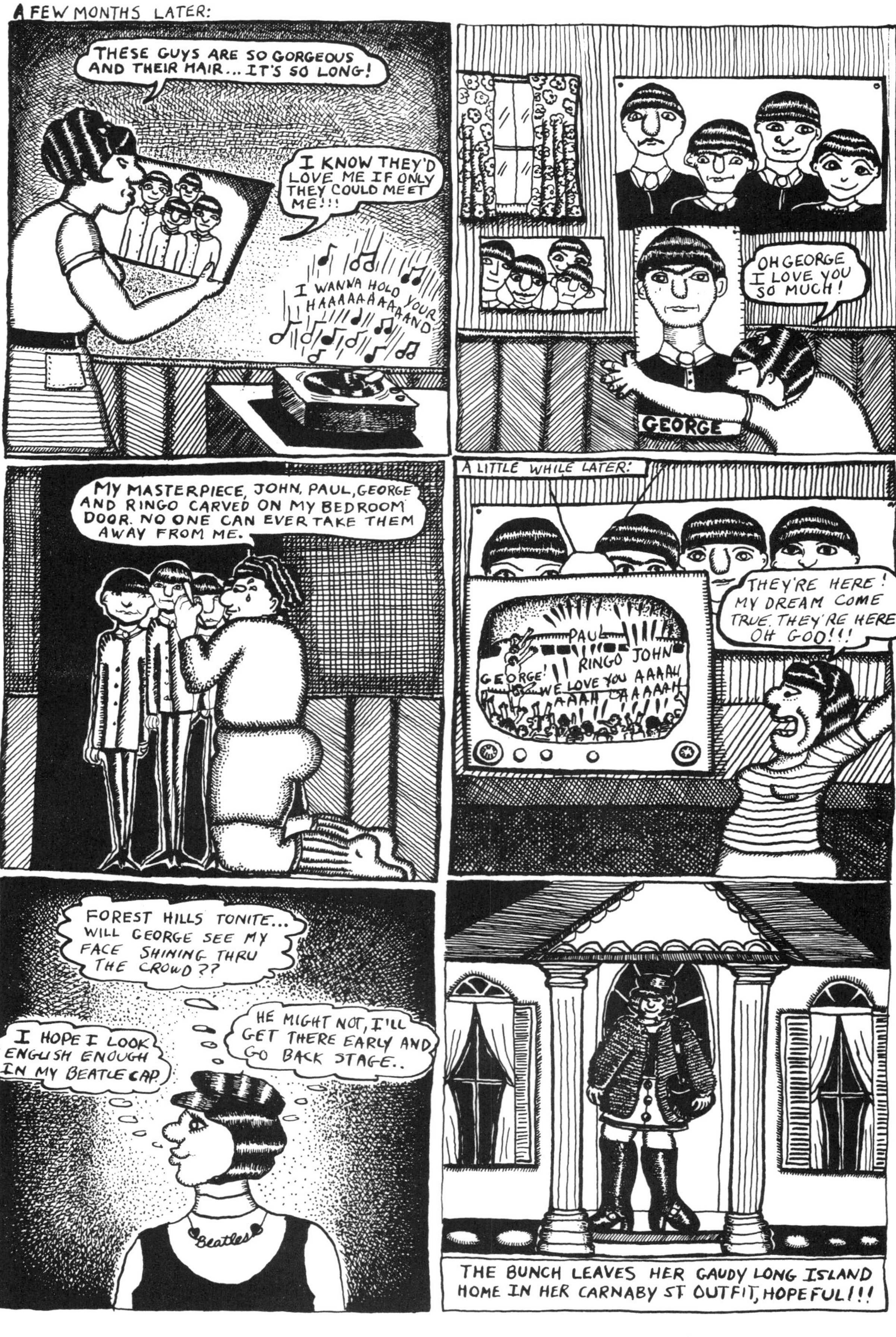
A FEW MONTHS LATER:
THESE GUYS ARE SO GORGEOUS AND THEIR HAIR... IT'S SO LONG!
I KNOW THEY'D LOVE ME IF ONLY THEY COULD MEET ME!!!
I WANNA HOLD YOUR HAAAAAAAAAAAND
OH GEORGE I LOVE YOU SO MUCH!
GEORGE
MY MASTERPIECE, JOHN, PAUL, GEORGE AND RINGO CARVED ON MY BEDROOM DOOR. NO ONE CAN EVER TAKE THEM AWAY FROM ME.
A LITTLE WHILE LATER:
THEY'RE HERE! MY DREAM COME TRUE. THEY'RE HERE! OH GOD!!!
PAUL RINGO JOHN GEORGE! WE LOVE YOU AAAAH AAAAH AAAAAH
FOREST HILLS TONITE... WILL GEORGE SEE MY FACE SHINING THRU THE CROWD??
I HOPE I LOOK ENGLISH ENOUGH IN MY BEATLE CAP.
HE MIGHT NOT, I'LL GET THERE EARLY AND GO BACK STAGE..
Beatles
THE BUNCH LEAVES HER GAUDY LONG ISLAND HOME IN HER CARNABY ST OUTFIT, HOPEFUL!!!

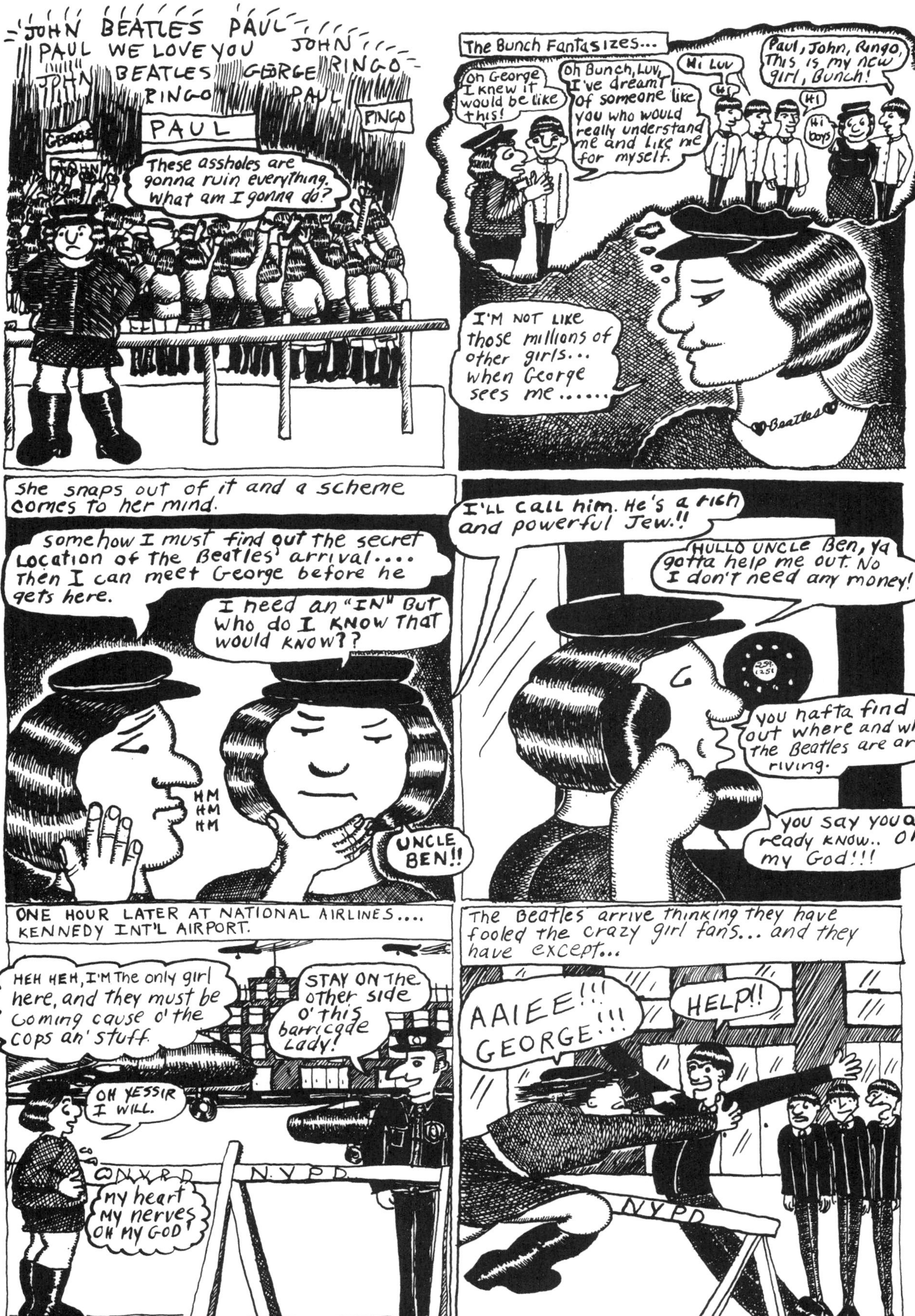
JOHN BEATLES PAUL
PAUL WE LOVE YOU JOHN
JOHN BEATLES GEORGE RINGO
RINGO PAUL
PAUL
GEORGE
JOHN
RINGO
These assholes are gonna ruin everything. What am I gonna do?
The Bunch Fantasizes...
Oh George I knew it would be like this!
Oh Bunch, Luv, I've dreamt of someone like you who would really understand me and like me for myself.
Hi Luv
Hi
Hi
Hi boys
Paul, John, Ringo, This is my new girl, Bunch!
I'M NOT LIKE those millions of other girls... when George sees me......
Beatles
She snaps out of it and a scheme comes to her mind.
somehow I must find out the secret Location of the Beatles' arrival.... Then I can meet George before he gets here.
I need an "IN" But who do I KNOW That would KNOW??
HM HM HM
UNCLE BEN!!
I'LL call him. He's a rich and powerful Jew!!
HULLO UNCLE Ben, ya gotta help me out. No I don't need any money!
you hafta find out where and when the Beatles are arriving.
you say you already know.. Oh my God!!!
ONE HOUR LATER AT NATIONAL AIRLINES.... KENNEDY INT'L AIRPORT.
HEH HEH, I'M The only girl here, and they must be coming cause o' the cops an' stuff.
STAY ON The other side o' this barricade Lady!
OH YESSIR I WILL.
NYPD
N.Y.P.D.
My heart My nerves OH MY GOD!
The Beatles arrive thinking they have fooled the crazy girl fans... and they have except...
AAIEE!!! GEORGE!!!
HELP!!
NYPD

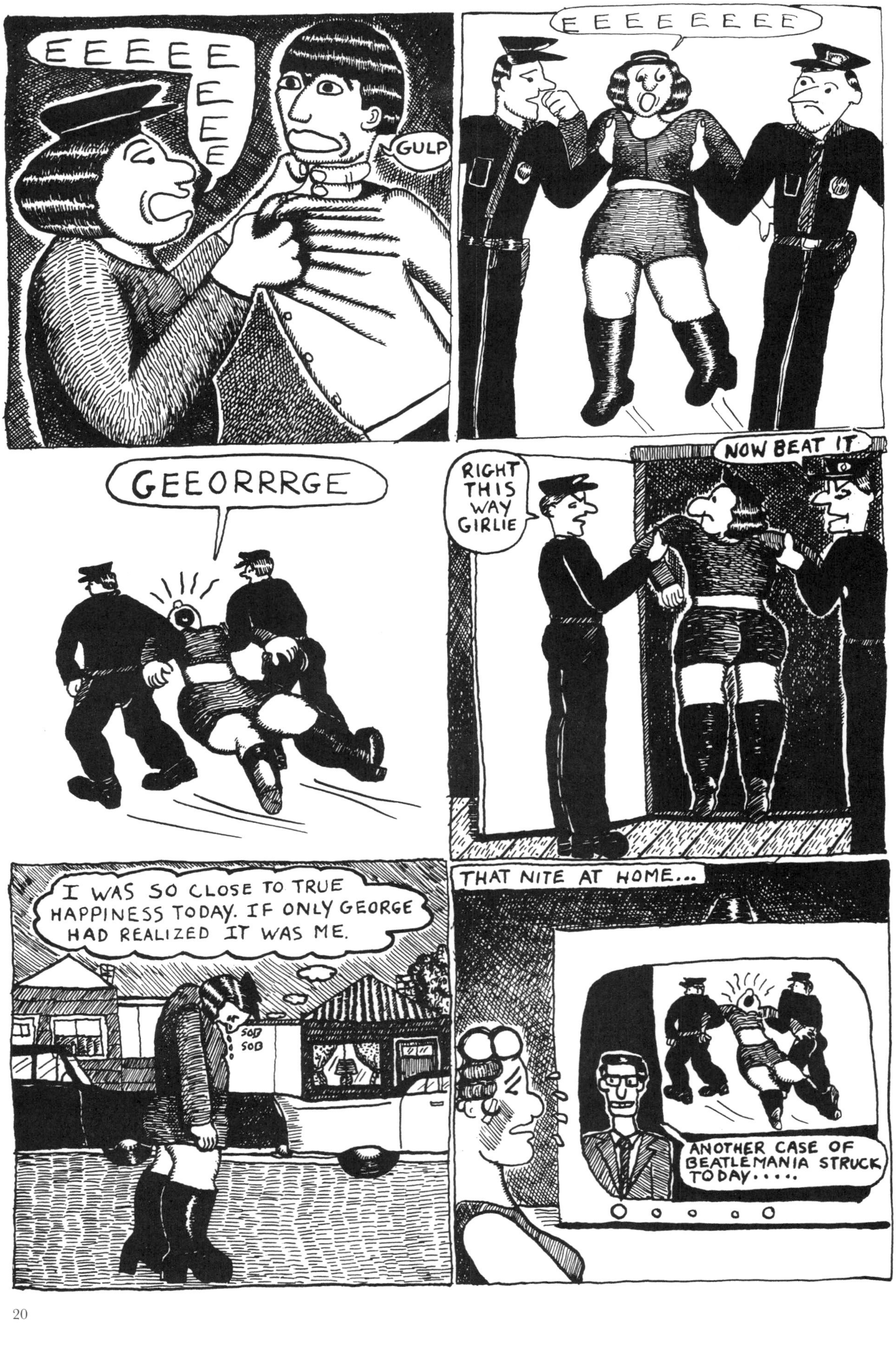
EEEEEEEEE
GULP
EEEEEEEE
GEEORRRGE
RIGHT THIS WAY GIRLIE
NOW BEAT IT
I WAS SO CLOSE TO TRUE HAPPINESS TODAY. IF ONLY GEORGE HAD REALIZED IT WAS ME.
SOB SOB
THAT NITE AT HOME...
ANOTHER CASE OF BEATLEMANIA STRUCK TODAY.....

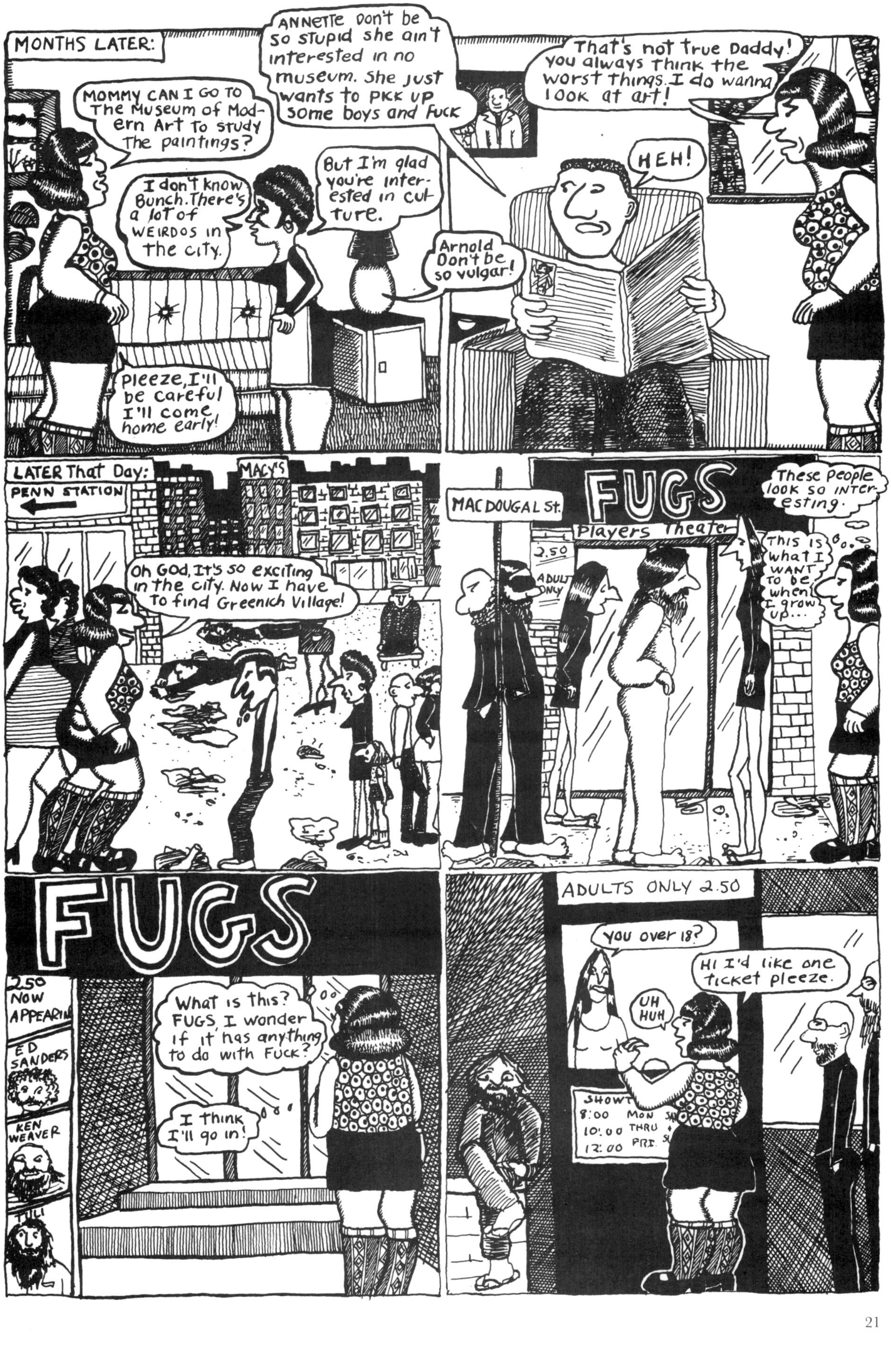
MONTHS LATER:
MOMMY CAN I GO TO THE MUSEUM OF MODERN ART TO STUDY THE PAINTINGS?
ANNETTE DON'T BE SO STUPID SHE AIN'T INTERESTED IN NO MUSEUM. SHE JUST WANTS TO PICK UP SOME BOYS AND FUCK
I DON'T KNOW BUNCH. THERE'S A LOT OF WEIRDOS IN THE CITY.
BUT I'M GLAD YOU'RE INTERESTED IN CULTURE.
ARNOLD DON'T BE SO VULGAR!
PLEEZE, I'LL BE CAREFUL I'LL COME HOME EARLY!
HEH!
THAT'S NOT TRUE DADDY! YOU ALWAYS THINK THE WORST THINGS. I DO WANNA LOOK AT ART!
LATER THAT DAY:
PENN STATION
MACY'S
OH GOD, IT'S SO EXCITING IN THE CITY. NOW I HAVE TO FIND GREENICH VILLAGE!
MACDOUGAL ST.
FUGS
PLAYERS THEATER
2.50
ADULTS ONLY
THESE PEOPLE LOOK SO INTERESTING.
THIS IS WHAT I WANT TO BE WHEN I GROW UP...
FUGS
2.50 NOW APPEARING
ED SANDERS
KEN WEAVER
TULI
WHAT IS THIS? FUGS, I WONDER IF IT HAS ANYTHING TO DO WITH FUCK?
I THINK I'LL GO IN!
ADULTS ONLY 2.50
YOU OVER 18?
HI I'D LIKE ONE TICKET PLEEZE.
UH HUH
SHOWT
8:00 MON
10:00 THRU
12:00 FRI.

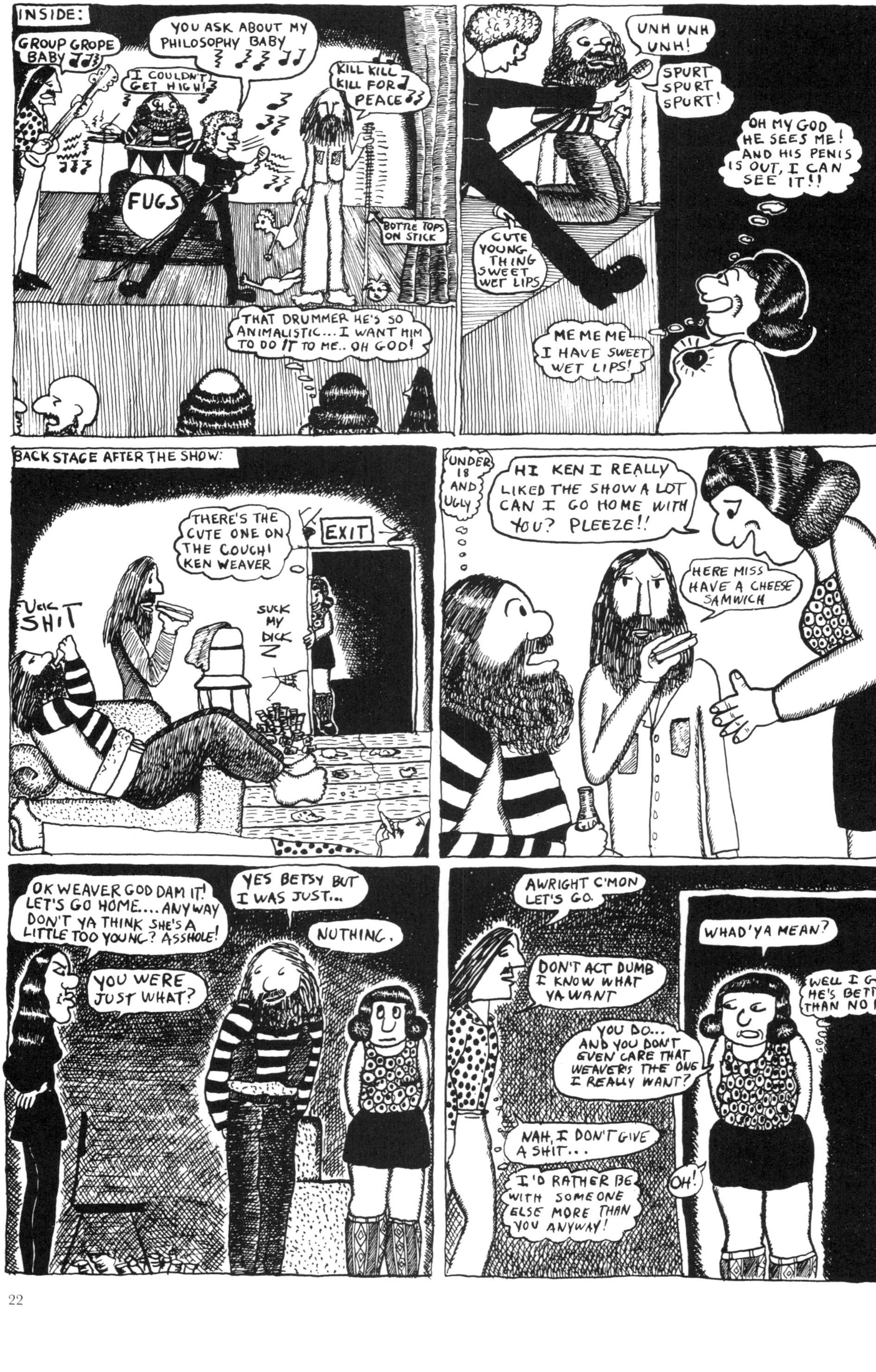
INSIDE:
GROUP GROPE BABY
YOU ASK ABOUT MY PHILOSOPHY BABY
I COULDN'T GET HIGH!
KILL KILL KILL FOR PEACE
FUGS
BOTTLE TOPS ON STICK
THAT DRUMMER HE'S SO ANIMALISTIC... I WANT HIM TO DO IT TO ME.. OH GOD!
UNH UNH UNH!
SPURT SPURT SPURT!
OH MY GOD HE SEES ME! AND HIS PENIS IS OUT, I CAN SEE IT!!
CUTE YOUNG THING SWEET WET LIPS
ME ME ME I HAVE SWEET WET LIPS!
BACK STAGE AFTER THE SHOW:
THERE'S THE CUTE ONE ON THE COUCH! KEN WEAVER
EXIT
UGH SHIT
SUCK MY DICK
UNDER 18 AND UGLY
HI KEN I REALLY LIKED THE SHOW A LOT CAN I GO HOME WITH YOU? PLEEZE!!
HERE MISS HAVE A CHEESE SAMWICH
OK WEAVER GOD DAM IT! LET'S GO HOME.... ANYWAY DON'T YA THINK SHE'S A LITTLE TOO YOUNG? ASSHOLE!
YES BETSY BUT I WAS JUST...
YOU WERE JUST WHAT?
NUTHING.
AWRIGHT C'MON LET'S GO.
WHAD'YA MEAN?
DON'T ACT DUMB I KNOW WHAT YA WANT
WELL I GUESS HE'S BETTER THAN NO FUG
YOU DO... AND YOU DON'T EVEN CARE THAT WEAVER'S THE ONE I REALLY WANT?
NAH, I DON'T GIVE A SHIT...
I'D RATHER BE WITH SOMEONE ELSE MORE THAN YOU ANYWAY!
OH!

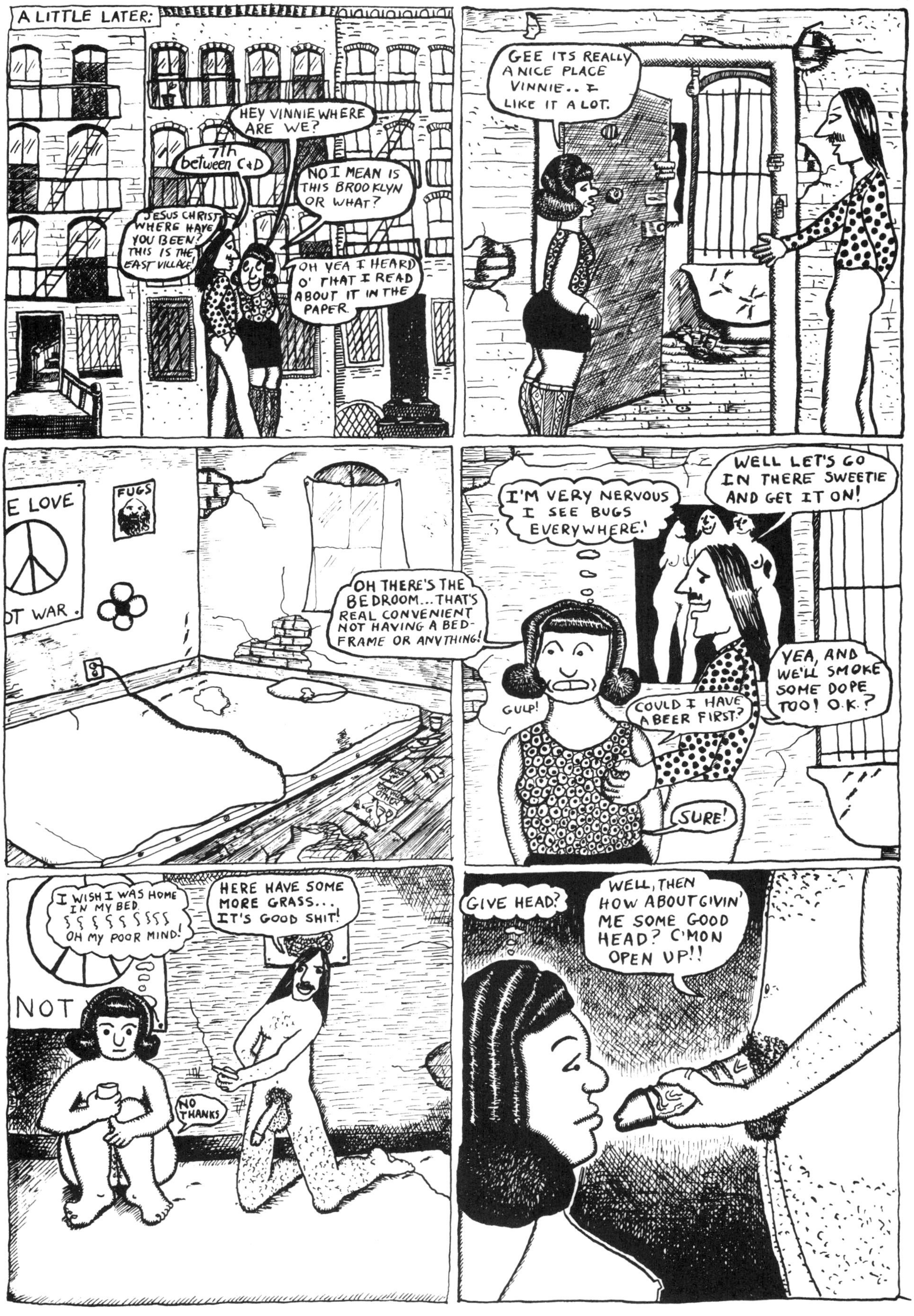
A LITTLE LATER:
HEY VINNIE WHERE ARE WE?
7th between C&D
NO I MEAN IS THIS BROOKLYN OR WHAT?
JESUS CHRIST WHERE HAVE YOU BEEN? THIS IS THE EAST VILLAGE!
OH YEA I HEARD O' THAT I READ ABOUT IT IN THE PAPER.
GEE ITS REALLY A NICE PLACE VINNIE.. I LIKE IT A LOT.
E LOVE
OT WAR.
FUGS
OH THERE'S THE BEDROOM... THAT'S REAL CONVENIENT NOT HAVING A BED-FRAME OR ANYTHING!
I'M VERY NERVOUS I SEE BUGS EVERYWHERE!
WELL LET'S GO IN THERE SWEETIE AND GET IT ON!
YEA, AND WE'LL SMOKE SOME DOPE TOO! O.K.?
GULP!
COULD I HAVE A BEER FIRST?
SURE!
I WISH I WAS HOME IN MY BED. OH MY POOR MIND!
HERE HAVE SOME MORE GRASS... IT'S GOOD SHIT!
NOT
NO THANKS
GIVE HEAD?
WELL, THEN HOW ABOUT GIVIN' ME SOME GOOD HEAD? C'MON OPEN UP!!

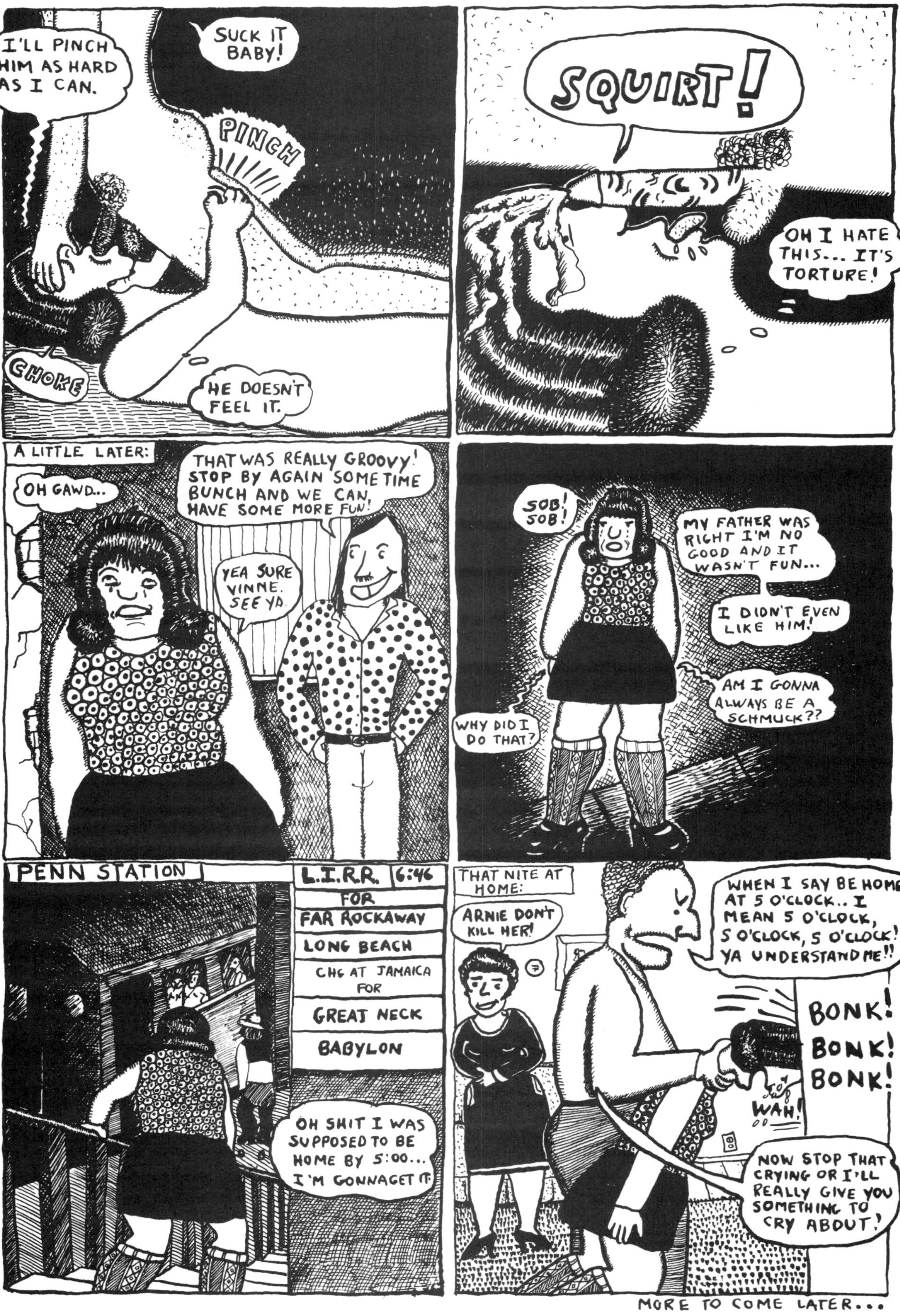
I'LL PINCH HIM AS HARD AS I CAN.
SUCK IT BABY!
PINCH
CHOKE
HE DOESN'T FEEL IT.
SQUIRT!
OH I HATE THIS... IT'S TORTURE!
A LITTLE LATER:
OH GAWD...
THAT WAS REALLY GROOVY! STOP BY AGAIN SOME TIME BUNCH AND WE CAN HAVE SOME MORE FUN!
YEA SURE VINNE. SEE YA.
SOB! SOB!
MY FATHER WAS RIGHT I'M NO GOOD AND IT WASN'T FUN...
I DIDN'T EVEN LIKE HIM!
AM I GONNA ALWAYS BE A SCHMUCK??
WHY DID I DO THAT?
PENN STATION
L.I.R.R. 6:46
FOR
FAR ROCKAWAY
LONG BEACH
CHG AT JAMAICA FOR
GREAT NECK
BABYLON
OH SHIT I WAS SUPPOSED TO BE HOME BY 5:00... I'M GONNA GET IT.
THAT NITE AT HOME:
ARNIE DON'T KILL HER!
WHEN I SAY BE HOME AT 5 O'CLOCK.. I MEAN 5 O'CLOCK, 5 O'CLOCK, 5 O'CLOCK! YA UNDERSTAND ME!!
BONK! BONK! BONK!
WAH!
NOW STOP THAT CRYING OR I'LL REALLY GIVE YOU SOMETHING TO CRY ABOUT!
MORE TO COME LATER...

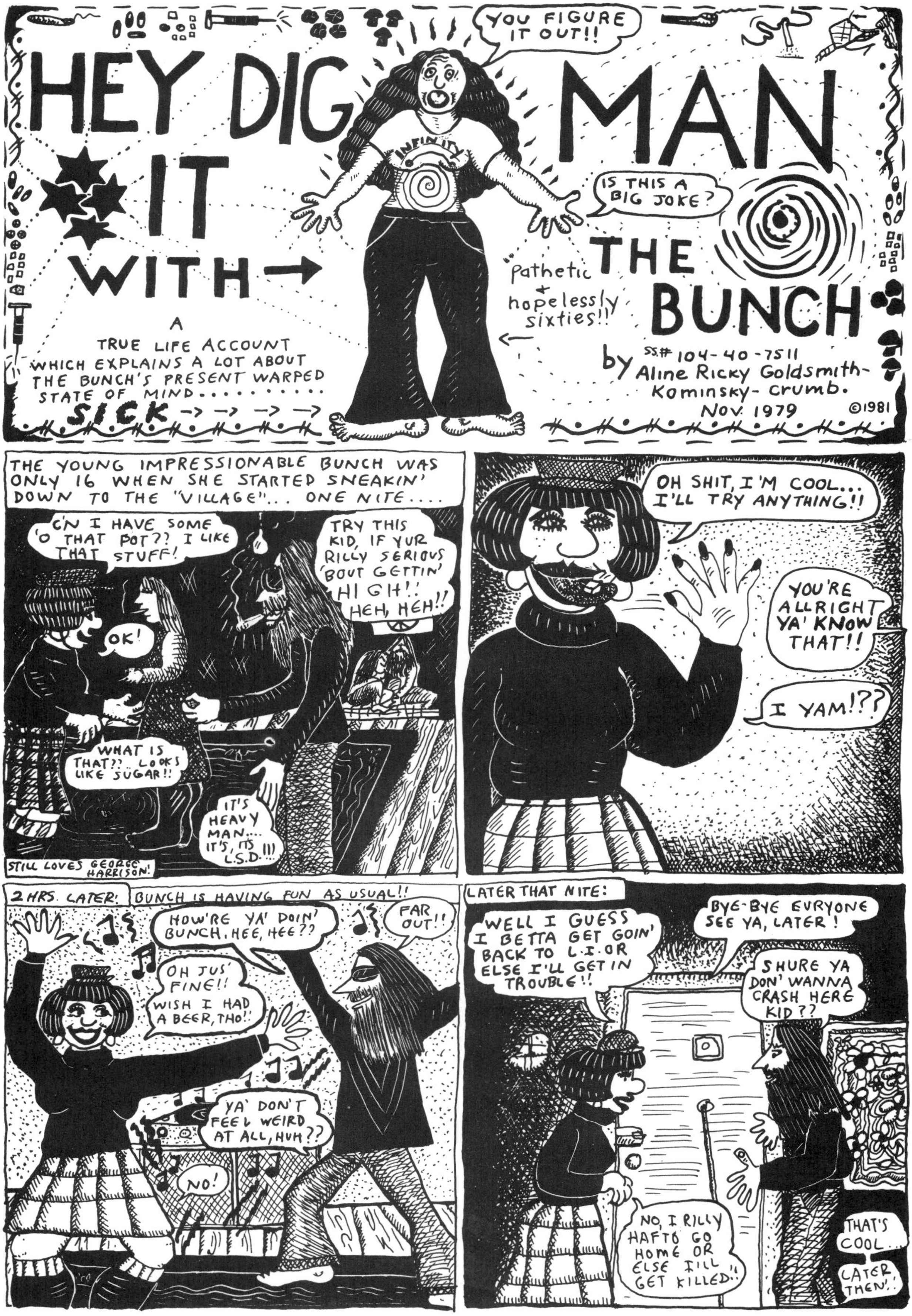

HEY DIG IT WITH → MAN THE BUNCH
YOU FIGURE IT OUT!!
INFINITY
IS THIS A BIG JOKE?
pathetic + hopelessly sixties!!
A TRUE LIFE ACCOUNT WHICH EXPLAINS A LOT ABOUT THE BUNCH'S PRESENT WARPED STATE OF MIND.........
SICK
by SS# 104-40-7511 Aline Ricky Goldsmith-Kominsky-crumb. Nov. 1979
©1981
THE YOUNG IMPRESSIONABLE BUNCH WAS ONLY 16 WHEN SHE STARTED SNEAKIN' DOWN TO THE "VILLAGE"... ONE NITE....
C'N I HAVE SOME 'O THAT POT?? I LIKE THAT STUFF!
TRY THIS KID, IF YUR RILLY SERIOUS 'BOUT GETTIN' HIGH!! HEH, HEH!!
OK!
WHAT IS THAT?? LOOKS LIKE SUGAR!!
IT'S HEAVY MAN... IT'S, IT'S L.S.D.!!!
STILL LOVES GEORGE HARRISON!
OH SHIT, I'M COOL... I'LL TRY ANYTHING!!
YOU'RE ALLRIGHT YA' KNOW THAT!!
I YAM!??
2 HRS. LATER:
BUNCH IS HAVING FUN AS USUAL!!
HOW'RE YA' DOIN' BUNCH, HEE, HEE??
FAR OUT!!
OH JUS' FINE!! WISH I HAD A BEER, THO!!
YA' DON'T FEEL WEIRD AT ALL, HUH??
NO!
LATER THAT NITE:
WELL I GUESS I BETTA GET GOIN' BACK TO L.I. OR ELSE I'LL GET IN TROUBLE!!
BYE-BYE EVRYONE SEE YA, LATER!
SHURE YA DON' WANNA CRASH HERE KID??
NO, I RILLY HAFTO GO HOME OR ELSE I'LL GET KILLED!!
THAT'S COOL.
LATER THEN!

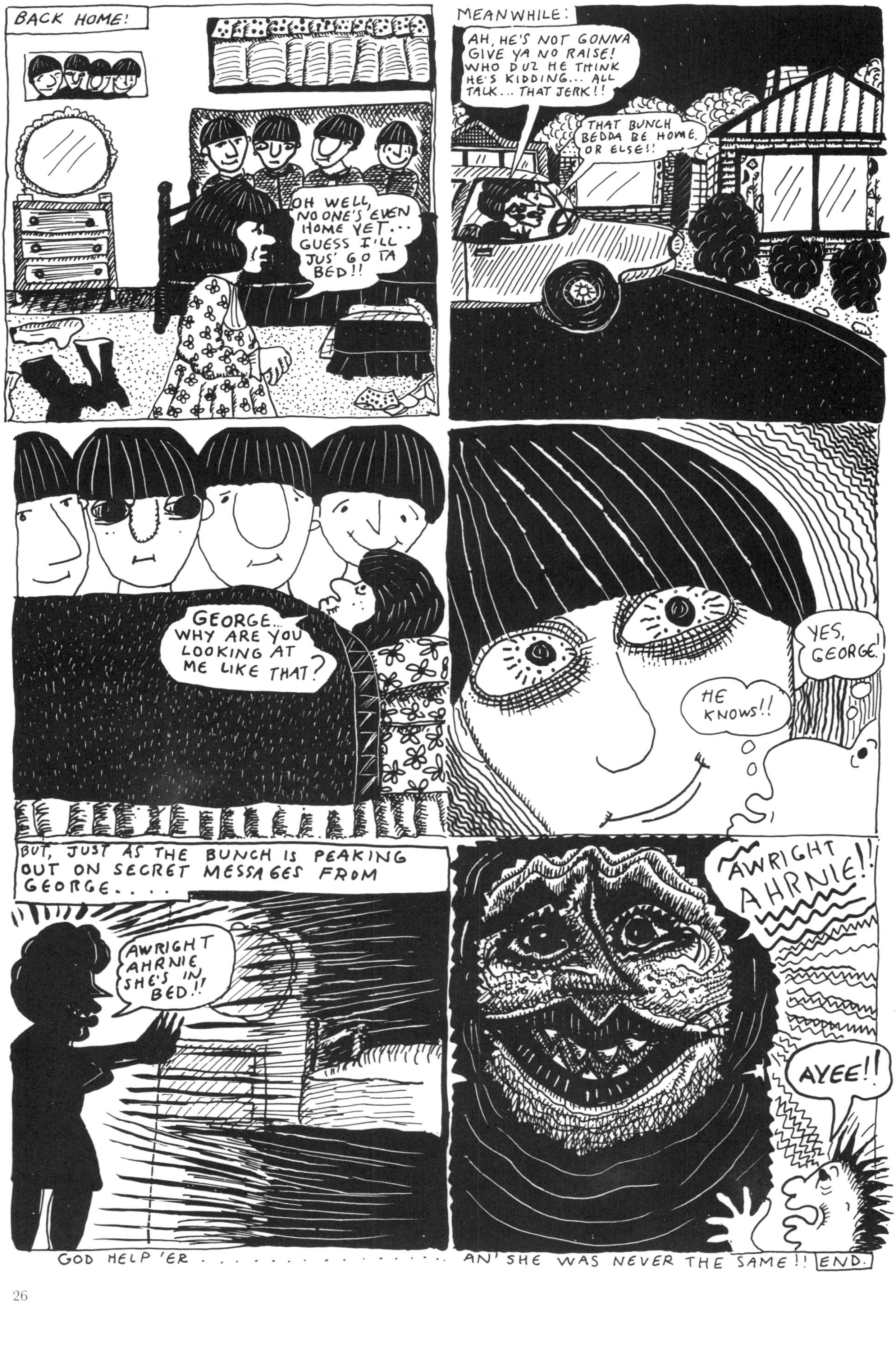
BACK HOME!
OH WELL, NO ONE'S EVEN HOME YET... GUESS I'LL JUS' GO TA BED!!
MEANWHILE:
AH, HE'S NOT GONNA GIVE YA NO RAISE! WHO DUZ HE THINK HE'S KIDDING... ALL TALK... THAT JERK!!
THAT BUNCH BEDDA BE HOME, OR ELSE!!
GEORGE... WHY ARE YOU LOOKING AT ME LIKE THAT?
YES, GEORGE!
HE KNOWS!!
BUT, JUST AS THE BUNCH IS PEAKING OUT ON SECRET MESSAGES FROM GEORGE....
AWRIGHT AHRNIE SHE'S IN BED!!
AWRIGHT AHRNIE!!
AYEE!!
GOD HELP 'ER ....
AN' SHE WAS NEVER THE SAME!!
END.

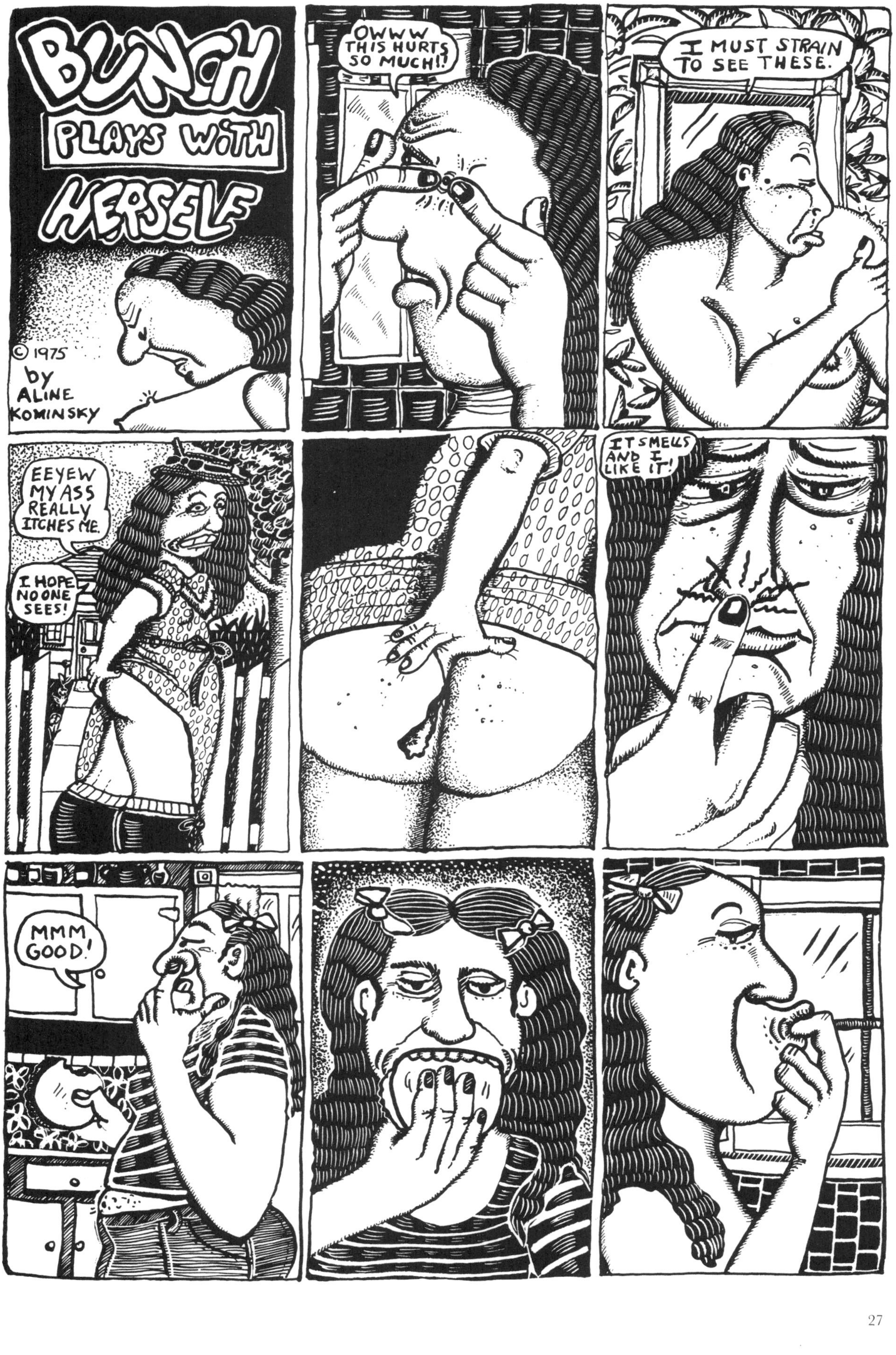
BUNCH PLAYS WITH HERSELF
© 1975
by ALINE KOMINSKY
OWWW THIS HURTS SO MUCH!!
I MUST STRAIN TO SEE THESE.
EEYEW MY ASS REALLY ITCHES ME.
I HOPE NO ONE SEES!
IT SMELLS AND I LIKE IT!
MMM, GOOD!

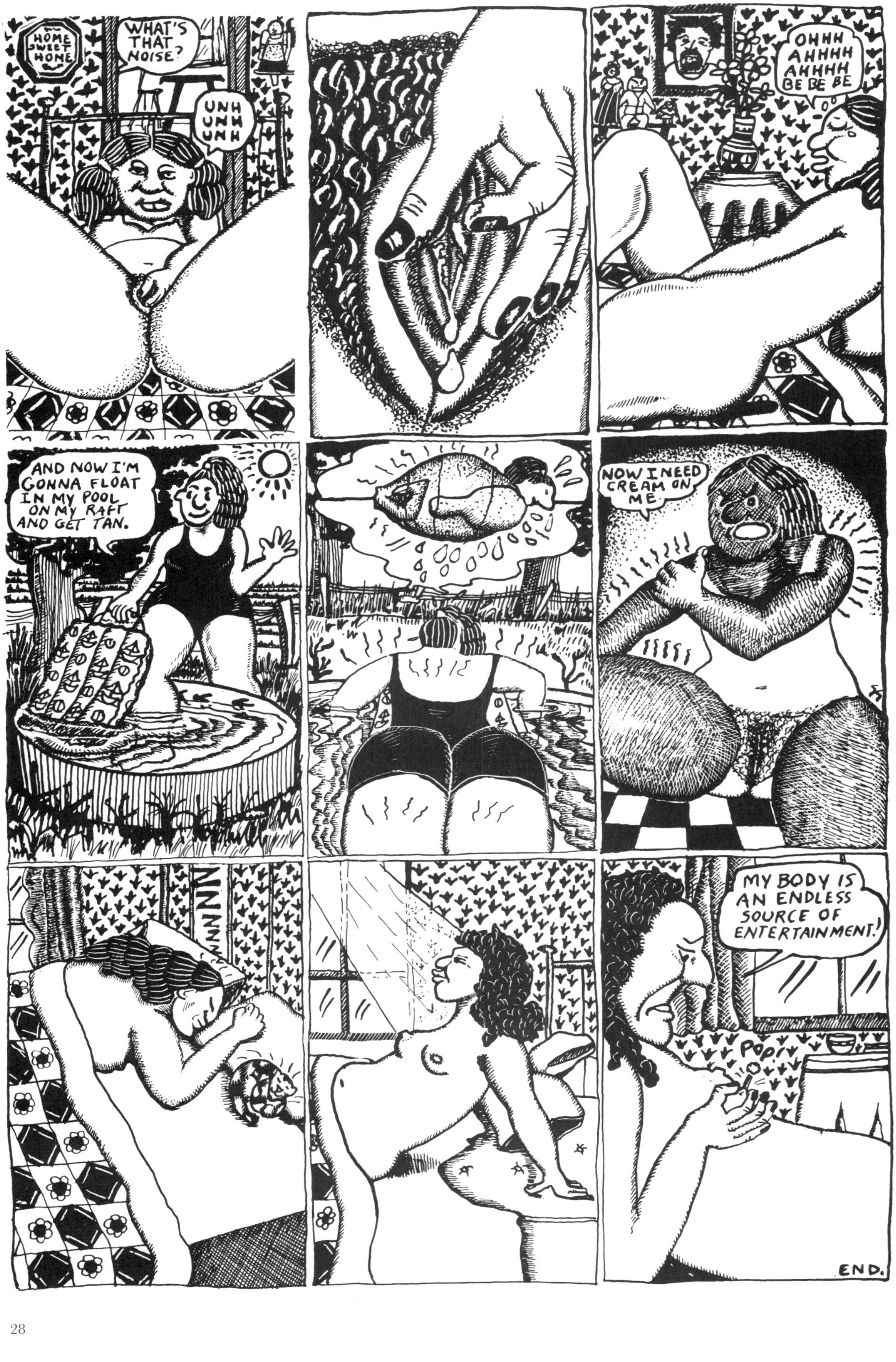
HOME SWEET HOME
WHAT'S THAT NOISE?
UNH UNH UNH
OHHH AHHHH AHHHH BE BE BE
AND NOW I'M GONNA FLOAT IN MY POOL ON MY RAFT AND GET TAN.
NOW I NEED CREAM ON ME.
MY BODY IS AN ENDLESS SOURCE OF ENTERTAINMENT!
POP!
END.

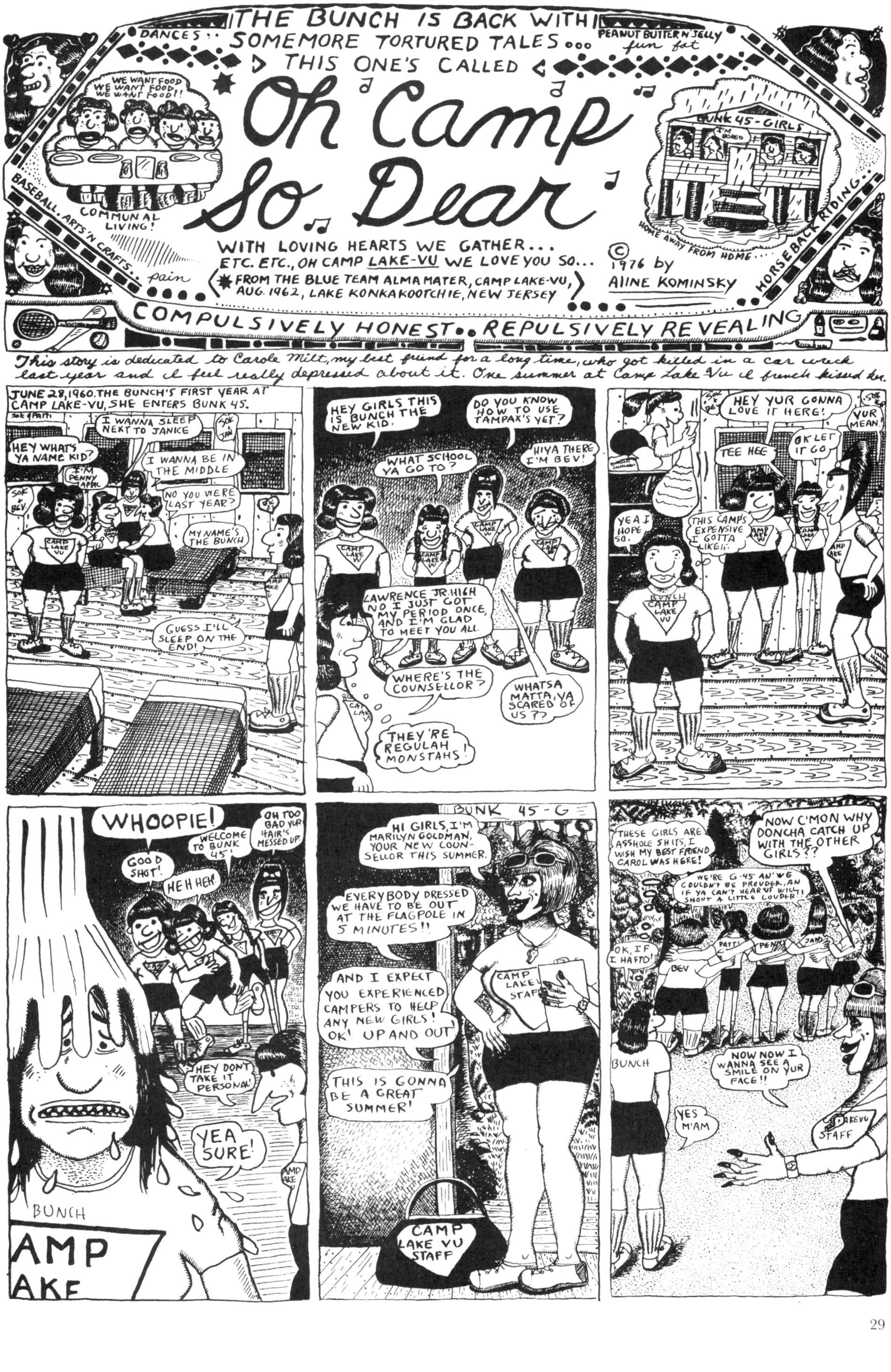
THE BUNCH IS BACK WITH SOMEMORE TORTURED TALES...
THIS ONE'S CALLED
Oh Camp So Dear
DANCES
PEANUT BUTTER N JELLY
fun fat
WE WANT FOOD WE WANT FOOD WE WANT FOOD!!
COMMUNAL LIVING!
BUNK 45 - GIRLS
I'M BORED
HOME AWAY FROM HOME
BASEBALL. ARTS 'N CRAFTS..
pain
HORSEBACK RIDING..
WITH LOVING HEARTS WE GATHER...
ETC. ETC., OH CAMP LAKE-VU WE LOVE YOU SO...
FROM THE BLUE TEAM ALMA MATER, CAMP LAKE-VU, AUG. 1962, LAKE KONKAKOOTCHIE, NEW JERSEY
© 1976 by AlINE KOMINSKY
COMPULSIVELY HONEST.. REPULSIVELY REVEALING
This story is dedicated to Carole Milt, my best friend for a long time, who got killed in a car wreck last year and I feel really depressed about it. One summer at Camp Lake Vu I french kissed her.
JUNE 28, 1960. THE BUNCH'S FIRST YEAR AT CAMP LAKE-VU, SHE ENTERS BUNK 45.
I WANNA SLEEP NEXT TO JANICE
HEY WHAT'S YA NAME KID?
I'M PENNY
I WANNA BE IN THE MIDDLE
NO YOU WERE LAST YEAR?
MY NAME'S THE BUNCH
GUESS I'LL SLEEP ON THE END!
HEY GIRLS THIS IS BUNCH THE NEW KID.
DO YOU KNOW HOW TO USE TAMPAX'S YET?
WHAT SCHOOL YA GO TO?
HIYA THERE I'M BEV!
LAWRENCE JR. HIGH NO I JUST GOT MY PERIOD ONCE, AND I'M GLAD TO MEET YOU ALL.
WHERE'S THE COUNSELLOR?
WHATSA MATTA, YA SCARED OF US??
THEY'RE REGULAH MONSTAHS!
HEY YUR GONNA LOVE IT HERE!
YUR MEAN!
TEE HEE
OK LET IT GO
YEA I HOPE SO.
THIS CAMP'S EXPENSIVE I GOTTA LIKE IT.
WHOOPIE!
WELCOME TO BUNK 45!
OH TOO BAD YUR HAIR'S MESSED UP.
GOOD SHOT!
HEH HEH
HEY DON'T TAKE IT PERSONAL!
YEA SURE!
BUNCH
BUNK 45 - G
HI GIRLS, I'M MARILYN GOLDMAN, YOUR NEW COUNSELLOR THIS SUMMER.
EVERYBODY DRESSED WE HAVE TO BE OUT AT THE FLAGPOLE IN 5 MINUTES!!
AND I EXPECT YOU EXPERIENCED CAMPERS TO HELP ANY NEW GIRLS! OK! UP AND OUT!
THIS IS GONNA BE A GREAT SUMMER!
CAMP LAKE STAFF
CAMP LAKE VU STAFF
THESE GIRLS ARE ASSHOLE SHITS, I WISH MY BEST FRIEND CAROL WAS HERE!
NOW C'MON WHY DONCHA CATCH UP WITH THE OTHER GIRLS??
WE'RE G-45 AN' WE COULDN'T BE PROUDER, AN IF YA CAN'T HEAR US WE'LL SHOUT A LITTLE LOUDER!
OK, IF I HAFTO!
BEV
PATTI
PENNY
JAN
BUNCH
NOW NOW I WANNA SEE A SMILE ON YUR FACE!!
YES M'AM
STAFF

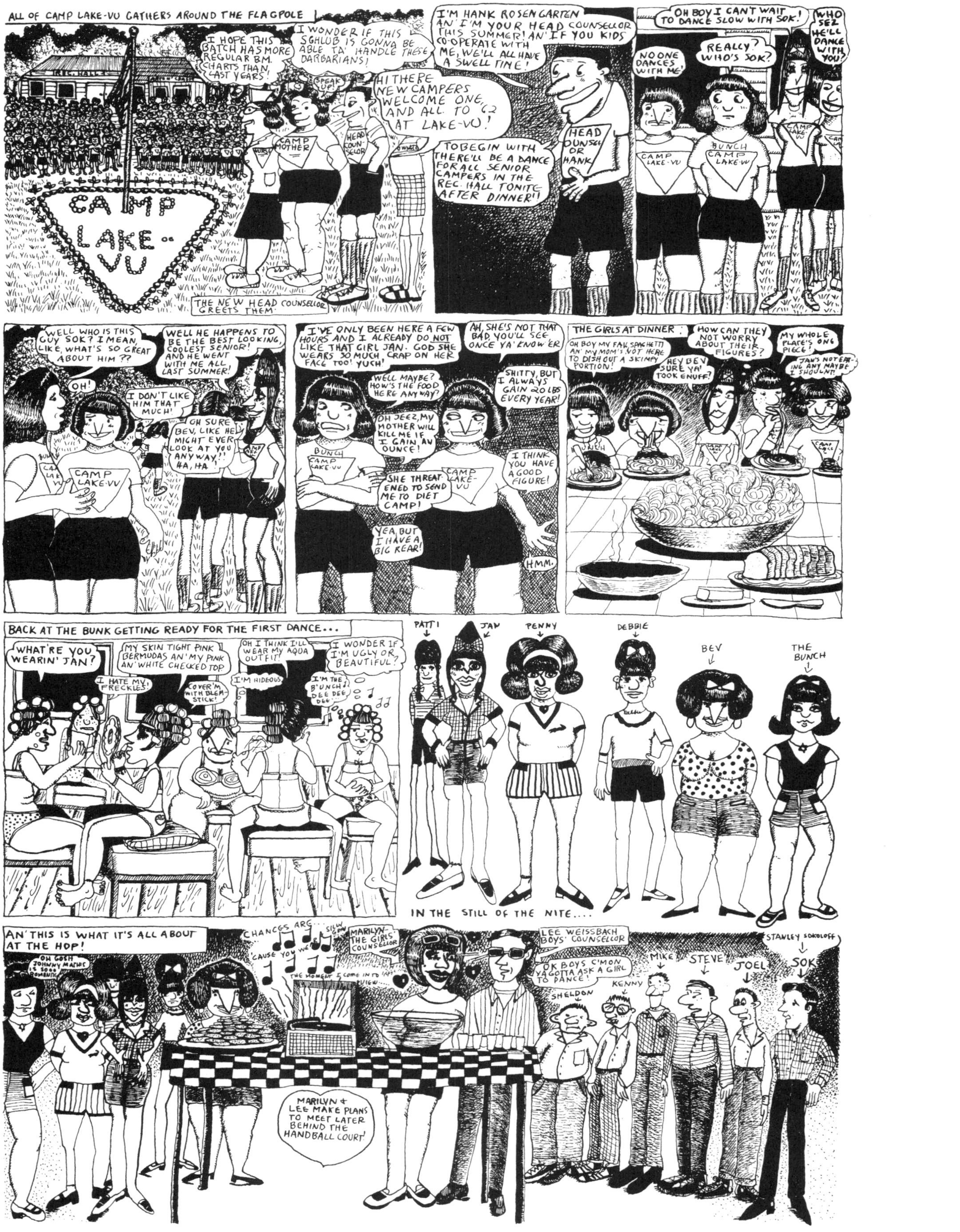

ALL OF CAMP LAKE-VU GATHERS AROUND THE FLAGPOLE
I HOPE THIS BATCH HAS MORE REGULAR B.M. CHARTS THAN LAST YEARS!
I WONDER IF THIS SCHLUB IS GONNA BE ABLE TA' HANDLE THESE BARBARIANS!
SPEAK UP!
HI THERE NEW CAMPERS WELCOME ONE, AND ALL TO '62 AT LAKE-VU!
REC. HALL
CAMP MOTHER
HEAD COUN-SELOR
CAMP LAKE-VU
THE NEW HEAD COUNSELLOR GREETS THEM.
I'M HANK ROSENGARTEN AN' I'M YOUR HEAD COUNSELLOR THIS SUMMER! AN' IF YOU KIDS CO-OPERATE WITH ME, WE'LL ALL HAVE A SWELL TIME!
TO BEGIN WITH THERE'LL BE A DANCE FOR ALL SENIOR CAMPERS IN THE REC. HALL TONITE AFTER DINNER!!
HEAD COUNSELLOR HANK
OH BOY I CAN'T WAIT TO DANCE SLOW WITH SOK!
WHO SEZ HE'LL DANCE WITH YOU?
NO ONE DANCES WITH ME!
REALLY? WHO'S SOK?
CAMP LAKE-VU
BUNCH
WELL WHO IS THIS GUY SOK? I MEAN, LIKE, WHAT'S SO GREAT ABOUT HIM??
WELL HE HAPPENS TO BE THE BEST LOOKING, COOLEST SENIOR! AND HE WENT WITH ME ALL LAST SUMMER!
OH!
I DON'T LIKE HIM THAT MUCH!
OH SURE BEV, LIKE HE MIGHT EVER LOOK AT YOU ANYWAY!! HA, HA!
I'VE ONLY BEEN HERE A FEW HOURS AND I ALREADY DO NOT LIKE THAT GIRL JAN. GOD SHE WEARS SO MUCH CRAP ON HER FACE TOO! YUCH!
AH, SHE'S NOT THAT BAD, YOU'LL SEE ONCE YA' KNOW 'ER
WELL MAYBE? HOW'S THE FOOD HERE ANYWAY?
SHITTY, BUT I ALWAYS GAIN 20 LBS EVERY YEAR!
OH JEEZ, MY MOTHER WILL KILL ME IF I GAIN AN OUNCE!
SHE THREATENED TO SEND ME TO DIET CAMP!
I THINK YOU HAVE A GOOD FIGURE!
YEA, BUT I HAVE A BIG REAR!
HMM.
THE GIRLS AT DINNER:
OH BOY MY FAV. SPAGHETTI AN' MY MOM'S NOT HERE TO DISH OUT A SKIMPY PORTION!
HOW CAN THEY NOT WORRY ABOUT THEIR FIGURES?
HEY BEV SURE YA' TOOK ENUFF?
MY WHOLE PLATE'S ONE PIECE!
JAN'S NOT EATING ANY MAYBE I SHOULN'T!
BACK AT THE BUNK GETTING READY FOR THE FIRST DANCE...
WHAT'RE YOU WEARIN' JAN?
MY SKIN TIGHT PINK BERMUDAS AN' MY PINK AN' WHITE CHECKED TOP
I HATE MY FRECKLES!
COVER 'M WITH BLEM-STICK!
OH I THINK I'LL WEAR MY AQUA OUTFIT!
I'M HIDEOUS
I WONDER IF I'M UGLY OR BEAUTIFUL?
I'M THE B'UNCH DEE DEE DEE...
PATTI
JAN
PENNY
DEBBIE
BEV
THE BUNCH
IN THE STILL OF THE NITE....
AN' THIS IS WHAT IT'S ALL ABOUT AT THE HOP!
OH GOSH JOHNNY MATHIS IS SOOO ROMANTIC
CHANCES ARE... 'CAUSE YOU WE'RE SILLY GRIN
THE MOMENT I COME INTO VIEW....
MARILYN THE GIRLS' COUNSELLOR
LEE WEISSBACH BOYS' COUNSELLOR
OK BOYS C'MON YA GOTTA ASK A GIRL TO DANCE!
SHELDON
KENNY
MIKE
STEVE
JOEL
STANLEY SOKOLOFF
SOK
MARILYN & LEE MAKE PLANS TO MEET LATER BEHIND THE HANDBALL COURT!

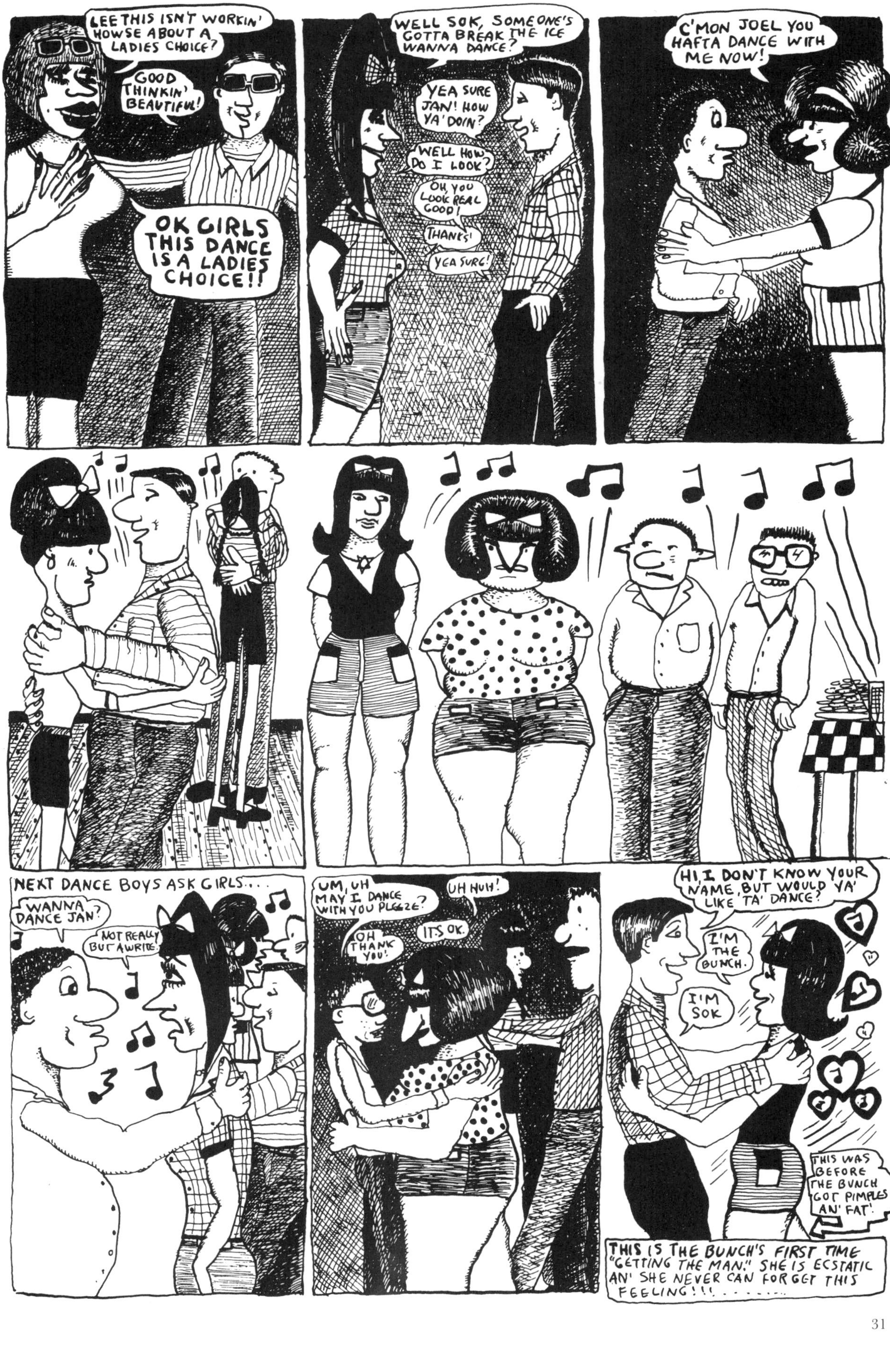
LEE THIS ISN'T WORKIN' HOWSE ABOUT A LADIES CHOICE?
GOOD THINKIN' BEAUTIFUL!
OK GIRLS THIS DANCE IS A LADIES CHOICE!!
WELL SOK, SOMEONE'S GOTTA BREAK THE ICE WANNA DANCE?
YEA SURE JAN! HOW YA' DOIN?
WELL HOW DO I LOOK?
OH, YOU LOOK REAL GOOD!
THANKS!
YEA SURE!
C'MON JOEL YOU HAFTA DANCE WITH ME NOW!
NEXT DANCE BOYS ASK GIRLS...
WANNA DANCE JAN?
NOT REALLY BUT AWRITE.
UM, UH MAY I DANCE WITH YOU PLEEZE?
UH HUH!
OH THANK YOU!
ITS OK.
HI, I DON'T KNOW YOUR NAME, BUT WOULD YA' LIKE TA' DANCE?
I'M THE BUNCH.
I'M SOK
THIS WAS BEFORE THE BUNCH GOT PIMPLES AN' FAT.
THIS IS THE BUNCH'S FIRST TIME "GETTING THE MAN." SHE IS ECSTATIC AN' SHE NEVER CAN FORGET THIS FEELING!!! . . . . . .

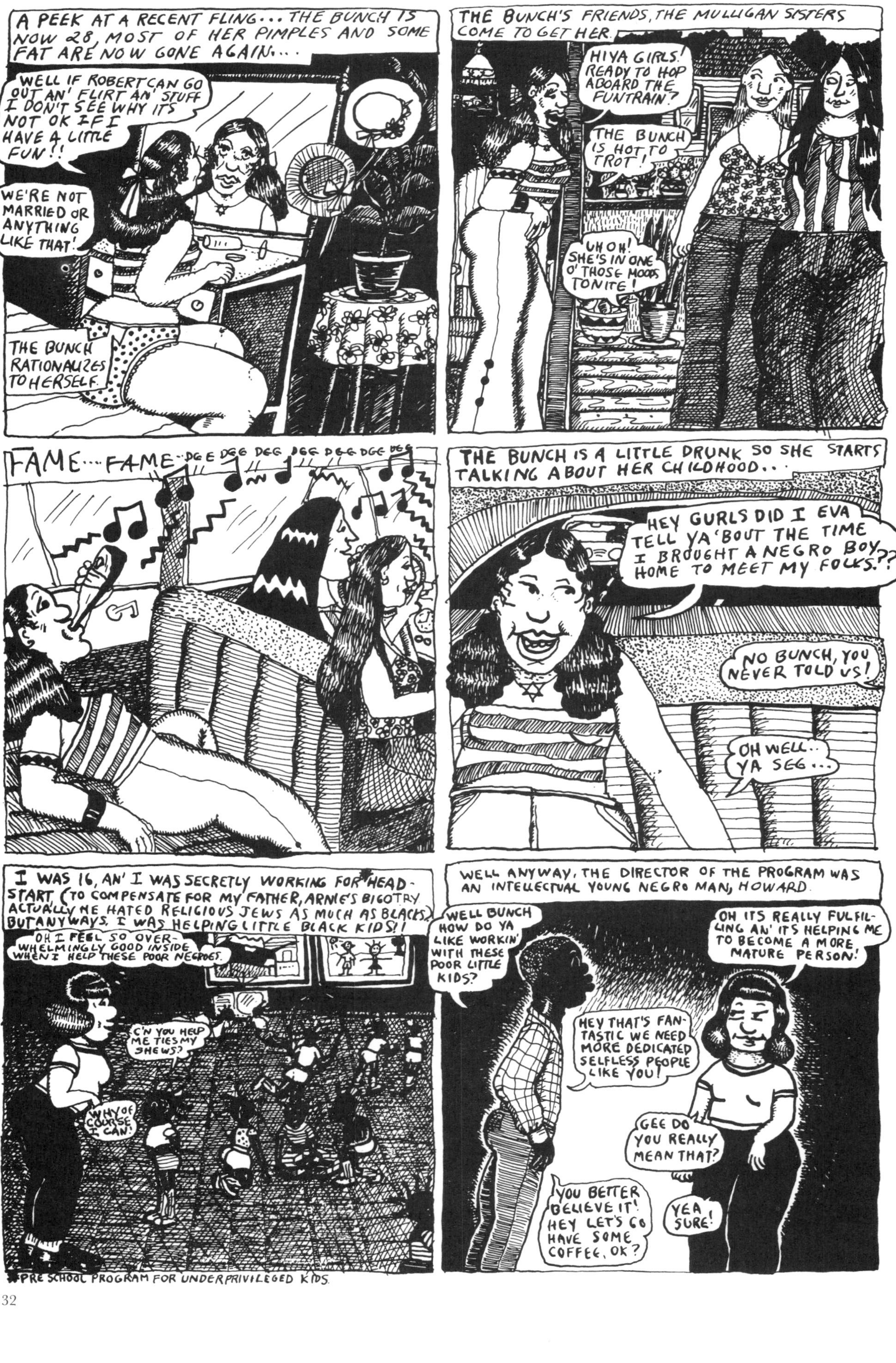

A PEEK AT A RECENT FLING... THE BUNCH IS NOW 28, MOST OF HER PIMPLES AND SOME FAT ARE NOW GONE AGAIN...
WELL IF ROBERT CAN GO OUT AN' FLIRT AN' STUFF I DON'T SEE WHY ITS NOT OK IF I HAVE A LITTLE FUN!!
WE'RE NOT MARRIED OR ANYTHING LIKE THAT!
THE BUNCH RATIONALIZES TO HERSELF.
THE BUNCH'S FRIENDS, THE MULLIGAN SISTERS COME TO GET HER.
HIYA GIRLS! READY TO HOP ABOARD THE FUNTRAIN?
THE BUNCH IS HOT TO TROT!
UH OH! SHE'S IN ONE O' THOSE MOODS TONITE!
FAME... FAME... DGE DGE DGE DGE DGE DGE DGE
THE BUNCH IS A LITTLE DRUNK SO SHE STARTS TALKING ABOUT HER CHILDHOOD..
HEY GURLS DID I EVA TELL YA 'BOUT THE TIME I BROUGHT A NEGRO BOY HOME TO MEET MY FOLKS??
NO BUNCH, YOU NEVER TOLD US!
OH WELL.. YA SEE...
I WAS 16, AN' I WAS SECRETLY WORKING FOR *HEAD-START (TO COMPENSATE FOR MY FATHER, ARNIE'S BIGOTRY ACTUALLY HE HATED RELIGIOUS JEWS AS MUCH AS BLACKS). BUT ANYWAYS, I WAS HELPING LITTLE BLACK KIDS!!
OH I FEEL SO OVER-WHELMINGLY GOOD INSIDE WHEN I HELP THESE POOR NEGROES.
C'N YOU HELP ME TIES MY SHEWS?
WHY OF COURSE I CAN!
*PRE SCHOOL PROGRAM FOR UNDERPRIVILEGED KIDS.
WELL ANYWAY, THE DIRECTOR OF THE PROGRAM WAS AN INTELLECTUAL YOUNG NEGRO MAN, HOWARD.
WELL BUNCH HOW DO YA LIKE WORKIN' WITH THESE POOR LITTLE KIDS?
OH ITS REALLY FULFIL-LING AN' IT'S HELPING ME TO BECOME A MORE NATURE PERSON!
HEY THAT'S FAN-TASTIC WE NEED MORE DEDICATED SELFLESS PEOPLE LIKE YOU!
GEE DO YOU REALLY MEAN THAT?
YOU BETTER BELIEVE IT! HEY LET'S GO HAVE SOME COFFEE, OK?
YEA SURE!

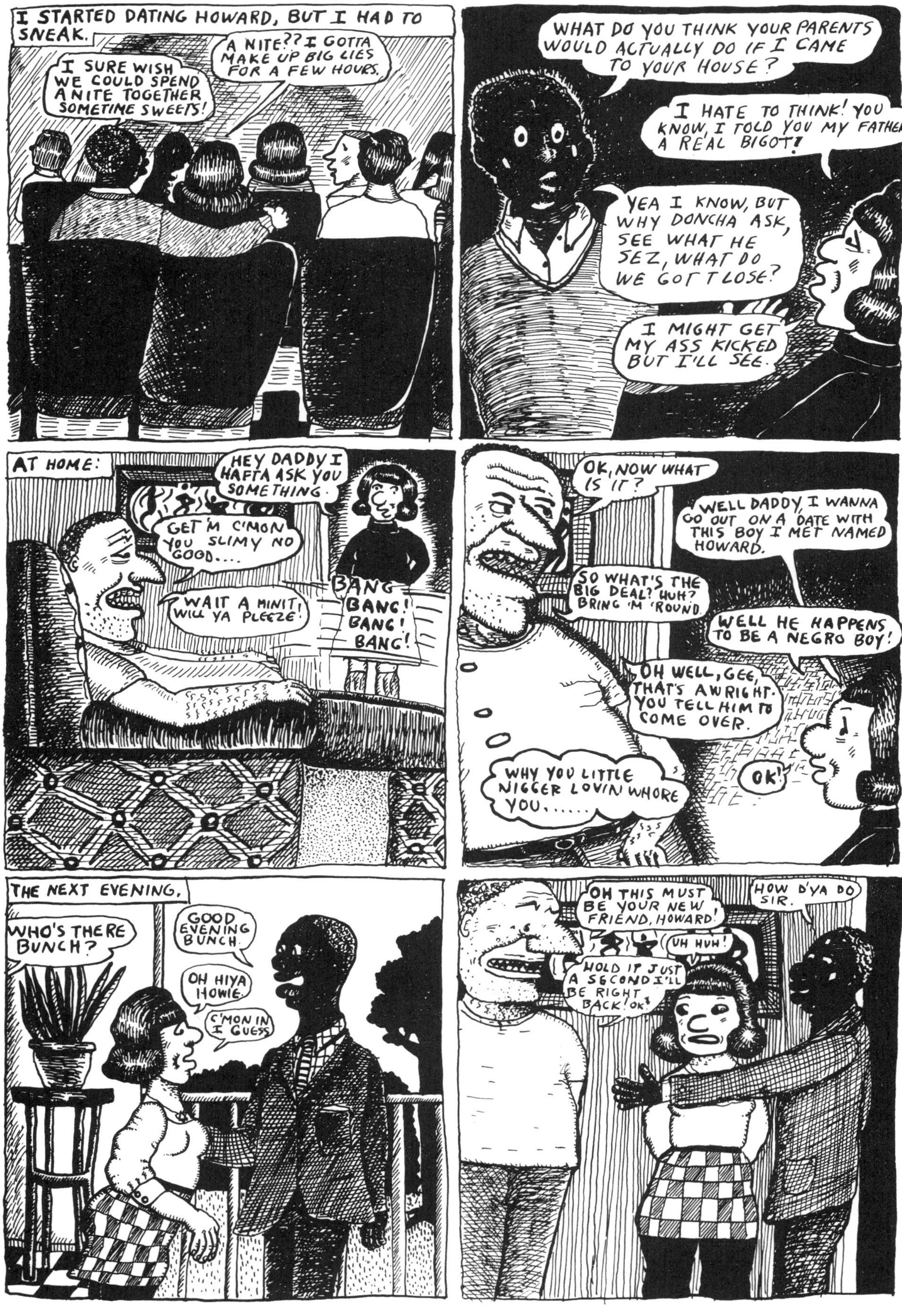
I STARTED DATING HOWARD, BUT I HAD TO SNEAK.
I SURE WISH WE COULD SPEND A NITE TOGETHER SOMETIME SWEETS!
A NITE?? I GOTTA MAKE UP BIG LIES FOR A FEW HOURS.
WHAT DO YOU THINK YOUR PARENTS WOULD ACTUALLY DO IF I CAME TO YOUR HOUSE?
I HATE TO THINK! YOU KNOW, I TOLD YOU MY FATHER'S A REAL BIGOT!
YEA I KNOW, BUT WHY DONCHA ASK, SEE WHAT HE SEZ, WHAT DO WE GOT T LOSE?
I MIGHT GET MY ASS KICKED BUT I'LL SEE.
AT HOME:
HEY DADDY I HAFTA ASK YOU SOMETHING.
GET'M C'MON YOU SLIMY NO GOOD....
WAIT A MINIT WILL YA PLEEZE!
BANG BANG! BANG! BANG!
OK, NOW WHAT IS IT?
WELL DADDY, I WANNA GO OUT ON A DATE WITH THIS BOY I MET NAMED HOWARD.
SO WHAT'S THE BIG DEAL? HUH? BRING 'M 'ROUND.
WELL HE HAPPENS TO BE A NEGRO BOY!
OH WELL, GEE, THAT'S AWRIGHT. YOU TELL HIM TO COME OVER.
WHY YOU LITTLE NIGGER LOVIN' WHORE YOU.....
OK!
THE NEXT EVENING.
WHO'S THERE BUNCH?
GOOD EVENING BUNCH.
OH HIYA HOWIE.
C'MON IN I GUESS.
OH THIS MUST BE YOUR NEW FRIEND, HOWARD!
HOW D'YA DO SIR.
UH HUH!
HOLD IT JUST A SECOND I'LL BE RIGHT BACK! OK?

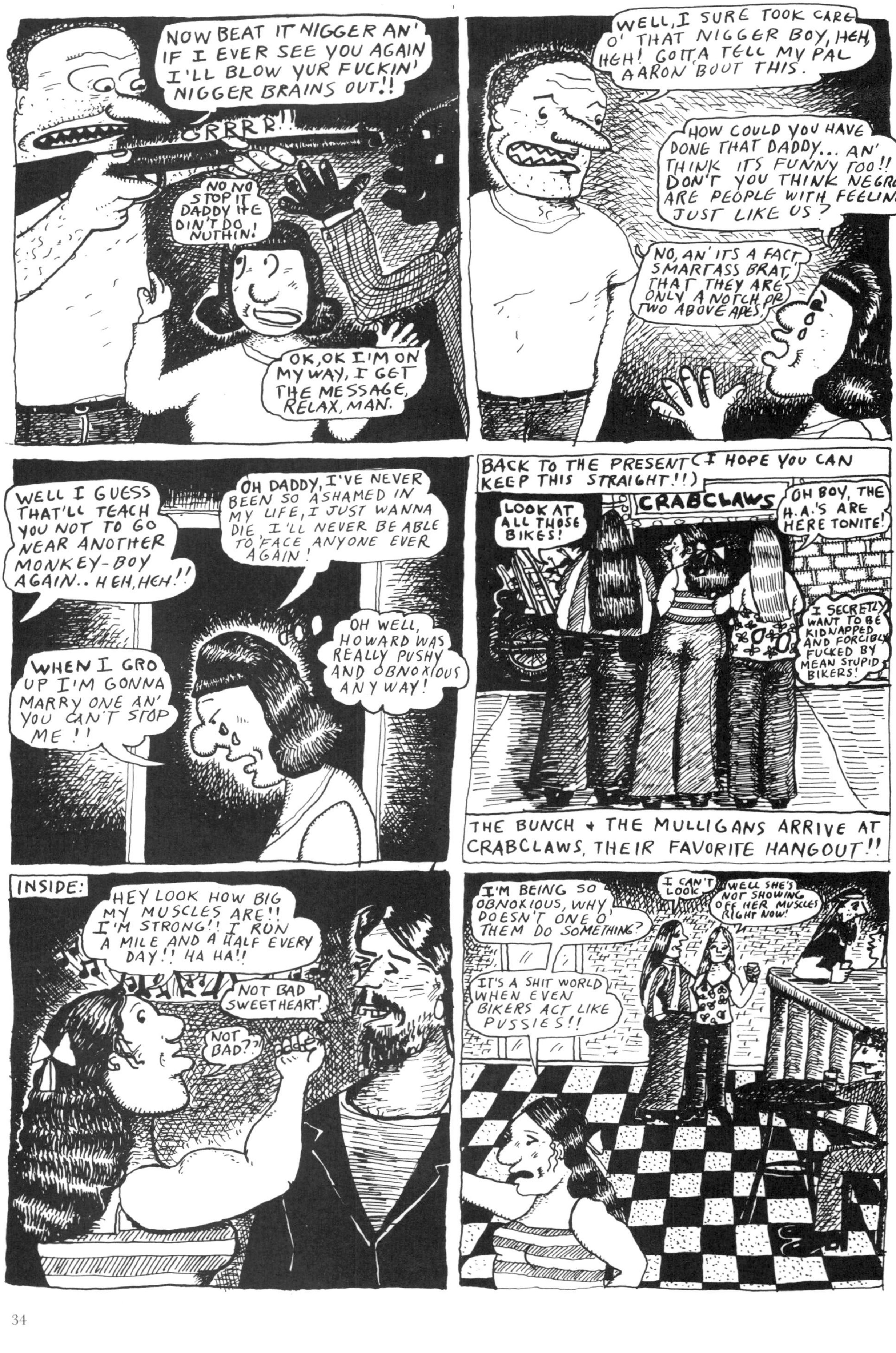
NOW BEAT IT NIGGER AN' IF I EVER SEE YOU AGAIN I'LL BLOW YUR FUCKIN' NIGGER BRAINS OUT!!
GRRRR!
NO NO STOP IT DADDY HE DIN'T DO NUTHIN!
OK, OK I'M ON MY WAY, I GET THE MESSAGE, RELAX, MAN.
WELL, I SURE TOOK CARE O' THAT NIGGER BOY, HEH, HEH! GOTTA TELL MY PAL AARON 'BOUT THIS.
HOW COULD YOU HAVE DONE THAT DADDY... AN' THINK ITS FUNNY TOO!! DON'T YOU THINK NEGROES ARE PEOPLE WITH FEELINGS JUST LIKE US?
NO, AN' ITS A FACT, SMARTASS BRAT, THAT THEY ARE ONLY A NOTCH OR TWO ABOVE APES!
WELL I GUESS THAT'LL TEACH YOU NOT TO GO NEAR ANOTHER MONKEY-BOY AGAIN.. HEH, HEH!!
OH DADDY, I'VE NEVER BEEN SO ASHAMED IN MY LIFE, I JUST WANNA DIE, I'LL NEVER BE ABLE TO FACE ANYONE EVER AGAIN!
WHEN I GRO UP I'M GONNA MARRY ONE AN' YOU CAN'T STOP ME!!
OH WELL, HOWARD WAS REALLY PUSHY AND OBNOXIOUS ANYWAY!
BACK TO THE PRESENT (I HOPE YOU CAN KEEP THIS STRAIGHT!!)
CRABCLAWS
LOOK AT ALL THOSE BIKES!
OH BOY, THE H.A.'S ARE HERE TONITE!
I SECRETLY WANT TO BE KIDNAPPED AND FORCIBLY FUCKED BY MEAN STUPID BIKERS!
THE BUNCH & THE MULLIGANS ARRIVE AT CRABCLAWS, THEIR FAVORITE HANGOUT!!
INSIDE:
HEY LOOK HOW BIG MY MUSCLES ARE!! I'M STRONG!! I RUN A MILE AND A HALF EVERY DAY!! HA HA!!
NOT BAD SWEETHEART!
NOT BAD??
I'M BEING SO OBNOXIOUS, WHY DOESN'T ONE O' THEM DO SOMETHING?
I CAN'T LOOK
WELL SHE'S NOT SHOWING OFF HER MUSCLES RIGHT NOW!
IT'S A SHIT WORLD WHEN EVEN BIKERS ACT LIKE PUSSIES!!

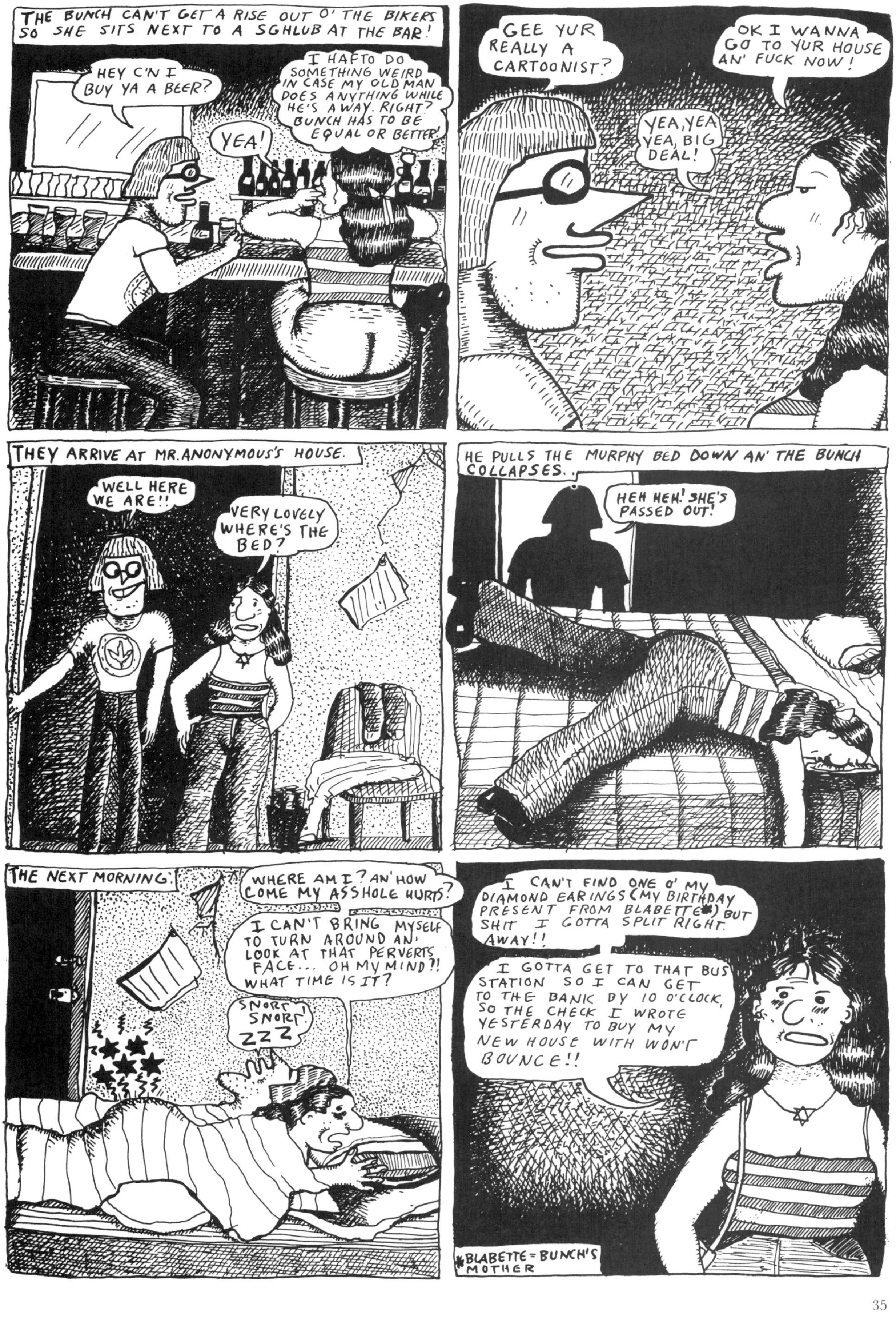
THE BUNCH CAN'T GET A RISE OUT O' THE BIKERS SO SHE SITS NEXT TO A SGHLUB AT THE BAR!
HEY C'N I BUY YA A BEER?
I HAFTO DO SOMETHING WEIRD IN CASE MY OLD MAN DOES ANYTHING WHILE HE'S AWAY. RIGHT? BUNCH HAS TO BE EQUAL OR BETTER!
YEA!
GEE YUR REALLY A CARTOONIST?
OK I WANNA GO TO YUR HOUSE AN' FUCK NOW!
YEA, YEA YEA, BIG DEAL!
THEY ARRIVE AT MR. ANONYMOUS'S HOUSE.
WELL HERE WE ARE!!
VERY LOVELY WHERE'S THE BED?
HE PULLS THE MURPHY BED DOWN AN' THE BUNCH COLLAPSES..
HEH HEH! SHE'S PASSED OUT!
THE NEXT MORNING.
WHERE AM I? AN' HOW COME MY ASSHOLE HURTS?
I CAN'T BRING MYSELF TO TURN AROUND AN' LOOK AT THAT PERVERTS FACE... OH MY MIND?! WHAT TIME IS IT?
SNORT! SNORT! ZZZ
I CAN'T FIND ONE O' MY DIAMOND EARINGS (MY BIRTHDAY PRESENT FROM BLABETTE*) BUT SHIT I GOTTA SPLIT RIGHT AWAY!!
I GOTTA GET TO THAT BUS STATION SO I CAN GET TO THE BANK BY 10 O'CLOCK, SO THE CHECK I WROTE YESTERDAY TO BUY MY NEW HOUSE WITH WON'T BOUNCE!!
*BLABETTE = BUNCH'S MOTHER

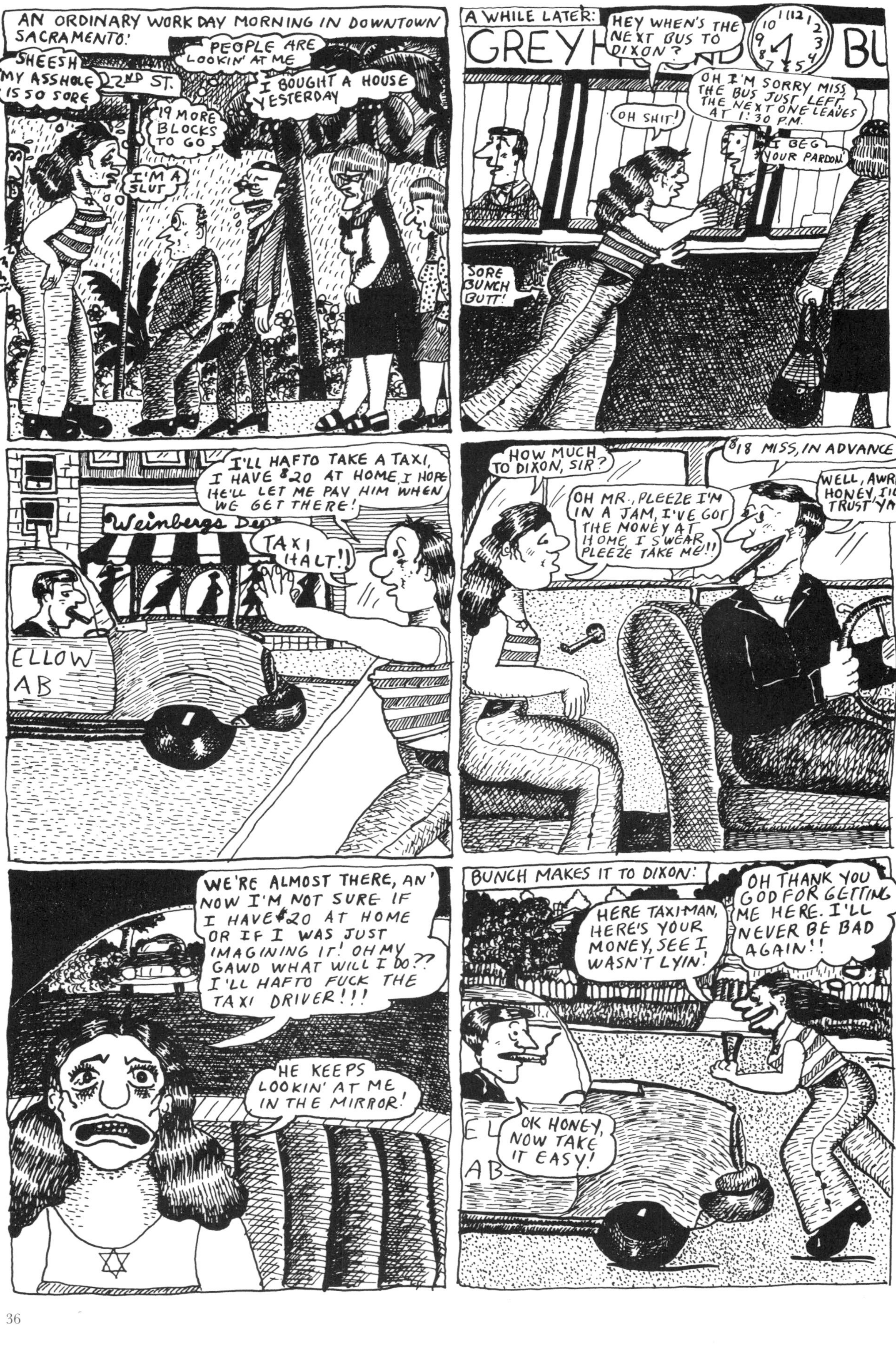
AN ORDINARY WORK DAY MORNING IN DOWNTOWN SACRAMENTO!
SHEESH MY ASSHOLE IS SO SORE
22ND ST.
PEOPLE ARE LOOKIN' AT ME
I BOUGHT A HOUSE YESTERDAY
19 MORE BLOCKS TO GO
I'M A SLUT
A WHILE LATER:
GREYH
BU
HEY WHEN'S THE NEXT BUS TO DIXON?
OH I'M SORRY MISS, THE BUS JUST LEFT, THE NEXT ONE LEAVES AT 1:30 P.M.
OH SHIT!
I BEG YOUR PARDON!
SORE BUNCH BUTT!
I'LL HAFTO TAKE A TAXI, I HAVE $20 AT HOME, I HOPE HE'LL LET ME PAY HIM WHEN WE GET THERE!
Weinbergs
TAXI HALT!!
ELLOW
AB
HOW MUCH TO DIXON, SIR?
$18 MISS, IN ADVANCE
OH MR., PLEEZE I'M IN A JAM, I'VE GOT THE MONEY AT HOME, I SWEAR, PLEEZE TAKE ME!!!
WELL, AWRIGHT HONEY, I'LL TRUST YA!
WE'RE ALMOST THERE, AN' NOW I'M NOT SURE IF I HAVE $20 AT HOME OR IF I WAS JUST IMAGINING IT! OH MY GAWD WHAT WILL I DO?? I'LL HAFTO FUCK THE TAXI DRIVER!!!
HE KEEPS LOOKIN' AT ME IN THE MIRROR!
BUNCH MAKES IT TO DIXON!
HERE TAXI-MAN, HERE'S YOUR MONEY, SEE I WASN'T LYIN'!
OH THANK YOU GOD FOR GETTING ME HERE. I'LL NEVER BE BAD AGAIN!!
OK HONEY, NOW TAKE IT EASY!
EL
AB

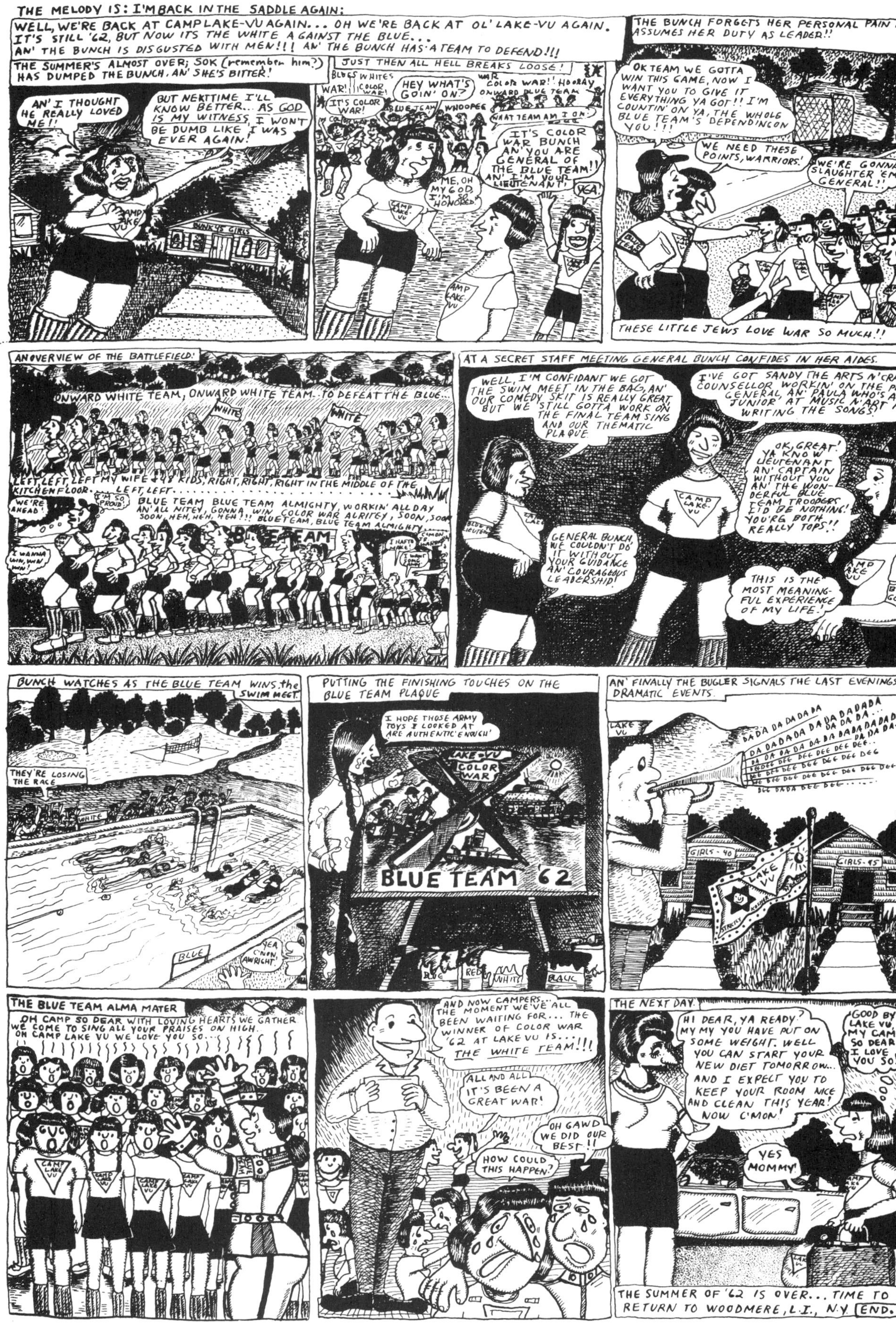

THE MELODY IS: I'M BACK IN THE SADDLE AGAIN:
WELL, WE'RE BACK AT CAMP LAKE-VU AGAIN... OH WE'RE BACK AT OL' LAKE-VU AGAIN. IT'S STILL '62, BUT NOW ITS THE WHITE AGAINST THE BLUE... AN' THE BUNCH IS DISGUSTED WITH MEN!!! AN' THE BUNCH HAS A TEAM TO DEFEND!!!
THE SUMMER'S ALMOST OVER; SOK (remember him?) HAS DUMPED THE BUNCH, AN' SHE'S BITTER!
AN' I THOUGHT HE REALLY LOVED ME!!
BUT NEXTTIME I'LL KNOW BETTER... AS GOD IS MY WITNESS, I WON'T BE DUMB LIKE I WAS EVER AGAIN!
BUNK 45 GIRLS
CAMP LAKE VU
JUST THEN ALL HELL BREAKS LOOSE!
BLUES WHITES
WAR!
COLOR WAR!
HEY WHAT'S GOIN' ON?
IT'S COLOR WAR!
BLUE TEAM
WHOOPEE
WAR
COLOR WAR!! HOORAY
ONWARD BLUE TEAM
WHAT TEAM AM I ON?
IT'S COLOR WAR BUNCH AN' YOU ARE GENERAL OF THE BLUE TEAM!! AN' I'M YOUR LIEUTENANT!
ME, OH MY GOD, I'M SO HONORED.
YEA!
THE BUNCH FORGETS HER PERSONAL PAIN AN' ASSUMES HER DUTY AS LEADER!!
OK TEAM WE GOTTA WIN THIS GAME, NOW I WANT YOU TO GIVE IT EVERYTHING YA GOT!! I'M COUNTIN' ON YA, THE WHOLE BLUE TEAM'S DEPENDIN' ON YOU!!!
WE NEED THESE POINTS, WARRIORS!
WE'RE GONNA SLAUGHTER 'EM GENERAL!!
BLUE TEAM
THESE LITTLE JEWS LOVE WAR SO MUCH!!
AN OVERVIEW OF THE BATTLEFIELD!
ONWARD WHITE TEAM, ONWARD WHITE TEAM. TO DEFEAT THE BLUE...
WHITE
WHITE
LEFT, LEFT, LEFT MY WIFE & 48 KIDS, RIGHT, RIGHT, RIGHT IN THE MIDDLE OF THE KITCHEN FLOOR. LEFT, LEFT...
WE'RE AHEAD!
I'M SO PROUD!
BLUE TEAM BLUE TEAM ALMIGHTY, WORKIN' ALL DAY AN' ALL NITEY, GONNA WIN COLOR WAR ALRITEY, SOON, SOON SOON, HEH, HEH, HEH!!! BLUE TEAM, BLUE TEAM ALMIGHTY...
BLUE TEAM
I WANNA WIN, WIN WIN!
I HAFTA MAKE!
I WANT SOME CANDY
C'MON
AT A SECRET STAFF MEETING GENERAL BUNCH CONFIDES IN HER AIDES.
WELL, I'M CONFIDANT WE GOT THE SWIM MEET IN THE BAG, AN' OUR COMEDY SKIT IS REALLY GREAT, BUT WE STILL GOTTA WORK ON THE FINAL TEAM SING AND OUR THEMATIC PLAQUE.
I'VE GOT SANDY THE ARTS N' CRAFTS COUNSELLOR WORKIN' ON THE PLAQUE GENERAL, AN' PAULA WHO'S A JUNIOR AT MUSIC N' ART IS WRITING THE SONGS!
OK, GREAT! YA KNOW LIEUTENANT AN' CAPTAIN WITHOUT YOU AN' THE WONDERFUL BLUE TEAM TROOPERS I'D BE NOTHING! YOU'RE BOTH REALLY TOPS!!
CAMP LAKE VU
GENERAL BUNCH, WE COULDN'T DO IT WITHOUT YOUR GUIDANCE AN' COURAGEOUS LEADERSHIP!
THIS IS THE MOST MEANINGFUL EXPERIENCE OF MY LIFE!
BUNCH WATCHES AS THE BLUE TEAM WINS the SWIM MEET.
THEY'RE LOSING THE RACE
WHITE
BLUE
YEA C'MON, AWRIGHT.
PUTTING THE FINISHING TOUCHES ON THE BLUE TEAM PLAQUE
I HOPE THOSE ARMY TOYS I LOOKED AT ARE AUTHENTIC ENOUGH!
LAKE-VU
COLOR WAR
BLUE TEAM '62
BLUE
RED
WHITE
BLACK
AN' FINALLY THE BUGLER SIGNALS THE LAST EVENINGS DRAMATIC EVENTS.
LAKE VU
DA DA DA DA DA DA
DA DA DA DA DA DA DA DA DA DA DA DA DA DA DA...
DA DA DA DA DA DA DA DA DA DA DA DA DA DA DA DA DA...
DEE DEE DEE DEE DEE DEE DEE DEE DEE DEE DEE DEE...
DEE DADA DEE DEE...
GIRLS-40
GIRLS-45
LAKE VU
THE BLUE TEAM ALMA MATER
OH CAMP SO DEAR WITH LOVING HEARTS WE GATHER WE COME TO SING ALL YOUR PRAISES ON HIGH. ON CAMP LAKE VU WE LOVE YOU SO...
CAMP LAKE VU
AND NOW CAMPERS... THE MOMENT WE'VE ALL BEEN WAITING FOR... THE WINNER OF COLOR WAR '62 AT LAKE VU IS... THE WHITE TEAM!!!
ALL AND ALL IT'S BEEN A GREAT WAR!
OH GAWD WE DID OUR BEST!!
HOW COULD THIS HAPPEN?
THE NEXT DAY.
HI DEAR, YA READY? MY MY YOU HAVE PUT ON SOME WEIGHT. WELL YOU CAN START YOUR NEW DIET TOMORROW... AND I EXPECT YOU TO KEEP YOUR ROOM NICE AND CLEAN THIS YEAR! NOW C'MON!
GOOD BY LAKE VU, MY CAMP SO DEAR, I LOVE YOU SO!
YES MOMMY!
THE SUMMER OF '62 IS OVER... TIME TO RETURN TO WOODMERE, L.I., N.Y.
END.

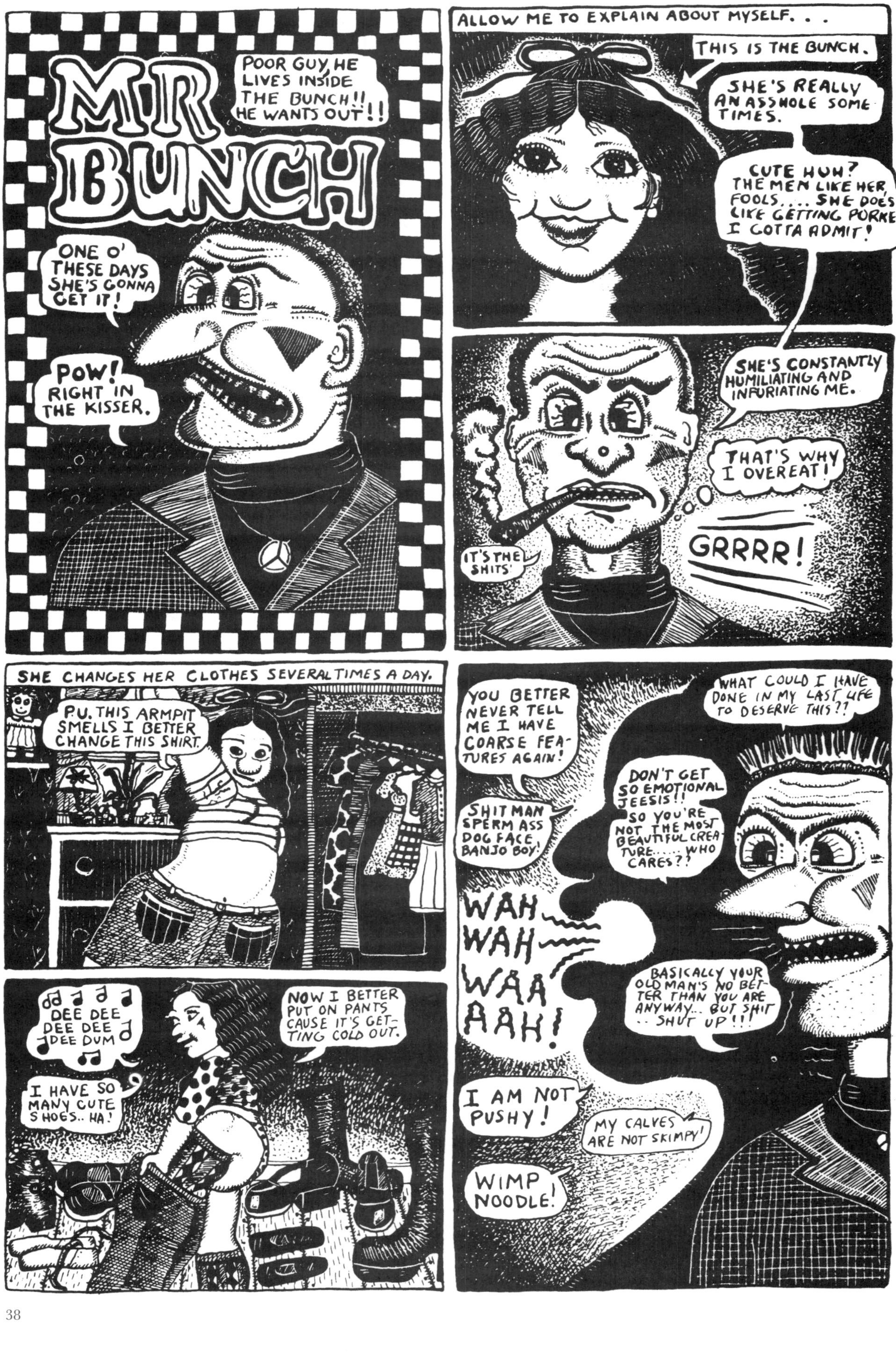

MR BUNCH
POOR GUY, HE LIVES INSIDE THE BUNCH!! HE WANTS OUT!!
ONE O' THESE DAYS SHE'S GONNA GET IT!
POW! RIGHT IN THE KISSER.
ALLOW ME TO EXPLAIN ABOUT MYSELF. . .
THIS IS THE BUNCH.
SHE'S REALLY AN ASSHOLE SOME TIMES.
CUTE HUH? THE MEN LIKE HER FOOLS.... SHE DOES LIKE GETTING PORKED I GOTTA ADMIT!
SHE'S CONSTANTLY HUMILIATING AND INFURIATING ME.
THAT'S WHY I OVEREAT!
IT'S THE SHITS
GRRRR!
SHE CHANGES HER CLOTHES SEVERAL TIMES A DAY.
P.U. THIS ARMPIT SMELLS I BETTER CHANGE THIS SHIRT.
DEE DEE DEE DEE DEE DUM
NOW I BETTER PUT ON PANTS CAUSE IT'S GETTING COLD OUT.
I HAVE SO MANY CUTE SHOES.. HA!
YOU BETTER NEVER TELL ME I HAVE COARSE FEATURES AGAIN!
WHAT COULD I HAVE DONE IN MY LAST LIFE TO DESERVE THIS??
SHITMAN SPERM ASS DOG FACE BANJO BOY!
DON'T GET SO EMOTIONAL JEESIS!! SO YOU'RE NOT THE MOST BEAUTIFUL CREATURE...... WHO CARES??
WAH WAH WAA AAH!
BASICALLY YOUR OLD MAN'S NO BETTER THAN YOU ARE ANYWAY.. BUT SHIT .. SHUT UP!!!
I AM NOT PUSHY!
MY CALVES ARE NOT SKIMPY!
WIMP NOODLE!

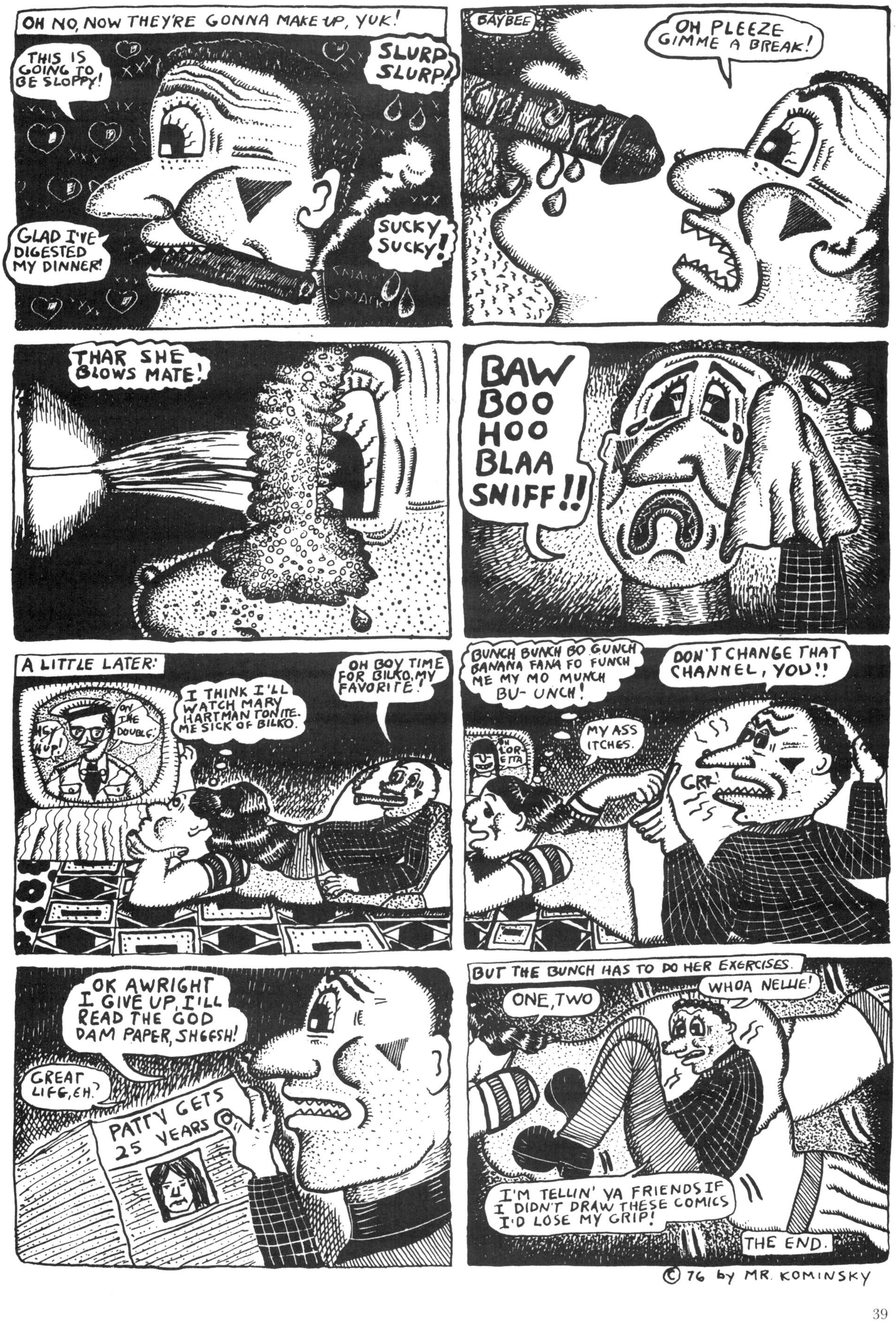

OH NO, NOW THEY'RE GONNA MAKE-UP, YUK!
THIS IS GOING TO BE SLOPPY!
SLURP SLURP!
GLAD I'VE DIGESTED MY DINNER!
SUCKY SUCKY!
SMACK SMACK
BAYBEE
OH PLEEZE GIMME A BREAK!
THAR SHE BLOWS MATE!
BAW BOO HOO BLAA SNIFF!!
A LITTLE LATER:
I THINK I'LL WATCH MARY HARTMAN TONITE. ME SICK OF BILKO.
OH BOY TIME FOR BILKO, MY FAVORITE!
HUP! HUP!
ON THE DOUBLE!
BUNCH BUNCH BO GUNCH BANANA FANA FO FUNCH ME MY MO MUNCH BU-UNCH!
DON'T CHANGE THAT CHANNEL, YOU!!
OH LORETTA
MY ASS ITCHES.
GRR!
OK AWRIGHT I GIVE UP, I'LL READ THE GOD DAM PAPER, SHEESH!
GREAT LIFE, EH?
PATTY GETS 25 YEARS
BUT THE BUNCH HAS TO DO HER EXERCISES.
ONE, TWO
WHOA NELLIE!
I'M TELLIN' YA FRIENDS IF I DIDN'T DRAW THESE COMICS I'D LOSE MY GRIP!
THE END.

© 76 by MR. KOMINSKY

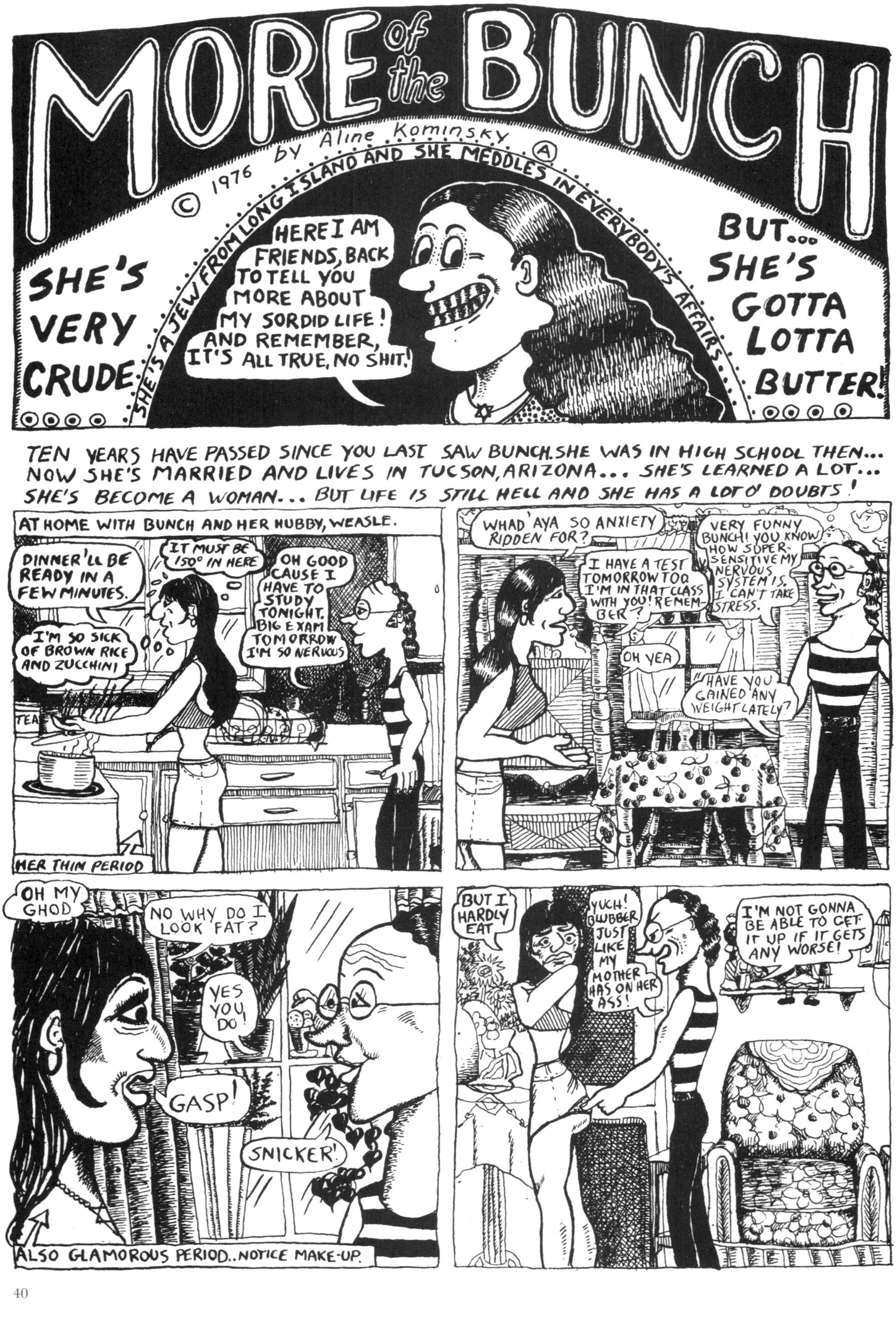

MORE of the BUNCH
by Aline Kominsky Ⓐ
© 1976
SHE'S A JEW FROM LONG ISLAND AND SHE MEDDLES IN EVERYBODY'S AFFAIRS
SHE'S VERY CRUDE
HERE I AM FRIENDS, BACK TO TELL YOU MORE ABOUT MY SORDID LIFE! AND REMEMBER, IT'S ALL TRUE, NO SHIT!
BUT... SHE'S GOTTA LOTTA BUTTER!
TEN YEARS HAVE PASSED SINCE YOU LAST SAW BUNCH. SHE WAS IN HIGH SCHOOL THEN... NOW SHE'S MARRIED AND LIVES IN TUCSON, ARIZONA... SHE'S LEARNED A LOT... SHE'S BECOME A WOMAN... BUT LIFE IS STILL HELL AND SHE HAS A LOT O' DOUBTS!
AT HOME WITH BUNCH AND HER HUBBY, WEASLE.
DINNER'LL BE READY IN A FEW MINUTES.
IT MUST BE 150° IN HERE
OH GOOD CAUSE I HAVE TO STUDY TONIGHT. BIG EXAM TOMORROW I'M SO NERVOUS
I'M SO SICK OF BROWN RICE AND ZUCCHINI
TEA
HER THIN PERIOD
WHAD'AYA SO ANXIETY RIDDEN FOR?
I HAVE A TEST TOMORROW TOO I'M IN THAT CLASS WITH YOU! REMEMBER?
VERY FUNNY BUNCH! YOU KNOW HOW SUPER-SENSITIVE MY NERVOUS SYSTEM IS. I CAN'T TAKE STRESS.
OH YEA
HAVE YOU GAINED ANY WEIGHT LATELY?
OH MY GHOD
NO WHY DO I LOOK FAT?
YES YOU DO!
GASP!
SNICKER!
ALSO GLAMOROUS PERIOD.. NOTICE MAKE-UP.
BUT I HARDLY EAT
YUCH! BLUBBER JUST LIKE MY MOTHER HAS ON HER ASS!
I'M NOT GONNA BE ABLE TO GET IT UP IF IT GETS ANY WORSE!

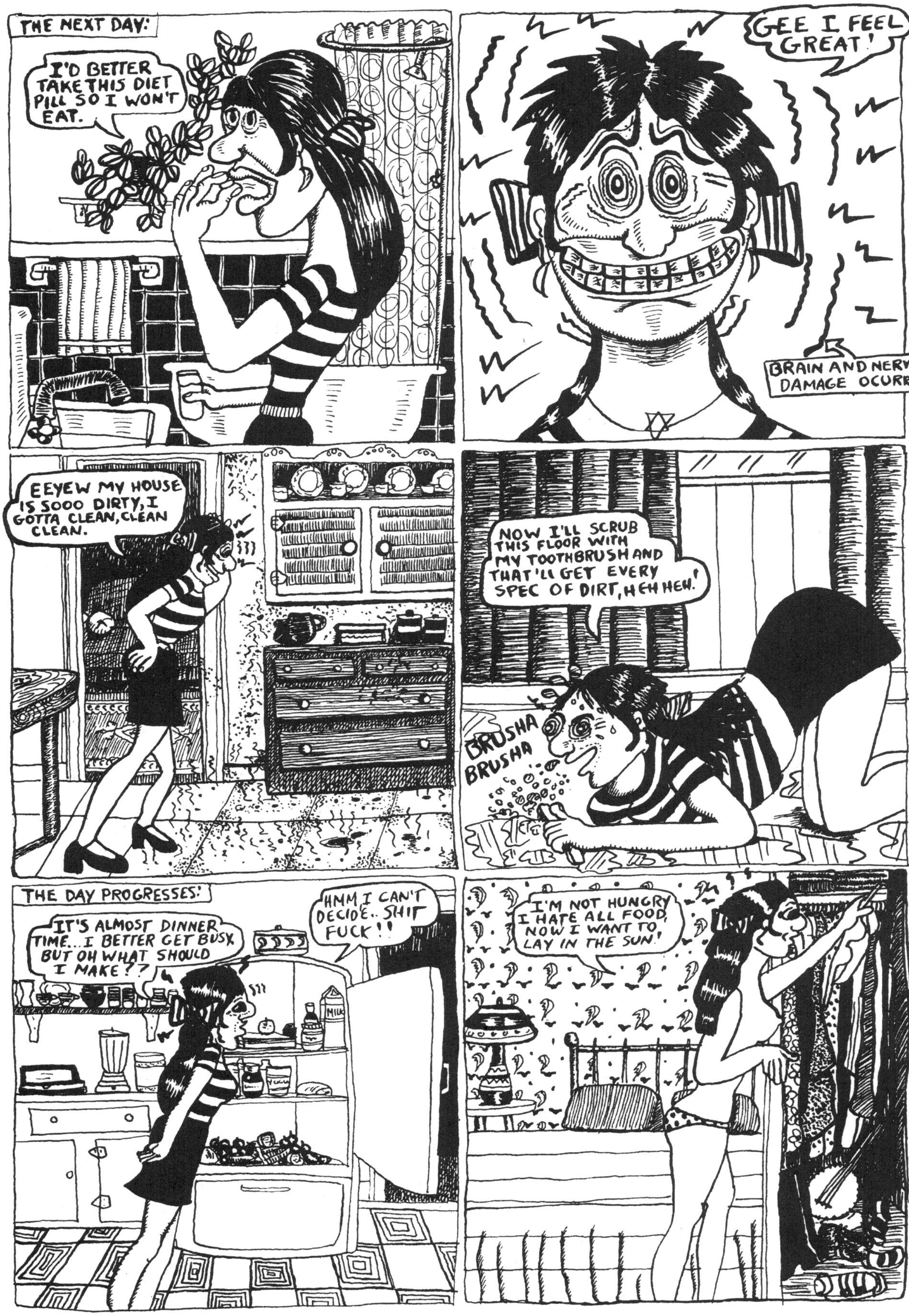
THE NEXT DAY:
I'D BETTER TAKE THIS DIET PILL SO I WON'T EAT.
GEE I FEEL GREAT!
BRAIN AND NERVE DAMAGE OCURRING
EEYEW MY HOUSE IS SOOO DIRTY, I GOTTA CLEAN, CLEAN CLEAN.
NOW I'LL SCRUB THIS FLOOR WITH MY TOOTHBRUSH AND THAT'LL GET EVERY SPEC OF DIRT, HEH HEH!
BRUSHA BRUSHA
THE DAY PROGRESSES:
IT'S ALMOST DINNER TIME... I BETTER GET BUSY, BUT OH WHAT SHOULD I MAKE??
HMM I CAN'T DECIDE.. SHIT FUCK!!
MILK
I'M NOT HUNGRY I HATE ALL FOOD, NOW I WANT TO LAY IN THE SUN!

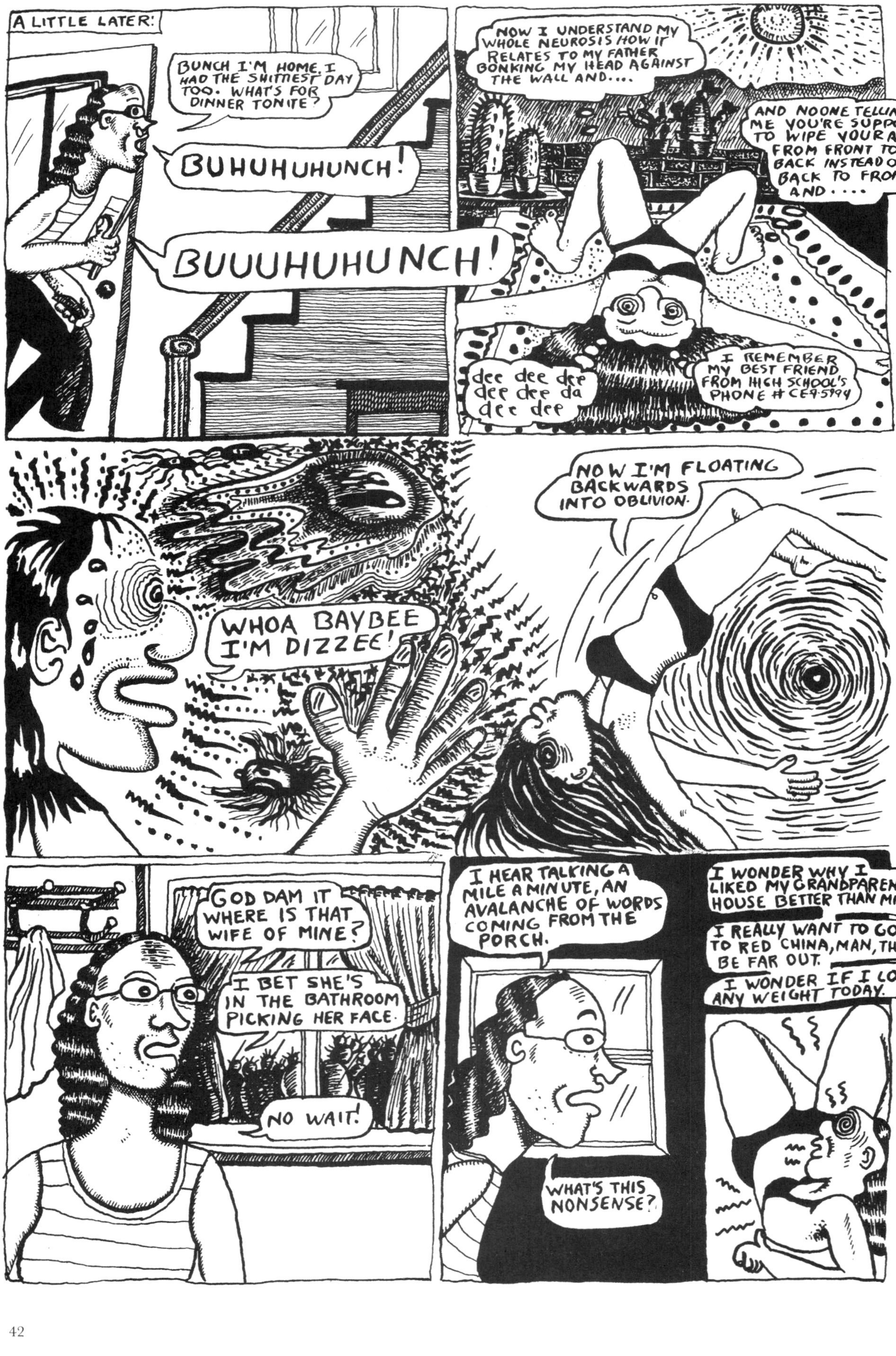
A LITTLE LATER:
BUNCH I'M HOME. I HAD THE SHITTIEST DAY TOO. WHAT'S FOR DINNER TONITE?
BUHUHUHUNCH!
BUUUHUHUNCH!
NOW I UNDERSTAND MY WHOLE NEUROSIS HOW IT RELATES TO MY FATHER BONKING MY HEAD AGAINST THE WALL AND....
AND NOONE TELLING ME YOU'RE SUPPOSED TO WIPE YOUR ASS FROM FRONT TO BACK INSTEAD OF BACK TO FRONT AND....
dee dee dee dee dee da dee dee
I REMEMBER MY BEST FRIEND FROM HIGH SCHOOL'S PHONE # CE9-5994
WHOA BAYBEE I'M DIZZEE!
NOW I'M FLOATING BACKWARDS INTO OBLIVION.
GOD DAM IT WHERE IS THAT WIFE OF MINE?
I BET SHE'S IN THE BATHROOM PICKING HER FACE.
NO WAIT!
I HEAR TALKING A MILE A MINUTE, AN AVALANCHE OF WORDS COMING FROM THE PORCH.
WHAT'S THIS NONSENSE?
I WONDER WHY I LIKED MY GRANDPARENTS' HOUSE BETTER THAN MINE?
I REALLY WANT TO GO TO RED CHINA, MAN, THAT'D BE FAR OUT.
I WONDER IF I LOST ANY WEIGHT TODAY.

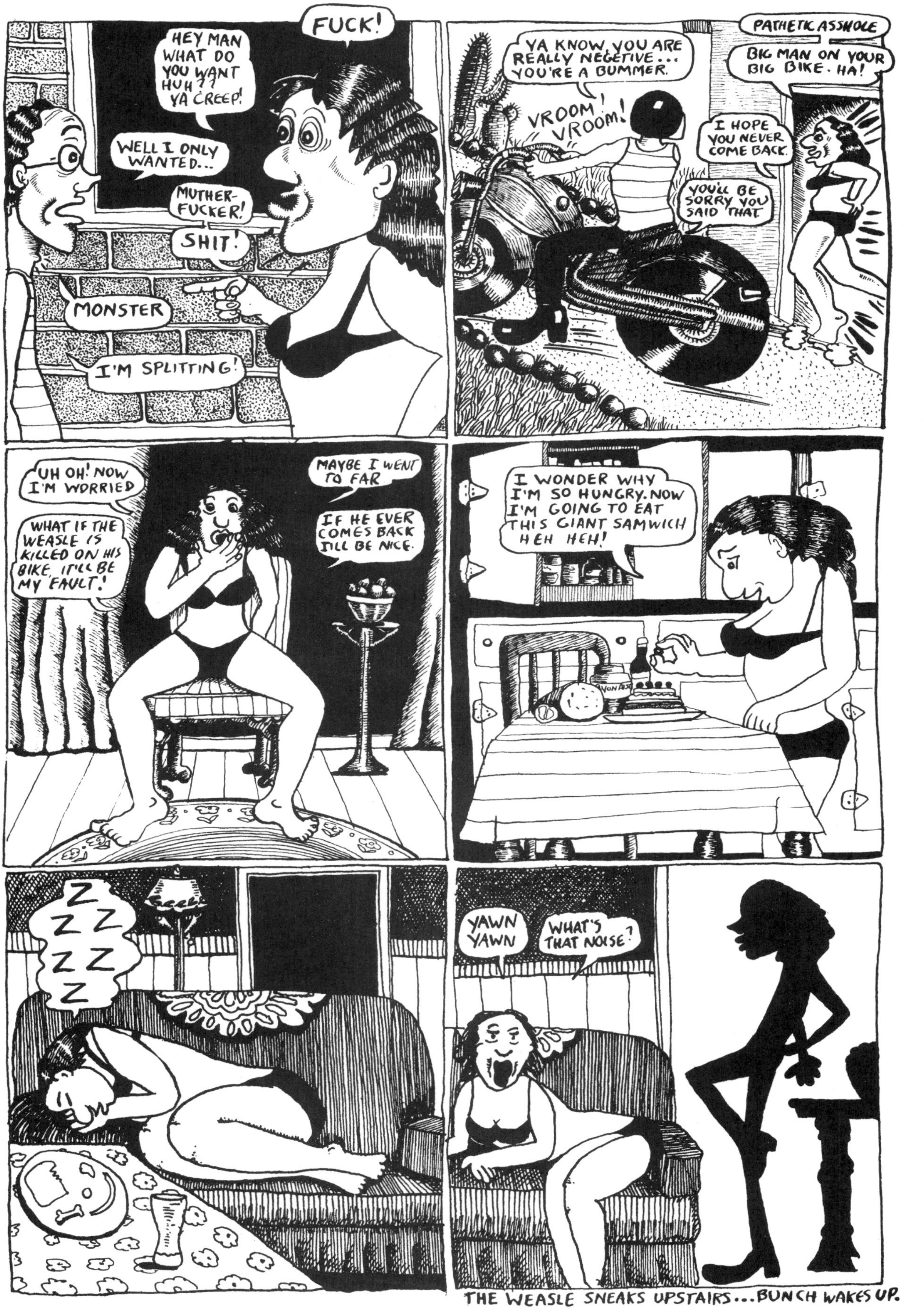
FUCK!
HEY MAN WHAT DO YOU WANT HUH?? YA CREEP!
WELL I ONLY WANTED...
MUTHER-FUCKER!
SHIT!
MONSTER
I'M SPLITTING!
PATHETIC ASSHOLE
YA KNOW, YOU ARE REALLY NEGETIVE... YOU'RE A BUMMER.
BIG MAN ON YOUR BIG BIKE. HA!
VROOM! VROOM!
I HOPE YOU NEVER COME BACK.
YOU'LL BE SORRY YOU SAID THAT.
UH OH! NOW I'M WORRIED
MAYBE I WENT TO FAR
WHAT IF THE WEASLE IS KILLED ON HIS BIKE, IT'LL BE MY FAULT!
IF HE EVER COMES BACK I'LL BE NICE.
I WONDER WHY I'M SO HUNGRY. NOW I'M GOING TO EAT THIS GIANT SAMWICH HEH HEH!
ZZZZZZ
YAWN YAWN
WHAT'S THAT NOISE?
THE WEASLE SNEAKS UPSTAIRS...BUNCH WAKES UP.

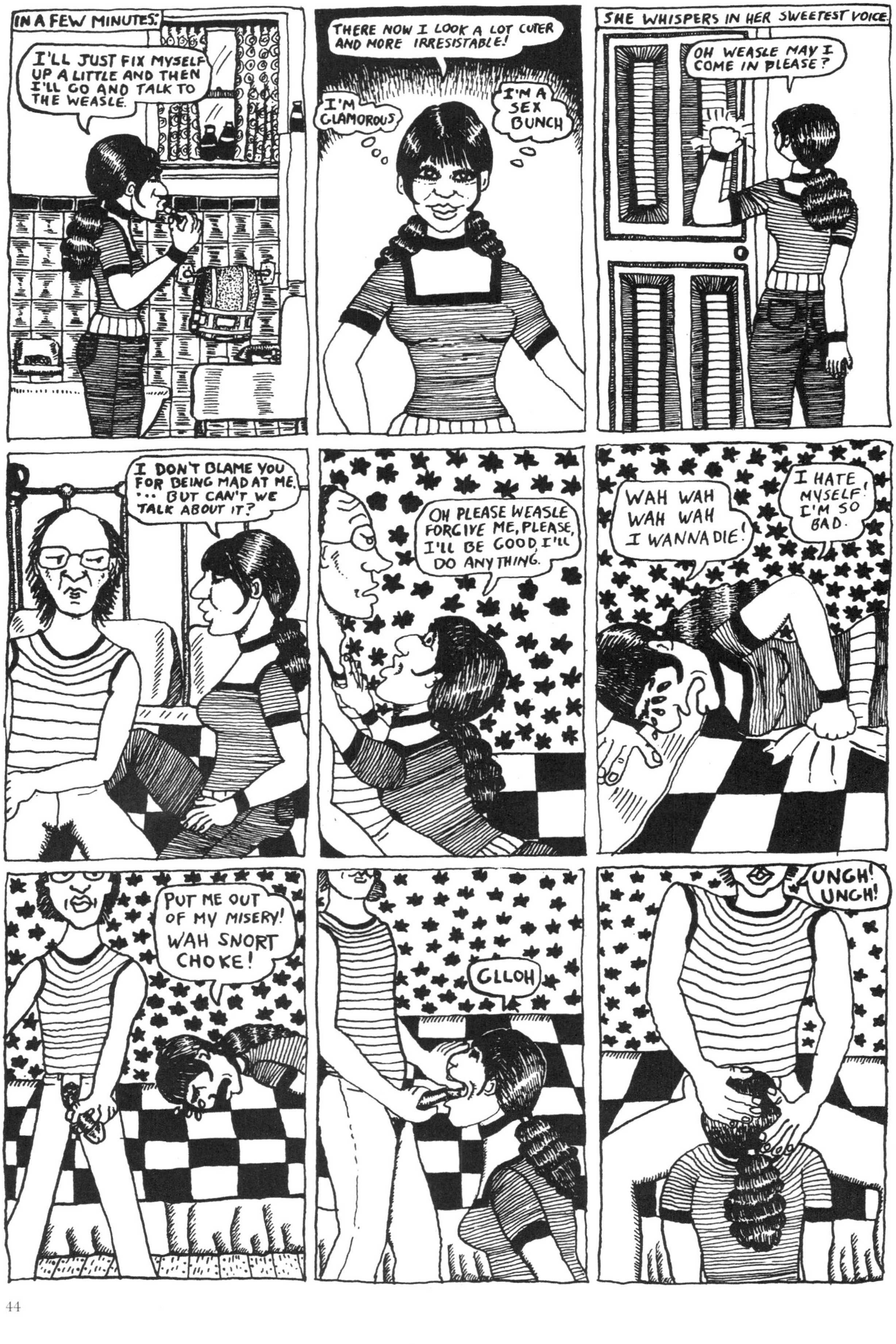
IN A FEW MINUTES:
I'LL JUST FIX MYSELF UP A LITTLE AND THEN I'LL GO AND TALK TO THE WEASLE.
THERE NOW I LOOK A LOT CUTER AND MORE IRRESISTABLE!
I'M GLAMOROUS
I'M A SEX BUNCH
SHE WHISPERS IN HER SWEETEST VOICE.
OH WEASLE MAY I COME IN PLEASE?
I DON'T BLAME YOU FOR BEING MAD AT ME. ... BUT CAN'T WE TALK ABOUT IT?
OH PLEASE WEASLE FORGIVE ME, PLEASE, I'LL BE GOOD I'LL DO ANYTHING.
WAH WAH WAH WAH I WANNA DIE!
I HATE MYSELF! I'M SO BAD.
PUT ME OUT OF MY MISERY! WAH SNORT CHOKE!
GLLOH
UNGH! UNGH!

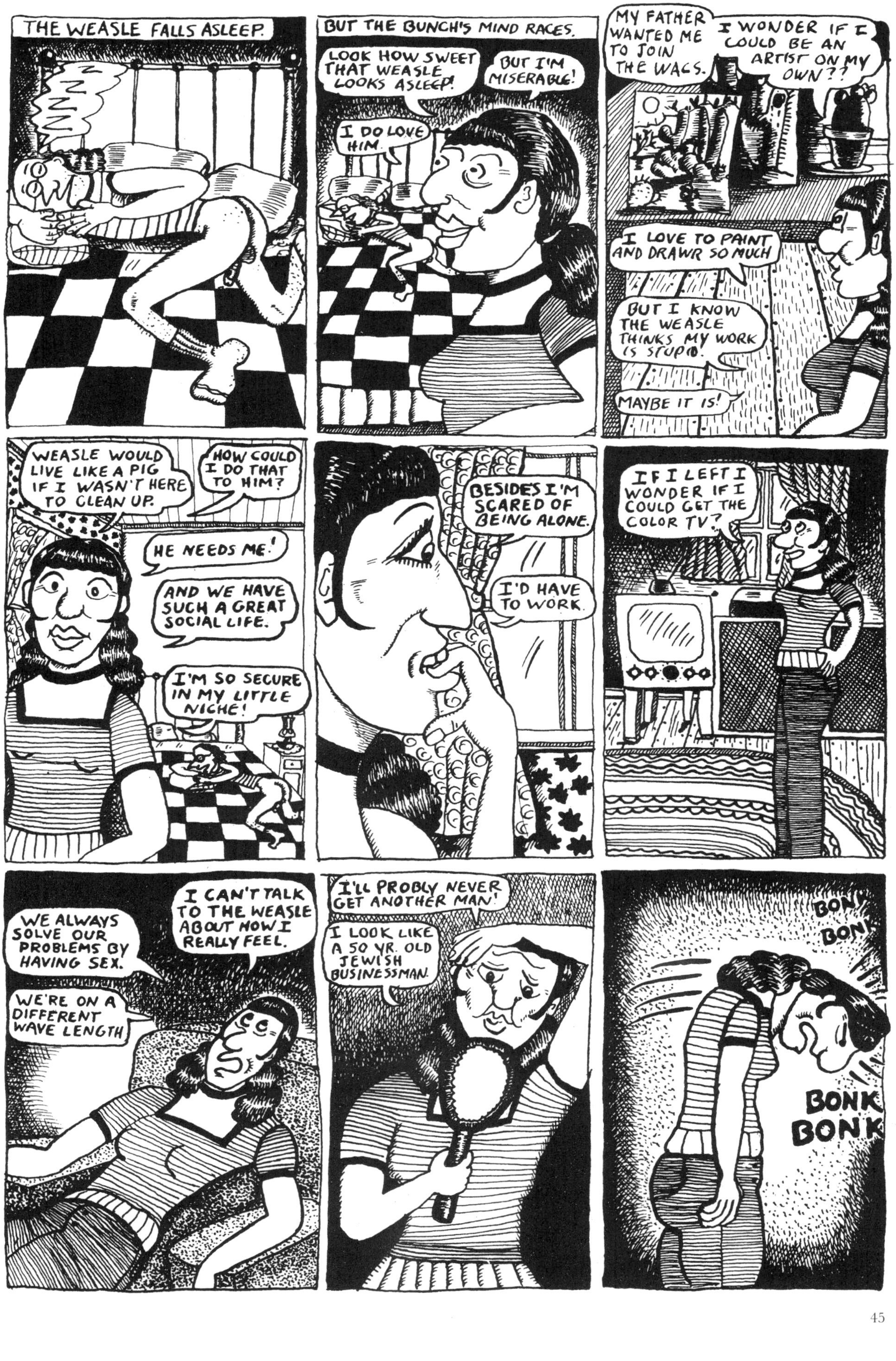
THE WEASLE FALLS ASLEEP.
ZZZZ
BUT THE BUNCH'S MIND RACES.
LOOK HOW SWEET THAT WEASLE LOOKS ASLEEP!
BUT I'M MISERABLE!
I DO LOVE HIM.
MY FATHER WANTED ME TO JOIN THE WACS.
I WONDER IF I COULD BE AN ARTIST ON MY OWN??
I LOVE TO PAINT AND DRAWR SO MUCH
BUT I KNOW THE WEASLE THINKS MY WORK IS STUPID.
MAYBE IT IS!
WEASLE WOULD LIVE LIKE A PIG IF I WASN'T HERE TO CLEAN UP.
HOW COULD I DO THAT TO HIM?
HE NEEDS ME!
AND WE HAVE SUCH A GREAT SOCIAL LIFE.
I'M SO SECURE IN MY LITTLE NICHE!
BESIDES I'M SCARED OF BEING ALONE.
I'D HAVE TO WORK.
IF I LEFT I WONDER IF I COULD GET THE COLOR TV?
WE ALWAYS SOLVE OUR PROBLEMS BY HAVING SEX.
I CAN'T TALK TO THE WEASLE ABOUT HOW I REALLY FEEL.
WE'RE ON A DIFFERENT WAVE LENGTH
I'LL PROBLY NEVER GET ANOTHER MAN!
I LOOK LIKE A 50 YR. OLD JEWISH BUSINESSMAN.
BONK BONK
BONK BONK

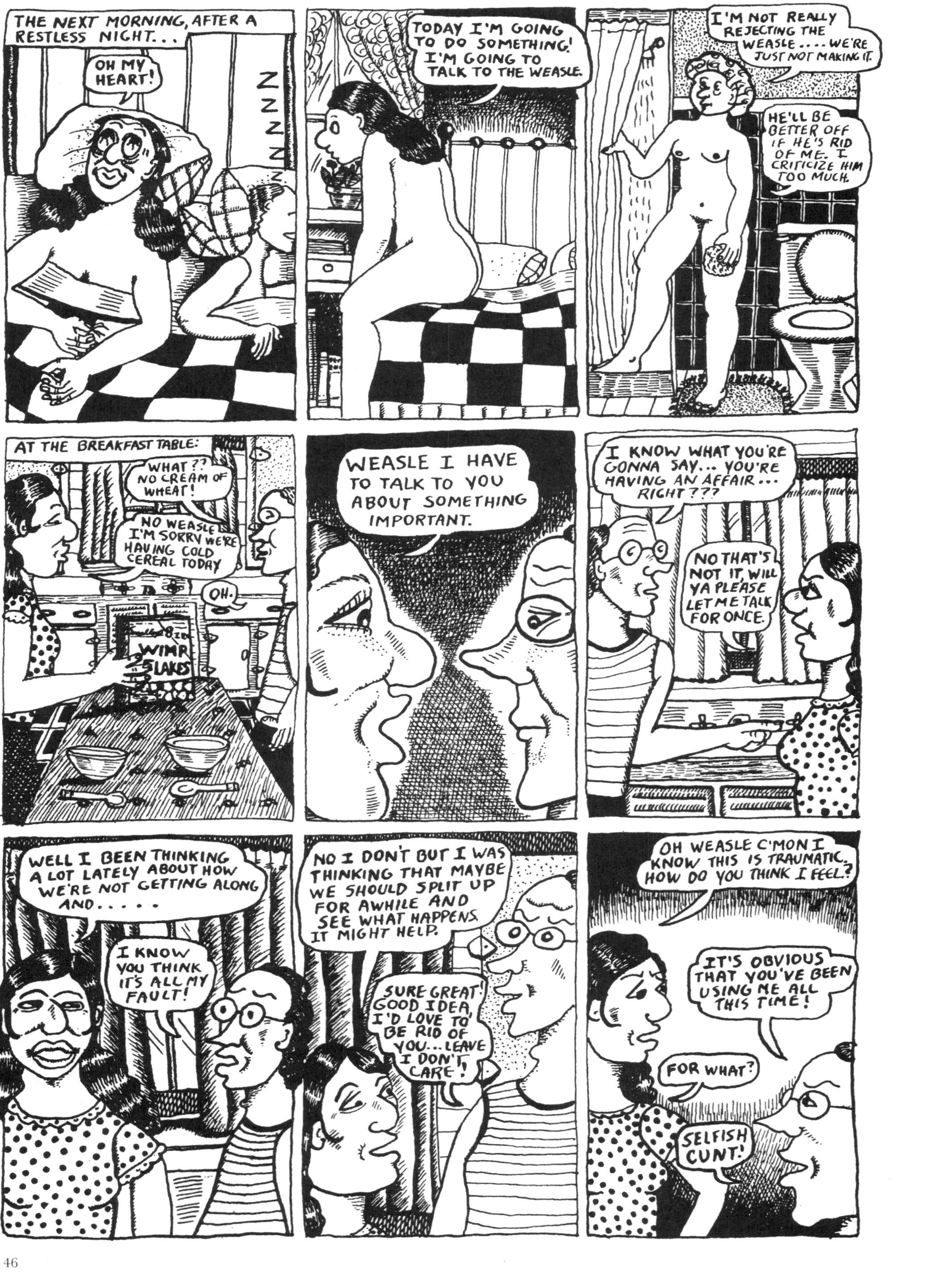
THE NEXT MORNING, AFTER A RESTLESS NIGHT...
OH MY HEART!
Z Z Z Z
TODAY I'M GOING TO DO SOMETHING! I'M GOING TO TALK TO THE WEASLE.
I'M NOT REALLY REJECTING THE WEASLE.... WE'RE JUST NOT MAKING IT.
HE'LL BE BETTER OFF IF HE'S RID OF ME. I CRITICIZE HIM TOO MUCH.
AT THE BREAKFAST TABLE:
WHAT?? NO CREAM OF WHEAT!
NO WEASLE I'M SORRY WE'RE HAVING COLD CEREAL TODAY
OH.
WIMP FLAKES
WEASLE I HAVE TO TALK TO YOU ABOUT SOMETHING IMPORTANT.
I KNOW WHAT YOU'RE GONNA SAY... YOU'RE HAVING AN AFFAIR... RIGHT???
NO THAT'S NOT IT, WILL YA PLEASE LET ME TALK FOR ONCE.
WELL I BEEN THINKING A LOT LATELY ABOUT HOW WE'RE NOT GETTING ALONG AND.....
I KNOW YOU THINK IT'S ALL MY FAULT!
NO I DON'T BUT I WAS THINKING THAT MAYBE WE SHOULD SPLIT UP FOR AWHILE AND SEE WHAT HAPPENS. IT MIGHT HELP.
SURE GREAT! GOOD IDEA, I'D LOVE TO BE RID OF YOU... LEAVE I DON'T CARE!
OH WEASLE C'MON I KNOW THIS IS TRAUMATIC. HOW DO YOU THINK I FEEL?
IT'S OBVIOUS THAT YOU'VE BEEN USING ME ALL THIS TIME!
FOR WHAT?
SELFISH CUNT!

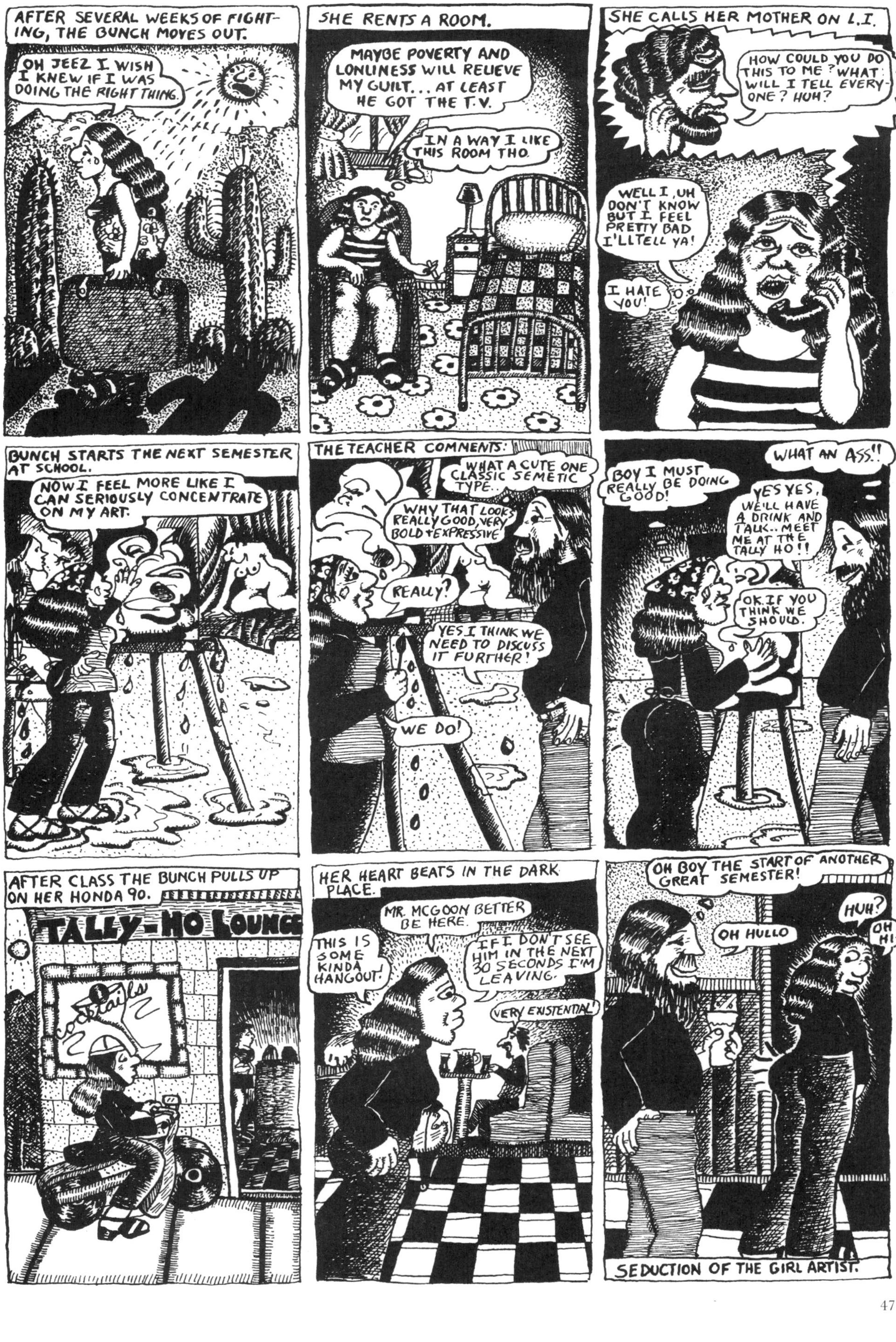

AFTER SEVERAL WEEKS OF FIGHTING, THE BUNCH MOVES OUT.
OH JEEZ I WISH I KNEW IF I WAS DOING THE RIGHT THING.
SHE RENTS A ROOM.
MAYBE POVERTY AND LONLINESS WILL RELIEVE MY GUILT... AT LEAST HE GOT THE T.V.
IN A WAY I LIKE THIS ROOM THO.
SHE CALLS HER MOTHER ON L.I.
HOW COULD YOU DO THIS TO ME? WHAT WILL I TELL EVERYONE? HUH?
WELL I, UH DON'T KNOW BUT I FEEL PRETTY BAD I'LL TELL YA!
I HATE YOU!
BUNCH STARTS THE NEXT SEMESTER AT SCHOOL.
NOW I FEEL MORE LIKE I CAN SERIOUSLY CONCENTRATE ON MY ART.
THE TEACHER COMMENTS:
WHAT A CUTE ONE CLASSIC SEMETIC TYPE.
WHY THAT LOOKS REALLY GOOD, VERY BOLD + EXPRESSIVE
REALLY?
YES I THINK WE NEED TO DISCUSS IT FURTHER!
WE DO!
WHAT AN ASS!!
BOY I MUST REALLY BE DOING GOOD!
YES YES, WE'LL HAVE A DRINK AND TALK.. MEET ME AT THE TALLY HO!!
OK IF YOU THINK WE SHOULD.
AFTER CLASS THE BUNCH PULLS UP ON HER HONDA 90.
TALLY-HO LOUNGE
cocktails
HER HEART BEATS IN THE DARK PLACE.
MR. MCGOON BETTER BE HERE.
THIS IS SOME KINDA HANGOUT!
IF I DON'T SEE HIM IN THE NEXT 30 SECONDS I'M LEAVING.
VERY EXISTENTIAL!
OH BOY THE START OF ANOTHER GREAT SEMESTER!
HUH?
OH HULLO
OH HI!
SEDUCTION OF THE GIRL ARTIST.

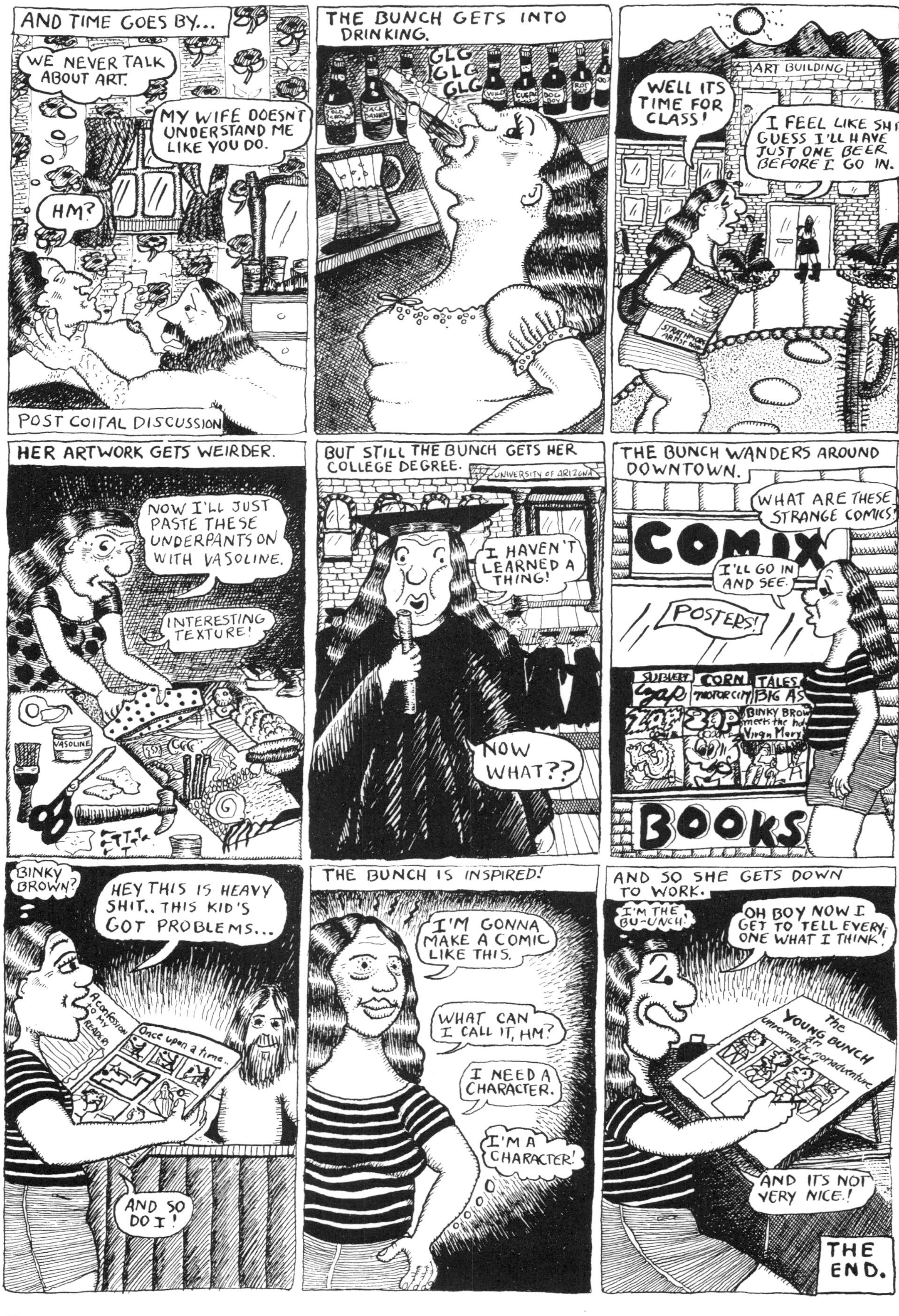
AND TIME GOES BY...
WE NEVER TALK ABOUT ART.
MY WIFE DOESN'T UNDERSTAND ME LIKE YOU DO.
HM?
POST COITAL DISCUSSION
THE BUNCH GETS INTO DRINKING.
GLG GLG GLG
WELL ITS TIME FOR CLASS!
ART BUILDING
I FEEL LIKE SHIT. GUESS I'LL HAVE JUST ONE BEER BEFORE I GO IN.
HER ARTWORK GETS WEIRDER.
NOW I'LL JUST PASTE THESE UNDERPANTS ON WITH VASOLINE.
INTERESTING TEXTURE!
VASOLINE
BUT STILL THE BUNCH GETS HER COLLEGE DEGREE.
UNIVERSITY OF ARIZONA
I HAVEN'T LEARNED A THING!
NOW WHAT??
THE BUNCH WANDERS AROUND DOWNTOWN.
WHAT ARE THESE STRANGE COMICS?
COMIX
I'LL GO IN AND SEE.
POSTERS!
CORN
TALES
BIG AS
BINKY BROW meets the ho Virgin Mary
BOOKS
BINKY BROWN?
HEY THIS IS HEAVY SHIT.. THIS KID'S GOT PROBLEMS...
A confession to my readers
Once upon a time..
AND SO DO I!
THE BUNCH IS INSPIRED!
I'M GONNA MAKE A COMIC LIKE THIS.
WHAT CAN I CALL IT, HM?
I NEED A CHARACTER.
I'M A CHARACTER!
AND SO SHE GETS DOWN TO WORK.
I'M THE BU-UNCH!
OH BOY NOW I GET TO TELL EVERY-ONE WHAT I THINK!
The YOUNG BUNCH an unromantic nonadventure story
AND ITS NOT VERY NICE!
THE END.

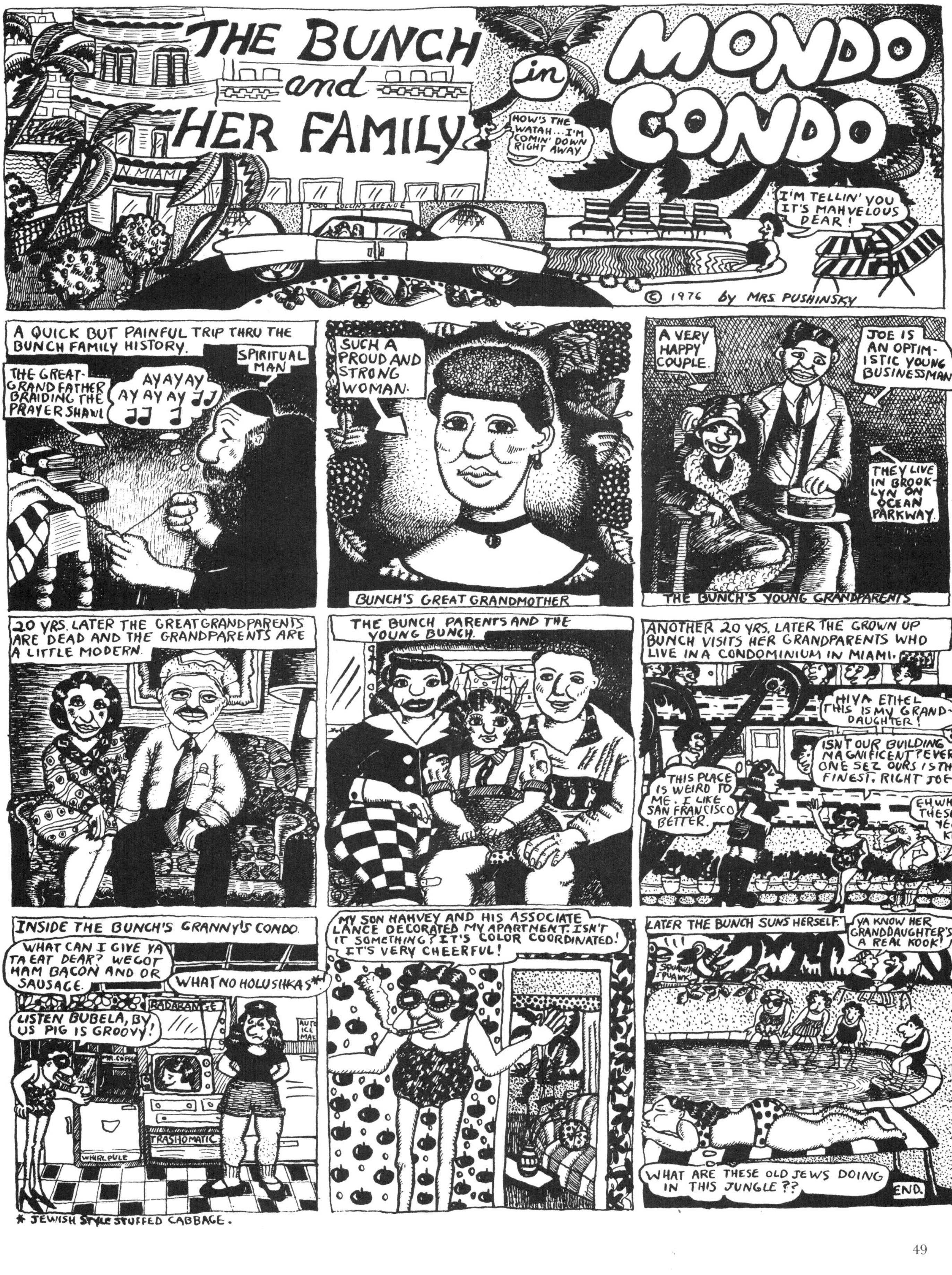
THE BUNCH and HER FAMILY in MONDO CONDO
HOW'S THE WATAH... I'M COMIN' DOWN RIGHT AWAY.
N. MIAMI
5000 COLLINS AVENUE
I'M TELLIN' YOU IT'S MAHVELOUS DEAR!
© 1976 by MRS PUSHINSKY
A QUICK BUT PAINFUL TRIP THRU THE BUNCH FAMILY HISTORY.
SPIRITUAL MAN
THE GREAT-GRAND FATHER BRAIDING THE PRAYER SHAWL
AY AY AY AY AY AY
SUCH A PROUD AND STRONG WOMAN.
BUNCH'S GREAT GRANDMOTHER
A VERY HAPPY COUPLE.
JOE IS AN OPTIMISTIC YOUNG BUSINESSMAN.
THEY LIVE IN BROOKLYN ON OCEAN PARKWAY.
THE BUNCH'S YOUNG GRANDPARENTS
20 YRS. LATER THE GREAT GRANDPARENTS ARE DEAD AND THE GRANDPARENTS ARE A LITTLE MODERN.
THE BUNCH PARENTS AND THE YOUNG BUNCH.
ANOTHER 20 YRS. LATER THE GROWN UP BUNCH VISITS HER GRANDPARENTS WHO LIVE IN A CONDOMINIUM IN MIAMI.
HIYA ETHEL THIS IS MY GRAND-DAUGHTER!
ISN'T OUR BUILDING MAGNIFICENT? EVERYONE SEZ OURS IS THE FINEST. RIGHT JOE?
THIS PLACE IS WEIRD TO ME. I LIKE SAN FRANCISCO BETTER.
EH, WHAD'A THESE YENTAS KNOW
INSIDE THE BUNCH'S GRANNY'S CONDO.
WHAT CAN I GIVE YA TA EAT DEAR? WE GOT HAM BACON AND OR SAUSAGE.
WHAT NO HOLUSHKAS*
LISTEN BUBELA, BY US PIG IS GROOVY!
RADARANGE
TRASHOMATIC
WHIRLPULE
MY SON HAHVEY AND HIS ASSOCIATE LANCE DECORATED MY APARTMENT. ISN'T IT SOMETHING? IT'S COLOR COORDINATED! IT'S VERY CHEERFUL!
LATER THE BUNCH SUNS HERSELF.
YA KNOW HER GRANDDAUGHTER'S A REAL KOOK!
SQUAWK SQUAWK
WHAT ARE THESE OLD JEWS DOING IN THIS JUNGLE??
END.
* JEWISH STYLE STUFFED CABBAGE.

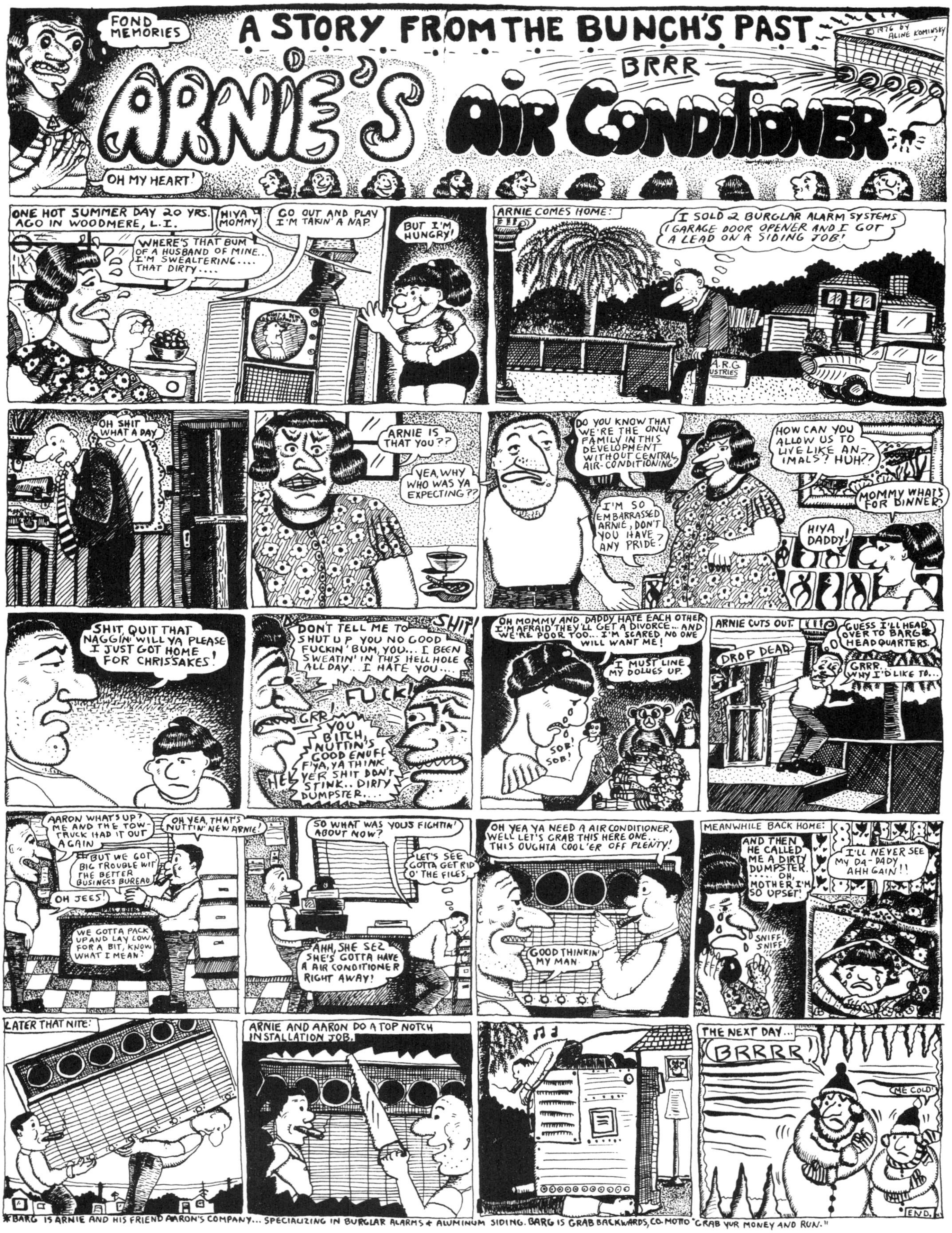

FOND MEMORIES
A STORY FROM THE BUNCH'S PAST
© 1976 by ALINE KOMINSKY
ARNIE'S
BRRR
AIR CONDITIONER
OH MY HEART!
ONE HOT SUMMER DAY 20 YRS. AGO IN WOODMERE, L.I.
HIYA MOMMY
GO OUT AND PLAY I'M TAKIN' A NAP.
WHERE'S THAT BUM OF A HUSBAND OF MINE.. I'M SWEALTERING.... THAT DIRTY....
BUT I'M HUNGRY!
ARNIE COMES HOME:
I SOLD 2 BURGLAR ALARM SYSTEMS 1 GARAGE DOOR OPENER AND I GOT A LEAD ON A SIDING JOB!
A.R.G. USTRIES
OH SHIT WHAT A DAY
ARNIE IS THAT YOU??
YEA, WHY WHO WAS YA EXPECTING??
DO YOU KNOW THAT WE'RE THE ONLY FAMILY IN THIS DEVELOPMENT WITHOUT CENTRAL AIR-CONDITIONING?
HOW CAN YOU ALLOW US TO LIVE LIKE AN-IMALS? HUH??
I'M SO EMBARRASSED ARNIE, DON'T YOU HAVE ANY PRIDE?
MOMMY WHATS FOR DINNER?
HIYA DADDY!
SHIT, QUIT THAT NAGGIN' WILL YA PLEASE I JUST GOT HOME FOR CHRISSAKES!
DON'T TELL ME TO SHUT UP YOU NO GOOD FUCKIN' BUM, YOU... I BEEN SWEATIN' IN THIS HELL HOLE ALL DAY... I HATE YOU....
SHIT!
FUCK!
GRR
YOU BITCH, NUTTIN'S GOOD ENUFF F'YA, YA THINK YER SHIT DON'T STINK.. DIRTY DUMPSTER....
HEH
OH MOMMY AND DADDY HATE EACH OTHER I'M AFRAID THEY'LL GET A DIVORCE... AND WE'RE POOR TOO... I'M SCARED NO ONE WILL WANT ME!
I MUST LINE MY DOLLIES UP.
SOB! SOB!
ARNIE CUTS OUT.
GUESS I'LL HEAD OVER TO BARG* HEADQUARTERS.
DROP DEAD
GRRR.. WHY I'D LIKE TO...
AARON WHAT'S UP? ME AND THE TOW-TRUCK HAD IT OUT AGAIN
OH YEA, THAT'S NUTTIN' NEW ARNIE!
BUT WE GOT BIG TROUBLE WIT THE BETTER BUSINESS BUREAU.
OH JEES!
WE GOTTA PACK UP AND LAY LOW FOR A BIT, KNOW WHAT I MEAN?
SO WHAT WAS YOUS FIGHTIN' ABOUT NOW?
LET'S SEE GOTTA GET RID O' THE FILES
AHH, SHE SEZ SHE'S GOTTA HAVE A AIR CONDITIONER RIGHT AWAY!
OH YEA YA NEED A AIR CONDITIONER, WELL LET'S GRAB THIS HERE ONE... THIS OUGHTA COOL'ER OFF PLENTY!
GOOD THINKIN' MY MAN.
MEANWHILE BACK HOME:
AND THEN HE CALLED ME A DIRTY DUMPSTER. ..... OH, MOTHER I'M SO UPSET!
I'LL NEVER SEE MY DA-DADY AHH GAIN!!
SNIFF, SNIFF
LATER THAT NITE:
ARNIE AND AARON DO A TOP NOTCH INSTALLATION JOB.
THE NEXT DAY...
BRRRR!
ME COLD!
END.
*BARG IS ARNIE AND HIS FRIEND AARON'S COMPANY... SPECIALIZING IN BURGLAR ALARMS & ALUMINUM SIDING. BARG IS GRAB BACKWARDS, CO. MOTTO "GRAB YUR MONEY AND RUN."

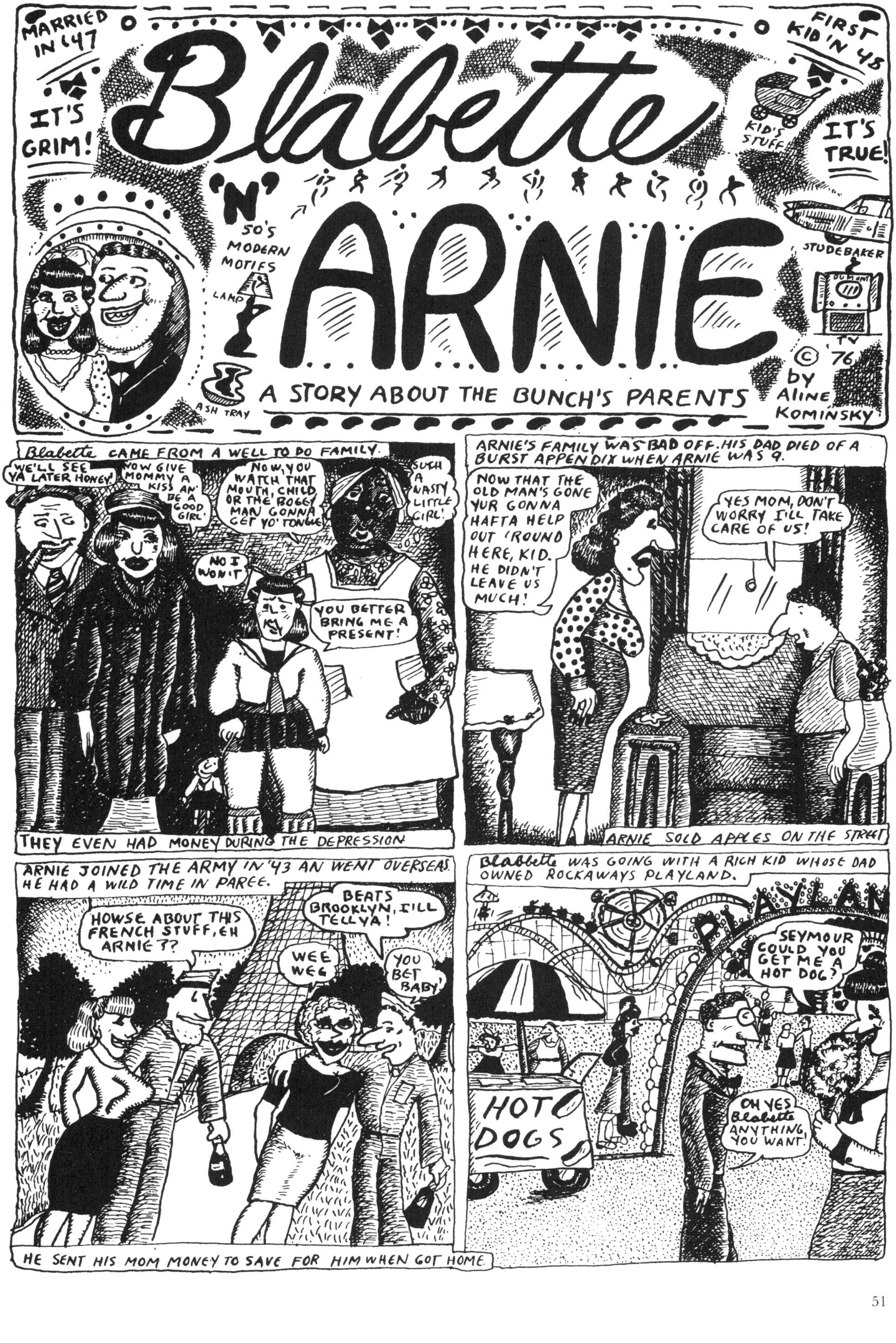

MARRIED IN '47
FIRST KID IN '48
Blabette 'N' ARNIE
IT'S GRIM!
IT'S TRUE!
KID'S STUFF
50'S MODERN MOTIFS
LAMP
ASH TRAY
STUDEBAKER
TV
© '76 by Aline Kominsky
A STORY ABOUT THE BUNCH'S PARENTS
Blabette CAME FROM A WELL TO DO FAMILY.
WE'LL SEE YA LATER HONEY!
NOW GIVE MOMMY A KISS AN' BE A GOOD GIRL!
NOW, YOU WATCH THAT MOUTH, CHILD, OR THE BOGGY MAN GONNA GET YO' TONGUE
SUCH A NASTY LITTLE GIRL!
NO I WON'T!
YOU BETTER BRING ME A PRESENT!
THEY EVEN HAD MONEY DURING THE DEPRESSION
ARNIE'S FAMILY WAS BAD OFF. HIS DAD DIED OF A BURST APPENDIX WHEN ARNIE WAS 9.
NOW THAT THE OLD MAN'S GONE YUR GONNA HAFTA HELP OUT 'ROUND HERE, KID. HE DIDN'T LEAVE US MUCH!
YES MOM, DON'T WORRY I'LL TAKE CARE OF US!
ARNIE SOLD APPLES ON THE STREET
ARNIE JOINED THE ARMY IN '43 AN WENT OVERSEAS. HE HAD A WILD TIME IN PAREE.
HOWSE ABOUT THIS FRENCH STUFF, EH ARNIE?
BEATS BROOKLYN, I'LL TELLYA!
WEE WEE
YOU BET BABY!
HE SENT HIS MOM MONEY TO SAVE FOR HIM WHEN GOT HOME
Blabette WAS GOING WITH A RICH KID WHOSE DAD OWNED ROCKAWAYS PLAYLAND.
PLAYLAN
SEYMOUR COULD YOU GET ME A HOT DOG?
HOT DOGS
OH YES Blabette ANYTHING YOU WANT!

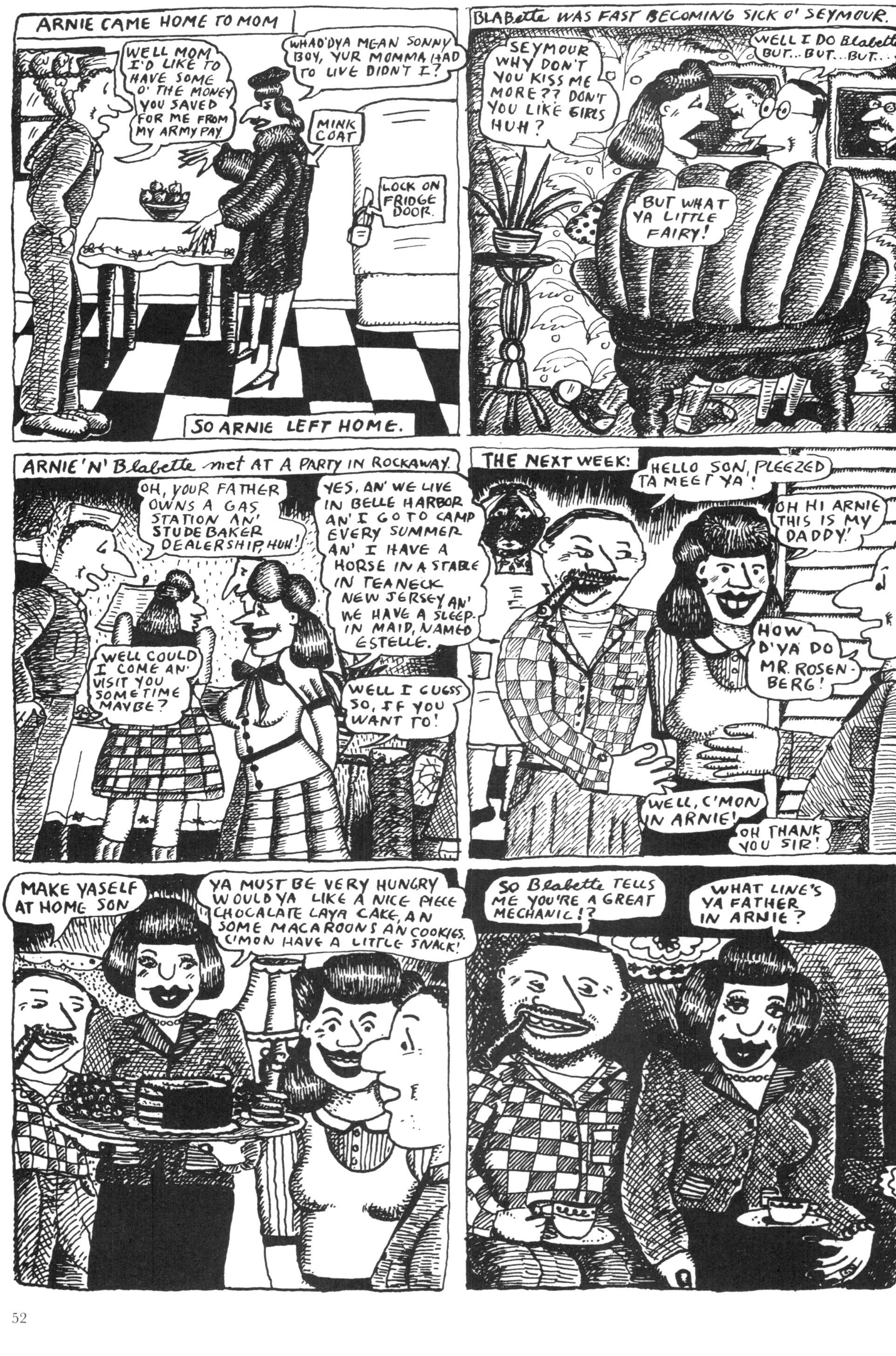
ARNIE CAME HOME TO MOM
WELL MOM I'D LIKE TO HAVE SOME O' THE MONEY YOU SAVED FOR ME FROM MY ARMY PAY
WHAD'DYA MEAN SONNY BOY, YUR MOMMA HAD TO LIVE DIDN'T I?
MINK COAT
LOCK ON FRIDGE DOOR.
SO ARNIE LEFT HOME.
BLABette WAS FAST BECOMING SICK O' SEYMOUR.
SEYMOUR WHY DON'T YOU KISS ME MORE?? DON'T YOU LIKE GIRLS HUH?
WELL I DO Blabette BUT...BUT...BUT...
BUT WHAT YA LITTLE FAIRY!
ARNIE 'N' Blabette met AT A PARTY IN ROCKAWAY.
OH, YOUR FATHER OWNS A GAS STATION AN' STUDEBAKER DEALERSHIP, HUH!
YES. AN' WE LIVE IN BELLE HARBOR AN' I GO TO CAMP EVERY SUMMER AN' I HAVE A HORSE IN A STABLE IN TEANECK NEW JERSEY AN' WE HAVE A SLEEP-IN MAID, NAMED ESTELLE.
WELL COULD I COME AN' VISIT YOU SOMETIME MAYBE?
WELL I GUESS SO, IF YOU WANT TO!
THE NEXT WEEK:
HELLO SON, PLEEZED TA MEET YA'!
OH HI ARNIE THIS IS MY DADDY!
HOW D'YA DO MR. ROSENBERG!
WELL, C'MON IN ARNIE!
OH THANK YOU SIR!
MAKE YASELF AT HOME SON
YA MUST BE VERY HUNGRY WOULD YA LIKE A NICE PIECE CHOCALATE LAYA CAKE, AN SOME MACAROONS AN COOKIES. C'MON HAVE A LITTLE SNACK!
SO Blabette TELLS ME YOU'RE A GREAT MECHANIC!?
WHAT LINE'S YA FATHER IN ARNIE?

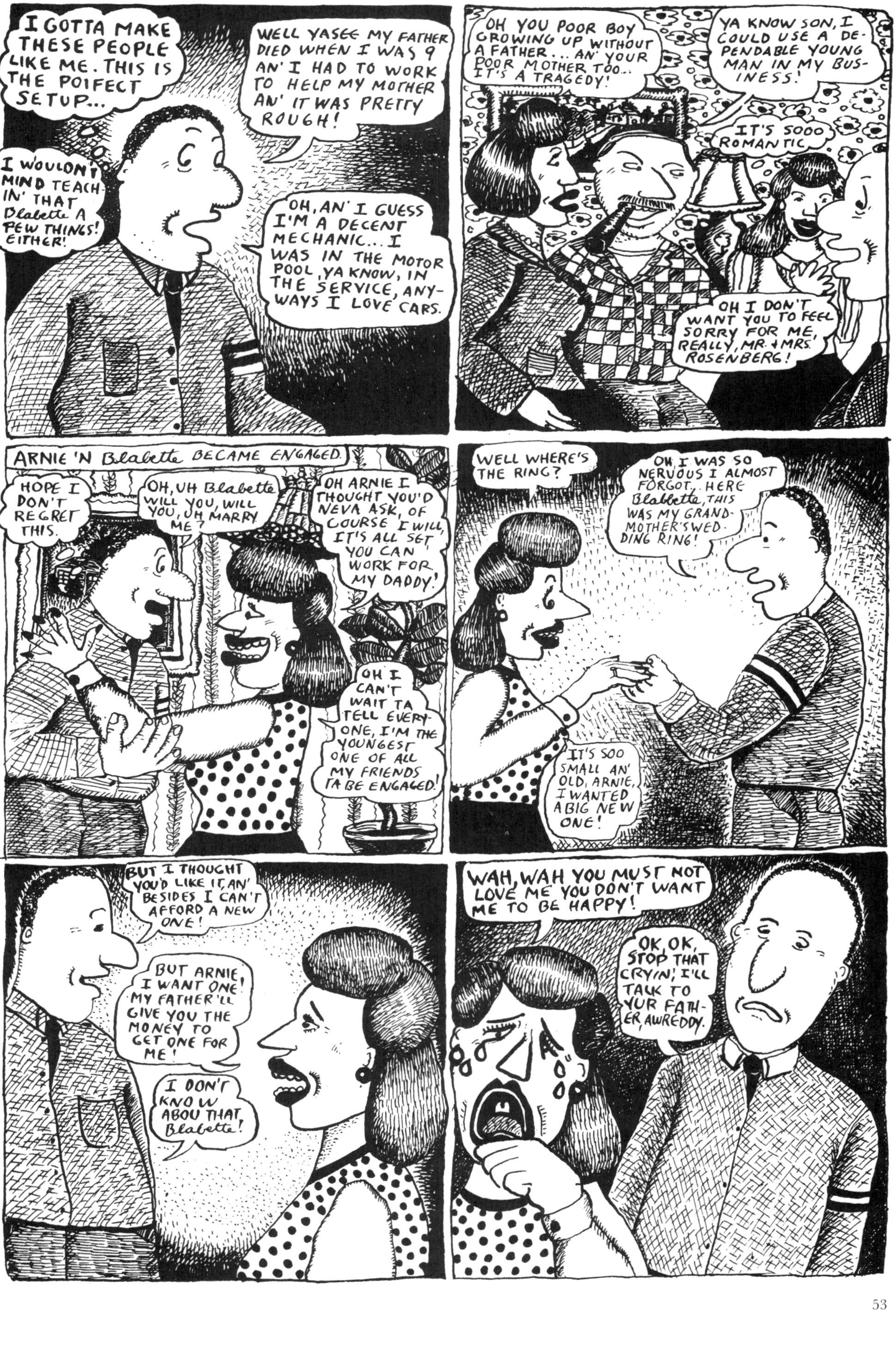
I GOTTA MAKE THESE PEOPLE LIKE ME. THIS IS THE POIFECT SETUP...
I WOULDN'T MIND TEACHIN' THAT Blabette A FEW THINGS! EITHER!
WELL YASEE MY FATHER DIED WHEN I WAS 9 AN' I HAD TO WORK TO HELP MY MOTHER AN' IT WAS PRETTY ROUGH!
OH, AN' I GUESS I'M A DECENT MECHANIC... I WAS IN THE MOTOR POOL, YA KNOW, IN THE SERVICE, ANYWAYS I LOVE CARS.
OH YOU POOR BOY GROWING UP WITHOUT A FATHER... AN' YOUR POOR MOTHER TOO... IT'S A TRAGEDY!
YA KNOW SON, I COULD USE A DEPENDABLE YOUNG MAN IN MY BUSINESS!
IT'S SOOO ROMANTIC
OH I DON'T WANT YOU TO FEEL SORRY FOR ME, REALLY, MR. + MRS. ROSENBERG!
ARNIE 'N Blabette BECAME ENGAGED.
HOPE I DON'T REGRET THIS.
OH, UH Blabette WILL YOU, WILL YOU, UH MARRY ME?
OH ARNIE I THOUGHT YOU'D NEVA ASK, OF COURSE I WILL, IT'S ALL SET YOU CAN WORK FOR MY DADDY!
OH I CAN'T WAIT TA TELL EVERYONE, I'M THE YOUNGEST ONE OF ALL MY FRIENDS TA BE ENGAGED!
WELL WHERE'S THE RING?
OH, I WAS SO NERVOUS I ALMOST FORGOT. HERE Blabette, THIS WAS MY GRANDMOTHER'S WEDDING RING!
IT'S SOO SMALL AN' OLD, ARNIE, I WANTED A BIG NEW ONE!
BUT I THOUGHT YOU'D LIKE IT, AN' BESIDES I CAN'T AFFORD A NEW ONE!
BUT ARNIE, I WANT ONE! MY FATHER'LL GIVE YOU THE MONEY TO GET ONE FOR ME!
I DON'T KNOW ABOU THAT, Blabette!
WAH, WAH YOU MUST NOT LOVE ME YOU DON'T WANT ME TO BE HAPPY!
OK, OK, STOP THAT CRYIN'! I'LL TALK TO YUR FATHER, AWREDDY.

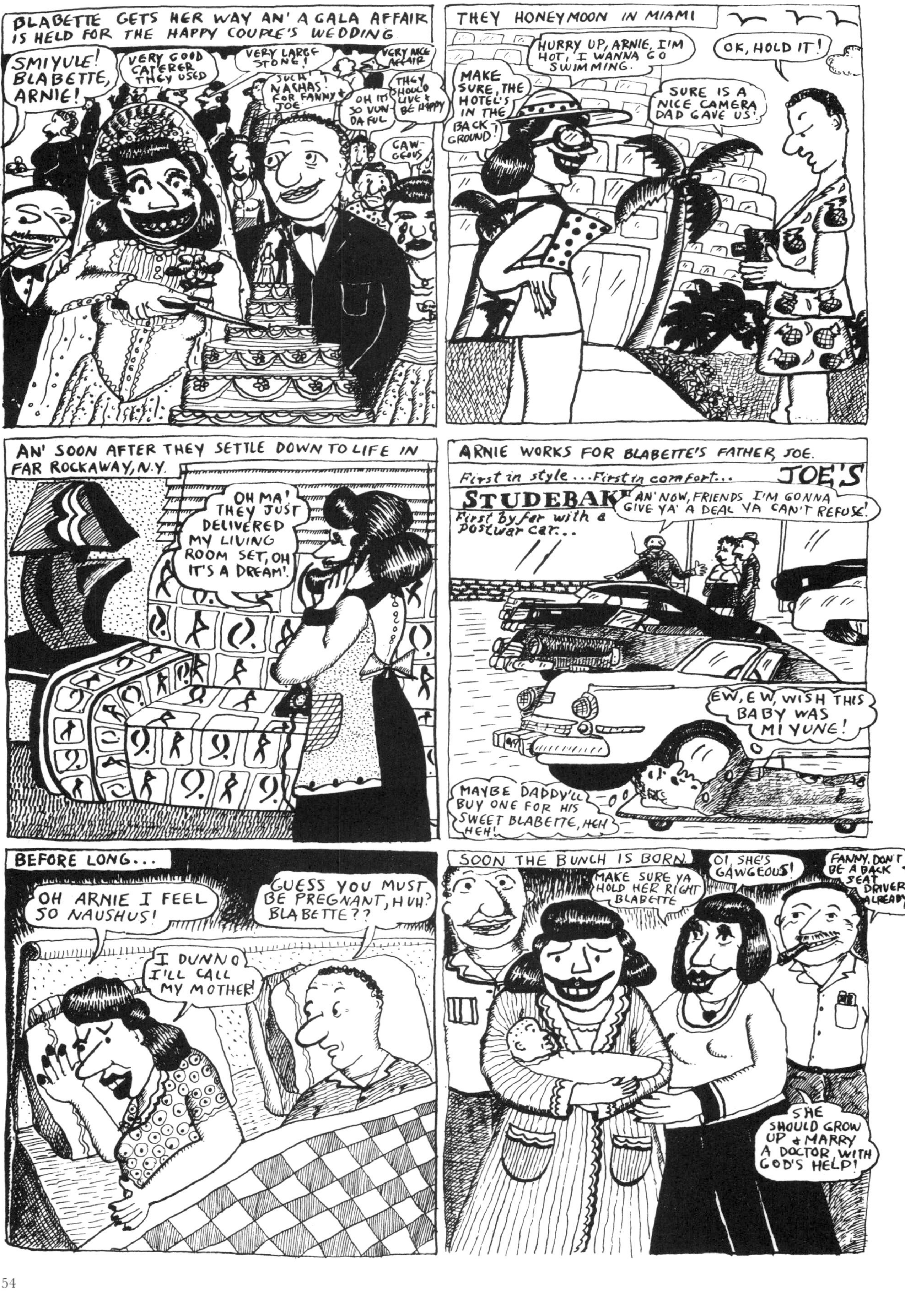
BLABETTE GETS HER WAY AN' A GALA AFFAIR IS HELD FOR THE HAPPY COUPLE'S WEDDING
SMIYULE! BLABETTE, ARNIE!
VERY GOOD CATERER THEY USED
VERY LARGE STONE!
VERY NICE AFFAIR
SUCH NACHAS! FOR FANNY + JOE
OH ITS SO VUN-DA FUL
THEY SHOULD LIVE + BE HAPPY
GAW-GEOUS
THEY HONEYMOON IN MIAMI
HURRY UP, ARNIE, I'M HOT, I WANNA GO SWIMMING.
MAKE SURE, THE HOTEL'S IN THE BACK-GROUND!
OK, HOLD IT!
SURE IS A NICE CAMERA DAD GAVE US!
AN' SOON AFTER THEY SETTLE DOWN TO LIFE IN FAR ROCKAWAY, N.Y.
OH MA! THEY JUST DELIVERED MY LIVING ROOM SET, OH IT'S A DREAM!
ARNIE WORKS FOR BLABETTE'S FATHER JOE.
First in style... First in comfort...
JOE'S
STUDEBAK
First by far with a postwar car...
AN' NOW, FRIENDS I'M GONNA GIVE YA' A DEAL YA CAN'T REFUSE!
EW, EW, WISH THIS BABY WAS MI YUNE!
MAYBE DADDY'LL BUY ONE FOR HIS SWEET BLABETTE, HEH HEH!
BEFORE LONG...
OH ARNIE I FEEL SO NAUSHUS!
GUESS YOU MUST BE PREGNANT, HUH? BLABETTE??
I DUNNO I'LL CALL MY MOTHER!
SOON THE BUNCH IS BORN.
MAKE SURE YA HOLD HER RIGHT BLABETTE
OI, SHE'S GAWGEOUS!
FANNY, DON'T BE A BACK SEAT DRIVER ALREADY
SHE SHOULD GROW UP & MARRY A DOCTOR WITH GOD'S HELP!

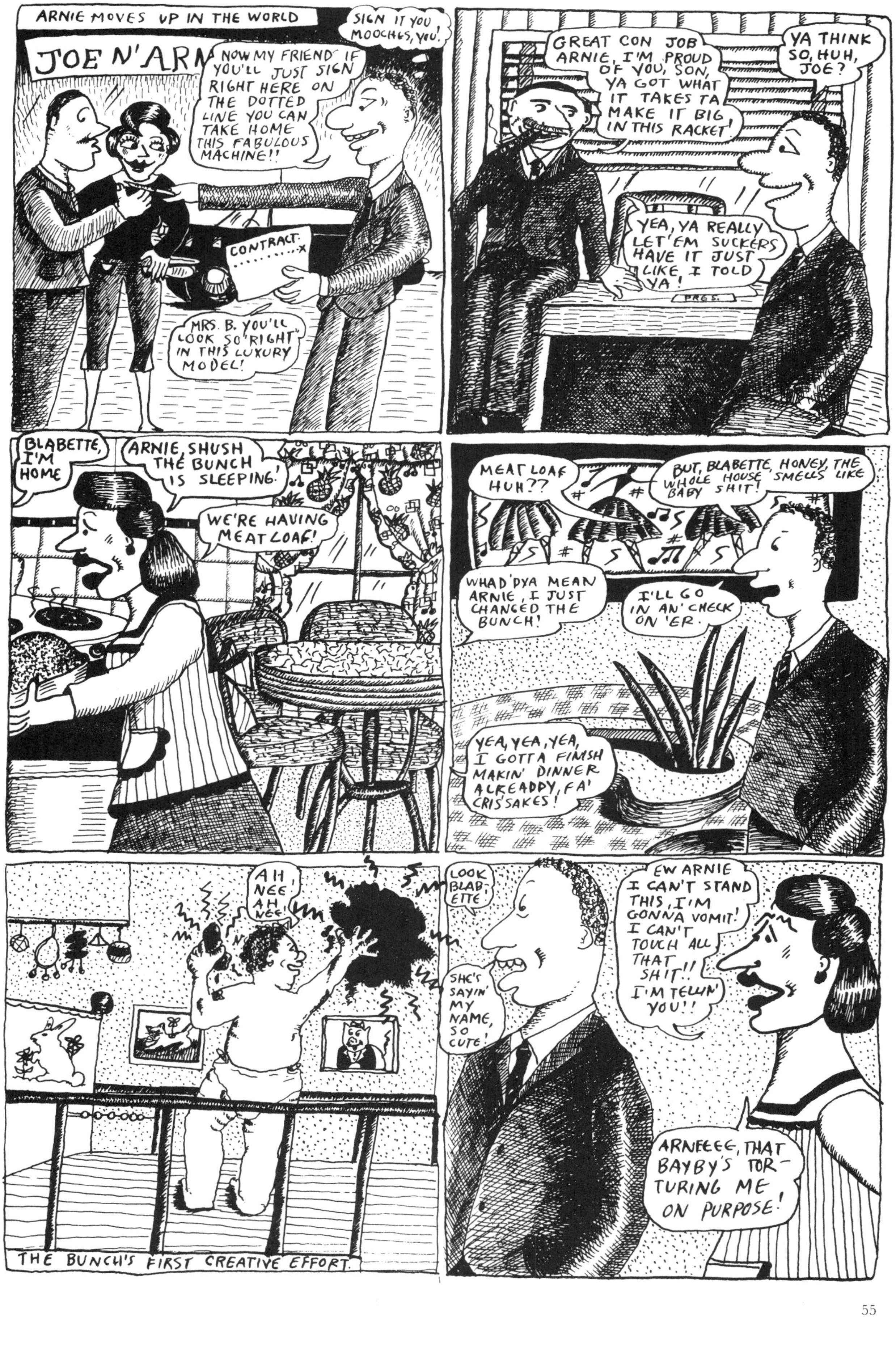
ARNIE MOVES UP IN THE WORLD
JOE N'ARN
SIGN IT YOU MOOCHES, YOU!
NOW MY FRIEND IF YOU'LL JUST SIGN RIGHT HERE ON THE DOTTED LINE YOU CAN TAKE HOME THIS FABULOUS MACHINE!!
CONTRACT
MRS. B. YOU'LL LOOK SO "RIGHT" IN THIS LUXURY MODEL!
GREAT CON JOB ARNIE, I'M PROUD OF YOU, SON, YA GOT WHAT IT TAKES TA MAKE IT BIG IN THIS RACKET!
YA THINK SO, HUH, JOE?
YEA, YA REALLY LET 'EM SUCKERS HAVE IT JUST LIKE I TOLD YA!
PRES.
BLABETTE, I'M HOME
ARNIE, SHUSH THE BUNCH IS SLEEPING!
WE'RE HAVING MEAT LOAF!
MEAT LOAF HUH??
BUT, BLABETTE, HONEY, THE WHOLE HOUSE SMELLS LIKE BABY SHIT!
WHAD'DYA MEAN ARNIE, I JUST CHANGED THE BUNCH!
I'LL GO IN AN' CHECK ON 'ER.
YEA, YEA, YEA, I GOTTA FINISH MAKIN' DINNER ALREADDY, FA' CRISSAKES!
AH NEE AH NEE!
THE BUNCH'S FIRST CREATIVE EFFORT.
LOOK BLABETTE
SHE'S SAYIN' MY NAME, SO CUTE!
EW ARNIE I CAN'T STAND THIS, I'M GONNA VOMIT! I CAN'T TOUCH ALL THAT SHIT!! I'M TELLIN' YOU!!
ARNEEEE, THAT BAYBY'S TORTURING ME ON PURPOSE!

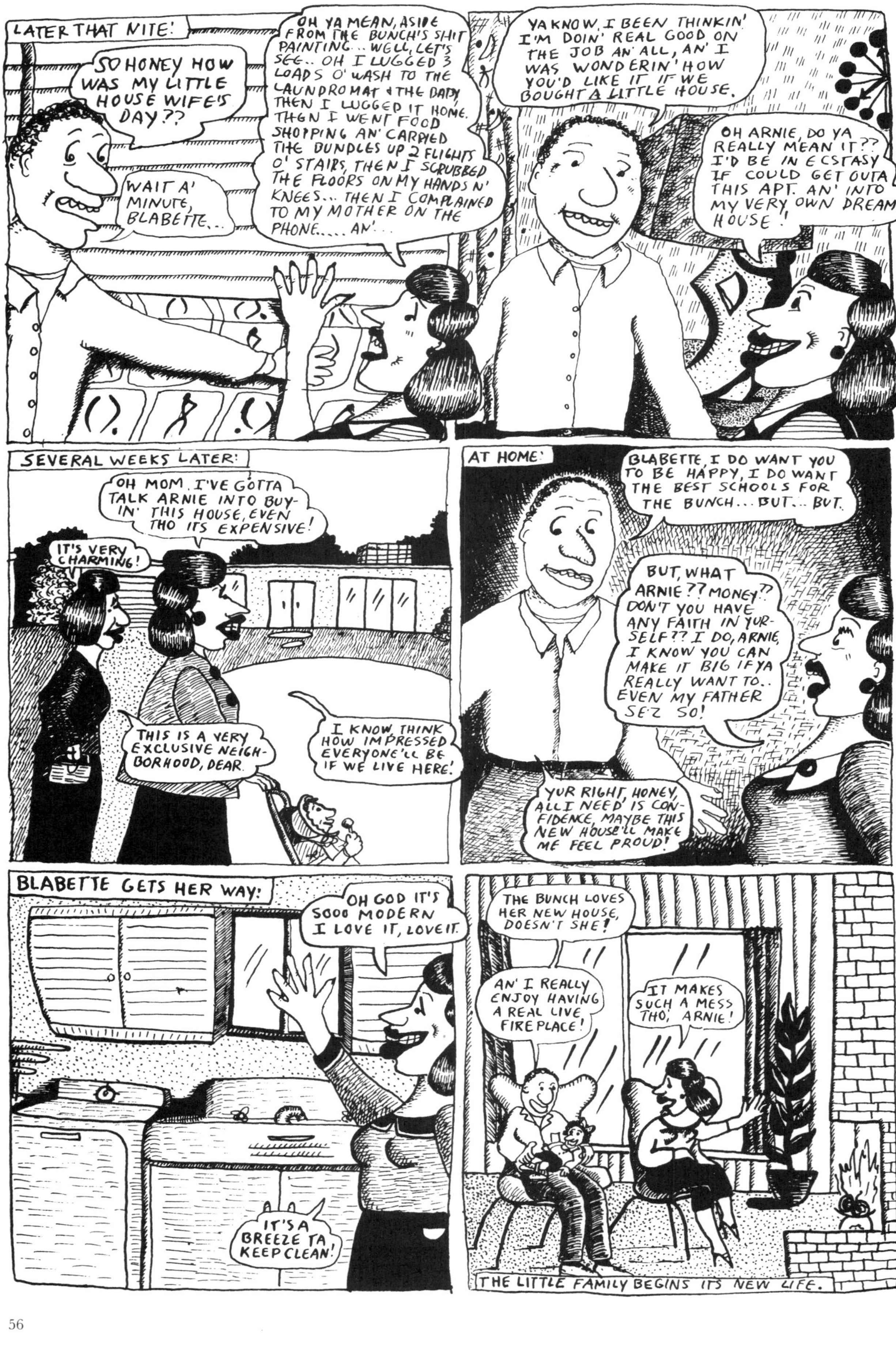
LATER THAT NITE:
SO HONEY HOW WAS MY LITTLE HOUSE WIFE'S DAY??
OH YA MEAN, ASIDE FROM THE BUNCH'S SHIT PAINTING... WELL, LET'S SEE.. OH I LUGGED 3 LOADS O' WASH TO THE LAUNDROMAT & THE DADY THEN I LUGGED IT HOME. THEN I WENT FOOD SHOPPING AN' CARRIED THE BUNDLES UP 2 FLIGHTS O' STAIRS, THEN I SCRUBBED THE FLOORS ON MY HANDS N' KNEES... THEN I COMPLAINED TO MY MOTHER ON THE PHONE..... AN'...
WAIT A' MINUTE, BLABETTE...
YA KNOW, I BEEN THINKIN' I'M DOIN' REAL GOOD ON THE JOB AN' ALL, AN' I WAS WONDERIN' HOW YOU'D LIKE IT IF WE BOUGHT A LITTLE HOUSE.
OH ARNIE, DO YA REALLY MEAN IT?? I'D BE IN ECSTASY IF COULD GET OUTA THIS APT. AN' INTO MY VERY OWN DREAM HOUSE!
SEVERAL WEEKS LATER:
OH MOM, I'VE GOTTA TALK ARNIE INTO BUY-IN' THIS HOUSE, EVEN THO ITS EXPENSIVE!
IT'S VERY CHARMING!
THIS IS A VERY EXCLUSIVE NEIGH-BORHOOD, DEAR.
I KNOW, THINK HOW IMPRESSED EVERYONE'LL BE IF WE LIVE HERE!
AT HOME:
BLABETTE, I DO WANT YOU TO BE HAPPY, I DO WANT THE BEST SCHOOLS FOR THE BUNCH... BUT... BUT.
BUT, WHAT ARNIE?? MONEY?? DON'T YOU HAVE ANY FAITH IN YUR-SELF?? I DO, ARNIE, I KNOW YOU CAN MAKE IT BIG IF YA REALLY WANT TO.. EVEN MY FATHER SEZ SO!
YUR RIGHT, HONEY, ALL I NEED IS CON-FIDENCE, MAYBE THIS NEW HOUSE'LL MAKE ME FEEL PROUD!
BLABETTE GETS HER WAY:
OH GOD IT'S SOOO MODERN I LOVE IT, LOVE IT.
IT'S A BREEZE TA KEEP CLEAN!
THE BUNCH LOVES HER NEW HOUSE, DOESN'T SHE!
AN' I REALLY ENJOY HAVING A REAL LIVE FIREPLACE!
IT MAKES SUCH A MESS THO, ARNIE!
THE LITTLE FAMILY BEGINS ITS NEW LIFE.

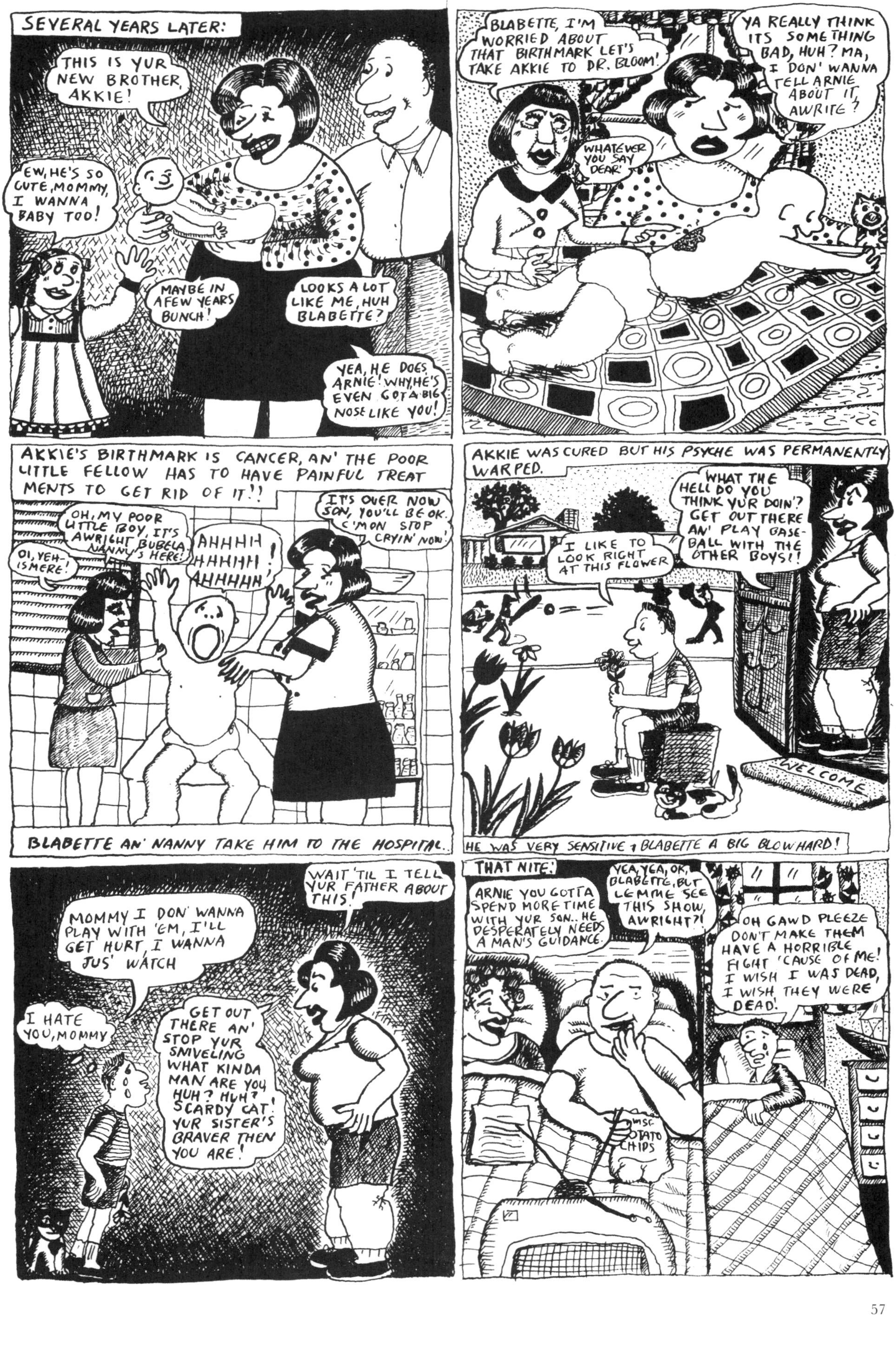
SEVERAL YEARS LATER:
THIS IS YUR NEW BROTHER, AKKIE!
EW, HE'S SO CUTE, MOMMY, I WANNA BABY TOO!
MAYBE IN AFEW YEARS, BUNCH!
LOOKS A LOT LIKE ME, HUH BLABETTE?
YEA, HE DOES, ARNIE! WHY HE'S EVEN GOT A BIG NOSE LIKE YOU!
BLABETTE, I'M WORRIED ABOUT THAT BIRTHMARK LET'S TAKE AKKIE TO DR. BLOOM!
YA REALLY THINK ITS SOMETHING BAD, HUH? MA, I DON' WANNA TELL ARNIE ABOUT IT, AWRITE?
WHATEVER YOU SAY DEAR!
AKKIE'S BIRTHMARK IS CANCER, AN' THE POOR LITTLE FELLOW HAS TO HAVE PAINFUL TREATMENTS TO GET RID OF IT!!
OI, YEH-ISMERE!
OH, MY POOR LITTLE BOY, IT'S AWRIGHT BUBELA, NANNY'S HERE!
AHHHH HHHHH! AHHHHH!
IT'S OVER NOW SON, YOU'LL BE OK. C'MON STOP CRYIN' NOW!
BLABETTE AN' NANNY TAKE HIM TO THE HOSPITAL.
AKKIE WAS CURED BUT HIS PSYCHE WAS PERMANENTLY WARPED.
WHAT THE HELL DO YOU THINK YUR DOIN'? GET OUT THERE AN' PLAY BASEBALL WITH THE OTHER BOYS!!
I LIKE TO LOOK RIGHT AT THIS FLOWER
WELCOME
HE WAS VERY SENSITIVE & BLABETTE A BIG BLOWHARD!
MOMMY I DON' WANNA PLAY WITH 'EM, I'LL GET HURT, I WANNA JUS' WATCH
WAIT 'TIL I TELL YUR FATHER ABOUT THIS!
I HATE YOU, MOMMY
GET OUT THERE AN' STOP YUR SNIVELING WHAT KINDA MAN ARE YOU HUH? HUH? SCARDY CAT! YUR SISTER'S BRAVER THEN YOU ARE!
THAT NITE:
ARNIE YOU GOTTA SPEND MORE TIME WITH YUR SON.. HE DESPERATELY NEEDS A MAN'S GUIDANCE.
YEA, YEA, OK, BLABETTE, BUT LEMME SEE THIS SHOW, AWRIGHT?!
OH GAWD PLEEZE DON'T MAKE THEM HAVE A HORRIBLE FIGHT 'CAUSE OF ME! I WISH I WAS DEAD, I WISH THEY WERE DEAD!
POTATO CHIPS

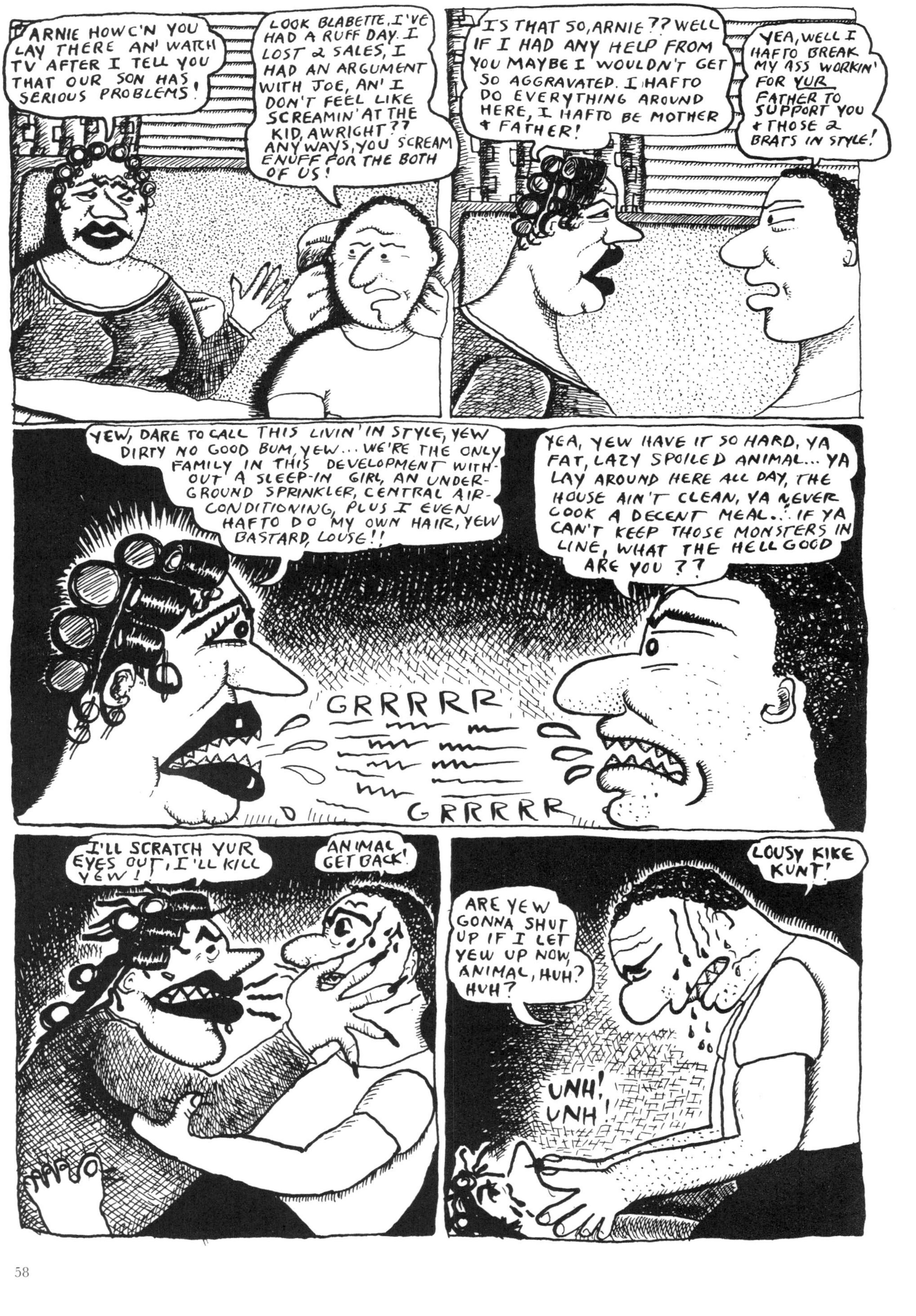
ARNIE HOWC'N YOU LAY THERE AN' WATCH TV AFTER I TELL YOU THAT OUR SON HAS SERIOUS PROBLEMS!
LOOK BLABETTE, I'VE HAD A RUFF DAY. I LOST 2 SALES, I HAD AN ARGUMENT WITH JOE, AN' I DON'T FEEL LIKE SCREAMIN' AT THE KID, AWRIGHT?? ANYWAYS, YOU SCREAM ENUFF FOR THE BOTH OF US!
IS THAT SO, ARNIE?? WELL IF I HAD ANY HELP FROM YOU MAYBE I WOULDN'T GET SO AGGRAVATED. I HAFTO DO EVERYTHING AROUND HERE, I HAFTO BE MOTHER & FATHER!
YEA, WELL I HAFTO BREAK MY ASS WORKIN' FOR YUR FATHER TO SUPPORT YOU & THOSE 2 BRATS IN STYLE!
YEW, DARE TO CALL THIS LIVIN' IN STYLE, YEW DIRTY NO GOOD BUM, YEW... WE'RE THE ONLY FAMILY IN THIS DEVELOPMENT WITHOUT A SLEEP-IN GIRL, AN UNDERGROUND SPRINKLER, CENTRAL AIR-CONDITIONING, PLUS I EVEN HAFTO DO MY OWN HAIR, YEW BASTARD, LOUSE!!
YEA, YEW HAVE IT SO HARD, YA FAT, LAZY SPOILED ANIMAL... YA LAY AROUND HERE ALL DAY, THE HOUSE AIN'T CLEAN, YA NEVER COOK A DECENT MEAL...! IF YA CAN'T KEEP THOSE MONSTERS IN LINE, WHAT THE HELL GOOD ARE YOU??
GRRRRR
GRRRRR
I'LL SCRATCH YUR EYES OUT, I'LL KILL YEW!
ANIMAL GET BACK!
LOUSY KIKE KUNT!
ARE YEW GONNA SHUT UP IF I LET YEW UP NOW, ANIMAL, HUH? HUH?
UNH! UNH!

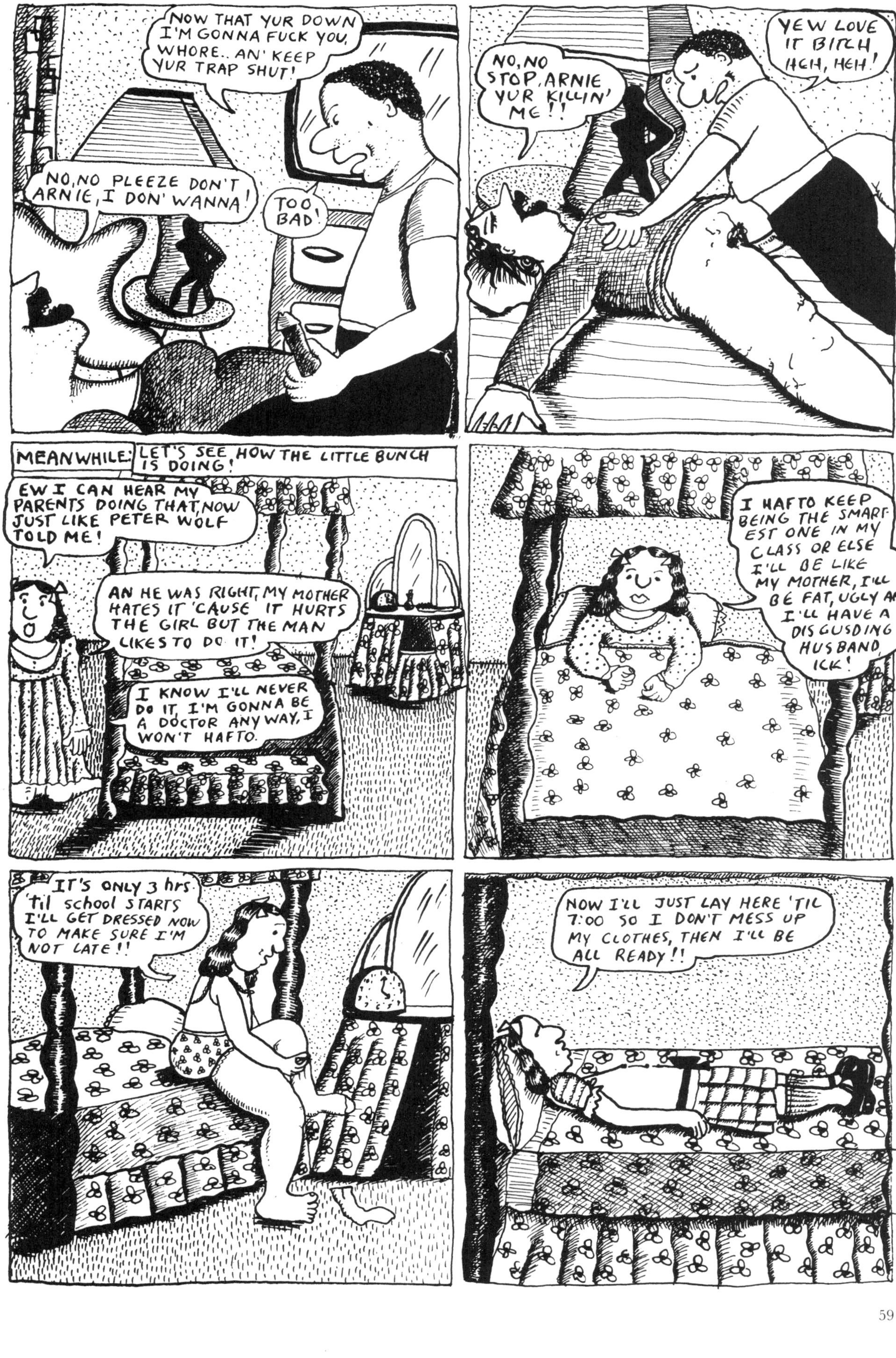
NOW THAT YUR DOWN I'M GONNA FUCK YOU, WHORE.. AN' KEEP YUR TRAP SHUT!
NO, NO PLEEZE DON'T ARNIE, I DON' WANNA!
TOO BAD!
NO, NO STOP, ARNIE YUR KILLIN' ME!!
YEW LOVE IT BITCH HEH, HEH!
MEANWHILE:
LET'S SEE HOW THE LITTLE BUNCH IS DOING!
EW I CAN HEAR MY PARENTS DOING THAT, NOW JUST LIKE PETER WOLF TOLD ME!
AN HE WAS RIGHT, MY MOTHER HATES IT 'CAUSE IT HURTS THE GIRL BUT THE MAN LIKES TO DO IT!
I KNOW I'LL NEVER DO IT, I'M GONNA BE A DOCTOR ANYWAY, I WON'T HAFTO.
I HAFTO KEEP BEING THE SMART-EST ONE IN MY CLASS OR ELSE I'LL BE LIKE MY MOTHER, I'LL BE FAT, UGLY AN' I'LL HAVE A DISGUSDING HUSBAND, ICK!
IT'S ONLY 3 hrs 'til school STARTS I'LL GET DRESSED NOW TO MAKE SURE I'M NOT LATE!!
NOW I'LL JUST LAY HERE 'TIL 7:00 SO I DON'T MESS UP MY CLOTHES, THEN I'LL BE ALL READY!!

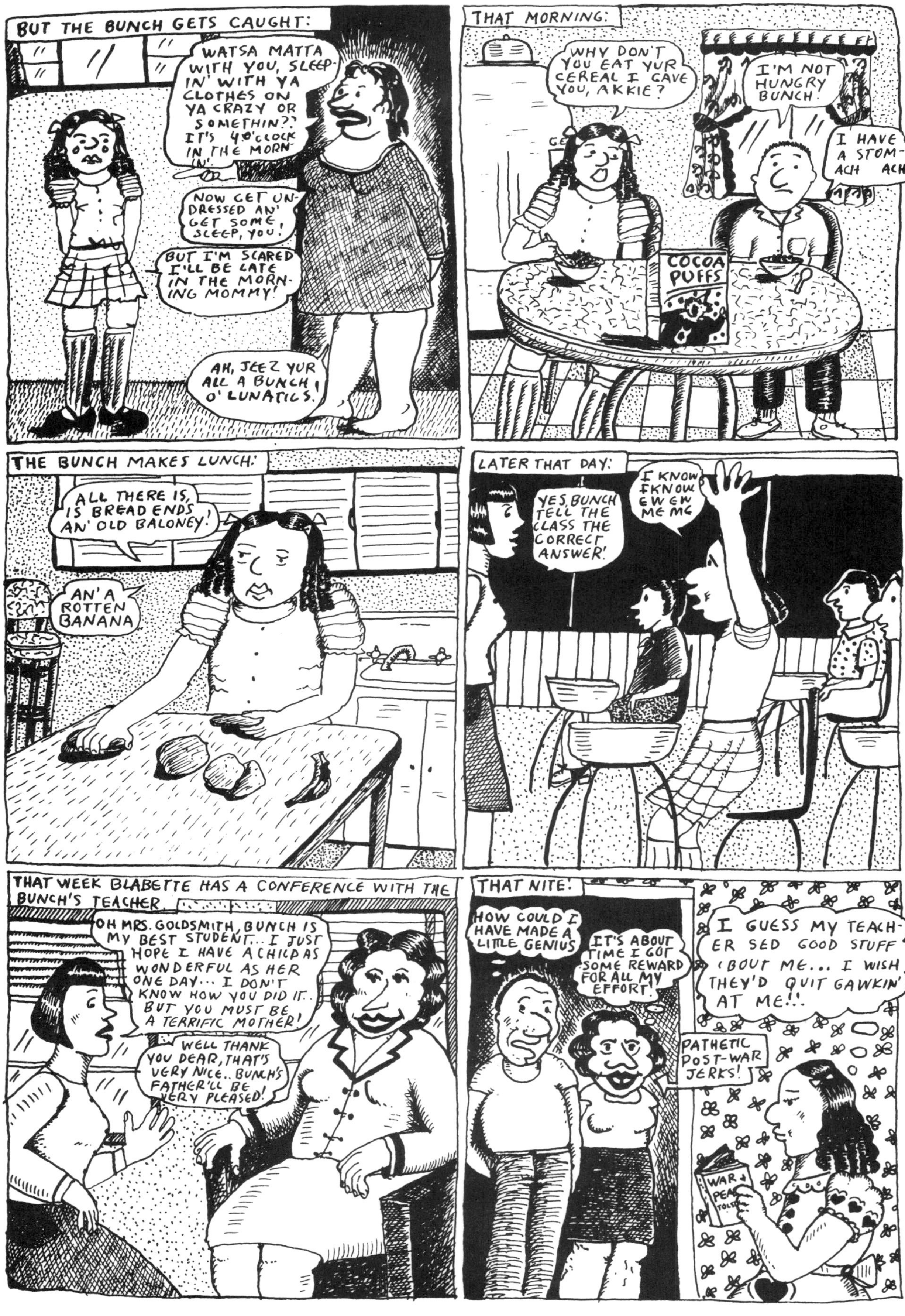
BUT THE BUNCH GETS CAUGHT:
WATSA MATTA WITH YOU, SLEEPIN' WITH YA CLOTHES ON YA CRAZY OR SOMETHIN?? IT'S 4 O'CLOCK IN THE MORNIN'!
NOW GET UNDRESSED AN' GET SOME SLEEP, YOU!
BUT I'M SCARED I'LL BE LATE IN THE MORNING MOMMY!
AH, JEEZ YUR ALL A BUNCH O' LUNATICS!
THAT MORNING:
WHY DON'T YOU EAT YUR CEREAL I GAVE YOU, AKKIE?
I'M NOT HUNGRY BUNCH.
I HAVE A STOMACH ACHE
COCOA PUFFS
THE BUNCH MAKES LUNCH:
ALL THERE IS, IS BREAD ENDS AN' OLD BALONEY!
AN' A ROTTEN BANANA
LATER THAT DAY:
YES, BUNCH TELL THE CLASS THE CORRECT ANSWER!
I KNOW I KNOW EW EW ME ME
THAT WEEK BLABETTE HAS A CONFERENCE WITH THE BUNCH'S TEACHER.
OH MRS. GOLDSMITH, BUNCH IS MY BEST STUDENT... I JUST HOPE I HAVE A CHILD AS WONDERFUL AS HER ONE DAY... I DON'T KNOW HOW YOU DID IT... BUT YOU MUST BE A TERRIFIC MOTHER!
WELL THANK YOU DEAR, THAT'S VERY NICE.. BUNCH'S FATHER'LL BE VERY PLEASED!
THAT NITE:
HOW COULD I HAVE MADE A LITTLE GENIUS
IT'S ABOUT TIME I GOT SOME REWARD FOR ALL MY EFFORT!
PATHETIC POST-WAR JERKS!
I GUESS MY TEACHER SED GOOD STUFF 'BOUT ME... I WISH THEY'D QUIT GAWKIN' AT ME!!.
WAR PEA

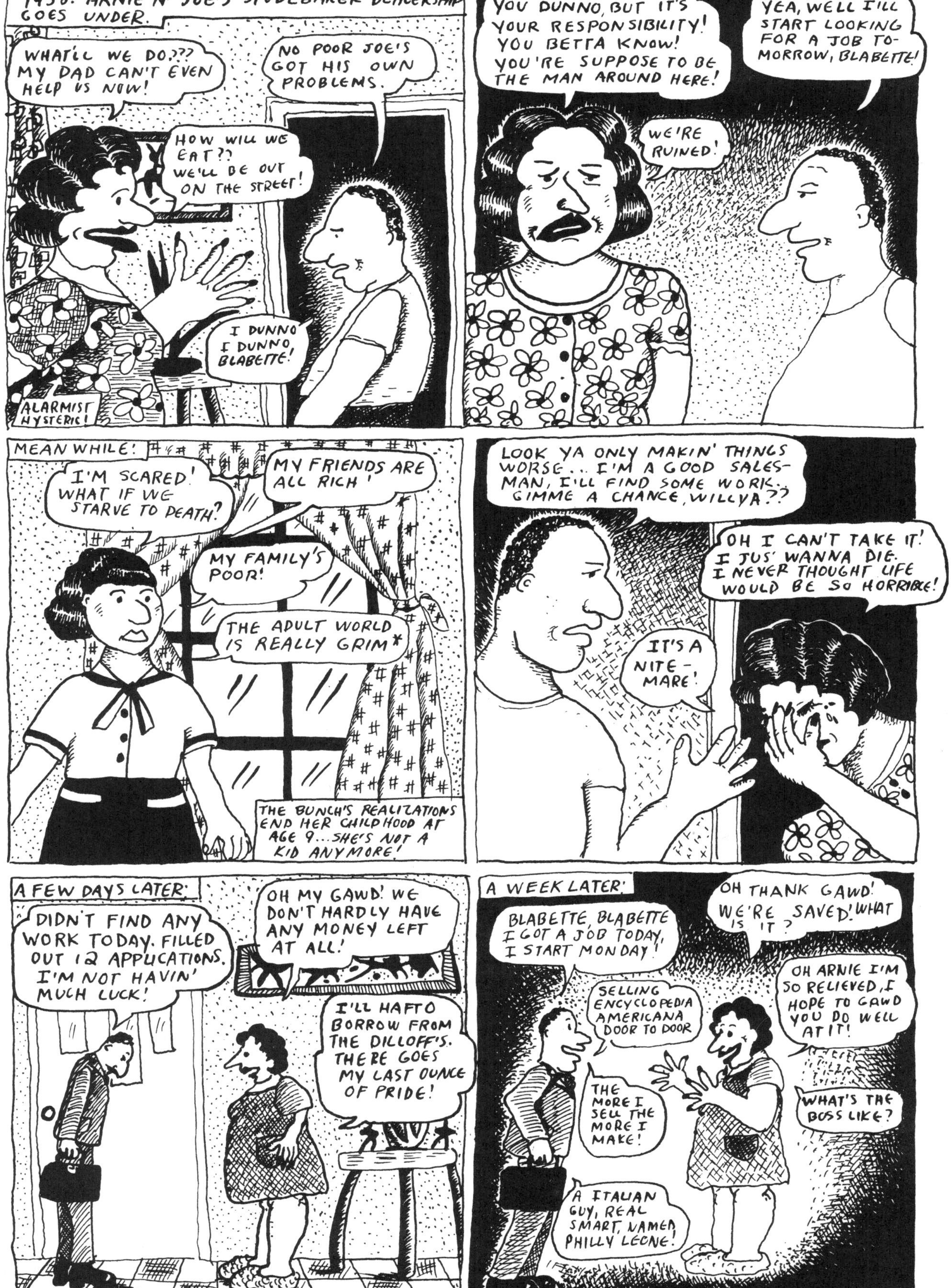

1958: ARNIE N' JOE'S STUDEBAKER DEALERSHIP GOES UNDER.
WHAT'LL WE DO??? MY DAD CAN'T EVEN HELP US NOW!
NO POOR JOE'S GOT HIS OWN PROBLEMS.
HOW WILL WE EAT?? WE'LL BE OUT ON THE STREET!
I DUNNO I DUNNO, BLABETTE!
ALARMIST HYSTERIC!
YOU DUNNO, BUT IT'S YOUR RESPONSIBILITY! YOU BETTA KNOW! YOU'RE SUPPOSE TO BE THE MAN AROUND HERE!
YEA, WELL I'LL START LOOKING FOR A JOB TOMORROW, BLABETTE!
WE'RE RUINED!
MEANWHILE!
I'M SCARED! WHAT IF WE STARVE TO DEATH?
MY FRIENDS ARE ALL RICH!
MY FAMILY'S POOR!
THE ADULT WORLD IS REALLY GRIM*
THE BUNCH'S REALIZATIONS END HER CHILDHOOD AT AGE 9... SHE'S NOT A KID ANYMORE!
LOOK YA ONLY MAKIN' THINGS WORSE... I'M A GOOD SALESMAN, I'LL FIND SOME WORK... GIMME A CHANCE, WILLYA??
OH I CAN'T TAKE IT! I JUS' WANNA DIE. I NEVER THOUGHT LIFE WOULD BE SO HORRIBLE!
IT'S A NITEMARE!
A FEW DAYS LATER:
DIDN'T FIND ANY WORK TODAY. FILLED OUT 12 APPLICATIONS. I'M NOT HAVIN' MUCH LUCK!
OH MY GAWD! WE DON'T HARDLY HAVE ANY MONEY LEFT AT ALL!
I'LL HAFTO BORROW FROM THE DILLOFF'S. THERE GOES MY LAST OUNCE OF PRIDE!
A WEEK LATER:
BLABETTE, BLABETTE I GOT A JOB TODAY, I START MONDAY!
OH THANK GAWD! WE'RE SAVED! WHAT IS IT?
SELLING ENCYCLOPEDIA AMERICANA DOOR TO DOOR
OH ARNIE I'M SO RELIEVED, I HOPE TO GAWD YOU DO WELL AT IT!
THE MORE I SELL THE MORE I MAKE!
WHAT'S THE BOSS LIKE?
A ITALIAN GUY, REAL SMART, NAMED PHILLY LEONE!
* THE BUNCH STILL FEELS THIS WAY AN' IS A CLASSIC CASE OF ARRESTED DEVELOPMENT!

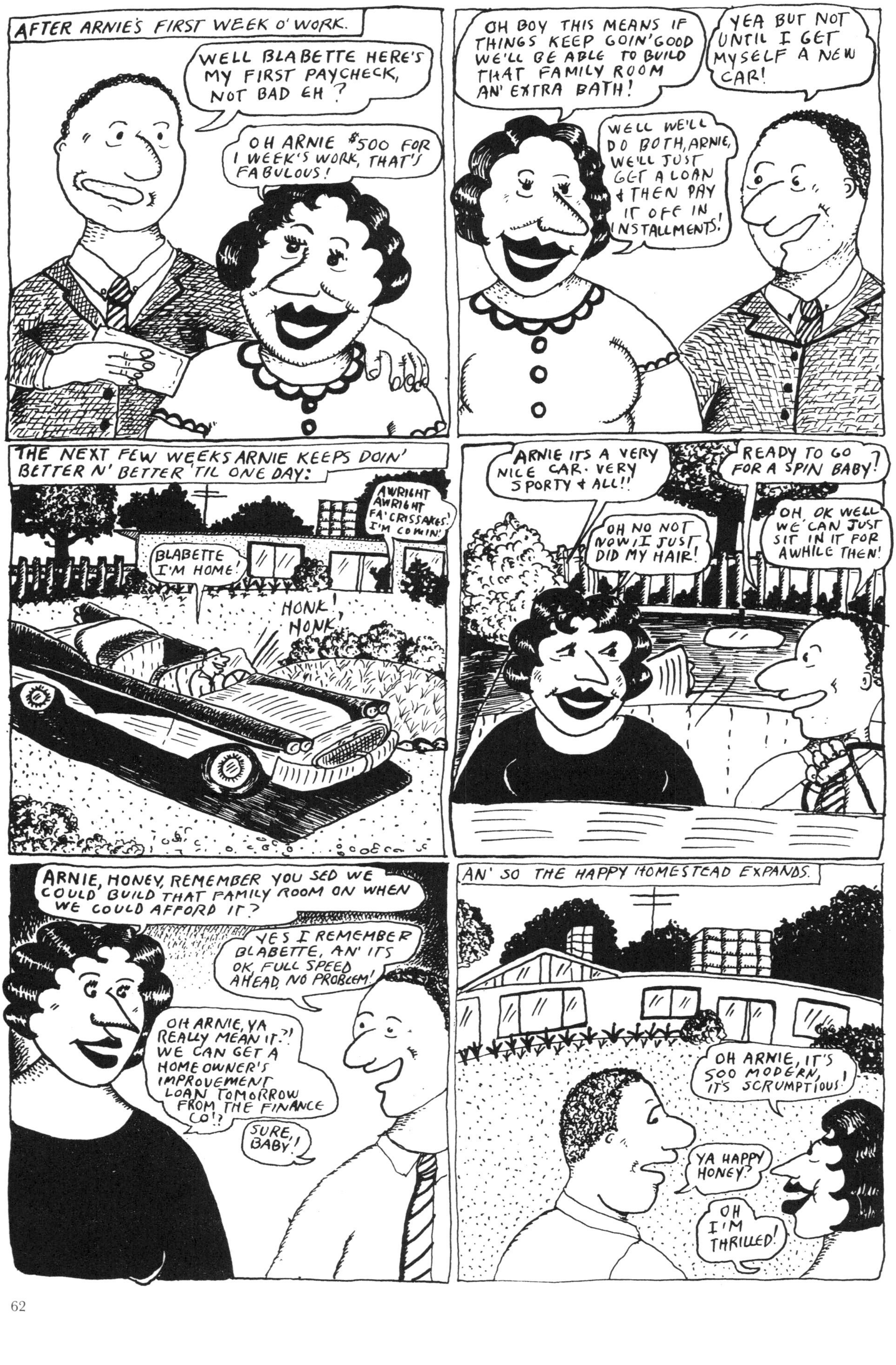
AFTER ARNIE'S FIRST WEEK O' WORK.
WELL BLABETTE HERE'S MY FIRST PAYCHECK, NOT BAD EH?
OH ARNIE $500 FOR 1 WEEK'S WORK, THAT'S FABULOUS!
OH BOY THIS MEANS IF THINGS KEEP GOIN' GOOD WE'LL BE ABLE TO BUILD THAT FAMILY ROOM AN' EXTRA BATH!
YEA BUT NOT UNTIL I GET MYSELF A NEW CAR!
WELL WE'LL DO BOTH, ARNIE, WE'LL JUST GET A LOAN & THEN PAY IT OFF IN INSTALLMENTS!
THE NEXT FEW WEEKS ARNIE KEEPS DOIN' BETTER N' BETTER 'TIL ONE DAY:
BLABETTE I'M HOME!
HONK! HONK!
AWRIGHT AWRIGHT FA'CRISSAKES! I'M COMIN'
ARNIE ITS A VERY NICE CAR. VERY SPORTY & ALL!!
READY TO GO FOR A SPIN BABY?
OH NO NOT NOW, I JUST DID MY HAIR!
OH, OK WELL WE CAN JUST SIT IN IT FOR AWHILE THEN!
ARNIE, HONEY, REMEMBER YOU SED WE COULD BUILD THAT FAMILY ROOM ON WHEN WE COULD AFFORD IT?
YES I REMEMBER BLABETTE, AN' ITS OK, FULL SPEED AHEAD, NO PROBLEM!
OH ARNIE, YA REALLY MEAN IT?! WE CAN GET A HOME OWNER'S IMPROVEMENT LOAN TOMORROW FROM THE FINANCE CO!?
SURE, BABY!
AN' SO THE HAPPY HOMESTEAD EXPANDS.
OH ARNIE, IT'S SOO MODERN, IT'S SCRUMPTIOUS!
YA HAPPY HONEY?
OH I'M THRILLED!

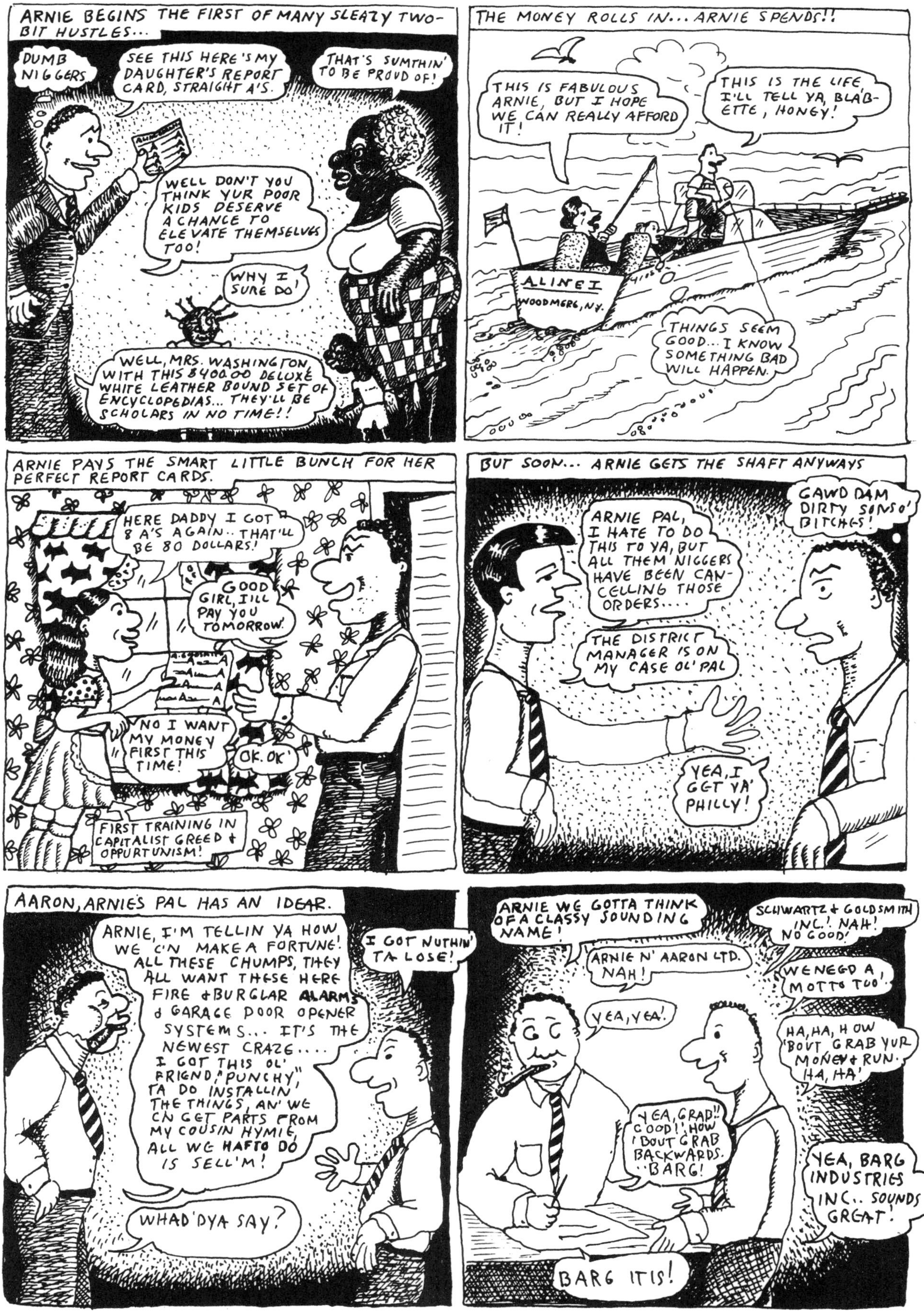
ARNIE BEGINS THE FIRST OF MANY SLEAZY TWO-BIT HUSTLES...
DUMB NIGGERS
SEE THIS HERE'S MY DAUGHTER'S REPORT CARD, STRAIGHT A'S.
THAT'S SUMTHIN' TO BE PROUD OF!
WELL DON'T YOU THINK YUR POOR KIDS DESERVE A CHANCE TO ELEVATE THEMSELVES TOO!
WHY I SURE DO!
WELL, MRS. WASHINGTON, WITH THIS $400.00 DELUXE WHITE LEATHER BOUND SET OF ENCYCLOPEDIAS... THEY'LL BE SCHOLARS IN NO TIME!!
THE MONEY ROLLS IN... ARNIE SPENDS!!
THIS IS FABULOUS ARNIE, BUT I HOPE WE CAN REALLY AFFORD IT!
THIS IS THE LIFE I'LL TELL YA, BLAB-ETTE, HONEY!
ALINE I
WOODMERE, N.Y.
THINGS SEEM GOOD... I KNOW SOMETHING BAD WILL HAPPEN.
ARNIE PAYS THE SMART LITTLE BUNCH FOR HER PERFECT REPORT CARDS.
HERE DADDY I GOT 8 A'S AGAIN.. THAT'LL BE 80 DOLLARS!
GOOD GIRL, I'LL PAY YOU TOMORROW.
NO I WANT MY MONEY FIRST THIS TIME!
OK. OK!
FIRST TRAINING IN CAPITALIST GREED & OPPURTUNISM!
BUT SOON... ARNIE GETS THE SHAFT ANYWAYS
ARNIE PAL, I HATE TO DO THIS TO YA, BUT ALL THEM NIGGERS HAVE BEEN CANCELLING THOSE ORDERS...
GAWD DAM DIRTY SONSO' BITCHES!
THE DISTRICT MANAGER IS ON MY CASE OL' PAL
YEA, I GET YA' PHILLY!
AARON, ARNIE'S PAL HAS AN IDEAR.
ARNIE, I'M TELLIN YA HOW WE C'N MAKE A FORTUNE! ALL THESE CHUMPS, THEY ALL WANT THESE HERE FIRE & BURGLAR ALARMS & GARAGE DOOR OPENER SYSTEMS... IT'S THE NEWEST CRAZE.... I GOT THIS OL' FRIEND, "PUNCHY," TA DO INSTALLIN THE THINGS, AN' WE C'N GET PARTS FROM MY COUSIN HYMIE, ALL WE HAFTO DO IS SELL'M!
I GOT NUTHIN' TA LOSE!
WHAD'DYA SAY?
ARNIE WE GOTTA THINK OF A CLASSY SOUNDING NAME!
SCHWARTZ & GOLDSMITH INC.! NAH! NO GOOD!
ARNIE N' AARON LTD. NAH!
WE NEED A MOTTO TOO!
YEA, YEA!
HA, HA, HOW 'BOUT GRAB YUR MONEY & RUN. HA, HA!
YEA, GRAB!! GOOD!! HOW 'BOUT GRAB BACKWARDS. BARG!
YEA, BARG INDUSTRIES INC.. SOUNDS GREAT!
BARG IT IS!

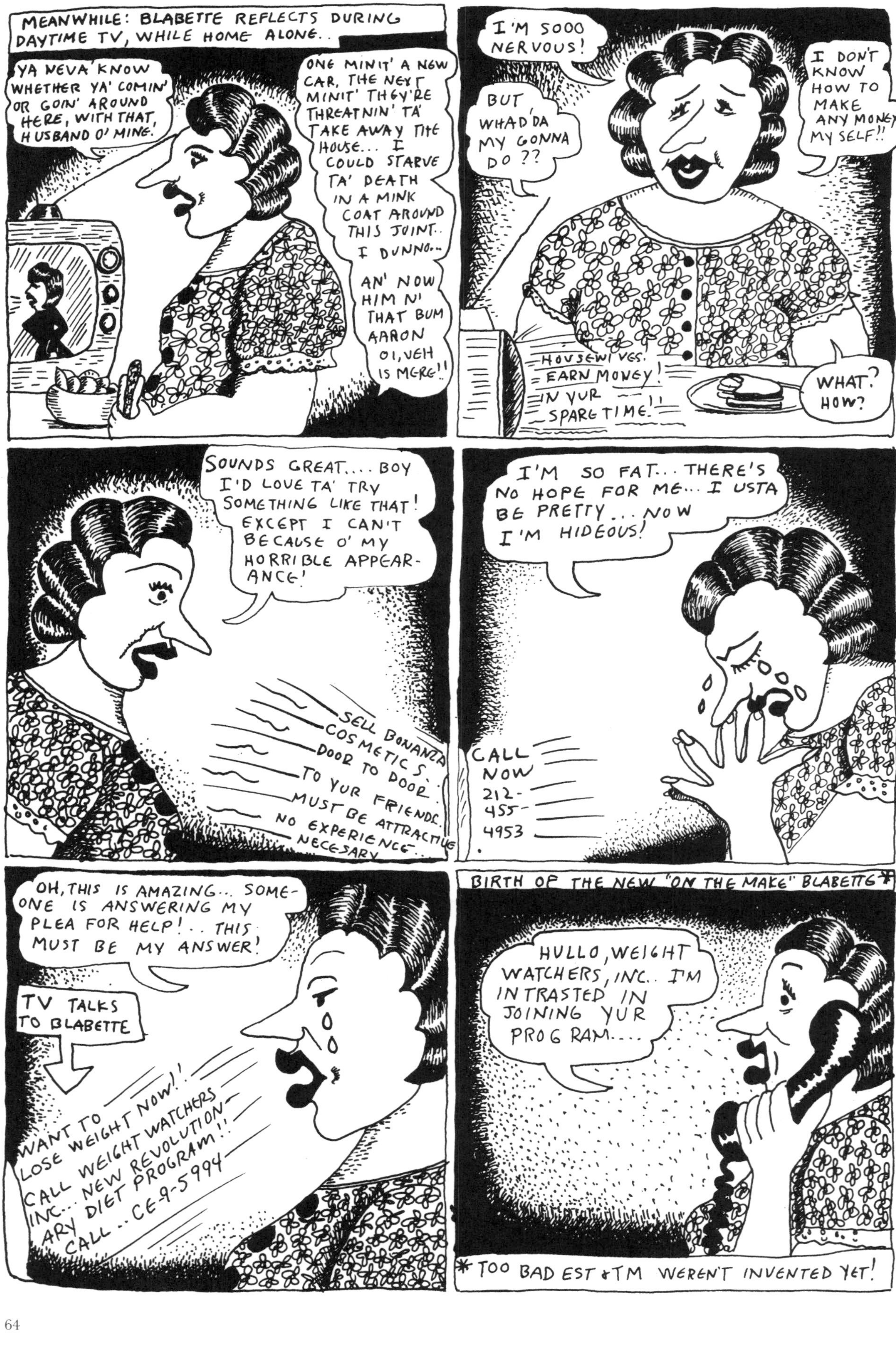

MEANWHILE: BLABETTE REFLECTS DURING DAYTIME TV, WHILE HOME ALONE..
YA NEVA KNOW WHETHER YA' COMIN' OR GOIN' AROUND HERE, WITH THAT, HUSBAND O' MINE.
ONE MINIT' A NEW CAR, THE NEXT MINIT' THEY'RE THREATNIN' TA' TAKE AWAY THE HOUSE... I COULD STARVE TA' DEATH IN A MINK COAT AROUND THIS JOINT.. I DUNNO...
AN' NOW HIM N' THAT BUM AARON OI, VEH IS MERE!!
I'M SOOO NERVOUS!
BUT, WHAD'DA MY GONNA DO??
I DON'T KNOW HOW TO MAKE ANY MONEY MYSELF!!
HOUSEWIVES. EARN MONEY! IN YUR SPARE TIME!!
WHAT? HOW?
SOUNDS GREAT.... BOY I'D LOVE TA' TRY SOMETHING LIKE THAT! EXCEPT I CAN'T BECAUSE O' MY HORRIBLE APPEARANCE!
SELL BONANZA COSMETICS. DOOR TO DOOR. TO YUR FRIENDS. MUST BE ATTRACTIVE NO EXPERIENCE NECESARY.
I'M SO FAT... THERE'S NO HOPE FOR ME... I USTA BE PRETTY... NOW I'M HIDEOUS!
CALL NOW 212-455-4953
OH, THIS IS AMAZING... SOMEONE IS ANSWERING MY PLEA FOR HELP!.. THIS MUST BE MY ANSWER!
TV TALKS TO BLABETTE
WANT TO LOSE WEIGHT NOW!! CALL WEIGHT WATCHERS INC.. NEW REVOLUTIONARY DIET PROGRAM!! CALL.. CE-9-5994
BIRTH OF THE NEW "ON THE MAKE" BLABETTE*
HULLO, WEIGHT WATCHERS, INC.. I'M INTRASTED IN JOINING YUR PROGRAM....
*TOO BAD EST & TM WEREN'T INVENTED YET!

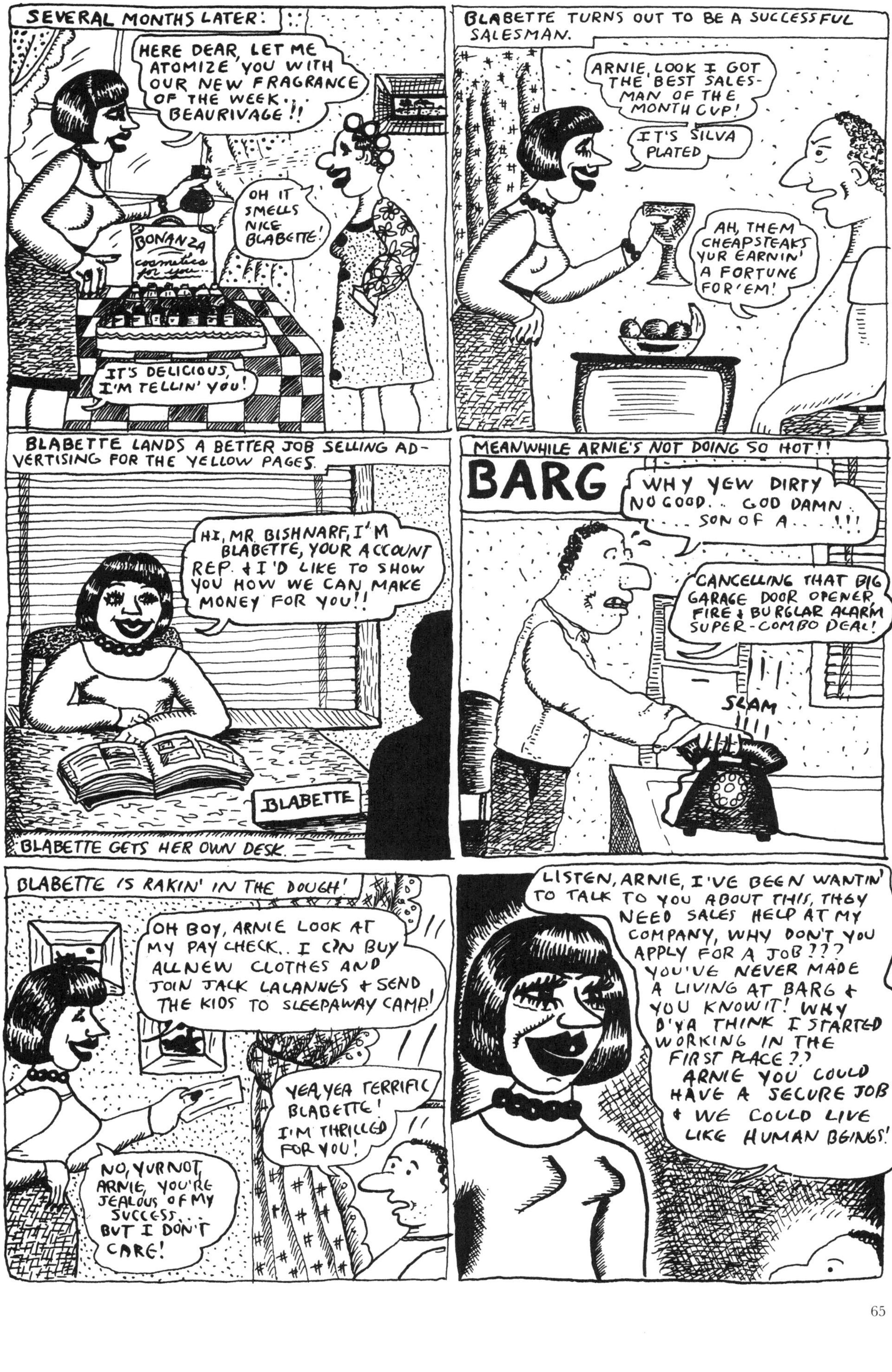

SEVERAL MONTHS LATER:
HERE DEAR, LET ME ATOMIZE YOU WITH OUR NEW FRAGRANCE OF THE WEEK. BEAURIVAGE!!
OH IT SMELLS NICE BLABETTE!
BONANZA cosmetics for you
IT'S DELICIOUS, I'M TELLIN' YOU!
BLABETTE TURNS OUT TO BE A SUCCESSFUL SALESMAN.
ARNIE, LOOK I GOT THE BEST SALES-MAN OF THE MONTH CUP!
IT'S SILVA PLATED
AH, THEM CHEAPSTEAKS YUR EARNIN' A FORTUNE FOR'EM!
BLABETTE LANDS A BETTER JOB SELLING AD-VERTISING FOR THE YELLOW PAGES.
HI, MR BISHNARF, I'M BLABETTE, YOUR ACCOUNT REP & I'D LIKE TO SHOW YOU HOW WE CAN MAKE MONEY FOR YOU!!
BLABETTE
BLABETTE GETS HER OWN DESK.
MEANWHILE ARNIE'S NOT DOING SO HOT!!
BARG
WHY YEW DIRTY NO GOOD.. GOD DAMN SON OF A...!!!
CANCELLING THAT BIG GARAGE DOOR OPENER FIRE & BURGLAR ALARM SUPER-COMBO DEAL!
SLAM
BLABETTE IS RAKIN' IN THE DOUGH!
OH BOY, ARNIE LOOK AT MY PAY CHECK.. I CAN BUY ALL NEW CLOTHES AND JOIN JACK LALANNES & SEND THE KIDS TO SLEEPAWAY CAMP!
YEA, YEA TERRIFIC BLABETTE! I'M THRILLED FOR YOU!
NO, YURNOT, ARNIE, YOU'RE JEALOUS OF MY SUCCESS. BUT I DON'T CARE!
LISTEN, ARNIE, I'VE BEEN WANTIN' TO TALK TO YOU ABOUT THIS, THEY NEED SALES HELP AT MY COMPANY, WHY DON'T YOU APPLY FOR A JOB??? YOU'VE NEVER MADE A LIVING AT BARG & YOU KNOW IT! WHY D'YA THINK I STARTED WORKING IN THE FIRST PLACE?? ARNIE YOU COULD HAVE A SECURE JOB & WE COULD LIVE LIKE HUMAN BEINGS!

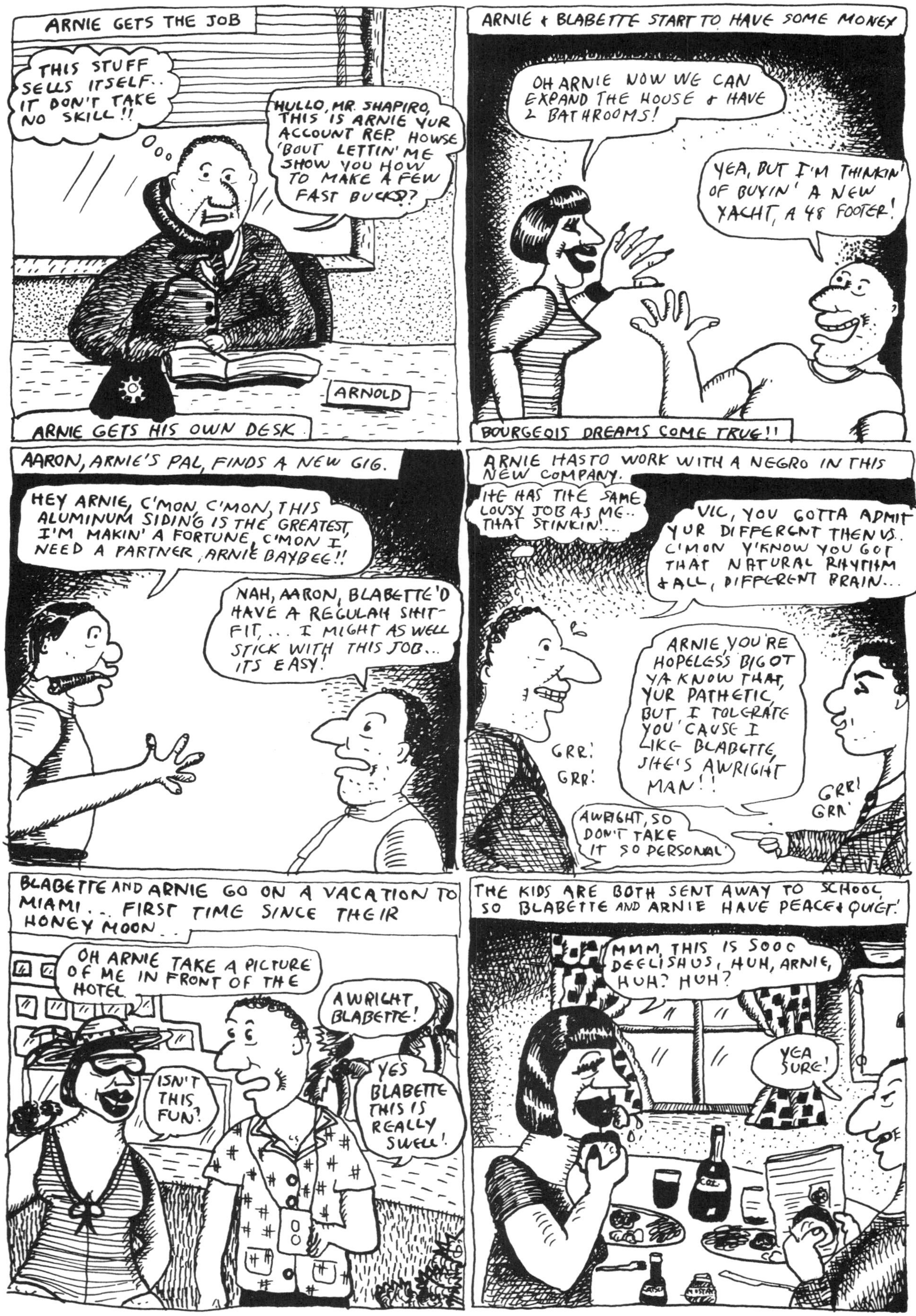
ARNIE GETS THE JOB
THIS STUFF SELLS ITSELF.. IT DON'T TAKE NO SKILL!!
HULLO, MR. SHAPIRO, THIS IS ARNIE YUR ACCOUNT REP. HOWSE 'BOUT LETTIN' ME SHOW YOU HOW TO MAKE A FEW FAST BUCKS?
ARNOLD
ARNIE GETS HIS OWN DESK
ARNIE & BLABETTE START TO HAVE SOME MONEY
OH ARNIE NOW WE CAN EXPAND THE HOUSE & HAVE 2 BATHROOMS!
YEA, BUT I'M THINKIN' OF BUYIN' A NEW YACHT, A 48 FOOTER!
BOURGEOIS DREAMS COME TRUE!!
AARON, ARNIE'S PAL, FINDS A NEW GIG.
HEY ARNIE, C'MON, C'MON, THIS ALUMINUM SIDING IS THE GREATEST, I'M MAKIN' A FORTUNE, C'MON I NEED A PARTNER, ARNIE BAYBEE!!
NAH, AARON, BLABETTE'D HAVE A REGULAH SHIT-FIT, ... I MIGHT AS WELL STICK WITH THIS JOB... ITS EASY!
ARNIE HAS TO WORK WITH A NEGRO IN THIS NEW COMPANY.
HE HAS THE SAME LOUSY JOB AS ME.. THAT STINKIN'...
VIC, YOU GOTTA ADMIT YUR DIFFERENT THEN US. C'MON Y'KNOW YOU GOT THAT NATURAL RHYTHM & ALL, DIFFERENT BRAIN...
ARNIE, YOU'RE HOPELESS BIGOT YA KNOW THAT, YUR PATHETIC, BUT, I TOLERATE YOU 'CAUSE I LIKE BLABETTE, SHE'S AWRIGHT MAN!!
GRR! GRR!
GRR! GRR!
AWRIGHT, SO DON'T TAKE IT SO PERSONAL!
BLABETTE AND ARNIE GO ON A VACATION TO MIAMI... FIRST TIME SINCE THEIR HONEYMOON...
OH ARNIE TAKE A PICTURE OF ME IN FRONT OF THE HOTEL
AWRIGHT, BLABETTE!
ISN'T THIS FUN?
YES BLABETTE THIS IS REALLY SWELL!
THE KIDS ARE BOTH SENT AWAY TO SCHOOL, SO BLABETTE AND ARNIE HAVE PEACE & QUIET!
MMM, THIS IS SOOO DEELISHUS, HUH, ARNIE, HUH? HUH?
YEA SURE!

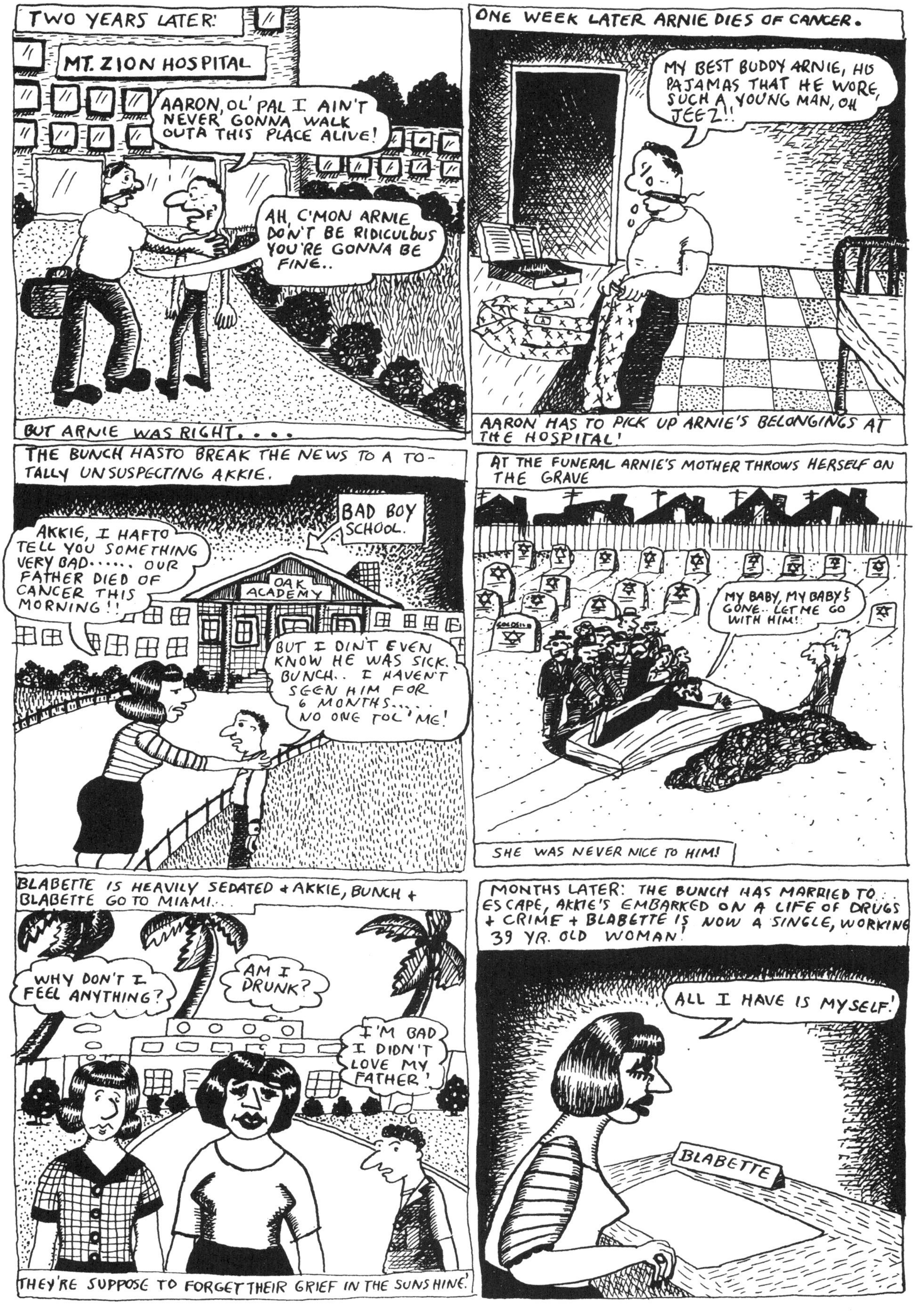
TWO YEARS LATER:
MT. ZION HOSPITAL
AARON, OL' PAL I AIN'T NEVER GONNA WALK OUTA THIS PLACE ALIVE!
AH, C'MON ARNIE DON'T BE RIDICULOUS YOU'RE GONNA BE FINE..
BUT ARNIE WAS RIGHT....
ONE WEEK LATER ARNIE DIES OF CANCER.
MY BEST BUDDY ARNIE, HIS PAJAMAS THAT HE WORE, SUCH A YOUNG MAN, OH JEEZ!!
AARON HAS TO PICK UP ARNIE'S BELONGINGS AT THE HOSPITAL!
THE BUNCH HASTO BREAK THE NEWS TO A TOTALLY UNSUSPECTING AKKIE.
BAD BOY SCHOOL.
OAK ACADEMY
AKKIE, I HAFTO TELL YOU SOMETHING VERY BAD...... OUR FATHER DIED OF CANCER THIS MORNING!!
BUT I DIN'T EVEN KNOW HE WAS SICK. BUNCH.. I HAVEN'T SEEN HIM FOR 6 MONTHS..... NO ONE TOL' ME!
AT THE FUNERAL ARNIE'S MOTHER THROWS HERSELF ON THE GRAVE
MY BABY, MY BABY'S GONE.. LET ME GO WITH HIM!
SHE WAS NEVER NICE TO HIM!
BLABETTE IS HEAVILY SEDATED + AKKIE, BUNCH + BLABETTE GO TO MIAMI...
WHY DON'T I FEEL ANYTHING?
AM I DRUNK?
I'M BAD I DIDN'T LOVE MY FATHER!
THEY'RE SUPPOSE TO FORGET THEIR GRIEF IN THE SUNSHINE!
MONTHS LATER: THE BUNCH HAS MARRIED TO ESCAPE, AKKIE'S EMBARKED ON A LIFE OF DRUGS + CRIME + BLABETTE IS NOW A SINGLE, WORKING 39 YR. OLD WOMAN!
ALL I HAVE IS MYSELF!
BLABETTE

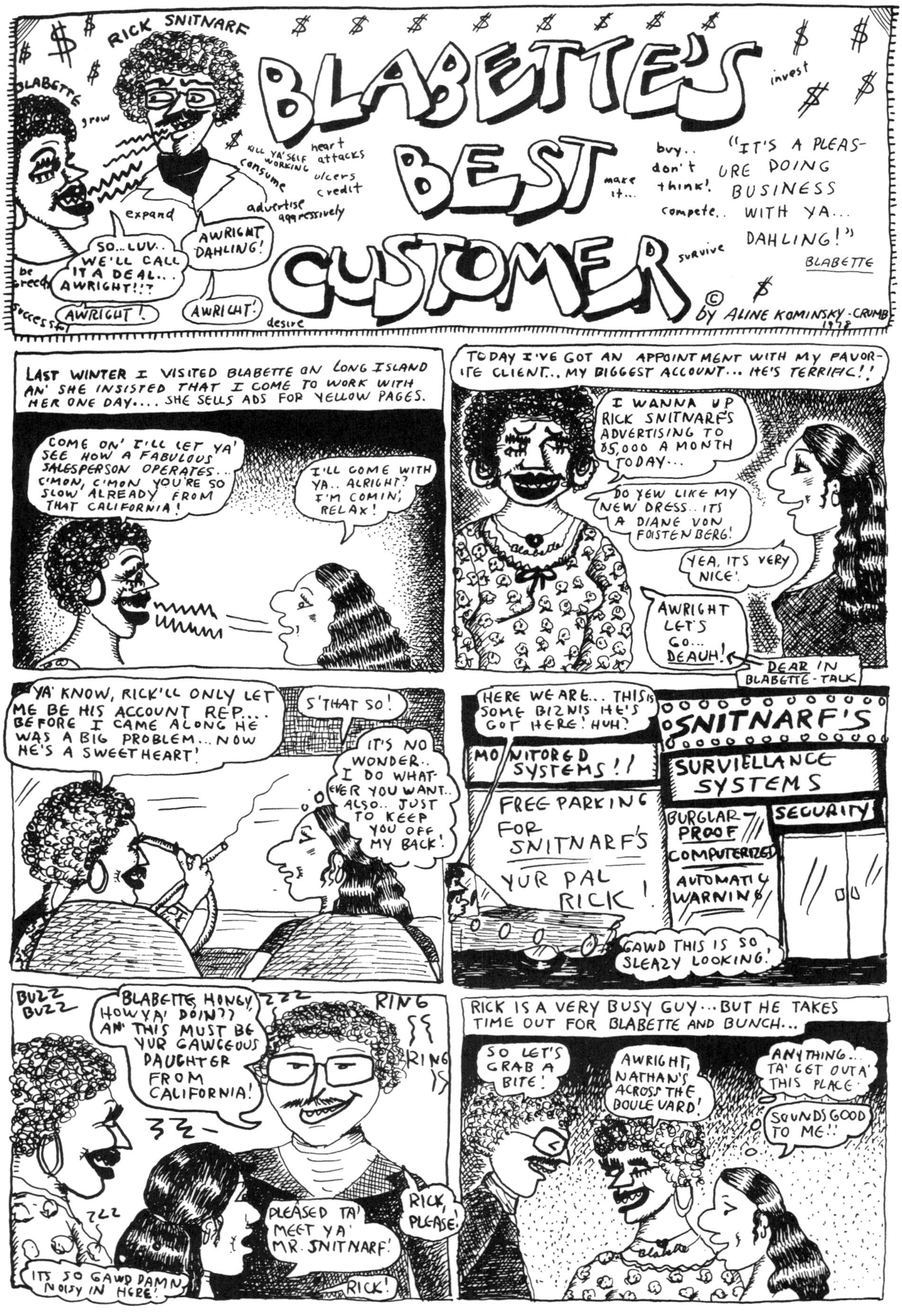
BLABETTE'S BEST CUSTOMER
© by ALINE KOMINSKY-CRUMB 1978
RICK SNITNARF
BLABETTE
grow
expand
KILL YA'SELF WORKING
consume
heart attacks
ulcers
credit
advertise aggressively
be greedy
successful
desire
buy.. don't think!
make it...
compete..
survive
invest
SO...LUV.. WE'LL CALL IT A DEAL... AWRIGHT!!?
AWRIGHT DAHLING!
AWRIGHT!
AWRIGHT!
"IT'S A PLEASURE DOING BUSINESS WITH YA... DAHLING!"
BLABETTE
LAST WINTER I VISITED BLABETTE ON LONG ISLAND AN' SHE INSISTED THAT I COME TO WORK WITH HER ONE DAY.... SHE SELLS ADS FOR YELLOW PAGES.
COME ON' I'LL LET YA' SEE HOW A FABULOUS SALESPERSON OPERATES... C'MON, C'MON YOU'RE SO SLOW ALREADY FROM THAT CALIFORNIA!
I'LL COME WITH YA.. ALRIGHT? I'M COMIN, RELAX!
TODAY I'VE GOT AN APPOINTMENT WITH MY FAVORITE CLIENT... MY BIGGEST ACCOUNT... HE'S TERRIFIC!!
I WANNA UP RICK SNITNARF'S ADVERTISING TO 85,000 A MONTH TODAY...
DO YEW LIKE MY NEW DRESS.. ITS A DIANE VON FOISTENBERG!
YEA, ITS VERY NICE.
AWRIGHT LET'S GO... DEAUH!
DEAR IN BLABETTE-TALK
YA' KNOW, RICK'LL ONLY LET ME BE HIS ACCOUNT REP... BEFORE I CAME ALONG HE WAS A BIG PROBLEM... NOW HE'S A SWEETHEART!
S'THAT SO!
IT'S NO WONDER.. I DO WHATEVER YOU WANT.. ALSO.. JUST TO KEEP YOU OFF MY BACK!
HERE WE ARE... THIS IS SOME BIZNIS HE'S GOT HERE! HUH?
SNITNARF'S
MONITORED SYSTEMS!!
SURVIELLANCE SYSTEMS
FREE PARKING FOR SNITNARF'S YUR PAL RICK!
BURGLAR PROOF
SECURITY
COMPUTERIZED
AUTOMATIC WARNING
GAWD THIS IS SO SLEAZY LOOKING!
BUZZ BUZZ
BLABETTE, HONEY, HOW YA' DOIN?? AN' THIS MUST BE YUR GAWGEOUS DAUGHTER FROM CALIFORNIA!
RING RING
PLEASED TA' MEET YA' MR. SNITNARF!
RICK, PLEASE!
RICK!
ITS SO GAWD DAMN NOISY IN HERE!
RICK IS A VERY BUSY GUY... BUT HE TAKES TIME OUT FOR BLABETTE AND BUNCH...
SO LET'S GRAB A BITE!
AWRIGHT, NATHAN'S ACROSS THE BOULEVARD!
ANYTHING... TA' GET OUTA' THIS PLACE.
SOUNDS GOOD TO ME!!

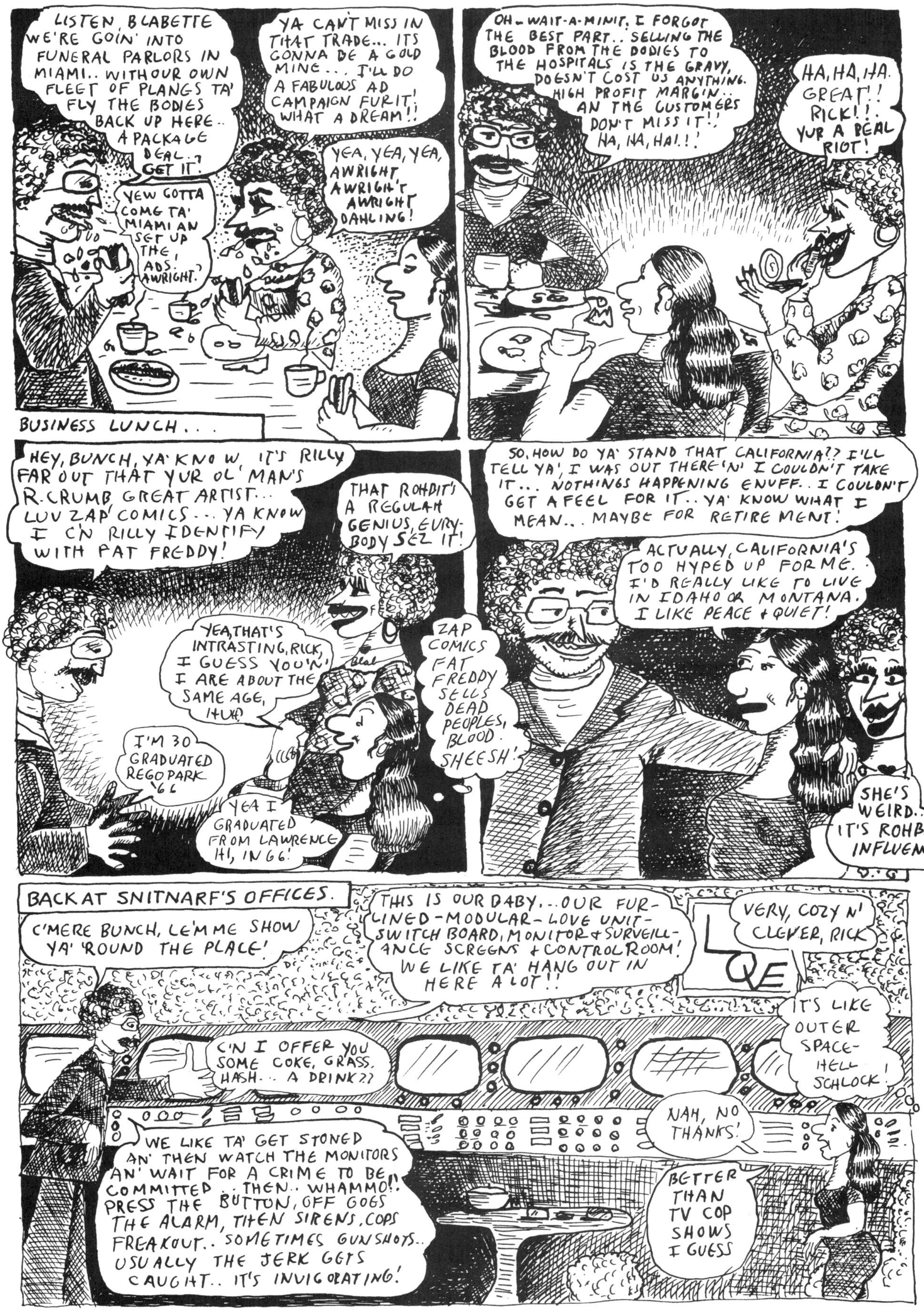

LISTEN, BLABETTE WE'RE GOIN' INTO FUNERAL PARLORS IN MIAMI.. WITH OUR OWN FLEET OF PLANES TA' FLY THE BODIES BACK UP HERE.. A PACKAGE DEAL.. GET IT.
YA CAN'T MISS IN THAT TRADE... ITS GONNA BE A GOLD MINE... I'LL DO A FABULOUS AD CAMPAIGN FUR IT! WHAT A DREAM!!
YEA, YEA, YEA, AWRIGHT AWRIGHT AWRIGHT DAHLING!
YEW GOTTA COME TA' MIAMI AN SET UP THE ADS. AWRIGHT.
BUSINESS LUNCH...
OH-WAIT-A-MINIT, I FORGOT THE BEST PART.. SELLING THE BLOOD FROM THE BODIES TO THE HOSPITALS IS THE GRAVY, DOESN'T COST US ANYTHING. HIGH PROFIT MARGIN.. AN THE CUSTOMERS DON'T MISS IT!! HA, HA, HA!!
HA, HA, HA. GREAT!! RICK!! YUR A REAL RIOT!
HEY, BUNCH, YA' KNOW, IT'S RILLY FAR OUT THAT YUR OL' MAN'S R. CRUMB GREAT ARTIST... LUV ZAP COMICS... YA KNOW I C'N RILLY IDENTIFY WITH FAT FREDDY!
THAT ROHBIT'S A REGULAH GENIUS, EVRY-BODY SEZ IT!
YEA, THAT'S INTRASTING, RICK, I GUESS YOU'N I ARE ABOUT THE SAME AGE, HUH?
I'M 30 GRADUATED REGO PARK '66
YEA I GRADUATED FROM LAWRENCE HI, IN 66.
ZAP COMICS FAT FREDDY SELLS DEAD PEOPLES BLOOD. SHEESH.
SO, HOW DO YA' STAND THAT CALIFORNIA?? I'LL TELL YA', I WAS OUT THERE 'N' I COULDN'T TAKE IT... NOTHINGS HAPPENING ENUFF.. I COULDN'T GET A FEEL FOR IT.. YA' KNOW WHAT I MEAN... MAYBE FOR RETIREMENT.
ACTUALLY, CALIFORNIA'S TOO HYPED UP FOR ME. I'D REALLY LIKE TO LIVE IN IDAHO OR MONTANA. I LIKE PEACE + QUIET!
SHE'S WEIRD.. IT'S ROHBIT'S INFLUENCE!
BACK AT SNITNARF'S OFFICES.
C'MERE BUNCH, LEM'ME SHOW YA' 'ROUND THE PLACE.
THIS IS OUR BABY...OUR FUR-LINED-MODULAR-LOVE UNIT-SWITCH BOARD, MONITOR + SURVEILL-ANCE SCREENS + CONTROL ROOM! WE LIKE TA' HANG OUT IN HERE A LOT!!
VERY, COZY N' CLEVER, RICK
LOVE
IT'S LIKE OUTER SPACE-HELL SCHLOCK!
C'N I OFFER YOU SOME COKE, GRASS, HASH... A DRINK??
NAH, NO THANKS!
WE LIKE TA' GET STONED AN' THEN WATCH THE MONITORS AN' WAIT FOR A CRIME TO BE COMMITTED.. THEN.. WHAMMO!! PRESS THE BUTTON, OFF GOES THE ALARM, THEN SIRENS, COPS FREAKOUT.. SOMETIMES GUNSHOTS.. USUALLY THE JERK GETS CAUGHT.. IT'S INVIGORATING!
BETTER THAN TV COP SHOWS I GUESS

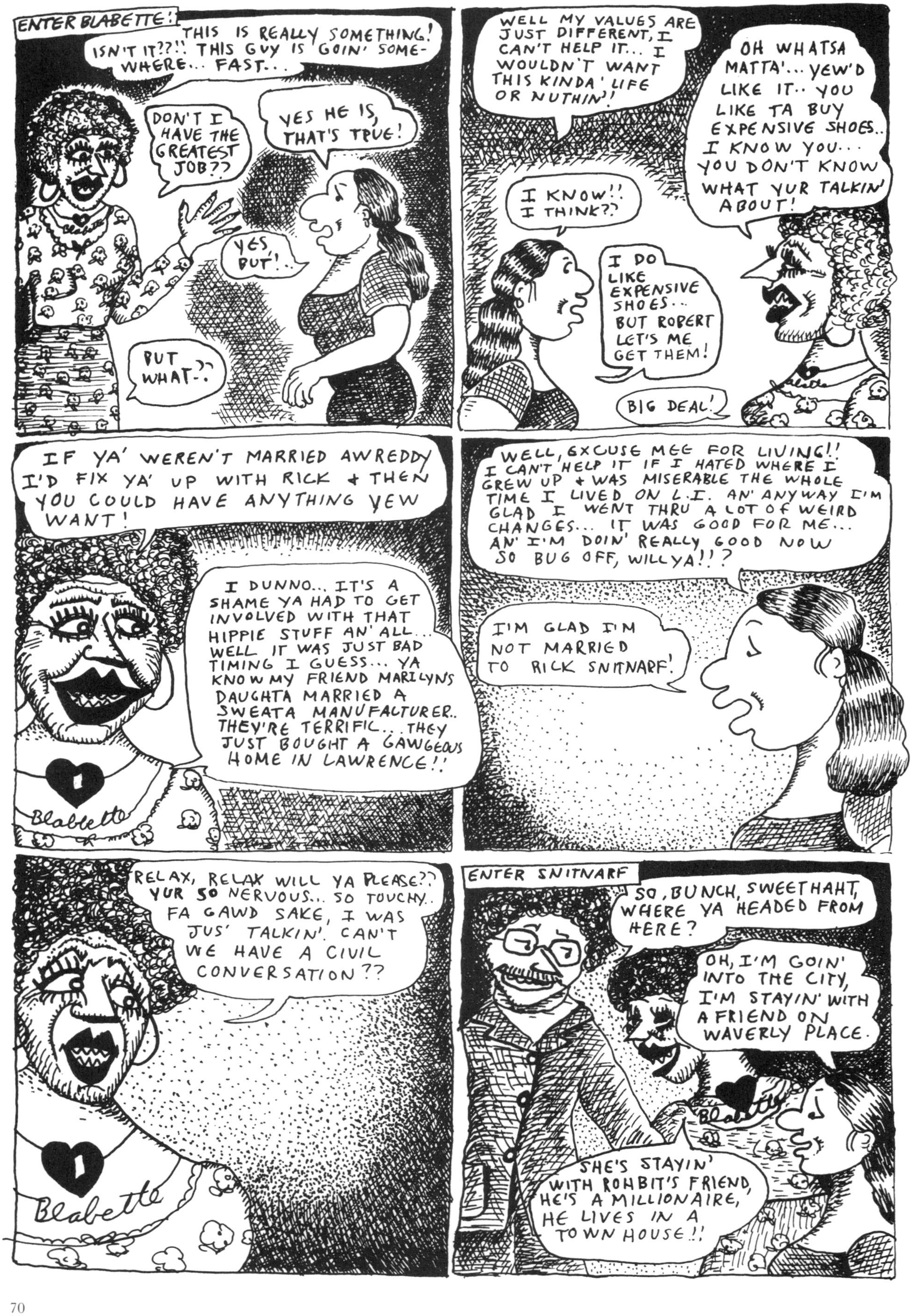
ENTER BLABETTE!
ISN'T IT??!! THIS IS REALLY SOMETHING! THIS GUY IS GOIN' SOME-WHERE... FAST...
DON'T I HAVE THE GREATEST JOB??
YES HE IS, THAT'S TRUE!
YES, BUT!..
BUT WHAT?..
WELL MY VALUES ARE JUST DIFFERENT, I CAN'T HELP IT... I WOULDN'T WANT THIS KINDA' LIFE OR NUTHIN'!
OH WHATSA MATTA'... YEW'D LIKE IT.. YOU LIKE TA BUY EXPENSIVE SHOES.. I KNOW YOU... YOU DON'T KNOW WHAT YUR TALKIN' ABOUT!
I KNOW!! I THINK??
I DO LIKE EXPENSIVE SHOES... BUT ROBERT LET'S ME GET THEM!
BIG DEAL!
IF YA' WEREN'T MARRIED AWREDDY I'D FIX YA' UP WITH RICK & THEN YOU COULD HAVE ANYTHING YEW WANT!
I DUNNO... IT'S A SHAME YA HAD TO GET INVOLVED WITH THAT HIPPIE STUFF AN' ALL... WELL IT WAS JUST BAD TIMING I GUESS... YA KNOW MY FRIEND MARILYN'S DAUGHTA MARRIED A SWEATA MANUFACTURER.. THEY'RE TERRIFIC... THEY JUST BOUGHT A GAWGEOUS HOME IN LAWRENCE!!
Blabette
WELL, EXCUSE MEE FOR LIVING!! I CAN'T HELP IT IF I HATED WHERE I GREW UP & WAS MISERABLE THE WHOLE TIME I LIVED ON L.I. AN' ANYWAY I'M GLAD I WENT THRU A LOT OF WEIRD CHANGES... IT WAS GOOD FOR ME... AN' I'M DOIN' REALLY GOOD NOW SO BUG OFF, WILLYA!!?
I'M GLAD I'M NOT MARRIED TO RICK SNITNARF!
RELAX, RELAX WILL YA PLEASE?? YUR SO NERVOUS... SO TOUCHY.. FA GAWD SAKE, I WAS JUS' TALKIN'. CAN'T WE HAVE A CIVIL CONVERSATION??
Blabette
ENTER SNITNARF
SO, BUNCH, SWEETHAHT, WHERE YA HEADED FROM HERE?
OH, I'M GOIN' INTO THE CITY, I'M STAYIN' WITH A FRIEND ON WAVERLY PLACE.
SHE'S STAYIN' WITH ROHBIT'S FRIEND, HE'S A MILLIONAIRE, HE LIVES IN A TOWN HOUSE!!

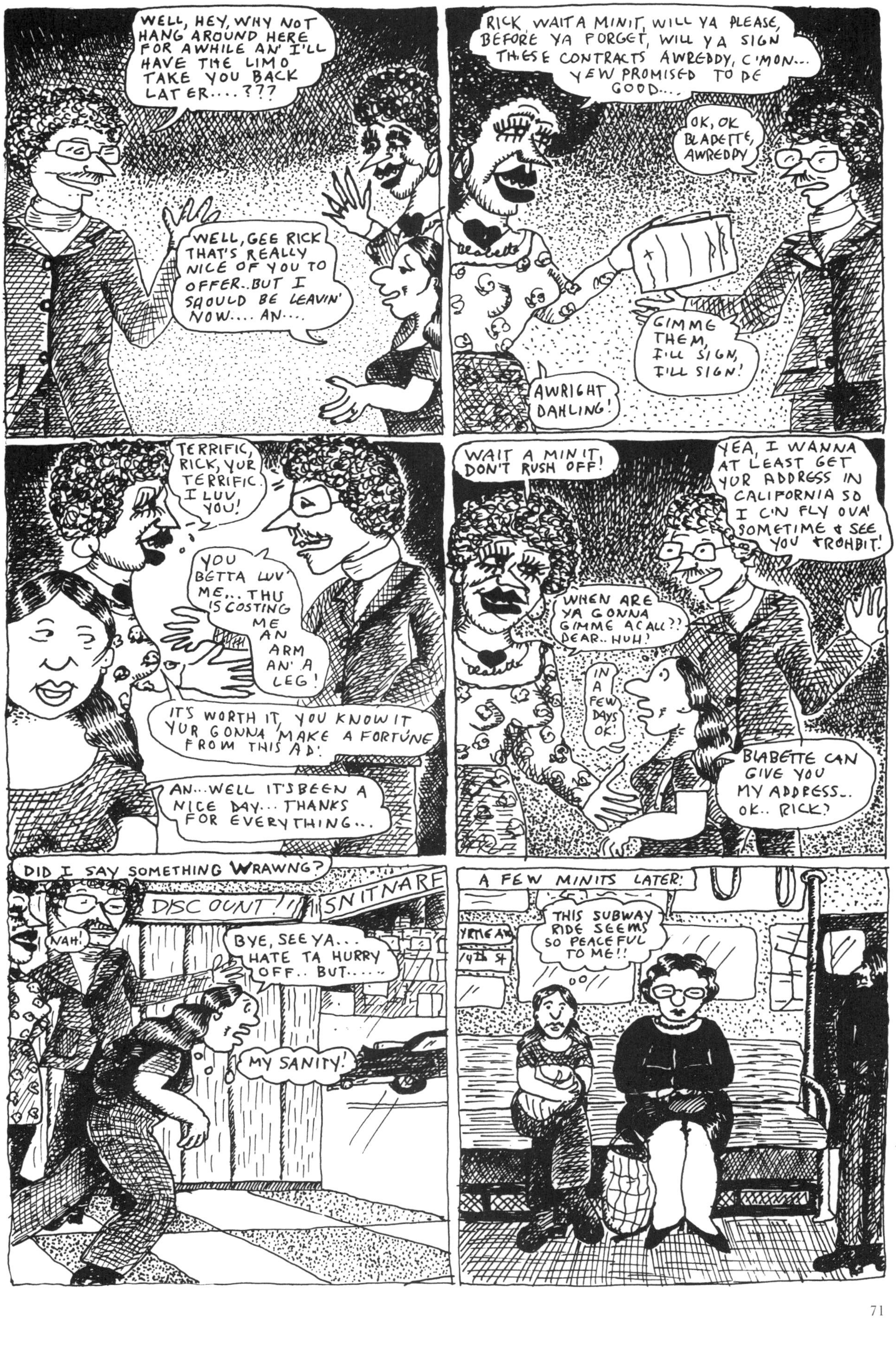
WELL, HEY, WHY NOT HANG AROUND HERE FOR AWHILE AN' I'LL HAVE THE LIMO TAKE YOU BACK LATER....???
WELL, GEE RICK THAT'S REALLY NICE OF YOU TO OFFER..BUT I SHOULD BE LEAVIN' NOW.... AN....
RICK, WAIT A MINIT, WILL YA PLEASE, BEFORE YA FORGET, WILL YA SIGN THESE CONTRACTS AWREDDY, C'MON... YEW PROMISED TO BE GOOD...
OK, OK BLADETTE, AWREDDY
GIMME THEM, I'LL SIGN, I'LL SIGN!
AWRIGHT DAHLING!
TERRIFIC, RICK, YUR TERRIFIC. I LUV YOU!
YOU BETTA LUV' ME... THU IS COSTING ME AN ARM AN' A LEG!
IT'S WORTH IT, YOU KNOW IT YUR GONNA MAKE A FORTUNE FROM THIS AD!
AN... WELL IT'S BEEN A NICE DAY... THANKS FOR EVERYTHING...
WAIT A MINIT, DON'T RUSH OFF!
YEA, I WANNA AT LEAST GET YUR ADDRESS IN CALIFORNIA SO I C'N FLY OVA' SOMETIME & SEE YOU t'ROHBIT!
WHEN ARE YA GONNA GIMME A CALL?? DEAR.. HUH!
IN A FEW DAYS OK!
BLABETTE CAN GIVE YOU MY ADDRESS.. OK.. RICK?
DID I SAY SOMETHING WRAWNG?
DISCOUNT!
SNITNARE
NAH!
BYE, SEE YA... HATE TA HURRY OFF.. BUT.....
MY SANITY!
A FEW MINITS LATER:
THIS SUBWAY RIDE SEEMS SO PEACEFUL TO ME!!
14th St

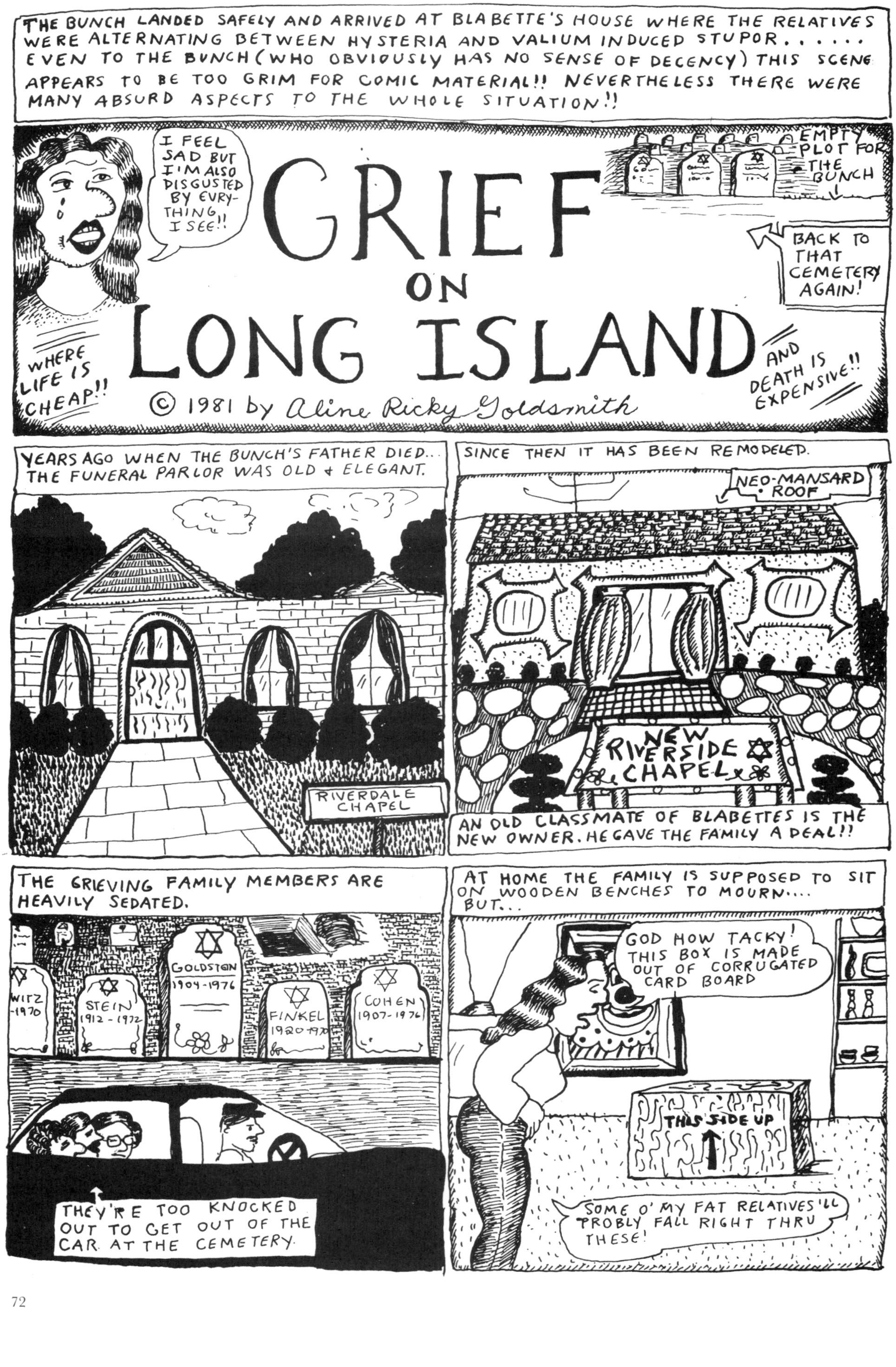
THE BUNCH LANDED SAFELY AND ARRIVED AT BLABETTE'S HOUSE WHERE THE RELATIVES WERE ALTERNATING BETWEEN HYSTERIA AND VALIUM INDUCED STUPOR...... EVEN TO THE BUNCH (WHO OBVIOUSLY HAS NO SENSE OF DECENCY) THIS SCENE APPEARS TO BE TOO GRIM FOR COMIC MATERIAL!! NEVERTHELESS THERE WERE MANY ABSURD ASPECTS TO THE WHOLE SITUATION!!
I FEEL SAD BUT I'M ALSO DISGUSTED BY EVRYTHING I SEE!!
EMPTY PLOT FOR THE BUNCH
BACK TO THAT CEMETERY AGAIN!
GRIEF ON LONG ISLAND
WHERE LIFE IS CHEAP!!
AND DEATH IS EXPENSIVE!!
© 1981 by Aline Ricky Goldsmith
YEARS AGO WHEN THE BUNCH'S FATHER DIED... THE FUNERAL PARLOR WAS OLD & ELEGANT.
RIVERDALE CHAPEL
SINCE THEN IT HAS BEEN REMODELED.
NEO-MANSARD ROOF
NEW RIVERSIDE CHAPEL
AN OLD CLASSMATE OF BLABETTES IS THE NEW OWNER. HE GAVE THE FAMILY A DEAL!!
THE GRIEVING FAMILY MEMBERS ARE HEAVILY SEDATED.
GOLDSTEIN 1904-1976
WITZ -1970
STEIN 1912-1972
FINKEL 1920-1970
COHEN 1907-1976
THEY'RE TOO KNOCKED OUT TO GET OUT OF THE CAR AT THE CEMETERY.
AT HOME THE FAMILY IS SUPPOSED TO SIT ON WOODEN BENCHES TO MOURN.... BUT...
GOD HOW TACKY! THIS BOX IS MADE OUT OF CORRUGATED CARD BOARD
THIS SIDE UP
SOME O' MY FAT RELATIVES'LL PROBLY FALL RIGHT THRU THESE!

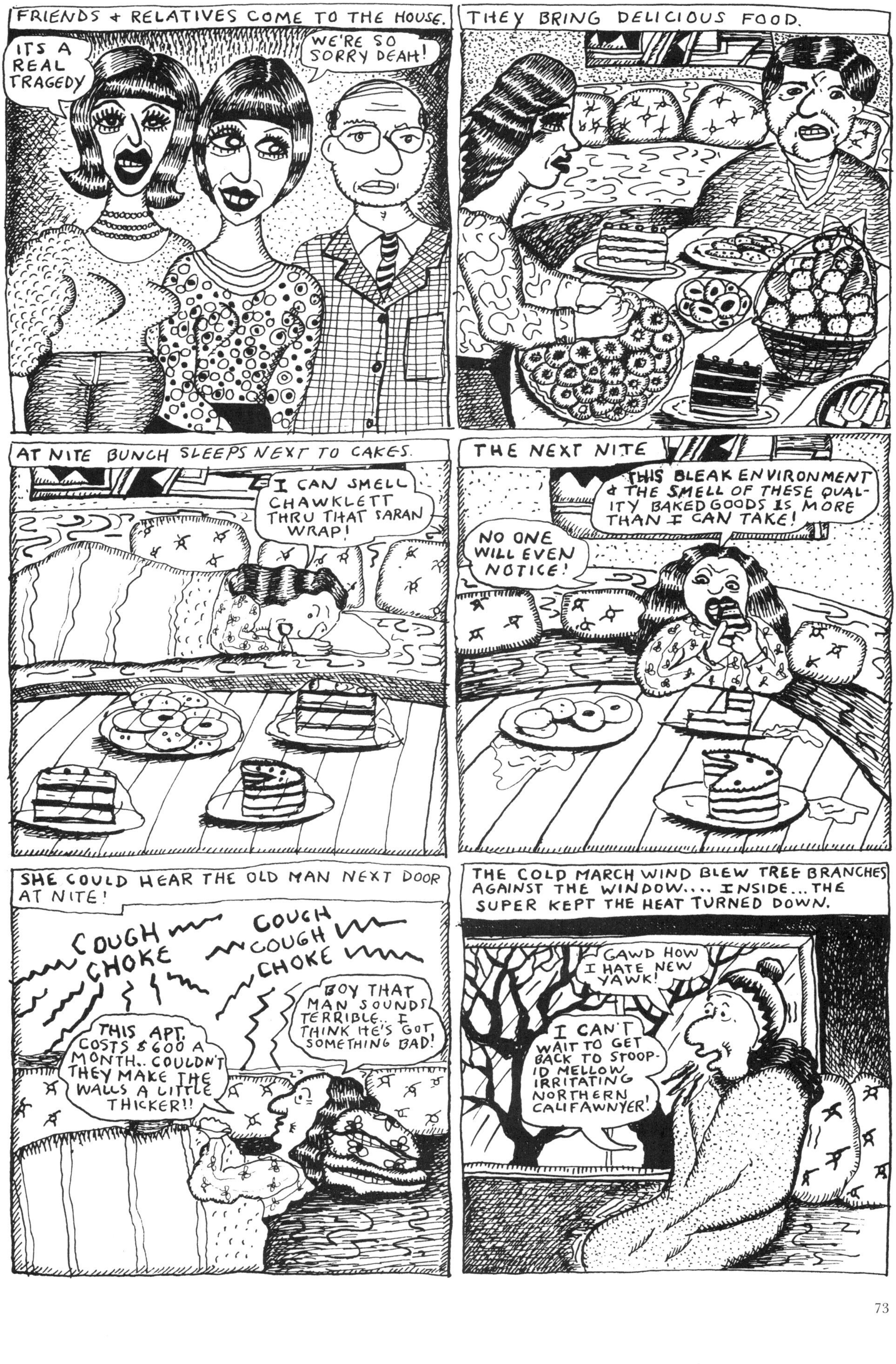
FRIENDS + RELATIVES COME TO THE HOUSE.
ITS A REAL TRAGEDY
WE'RE SO SORRY DEAH!
THEY BRING DELICIOUS FOOD.
AT NITE BUNCH SLEEPS NEXT TO CAKES.
I CAN SMELL CHAWKLETT THRU THAT SARAN WRAP!
THE NEXT NITE
THIS BLEAK ENVIRONMENT & THE SMELL OF THESE QUALITY BAKED GOODS IS MORE THAN I CAN TAKE!
NO ONE WILL EVEN NOTICE!
SHE COULD HEAR THE OLD MAN NEXT DOOR AT NITE!
COUGH CHOKE
COUGH COUGH CHOKE
BOY THAT MAN SOUNDS TERRIBLE.. I THINK HE'S GOT SOMETHING BAD!
THIS APT. COSTS $600 A MONTH.. COULDN'T THEY MAKE THE WALLS A LITTLE THICKER!!
THE COLD MARCH WIND BLEW TREE BRANCHES AGAINST THE WINDOW.... INSIDE... THE SUPER KEPT THE HEAT TURNED DOWN.
GAWD HOW I HATE NEW YAWK!
I CAN'T WAIT TO GET BACK TO STOOP-ID MELLOW IRRITATING NORTHERN CALIFAWNYER!

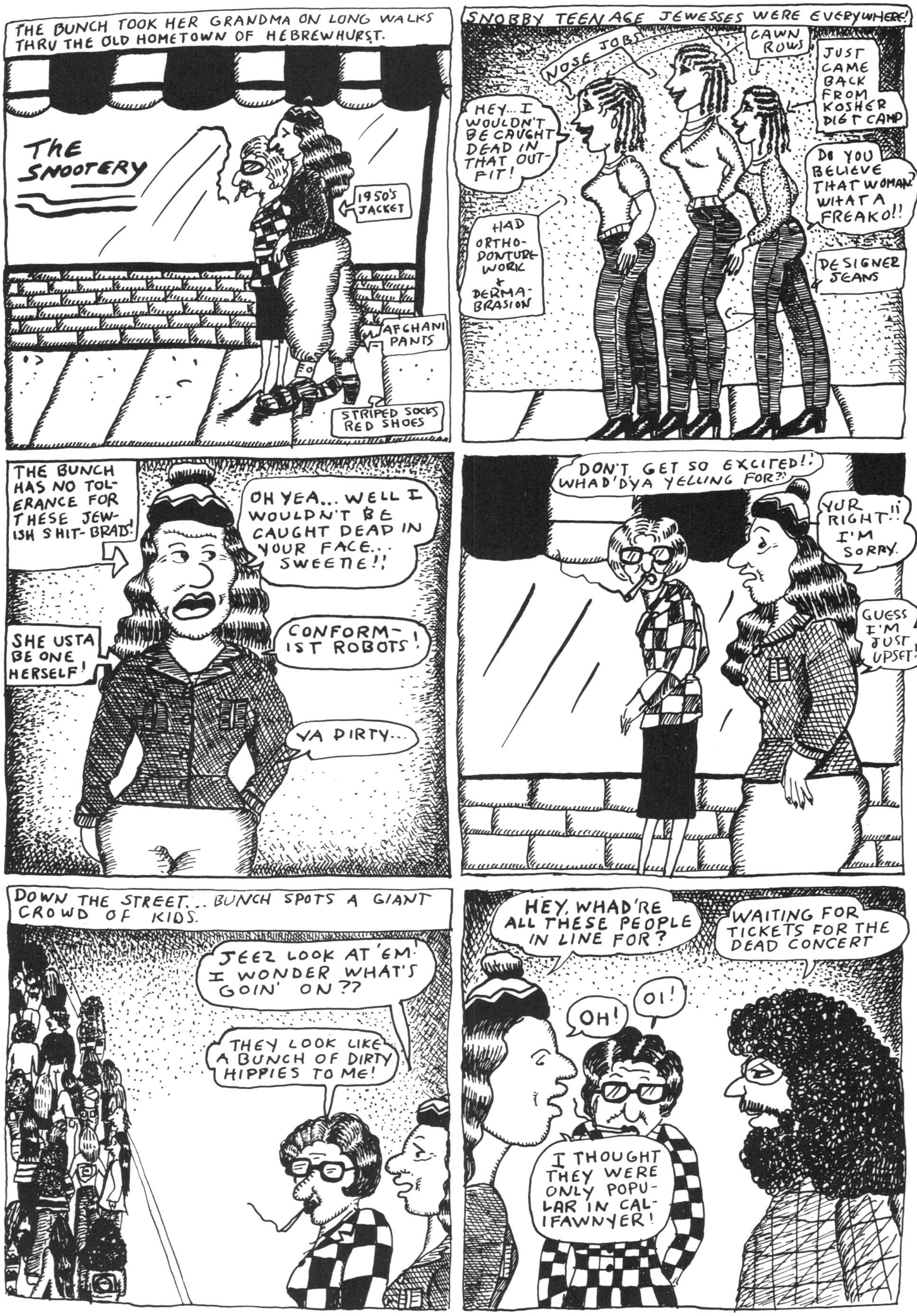
THE BUNCH TOOK HER GRANDMA ON LONG WALKS THRU THE OLD HOMETOWN OF HEBREWHURST.
THE SNOOTERY
1950'S JACKET
AFGHANI PANTS
STRIPED SOCKS RED SHOES
SNOBBY TEEN AGE JEWESSES WERE EVERYWHERE!
NOSE JOBS
CAWN ROWS
JUST CAME BACK FROM KOSHER DIET CAMP
HEY... I WOULDN'T BE CAUGHT DEAD IN THAT OUTFIT!
DO YOU BELIEVE THAT WOMAN? WHAT A FREAKO!!
HAD ORTHODONTURE WORK + DERMABRASION
DESIGNER JEANS
THE BUNCH HAS NO TOLERANCE FOR THESE JEWISH SHIT-BRATS!
OH YEA... WELL I WOULDN'T BE CAUGHT DEAD IN YOUR FACE... SWEETIE!!
SHE USTA BE ONE HERSELF!
CONFORMIST ROBOTS!
YA DIRTY...
DON'T GET SO EXCITED!! WHAD'DYA YELLING FOR?!
YUR RIGHT!! I'M SORRY.
GUESS I'M JUST UPSET!
DOWN THE STREET... BUNCH SPOTS A GIANT CROWD OF KIDS.
JEEZ LOOK AT 'EM. I WONDER WHAT'S GOIN' ON??
THEY LOOK LIKE A BUNCH OF DIRTY HIPPIES TO ME!
HEY, WHAD'RE ALL THESE PEOPLE IN LINE FOR?
WAITING FOR TICKETS FOR THE DEAD CONCERT
OH!
OI!
I THOUGHT THEY WERE ONLY POPULAR IN CALIFAWNYER!

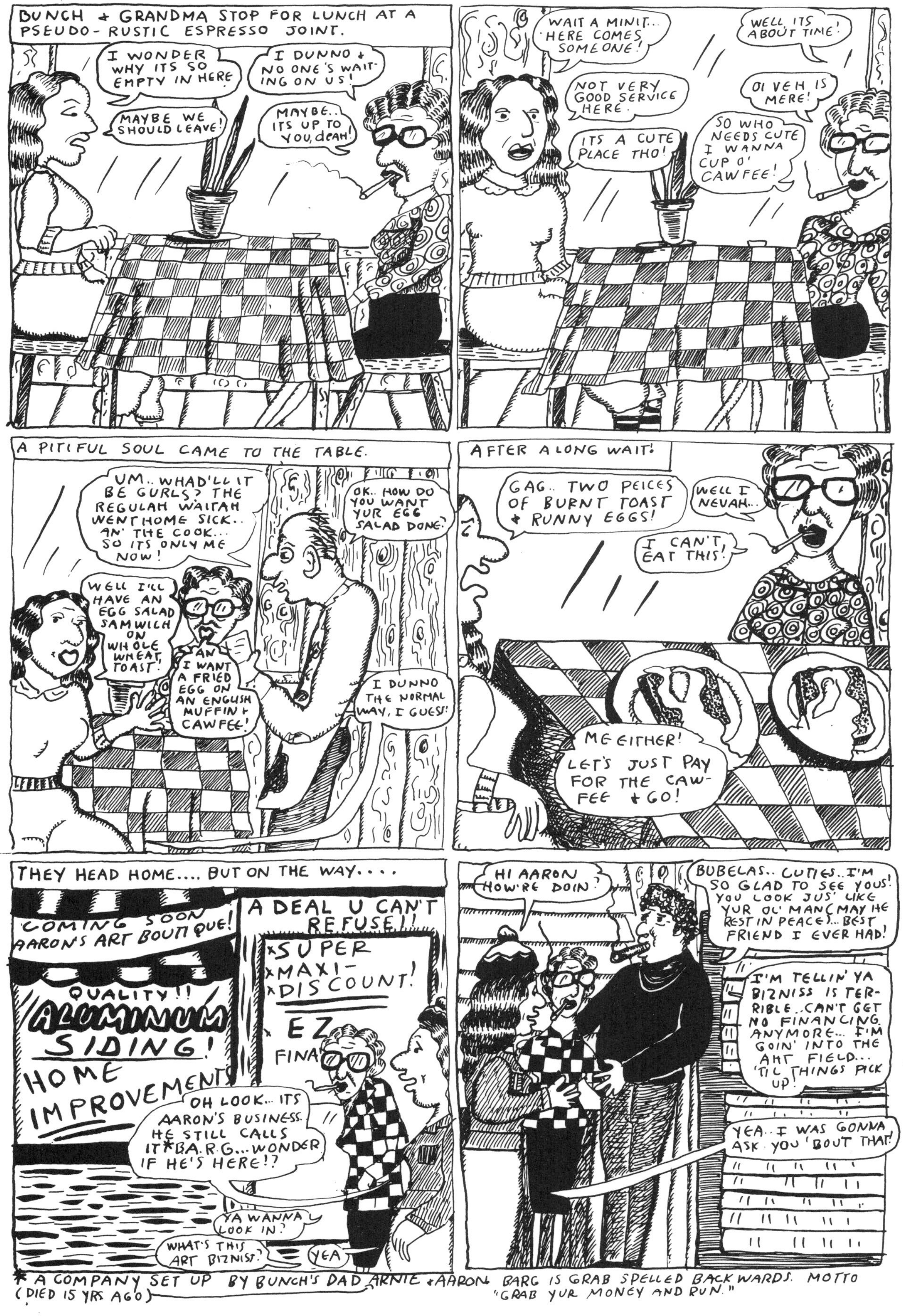

BUNCH + GRANDMA STOP FOR LUNCH AT A PSEUDO-RUSTIC ESPRESSO JOINT.
I WONDER WHY ITS SO EMPTY IN HERE
I DUNNO + NO ONE'S WAITING ON US!
MAYBE WE SHOULD LEAVE!
MAYBE.. ITS UP TO YOU, DEAH!
WAIT A MINIT... HERE COMES SOMEONE!
WELL ITS ABOUT TIME!
NOT VERY GOOD SERVICE HERE.
OI VEH IS MERE!
ITS A CUTE PLACE THO!
SO WHO NEEDS CUTE I WANNA CUP O' CAWFEE!
A PITIFUL SOUL CAME TO THE TABLE.
UM.. WHAD'LL IT BE GURLS? THE REGULAH WAITAH WENT HOME SICK.. AN' THE COOK... SO ITS ONLY ME NOW!
OK.. HOW DO YOU WANT YUR EGG SALAD DONE?
WELL I'LL HAVE AN EGG SALAD SAMWICH ON WHOLE WHEAT TOAST!
AN I WANT A FRIED EGG ON AN ENGLISH MUFFIN + CAWFEE!
I DUNNO THE NORMAL WAY, I GUESS!
AFTER A LONG WAIT!
GAG.. TWO PEICES OF BURNT TOAST + RUNNY EGGS!
WELL I NEVAH...
I CAN'T EAT THIS!
ME EITHER! LET'S JUST PAY FOR THE CAWFEE + GO!
THEY HEAD HOME.... BUT ON THE WAY....
COMING SOON AARON'S ART BOUTIQUE!
A DEAL U CAN'T REFUSE!!
SUPER MAXI-DISCOUNT!
QUALITY!! ALUMINUM SIDING!
HOME IMPROVEMENTS
EZ FINA
OH LOOK... ITS AARON'S BUSINESS. HE STILL CALLS IT*B.A.R.G... WONDER IF HE'S HERE!?
YA WANNA LOOK IN?
WHAT'S THIS ART BIZNISS?
YEA
HI AARON HOW'RE DOIN?
BUBELAS.. CUTIES.. I'M SO GLAD TO SEE YOUS! YOU LOOK JUS' LIKE YUR OL' MAN (MAY HE REST IN PEACE)... BEST FRIEND I EVER HAD!
I'M TELLIN' YA BIZNISS IS TERRIBLE.. CAN'T GET NO FINANCING ANYMORE... I'M GOIN' INTO THE ART FIELD... 'TIL THINGS PICK UP!
YEA.. I WAS GONNA ASK YOU 'BOUT THAT!
* A COMPANY SET UP BY BUNCH'S DAD ARNIE (DIED 15 YRS AGO) + AARON. BARG IS GRAB SPELLED BACKWARDS. MOTTO "GRAB YUR MONEY AND RUN."

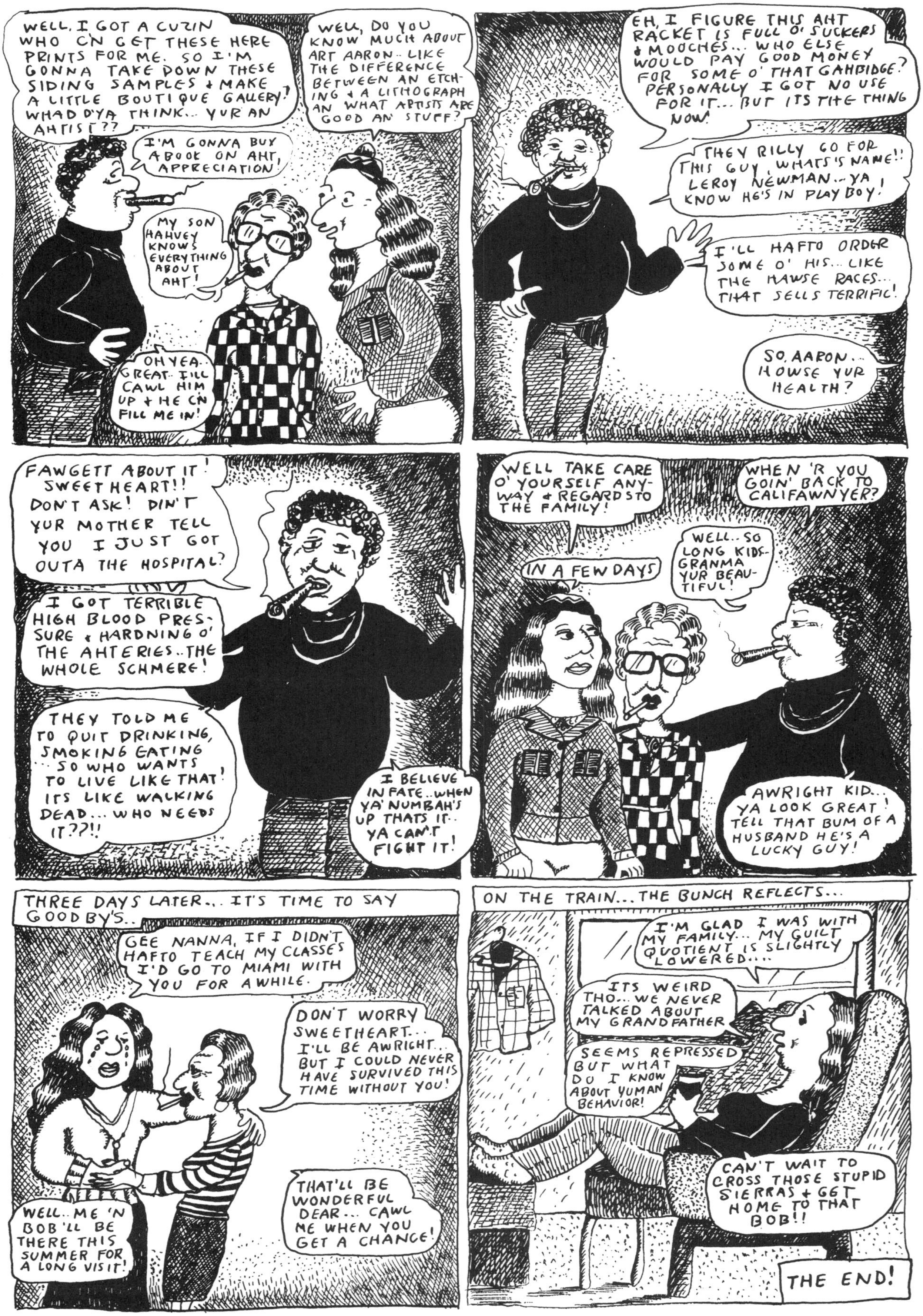
WELL, I GOT A CUZIN WHO CN GET THESE HERE PRINTS FOR ME. SO I'M GONNA TAKE DOWN THESE SIDING SAMPLES & MAKE A LITTLE BOUTIQUE GALLERY! WHAD D'YA THINK... YUR AN AHTIST??
WELL, DO YOU KNOW MUCH ABOUT ART AARON.. LIKE THE DIFFERENCE BETWEEN AN ETCHING & A LITHOGRAPH AN WHAT ARTISTS ARE GOOD AN STUFF?
I'M GONNA BUY A BOOK ON AHT, APPRECIATION!
MY SON HAHVEY KNOWS EVERYTHING ABOUT AHT!
OH YEA. GREAT. I'LL CAWL HIM UP & HE CN FILL ME IN!
EH, I FIGURE THIS AHT RACKET IS FULL O' SUCKERS & MOOCHES... WHO ELSE WOULD PAY GOOD MONEY FOR SOME O' THAT GAHBIDGE? PERSONALLY I GOT NO USE FOR IT... BUT ITS THE THING NOW!
THEY RILLY GO FOR THIS GUY, WHAT'S'S NAME!! LEROY NEWMAN.. YA KNOW HE'S IN PLAYBOY!
I'LL HAFTO ORDER SOME O' HIS... LIKE THE HAWSE RACES... THAT SELLS TERRIFIC!
SO, AARON... HOWSE YUR HEALTH?
FAWGETT ABOUT IT! SWEETHEART!! DON'T ASK! DIN'T YUR MOTHER TELL YOU I JUST GOT OUTA THE HOSPITAL?
I GOT TERRIBLE HIGH BLOOD PRESSURE & HARDNING O' THE AHTERIES.. THE WHOLE SCHMERE!
THEY TOLD ME TO QUIT DRINKING, SMOKING EATING ... SO WHO WANTS TO LIVE LIKE THAT! ITS LIKE WALKING DEAD... WHO NEEDS IT??!!
I BELIEVE IN FATE.. WHEN YA' NUMBAH'S UP THATS IT.. YA CAN'T FIGHT IT!
WELL TAKE CARE O' YOURSELF ANYWAY & REGARDS TO THE FAMILY!
WHEN 'R YOU GOIN' BACK TO CALIFAWNYER?
IN A FEW DAYS
WELL.. SO LONG KIDS.. GRANMA YUR BEAUTIFUL!
AWRIGHT KID... YA LOOK GREAT! TELL THAT BUM OF A HUSBAND HE'S A LUCKY GUY!
THREE DAYS LATER... IT'S TIME TO SAY GOODBY'S..
GEE NANNA, IF I DIDN'T HAFTO TEACH MY CLASSES I'D GO TO MIAMI WITH YOU FOR AWHILE.
DON'T WORRY SWEETHEART... I'LL BE AWRIGHT... BUT I COULD NEVER HAVE SURVIVED THIS TIME WITHOUT YOU!
WELL.. ME 'N BOB'LL BE THERE THIS SUMMER FOR A LONG VISIT!
THAT'LL BE WONDERFUL DEAR... CAWL ME WHEN YOU GET A CHANCE!
ON THE TRAIN... THE BUNCH REFLECTS...
I'M GLAD I WAS WITH MY FAMILY... MY GUILT QUOTIENT IS SLIGHTLY LOWERED....
ITS WEIRD THO... WE NEVER TALKED ABOUT MY GRANDFATHER
SEEMS REPRESSED BUT WHAT DO I KNOW ABOUT YUMAN BEHAVIOR!
CAN'T WAIT TO CROSS THOSE STUPID SIERRAS & GET HOME TO THAT BOB!!
THE END!

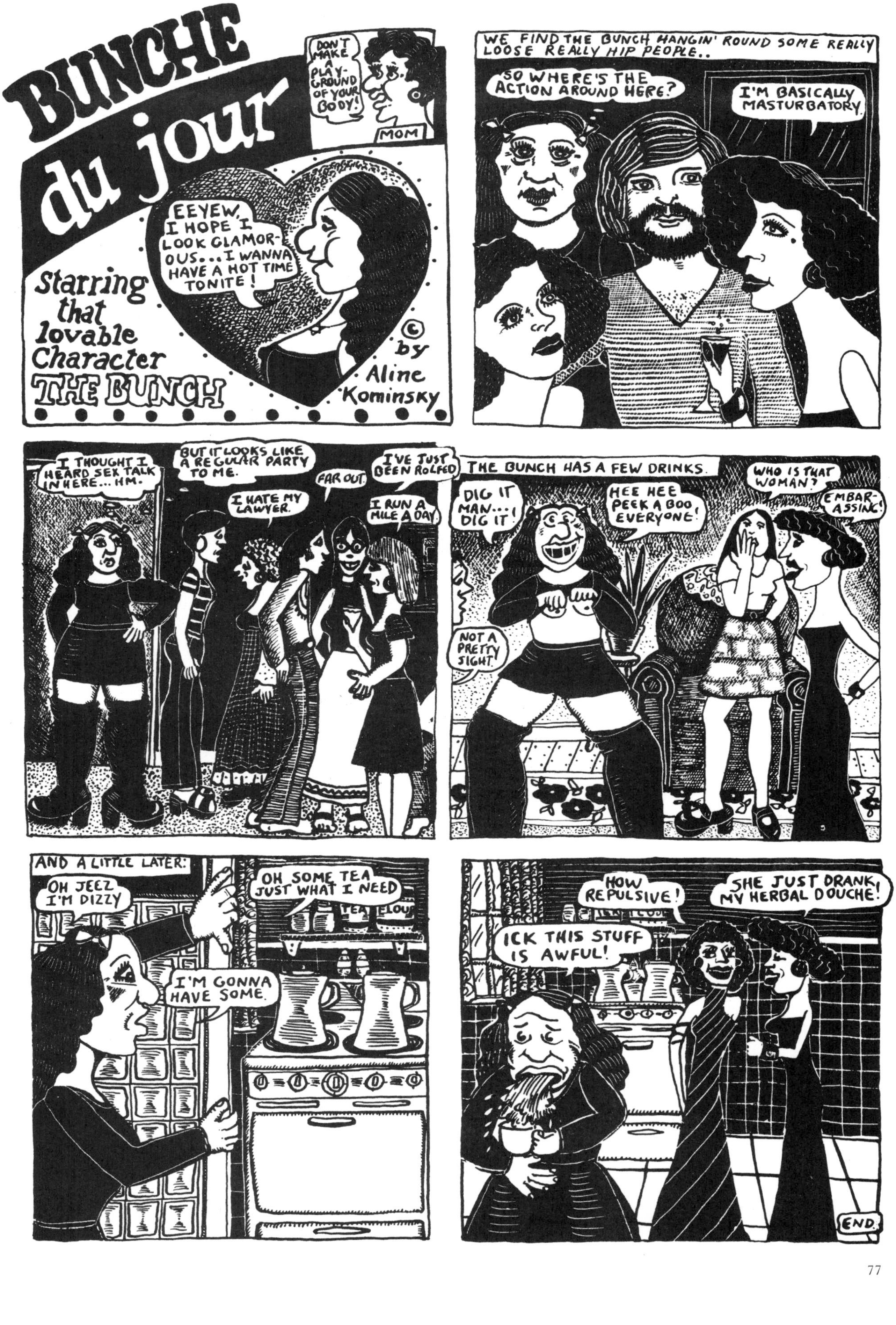
BUNCHE du jour
DON'T MAKE A PLAY-GROUND OF YOUR BODY!
MOM
EEYEW, I HOPE I LOOK GLAMOR-OUS... I WANNA HAVE A HOT TIME TONITE!
Starring that lovable Character THE BUNCH
© by Aline Kominsky
WE FIND THE BUNCH HANGIN' ROUND SOME REALLY LOOSE REALLY HIP PEOPLE..
SO WHERE'S THE ACTION AROUND HERE?
I'M BASICALLY MASTURBATORY.
I THOUGHT I HEARD SEX TALK IN HERE... HM.
BUT IT LOOKS LIKE A REGULAR PARTY TO ME.
I'VE JUST BEEN ROLFED
FAR OUT
I HATE MY LAWYER.
I RUN A MILE A DAY
THE BUNCH HAS A FEW DRINKS.
DIG IT MAN... DIG IT!
HEE HEE PEEK A BOO EVERYONE!
WHO IS THAT WOMAN?
EMBAR-ASSING!
NOT A PRETTY SIGHT.
AND A LITTLE LATER:
OH JEEZ I'M DIZZY
OH SOME TEA JUST WHAT I NEED
I'M GONNA HAVE SOME.
HOW REPULSIVE!
SHE JUST DRANK MY HERBAL DOUCHE!
ICK THIS STUFF IS AWFUL!
END.

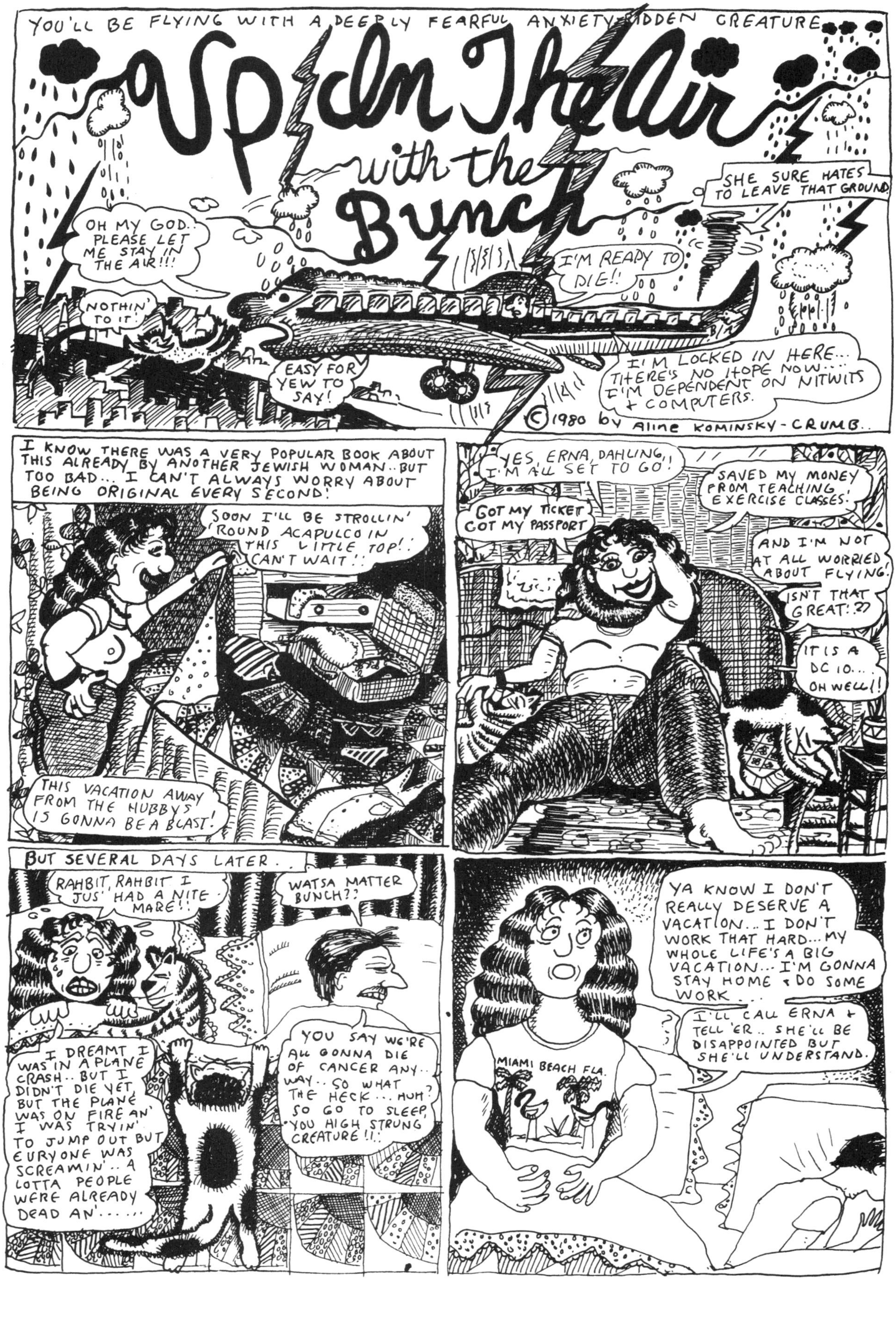

YOU'LL BE FLYING WITH A DEEPLY FEARFUL ANXIETY-RIDDEN CREATURE
Up In The Air with the Bunch
OH MY GOD.. PLEASE LET ME STAY IN THE AIR!!!
NOTHIN' TO IT!
EASY FOR YEW TO SAY!
I'M READY TO DIE!!
SHE SURE HATES TO LEAVE THAT GROUND
I'M LOCKED IN HERE... THERE'S NO HOPE NOW.... I'M DEPENDENT ON NITWITS + COMPUTERS.
© 1980 by Aline Kominsky-Crumb..
I KNOW THERE WAS A VERY POPULAR BOOK ABOUT THIS ALREADY BY ANOTHER JEWISH WOMAN.. BUT TOO BAD... I CAN'T ALWAYS WORRY ABOUT BEING ORIGINAL EVERY SECOND!
SOON I'LL BE STROLLIN' 'ROUND ACAPULCO IN THIS LITTLE TOP!. CAN'T WAIT!.!
THIS VACATION AWAY FROM THE HUBBYS IS GONNA BE A BLAST!
YES, ERNA, DAHLING, I'M ALL SET TO GO!
GOT MY TICKET GOT MY PASSPORT
SAVED MY MONEY FROM TEACHING EXERCISE CLASSES!
AND I'M NOT AT ALL WORRIED ABOUT FLYING!
ISN'T THAT GREAT!??
IT IS A DC 10.... OH WELL!!
BUT SEVERAL DAYS LATER..
RAHBIT, RAHBIT I JUS' HAD A NITE MARE!!
WATSA MATTER BUNCH??
I DREAMT I WAS IN A PLANE CRASH.. BUT I DIDN'T DIE YET, BUT THE PLANE WAS ON FIRE AN' I WAS TRYIN' TO JUMP OUT BUT EVRYONE WAS SCREAMIN'.. A LOTTA PEOPLE WERE ALREADY DEAD AN'.....
YOU SAY WE'RE ALL GONNA DIE OF CANCER ANY.. WAY.. SO WHAT THE HECK... HUH? SO GO TO SLEEP, YOU HIGH STRUNG CREATURE!!.
YA KNOW I DON'T REALLY DESERVE A VACATION... I DON'T WORK THAT HARD... MY WHOLE LIFE'S A BIG VACATION... I'M GONNA STAY HOME + DO SOME WORK...
I'LL CALL ERNA + TELL 'ER.. SHE'LL BE DISAPPOINTED BUT SHE'LL UNDERSTAND.
MIAMI BEACH FLA.

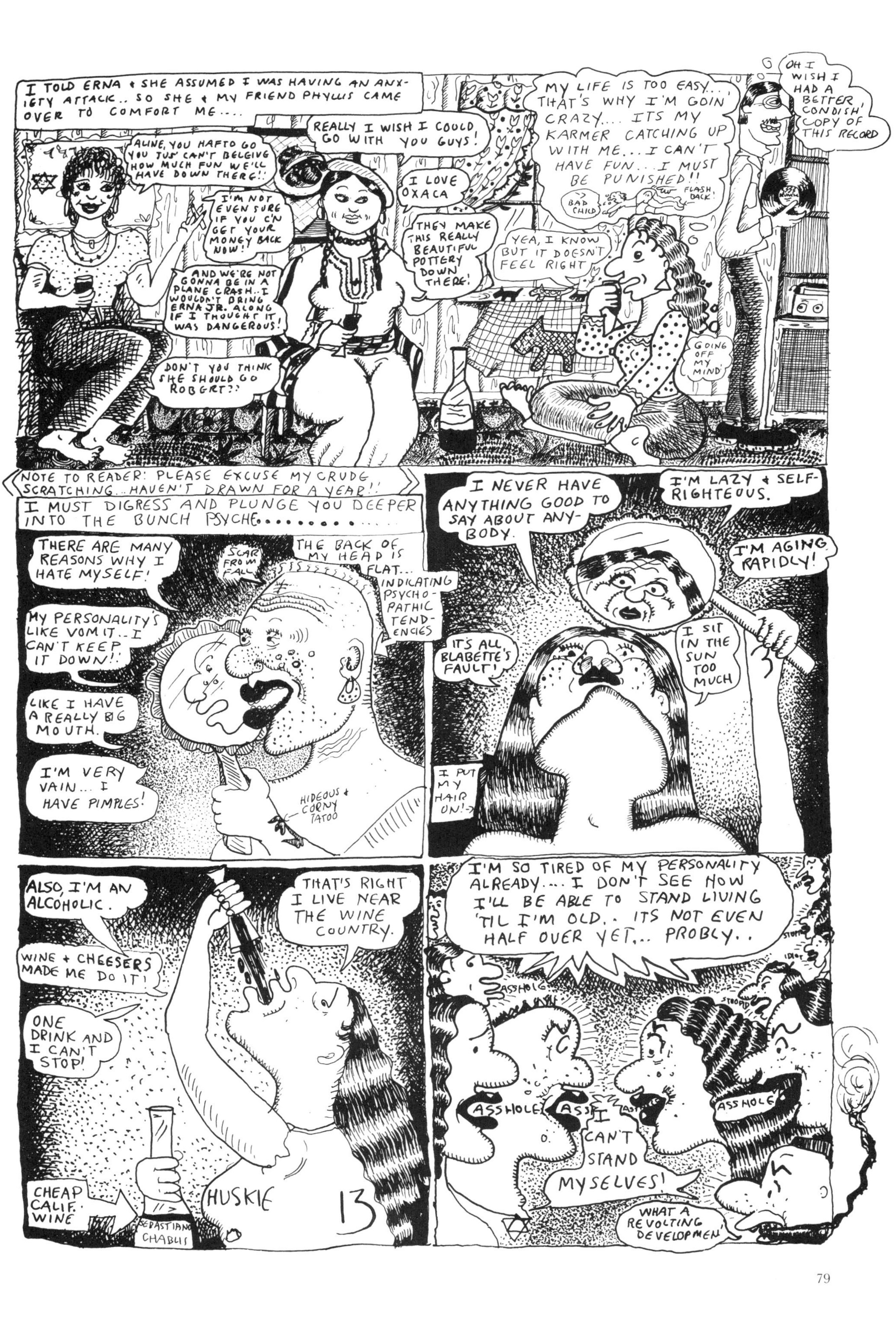
I TOLD ERNA & SHE ASSUMED I WAS HAVING AN ANXIETY ATTACK.. SO SHE & MY FRIEND PHYLLIS CAME OVER TO COMFORT ME....
ALINE, YOU HAFTO GO YOU JUS' CAN'T BELEIVE HOW MUCH FUN WE'LL HAVE DOWN THERE!!
I'M NOT EVEN SURE IF YOU C'N GET YOUR MONEY BACK NOW!
AND WE'RE NOT GONNA BE IN A PLANE CRASH.. I WOULDN'T BRING ERNA JR. ALONG IF I THOUGHT IT WAS DANGEROUS!
DON'T YOU THINK SHE SHOULD GO ROBERT??
REALLY I WISH I COULD GO WITH YOU GUYS!
I LOVE OXACA
THEY MAKE THIS REALLY BEAUTIFUL POTTERY DOWN THERE!
MY LIFE IS TOO EASY... THAT'S WHY I'M GOIN' CRAZY.... ITS MY KARMER CATCHING UP WITH ME... I CAN'T HAVE FUN... I MUST BE PUNISHED!!
BAD CHILD
FLASH BACK!
YEA, I KNOW BUT IT DOESN'T FEEL RIGHT
GOING OFF MY MIND
OH I WISH I HAD A BETTER, CONDISH' COPY OF THIS RECORD
NOTE TO READER: PLEASE EXCUSE MY CRUDE SCRATCHING.. HAVEN'T DRAWN FOR A YEAR!
I MUST DIGRESS AND PLUNGE YOU DEEPER INTO THE BUNCH PSYCHE..........
THERE ARE MANY REASONS WHY I HATE MYSELF!
SCAR FROM FALL
THE BACK OF MY HEAD IS FLAT... INDICATING PSYCHOPATHIC TENDENCIES
MY PERSONALITY'S LIKE VOMIT.. I CAN'T KEEP IT DOWN!
LIKE I HAVE A REALLY BIG MOUTH.
I'M VERY VAIN... I HAVE PIMPLES!
HIDEOUS & CORNY TATOO
I NEVER HAVE ANYTHING GOOD TO SAY ABOUT ANYBODY.
I'M LAZY & SELF-RIGHTEOUS.
I'M AGING RAPIDLY!
IT'S ALL BLABETTE'S FAULT!
I SIT IN THE SUN TOO MUCH
I PUT MY HAIR ON!
ALSO, I'M AN ALCOHOLIC.
WINE & CHEESERS MADE ME DO IT!
ONE DRINK AND I CAN'T STOP!
THAT'S RIGHT I LIVE NEAR THE WINE COUNTRY.
CHEAP CALIF. WINE
SEBASTIANO CHABLIS
HUSKIE
13
I'M SO TIRED OF MY PERSONALITY ALREADY.... I DON'T SEE HOW I'LL BE ABLE TO STAND LIVING 'TIL I'M OLD.. ITS NOT EVEN HALF OVER YET,.. PROBLY..
STUPID
IDIOT
ASSHOLE
STOOPID
ASSHOLE
ASSHOLE
I CAN'T STAND MYSELVES!
WHAT A REVOLTING DEVELOPMEN'

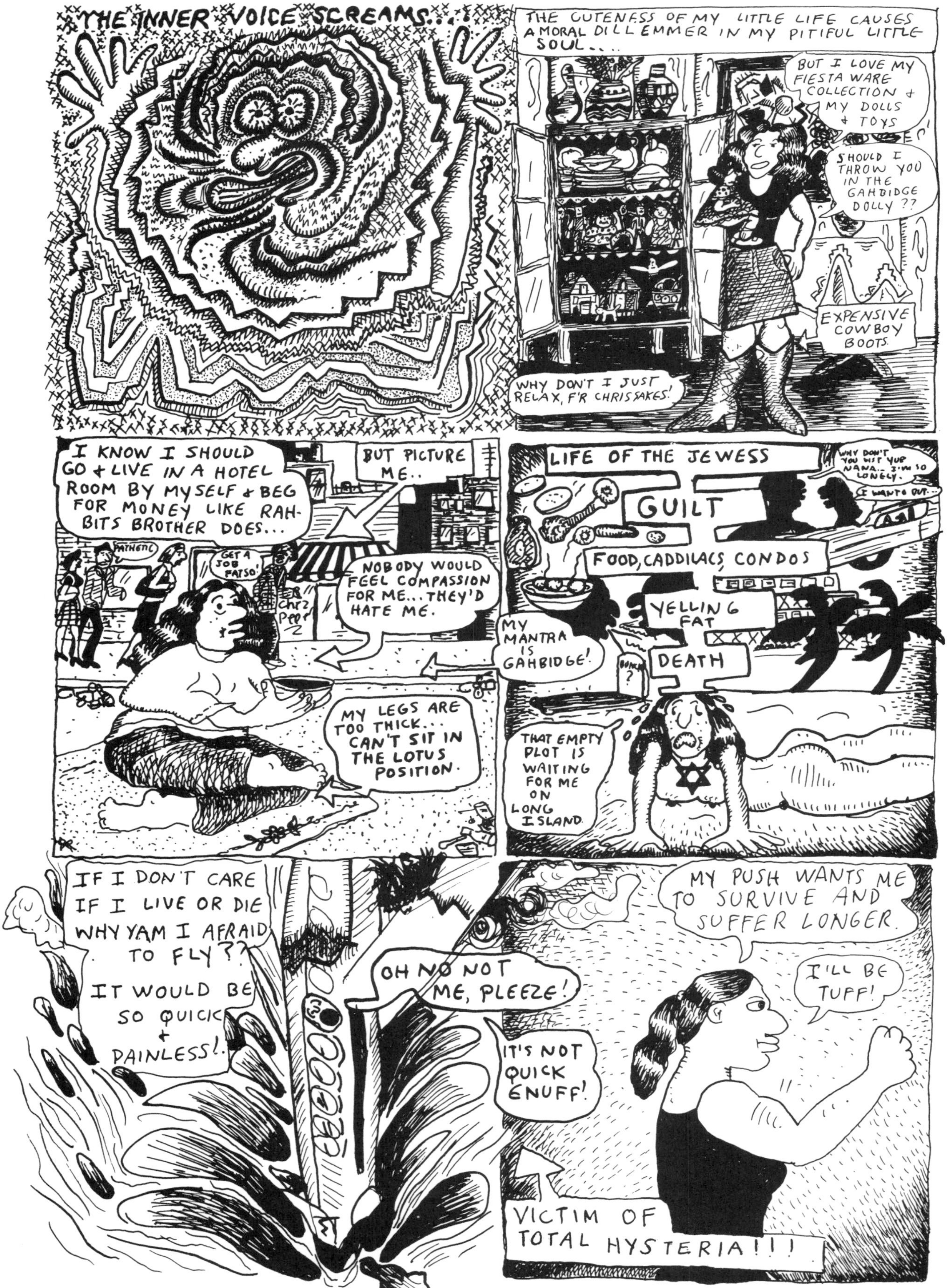
THE INNER VOICE SCREAMS...!
THE CUTENESS OF MY LITTLE LIFE CAUSES A MORAL DILLEMMER IN MY PITIFUL LITTLE SOUL...
BUT I LOVE MY FIESTA WARE COLLECTION & MY DOLLS & TOYS
SHOULD I THROW YOU IN THE GAHBIDGE DOLLY??
EXPENSIVE COWBOY BOOTS
WHY DON'T I JUST RELAX, F'R CHRISSAKES!
I KNOW I SHOULD GO & LIVE IN A HOTEL ROOM BY MYSELF & BEG FOR MONEY LIKE RAH-BITS BROTHER DOES...
BUT PICTURE ME..
PATHETIC
GET A JOB FATSO!
NOBODY WOULD FEEL COMPASSION FOR ME... THEY'D HATE ME.
MY LEGS ARE TOO THICK... CAN'T SIT IN THE LOTUS POSITION.
LIFE OF THE JEWESS
WHY DON'T YOU VISIT YUR NANA... I'M SO LONELY.
I WANTO OUT...
GUILT
FOOD, CADDILACS, CONDOS
YELLING FAT
DEATH
MY MANTRA IS GAHBIDGE!
THAT EMPTY PLOT IS WAITING FOR ME ON LONG ISLAND.
IF I DON'T CARE IF I LIVE OR DIE WHY YAM I AFRAID TO FLY??
IT WOULD BE SO QUICK + PAINLESS!
OH NO NOT ME, PLEEZE!
IT'S NOT QUICK ENUFF!
MY PUSH WANTS ME TO SURVIVE AND SUFFER LONGER.
I'LL BE TUFF!
VICTIM OF TOTAL HYSTERIA!!!

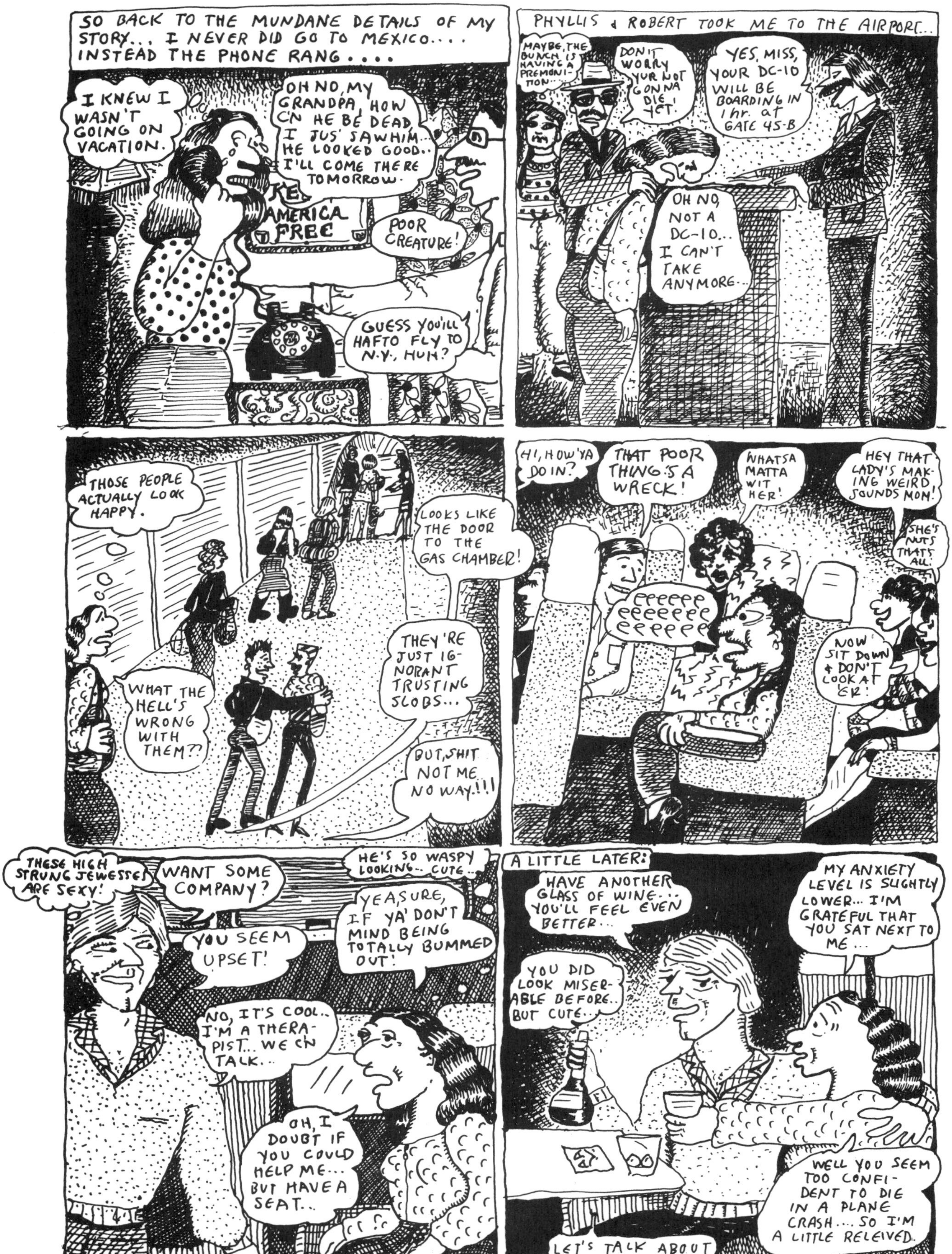
SO BACK TO THE MUNDANE DETAILS OF MY STORY... I NEVER DID GO TO MEXICO.... INSTEAD THE PHONE RANG....
I KNEW I WASN'T GOING ON VACATION.
OH NO, MY GRANDPA, HOW C'N HE BE DEAD, I JUS' SAW HIM.. HE LOOKED GOOD.. I'LL COME THERE TOMORROW.
AMERICA FREE
POOR CREATURE!
GUESS YOU'LL HAFTO FLY TO N.Y., HUH?
PHYLLIS & ROBERT TOOK ME TO THE AIRPORT...
MAYBE THE BUNCH IS HAVING A PREMONITION...
DON'T WORRY YUR NOT GONNA DIE YET.
YES, MISS, YOUR DC-10 WILL BE BOARDING IN 1 hr. at GATE 45-B
OH NO, NOT A DC-10.. I CAN'T TAKE ANYMORE...
THOSE PEOPLE ACTUALLY LOOK HAPPY.
LOOKS LIKE THE DOOR TO THE GAS CHAMBER!
THEY'RE JUST IGNORANT TRUSTING SLOBS...
WHAT THE HELL'S WRONG WITH THEM??
BUT, SHIT NOT ME NO WAY!!!
HI, HOW'YA DOIN?
THAT POOR THING'S A WRECK!
WHATSA MATTA WIT HER!
HEY THAT LADY'S MAKING WEIRD SOUNDS MOM!
SHE'S NUTS THAT'S ALL.
EEEEEE EEEEEE EEEEEE
NOW SIT DOWN & DON'T LOOK AT 'ER!
THESE HIGH STRUNG JEWESSES ARE SEXY!
WANT SOME COMPANY?
HE'S SO WASPY LOOKING.. CUTE..
YOU SEEM UPSET!
YEA SURE, IF YA' DON'T MIND BEING TOTALLY BUMMED OUT!
NO, IT'S COOL.. I'M A THERAPIST... WE C'N TALK..
OH, I DOUBT IF YOU COULD HELP ME... BUT HAVE A SEAT..
A LITTLE LATER:
HAVE ANOTHER GLASS OF WINE... YOU'LL FEEL EVEN BETTER...
MY ANXIETY LEVEL IS SLIGHTLY LOWER... I'M GRATEFUL THAT YOU SAT NEXT TO ME...
YOU DID LOOK MISERABLE BEFORE.. BUT CUTE..
WELL YOU SEEM TOO CONFIDENT TO DIE IN A PLANE CRASH.... SO I'M A LITTLE RELEIVED.
LET'S TALK ABOUT THIS FEAR....

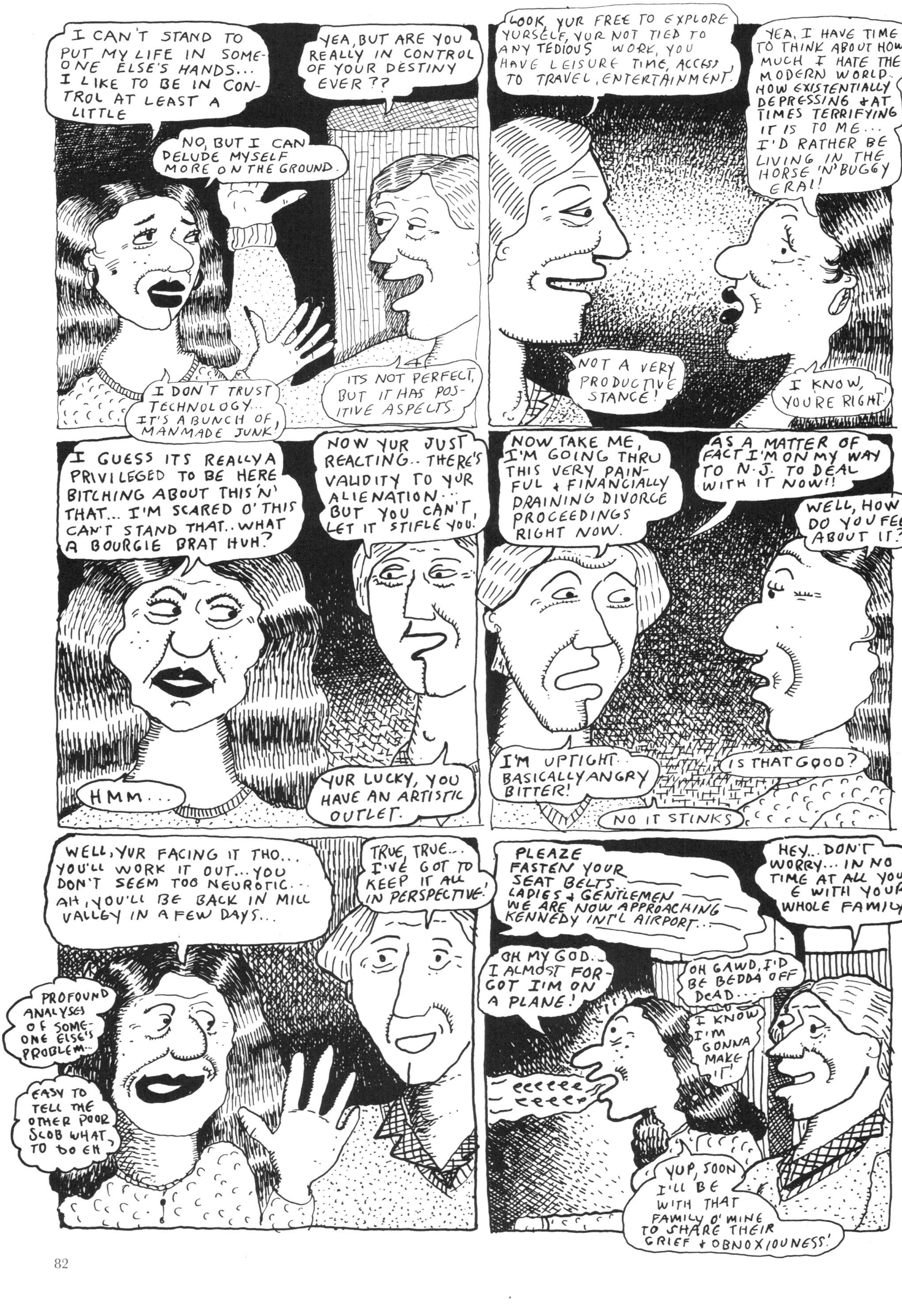
I CAN'T STAND TO PUT MY LIFE IN SOMEONE ELSE'S HANDS... I LIKE TO BE IN CONTROL AT LEAST A LITTLE
YEA, BUT ARE YOU REALLY IN CONTROL OF YOUR DESTINY EVER??
NO, BUT I CAN DELUDE MYSELF MORE ON THE GROUND.
I DON'T TRUST TECHNOLOGY.. IT'S A BUNCH OF MANMADE JUNK!
ITS NOT PERFECT, BUT IT HAS POSITIVE ASPECTS.
LOOK, YUR FREE TO EXPLORE YURSELF, YUR NOT TIED TO ANY TEDIOUS WORK, YOU HAVE LEISURE TIME, ACCESS TO TRAVEL, ENTERTAINMENT.
YEA, I HAVE TIME TO THINK ABOUT HOW MUCH I HATE THE MODERN WORLD.. HOW EXISTENTIALLY DEPRESSING & AT TIMES TERRIFYING IT IS TO ME... I'D RATHER BE LIVING IN THE HORSE 'N' BUGGY ERA!
NOT A VERY PRODUCTIVE STANCE!
I KNOW, YOU'RE RIGHT.
I GUESS ITS REALLY A PRIVILEGED TO BE HERE BITCHING ABOUT THIS 'N' THAT... I'M SCARED O' THIS CAN'T STAND THAT.. WHAT A BOURGIE BRAT HUH?
NOW YUR JUST REACTING.. THERE'S VALIDITY TO YUR ALIENATION... BUT YOU CAN'T LET IT STIFLE YOU!
HMM...
YUR LUCKY, YOU HAVE AN ARTISTIC OUTLET.
NOW TAKE ME, I'M GOING THRU THIS VERY PAINFUL & FINANCIALLY DRAINING DIVORCE PROCEEDINGS RIGHT NOW.
AS A MATTER OF FACT I'M ON MY WAY TO N.J. TO DEAL WITH IT NOW!!
WELL, HOW DO YOU FEEL ABOUT IT?
I'M UPTIGHT. BASICALLY ANGRY BITTER!
IS THAT GOOD?
NO IT STINKS
WELL, YUR FACING IT THO... YOU'LL WORK IT OUT... YOU DON'T SEEM TOO NEUROTIC.. AH, YOU'LL BE BACK IN MILL VALLEY IN A FEW DAYS...
TRUE, TRUE.. I'VE GOT TO KEEP IT ALL IN PERSPECTIVE!
PROFOUND ANALYSES OF SOMEONE ELSE'S PROBLEM..
EASY TO TELL THE OTHER POOR SLOB WHAT TO DO EH
PLEAZE FASTEN YOUR SEAT BELTS LADIES & GENTLEMEN WE ARE NOW APPROACHING KENNEDY INT'L AIRPORT...
HEY... DON'T WORRY... IN NO TIME AT ALL YOU'LL E WITH YOUR WHOLE FAMILY!
OH MY GOD.. I ALMOST FORGOT I'M ON A PLANE!
OH GAWD, I'D BE BEDDA OFF DEAD...
I KNOW I'M GONNA MAKE IT!
eeeeee eeeee
YUP, SOON I'LL BE WITH THAT FAMILY O' MINE TO SHARE THEIR GRIEF & OBNOXIOUNESS!

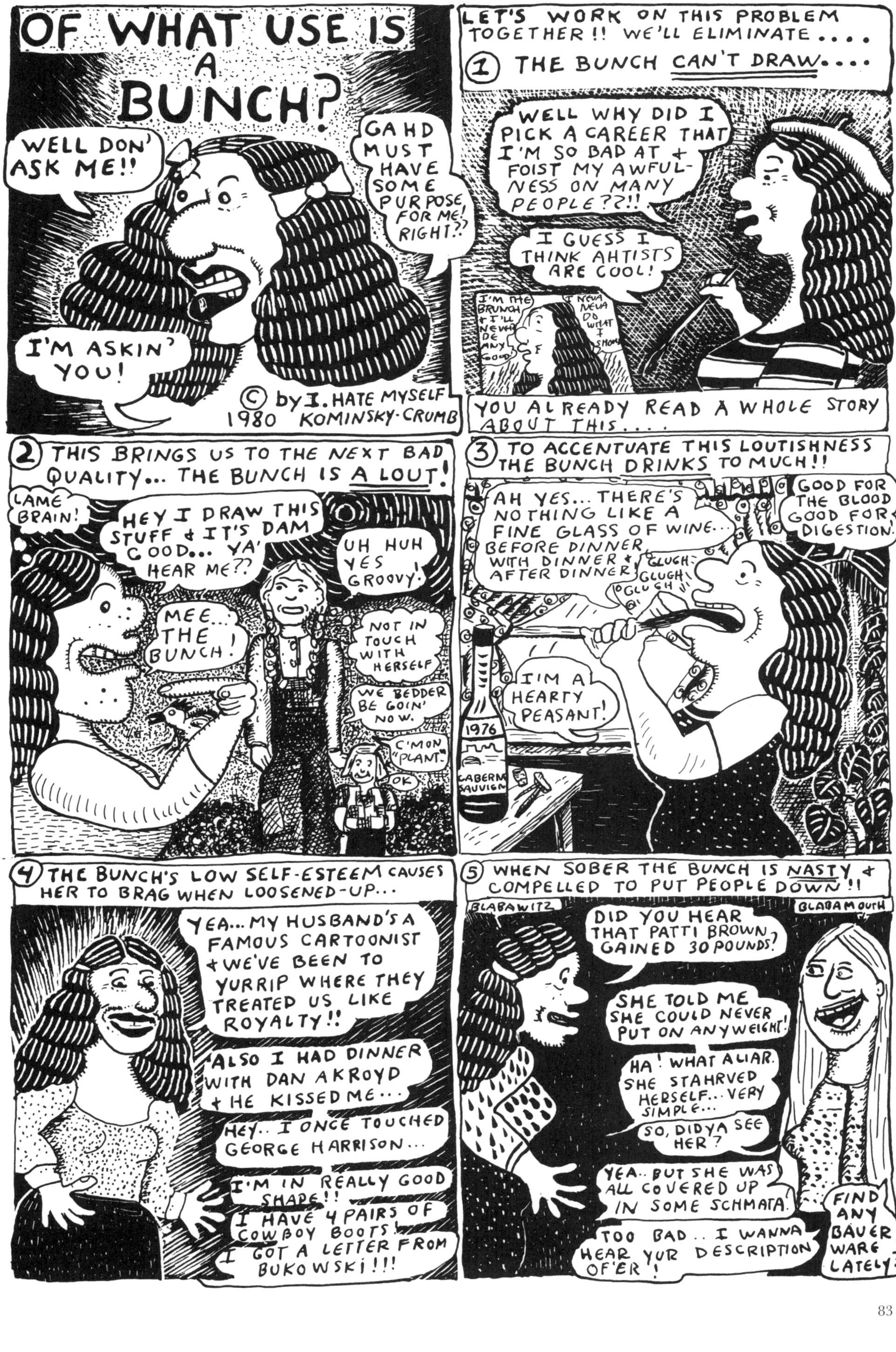
OF WHAT USE IS A BUNCH?
WELL DON' ASK ME!!
GAHD MUST HAVE SOME PURPOSE FOR ME! RIGHT??
I'M ASKIN' YOU!
© by I. HATE MYSELF 1980 KOMINSKY-CRUMB
LET'S WORK ON THIS PROBLEM TOGETHER!! WE'LL ELIMINATE....
1 THE BUNCH CAN'T DRAW....
WELL WHY DID I PICK A CAREER THAT I'M SO BAD AT & FOIST MY AWFULNESS ON MANY PEOPLE??!!
I GUESS I THINK AHTISTS ARE COOL!
I'M THE BRUNCH & I'LL NEVER BE ANY GOOD!
I NEVA NEVA DO WHAT I SHOW
YOU ALREADY READ A WHOLE STORY ABOUT THIS....
2 THIS BRINGS US TO THE NEXT BAD QUALITY... THE BUNCH IS A LOUT!
LAME BRAIN!
HEY I DRAW THIS STUFF & IT'S DAM GOOD... YA' HEAR ME??
UH HUH YES GROOVY!
MEE... THE BUNCH!
NOT IN TOUCH WITH HERSELF
WE BEDDER BE GOIN' NOW.
C'MON "PLANT"
OK
3 TO ACCENTUATE THIS LOUTISHNESS THE BUNCH DRINKS TO MUCH!!
AH YES... THERE'S NOTHING LIKE A FINE GLASS OF WINE... BEFORE DINNER WITH DINNER & AFTER DINNER!
GOOD FOR THE BLOOD GOOD FOR DIGESTION!
GLUGH GLUGH GLUGH
I'M A HEARTY PEASANT!
1976
CABERN SAUVIGN
4 THE BUNCH'S LOW SELF-ESTEEM CAUSES HER TO BRAG WHEN LOOSENED-UP...
YEA... MY HUSBAND'S A FAMOUS CARTOONIST & WE'VE BEEN TO YURRIP WHERE THEY TREATED US LIKE ROYALTY!!
ALSO I HAD DINNER WITH DAN AKROYD & HE KISSED ME...
HEY.. I ONCE TOUCHED GEORGE HARRISON...
I'M IN REALLY GOOD SHAPE!!
I HAVE 4 PAIRS OF COWBOY BOOTS!
I GOT A LETTER FROM BUKOWSKI!!!
5 WHEN SOBER THE BUNCH IS NASTY & COMPELLED TO PUT PEOPLE DOWN!!
BLABAWITZ
BLABAMOUTH
DID YOU HEAR THAT PATTI BROWN GAINED 30 POUNDS?
SHE TOLD ME SHE COULD NEVER PUT ON ANYWEIGHT!
HA! WHAT A LIAR. SHE STAHRVED HERSELF... VERY SIMPLE...
SO, DIDYA SEE HER?
YEA.. BUT SHE WAS ALL COVERED UP IN SOME SCHMATA!
TOO BAD.. I WANNA HEAR YUR DESCRIPTION OF'ER!
FIND ANY BAUER WARE LATELY?

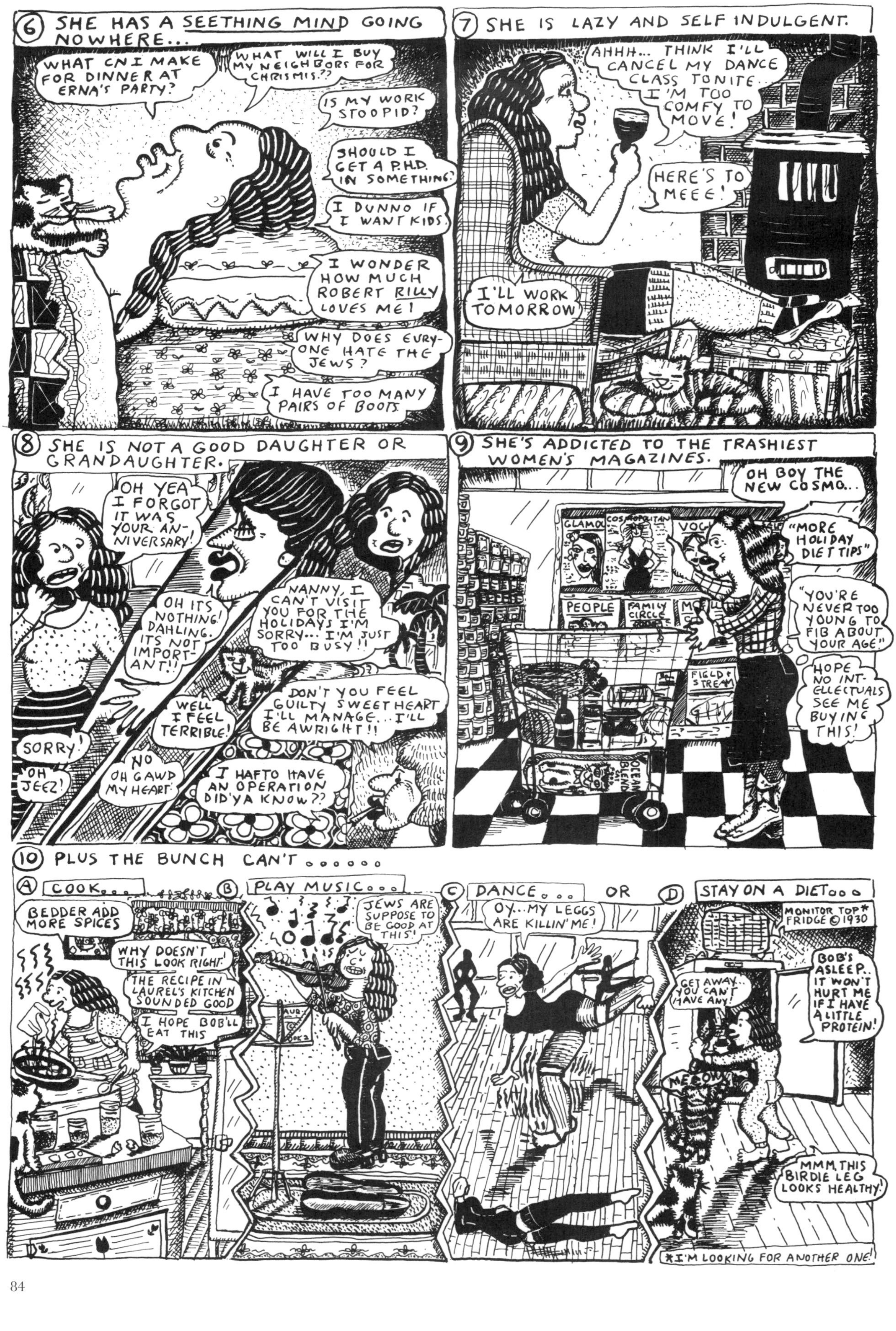
6 SHE HAS A SEETHING MIND GOING NOWHERE...
WHAT CN I MAKE FOR DINNER AT ERNA'S PARTY?
WHAT WILL I BUY MY NEIGHBORS FOR CHRISMIS.??
IS MY WORK STOOPID?
SHOULD I GET A P.H.D. IN SOMETHING?
I DUNNO IF I WANT KIDS.
I WONDER HOW MUCH ROBERT RILLY LOVES ME!
WHY DOES EVRY-ONE HATE THE JEWS?
I HAVE TOO MANY PAIRS OF BOOTS.
7 SHE IS LAZY AND SELF INDULGENT.
AHHH... THINK I'LL CANCEL MY DANCE CLASS TONITE. I'M TOO COMFY TO MOVE!
HERE'S TO MEEE!
I'LL WORK TOMORROW
8 SHE IS NOT A GOOD DAUGHTER OR GRANDAUGHTER.
OH YEA I FORGOT IT WAS YOUR AN-NIVERSARY!
OH ITS NOTHING! DAHLING. ITS NOT IMPORT-ANT!!
NANNY, I CAN'T VISIT YOU FOR THE HOLIDAYS I'M SORRY... I'M JUST TOO BUSY!!
WELL I FEEL TERRIBLE!
DON'T YOU FEEL GUILTY SWEETHEART I'LL MANAGE... I'LL BE AWRIGHT!!
SORRY!
OH JEEZ!
NO OH GAWD MY HEART
I HAFTO HAVE AN OPERATION DID'YA KNOW??
9 SHE'S ADDICTED TO THE TRASHIEST WOMEN'S MAGAZINES.
OH BOY THE NEW COSMO...
"MORE HOLIDAY DIET TIPS"
"YOU'RE NEVER TOO YOUNG TO FIB ABOUT YOUR AGE"
HOPE NO INT-ELLECTUALS SEE ME BUYING THIS!
PEOPLE
FAMILY CIRCLE
FIELD + STREAM
10 PLUS THE BUNCH CAN'T......
A COOK...
BEDDER ADD MORE SPICES
WHY DOESN'T THIS LOOK RIGHT!
THE RECIPE IN LAUREL'S KITCHEN SOUNDED GOOD
I HOPE BOB'LL EAT THIS
B PLAY MUSIC....
JEWS ARE SUPPOSE TO BE GOOD AT THIS!
C DANCE... OR
OY.. MY LEGGS ARE KILLIN' ME!
D STAY ON A DIET...
MONITOR TOP* FRIDGE © 1930
BOB'S ASLEEP.. IT WON'T HURT ME IF I HAVE A LITTLE PROTEIN!
GET AWAY.. YOU CAN'T HAVE ANY!
MEOW
MMM, THIS BIRDIE LEG LOOKS HEALTHY!
*I'M LOOKING FOR ANOTHER ONE!

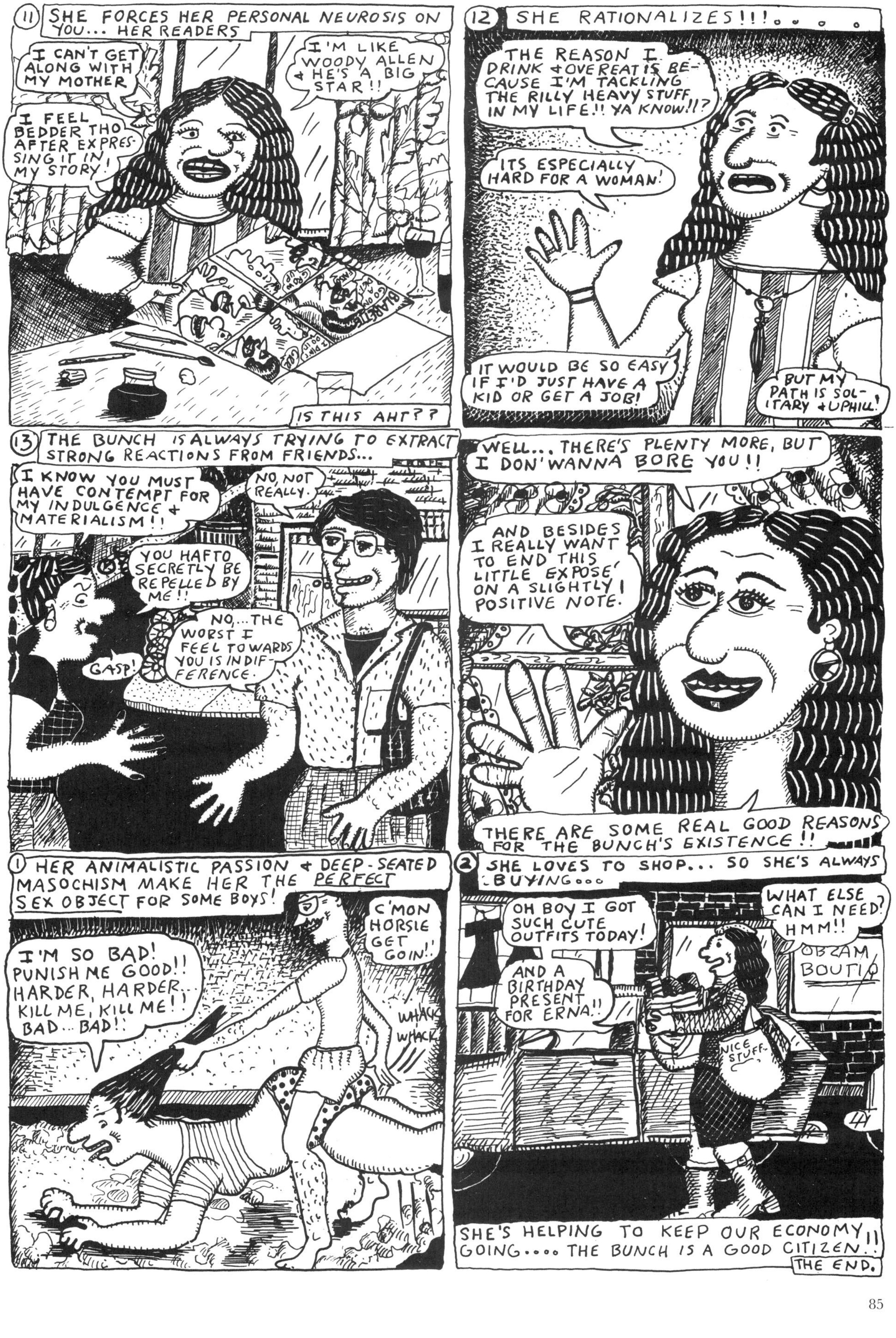
11 SHE FORCES HER PERSONAL NEUROSIS ON YOU... HER READERS
I CAN'T GET ALONG WITH MY MOTHER
I FEEL BEDDER THO AFTER EXPRESSING IT IN MY STORY!
I'M LIKE WOODY ALLEN & HE'S A BIG STAR!!
IS THIS AHT??
12 SHE RATIONALIZES!!!....
THE REASON I DRINK & OVEREAT IS BECAUSE I'M TACKLING THE RILLY HEAVY STUFF IN MY LIFE!! YA KNOW!!?
ITS ESPECIALLY HARD FOR A WOMAN!
IT WOULD BE SO EASY IF I'D JUST HAVE A KID OR GET A JOB!
BUT MY PATH IS SOLITARY & UPHILL!
13 THE BUNCH IS ALWAYS TRYING TO EXTRACT STRONG REACTIONS FROM FRIENDS...
I KNOW YOU MUST HAVE CONTEMPT FOR MY INDULGENCE & MATERIALISM!!
NO, NOT REALLY.
YOU HAFTO SECRETLY BE REPELLED BY ME!!
NO,...THE WORST I FEEL TOWARDS YOU IS INDIFFERENCE.
GASP!
WELL... THERE'S PLENTY MORE, BUT I DON'WANNA BORE YOU!!
AND BESIDES I REALLY WANT TO END THIS LITTLE EXPOSE' ON A SLIGHTLY POSITIVE NOTE.
THERE ARE SOME REAL GOOD REASONS FOR THE BUNCH'S EXISTENCE!!
1 HER ANIMALISTIC PASSION & DEEP-SEATED MASOCHISM MAKE HER THE PERFECT SEX OBJECT FOR SOME BOYS!
I'M SO BAD! PUNISH ME GOOD!! HARDER, HARDER.. KILL ME, KILL ME!! BAD...BAD!
C'MON HORSIE GET GOIN'.
WHACK
WHACK
2 SHE LOVES TO SHOP... SO SHE'S ALWAYS BUYING...
OH BOY I GOT SUCH CUTE OUTFITS TODAY!
AND A BIRTHDAY PRESENT FOR ERNA!!
WHAT ELSE CAN I NEED? HMM!!
NICE STUFF
SHE'S HELPING TO KEEP OUR ECONOMY GOING.... THE BUNCH IS A GOOD CITIZEN!!
THE END.

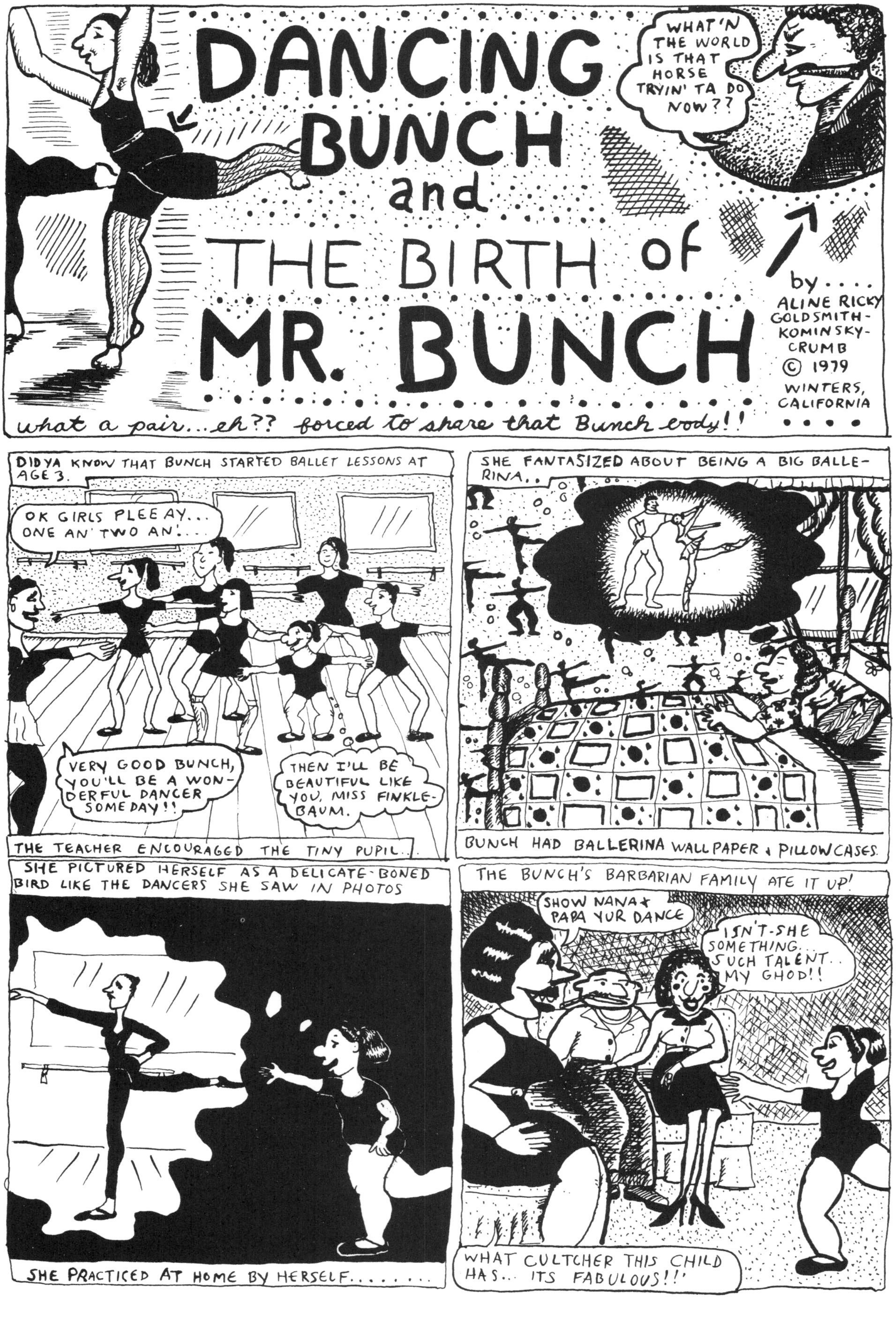
DANCING BUNCH and THE BIRTH of MR. BUNCH
WHAT'N THE WORLD IS THAT HORSE TRYIN' TA DO NOW??
by.... ALINE RICKY GOLDSMITH-KOMINSKY-CRUMB © 1979 WINTERS, CALIFORNIA
what a pair...eh?? forced to share that Bunch body!!
DIDYA KNOW THAT BUNCH STARTED BALLET LESSONS AT AGE 3.
OK GIRLS PLEEAY... ONE AN' TWO AN'...
VERY GOOD BUNCH, YOU'LL BE A WONDERFUL DANCER SOMEDAY!!
THEN I'LL BE BEAUTIFUL LIKE YOU, MISS FINKLEBAUM.
THE TEACHER ENCOURAGED THE TINY PUPIL.
SHE FANTASIZED ABOUT BEING A BIG BALLERINA..
BUNCH HAD BALLERINA WALLPAPER & PILLOWCASES.
SHE PICTURED HERSELF AS A DELICATE-BONED BIRD LIKE THE DANCERS SHE SAW IN PHOTOS
SHE PRACTICED AT HOME BY HERSELF.......
THE BUNCH'S BARBARIAN FAMILY ATE IT UP!
SHOW NANA & PAPA YUR DANCE
ISN'T-SHE SOMETHING.. SUCH TALENT.. MY GHOD!!
WHAT CULTCHER THIS CHILD HAS... ITS FABULOUS!!'

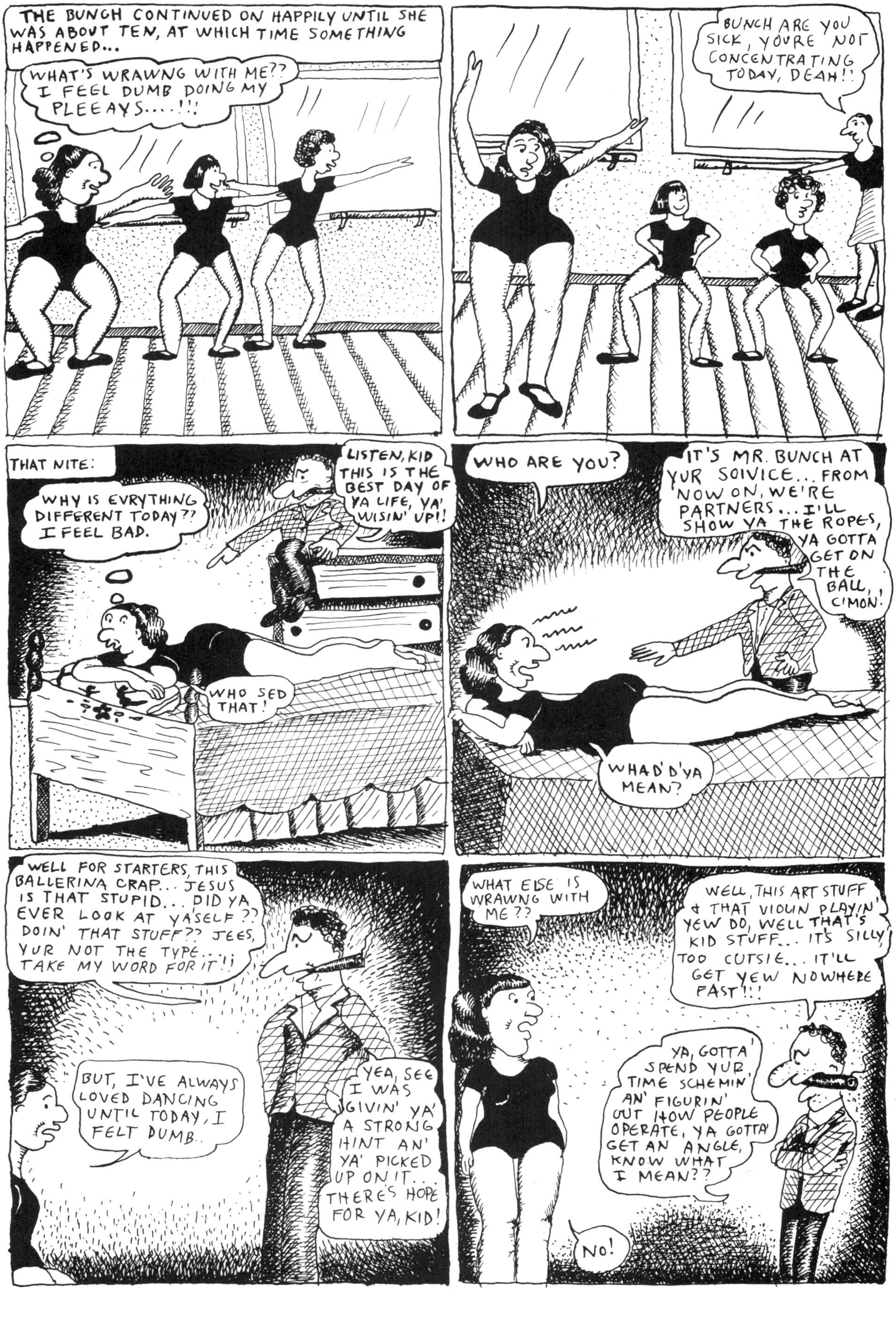
THE BUNCH CONTINUED ON HAPPILY UNTIL SHE WAS ABOUT TEN, AT WHICH TIME SOMETHING HAPPENED...
WHAT'S WRAWNG WITH ME?? I FEEL DUMB DOING MY PLEEAYS....!!
BUNCH ARE YOU SICK, YOU'RE NOT CONCENTRATING TODAY, DEAH!!
THAT NITE:
WHY IS EVRYTHING DIFFERENT TODAY?? I FEEL BAD.
LISTEN, KID THIS IS THE BEST DAY OF YA LIFE, YA' WISIN' UP!!
WHO SED THAT!
WHO ARE YOU?
IT'S MR. BUNCH AT YUR SOIVICE... FROM NOW ON, WE'RE PARTNERS... I'LL SHOW YA THE ROPES, YA GOTTA GET ON THE BALL, C'MON!
WHAD'D'YA MEAN?
WELL FOR STARTERS, THIS BALLERINA CRAP... JESUS IS THAT STUPID... DID YA EVER LOOK AT YA'SELF?? DOIN' THAT STUFF?? JEES, YUR NOT THE TYPE... TAKE MY WORD FOR IT!!
BUT, I'VE ALWAYS LOVED DANCING UNTIL TODAY, I FELT DUMB.
YEA, SEE I WAS GIVIN' YA' A STRONG HINT AN' YA' PICKED UP ON IT... THERE'S HOPE FOR YA, KID!
WHAT ELSE IS WRAWNG WITH ME??
WELL, THIS ART STUFF & THAT VIOLIN PLAYIN' YEW DO, WELL THAT'S KID STUFF... IT'S SILLY TOO CUTSIE... IT'LL GET YEW NOWHERE FAST!!!
YA, GOTTA SPEND YUR TIME SCHEMIN' AN' FIGURIN' OUT HOW PEOPLE OPERATE, YA GOTTA GET AN ANGLE, KNOW WHAT I MEAN??
NO!

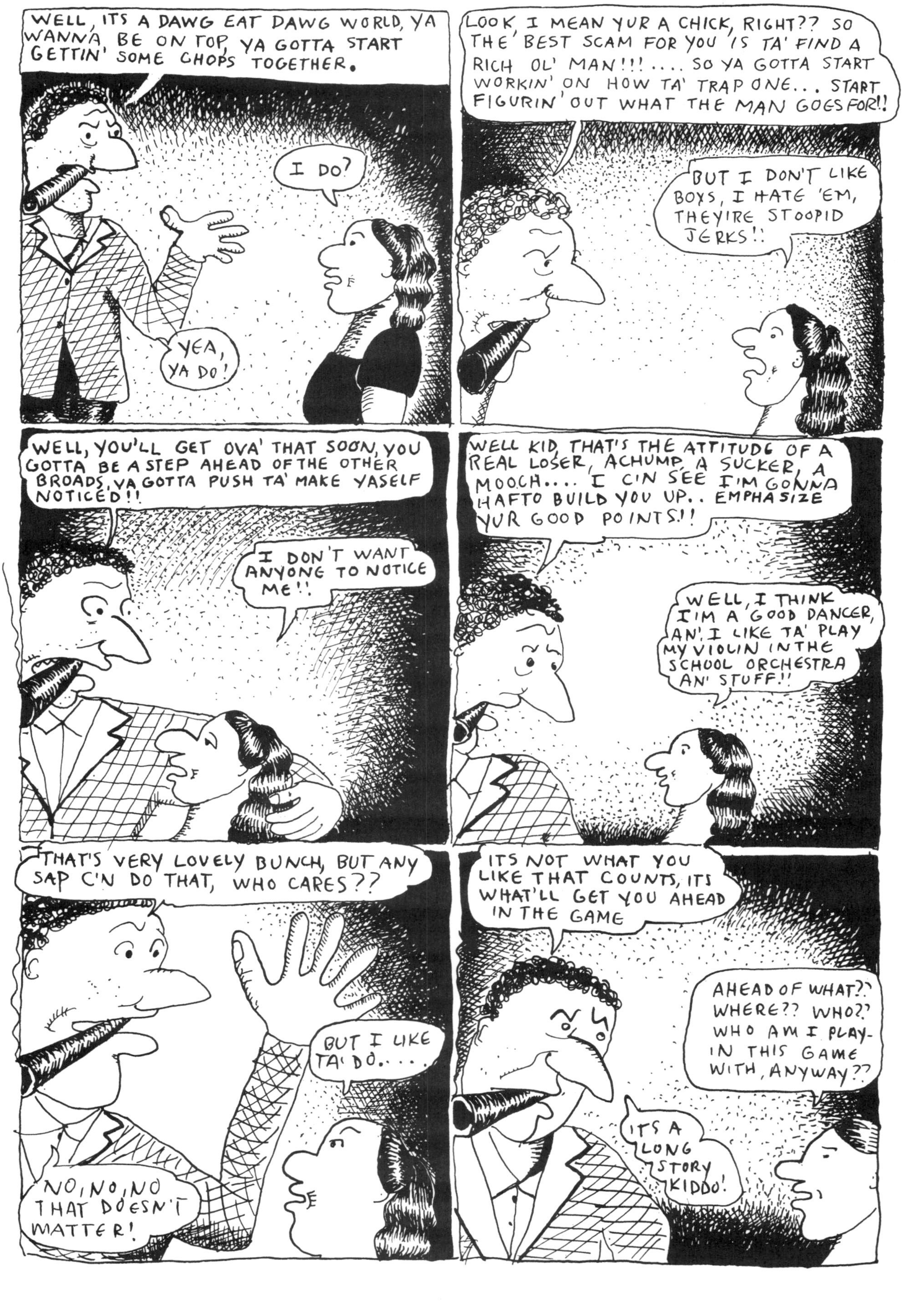
WELL, ITS A DAWG EAT DAWG WORLD, YA WANNA BE ON TOP, YA GOTTA START GETTIN' SOME CHOPS TOGETHER.
I DO?
YEA, YA DO!
LOOK, I MEAN YUR A CHICK, RIGHT?? SO THE BEST SCAM FOR YOU IS TA' FIND A RICH OL' MAN!!! .... SO YA GOTTA START WORKIN' ON HOW TA' TRAP ONE... START FIGURIN' OUT WHAT THE MAN GOES FOR!!
BUT I DON'T LIKE BOYS, I HATE 'EM, THEY'RE STOOPID JERKS!!
WELL, YOU'LL GET OVA' THAT SOON, YOU GOTTA BE A STEP AHEAD OF THE OTHER BROADS, YA GOTTA PUSH TA' MAKE YASELF NOTICED!!
I DON'T WANT ANYONE TO NOTICE ME!!
WELL KID, THAT'S THE ATTITUDE OF A REAL LOSER, A CHUMP, A SUCKER, A MOOCH.... I C'N SEE I'M GONNA HAFTO BUILD YOU UP.. EMPHASIZE YUR GOOD POINTS!!
WELL, I THINK I'M A GOOD DANCER, AN' I LIKE TA' PLAY MY VIOLIN IN THE SCHOOL ORCHESTRA AN' STUFF!!
THAT'S VERY LOVELY BUNCH, BUT ANY SAP C'N DO THAT, WHO CARES??
BUT I LIKE TA' DO....
NO, NO, NO THAT DOESN'T MATTER!
ITS NOT WHAT YOU LIKE THAT COUNTS, ITS WHAT'LL GET YOU AHEAD IN THE GAME
AHEAD OF WHAT?? WHERE?? WHO?? WHO AM I PLAY-IN THIS GAME WITH, ANYWAY??
ITS A LONG STORY KIDDO!

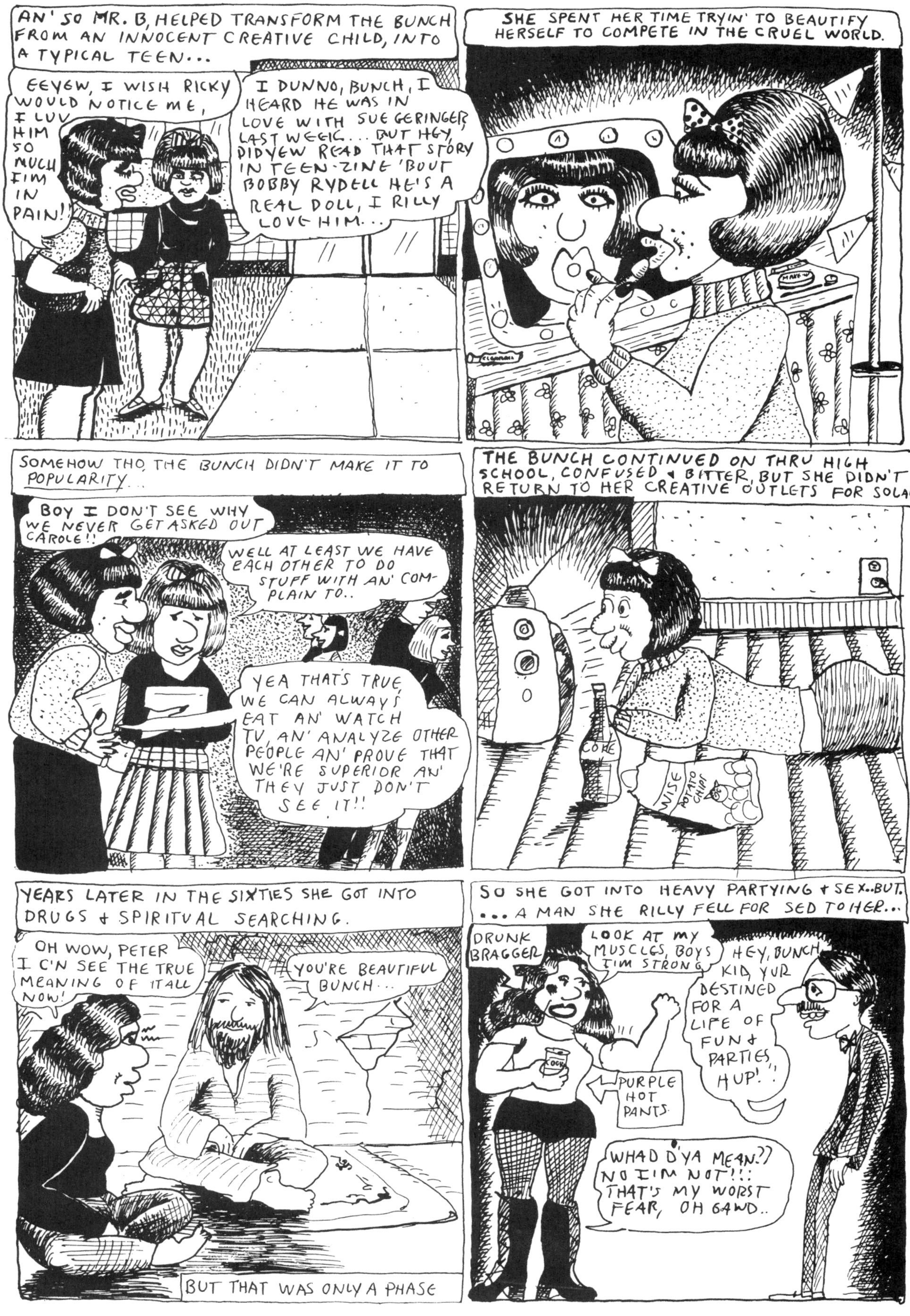

AN' SO MR. B, HELPED TRANSFORM THE BUNCH FROM AN INNOCENT CREATIVE CHILD, INTO A TYPICAL TEEN...
EEYEW, I WISH RICKY WOULD NOTICE ME, I LUV HIM SO MUCH I'M IN PAIN!
I DUNNO, BUNCH, I HEARD HE WAS IN LOVE WITH SUE GERINGER, LAST WEEK... BUT HEY, DIDYEW READ THAT STORY IN TEEN-ZINE 'BOUT BOBBY RYDELL HE'S A REAL DOLL, I RILLY LOVE HIM...
SHE SPENT HER TIME TRYIN' TO BEAUTIFY HERSELF TO COMPETE IN THE CRUEL WORLD.
SOMEHOW THO, THE BUNCH DIDN'T MAKE IT TO POPULARITY...
BOY I DON'T SEE WHY WE NEVER GET ASKED OUT CAROLE!!
WELL AT LEAST WE HAVE EACH OTHER TO DO STUFF WITH AN' COMPLAIN TO..
YEA THAT'S TRUE, WE CAN ALWAYS EAT AN' WATCH TV, AN' ANALYZE OTHER PEOPLE AN' PROVE THAT WE'RE SUPERIOR AN' THEY JUST DON'T SEE IT!!
THE BUNCH CONTINUED ON THRU HIGH SCHOOL, CONFUSED & BITTER, BUT SHE DIDN'T RETURN TO HER CREATIVE OUTLETS FOR SOLACE.
COKE
WISE POTATO CHIPS
YEARS LATER IN THE SIXTIES SHE GOT INTO DRUGS & SPIRITUAL SEARCHING.
OH WOW, PETER I C'N SEE THE TRUE MEANING OF IT ALL NOW!
YOU'RE BEAUTIFUL BUNCH...
BUT THAT WAS ONLY A PHASE
SO SHE GOT INTO HEAVY PARTYING & SEX..BUT. ...A MAN SHE RILLY FELL FOR SED TO HER...
DRUNK BRAGGER
LOOK AT MY MUSCLES, BOYS I'M STRONG
HEY, BUNCH KID YUR DESTINED FOR A LIFE OF FUN & PARTIES, HUP!
PURPLE HOT PANTS
WHAD D'YA MEAN?? NO I'M NOT!!: THAT'S MY WORST FEAR, OH GAWD..

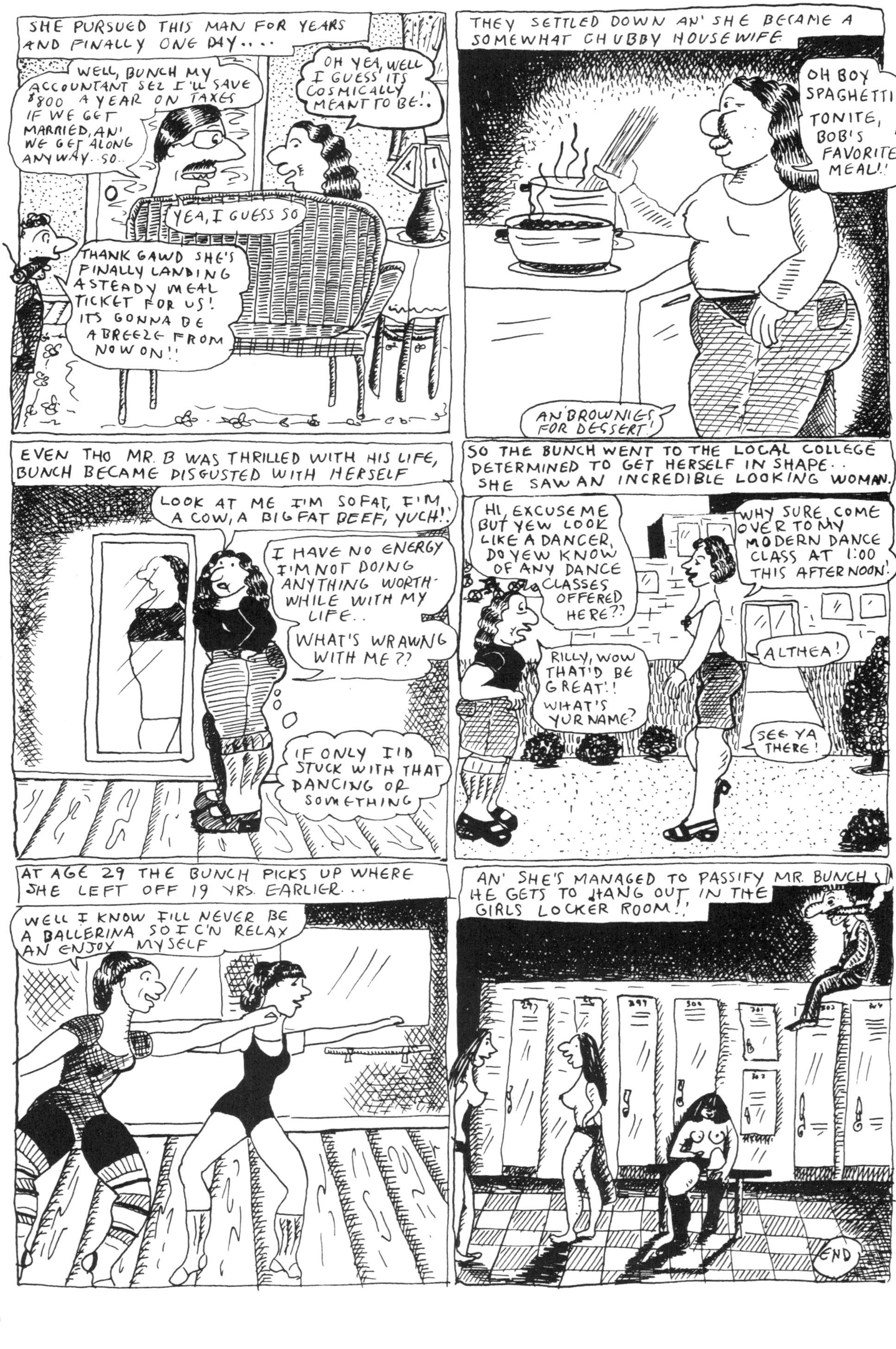

SHE PURSUED THIS MAN FOR YEARS AND FINALLY ONE DAY...
WELL, BUNCH MY ACCOUNTANT SEZ I'LL SAVE $800 A YEAR ON TAXES IF WE GET MARRIED, AN' WE GET ALONG ANYWAY.. SO..
OH YEA, WELL I GUESS ITS COSMICALLY MEANT TO BE!
YEA, I GUESS SO
THANK GAWD SHE'S FINALLY LANDING A STEADY MEAL TICKET FOR US! ITS GONNA BE A BREEZE FROM NOW ON!!
THEY SETTLED DOWN AN' SHE BECAME A SOMEWHAT CHUBBY HOUSEWIFE
OH BOY SPAGHETTI TONITE, BOB'S FAVORITE MEAL!!
AN' BROWNIES FOR DESSERT!
EVEN THO MR. B WAS THRILLED WITH HIS LIFE, BUNCH BECAME DISGUSTED WITH HERSELF
LOOK AT ME I'M SO FAT, I'M A COW, A BIG FAT BEEF, YUCH!!
I HAVE NO ENERGY I'M NOT DOING ANYTHING WORTHWHILE WITH MY LIFE..
WHAT'S WRAWNG WITH ME??
IF ONLY I'D STUCK WITH THAT DANCING OR SOMETHING
SO THE BUNCH WENT TO THE LOCAL COLLEGE DETERMINED TO GET HERSELF IN SHAPE.. SHE SAW AN INCREDIBLE LOOKING WOMAN.
HI, EXCUSE ME BUT YEW LOOK LIKE A DANCER, DO YEW KNOW OF ANY DANCE CLASSES OFFERED HERE??
WHY SURE COME OVER TO MY MODERN DANCE CLASS AT 1:00 THIS AFTERNOON!
RILLY, WOW THAT'D BE GREAT!! WHAT'S YUR NAME?
ALTHEA!
SEE YA THERE!
AT AGE 29 THE BUNCH PICKS UP WHERE SHE LEFT OFF 19 YRS. EARLIER..
WELL I KNOW I'LL NEVER BE A BALLERINA SO I C'N RELAX AN ENJOY MYSELF
AN' SHE'S MANAGED TO PASSIFY MR. BUNCH! HE GETS TO HANG OUT IN THE GIRLS LOCKER ROOM!!
END

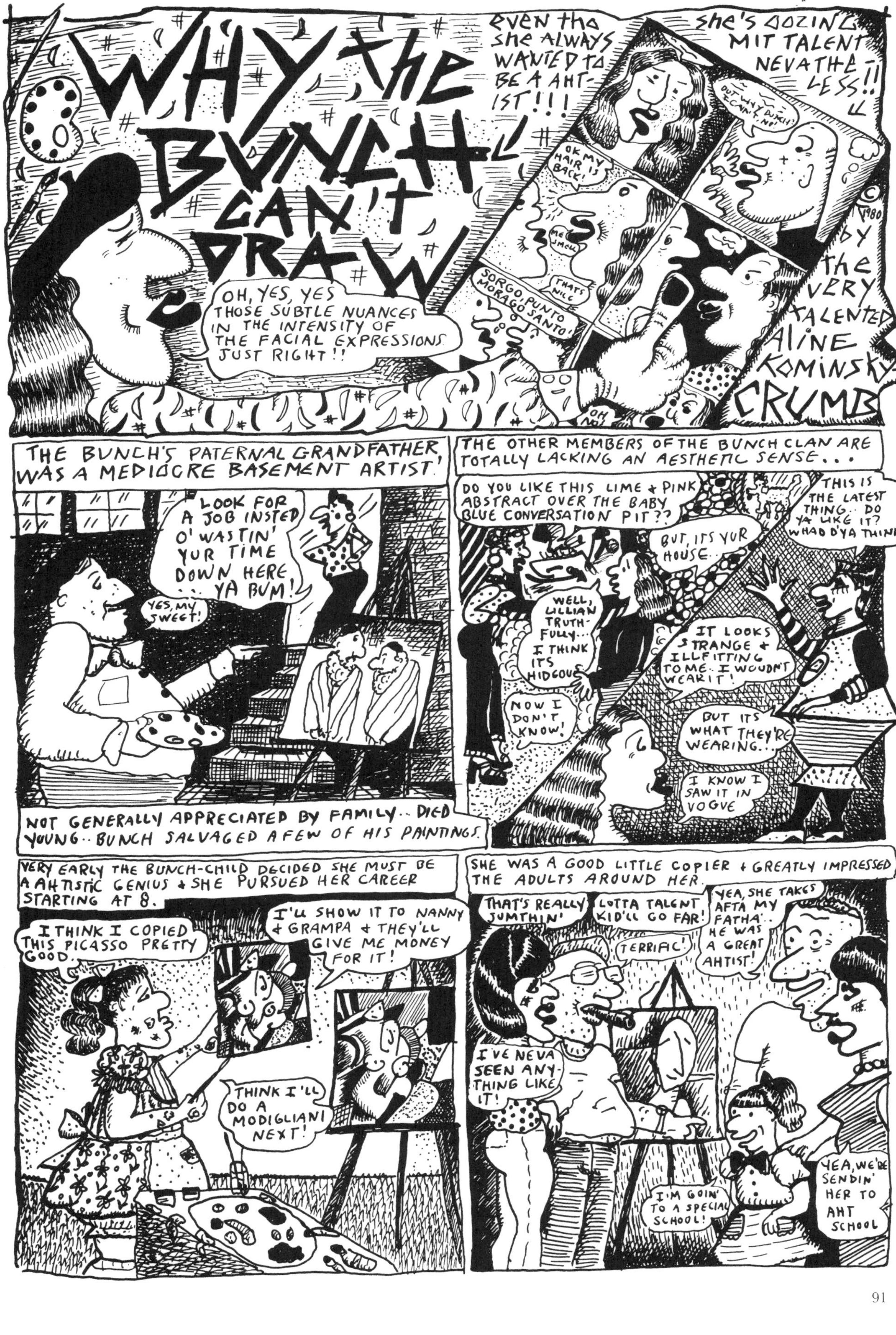

WHY the BUNCH CAN'T DRAW
even tho she ALWAYS WANTED TO BE A AHT-IST!!!
she's OOZING MIT TALENT NEVATHE-LESS!!
OK MY HAIR IS BACK!
THATS NICE
SORGO, PUNTO MORAGO SANTO!
OH NO!
OH, YES, YES THOSE SUBTLE NUANCES IN THE INTENSITY OF THE FACIAL EXPRESSIONS JUST RIGHT!!
© 1980 by the very talented Aline Kominsky-Crumb
THE BUNCH'S PATERNAL GRANDFATHER WAS A MEDIOCRE BASEMENT ARTIST
LOOK FOR A JOB INSTED O' WASTIN' YUR TIME DOWN HERE, YA BUM!
YES, MY SWEET!
NOT GENERALLY APPRECIATED BY FAMILY.. DIED YOUNG.. BUNCH SALVAGED A FEW OF HIS PAINTINGS.
THE OTHER MEMBERS OF THE BUNCH CLAN ARE TOTALLY LACKING AN AESTHETIC SENSE...
DO YOU LIKE THIS LIME + PINK ABSTRACT OVER THE BABY BLUE CONVERSATION PIT??
BUT, ITS YUR HOUSE...
WELL, LILLIAN TRUTHFULLY.. I THINK ITS HIDEOUS
NOW I DON'T KNOW!
THIS IS THE LATEST THING.. DO YA LIKE IT? WHAD D'YA THINK?
IT LOOKS STRANGE + ILLFITTING TO ME.. I WOUDN'T WEAR IT!
BUT ITS WHAT THEY'RE WEARING...
I KNOW I SAW IT IN VOGUE
VERY EARLY THE BUNCH-CHILD DECIDED SHE MUST BE A AHTISTIC GENIUS + SHE PURSUED HER CAREER STARTING AT 8.
I THINK I COPIED THIS PICASSO PRETTY GOOD.
I'LL SHOW IT TO NANNY + GRAMPA + THEY'LL GIVE ME MONEY FOR IT!
THINK I'LL DO A MODIGLIANI NEXT!
SHE WAS A GOOD LITTLE COPIER + GREATLY IMPRESSED THE ADULTS AROUND HER.
THAT'S REALLY JUMTHIN'
LOTTA TALENT KID'LL GO FAR!
TERRIFIC!
YEA, SHE TAKES AFTA MY FATHA. HE WAS A GREAT AHTIST!
I'VE NEVA SEEN ANYTHING LIKE IT!
I'M GOIN' TO A SPECIAL SCHOOL!
YEA, WE'RE SENDIN' HER TO AHT SCHOOL

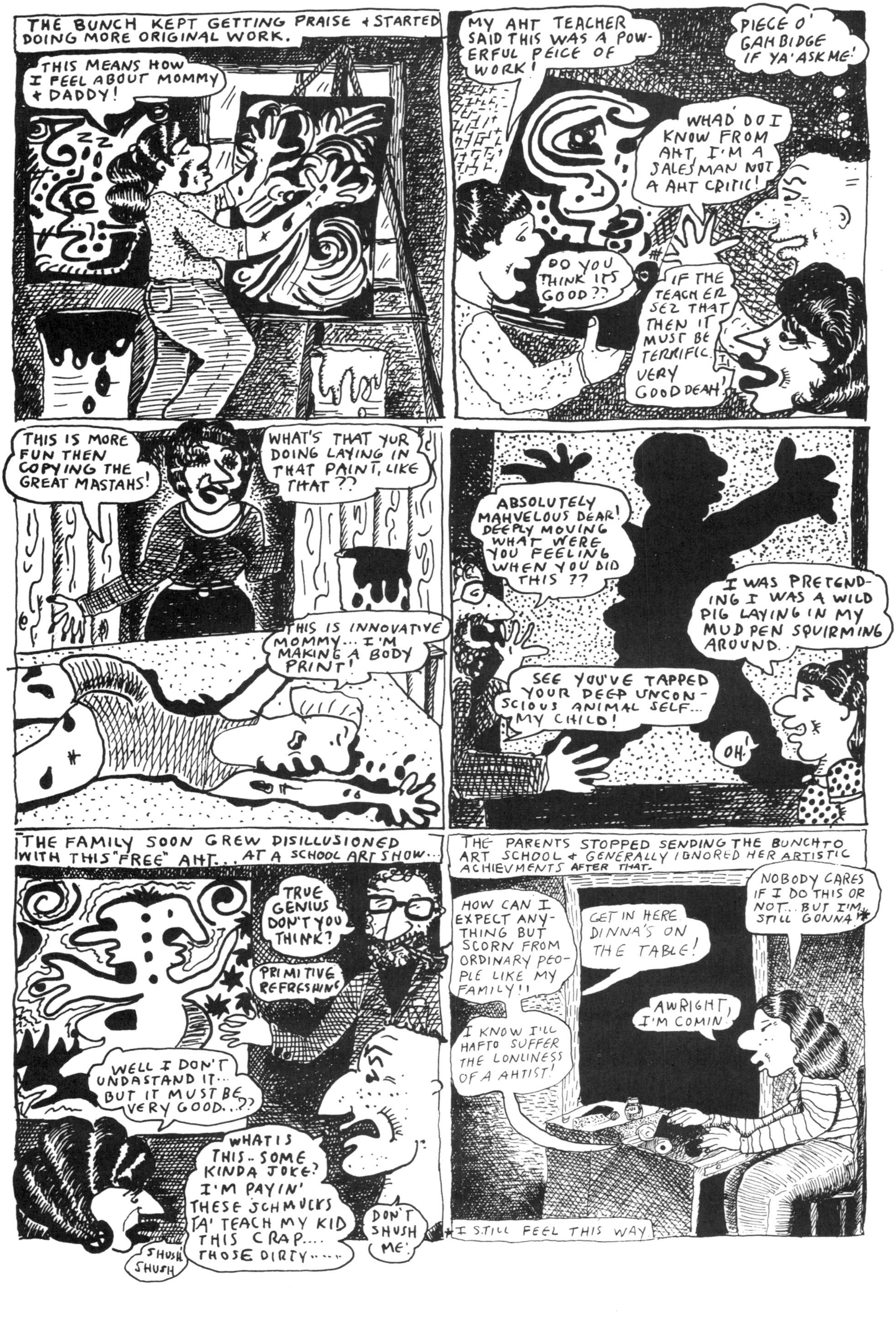
THE BUNCH KEPT GETTING PRAISE & STARTED DOING MORE ORIGINAL WORK.
THIS MEANS HOW I FEEL ABOUT MOMMY & DADDY!
MY AHT TEACHER SAID THIS WAS A POWERFUL PEICE OF WORK!
PIECE O' GAHBIDGE IF YA' ASK ME!
WHAD DO I KNOW FROM AHT, I'M A SALESMAN NOT A AHT CRITIC!
DO YOU THINK ITS GOOD??
IF THE TEACHER SEZ THAT THEN IT MUST BE TERRIFIC. VERY GOOD DEAH!
THIS IS MORE FUN THEN COPYING THE GREAT MASTAHS!
WHAT'S THAT YUR DOING LAYING IN THAT PAINT, LIKE THAT??
THIS IS INNOVATIVE MOMMY... I'M MAKING A BODY PRINT!
ABSOLUTELY MAHVELOUS DEAR! DEEPLY MOVING WHAT WERE YOU FEELING WHEN YOU DID THIS??
I WAS PRETENDING I WAS A WILD PIG LAYING IN MY MUD PEN SQUIRMING AROUND.
SEE YOU'VE TAPPED YOUR DEEP UNCONSCIOUS ANIMAL SELF... MY CHILD!
OH!
THE FAMILY SOON GREW DISILLUSIONED WITH THIS "FREE" AHT... AT A SCHOOL ART SHOW...
TRUE GENIUS DON'T YOU THINK?
PRIMITIVE REFRESHING
WELL I DON'T UNDASTAND IT... BUT IT MUST BE VERY GOOD...??
WHAT IS THIS.. SOME KINDA JOKE? I'M PAYIN' THESE SCHMUCKS TA' TEACH MY KID THIS CRAP.... THOSE DIRTY.....
DON'T SHUSH ME!
SHUSH SHUSH
THE PARENTS STOPPED SENDING THE BUNCH TO ART SCHOOL & GENERALLY IGNORED HER ARTISTIC ACHIEVMENTS AFTER THAT.
HOW CAN I EXPECT ANYTHING BUT SCORN FROM ORDINARY PEOPLE LIKE MY FAMILY!!
GET IN HERE DINNA'S ON THE TABLE!
NOBODY CARES IF I DO THIS OR NOT... BUT I'M STILL GONNA!*
I KNOW I'LL HAFTO SUFFER THE LONLINESS OF A AHTIST!
AWRIGHT, I'M COMIN'
*I STILL FEEL THIS WAY

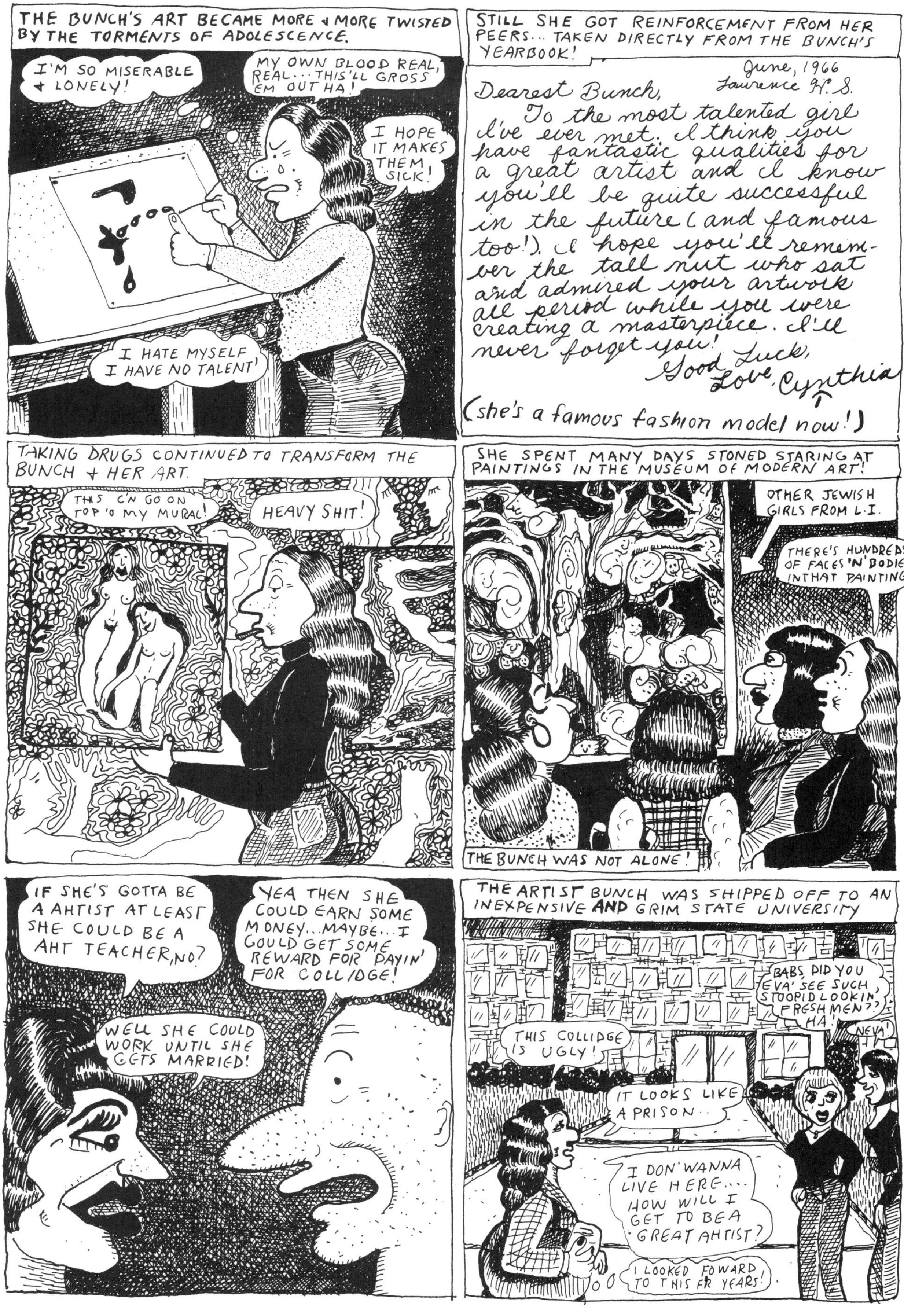
THE BUNCH'S ART BECAME MORE & MORE TWISTED BY THE TORMENTS OF ADOLESCENCE.
I'M SO MISERABLE & LONELY!
MY OWN BLOOD REAL, REAL... THIS'LL GROSS EM OUT HA!
I HOPE IT MAKES THEM SICK!
I HATE MYSELF I HAVE NO TALENT!
STILL SHE GOT REINFORCEMENT FROM HER PEERS... TAKEN DIRECTLY FROM THE BUNCH'S YEARBOOK!
June, 1966
Lawrence H. S.
Dearest Bunch,
To the most talented girl I've ever met. I think you have fantastic qualities for a great artist and I know you'll be quite successful in the future (and famous too!). I hope you'll remember the tall nut who sat and admired your artwork all period while you were creating a masterpiece. I'll never forget you!
Good Luck,
Love, Cynthia
(she's a famous fashion model now!)
TAKING DRUGS CONTINUED TO TRANSFORM THE BUNCH & HER ART.
THIS C'N GO ON TOP 'O MY MURAL!
HEAVY SHIT!
SHE SPENT MANY DAYS STONED STARING AT PAINTINGS IN THE MUSEUM OF MODERN ART!
OTHER JEWISH GIRLS FROM L.I.
THERE'S HUNDREDS OF FACES 'N' BODIES IN THAT PAINTING
THE BUNCH WAS NOT ALONE!
IF SHE'S GOTTA BE A AHTIST AT LEAST SHE COULD BE A AHT TEACHER, NO?
YEA THEN SHE COULD EARN SOME MONEY... MAYBE... I COULD GET SOME REWARD FOR PAYIN' FOR COLLIDGE!
WELL SHE COULD WORK UNTIL SHE GETS MARRIED!
THE ARTIST BUNCH WAS SHIPPED OFF TO AN INEXPENSIVE AND GRIM STATE UNIVERSITY
BABS, DID YOU EVA' SEE SUCH STOOPID LOOKIN' FRESHMEN?? HA!
NEVA!
THIS COLLIDGE IS UGLY!
IT LOOKS LIKE A PRISON..
I DON' WANNA LIVE HERE... HOW WILL I GET TO BE A GREAT AHTIST?
I LOOKED FOWARD TO THIS FR YEARS!

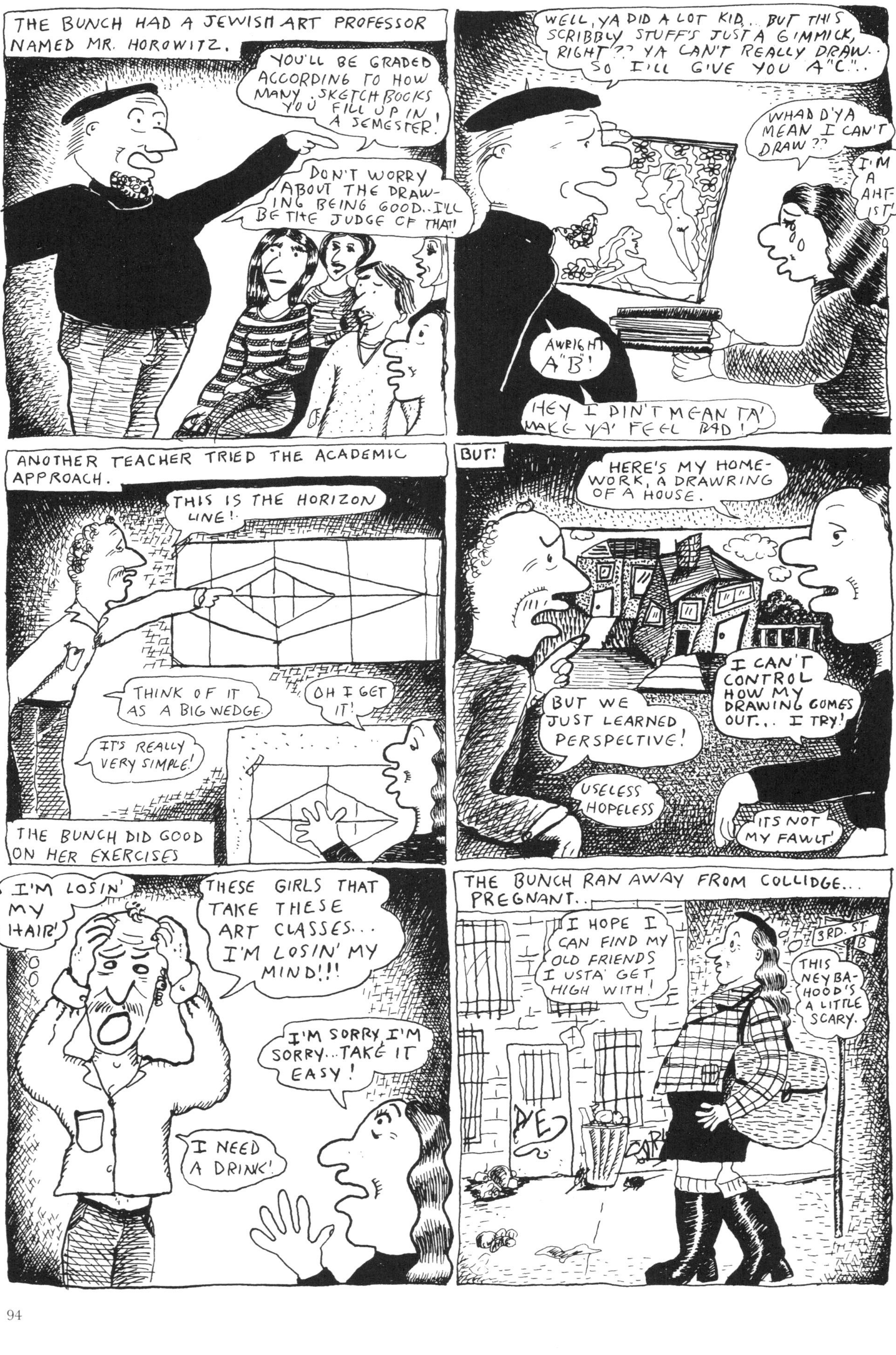
THE BUNCH HAD A JEWISH ART PROFESSOR NAMED MR. HOROWITZ.
YOU'LL BE GRADED ACCORDING TO HOW MANY SKETCHBOOKS YOU FILL UP IN A SEMESTER!
DON'T WORRY ABOUT THE DRAWING BEING GOOD.. I'LL BE THE JUDGE OF THAT!
WELL, YA DID A LOT KID.. BUT THIS SCRIBBLY STUFF'S JUST A GIMMICK, RIGHT?? YA CAN'T REALLY DRAW.. SO I'LL GIVE YOU A "C"..
WHADD'YA MEAN I CAN'T DRAW??
I'M A AHTIST!
AWRIGHT A "B"!
HEY I DIN'T MEAN TA' MAKE YA' FEEL BAD!
ANOTHER TEACHER TRIED THE ACADEMIC APPROACH.
THIS IS THE HORIZON LINE!
THINK OF IT AS A BIG WEDGE.
OH I GET IT!
IT'S REALLY VERY SIMPLE!
THE BUNCH DID GOOD ON HER EXERCISES
BUT!
HERE'S MY HOMEWORK, A DRAWRING OF A HOUSE.
BUT WE JUST LEARNED PERSPECTIVE!
I CAN'T CONTROL HOW MY DRAWING COMES OUT.. I TRY!
USELESS HOPELESS
ITS NOT MY FAWLT!
I'M LOSIN' MY HAIR!
THESE GIRLS THAT TAKE THESE ART CLASSES... I'M LOSIN' MY MIND!!!
I'M SORRY I'M SORRY.. TAKE IT EASY!
I NEED A DRINK!
THE BUNCH RAN AWAY FROM COLLIDGE... PREGNANT..
I HOPE I CAN FIND MY OLD FRIENDS I USTA' GET HIGH WITH!
3RD. ST
B
THIS NEYBAHOOD'S A LITTLE SCARY.

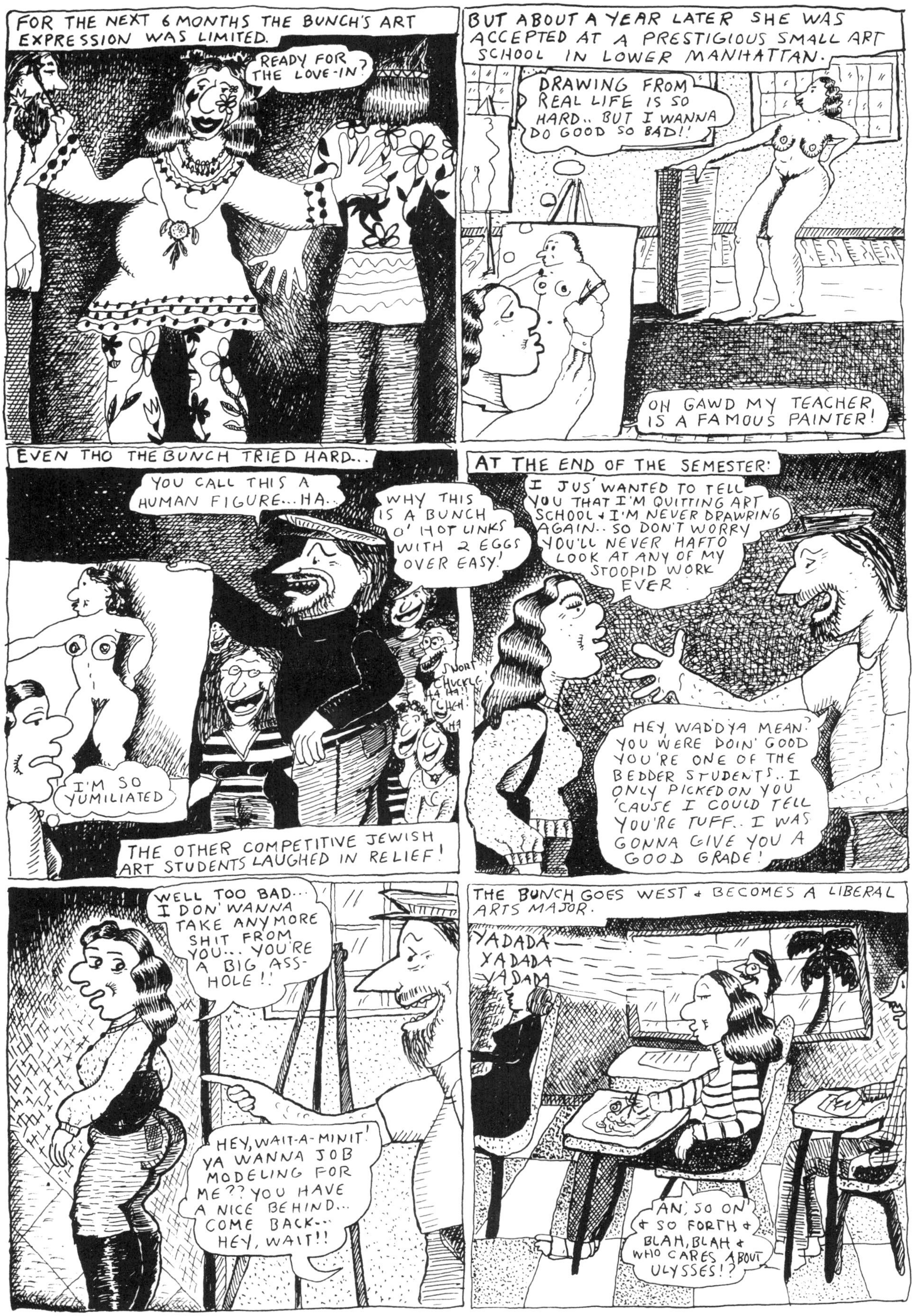
FOR THE NEXT 6 MONTHS THE BUNCH'S ART EXPRESSION WAS LIMITED.
READY FOR THE LOVE-IN?
BUT ABOUT A YEAR LATER SHE WAS ACCEPTED AT A PRESTIGIOUS SMALL ART SCHOOL IN LOWER MANHATTAN.
DRAWING FROM REAL LIFE IS SO HARD.. BUT I WANNA DO GOOD SO BAD!!
OH GAWD MY TEACHER IS A FAMOUS PAINTER!
EVEN THO THE BUNCH TRIED HARD..
YOU CALL THIS A HUMAN FIGURE... HA..
WHY THIS IS A BUNCH O' HOT LINKS WITH 2 EGGS OVER EASY!
SNORT CHUCKLE HA HA! CHCH! HA
I'M SO YUMILIATED
THE OTHER COMPETITIVE JEWISH ART STUDENTS LAUGHED IN RELIEF!
AT THE END OF THE SEMESTER:
I JUS' WANTED TO TELL YOU THAT I'M QUITTING ART SCHOOL & I'M NEVER DRAWRING AGAIN.. SO DON'T WORRY YOU'LL NEVER HAFTO LOOK AT ANY OF MY STOOPID WORK EVER
HEY, WADDYA MEAN? YOU WERE DOIN' GOOD YOU'RE ONE OF THE BEDDER STUDENTS.. I ONLY PICKED ON YOU 'CAUSE I COULD TELL YOU'RE TUFF.. I WAS GONNA GIVE YOU A GOOD GRADE!
WELL TOO BAD.. I DON' WANNA TAKE ANYMORE SHIT FROM YOU... YOU'RE A BIG ASS-HOLE!!
HEY, WAIT-A-MINIT! YA WANNA JOB MODELING FOR ME?? YOU HAVE A NICE BEHIND.. COME BACK.. HEY, WAIT!!
THE BUNCH GOES WEST & BECOMES A LIBERAL ARTS MAJOR.
YADADA— YADADA YADADA
AN' SO ON & SO FORTH & BLAH, BLAH & WHO CARES ABOUT ULYSSES!?

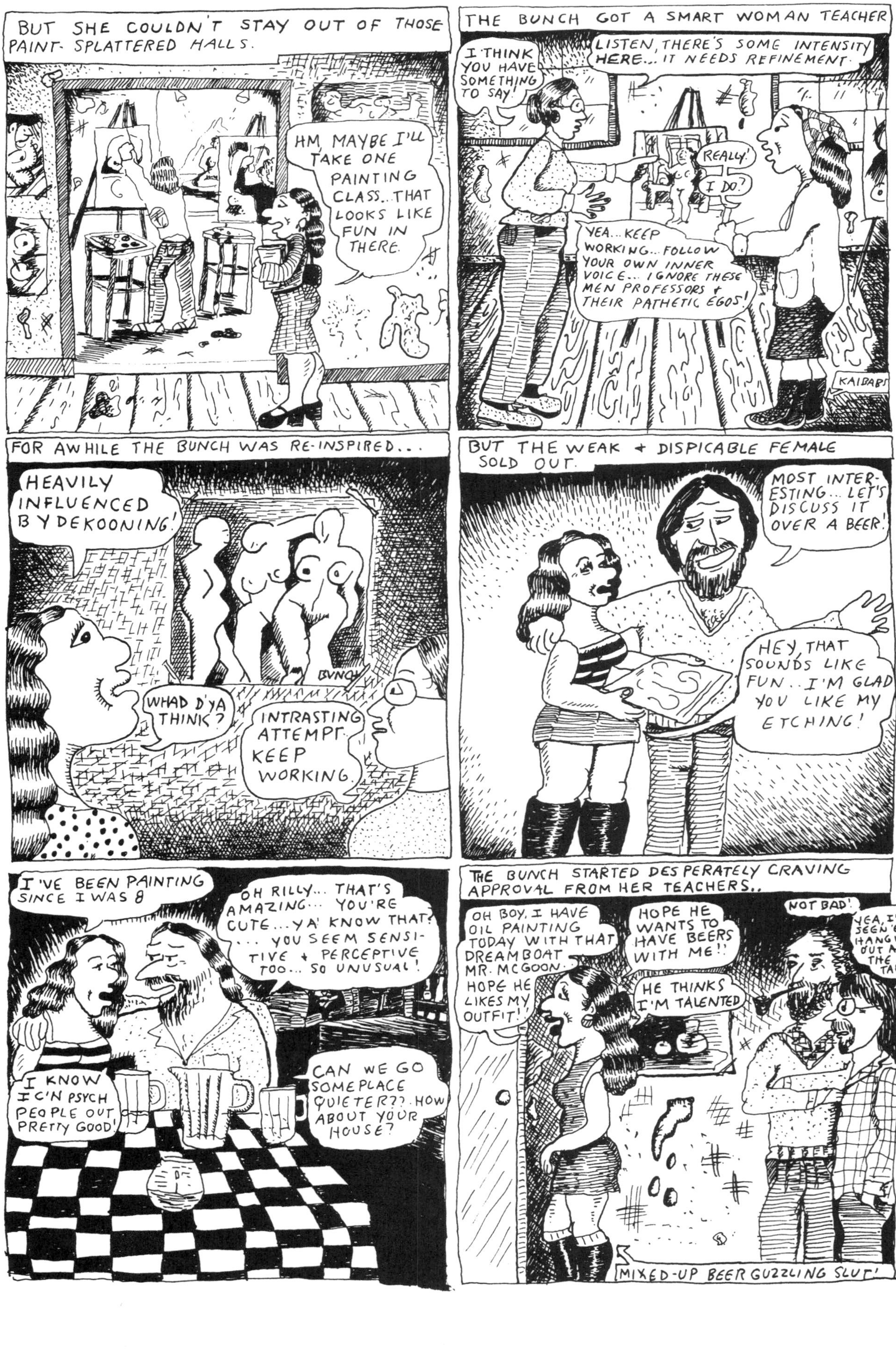

BUT SHE COULDN'T STAY OUT OF THOSE PAINT-SPLATTERED HALLS.
HM, MAYBE I'LL TAKE ONE PAINTING CLASS.. THAT LOOKS LIKE FUN IN THERE.
THE BUNCH GOT A SMART WOMAN TEACHER
I THINK YOU HAVE SOMETHING TO SAY!
LISTEN, THERE'S SOME INTENSITY HERE... IT NEEDS REFINEMENT.
REALLY!
I DO?
YEA... KEEP WORKING... FOLLOW YOUR OWN INNER VOICE... IGNORE THESE MEN PROFESSORS + THEIR PATHETIC EGOS!
KALBABS
FOR AWHILE THE BUNCH WAS RE-INSPIRED...
HEAVILY INFLUENCED BY DEKOONING!
BUNCH
WHAD D'YA THINK?
INTRASTING ATTEMPT. KEEP WORKING.
BUT THE WEAK + DISPICABLE FEMALE SOLD OUT.
MOST INTERESTING... LET'S DISCUSS IT OVER A BEER!
HEY, THAT SOUNDS LIKE FUN.. I'M GLAD YOU LIKE MY ETCHING!
I'VE BEEN PAINTING SINCE I WAS 8
OH RILLY... THAT'S AMAZING... YOU'RE CUTE... YA' KNOW THAT? ... YOU SEEM SENSITIVE + PERCEPTIVE TOO... SO UNUSUAL!
I KNOW I C'N PSYCH PEOPLE OUT PRETTY GOOD!
CAN WE GO SOMEPLACE QUIETER?? HOW ABOUT YOUR HOUSE?
THE BUNCH STARTED DESPERATELY CRAVING APPROVAL FROM HER TEACHERS..
OH BOY, I HAVE OIL PAINTING TODAY WITH THAT DREAMBOAT MR. MCGOON. HOPE HE LIKES MY OUTFIT!
HOPE HE WANTS TO HAVE BEERS WITH ME!
HE THINKS I'M TALENTED
NOT BAD!
YEA, I'VE SEEN 'ER HANGIN' OUT AT THE TALLY HO!
MIXED-UP BEER GUZZLING SLUT!

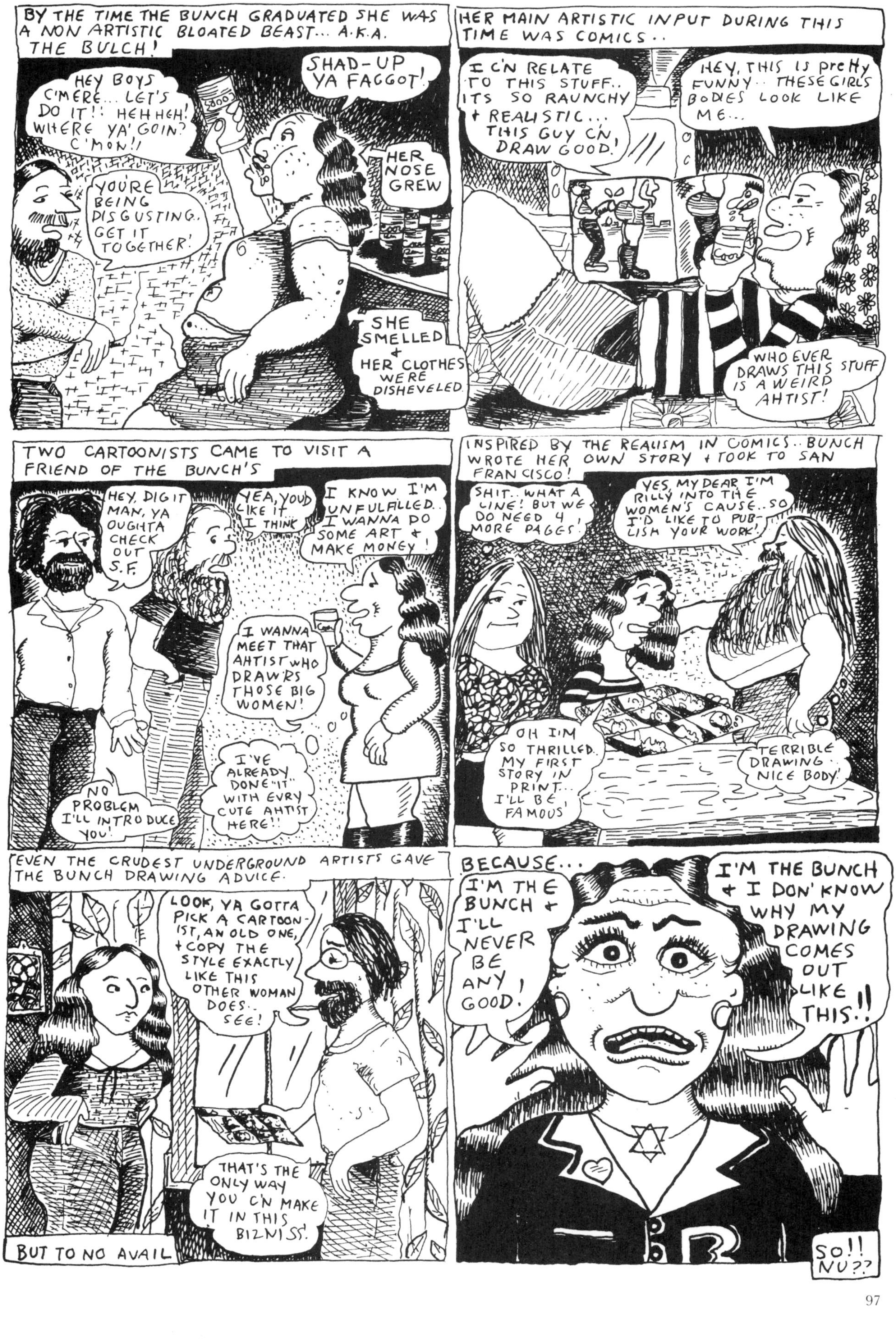
BY THE TIME THE BUNCH GRADUATED SHE WAS A NON ARTISTIC BLOATED BEAST... A.K.A. THE BULCH!
HEY BOYS C'MERE... LET'S DO IT!! HEH HEH! WHERE YA' GOIN? C'MON!!
SHAD-UP YA FAGGOT!
YOU'RE BEING DISGUSTING.. GET IT TOGETHER!
HER NOSE GREW
SHE SMELLED + HER CLOTHES WERE DISHEVELED.
HER MAIN ARTISTIC INPUT DURING THIS TIME WAS COMICS..
I C'N RELATE TO THIS STUFF.. ITS SO RAUNCHY + REALISTIC... THIS GUY C'N DRAW GOOD!
HEY, THIS IS pretty FUNNY.. THESE GIRLS BODIES LOOK LIKE ME...
WHO EVER DRAWS THIS STUFF IS A WEIRD AHTIST!
TWO CARTOONISTS CAME TO VISIT A FRIEND OF THE BUNCH'S
HEY, DIG IT MAN, YA OUGHTA CHECK OUT S.F.
YEA, YOU'D LIKE IT.. I THINK
I KNOW I'M UNFULFILLED.. I WANNA DO SOME ART + MAKE MONEY!
I WANNA MEET THAT AHTIST WHO DRAW'RS THOSE BIG WOMEN!
I'VE ALREADY DONE "IT" WITH EVRY CUTE AHTIST HERE!!
NO PROBLEM I'LL INTRODUCE YOU!
INSPIRED BY THE REALISM IN COMICS.. BUNCH WROTE HER OWN STORY + TOOK TO SAN FRANCISCO!
SHIT.. WHAT A LINE! BUT WE DO NEED 4 MORE PAGES!
YES, MY DEAR I'M RILLY INTO THE WOMEN'S CAUSE.. SO I'D LIKE TO PUBLISH YOUR WORK!
OH I'M SO THRILLED.. MY FIRST STORY IN PRINT.. I'LL BE FAMOUS!
TERRIBLE DRAWING.. NICE BODY!
EVEN THE CRUDEST UNDERGROUND ARTISTS GAVE THE BUNCH DRAWING ADVICE.
LOOK, YA GOTTA PICK A CARTOONIST, AN OLD ONE, + COPY THE STYLE EXACTLY LIKE THIS OTHER WOMAN DOES.. SEE!
THAT'S THE ONLY WAY YOU C'N MAKE IT IN THIS BIZNISS!
BUT TO NO AVAIL
BECAUSE...
I'M THE BUNCH + I'LL NEVER BE ANY GOOD!
I'M THE BUNCH + I DON' KNOW WHY MY DRAWING COMES OUT LIKE THIS!!
SO!! NU??

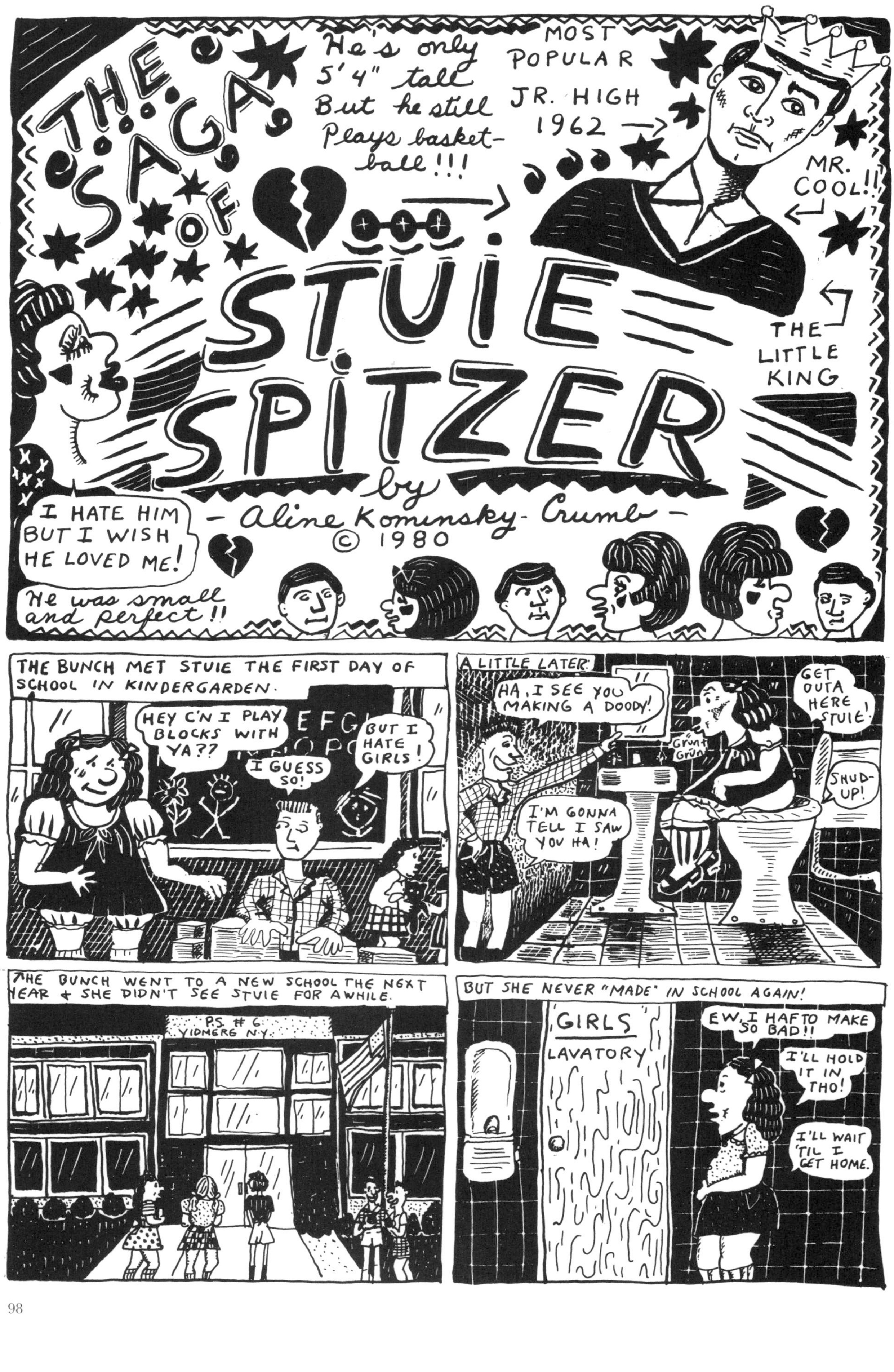
THE SAGA OF
STUIE SPITZER
by
- Aline Kominsky-Crumb -
© 1980
He's only 5'4" tall But he still Plays basket-ball!!!
MOST POPULAR JR. HIGH 1962
MR. COOL!!
THE LITTLE KING
I HATE HIM BUT I WISH HE LOVED ME!
He was small and perfect!!
THE BUNCH MET STUIE THE FIRST DAY OF SCHOOL IN KINDERGARDEN.
HEY C'N I PLAY BLOCKS WITH YA??
I GUESS SO!
BUT I HATE GIRLS!
A LITTLE LATER
HA, I SEE YOU MAKING A DOODY!
GET OUTA HERE STUIE!
Grunt Grunt
I'M GONNA TELL I SAW YOU HA!
SHUD-UP!
THE BUNCH WENT TO A NEW SCHOOL THE NEXT YEAR & SHE DIDN'T SEE STUIE FOR AWHILE.
P.S. # 6 YIDMERG N.Y.
BUT SHE NEVER "MADE" IN SCHOOL AGAIN!
GIRLS LAVATORY
EW, I HAFTO MAKE SO BAD!!
I'LL HOLD IT IN THO!
I'LL WAIT 'TIL I GET HOME.

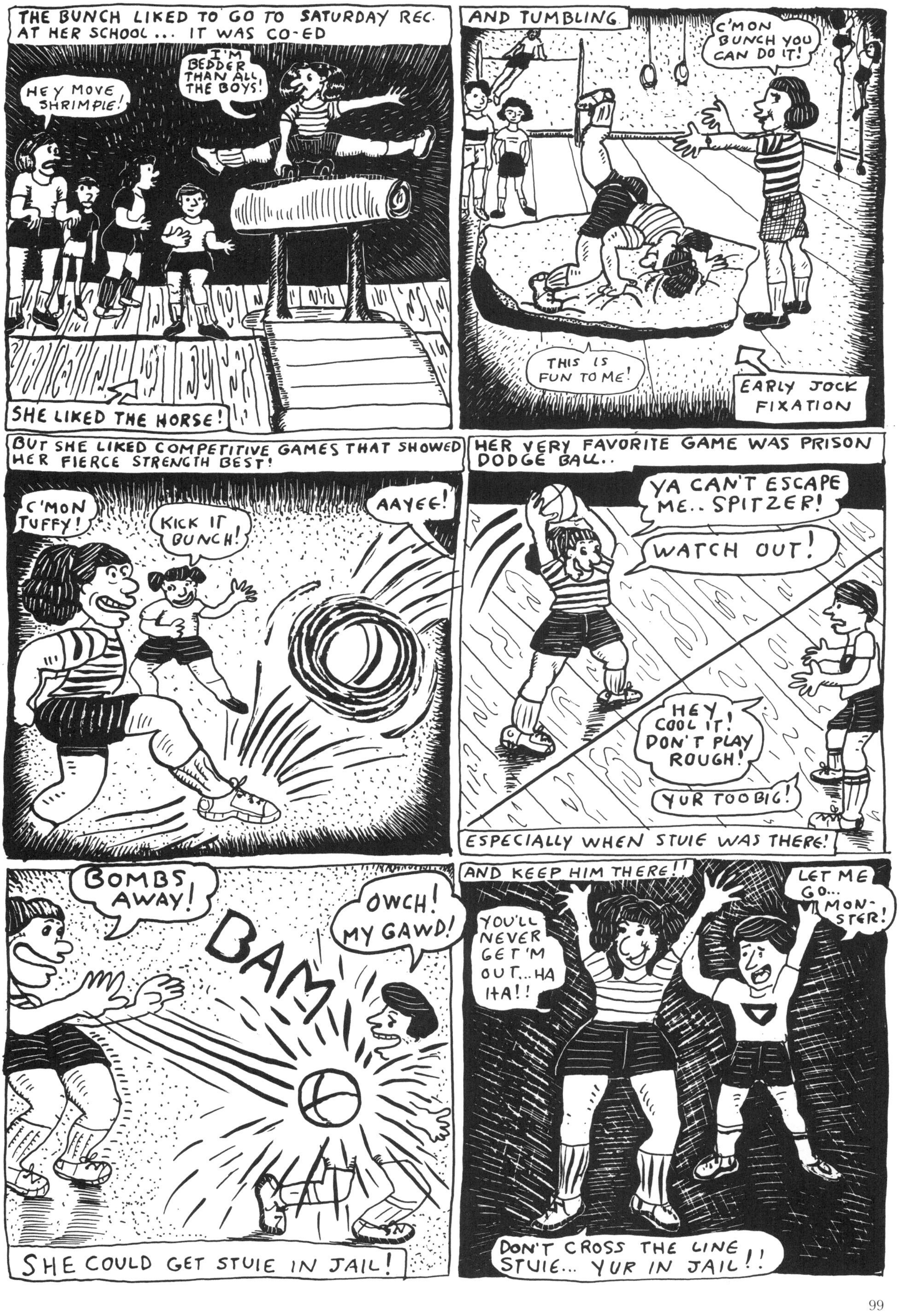
THE BUNCH LIKED TO GO TO SATURDAY REC. AT HER SCHOOL... IT WAS CO-ED
HEY MOVE SHRIMPIE!
I'M BEDDER THAN ALL THE BOYS!
SHE LIKED THE HORSE!
AND TUMBLING
C'MON BUNCH YOU CAN DO IT!
THIS IS FUN TO ME!
EARLY JOCK FIXATION
BUT SHE LIKED COMPETITIVE GAMES THAT SHOWED HER FIERCE STRENGTH BEST!
C'MON TUFFY!
KICK IT BUNCH!
AAYEE!
HER VERY FAVORITE GAME WAS PRISON DODGE BALL..
YA CAN'T ESCAPE ME.. SPITZER!
WATCH OUT!
HEY COOL IT! DON'T PLAY ROUGH!
YUR TOO BIG!
ESPECIALLY WHEN STUIE WAS THERE!
BOMBS AWAY!
OWCH! MY GAWD!
BAM
SHE COULD GET STUIE IN JAIL!
AND KEEP HIM THERE!!
YOU'LL NEVER GET 'M OUT...HA HA!!
LET ME GO... MONSTER!
DON'T CROSS THE LINE STUIE... YUR IN JAIL!!

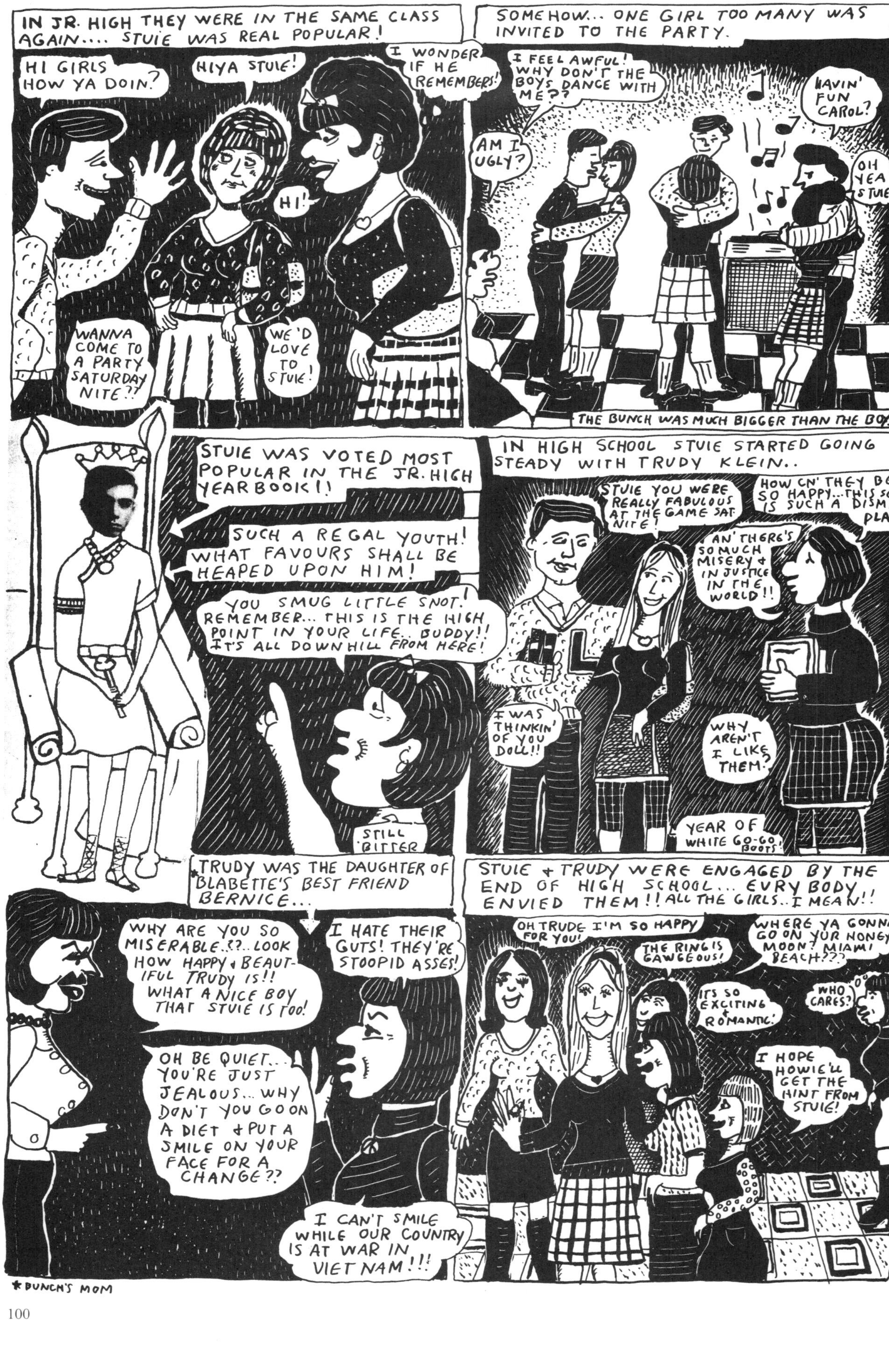
IN JR. HIGH THEY WERE IN THE SAME CLASS AGAIN.... STUIE WAS REAL POPULAR!
HI GIRLS HOW YA DOIN?
HIYA STUIE!
I WONDER IF HE REMEMBERS!
HI!
WANNA COME TO A PARTY SATURDAY NITE??
WE'D LOVE TO STUIE!
SOMEHOW... ONE GIRL TOO MANY WAS INVITED TO THE PARTY.
I FEEL AWFUL! WHY DON'T THE BOYS DANCE WITH ME??
AM I UGLY?
HAVIN' FUN CAROL?
OH YEA STUIE!
THE BUNCH WAS MUCH BIGGER THAN THE BOYS
STUIE WAS VOTED MOST POPULAR IN THE JR. HIGH YEARBOOK!!
SUCH A REGAL YOUTH! WHAT FAVOURS SHALL BE HEAPED UPON HIM!
YOU SMUG LITTLE SNOT! REMEMBER... THIS IS THE HIGH POINT IN YOUR LIFE.. BUDDY!! IT'S ALL DOWNHILL FROM HERE!
STILL BITTER
IN HIGH SCHOOL STUIE STARTED GOING STEADY WITH TRUDY KLEIN..
STUIE YOU WERE REALLY FABULOUS AT THE GAME SAT. NITE!
HOW CN' THEY BE SO HAPPY... THIS SCHOOL IS SUCH A DISMAL PLACE?
AN' THERE'S SO MUCH MISERY & INJUSTICE IN THE WORLD!!
I WAS THINKIN' OF YOU DOLL!!
WHY AREN'T I LIKE THEM?
YEAR OF WHITE GO-GO BOOTS!
*TRUDY WAS THE DAUGHTER OF BLABETTE'S BEST FRIEND BERNICE...
WHY ARE YOU SO MISERABLE.??.. LOOK HOW HAPPY & BEAUTIFUL TRUDY IS!! WHAT A NICE BOY THAT STUIE IS TOO!
I HATE THEIR GUTS! THEY'RE STOOPID ASSES!
OH BE QUIET... YOU'RE JUST JEALOUS... WHY DON'T YOU GO ON A DIET & PUT A SMILE ON YOUR FACE FOR A CHANGE??
I CAN'T SMILE WHILE OUR COUNTRY IS AT WAR IN VIETNAM!!!
STUIE & TRUDY WERE ENGAGED BY THE END OF HIGH SCHOOL... EVRYBODY ENVIED THEM!! ALL THE GIRLS.. I MEAN!!
OH TRUDE I'M SO HAPPY FOR YOU!
THE RING IS GAWGEOUS!
WHERE YA GONNA GO ON YUR HONEYMOON? MIAMI BEACH??
IT'S SO EXCITING & ROMANTIC!
WHO CARES?
I HOPE HOWIE'LL GET THE HINT FROM STUIE!

*BUNCH'S MOM

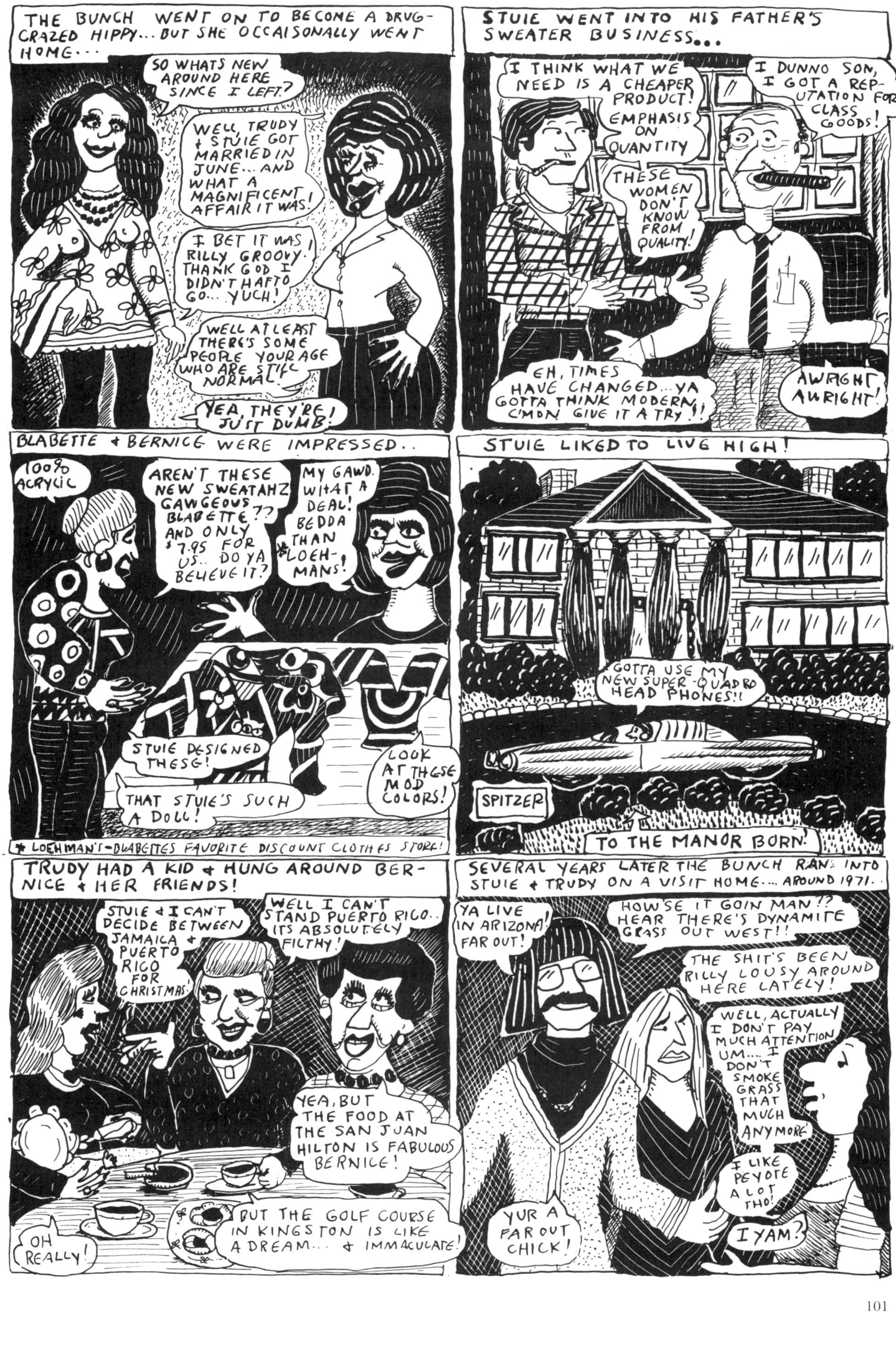
THE BUNCH WENT ON TO BECOME A DRUG-CRAZED HIPPY... BUT SHE OCCAISONALLY WENT HOME...
SO WHATS NEW AROUND HERE SINCE I LEFT?
WELL, TRUDY & STUIE GOT MARRIED IN JUNE... AND WHAT A MAGNIFICENT AFFAIR IT WAS!
I BET IT WAS RILLY GROOVY. THANK GOD I DIDN'T HAFTO GO... YUCH!
WELL AT LEAST THERE'S SOME PEOPLE YOUR AGE WHO ARE STILL NORMAL!
YEA, THEY'RE JUST DUMB!
STUIE WENT INTO HIS FATHER'S SWEATER BUSINESS...
I THINK WHAT WE NEED IS A CHEAPER PRODUCT!
EMPHASIS ON QUANTITY
THESE WOMEN DON'T KNOW FROM QUALITY!
I DUNNO SON, I GOT A REPUTATION FOR CLASS GOODS!
EH, TIMES HAVE CHANGED... YA GOTTA THINK MODERN, C'MON GIVE IT A TRY!!
AWRIGHT, AWRIGHT!
BLABETTE & BERNICE WERE IMPRESSED..
100% ACRYLIC
AREN'T THESE NEW SWEATAHZ GAWGEOUS BLABETTE?? AND ONLY $7.95 FOR US.. DO YA BELIEVE IT?
MY GAWD. WHAT A DEAL! BEDDA THAN *LOEHMANS!
STUIE DESIGNED THESE!
THAT STUIE'S SUCH A DOLL!
LOOK AT THESE MOD COLORS!
* LOEHMAN'S—BLABETTES FAVORITE DISCOUNT CLOTHES STORE!
STUIE LIKED TO LIVE HIGH!
GOTTA USE MY NEW SUPER-QUADRO HEAD PHONES!!
SPITZER
TO THE MANOR BORN.
TRUDY HAD A KID & HUNG AROUND BERNICE & HER FRIENDS!
STUIE & I CAN'T DECIDE BETWEEN JAMAICA & PUERTO RICO FOR CHRISTMAS.
WELL I CAN'T STAND PUERTO RICO.. ITS ABSOLUTELY FILTHY!
YEA, BUT THE FOOD AT THE SAN JUAN HILTON IS FABULOUS BERNICE!
OH REALLY!
BUT THE GOLF COURSE IN KINGSTON IS LIKE A DREAM... & IMMACULATE!
SEVERAL YEARS LATER THE BUNCH RAN INTO STUIE & TRUDY ON A VISIT HOME.... AROUND 1971.
YA LIVE IN ARIZONA! FAR OUT!
HOW'SE IT GOIN MAN!? HEAR THERE'S DYNAMITE GRASS OUT WEST!!
THE SHIT'S BEEN RILLY LOUSY AROUND HERE LATELY!
WELL, ACTUALLY I DON'T PAY MUCH ATTENTION UM.... I DON'T SMOKE GRASS THAT MUCH ANYMORE.
I LIKE PEYOTE A LOT THO!
YUR A FAR OUT CHICK!
I YAM?

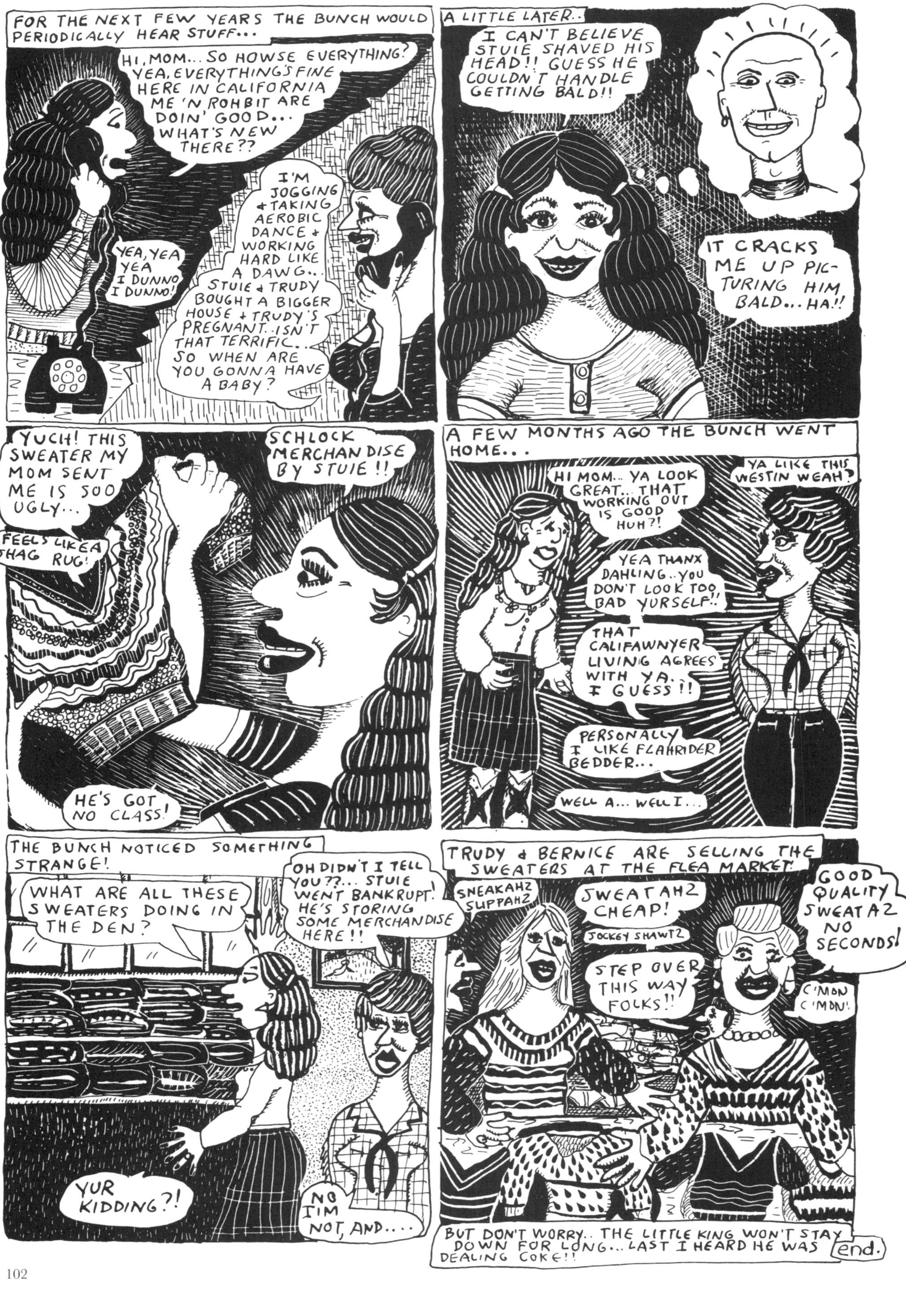

FOR THE NEXT FEW YEARS THE BUNCH WOULD PERIODICALLY HEAR STUFF...
HI, MOM... SO HOWSE EVERYTHING? YEA, EVERYTHING'S FINE HERE IN CALIFORNIA ME 'N ROHBIT ARE DOIN' GOOD... WHAT'S NEW THERE??
I'M JOGGING & TAKING AEROBIC DANCE & WORKING HARD LIKE A DAWG.. STUIE & TRUDY BOUGHT A BIGGER HOUSE & TRUDY'S PREGNANT.. ISN'T THAT TERRIFIC.. SO WHEN ARE YOU GONNA HAVE A BABY?
YEA, YEA YEA I DUNNO I DUNNO!
A LITTLE LATER..
I CAN'T BELIEVE STUIE SHAVED HIS HEAD!! GUESS HE COULDN'T HANDLE GETTING BALD!!
IT CRACKS ME UP PICTURING HIM BALD... HA!!
YUCH! THIS SWEATER MY MOM SENT ME IS SOO UGLY...
SCHLOCK MERCHANDISE BY STUIE!!
FEELS LIKE A SHAG RUG!
HE'S GOT NO CLASS!
A FEW MONTHS AGO THE BUNCH WENT HOME...
HI MOM.. YA LOOK GREAT... THAT WORKING OUT IS GOOD HUH?!
YA LIKE THIS WESTIN WEAH?
YEA THANX DAHLING.. YOU DON'T LOOK TOO BAD YURSELF!!
THAT CALIFAWNYER LIVING AGREES WITH YA.. I GUESS!!
PERSONALLY I LIKE FLAHRIDER BEDDER...
WELL A... WELL I...
THE BUNCH NOTICED SOMETHING STRANGE!
WHAT ARE ALL THESE SWEATERS DOING IN THE DEN?
OH DIDN'T I TELL YOU??... STUIE WENT BANKRUPT! HE'S STORING SOME MERCHANDISE HERE!!
YUR KIDDING?!
NO I'M NOT, AND....
TRUDY & BERNICE ARE SELLING THE SWEATERS AT THE FLEA MARKET.
SNEAKAHZ SUPPAHZ
SWEATAHZ CHEAP!
JOCKEY SHAWTZ
GOOD QUALITY SWEATAZ NO SECONDS!
STEP OVER THIS WAY FOLKS!!
C'MON C'MON!
BUT DON'T WORRY.. THE LITTLE KING WON'T STAY DOWN FOR LONG... LAST I HEARD HE WAS DEALING COKE!!
end.

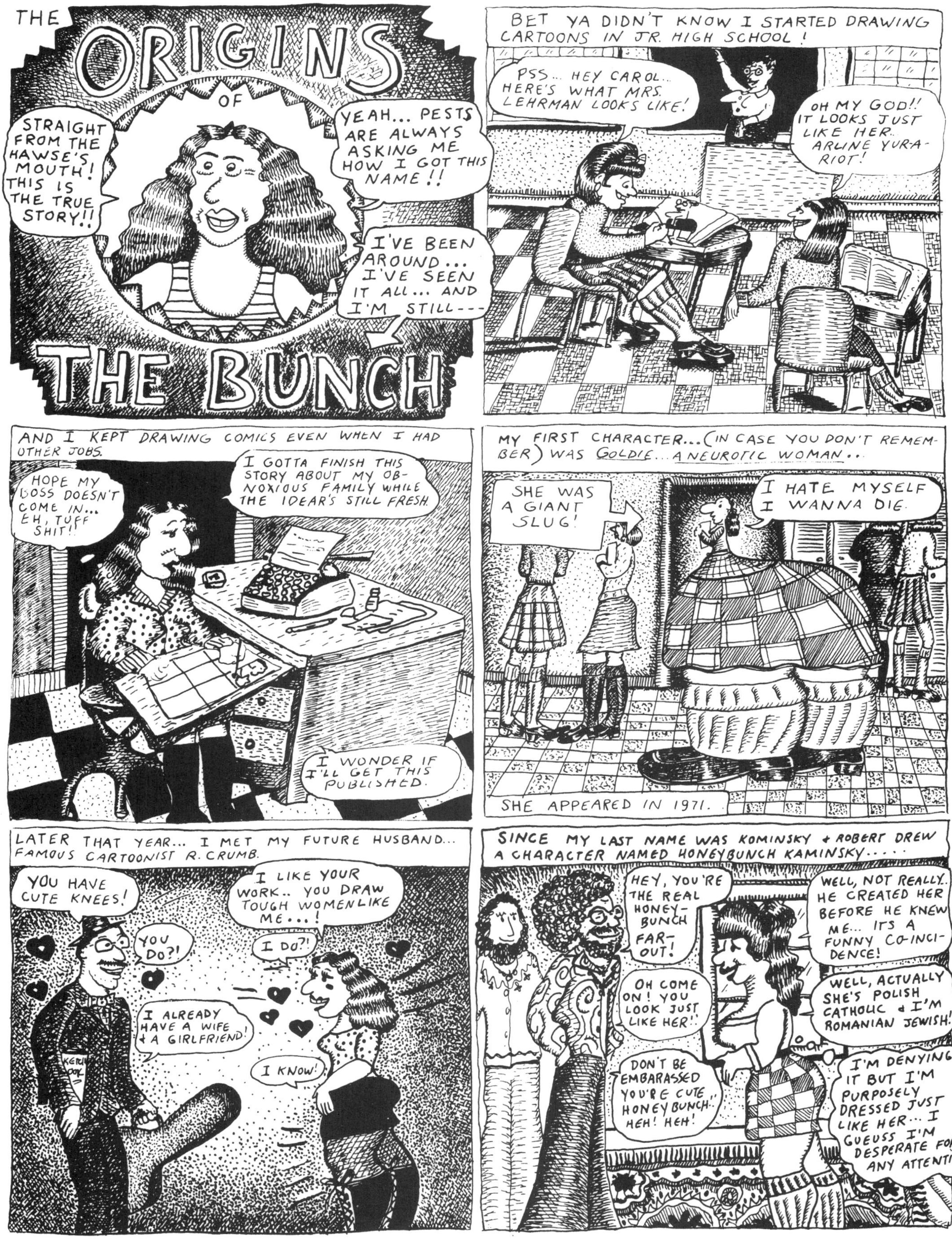
THE ORIGINS OF THE BUNCH
STRAIGHT FROM THE HAWSE'S MOUTH! THIS IS THE TRUE STORY!!
YEAH... PESTS ARE ALWAYS ASKING ME HOW I GOT THIS NAME!!
I'VE BEEN AROUND... I'VE SEEN IT ALL... AND I'M STILL---
BET YA DIDN'T KNOW I STARTED DRAWING CARTOONS IN JR. HIGH SCHOOL!
PSS... HEY CAROL... HERE'S WHAT MRS. LEHRMAN LOOKS LIKE!
OH MY GOD!! IT LOOKS JUST LIKE HER. ARLINE YUR-A-RIOT!
AND I KEPT DRAWING COMICS EVEN WHEN I HAD OTHER JOBS.
HOPE MY BOSS DOESN'T COME IN... EH, TUFF SHIT!!
I GOTTA FINISH THIS STORY ABOUT MY OBNOXIOUS FAMILY WHILE THE IDEAR'S STILL FRESH.
I WONDER IF I'LL GET THIS PUBLISHED.
MY FIRST CHARACTER... (IN CASE YOU DON'T REMEMBER) WAS GOLDIE... A NEUROTIC WOMAN..
SHE WAS A GIANT SLUG!
I HATE MYSELF I WANNA DIE.
SHE APPEARED IN 1971.
LATER THAT YEAR... I MET MY FUTURE HUSBAND... FAMOUS CARTOONIST R. CRUMB.
YOU HAVE CUTE KNEES!
YOU DO?!
I LIKE YOUR WORK.. YOU DRAW TOUGH WOMEN LIKE ME...!
I DO?!
I ALREADY HAVE A WIFE + A GIRLFRIEND!
I KNOW!
SINCE MY LAST NAME WAS KOMINSKY + ROBERT DREW A CHARACTER NAMED HONEYBUNCH KAMINSKY.....
HEY, YOU'RE THE REAL HONEYBUNCH FAR-OUT!
WELL, NOT REALLY.. HE CREATED HER BEFORE HE KNEW ME... ITS A FUNNY CO-INCIDENCE!
OH COME ON! YOU LOOK JUST LIKE HER!
WELL, ACTUALLY SHE'S POLISH CATHOLIC + I'M ROMANIAN JEWISH!
DON'T BE EMBARASSED YOU'RE CUTE, HONEY BUNCH.. HEH! HEH!
I'M DENYING IT BUT I'M PURPOSELY DRESSED JUST LIKE HER... I GUESS I'M DESPERATE FOR ANY ATTENTION!

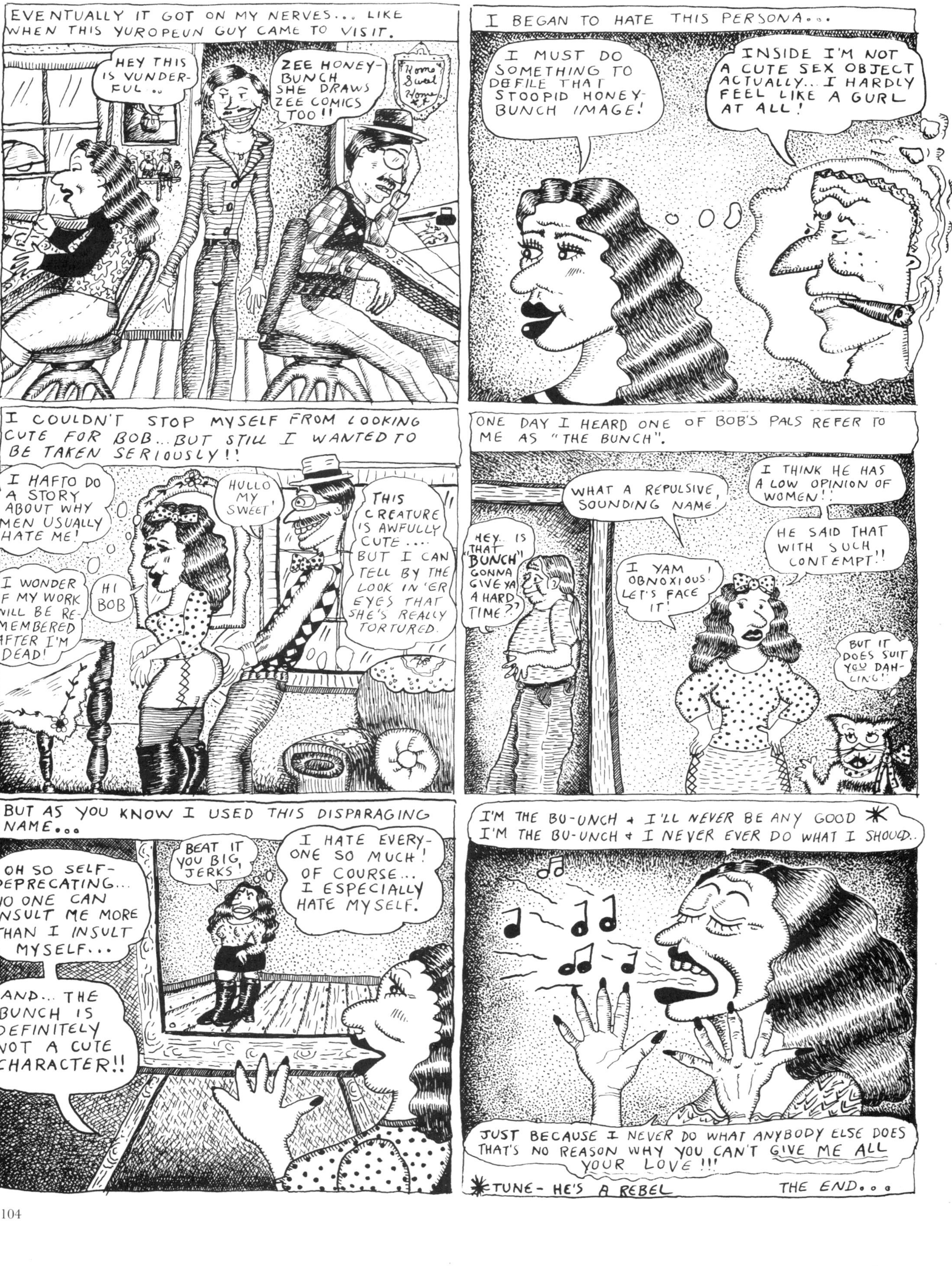
EVENTUALLY IT GOT ON MY NERVES... LIKE WHEN THIS YUROPEUN GUY CAME TO VISIT.
HEY THIS IS VUNDERFUL..
ZEE HONEY-BUNCH SHE DRAWS ZEE COMICS TOO!!
Home Sweet Home
I BEGAN TO HATE THIS PERSONA...
I MUST DO SOMETHING TO DEFILE THAT STOOPID HONEY-BUNCH IMAGE!
INSIDE I'M NOT A CUTE SEX OBJECT ACTUALLY... I HARDLY FEEL LIKE A GURL AT ALL!
I COULDN'T STOP MYSELF FROM LOOKING CUTE FOR BOB... BUT STILL I WANTED TO BE TAKEN SERIOUSLY!!
I HAFTO DO A STORY ABOUT WHY MEN USUALLY HATE ME!
HULLO MY SWEET!
THIS CREATURE IS AWFULLY CUTE.... BUT I CAN TELL BY THE LOOK IN 'ER EYES THAT SHE'S REALLY TORTURED.
I WONDER IF MY WORK WILL BE REMEMBERED AFTER I'M DEAD!
HI BOB
ONE DAY I HEARD ONE OF BOB'S PALS REFER TO ME AS "THE BUNCH".
WHAT A REPULSIVE, SOUNDING NAME.
I THINK HE HAS A LOW OPINION OF WOMEN!!
HEY.. IS THAT "BUNCH" GONNA GIVE YA A HARD TIME??
HE SAID THAT WITH SUCH CONTEMPT!!
I YAM OBNOXIOUS! LET'S FACE IT!
BUT IT DOES SUIT YOU DAHLING!
BUT AS YOU KNOW I USED THIS DISPARAGING NAME...
OH SO SELF-DEPRECATING... NO ONE CAN INSULT ME MORE THAN I INSULT MYSELF...
BEAT IT YOU BIG JERKS!
I HATE EVERYONE SO MUCH! OF COURSE... I ESPECIALLY HATE MYSELF.
AND... THE BUNCH IS DEFINITELY NOT A CUTE CHARACTER!!
I'M THE BU-UNCH & I'LL NEVER BE ANY GOOD *
I'M THE BU-UNCH & I NEVER EVER DO WHAT I SHOULD..
JUST BECAUSE I NEVER DO WHAT ANYBODY ELSE DOES THAT'S NO REASON WHY YOU CAN'T GIVE ME ALL YOUR LOVE!!!
*TUNE- HE'S A REBEL
THE END...

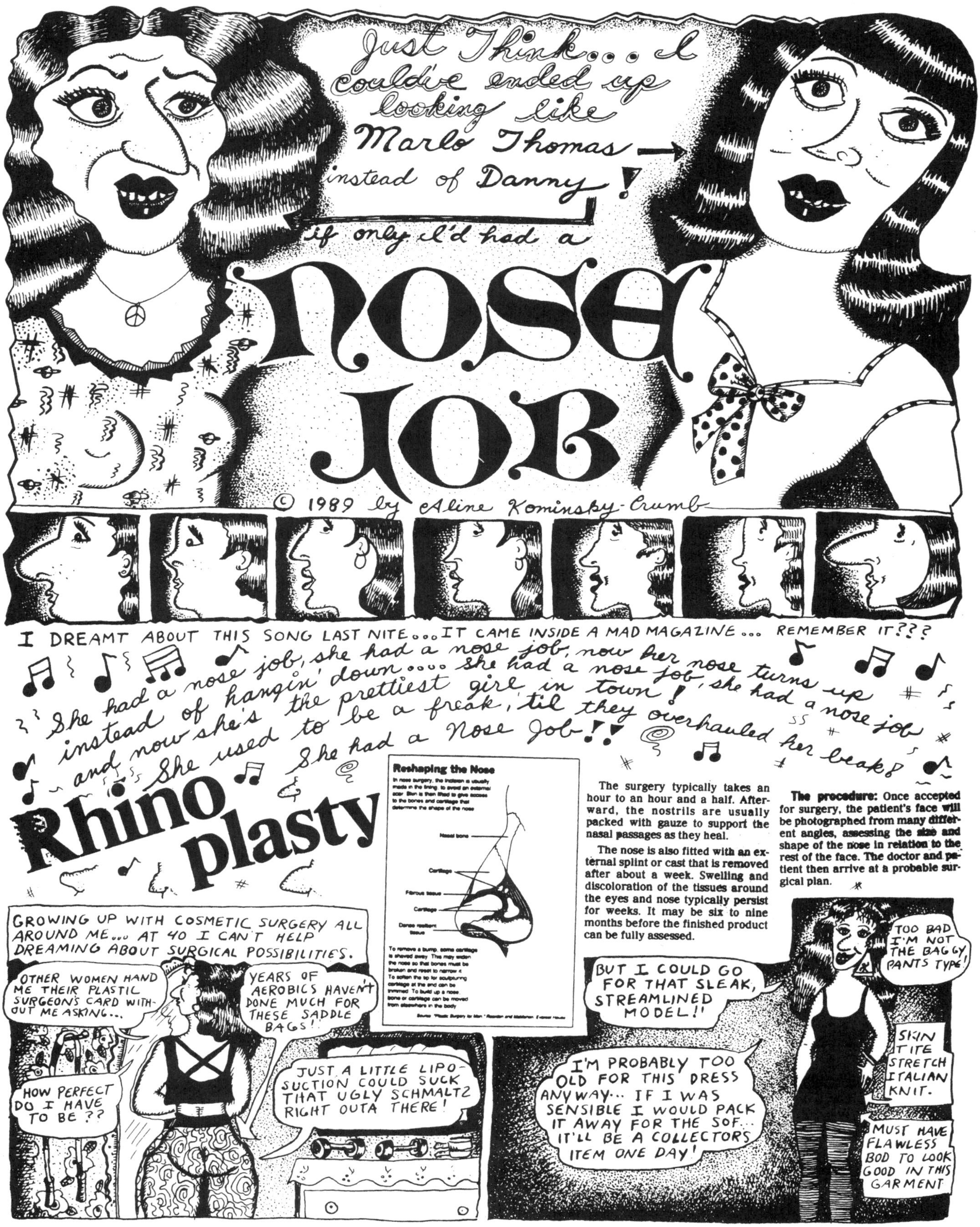

Just Think... I could've ended up looking like Marlo Thomas → instead of Danny!
if only I'd had a
NOSE JOB
© 1989 by Aline Kominsky-Crumb
I DREAMT ABOUT THIS SONG LAST NITE... IT CAME INSIDE A MAD MAGAZINE... REMEMBER IT???
"She had a nose job, she had a nose job, now her nose turns up instead of hangin' down.... She had a nose job, her nose turns up and now she's the prettiest girl in town! She had a nose job She used to be a freak, til they overhauled her beak!"
She had a Nose Job!!
Rhino plasty
Reshaping the Nose
In nose surgery, the incision is usually made in the lining, to avoid an external scar. Skin is then lifted to give access to the bones and cartilage that determine the shape of the nose
Nasal bone
Cartilage
Fibrous tissue
Cartilage
Dense resilient tissue
To remove a bump, some cartilage is shaved away. This may widen the nose so that bones must be broken and reset to narrow it. To soften the tip for sculpturing cartilage at the end can be trimmed. To build up a nose, bone or cartilage can be moved from elsewhere in the body
Source: "Plastic Surgery for Men."
The surgery typically takes an hour to an hour and a half. Afterward, the nostrils are usually packed with gauze to support the nasal passages as they heal.
The nose is also fitted with an external splint or cast that is removed after about a week. Swelling and discoloration of the tissues around the eyes and nose typically persist for weeks. It may be six to nine months before the finished product can be fully assessed.
The procedure: Once accepted for surgery, the patient's face will be photographed from many different angles, assessing the size and shape of the nose in relation to the rest of the face. The doctor and patient then arrive at a probable surgical plan.
GROWING UP WITH COSMETIC SURGERY ALL AROUND ME... AT 40 I CAN'T HELP DREAMING ABOUT SURGICAL POSSIBILITIES.
OTHER WOMEN HAND ME THEIR PLASTIC SURGEON'S CARD WITHOUT ME ASKING...
YEARS OF AEROBICS HAVEN'T DONE MUCH FOR THESE SADDLE BAGS!
HOW PERFECT DO I HAVE TO BE??
JUST A LITTLE LIPO-SUCTION COULD SUCK THAT UGLY SCHMALTZ RIGHT OUTA THERE!
BUT I COULD GO FOR THAT SLEAK, STREAMLINED MODEL!!
TOO BAD I'M NOT THE BAGGY PANTS TYPE!
I'M PROBABLY TOO OLD FOR THIS DRESS ANYWAY... IF I WAS SENSIBLE I WOULD PACK IT AWAY FOR THE SOF... IT'LL BE A COLLECTORS ITEM ONE DAY!
SKIN TITE STRETCH ITALIAN KNIT.
MUST HAVE FLAWLESS BOD TO LOOK GOOD IN THIS GARMENT

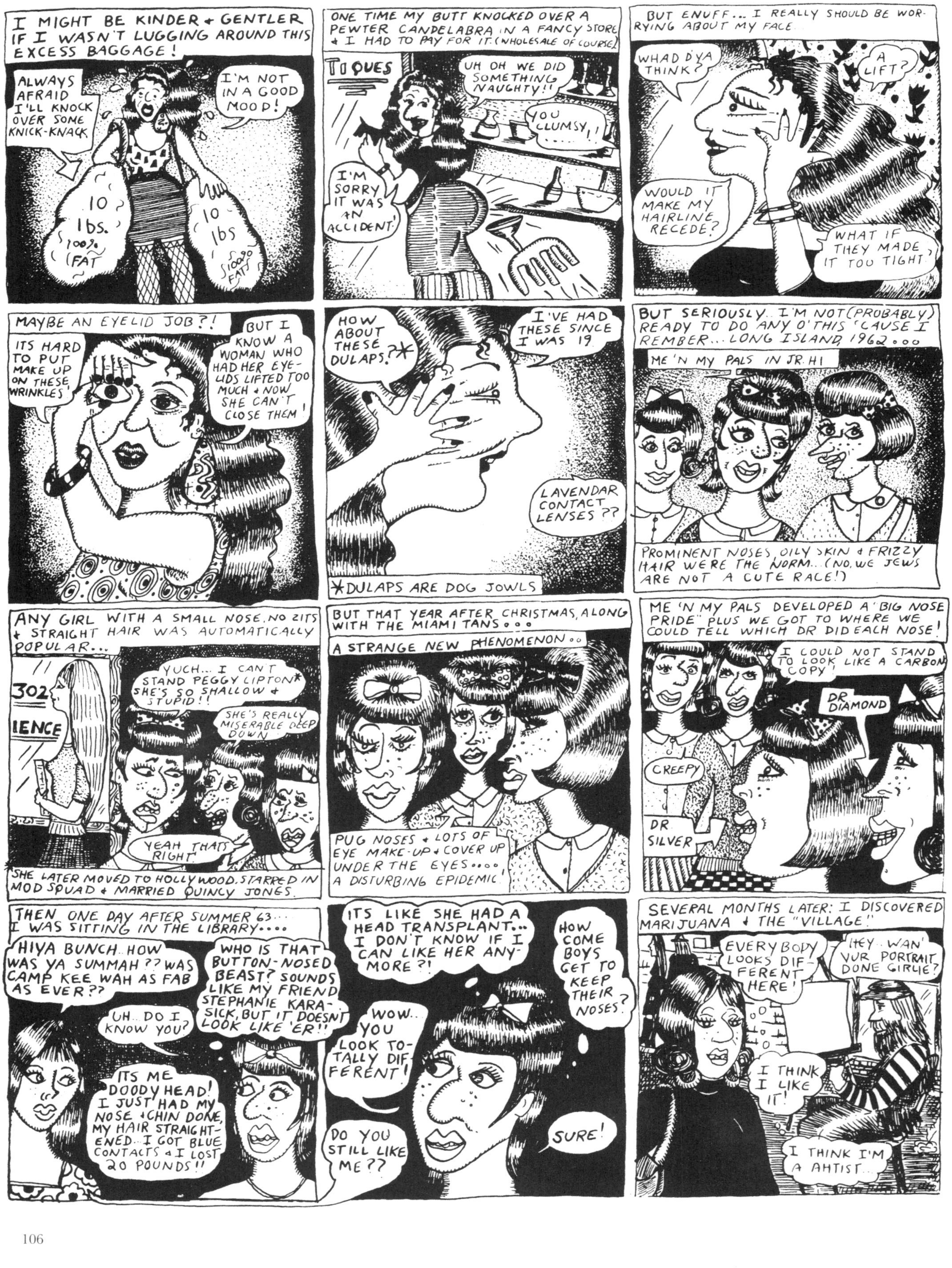

I MIGHT BE KINDER + GENTLER IF I WASN'T LUGGING AROUND THIS EXCESS BAGGAGE!
ALWAYS AFRAID I'LL KNOCK OVER SOME KNICK-KNACK
I'M NOT IN A GOOD MOOD!
10 lbs. 100% FAT
10 lbs 100% FAT
ONE TIME MY BUTT KNOCKED OVER A PEWTER CANDELABRA IN A FANCY STORE + I HAD TO PAY FOR IT. (WHOLESALE OF COURSE)
TIQUES
UH OH WE DID SOMETHING NAUGHTY!!
YOU CLUMSY!! ......
I'M SORRY IT WAS AN ACCIDENT!
BUT ENUFF... I REALLY SHOULD BE WORRYING ABOUT MY FACE
WHAD D'YA THINK?
A LIFT?
WOULD IT MAKE MY HAIRLINE RECEDE?
WHAT IF THEY MADE IT TOO TIGHT
MAYBE AN EYELID JOB?!
ITS HARD TO PUT MAKE UP ON THESE WRINKLES!
BUT I KNOW A WOMAN WHO HAD HER EYELIDS LIFTED TOO MUCH + NOW SHE CAN'T CLOSE THEM!
HOW ABOUT THESE DULAPS?*
I'VE HAD THESE SINCE I WAS 19.
LAVENDAR CONTACT LENSES??
*DULAPS ARE DOG JOWLS
BUT SERIOUSLY.. I'M NOT (PROBABLY) READY TO DO ANY O'THIS 'CAUSE I REMBER... LONG ISLAND, 1962...
ME 'N MY PALS IN JR. HI
PROMINENT NOSES, OILY SKIN + FRIZZY HAIR WERE THE NORM... (NO, WE JEWS ARE NOT A CUTE RACE!)
ANY GIRL WITH A SMALL NOSE, NO ZITS + STRAIGHT HAIR WAS AUTOMATICALLY POPULAR...
302
IENCE
YUCH... I CAN'T STAND PEGGY LIPTON* SHE'S SO SHALLOW + STUPID!!
SHE'S REALLY MISERABLE DEEP DOWN
YEAH THATS RIGHT!
*SHE LATER MOVED TO HOLLYWOOD, STARRED IN MOD SQUAD + MARRIED QUINCY JONES.
BUT THAT YEAR AFTER CHRISTMAS, ALONG WITH THE MIAMI TANS...
A STRANGE NEW PHENOMENON..
PUG NOSES + LOTS OF EYE MAKE-UP + COVER UP UNDER THE EYES.... A DISTURBING EPIDEMIC
ME 'N MY PALS DEVELOPED A "BIG NOSE PRIDE" PLUS WE GOT TO WHERE WE COULD TELL WHICH DR DID EACH NOSE!
I COULD NOT STAND TO LOOK LIKE A CARBON COPY!
DR DIAMOND
CREEPY
DR SILVER
THEN ONE DAY AFTER SUMMER 63... I WAS SITTING IN THE LIBRARY....
HIYA BUNCH.. HOW WAS YA SUMMAH?? WAS CAMP KEE WAH AS FAB AS EVER??
WHO IS THAT BUTTON-NOSED BEAST? SOUNDS LIKE MY FRIEND STEPHANIE KARASICK, BUT IT DOESN'T LOOK LIKE 'ER!!
UH.. DO I KNOW YOU?
ITS ME DOODY HEAD! I JUST HAD MY NOSE + CHIN DONE, MY HAIR STRAIGHTENED.. I GOT BLUE CONTACTS + I LOST 20 POUNDS!!
ITS LIKE SHE HAD A HEAD TRANSPLANT... I DON'T KNOW IF I CAN LIKE HER ANYMORE?!
HOW COME BOYS GET TO KEEP THEIR NOSES?
WOW.. YOU LOOK TOTALLY DIFFERENT!
DO YOU STILL LIKE ME??
SURE!
SEVERAL MONTHS LATER: I DISCOVERED MARIJUANA + THE "VILLAGE"
EVERYBODY LOOKS DIFFERENT HERE!
HEY.. WAN' YUR PORTRAIT DONE GIRLIE?
I THINK I LIKE IT!
I THINK I'M A AHTIST...

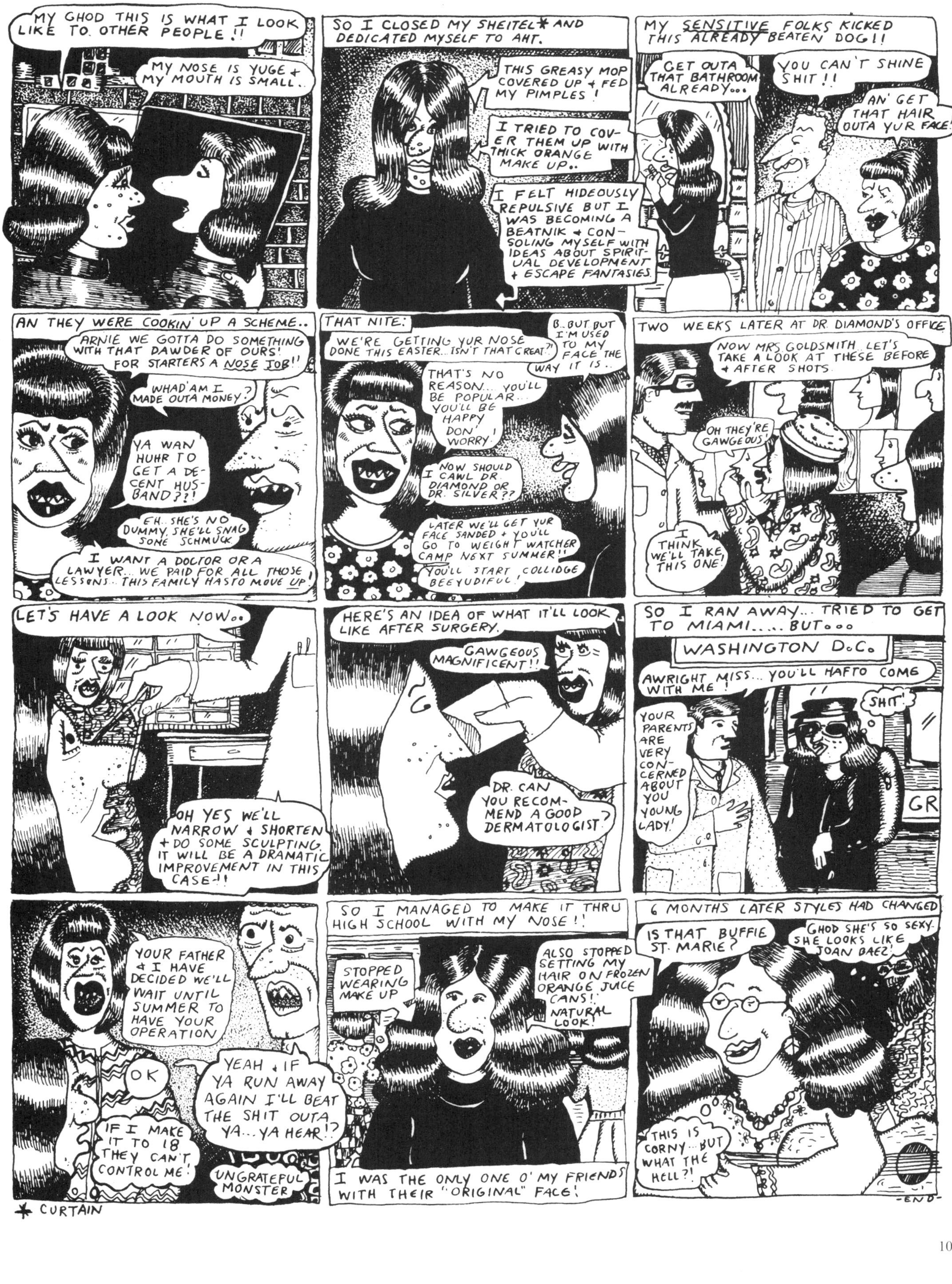
MY GHOD THIS IS WHAT I LOOK LIKE TO OTHER PEOPLE!!
MY NOSE IS YUGE + MY MOUTH IS SMALL..
SO I CLOSED MY SHEITEL* AND DEDICATED MYSELF TO AHT.
THIS GREASY MOP COVERED UP + FED MY PIMPLES!
I TRIED TO COVER THEM UP WITH THICK ORANGE MAKE UP..
I FELT HIDEOUSLY REPULSIVE BUT I WAS BECOMING A BEATNIK + CONSOLING MYSELF WITH IDEAS ABOUT SPIRITUAL DEVELOPMENT + ESCAPE FANTASIES.
MY SENSITIVE FOLKS KICKED THIS ALREADY BEATEN DOG!!
GET OUTA THAT BATHROOM ALREADY...
YOU CAN'T SHINE SHIT!!
AN' GET THAT HAIR OUTA YUR FACE!
AN THEY WERE COOKIN' UP A SCHEME..
ARNIE WE GOTTA DO SOMETHING WITH THAT DAWDER OF OURS! FOR STARTERS A NOSE JOB!!
WHAD'AM I MADE OUTA MONEY?
YA WAN HUHR TO GET A DECENT HUSBAND??!
EH.. SHE'S NO DUMMY. SHE'LL SNAG SOME SCHMUCK
I WANT A DOCTOR OR A LAWYER... WE PAID FOR ALL THOSE LESSONS... THIS FAMILY HAS TO MOVE UP!
THAT NITE:
WE'RE GETTING YUR NOSE DONE THIS EASTER... ISN'T THAT GREAT?!
B..BUT BUT I'M USED TO MY FACE THE WAY IT IS...
THAT'S NO REASON... YOU'LL BE POPULAR... YOU'LL BE HAPPY DON' WORRY!
I NOW SHOULD CAWL DR. DIAMOND OR DR. SILVER??
LATER WE'LL GET YUR FACE SANDED + YOU'LL GO TO WEIGHT WATCHER CAMP NEXT SUMMER!!
YOU'LL START COLLIDGE BEEYUDIFUL!
TWO WEEKS LATER AT DR. DIAMOND'S OFFICE
NOW MRS GOLDSMITH LET'S TAKE A LOOK AT THESE BEFORE + AFTER SHOTS.
OH THEY'RE GAWGEOUS!
I THINK WE'LL TAKE THIS ONE!
LET'S HAVE A LOOK NOW...
OH YES WE'LL NARROW + SHORTEN + DO SOME SCULPTING. IT WILL BE A DRAMATIC IMPROVEMENT IN THIS CASE!!
HERE'S AN IDEA OF WHAT IT'LL LOOK LIKE AFTER SURGERY.
GAWGEOUS MAGNIFICENT!!
DR. CAN YOU RECOMMEND A GOOD DERMATOLOGIST?
SO I RAN AWAY... TRIED TO GET TO MIAMI..... BUT...
WASHINGTON D.C.
AWRIGHT MISS... YOU'LL HAFTO COME WITH ME!
SHIT!
YOUR PARENTS ARE VERY CONCERNED ABOUT YOU YOUNG LADY!
GR
YOUR FATHER + I HAVE DECIDED WE'LL WAIT UNTIL SUMMER TO HAVE YOUR OPERATION
OK
IF I MAKE IT TO 18 THEY CAN'T CONTROL ME!
YEAH + IF YA RUN AWAY AGAIN I'LL BEAT THE SHIT OUTA YA... YA HEAR!?
UNGRATEFUL MONSTER
SO I MANAGED TO MAKE IT THRU HIGH SCHOOL WITH MY NOSE!!
STOPPED WEARING MAKE UP
ALSO STOPPED SETTING MY HAIR ON FROZEN ORANGE JUCE CANS!
NATURAL LOOK!
I WAS THE ONLY ONE O' MY FRIENDS WITH THEIR "ORIGINAL" FACE!
6 MONTHS LATER STYLES HAD CHANGED
IS THAT BUFFIE ST. MARIE?
GHOD SHE'S SO SEXY. SHE LOOKS LIKE JOAN BAEZ!
THIS IS CORNY... BUT WHAT THE HELL?!
-END-

* CURTAIN

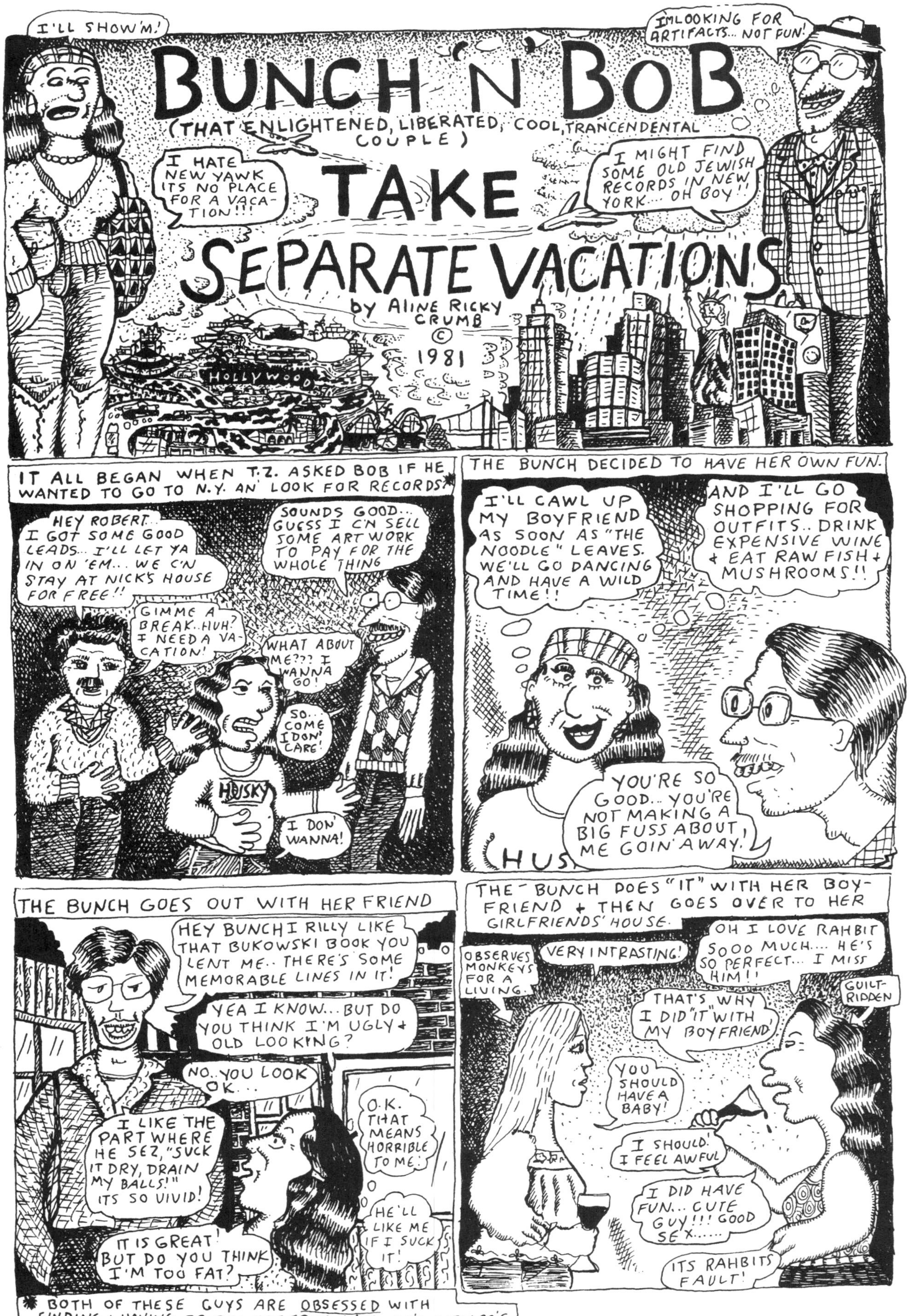
I'LL SHOW'M!
I'M LOOKING FOR ARTIFACTS... NOT FUN!
BUNCH 'N' BOB
(THAT ENLIGHTENED, LIBERATED, COOL, TRANCENDENTAL COUPLE)
I HATE NEW YAWK ITS NO PLACE FOR A VACATION!!!
I MIGHT FIND SOME OLD JEWISH RECORDS IN NEW YORK... OH BOY!!
TAKE
SEPARATE VACATIONS
by ALINE RICKY CRUMB © 1981
HOLLYWOOD
IT ALL BEGAN WHEN T.Z. ASKED BOB IF HE WANTED TO GO TO N.Y. AN' LOOK FOR RECORDS.*
HEY ROBERT... I GOT SOME GOOD LEADS... I'LL LET YA IN ON 'EM... WE C'N STAY AT NICK'S HOUSE FOR FREE!!
SOUNDS GOOD... GUESS I C'N SELL SOME ART WORK TO PAY FOR THE WHOLE THING
GIMME A BREAK..HUH? I NEED A VACATION!
WHAT ABOUT ME??? I WANNA GO!
SO... COME I DON' CARE!
HUSKY
I DON' WANNA!
THE BUNCH DECIDED TO HAVE HER OWN FUN.
I'LL CAWL UP MY BOYFRIEND AS SOON AS "THE NOODLE" LEAVES. WE'LL GO DANCING AND HAVE A WILD TIME!!
AND I'LL GO SHOPPING FOR OUTFITS.. DRINK EXPENSIVE WINE & EAT RAW FISH + MUSHROOMS!!
YOU'RE SO GOOD... YOU'RE NOT MAKING A BIG FUSS ABOUT ME GOIN' AWAY.
HUS
THE BUNCH GOES OUT WITH HER FRIEND
HEY BUNCH I RILLY LIKE THAT BUKOWSKI BOOK YOU LENT ME.. THERE'S SOME MEMORABLE LINES IN IT!
YEA I KNOW... BUT DO YOU THINK I'M UGLY + OLD LOOKING?
NO.. YOU LOOK OK...
O.K. THAT MEANS HORRIBLE TO ME.
I LIKE THE PART WHERE HE SEZ, "SUCK IT DRY, DRAIN MY BALLS!" ITS SO VIVID!
HE'LL LIKE ME IF I SUCK IT!
IT IS GREAT! BUT DO YOU THINK I'M TOO FAT?
THE BUNCH DOES "IT" WITH HER BOYFRIEND + THEN GOES OVER TO HER GIRLFRIENDS' HOUSE.
OBSERVES MONKEYS FOR A LIVING.
VERY INTRASTING!
OH I LOVE RAHBIT SOOO MUCH.... HE'S SO PERFECT... I MISS HIM!!
GUILT-RIDDEN
THAT'S WHY I DID "IT" WITH MY BOYFRIEND.
YOU SHOULD HAVE A BABY!
I SHOULD! I FEEL AWFUL
I DID HAVE FUN... CUTE GUY!!! GOOD SEX......
ITS RAHBITS FAULT!
* BOTH OF THESE GUYS ARE OBSESSED WITH FINDING + HAVING 78 RECORDS FROM LATE 20'S - EARLY 30'S.

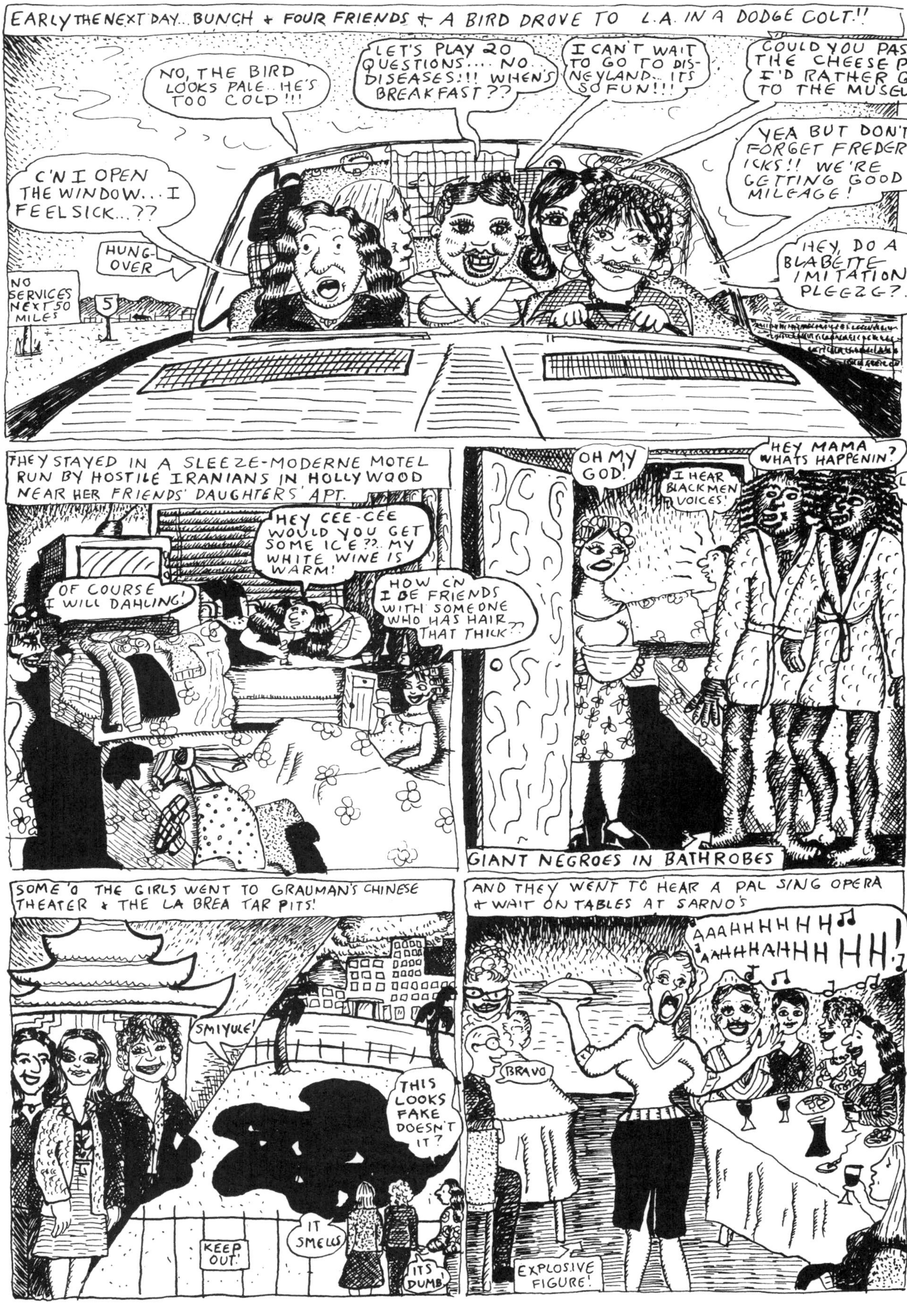

EARLY THE NEXT DAY.. BUNCH + FOUR FRIENDS + A BIRD DROVE TO L.A. IN A DODGE COLT!!
C'N I OPEN THE WINDOW... I FEEL SICK...??
HUNG-OVER
NO, THE BIRD LOOKS PALE.. HE'S TOO COLD!!!
LET'S PLAY 20 QUESTIONS... NO.. DISEASES!!! WHEN'S BREAKFAST??
I CAN'T WAIT TO GO TO DISNEYLAND.. ITS SO FUN!!!
COULD YOU PASS THE CHEESE PUFFS? I'D RATHER GO TO THE MUSEUM!
YEA BUT DON'T FORGET FREDERICKS!! WE'RE GETTING GOOD MILEAGE!
HEY, DO A BLABETTE IMITATION PLEEZE?!
NO SERVICES NEXT 50 MILES
5
THEY STAYED IN A SLEEZE-MODERNE MOTEL RUN BY HOSTILE IRANIANS IN HOLLYWOOD NEAR HER FRIENDS' DAUGHTERS' APT.
HEY CEE-CEE WOULD YOU GET SOME ICE?? MY WHITE WINE IS WARM!
OF COURSE I WILL DAHLING!
HOW C'N I BE FRIENDS WITH SOMEONE WHO HAS HAIR THAT THICK??
OH MY GOD!
I HEAR BLACK MEN VOICES!
HEY MAMA WHATS HAPPENIN?
LOOKIN' GOOD!
GIANT NEGROES IN BATHROBES
SOME 'O THE GIRLS WENT TO GRAUMAN'S CHINESE THEATER + THE LA BREA TAR PITS!
SMIYULE!
THIS LOOKS FAKE DOESN'T IT?
IT SMELLS
ITS DUMB
KEEP OUT
AND THEY WENT TO HEAR A PAL SING OPERA + WAIT ON TABLES AT SARNO'S
AAAHHHHHHH AAHHHAHHHH HH!
BRAVO
EXPLOSIVE FIGURE!

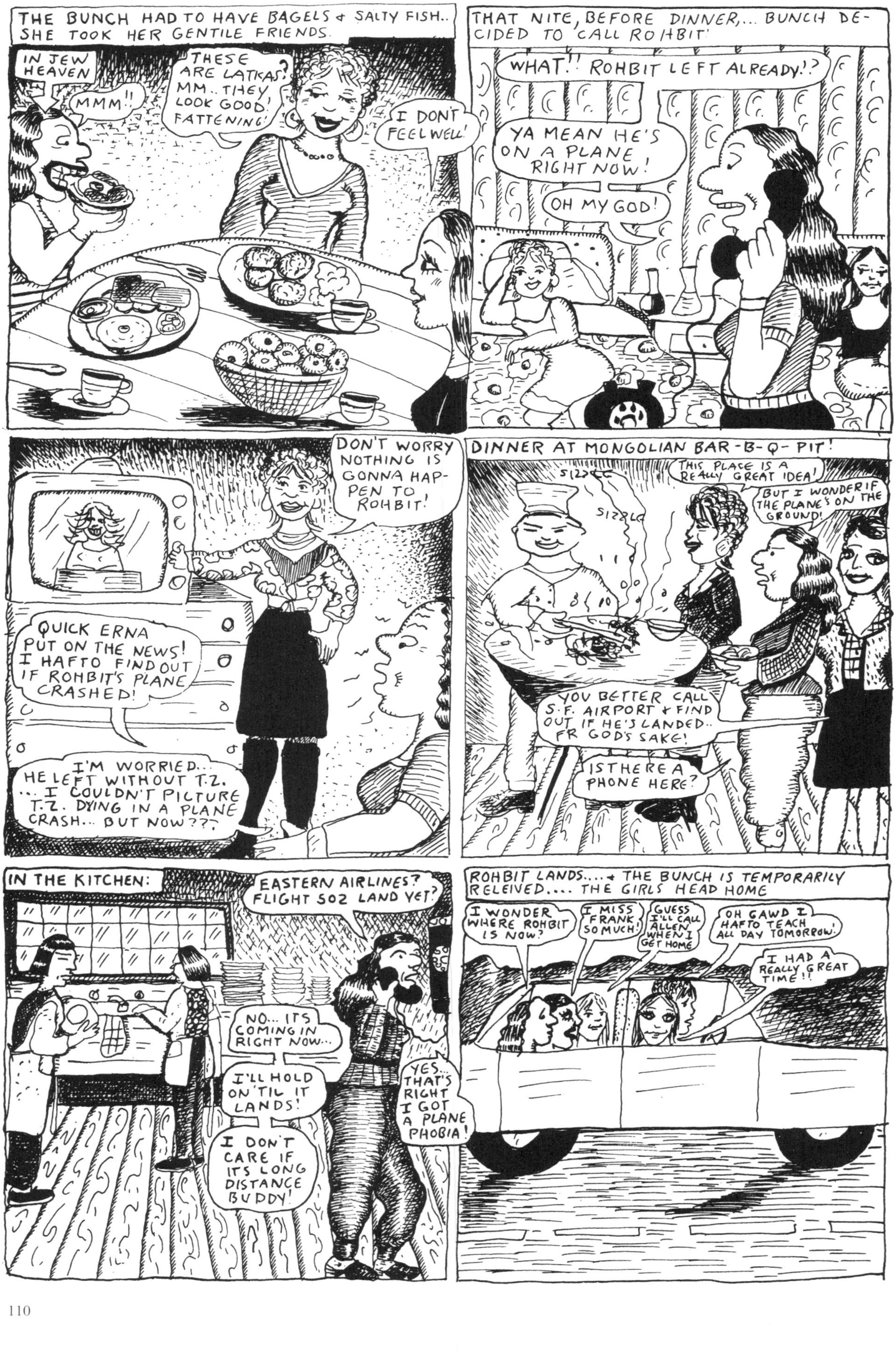
THE BUNCH HAD TO HAVE BAGELS & SALTY FISH.. SHE TOOK HER GENTILE FRIENDS.
IN JEW HEAVEN
MMM!!
THESE ARE LATKAS? MM.. THEY LOOK GOOD! FATTENING!
I DON'T FEEL WELL!
THAT NITE, BEFORE DINNER,... BUNCH DECIDED TO CALL ROHBIT
WHAT!! ROHBIT LEFT ALREADY!?
YA MEAN HE'S ON A PLANE RIGHT NOW!
OH MY GOD!
DON'T WORRY NOTHING IS GONNA HAPPEN TO ROHBIT!
QUICK ERNA PUT ON THE NEWS! I HAFTO FIND OUT IF ROHBIT'S PLANE CRASHED!
I'M WORRIED.. HE LEFT WITHOUT T.Z. ... I COULDN'T PICTURE T.Z. DYING IN A PLANE CRASH... BUT NOW???
DINNER AT MONGOLIAN BAR-B-Q-PIT!
SIZZLE
SIZZLE
THIS PLACE IS A REALLY GREAT IDEA!
BUT I WONDER IF THE PLANE'S ON THE GROUND!
YOU BETTER CALL S.F. AIRPORT & FIND OUT IF HE'S LANDED.. FR GOD'S SAKE!
IS THERE A PHONE HERE?
IN THE KITCHEN:
EASTERN AIRLINES? FLIGHT 502 LAND YET?
NO... ITS COMING IN RIGHT NOW...
I'LL HOLD ON 'TIL IT LANDS!
YES... THAT'S RIGHT I GOT A PLANE PHOBIA!
I DON'T CARE IF ITS LONG DISTANCE BUDDY!
ROHBIT LANDS.... & THE BUNCH IS TEMPORARILY RELEIVED.... THE GIRLS HEAD HOME
I WONDER WHERE ROHBIT IS NOW?
I MISS FRANK SO MUCH!
GUESS I'LL CALL ALLEN WHEN I GET HOME
OH GAWD I HAFTO TEACH ALL DAY TOMORROW!
I HAD A REALLY GREAT TIME!!

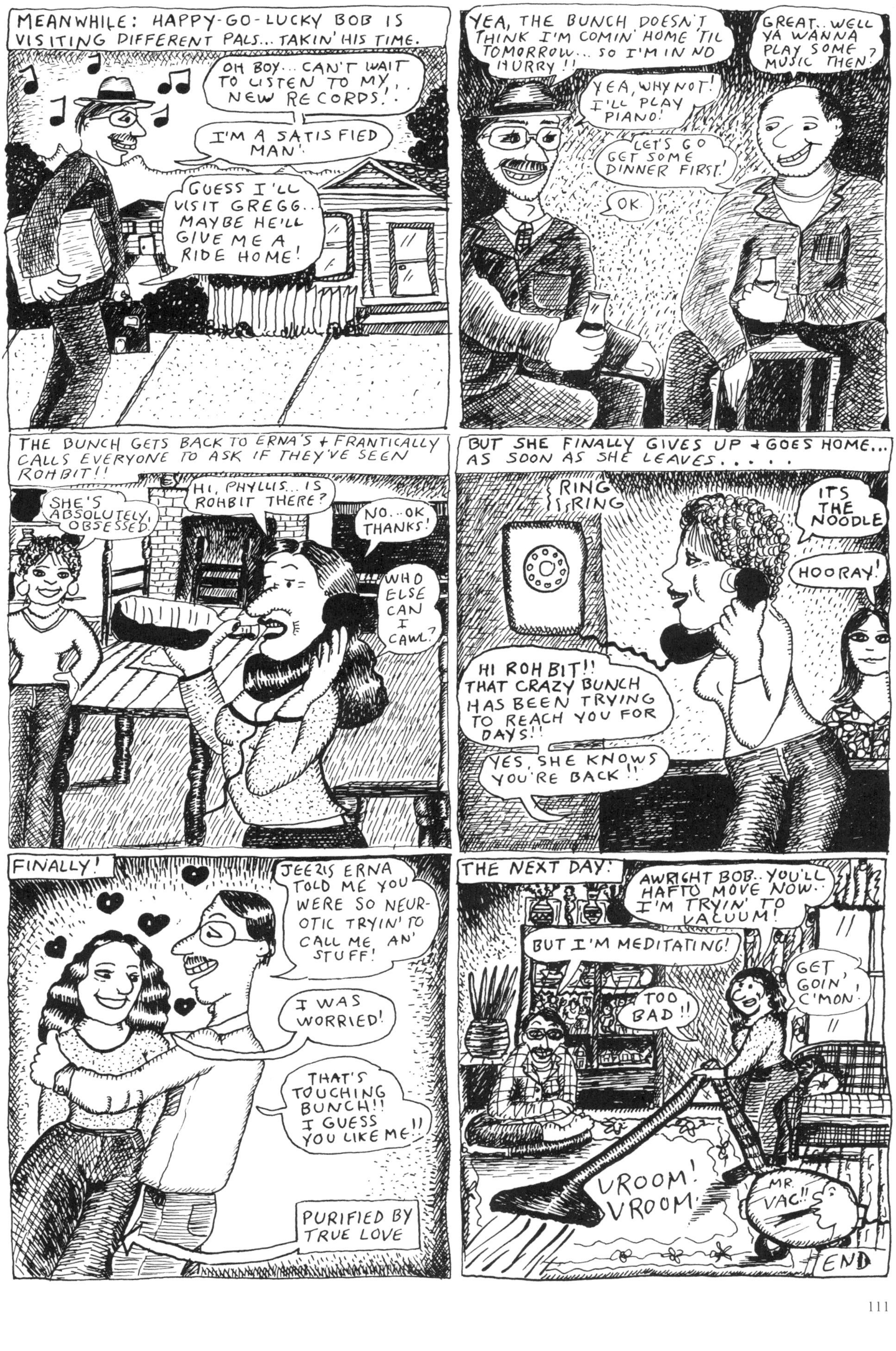
MEANWHILE: HAPPY-GO-LUCKY BOB IS VISITING DIFFERENT PALS... TAKIN' HIS TIME.
OH BOY... CAN'T WAIT TO LISTEN TO MY NEW RECORDS!
I'M A SATISFIED MAN!
GUESS I'LL VISIT GREGG.. MAYBE HE'LL GIVE ME A RIDE HOME!
YEA, THE BUNCH DOESN'T THINK I'M COMIN' HOME 'TIL TOMORROW... SO I'M IN NO HURRY!!
GREAT.. WELL YA WANNA PLAY SOME MUSIC THEN?
YEA, WHY NOT! I'LL PLAY PIANO!
LET'S GO GET SOME DINNER FIRST!
OK.
THE BUNCH GETS BACK TO ERNA'S + FRANTICALLY CALLS EVERYONE TO ASK IF THEY'VE SEEN ROHBIT!!
SHE'S ABSOLUTELY OBSESSED!
HI, PHYLLIS... IS ROHBIT THERE?
NO...OK THANKS!
WHO ELSE CAN I CAWL?
BUT SHE FINALLY GIVES UP + GOES HOME... AS SOON AS SHE LEAVES....
RING RING
ITS THE NOODLE
HOORAY!
HI ROHBIT!! THAT CRAZY BUNCH HAS BEEN TRYING TO REACH YOU FOR DAYS!!
YES, SHE KNOWS YOU'RE BACK!!
FINALLY!
JEEZ'S ERNA TOLD ME YOU WERE SO NEUROTIC TRYIN' TO CALL ME, AN' STUFF!
I WAS WORRIED!
THAT'S TOUCHING BUNCH!! I GUESS YOU LIKE ME!!
PURIFIED BY TRUE LOVE
THE NEXT DAY:
AWRIGHT BOB.. YOU'LL HAFTO MOVE NOW.. I'M TRYIN' TO VACUUM!
BUT I'M MEDITATING!
GET GOIN', C'MON!
TOO BAD!!
VROOM! VROOM!
MR. VAC!!
END

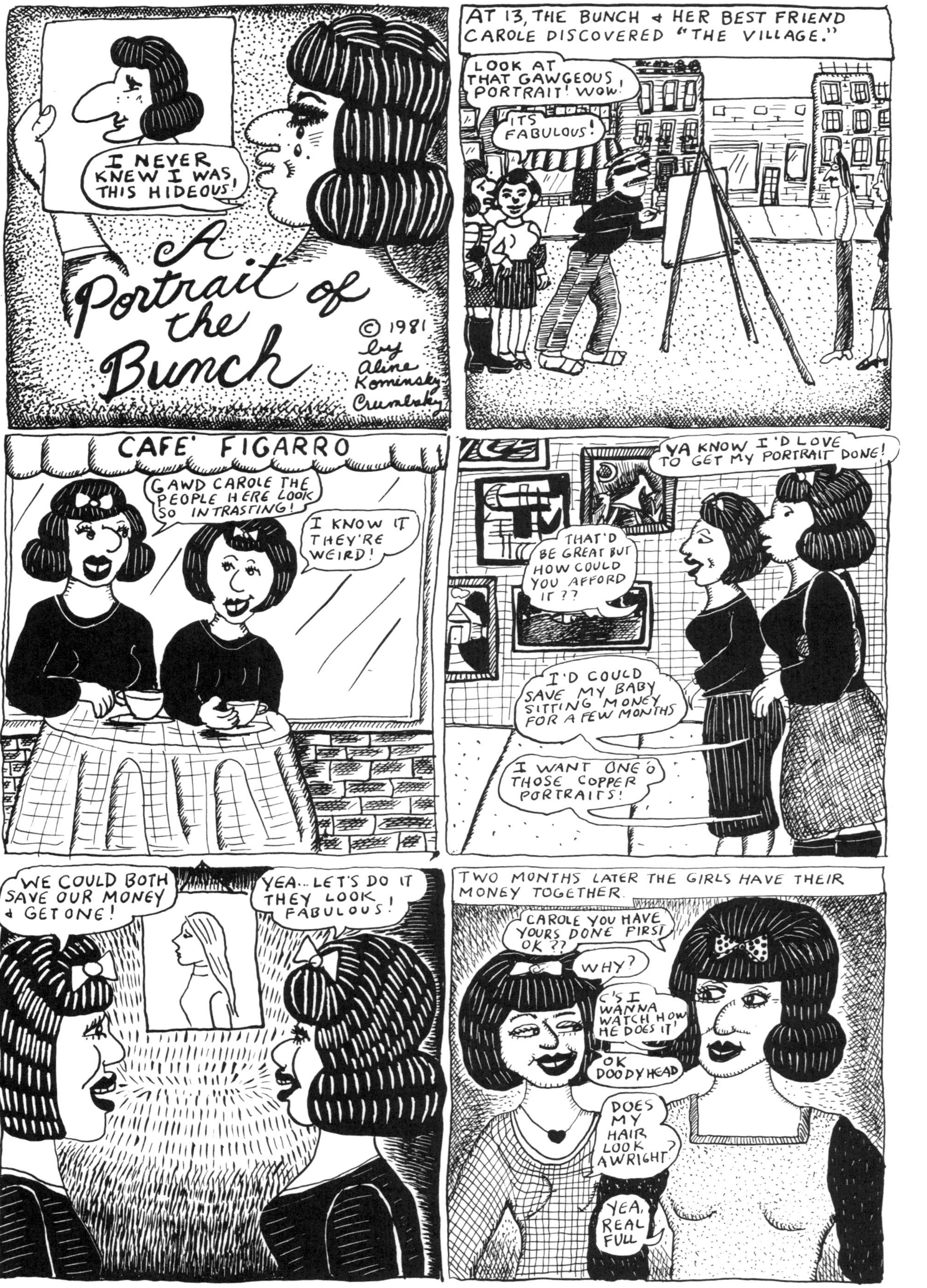
I NEVER KNEW I WAS THIS HIDEOUS!
A Portrait of the Bunch
© 1981 by Aline Kominsky-Crumbsky
AT 13, THE BUNCH & HER BEST FRIEND CAROLE DISCOVERED "THE VILLAGE."
LOOK AT THAT GAWGEOUS PORTRAIT! WOW!
ITS FABULOUS!
CAFE' FIGARRO
GAWD CAROLE THE PEOPLE HERE LOOK SO INTRASTING!
I KNOW IT THEY'RE WEIRD!
YA KNOW I'D LOVE TO GET MY PORTRAIT DONE!
THAT'D BE GREAT BUT HOW COULD YOU AFFORD IT??
I'D COULD SAVE MY BABY SITTING MONEY FOR A FEW MONTHS
I WANT ONE O' THOSE COPPER PORTRAITS!
WE COULD BOTH SAVE OUR MONEY & GET ONE!
YEA... LET'S DO IT THEY LOOK FABULOUS!
TWO MONTHS LATER THE GIRLS HAVE THEIR MONEY TOGETHER.
CAROLE YOU HAVE YOURS DONE FIRST OK??
WHY?
C'S I WANNA WATCH HOW HE DOES IT!
OK DOODYHEAD
DOES MY HAIR LOOK AWRIGHT?
YEA, REAL FULL

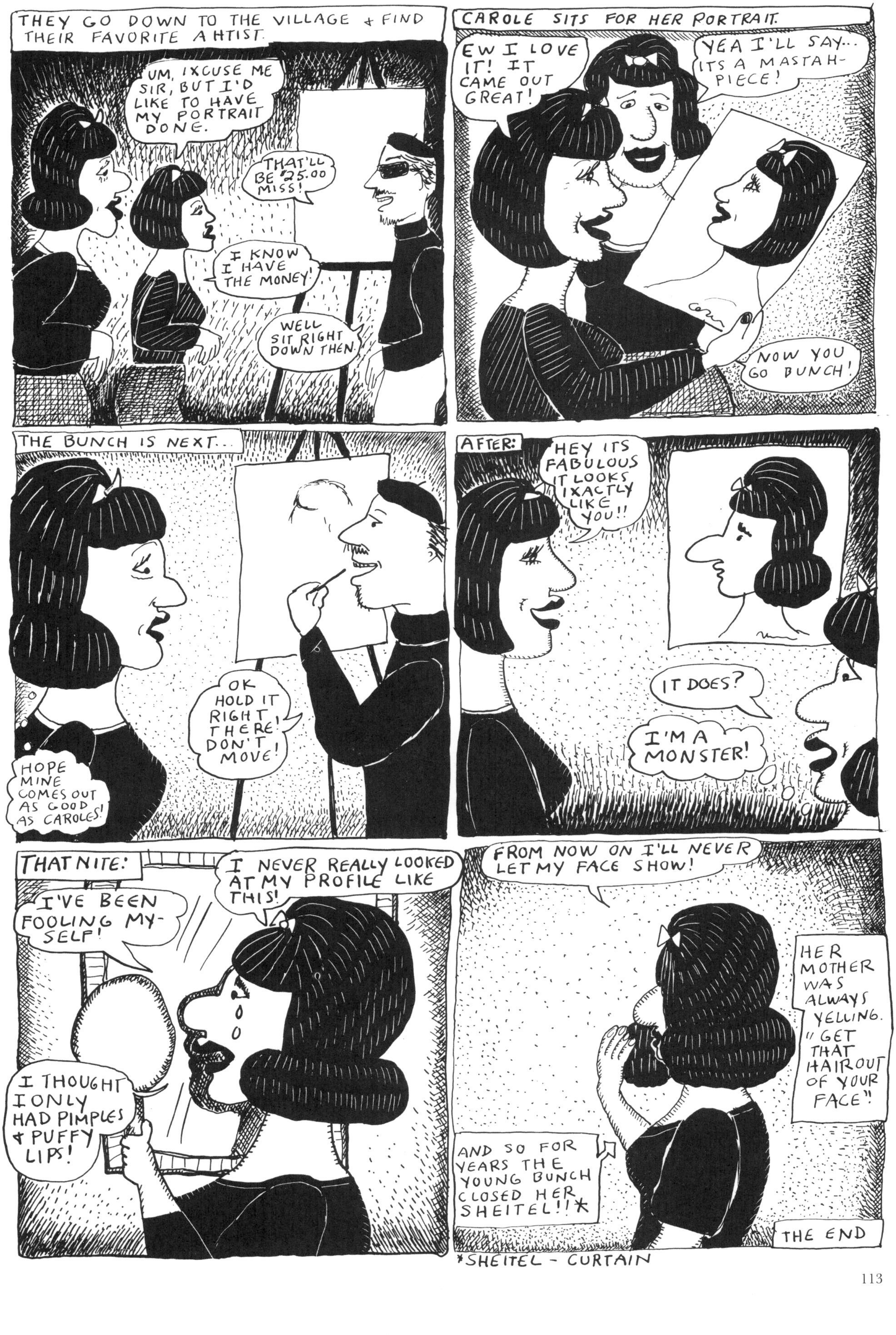
THEY GO DOWN TO THE VILLAGE & FIND THEIR FAVORITE AHTIST.
UM, IXCUSE ME SIR, BUT I'D LIKE TO HAVE MY PORTRAIT DONE.
THAT'LL BE $25.00 MISS!
I KNOW I HAVE THE MONEY!
WELL SIT RIGHT DOWN THEN.
CAROLE SITS FOR HER PORTRAIT.
EW I LOVE IT! IT CAME OUT GREAT!
YEA I'LL SAY... ITS A MASTAH-PIECE!
NOW YOU GO BUNCH!
THE BUNCH IS NEXT...
HOPE MINE COMES OUT AS GOOD AS CAROLES!
OK HOLD IT RIGHT THERE! DON'T MOVE!
AFTER:
HEY ITS FABULOUS IT LOOKS IXACTLY LIKE YOU!!
IT DOES?
I'M A MONSTER!
THAT NITE:
I'VE BEEN FOOLING MY-SELF!
I NEVER REALLY LOOKED AT MY PROFILE LIKE THIS!
I THOUGHT I ONLY HAD PIMPLES & PUFFY LIPS!
FROM NOW ON I'LL NEVER LET MY FACE SHOW!
HER MOTHER WAS ALWAYS YELLING. "GET THAT HAIR OUT OF YOUR FACE"!
AND SO FOR YEARS THE YOUNG BUNCH CLOSED HER SHEITEL!!*
THE END
*SHEITEL - CURTAIN

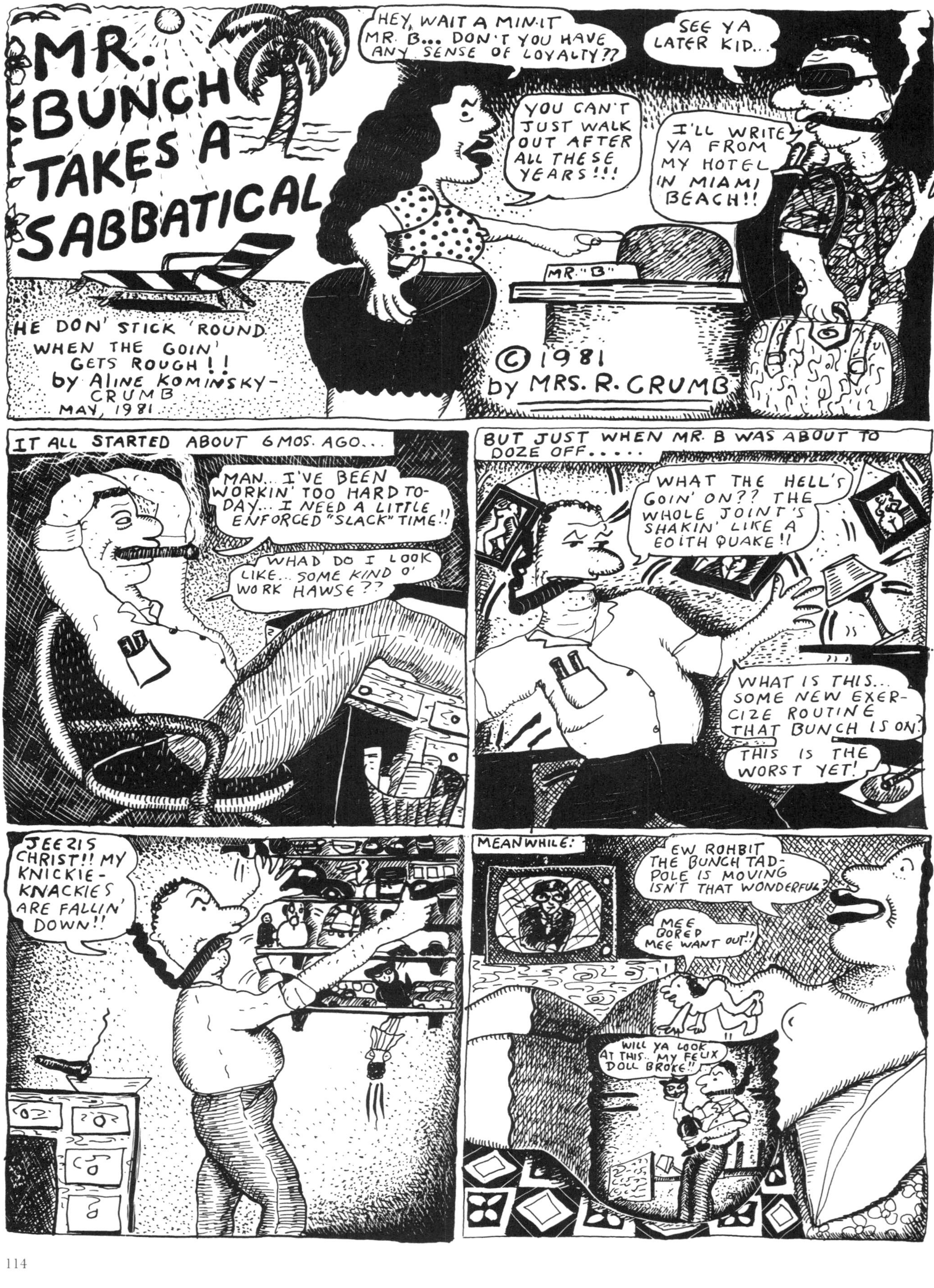
MR. BUNCH TAKES A SABBATICAL
HE DON' STICK 'ROUND WHEN THE GOIN' GETS ROUGH!! by ALINE KOMINSKY-CRUMB MAY, 1981
HEY, WAIT A MIN.IT MR. B... DON'T YOU HAVE ANY SENSE OF LOYALTY??
YOU CAN'T JUST WALK OUT AFTER ALL THESE YEARS!!!
SEE YA LATER KID...
I'LL WRITE YA FROM MY HOTEL IN MIAMI BEACH!!
MR. "B"
© 1981 by MRS. R. CRUMB
IT ALL STARTED ABOUT 6 MOS. AGO...
MAN... I'VE BEEN WORKIN' TOO HARD TO-DAY... I NEED A LITTLE ENFORCED "SLACK" TIME!!
WHAD DO I LOOK LIKE... SOME KIND O' WORK HAWSE??
BUT JUST WHEN MR. B WAS ABOUT TO DOZE OFF....
WHAT THE HELL'S GOIN' ON?? THE WHOLE JOINT'S SHAKIN' LIKE A EOITH QUAKE!!
WHAT IS THIS... SOME NEW EXER-CIZE ROUTINE THAT BUNCH IS ON?
THIS IS THE WORST YET!
JEEZIS CHRIST!! MY KNICKIE-KNACKIES ARE FALLIN' DOWN!!
MEANWHILE:
EW ROHBIT THE BUNCH TAD-POLE IS MOVING ISN'T THAT WONDERFUL
MEE BORED MEE WANT OUT!!
WILL YA LOOK AT THIS.. MY FELIX DOLL BROKE!!

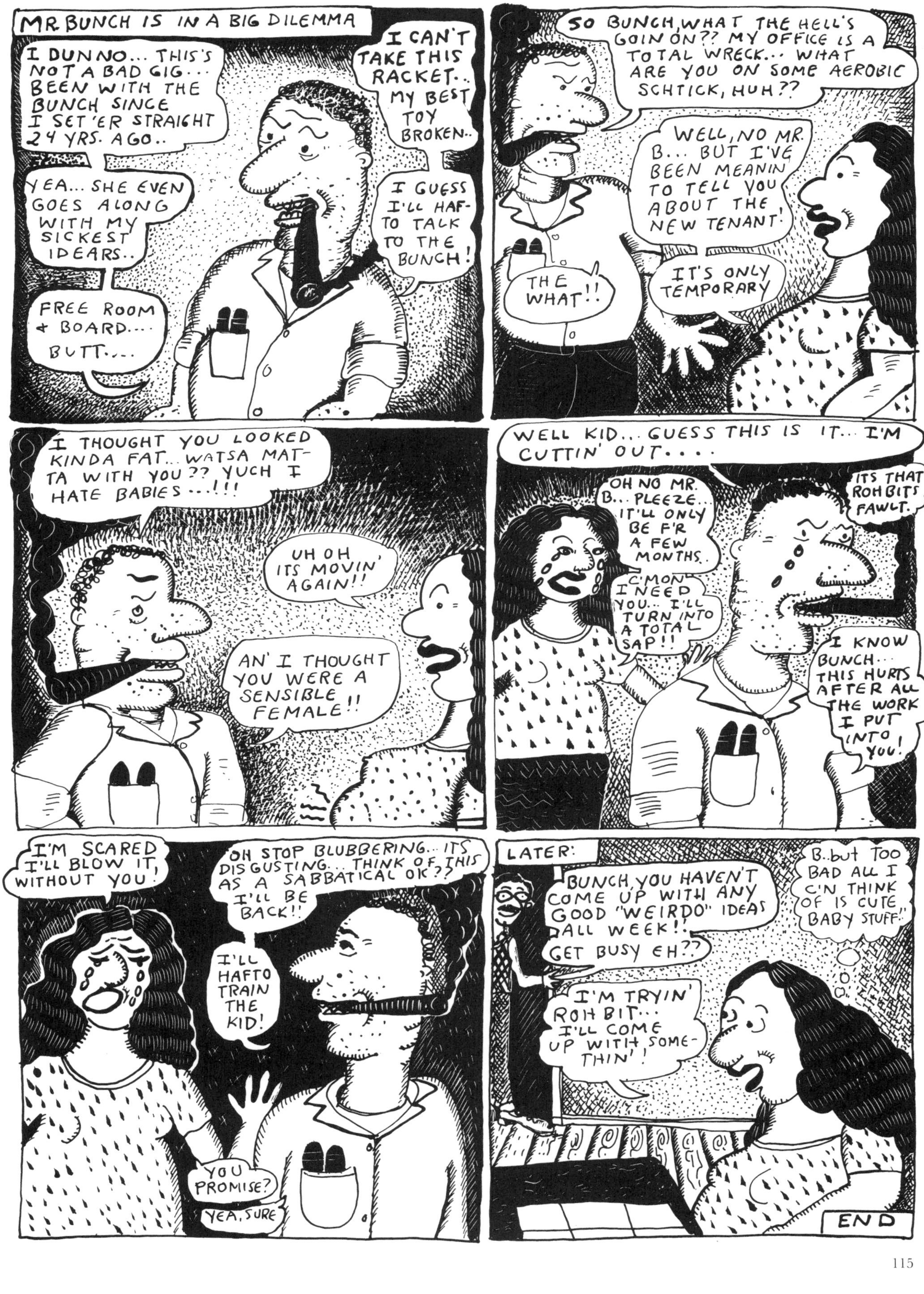
MR BUNCH IS IN A BIG DILEMMA
I DUNNO... THIS'S NOT A BAD GIG.. BEEN WITH THE BUNCH SINCE I SET 'ER STRAIGHT 24 YRS. AGO..
YEA... SHE EVEN GOES ALONG WITH MY SICKEST IDEARS..
FREE ROOM & BOARD.... BUTT....
I CAN'T TAKE THIS RACKET.. MY BEST TOY BROKEN..
I GUESS I'LL HAF-TO TALK TO THE BUNCH!
SO BUNCH, WHAT THE HELL'S GOIN ON?? MY OFFICE IS A TOTAL WRECK... WHAT ARE YOU ON SOME AEROBIC SCHTICK, HUH??
WELL, NO MR. B... BUT I'VE BEEN MEANIN TO TELL YOU ABOUT THE NEW TENANT!
THE WHAT!!
IT'S ONLY TEMPORARY
I THOUGHT YOU LOOKED KINDA FAT... WATSA MAT-TA WITH YOU?? YUCH I HATE BABIES...!!!
UH OH ITS MOVIN' AGAIN!!
AN' I THOUGHT YOU WERE A SENSIBLE FEMALE!!
WELL KID... GUESS THIS IS IT... I'M CUTTIN' OUT....
OH NO MR. B... PLEEZE.. IT'LL ONLY BE F'R A FEW MONTHS.
C'MON I NEED YOU... I'LL TURN INTO A TOTAL SAP!!
ITS THAT ROHBITS FAWLT.
I KNOW BUNCH.. THIS HURTS AFTER ALL THE WORK I PUT INTO YOU!
I'M SCARED I'LL BLOW IT, WITHOUT YOU!
OH STOP BLUBBERING... ITS DISGUSTING... THINK OF THIS AS A SABBATICAL OK?? I'LL BE BACK!!
I'LL HAFTO TRAIN THE KID!
YOU PROMISE?
YEA, SURE
LATER:
BUNCH, YOU HAVEN'T COME UP WITH ANY GOOD "WEIRDO" IDEAS ALL WEEK!
GET BUSY EH??
I'M TRYIN' ROHBIT... I'LL COME UP WITH SOME-THIN'!
B..but TOO BAD ALL I C'N THINK OF IS CUTE BABY STUFF!
END

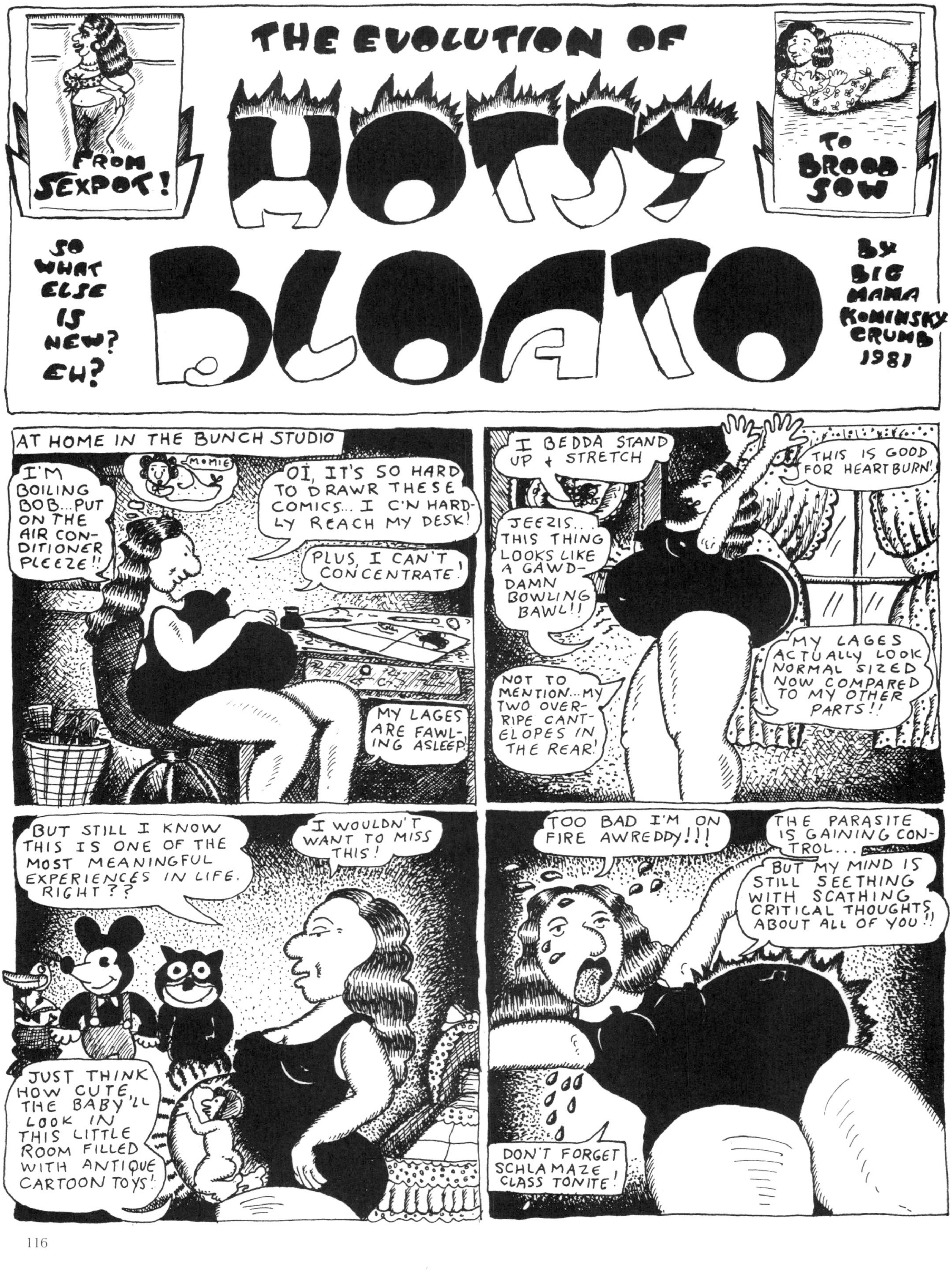
THE EVOLUTION OF
HOTSY BLOATO
FROM SEXPOT!
TO BROOD-SOW
SO WHAT ELSE IS NEW? EH?
BY BIG MAMA KOMINSKY CRUMB 1981
AT HOME IN THE BUNCH STUDIO
MOMIE
I'M BOILING BOB... PUT ON THE AIR CONDITIONER PLEEZE!!
OÏ, IT'S SO HARD TO DRAWR THESE COMICS... I C'N HARDLY REACH MY DESK!
PLUS, I CAN'T CONCENTRATE!
MY LAGES ARE FAWLING ASLEEP!
I BEDDA STAND UP + STRETCH
THIS IS GOOD FOR HEARTBURN!
JEEZIS... THIS THING LOOKS LIKE A GAWD-DAMN BOWLING BAWL!!
MY LAGES ACTUALLY LOOK NORMAL SIZED NOW COMPARED TO MY OTHER PARTS!!
NOT TO MENTION... MY TWO OVER-RIPE CANT-ELOPES IN THE REAR!
BUT STILL I KNOW THIS IS ONE OF THE MOST MEANINGFUL EXPERIENCES IN LIFE. RIGHT??
I WOULDN'T WANT TO MISS THIS!
JUST THINK HOW CUTE THE BABY'LL LOOK IN THIS LITTLE ROOM FILLED WITH ANTIQUE CARTOON TOYS!
TOO BAD I'M ON FIRE AWREDDY!!!
THE PARASITE IS GAINING CONTROL...
BUT MY MIND IS STILL SEETHING WITH SCATHING CRITICAL THOUGHTS ABOUT ALL OF YOU!!
DON'T FORGET SCHLAMAZE CLASS TONITE!

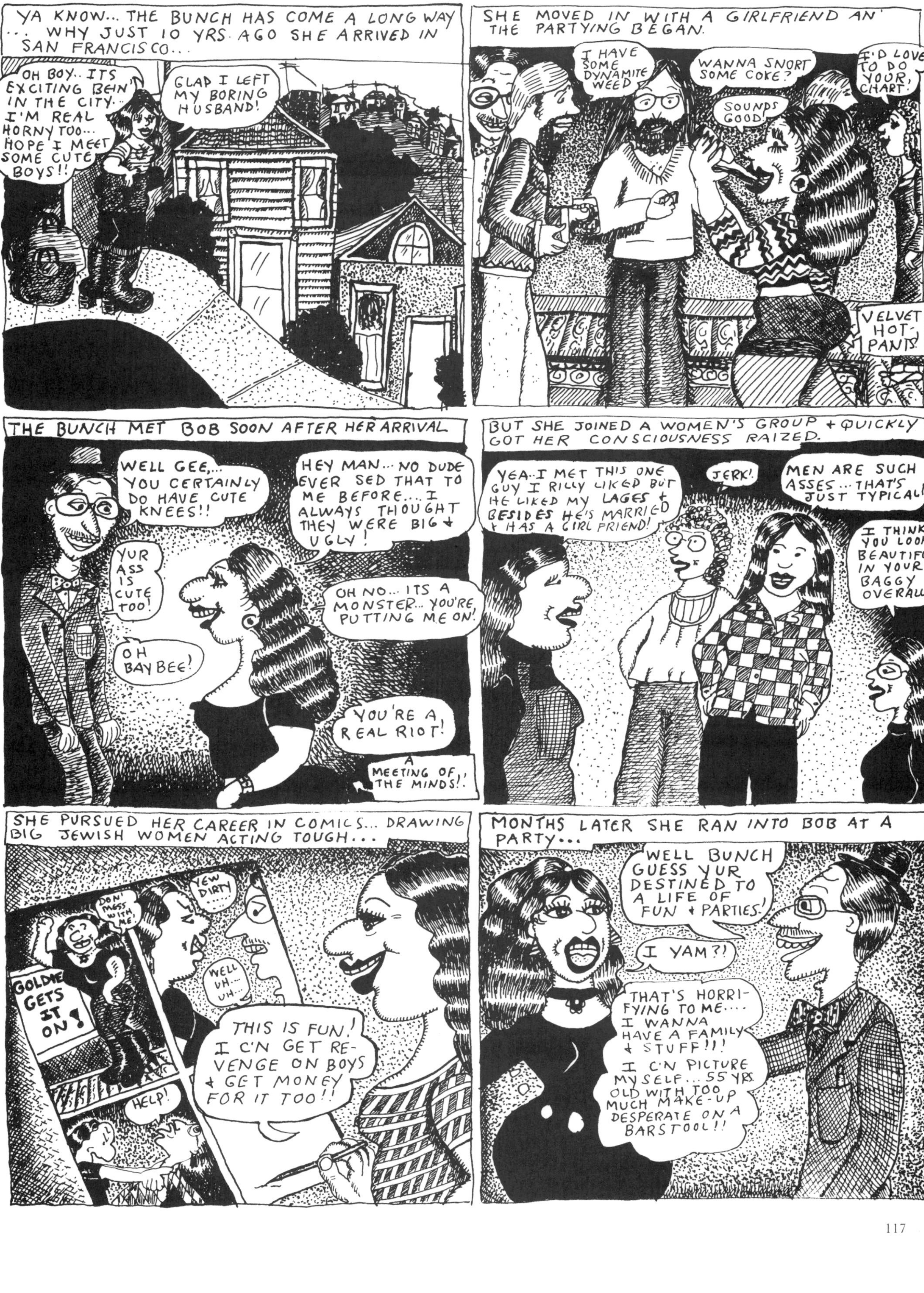

YA KNOW... THE BUNCH HAS COME A LONG WAY ... WHY JUST 10 YRS. AGO SHE ARRIVED IN SAN FRANCISCO...
OH BOY.. ITS EXCITING BEIN' IN THE CITY.. I'M REAL HORNY TOO... HOPE I MEET SOME CUTE BOYS!!
GLAD I LEFT MY BORING HUSBAND!
SHE MOVED IN WITH A GIRLFRIEND AN' THE PARTYING BEGAN.
I HAVE SOME DYNAMITE WEED
WANNA SNORT SOME COKE?
I'D LOVE TO DO YOUR CHART!
SOUNDS GOOD!
VELVET HOT-PANTS!
THE BUNCH MET BOB SOON AFTER HER ARRIVAL
WELL GEE,... YOU CERTAINLY DO HAVE CUTE KNEES!!
HEY MAN... NO DUDE EVER SED THAT TO ME BEFORE.... I ALWAYS THOUGHT THEY WERE BIG + UGLY!
YUR ASS IS CUTE TOO!
OH NO... ITS A MONSTER... YOU'RE PUTTING ME ON!
OH BAYBEE!
YOU'RE A REAL RIOT!
A MEETING OF THE MINDS!
BUT SHE JOINED A WOMEN'S GROUP + QUICKLY GOT HER CONSCIOUSNESS RAIZED.
YEA..I MET THIS ONE GUY I RILLY LIKED BUT HE LIKED MY LAGES + BESIDES HE'S MARRIED + HAS A GIRL FRIEND!
JERK!
MEN ARE SUCH ASSES... THAT'S JUST TYPICAL!
I THINK YOU LOOK BEAUTIFUL IN YOUR BAGGY OVERALLS!
SHE PURSUED HER CAREER IN COMICS... DRAWING BIG JEWISH WOMEN ACTING TOUGH...
DON'T MESS WITH ME!
YEW DIRTY...
WELL UH... UH...
GOLDIE GETS IT ON!
HELP!
THIS IS FUN! I C'N GET REVENGE ON BOYS + GET MONEY FOR IT TOO!!
MONTHS LATER SHE RAN INTO BOB AT A PARTY...
WELL BUNCH GUESS YUR DESTINED TO A LIFE OF FUN + PARTIES!
I YAM?!
THAT'S HORRIFYING TO ME.... I WANNA HAVE A FAMILY + STUFF!!! I C'N PICTURE MYSELF... 55 YRS. OLD WITH TOO MUCH MAKE-UP DESPERATE ON A BARSTOOL!!

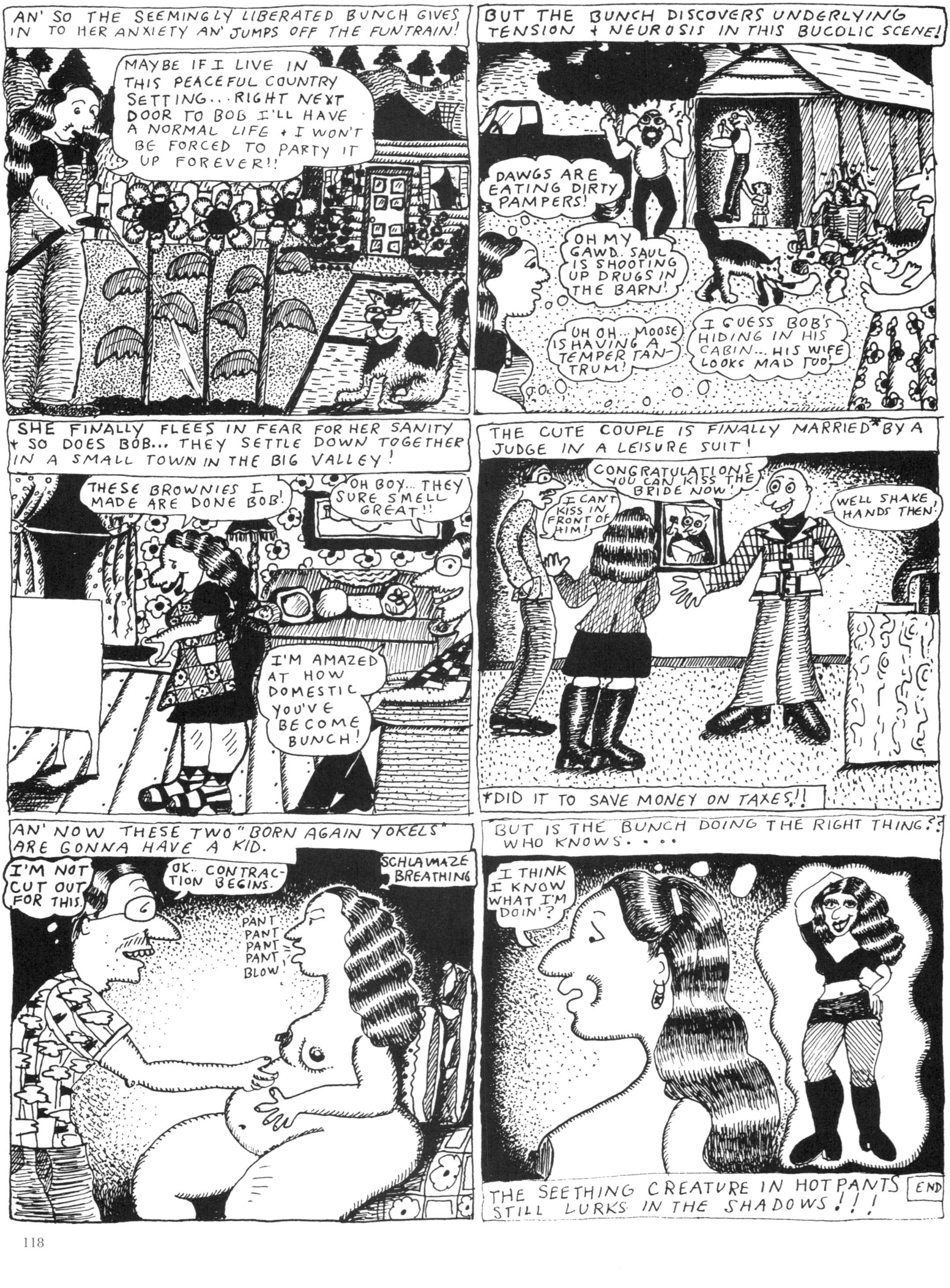

AN' SO THE SEEMINGLY LIBERATED BUNCH GIVES IN TO HER ANXIETY AN' JUMPS OFF THE FUNTRAIN!
MAYBE IF I LIVE IN THIS PEACEFUL COUNTRY SETTING... RIGHT NEXT DOOR TO BOB I'LL HAVE A NORMAL LIFE + I WON'T BE FORCED TO PARTY IT UP FOREVER!!
BUT THE BUNCH DISCOVERS UNDERLYING TENSION + NEUROSIS IN THIS BUCOLIC SCENE!
DAWGS ARE EATING DIRTY PAMPERS!
OH MY GAWD. SAUL IS SHOOTING UP DRUGS IN THE BARN!
UH OH... MOOSE IS HAVING A TEMPER TANTRUM!
I GUESS BOB'S HIDING IN HIS CABIN... HIS WIFE LOOKS MAD TOO!
SHE FINALLY FLEES IN FEAR FOR HER SANITY + SO DOES BOB... THEY SETTLE DOWN TOGETHER IN A SMALL TOWN IN THE BIG VALLEY!
THESE BROWNIES I MADE ARE DONE BOB!
OH BOY... THEY SURE SMELL GREAT!!
I'M AMAZED AT HOW DOMESTIC YOU'VE BECOME BUNCH!
THE CUTE COUPLE IS FINALLY MARRIED* BY A JUDGE IN A LEISURE SUIT!
CONGRATULATIONS YOU CAN KISS THE BRIDE NOW!
I CANT KISS IN FRONT OF HIM!
WELL SHAKE HANDS THEN!
*DID IT TO SAVE MONEY ON TAXES!!
AN' NOW THESE TWO "BORN AGAIN YOKELS" ARE GONNA HAVE A KID.
I'M NOT CUT OUT FOR THIS.
OK.. CONTRACTION BEGINS.
SCHLAMAZE BREATHING
PANT PANT PANT PANT BLOW
BUT IS THE BUNCH DOING THE RIGHT THING?? WHO KNOWS....
I THINK I KNOW WHAT I'M DOIN'?
THE SEETHING CREATURE IN HOTPANTS STILL LURKS IN THE SHADOWS!!!
END

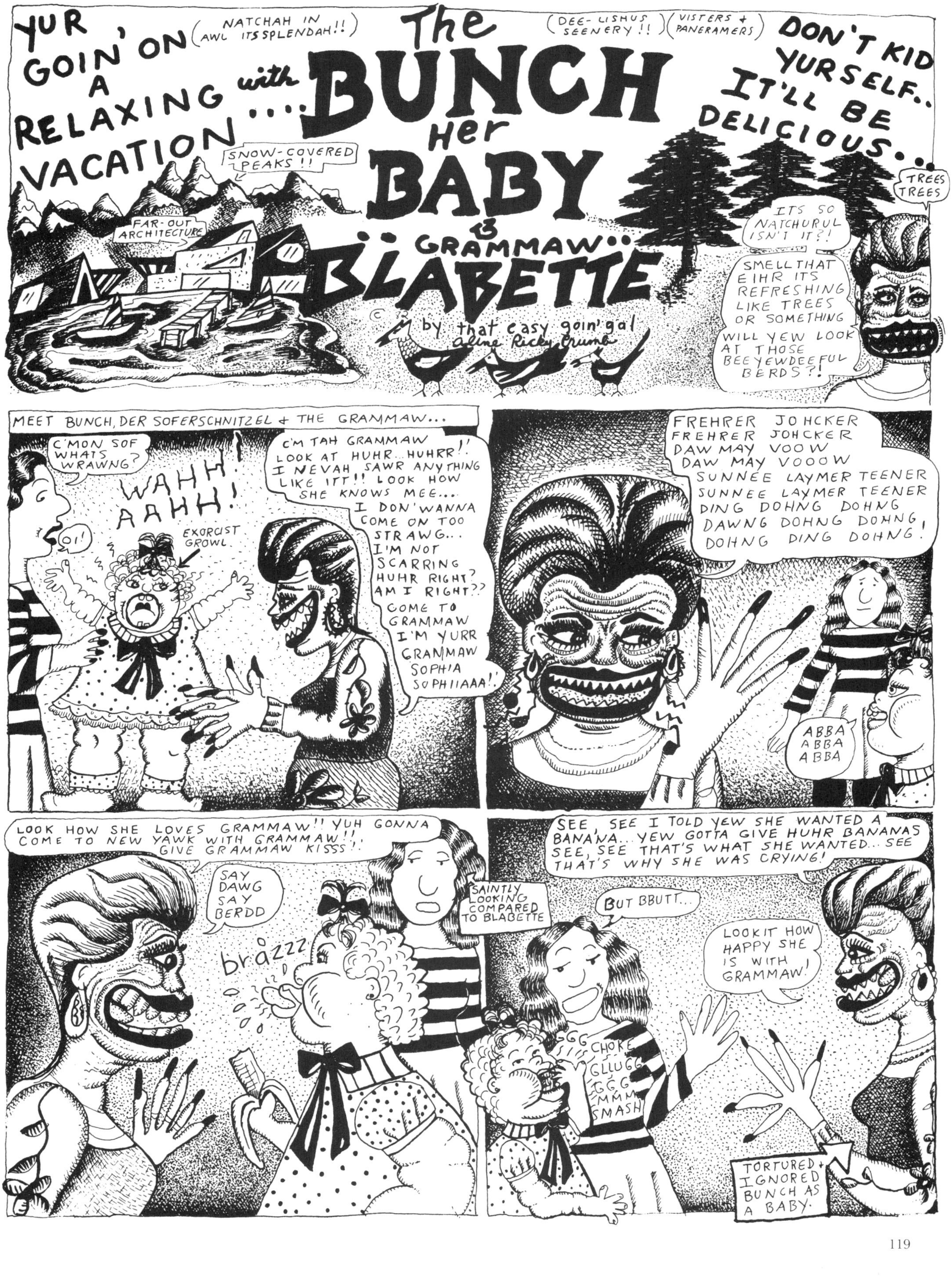
YUR GOIN' ON A RELAXING VACATION...
(NATCHAH IN AWL ITS SPLENDAH!!)
with
The BUNCH Her BABY & GRAMMAW.. BLABETTE
(DEE-LISHUS SEENERY!!)
(VISTERS + PANERAMERS)
DON'T KID YURSELF.. IT'LL BE DELICIOUS...
SNOW-COVERED PEAKS!!
FAR-OUT ARCHITECTURE
© by that easy goin' gal Aline Ricky Crumb
TREES TREES
ITS SO NATCHURUL ISN'T IT?!
SMELL THAT EIHR ITS REFRESHING LIKE TREES OR SOMETHING
WILL YEW LOOK AT THOSE BEEYEWDEEFUL BERDS?!
MEET BUNCH, DER SOFERSCHNITZEL + THE GRAMMAW...
C'MON SOF WHATS WRAWNG?
WAHH! AAHH!
OI!
EXORCIST GROWL
C'M TAH GRAMMAW LOOK AT HUHR.. HUHRR!! I NEVAH SAWR ANYTHING LIKE ITT!! LOOK HOW SHE KNOWS MEE...
I DON'WANNA COME ON TOO STRAWG... I'M NOT SCARRING HUHR RIGHT? AM I RIGHT??
COME TO GRAMMAW I'M YURR GRAMMAW SOPHIA SOPHIIAAA!
FREHRER JOHCKER FREHRER JOHCKER DAW MAY VOOW DAW MAY VOOOW SUNNEE LAYMER TEENER SUNNEE LAYMER TEENER DING DOHNG DOHNG DAWNG DOHNG DOHNG, DOHNG DING DOHNG!
ABBA ABBA ABBA
LOOK HOW SHE LOVES GRAMMAW!! YUH GONNA COME TO NEW YAWK WITH GRAMMAW!! GIVE GRAMMAW KISSS!
SAY DAWG SAY BERDD
SAINTLY LOOKING COMPARED TO BLABETTE
brazzz
SEE, SEE I TOLD YEW SHE WANTED A BANANA... YEW GOTTA GIVE HUHR BANANAS SEE, SEE THAT'S WHAT SHE WANTED... SEE THAT'S WHY SHE WAS CRYING!
BUT BBUTT...
LOOKIT HOW HAPPY SHE IS WITH GRAMMAW!
GGG CHOKE GLLUGG GGG MMM SMASH
TORTURED + IGNORED BUNCH AS A BABY.

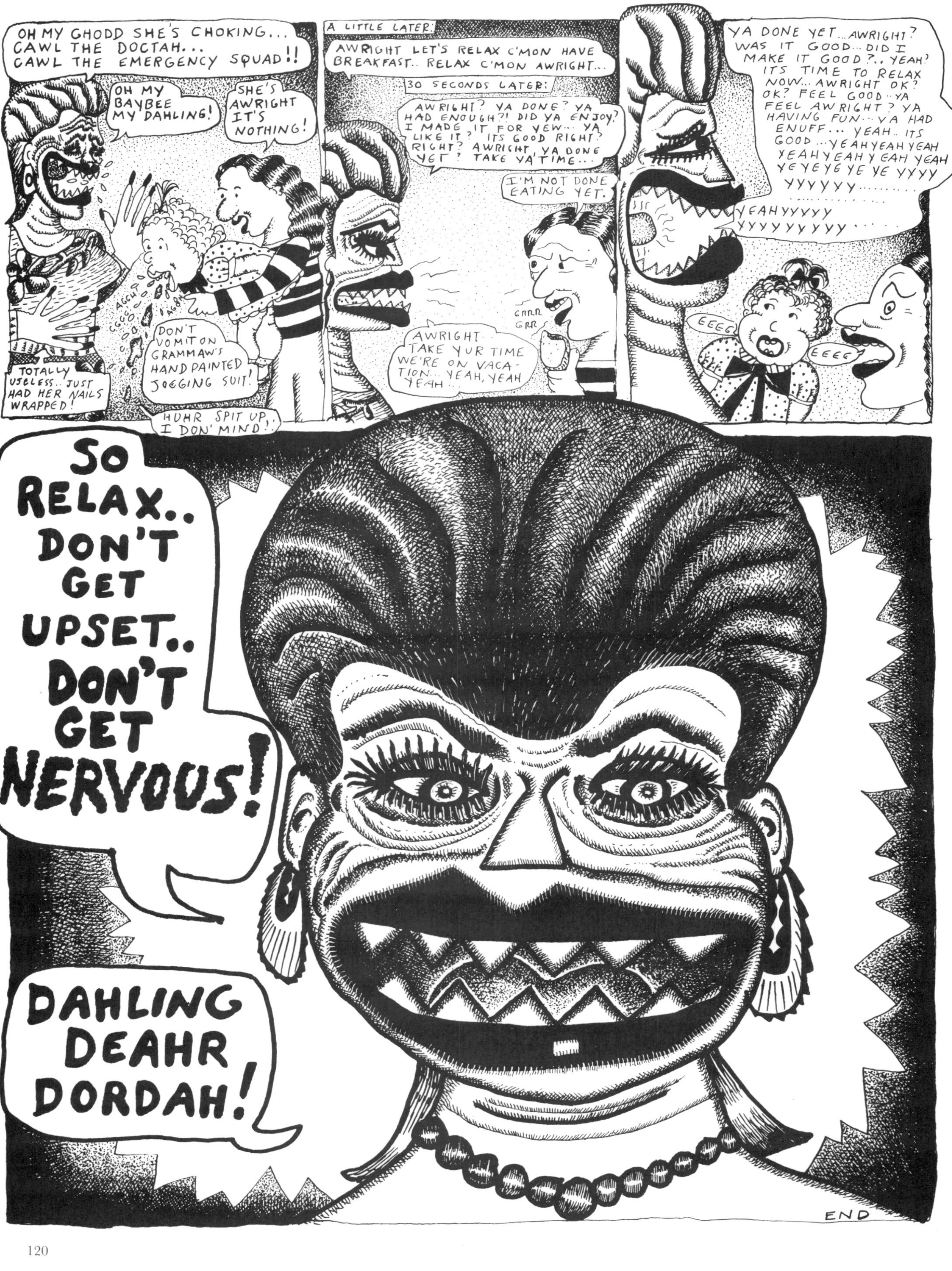

OH MY GHODD SHE'S CHOKING... CAWL THE DOCTAH... CAWL THE EMERGENCY SQUAD!!
OH MY BAYBEE MY DAHLING!
SHE'S AWRIGHT IT'S NOTHING!
AGGH
DON'T VOMIT ON GRAMMAW'S HAND PAINTED JOGGING SUIT!
TOTALLY USELESS.. JUST HAD HER NAILS WRAPPED!
HUHR SPIT UP, I DON' MIND!
A LITTLE LATER:
AWRIGHT LET'S RELAX C'MON HAVE BREAKFAST.. RELAX C'MON AWRIGHT...
30 SECONDS LATER:
AWRIGHT? YA DONE? YA HAD ENOUGH?! DID YA ENJOY? I MADE IT FOR YEW... YA LIKE IT? ITS GOOD RIGHT? RIGHT? AWRIGHT, YA DONE YET? TAKE YA'TIME...
I'M NOT DONE EATING YET.
GRRR GRR
AWRIGHT TAKE YUR TIME WE'RE ON VACATION... YEAH, YEAH YEAH...
YA DONE YET... AWRIGHT? WAS IT GOOD... DID I MAKE IT GOOD?.. YEAH? ITS TIME TO RELAX NOW... AWRIGHT OK? OK? FEEL GOOD.. YA FEEL AWRIGHT? YA HAVING FUN... YA HAD ENUFF... YEAH.. ITS GOOD... YEAH YEAH YEAH YEAH YEAH YEAH YEAH YE YE YG YE YE YYYY YYYYY.........
YEAH YYYYY YYYYYYYYY...
EEEG
EEEG
SO RELAX.. DON'T GET UPSET.. DON'T GET NERVOUS!
DAHLING DEAHR DORDAH!
END

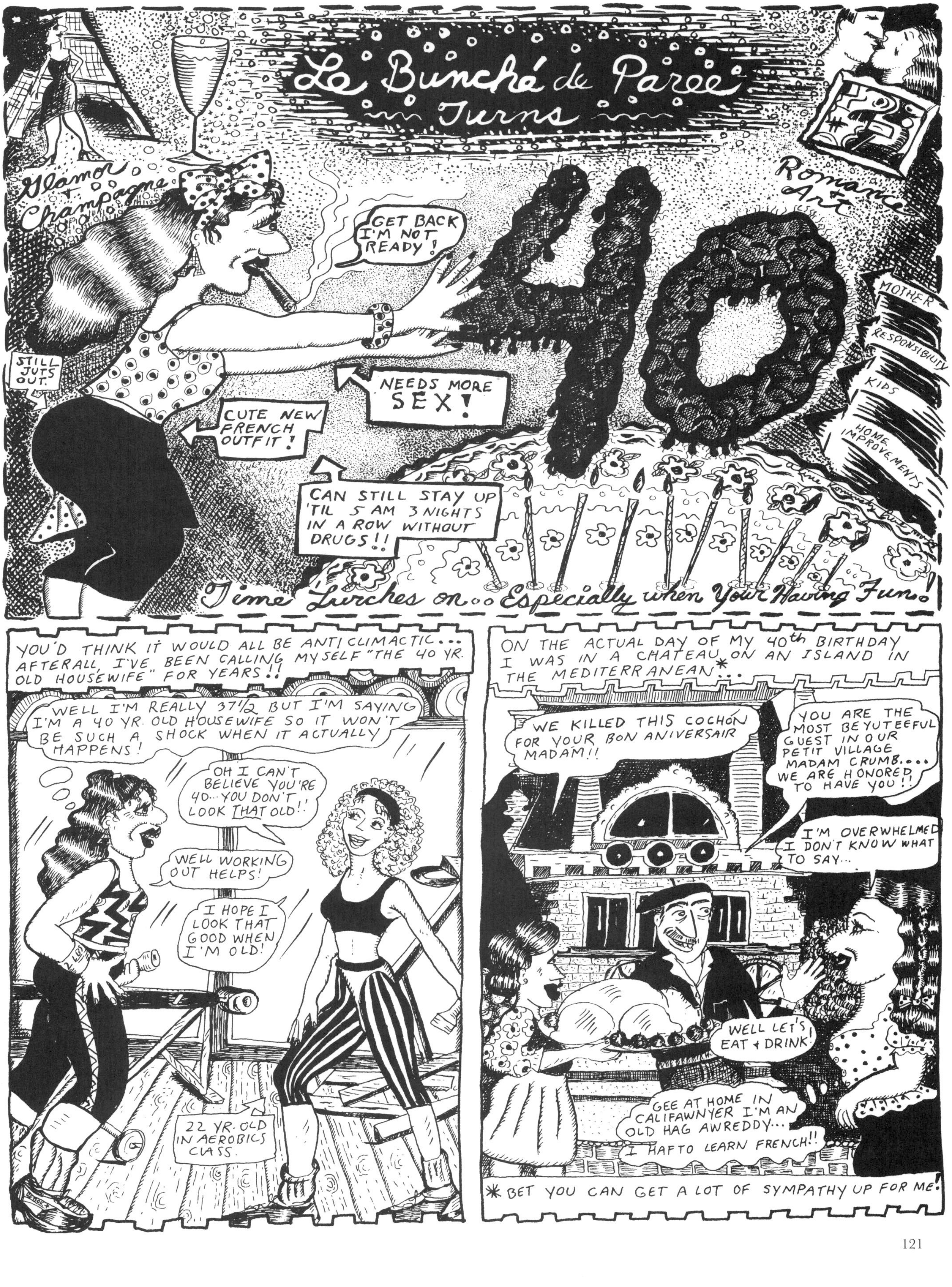
Le Bunché de Paree
Turns
40
Glamor + Champagne
Romance Art
GET BACK I'M NOT READY!
MOTHER
RESPONSIBILITY
KIDS
HOME IMPROVEMENTS
STILL JUTS OUT.
NEEDS MORE SEX!
CUTE NEW FRENCH OUTFIT!
CAN STILL STAY UP 'TIL 5 AM 3 NIGHTS IN A ROW WITHOUT DRUGS!!
Time Lurches on... Especially when Your Having Fun!
YOU'D THINK IT WOULD ALL BE ANTICLIMACTIC... AFTERALL, I'VE BEEN CALLING MYSELF "THE 40 YR. OLD HOUSEWIFE" FOR YEARS!!
WELL I'M REALLY 37½ BUT I'M SAYING I'M A 40 YR. OLD HOUSEWIFE SO IT WON'T BE SUCH A SHOCK WHEN IT ACTUALLY HAPPENS!
OH I CAN'T BELIEVE YOU'RE 40... YOU DON'T LOOK THAT OLD!!
WELL WORKING OUT HELPS!
I HOPE I LOOK THAT GOOD WHEN I'M OLD!
22 YR. OLD IN AEROBICS CLASS.
ON THE ACTUAL DAY OF MY 40th BIRTHDAY I WAS IN A CHATEAU* ON AN ISLAND IN THE MEDITERRANEAN...
WE KILLED THIS COCHÓN FOR YOUR BON ANIVERSAIR MADAM!!
YOU ARE THE MOST BEYUTEEFUL GUEST IN OUR PETIT VILLAGE MADAM CRUMB.... WE ARE HONORED TO HAVE YOU!!
I'M OVERWHELMED I DON'T KNOW WHAT TO SAY...
WELL LET'S EAT & DRINK!
GEE AT HOME IN CALIFAWNYER I'M AN OLD HAG AWREDDY... I HAFTO LEARN FRENCH!!
* BET YOU CAN GET A LOT OF SYMPATHY UP FOR ME!

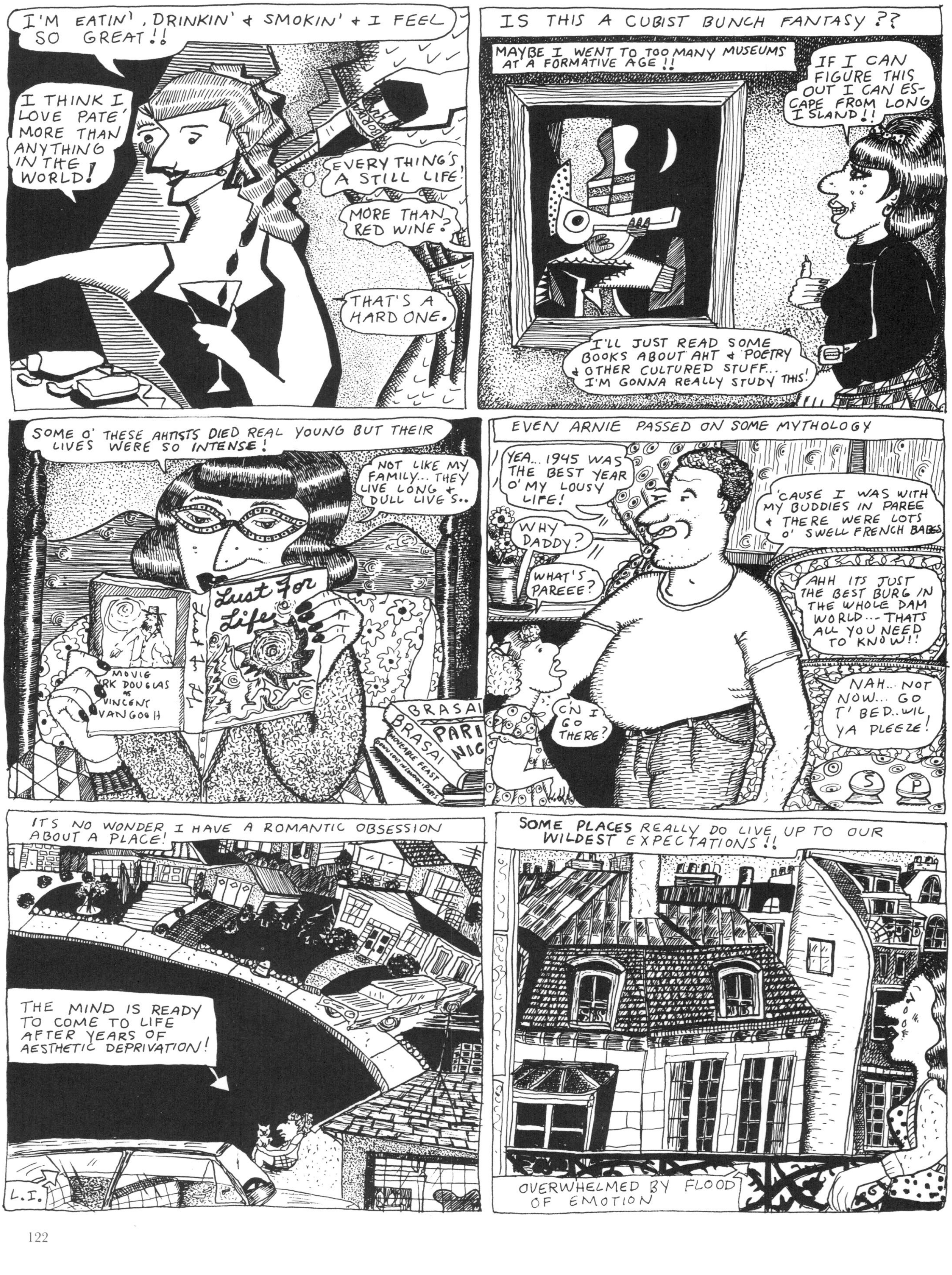
I'M EATIN', DRINKIN' & SMOKIN' + I FEEL SO GREAT!!
I THINK I LOVE PATE' MORE THAN ANYTHING IN THE WORLD!
EVERYTHING'S A STILL LIFE!
MORE THAN RED WINE?
THAT'S A HARD ONE.
IS THIS A CUBIST BUNCH FANTASY??
MAYBE I WENT TO TOO MANY MUSEUMS AT A FORMATIVE AGE!!
IF I CAN FIGURE THIS OUT I CAN ES-CAPE FROM LONG ISLAND!!
I'LL JUST READ SOME BOOKS ABOUT AHT & POETRY & OTHER CULTURED STUFF... I'M GONNA REALLY STUDY THIS!
SOME O' THESE AHTISTS DIED REAL YOUNG BUT THEIR LIVES WERE SO INTENSE!
NOT LIKE MY FAMILY... THEY LIVE LONG & DULL LIVE'S..
Lust For Life
MOVIE
RK DOUGLAS AS VINCENT VANGOGH
BRASAI
BRASAI
PARI
NIG
MOVEABLE FEAST
EVEN ARNIE PASSED ON SOME MYTHOLOGY
YEA... 1945 WAS THE BEST YEAR O' MY LOUSY LIFE!
'CAUSE I WAS WITH MY BUDDIES IN PAREE + THERE WERE LOTS O' SWELL FRENCH BABES
WHY DADDY?
WHAT'S PAREEE?
AHH ITS JUST THE BEST BURG IN THE WHOLE DAM WORLD...-THATS ALL YOU NEED TO KNOW!!
C'N I GO THERE?
NAH... NOT NOW... GO T' BED..WIL YA PLEEZE!
S
P
ITS NO WONDER I HAVE A ROMANTIC OBSESSION ABOUT A PLACE!
THE MIND IS READY TO COME TO LIFE AFTER YEARS OF AESTHETIC DEPRIVATION!
L.I.
SOME PLACES REALLY DO LIVE UP TO OUR WILDEST EXPECTATIONS!!
OVERWHELMED BY FLOOD OF EMOTION

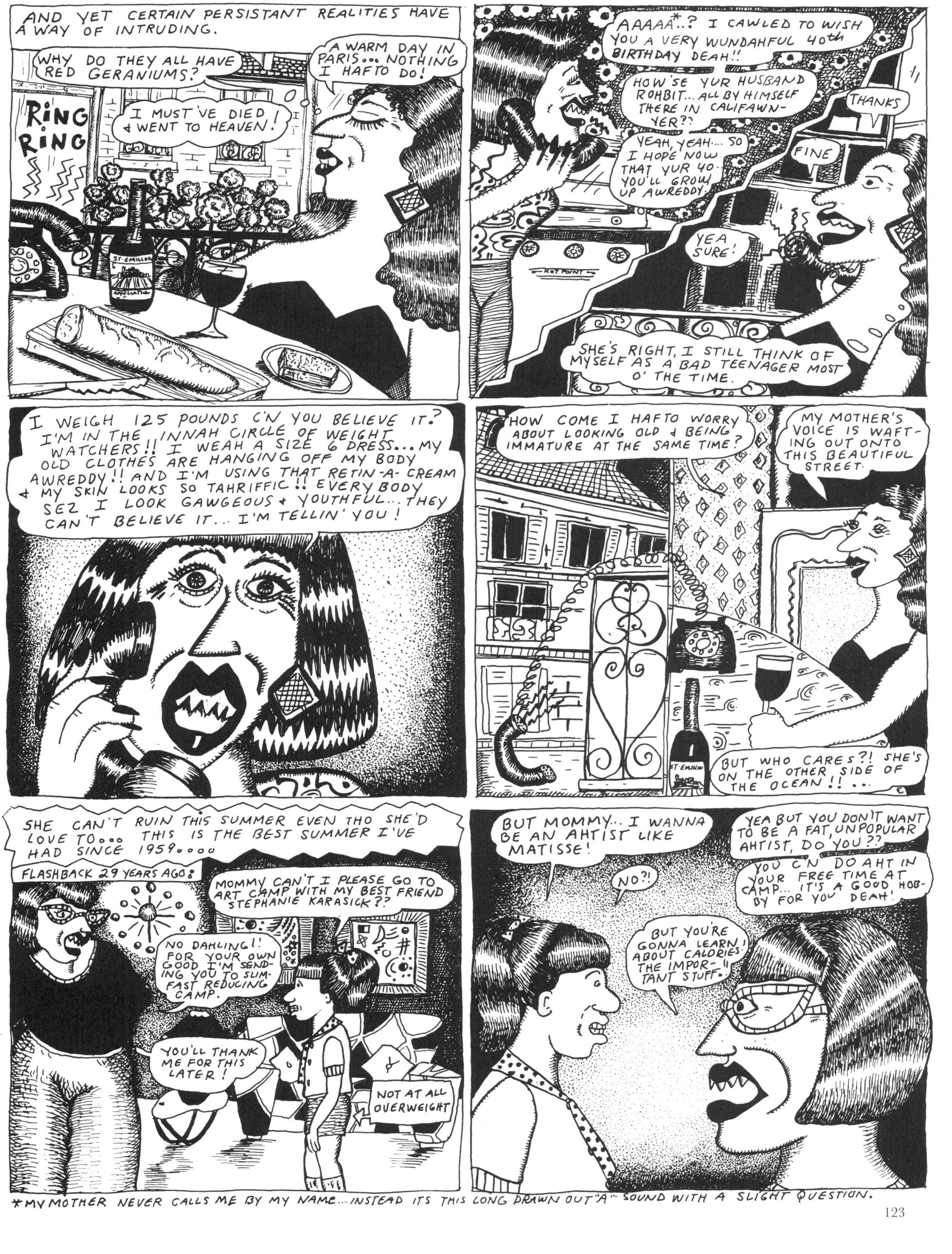
AND YET CERTAIN PERSISTANT REALITIES HAVE A WAY OF INTRUDING.
WHY DO THEY ALL HAVE RED GERANIUMS?
A WARM DAY IN PARIS... NOTHING I HAFTO DO!
I MUST'VE DIED & WENT TO HEAVEN!
RING RING
AAAAA*..? I CAWLED TO WISH YOU A VERY WUNDAHFUL 40th BIRTHDAY DEAH!!
HOW'SE YUR HUSBAND ROHBIT... ALL BY HIMSELF THERE IN CALIFAWNYER??
THANKS
FINE
YEAH, YEAH... SO I HOPE NOW THAT YUR 40 YOU'LL GROW UP AWREDDY.
YEA SURE!
SHE'S RIGHT, I STILL THINK OF MYSELF AS A BAD TEENAGER MOST O' THE TIME.
I WEIGH 125 POUNDS C'N YOU BELIEVE IT? I'M IN THE INNAH CIRCLE OF WEIGHT WATCHERS!! I WEAH A SIZE 6 DRESS... MY OLD CLOTHES ARE HANGING OFF MY BODY AWREDDY!! AND I'M USING THAT RETIN-A-CREAM & MY SKIN LOOKS SO TAHRIFFIC!! EVERYBODY SEZ I LOOK GAWGEOUS & YOUTHFUL... THEY CAN'T BELIEVE IT... I'M TELLIN' YOU!
HOW COME I HAFTO WORRY ABOUT LOOKING OLD & BEING IMMATURE AT THE SAME TIME?
MY MOTHER'S VOICE IS WAFTING OUT ONTO THIS BEAUTIFUL STREET.
BUT WHO CARES?! SHE'S ON THE OTHER SIDE OF THE OCEAN!!...
SHE CAN'T RUIN THIS SUMMER EVEN THO SHE'D LOVE TO... THIS IS THE BEST SUMMER I'VE HAD SINCE 1959...
FLASHBACK 29 YEARS AGO:
MOMMY CAN'T I PLEASE GO TO ART CAMP WITH MY BEST FRIEND STEPHANIE KARASICK??
NO DAHLING! FOR YOUR OWN GOOD I'M SENDING YOU TO SLIM-FAST REDUCING CAMP.
YOU'LL THANK ME FOR THIS LATER!
NOT AT ALL OVERWEIGHT
BUT MOMMY... I WANNA BE AN AHTIST LIKE MATISSE!
YEA BUT YOU DON'T WANT TO BE A FAT, UNPOPULAR AHTIST, DO YOU??
NO?!
YOU C'N DO AHT IN YOUR FREE TIME AT CAMP... IT'S A GOOD HOBBY FOR YOU DEAH!
BUT YOU'RE GONNA LEARN ABOUT CALORIES THE IMPORTANT STUFF.

*MY MOTHER NEVER CALLS ME BY MY NAME.... INSTEAD ITS THIS LONG DRAWN OUT "A" SOUND WITH A SLIGHT QUESTION.

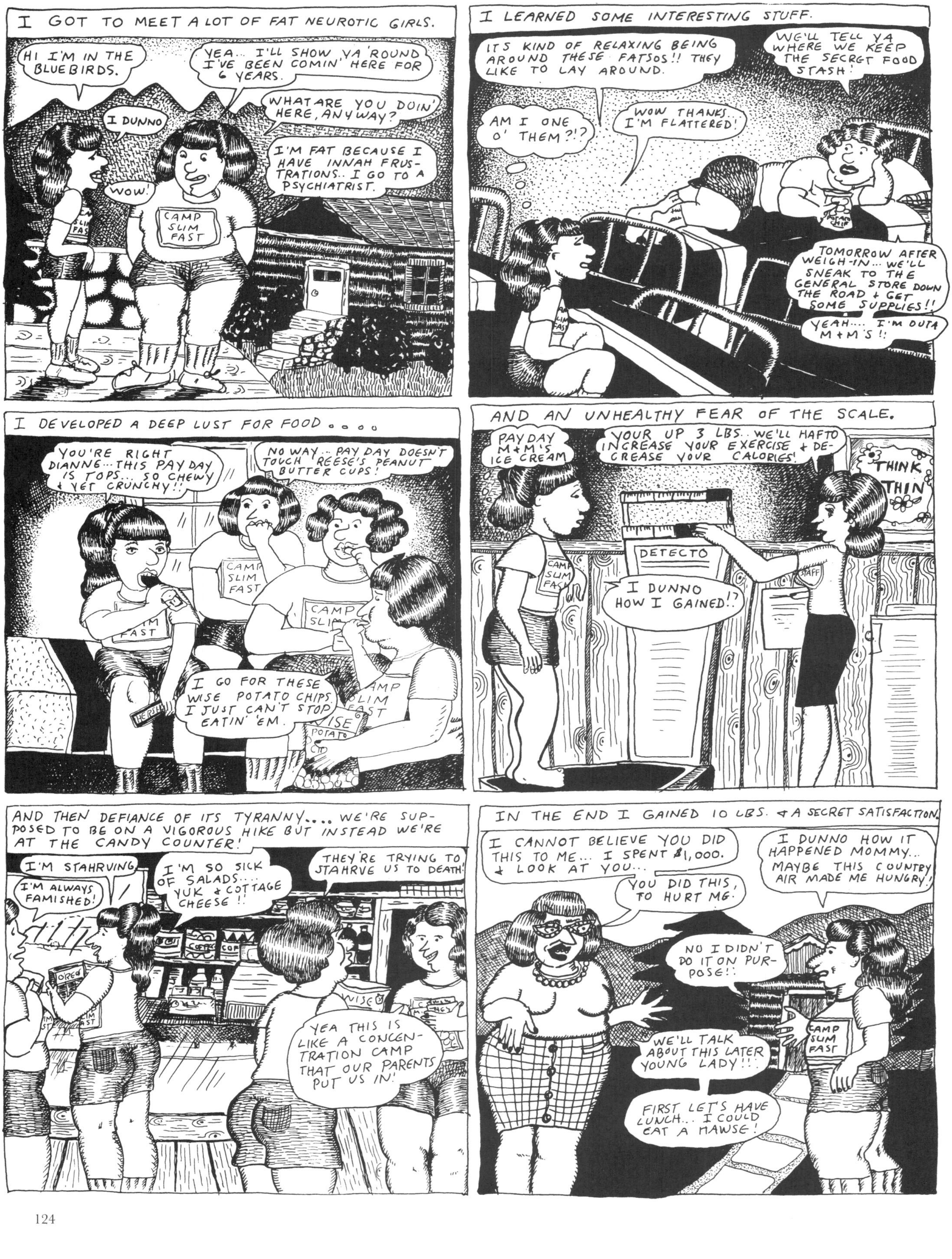
I GOT TO MEET A LOT OF FAT NEUROTIC GIRLS.
HI I'M IN THE BLUEBIRDS.
YEA.. I'LL SHOW YA 'ROUND I'VE BEEN COMIN' HERE FOR 6 YEARS.
I DUNNO
WHATARE YOU DOIN' HERE, ANYWAY?
I'M FAT BECAUSE I HAVE INNAH FRUSTRATIONS.. I GO TO A PSYCHIATRIST.
WOW!
CAMP SLIM FAST
I LEARNED SOME INTERESTING STUFF.
ITS KIND OF RELAXING BEING AROUND THESE FATSOS!! THEY LIKE TO LAY AROUND.
WE'LL TELL YA WHERE WE KEEP THE SECRET FOOD STASH!
AM I ONE O' THEM?!?
WOW THANKS. I'M FLATTERED!
TOMORROW AFTER WEIGH-IN... WE'LL SNEAK TO THE GENERAL STORE DOWN THE ROAD & GET SOME SUPPLIES!!
YEAH.... I'M OUTA M+M'S!!
I DEVELOPED A DEEP LUST FOR FOOD....
YOU'RE RIGHT DIANNE...THIS PAYDAY IS TOPS... SO CHEWY & YET CRUNCHY!!
NO WAY... PAY DAY DOESN'T TOUCH REESE'S PEANUT BUTTER CUPS!
CAMP SLIM FAST
I GO FOR THESE WISE POTATO CHIPS. I JUST CAN'T STOP EATIN' 'EM.
AND AN UNHEALTHY FEAR OF THE SCALE.
PAYDAY M+M'S ICE CREAM
YOUR UP 3 LBS. WE'LL HAFTO INCREASE YOUR EXERCISE & DECREASE YOUR CALORIES!
THINK THIN
DETECTO
I DUNNO HOW I GAINED!?
AND THEN DEFIANCE OF ITS TYRANNY.... WE'RE SUPPOSED TO BE ON A VIGOROUS HIKE BUT INSTEAD WE'RE AT THE CANDY COUNTER!
I'M STAHRVING
I'M ALWAYS FAMISHED!
I'M SO SICK OF SALADS.... YUK & COTTAGE CHEESE!!
THEY'RE TRYING TO STAHRVE US TO DEATH!
YEA THIS IS LIKE A CONCENTRATION CAMP THAT OUR PARENTS PUT US IN!
IN THE END I GAINED 10 LBS. & A SECRET SATISFACTION.
I CANNOT BELIEVE YOU DID THIS TO ME... I SPENT $1,000. & LOOK AT YOU...
YOU DID THIS TO HURT ME.
I DUNNO HOW IT HAPPENED MOMMY... MAYBE THIS COUNTRY AIR MADE ME HUNGRY!
NO I DIDN'T DO IT ON PURPOSE!
WE'LL TALK ABOUT THIS LATER YOUNG LADY!!
CAMP SLIM FAST
FIRST LET'S HAVE LUNCH... I COULD EAT A HAWSE!

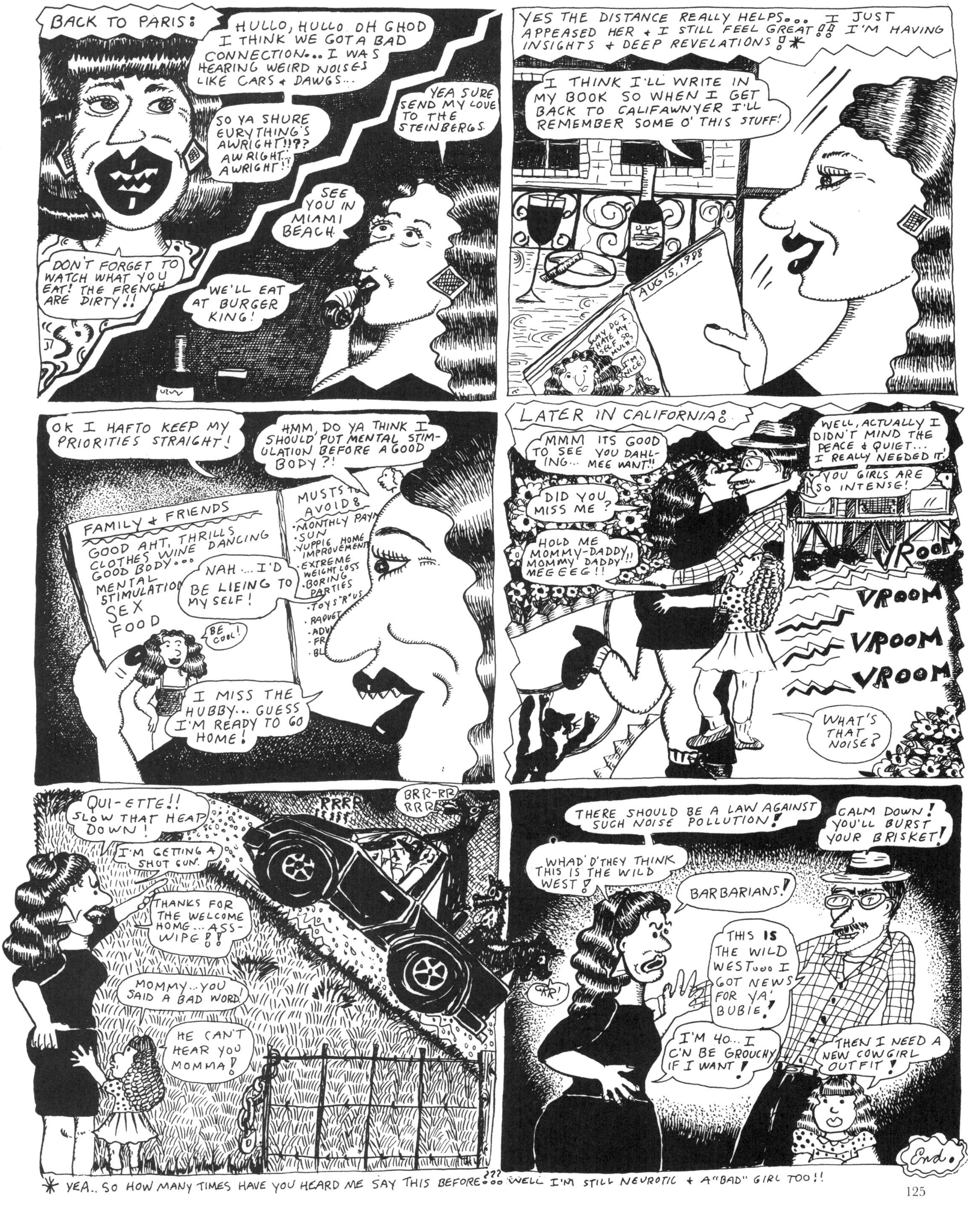
BACK TO PARIS:
HULLO, HULLO OH GHOD I THINK WE GOT A BAD CONNECTION... I WAS HEARING WEIRD NOISES LIKE CARS & DAWGS...
SO YA SHURE EVRYTHING'S AWRIGHT!!?? AWRIGHT... AWRIGHT!!
YEA SURE SEND MY LOVE TO THE STEINBERGS.
SEE YOU IN MIAMI BEACH.
DON'T FORGET TO WATCH WHAT YOU EAT! THE FRENCH ARE DIRTY!!
WE'LL EAT AT BURGER KING!
YES THE DISTANCE REALLY HELPS... I JUST APPEASED HER & I STILL FEEL GREAT!! I'M HAVING INSIGHTS & DEEP REVELATIONS!*
I THINK I'LL WRITE IN MY BOOK SO WHEN I GET BACK TO CALIFAWNYER I'LL REMEMBER SOME O' THIS STUFF!
AUG 15, 1988
WHY DO I HATE MY SELF SO MUCH?
I'M NICE!
OK I HAFTO KEEP MY PRIORITIES STRAIGHT!
HMM, DO YA THINK I SHOULD PUT MENTAL STIMULATION BEFORE A GOOD BODY?!
FAMILY & FRIENDS
GOOD AHT, THRILLS CLOTHES WINE DANCING GOOD BODY... MENTAL STIMULATION SEX FOOD
MUSTS TO AVOID:
MONTHLY PAY
SUN
YUPPIE HOME IMPROVEMENT
EXTREME WEIGHT LOSS
BORING PARTIES
TOYS "R" US
NAH... I'D BE LIEING TO MY SELF!
BE COOL!
I MISS THE HUBBY... GUESS I'M READY TO GO HOME!
LATER IN CALIFORNIA:
MMM ITS GOOD TO SEE YOU DAHLING... MEE WANT!!
WELL, ACTUALLY I DIDN'T MIND THE PEACE & QUIET... I REALLY NEEDED IT!
YOU GIRLS ARE SO INTENSE!
DID YOU MISS ME?
HOLD ME MOMMY-DADDY MOMMY DADDY!! MEEEEG!!
VROOM
VROOM
VROOM
VROOM
WHAT'S THAT NOISE?
QUI-ETTE!! SLOW THAT HEAP DOWN!
RRRR
BRR-RR RRR
I'M GETTING A SHOT GUN.
THANKS FOR THE WELCOME HOME... ASS-WIPE!!
MOMMY... YOU SAID A BAD WORD!
HE CAN'T HEAR YOU MOMMA!
THERE SHOULD BE A LAW AGAINST SUCH NOISE POLLUTION!
CALM DOWN! YOU'LL BURST YOUR BRISKET!
WHAD'D'THEY THINK THIS IS THE WILD WEST!
BARBARIANS!
THIS IS THE WILD WEST... I GOT NEWS FOR YA' BUBIE!
GRR!
I'M 40... I C'N BE GROUCHY IF I WANT!
THEN I NEED A NEW COWGIRL OUTFIT!
End.

* YEA.. SO HOW MANY TIMES HAVE YOU HEARD ME SAY THIS BEFORE???... WELL I'M STILL NEUROTIC & A "BAD" GIRL TOO!!

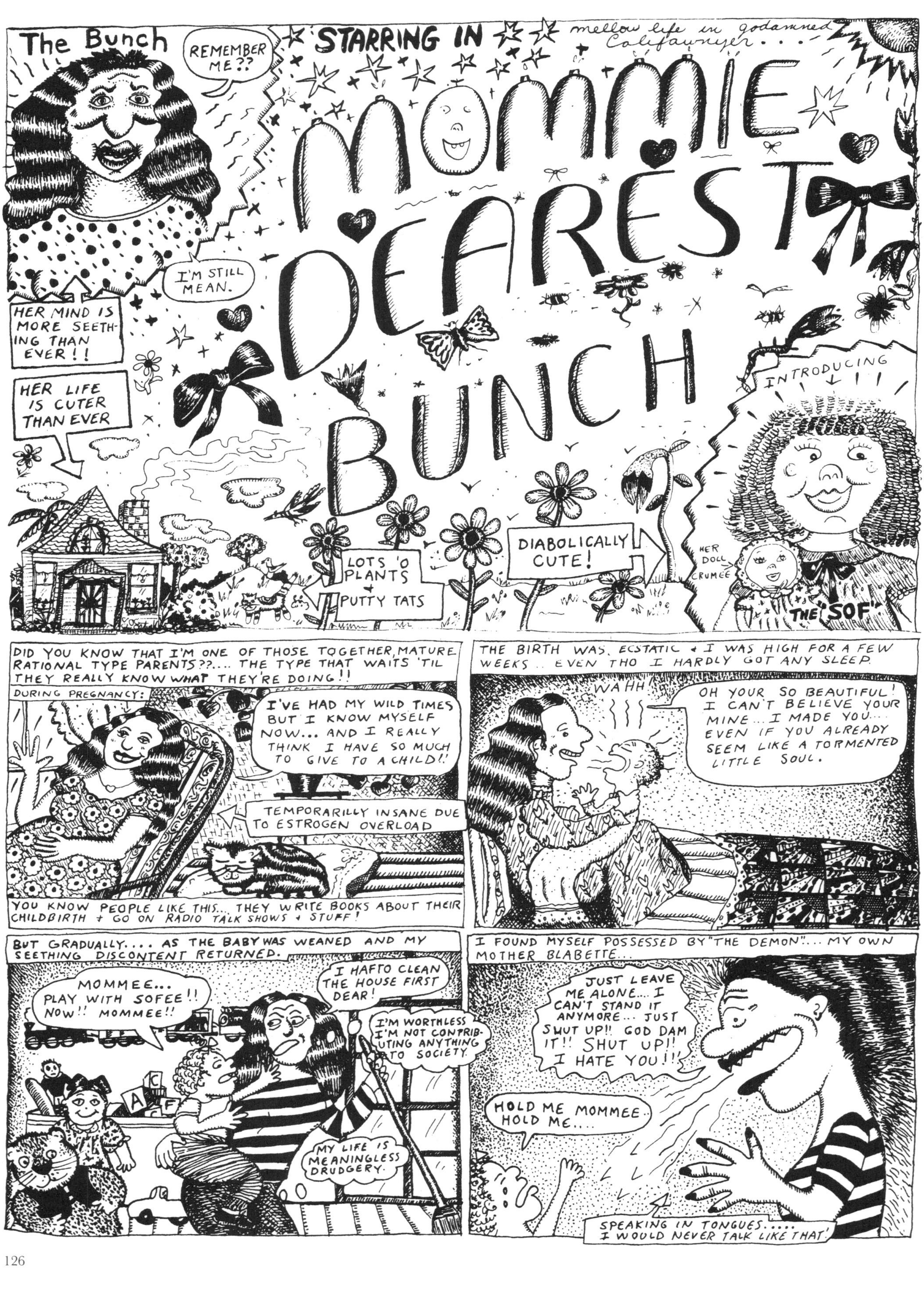
The Bunch
REMEMBER ME??
STARRING IN
mellow life in godamned Califaunyer...
MOMMIE DEAREST BUNCH
I'M STILL MEAN.
HER MIND IS MORE SEETHING THAN EVER!!
HER LIFE IS CUTER THAN EVER
LOTS 'O PLANTS + PUTTY TATS
DIABOLICALLY CUTE!
INTRODUCING
HER DOLL CRUMEE
THE "SOF"
DID YOU KNOW THAT I'M ONE OF THOSE TOGETHER, MATURE RATIONAL TYPE PARENTS??... THE TYPE THAT WAITS 'TIL THEY REALLY KNOW WHAT THEY'RE DOING!!
DURING PREGNANCY:
I'VE HAD MY WILD TIMES BUT I KNOW MYSELF NOW... AND I REALLY THINK I HAVE SO MUCH TO GIVE TO A CHILD!
TEMPORARILLY INSANE DUE TO ESTROGEN OVERLOAD
YOU KNOW PEOPLE LIKE THIS... THEY WRITE BOOKS ABOUT THEIR CHILDBIRTH + GO ON RADIO TALK SHOWS + STUFF!
THE BIRTH WAS ECSTATIC + I WAS HIGH FOR A FEW WEEKS.. EVEN THO I HARDLY GOT ANY SLEEP.
WAHH
OH YOUR SO BEAUTIFUL! I CAN'T BELIEVE YOUR MINE... I MADE YOU... EVEN IF YOU ALREADY SEEM LIKE A TORMENTED LITTLE SOUL.
BUT GRADUALLY.... AS THE BABY WAS WEANED AND MY SEETHING DISCONTENT RETURNED.
MOMMEE... PLAY WITH SOFEE!! NOW!! MOMMEE!!
I HAFTO CLEAN THE HOUSE FIRST DEAR!
I'M WORTHLESS I'M NOT CONTRIBUTING ANYTHING TO SOCIETY.
MY LIFE IS MEANINGLESS DRUDGERY.
I FOUND MYSELF POSSESSED BY "THE DEMON"... MY OWN MOTHER BLABETTE...
JUST LEAVE ME ALONE... I CAN'T STAND IT ANYMORE... JUST SHUT UP!! GOD DAM IT!! SHUT UP!! I HATE YOU!!
HOLD ME MOMMEE.. HOLD ME...
SPEAKING IN TONGUES..... I WOULD NEVER TALK LIKE THAT!

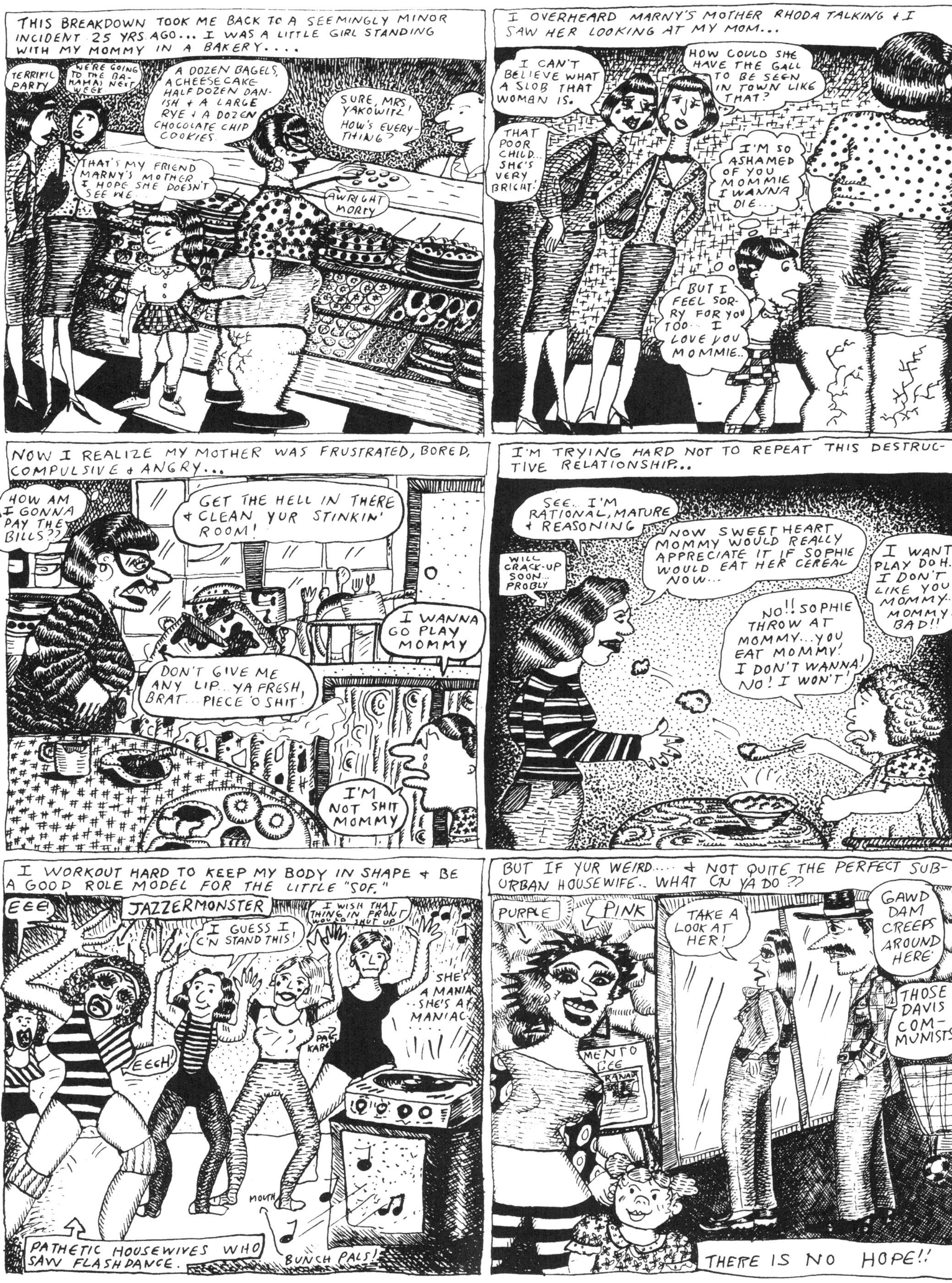
THIS BREAKDOWN TOOK ME BACK TO A SEEMINGLY MINOR INCIDENT 25 YRS AGO... I WAS A LITTLE GIRL STANDING WITH MY MOMMY IN A BAKERY....
TERRIFIC PARTY
WE'RE GOING TO THE BAHAMAS NEXT WEEK
A DOZEN BAGELS, A CHEESECAKE HALF DOZEN DANISH & A LARGE RYE & A DOZEN CHOCOLATE CHIP COOKIES
SURE, MRS. YAKOWITZ! HOW'S EVERYTHING?
THAT'S MY FRIEND MARNY'S MOTHER I HOPE SHE DOESN'T SEE ME
AWRIGHT MORTY
I OVERHEARD MARNY'S MOTHER RHODA TALKING & I SAW HER LOOKING AT MY MOM...
I CAN'T BELIEVE WHAT A SLOB THAT WOMAN IS.
HOW COULD SHE HAVE THE GALL TO BE SEEN IN TOWN LIKE THAT?
THAT POOR CHILD.. SHE'S VERY BRIGHT.
I'M SO ASHAMED OF YOU MOMMIE I WANNA DIE...
BUT I FEEL SORRY FOR YOU TOO... I LOVE YOU MOMMIE..
NOW I REALIZE MY MOTHER WAS FRUSTRATED, BORED, COMPULSIVE & ANGRY...
HOW AM I GONNA PAY THE BILLS??
GET THE HELL IN THERE & CLEAN YUR STINKIN' ROOM!
I WANNA GO PLAY MOMMY
DON'T GIVE ME ANY LIP.. YA FRESH, BRAT... PIECE 'O SHIT!
I'M NOT SHIT MOMMY
I'M TRYING HARD NOT TO REPEAT THIS DESTRUCTIVE RELATIONSHIP..
SEE.. I'M RATIONAL, MATURE & REASONING
WILL CRACK-UP SOON... PROBLY
NOW SWEETHEART MOMMY WOULD REALLY APPRECIATE IT IF SOPHIE WOULD EAT HER CEREAL NOW...
I WANT PLAY DOH.. I DON'T LIKE YOU MOMMY... MOMMY'S BAD!!
NO!! SOPHIE THROW AT MOMMY...YOU EAT MOMMY! I DON'T WANNA! NO! I WON'T!
I WORKOUT HARD TO KEEP MY BODY IN SHAPE & BE A GOOD ROLE MODEL FOR THE LITTLE "SOF."
EEE
JAZZERMONSTER
I GUESS I C'N STAND THIS!
I WISH THAT THING IN FRONT WOULD SHUT UP
SHE'S A MANIAC ..SHE'S A MANIAC
EECH
PAC KARS
MOUTH
PATHETIC HOUSEWIVES WHO SAW FLASHDANCE.
BUNCH PALS!
BUT IF YUR WEIRD.... & NOT QUITE THE PERFECT SUBURBAN HOUSEWIFE.. WHAT C'N YA DO??
PURPLE
PINK
TAKE A LOOK AT HER!
GAWD DAM CREEPS AROUND HERE
THOSE DAVIS COMMUNISTS
MENTO
THERE IS NO HOPE!!

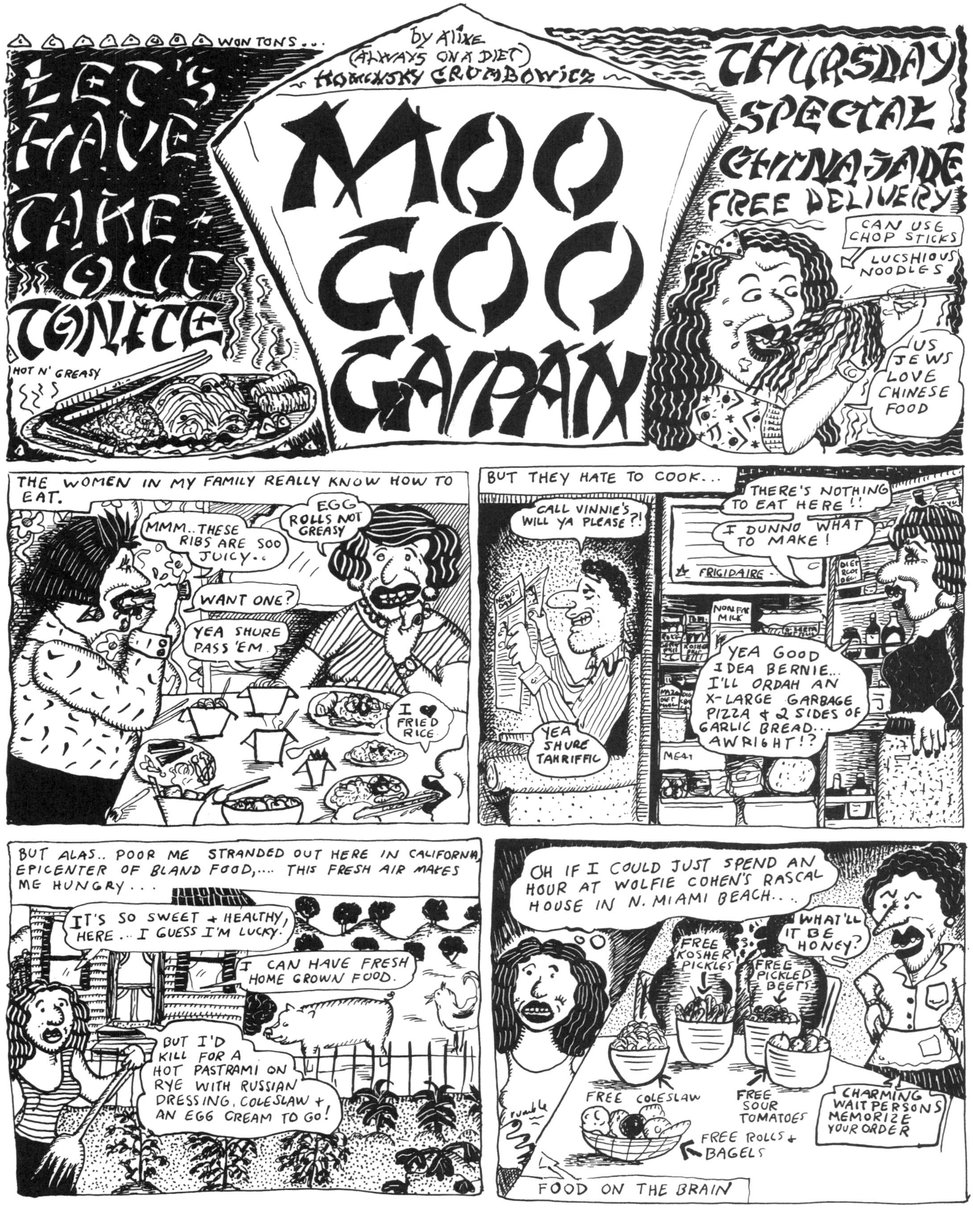
WON TONS...
LET'S HAVE TAKE OUT TONITE
HOT N' GREASY
By Aline (ALWAYS ON A DIET) KOMINSKY CRUMBOWICZ
MOO GOO GAIPAN
THURSDAY SPECIAL
CHINA JADE FREE DELIVERY
CAN USE CHOP STICKS
LUCSHIOUS NOODLES
US JEWS LOVE CHINESE FOOD
THE WOMEN IN MY FAMILY REALLY KNOW HOW TO EAT.
MMM.. THESE RIBS ARE SOO JUICY..
EGG ROLLS NOT GREASY
WANT ONE?
YEA SHURE PASS 'EM.
I ♥ FRIED RICE.
BUT THEY HATE TO COOK...
CALL VINNIE'S WILL YA PLEASE?!
THERE'S NOTHING TO EAT HERE!!
I DUNNO WHAT TO MAKE!
FRIGIDAIRE
NON FAT MILK
YEA GOOD IDEA BERNIE... I'LL ORDAH AN X-LARGE GARBAGE PIZZA & 2 SIDES OF GARLIC BREAD... AWRIGHT!?
YEA SHURE TAHRIFFIC
MEAT
BUT ALAS.. POOR ME STRANDED OUT HERE IN CALIFORNIA, EPICENTER OF BLAND FOOD,.... THIS FRESH AIR MAKES ME HUNGRY...
IT'S SO SWEET + HEALTHY, HERE... I GUESS I'M LUCKY.
I CAN HAVE FRESH HOME GROWN FOOD.
BUT I'D KILL FOR A HOT PASTRAMI ON RYE WITH RUSSIAN DRESSING, COLESLAW + AN EGG CREAM TO GO!
OH IF I COULD JUST SPEND AN HOUR AT WOLFIE COHEN'S RASCAL HOUSE IN N. MIAMI BEACH...
WHAT'LL IT BE HONEY?
FREE KOSHER PICKLES
FREE PICKLED BEETS
FREE COLESLAW
FREE SOUR TOMATOES
CHARMING WAITPERSONS MEMORIZE YOUR ORDER
rumble
FREE ROLLS + BAGELS
FOOD ON THE BRAIN

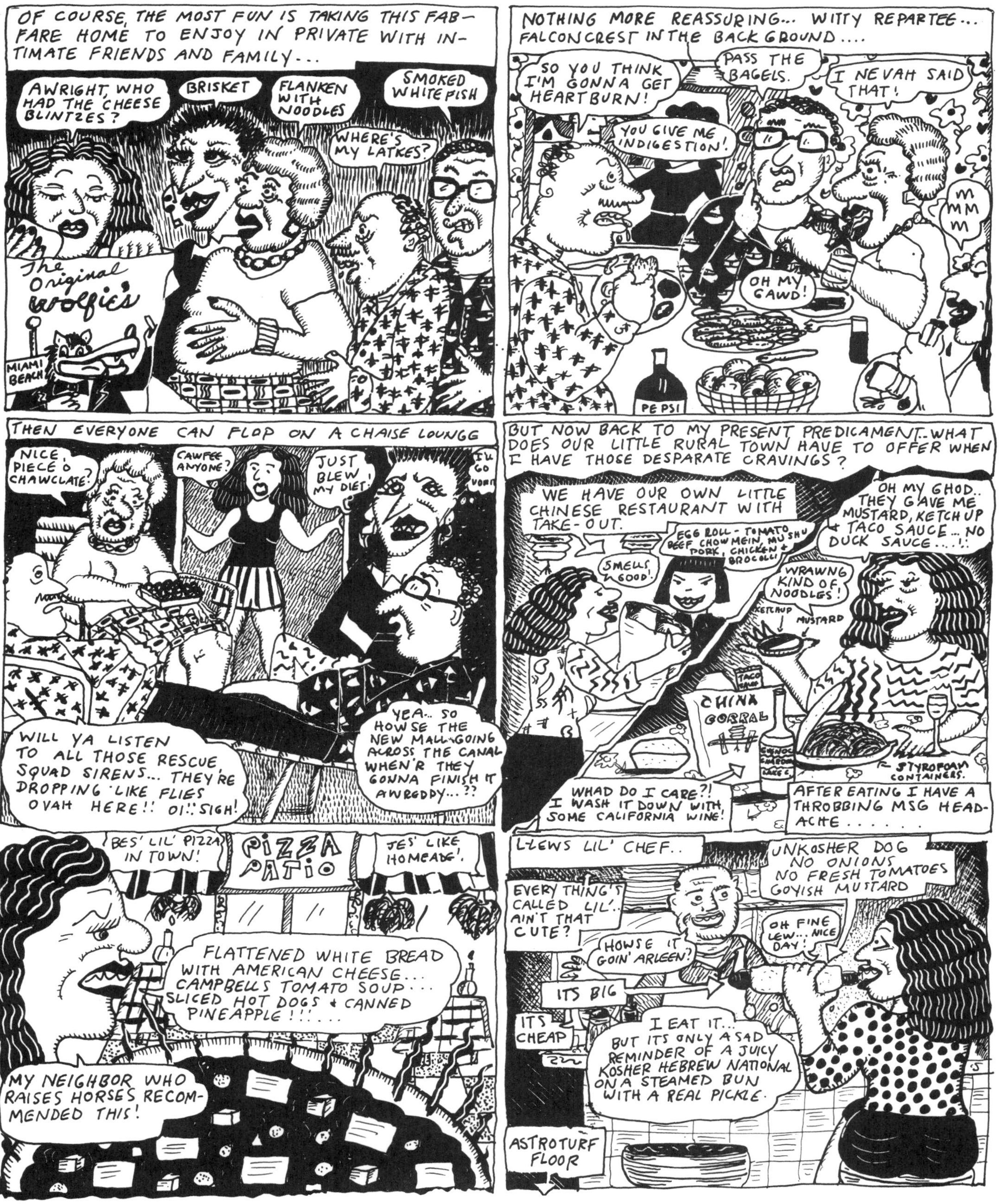

OF COURSE, THE MOST FUN IS TAKING THIS FAB-FARE HOME TO ENJOY IN PRIVATE WITH INTIMATE FRIENDS AND FAMILY...
AWRIGHT, WHO HAD THE CHEESE BLINTZES?
BRISKET
FLANKEN WITH NOODLES
SMOKED WHITEFISH
WHERE'S MY LATKES?
The Original Wolfie's
MIAMI BEACH
NOTHING MORE REASSURING... WITTY REPARTEE... FALCONCREST IN THE BACKGROUND....
SO YOU THINK I'M GONNA GET HEARTBURN!
PASS THE BAGELS.
I NEVAH SAID THAT!
YOU GIVE ME INDIGESTION!
MMMM
OH MY GAWD!
PEPSI
THEN EVERYONE CAN FLOP ON A CHAISE LOUNGE
NICE PIECE O CHAWCLATE?
CAWFEE ANYONE?
JUST BLEW MY DIET!
I'LL GO VOMIT
WILL YA LISTEN TO ALL THOSE RESCUE SQUAD SIRENS... THEY'RE DROPPING LIKE FLIES OVAH HERE!! OI!! SIGH!
YEA.. SO HOWSE THE NEW MALL GOING ACROSS THE CANAL WHEN'R THEY GONNA FINISH IT AWREDDY...??
BUT NOW BACK TO MY PRESENT PREDICAMENT.. WHAT DOES OUR LITTLE RURAL TOWN HAVE TO OFFER WHEN I HAVE THOSE DESPARATE CRAVINGS?
WE HAVE OUR OWN LITTLE CHINESE RESTAURANT WITH TAKE-OUT.
EGG ROLL - TOMATO BEEF CHOW MEIN, MU SHU PORK, CHICKEN & BROCOLLI
SMELLS GOOD!
OH MY GHOD.. THEY GAVE ME MUSTARD, KETCHUP & TACO SAUCE... NO DUCK SAUCE...!!
WRAWNG KIND OF NOODLES!
KETCHUP
MUSTARD
TACO SAUCE
CHINA CORRAL
STYROFOAM CONTAINERS.
WHAD DO I CARE?! I WASH IT DOWN WITH SOME CALIFORNIA WINE!
AFTER EATING I HAVE A THROBBING MSG HEADACHE.....
BES' LIL' PIZZA IN TOWN!
PIZZA PATIO
JES' LIKE HOMEADE!
FLATTENED WHITE BREAD WITH AMERICAN CHEESE... CAMPBELLS TOMATO SOUP... SLICED HOT DOGS & CANNED PINEAPPLE!!!....
MY NEIGHBOR WHO RAISES HORSES RECOMMENDED THIS!
LLEWS LIL' CHEF..
UNKOSHER DOG NO ONIONS NO FRESH TOMATOES GOYISH MUSTARD
EVERYTHING'S CALLED LIL'.. AIN'T THAT CUTE?
HOWSE IT GOIN' ARLEEN?
OH FINE LEW... NICE DAY!
ITS BIG
ITS CHEAP
I EAT IT... BUT ITS ONLY A SAD REMINDER OF A JUICY KOSHER HEBREW NATIONAL ON A STEAMED BUN WITH A REAL PICKLE.
ASTROTURF FLOOR

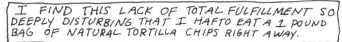

I FIND THIS LACK OF TOTAL FULFILLMENT SO DEEPLY DISTURBING THAT I HAFTO EAT A 1 POUND BAG OF NATURAL TORTILLA CHIPS RIGHT AWAY.

SO DO YOU FIND YURSELF ASKING... IF SHE'S SO MISERABLE WHY DOES SHE STAY IN SUCH A CULTURAL DESERT?? SHE'S AN AHTIST SHE COULD LIVE IN PARIS FOR GOD SAKE!!

NOW I'M A BLOATED FEEDBAG FROM ALL THIS SALT & GREASE...

MAYBE I'M JUST COMFORTABLE WITH MY ALIENATION

PERHAPS I JUST LOVE TO COMPLAIN?!

VERY NEGATIVE BEHAVIOR PATTERN... BUT IF IT WORKS??

MAYBE I SHOULD LEAVE FOR AWHIE.. A TRIP EAST BACK TO MY ETHNIC ROOTS!

SO INSTEAD OF FRUITLESS FANTASIES I GO DIRECTLY TO LONG ISLAND AND END UP AT MY COUSIN IRENE'S HOUSE..

WHAD'RE WE GONNA DO FUR DINNER

SO HOWSE THE HICKS OUT THERE IN CALIFAWNYA? WHADDYA THINK OF MY NEW KITCHEN?

WE'LL ORDAH TAKE-OUT HOW 'BOUT SUSHI?

NAH, ITS NOT FILLING.. I LIKE THAT NEW ETHIOPIAN THEY GIVE YA ALOT!

IT LOOKS GREAT.. THE FRIDGE IS YUGE...

HOW ABOUT DELI?

OI, WE'RE SICK O' DELI... WE HAD IT 4 TIMES LAST WEEK!

HOW 'BOUT THAT WESTUHN BAR-B-QUE. THEY GOT STEAK 'N CHILI, RIBS & MISQUITE GRILLES!! ITS THE LATEST THING!!

THEY GIVE YA ALOT TA' EAT... GOOD VALUE.. VERY FILLING!

ITS SOMETHING DIFFERENT FOR A CHANGE.

YOU'LL LIKE IT.. YA LOVE THAT WESTUHN LIFE DONCHA?!

THEY IGNORE ME... THEY'RE TOO USED TO OUT-ARGUEING EACH OTHER!

WELL I WOULDN'T MIND CHINESE OR EQUADORIAN OR ARMENIAN

AWRIGHT... QUIET AWREDDY.. I'M CALLING BUCKAROO BAR-B-QUE....

SO I HAVE A CHILI DOG THAT TASTES ALL WRONG BUT FOR TOTALLY DIFFERENT REASONS. IT TASTES TOO JEWISH!

THE DOG IS HIGH QUALITY KOSHER BUT THE CHILI IS TASTELESS LIKE MY GRAND-MOTHER'S ITALIAN FOOD... THIS IS KINDA LIKE KETCHUP & OVERCOOKED MEATLOAF WITH A FEW BAKED BEANS THROWNIN!

THIS HOT DOG GIVES ME DEEP INSIGHT.......

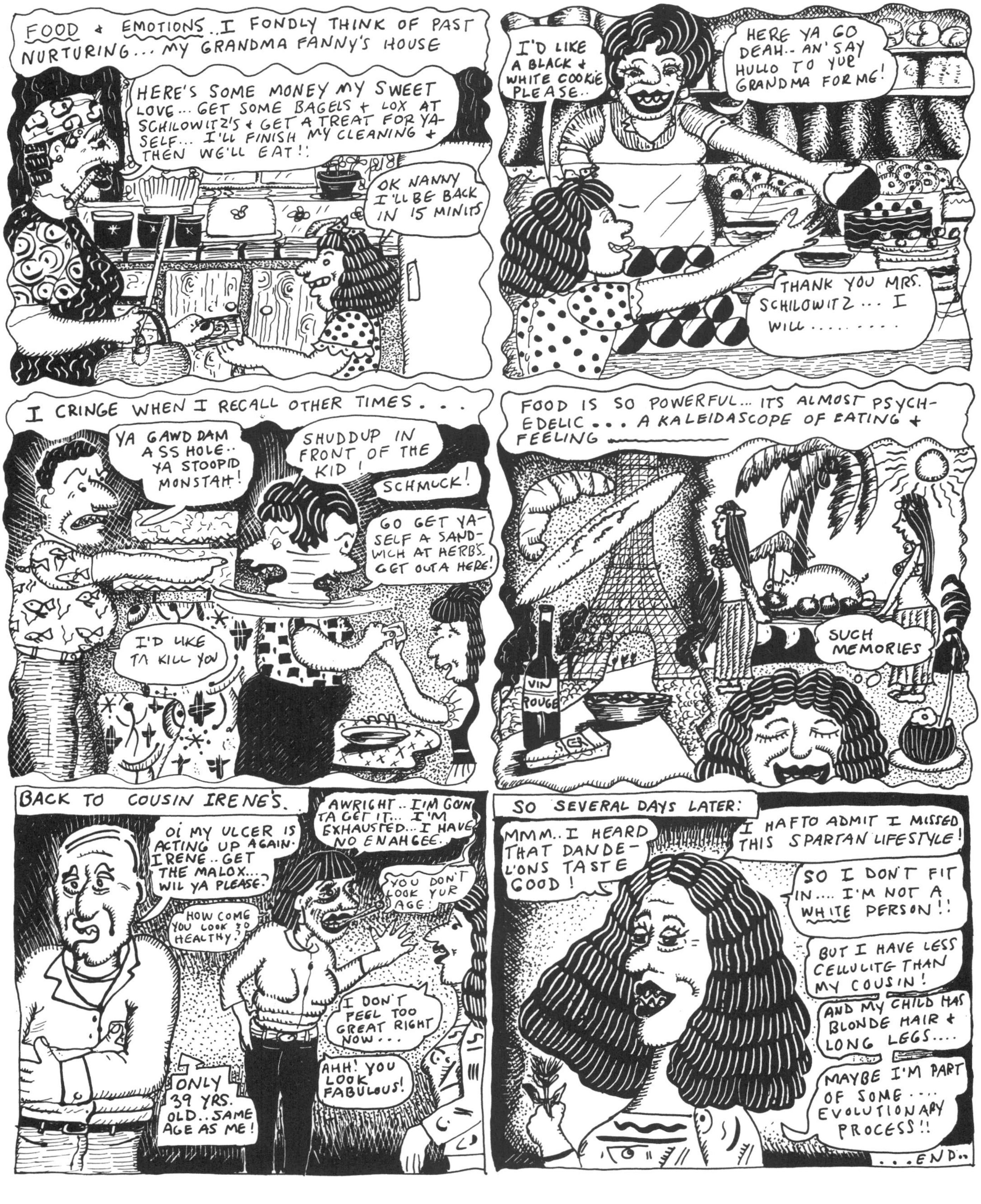
FOOD + EMOTIONS.. I FONDLY THINK OF PAST NURTURING... MY GRANDMA FANNY'S HOUSE
HERE'S SOME MONEY MY SWEET LOVE... GET SOME BAGELS + LOX AT SCHILOWITZ'S + GET A TREAT FOR YA-SELF... I'LL FINISH MY CLEANING + THEN WE'LL EAT!!
OK NANNY I'LL BE BACK IN 15 MINUTS
I'D LIKE A BLACK + WHITE COOKIE PLEASE..
HERE YA GO DEAH.. AN' SAY HULLO TO YUR GRANDMA FOR ME!
THANK YOU MRS. SCHILOWITZ... I WILL.........
I CRINGE WHEN I RECALL OTHER TIMES...
YA GAWD DAM ASSHOLE.. YA STOOPID MONSTAH!
SHUDDUP IN FRONT OF THE KID!
SCHMUCK!
GO GET YA-SELF A SAND-WICH AT HERB'S. GET OUTA HERE!
I'D LIKE TA KILL YOU
FOOD IS SO POWERFUL... ITS ALMOST PSYCH-EDELIC... A KALEIDASCOPE OF EATING + FEELING
VIN ROUGE
SUCH MEMORIES
BACK TO COUSIN IRENE'S.
OI MY ULCER IS ACTING UP AGAIN. IRENE.. GET THE MALOX... WIL YA PLEASE?
AWRIGHT.. I'M GOIN TA GET IT... I'M EXHAUSTED... I HAVE NO ENAHGEE.
YOU DON'T LOOK YUR AGE!
HOW COME YOU LOOK SO HEALTHY?
I DON'T FEEL TOO GREAT RIGHT NOW...
AHH! YOU LOOK FABULOUS!
ONLY 39 YRS. OLD.. SAME AGE AS ME!
SO SEVERAL DAYS LATER:
MMM.. I HEARD THAT DANDE-L'ONS TASTE GOOD!
I HAFTO ADMIT I MISSED THIS SPARTAN LIFESTYLE!
SO I DON'T FIT IN.... I'M NOT A WHITE PERSON!!
BUT I HAVE LESS CELLULITE THAN MY COUSIN!
AND MY CHILD HAS BLONDE HAIR + LONG LEGS....
MAYBE I'M PART OF SOME.... EVOLUTIONARY PROCESS!!
...END..

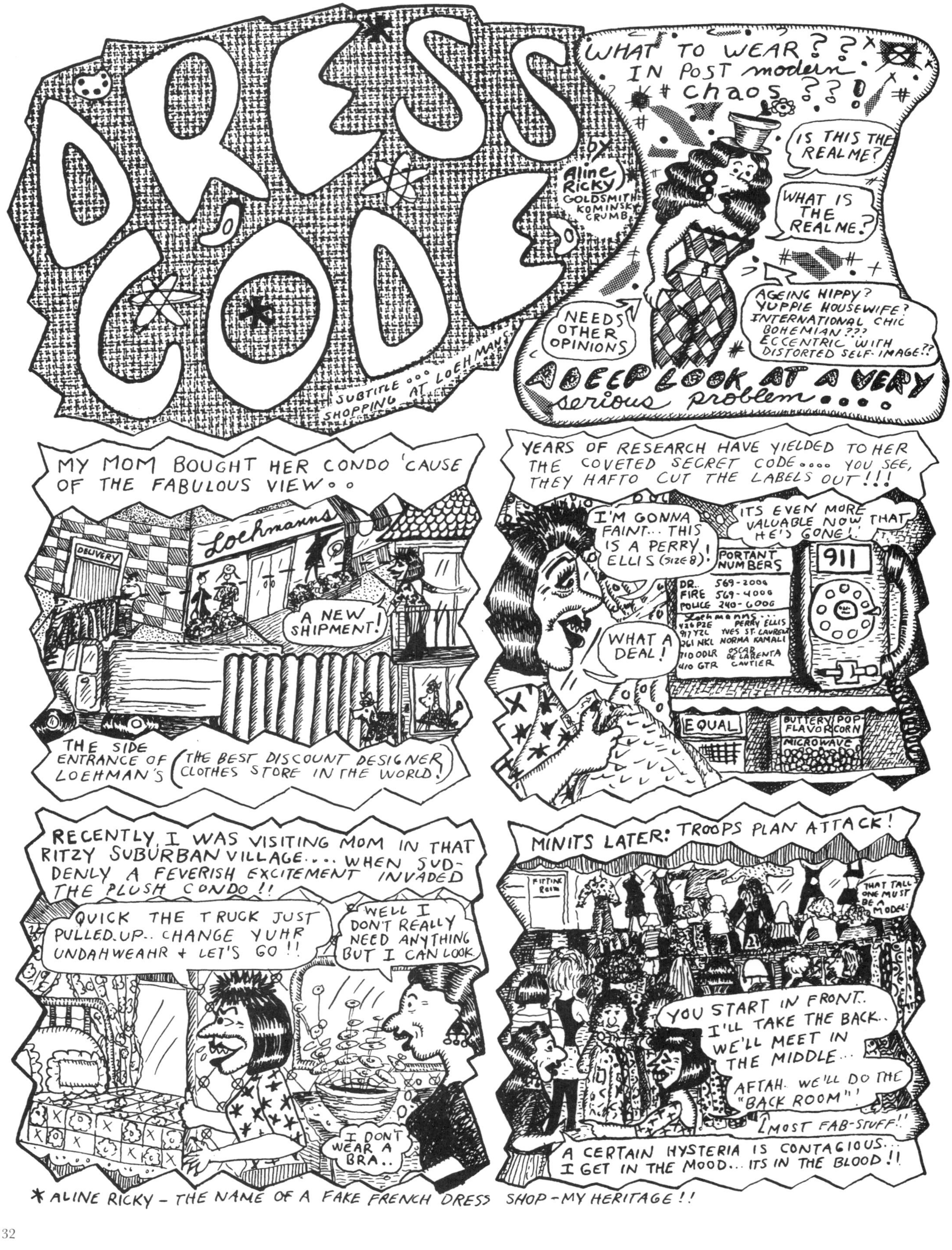
DRESS CODE*
BY Aline Ricky GOLDSMITH KOMINSKY CRUMB
SUBTITLE ... SHOPPING AT LOEHMANS
WHAT TO WEAR??? IN POST modern chaos???!
IS THIS THE REAL ME?
WHAT IS THE REAL ME?
NEEDS OTHER OPINIONS
AGEING HIPPY? YUPPIE HOUSEWIFE? INTERNATIONAL CHIC BOHEMIAN??? ECCENTRIC WITH DISTORTED SELF-IMAGE??
A DEEP LOOK AT A VERY serious problem....
MY MOM BOUGHT HER CONDO 'CAUSE OF THE FABULOUS VIEW..
Lochmanns
DELIVERY
A NEW SHIPMENT!
THE SIDE ENTRANCE OF LOEHMAN'S (THE BEST DISCOUNT DESIGNER CLOTHES STORE IN THE WORLD!)
YEARS OF RESEARCH HAVE YIELDED TO HER THE COVETED SECRET CODE.... YOU SEE, THEY HAFTO CUT THE LABELS OUT!!!
I'M GONNA FAINT... THIS IS A PERRY ELLIS (SIZE 8)!
ITS EVEN MORE VALUABLE NOW THAT HE'S GONE!
PORTANT NUMBERS
DR.. 569-2000
FIRE 569-4000
POLICE 240-6000
Loehmanns...
426 PZE PERRY ELLIS
917 YZL YVES ST. LAURENT
261 NKL NORMA KAMALI
710 ODLR OSCAR DE LARENTA
410 GTR GAUTIER
911
WHAT A DEAL!
EQUAL
BUTTERY FLAVOR POPCORN
MICROWAVE
RECENTLY I WAS VISITING MOM IN THAT RITZY SUBURBAN VILLAGE.... WHEN SUDDENLY A FEVERISH EXCITEMENT INVADED THE PLUSH CONDO!!
QUICK THE TRUCK JUST PULLED UP.. CHANGE YUHR UNDAHWEAHR + LET'S GO!!
WELL I DON'T REALLY NEED ANYTHING BUT I CAN LOOK.
I DONT WEAR A BRA..
MINITS LATER: TROOPS PLAN ATTACK!
FITTING ROOM
THAT TALL ONE MUST BE A MODEL!
YOU START IN FRONT.. I'LL TAKE THE BACK.. WE'LL MEET IN THE MIDDLE...
AFTAH.. WE'LL DO THE "BACK ROOM"!
(MOST FAB-STUFF!!
A CERTAIN HYSTERIA IS CONTAGIOUS... I GET IN THE MOOD... ITS IN THE BLOOD!!

* ALINE RICKY - THE NAME OF A FAKE FRENCH DRESS SHOP - MY HERITAGE!!

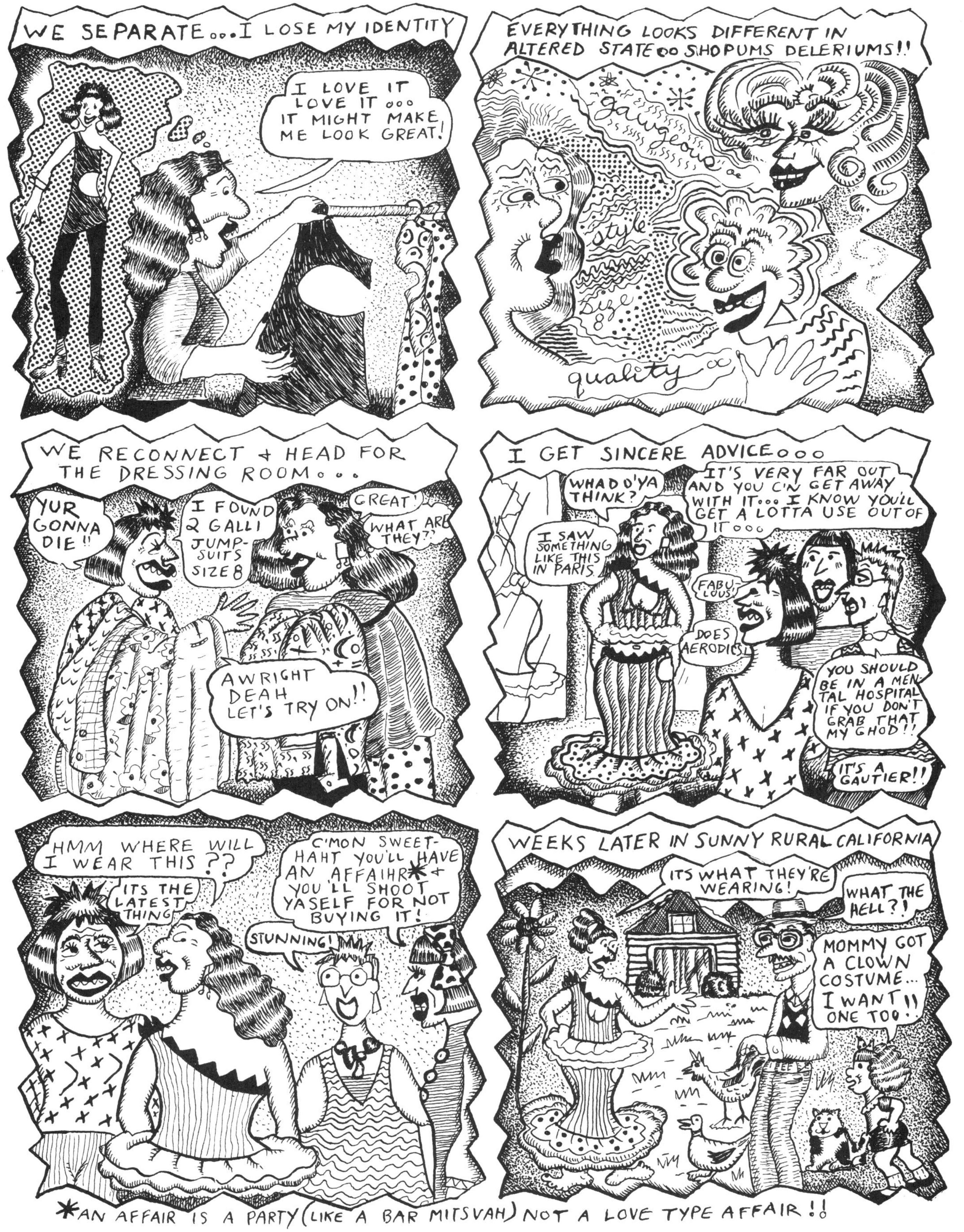
WE SEPARATE... I LOSE MY IDENTITY
I LOVE IT LOVE IT... IT MIGHT MAKE ME LOOK GREAT!
EVERYTHING LOOKS DIFFERENT IN ALTERED STATE.. SHOPUMS DELERIUMS!!
gaugeous
style
size 8
quality
WE RECONNECT + HEAD FOR THE DRESSING ROOM...
YUR GONNA DIE!!
I FOUND 2 GALLI JUMP-SUITS SIZE 8
GREAT!
WHAT ARE THEY??
AWRIGHT DEAH LET'S TRY ON!!
I GET SINCERE ADVICE...
WHAD D'YA THINK?
IT'S VERY FAR OUT AND YOU C'N GET AWAY WITH IT... I KNOW YOU'LL GET A LOTTA USE OUT OF IT...
I SAW SOMETHING LIKE THIS IN PARIS
FABULOUS!
DOES AERODICS!
YOU SHOULD BE IN A MENTAL HOSPITAL IF YOU DON'T GRAB THAT MY GHOD!!
IT'S A GAUTIER!!
HMM WHERE WILL I WEAR THIS??
ITS THE LATEST THING!
C'MON SWEET-HAHT YOU'LL HAVE AN AFFAIHR* + YOU'LL SHOOT YASELF FOR NOT BUYING IT!
STUNNING!
WEEKS LATER IN SUNNY RURAL CALIFORNIA
ITS WHAT THEY'RE WEARING!
WHAT THE HELL?!
MOMMY GOT A CLOWN COSTUME... I WANT ONE TOO!!
*AN AFFAIR IS A PARTY (LIKE A BAR MITSVAH) NOT A LOVE TYPE AFFAIR!!

Deep Thoughts
Do women who bake get more love?
From My Kitchen
MR. COFFEE
THIS IS ME.. I HAVE IT ALL!
MICROWAVES
SEXUAL FRUSTRATION
EXISTENTIAL ANGST
FEAR OF FALLEN SOUFFLETS
WEAK MATERNAL INSTINCT
CUTE 1930'S KNICK-KNACKS
LOW SELF ESTEEM
DESIRE TO TRAVEL..
MEMORIES...
I CAN ONLY THINK AT THE KITCHEN TABLE!
YES....
I WAS ONCE A WILD + CRAZY GIRL...
MMM
FEEL MY MUSCLE!
AND NOW MY SOUL HAS WITHERED...
EVERY-BODY LIKE'S ME NOW!
WANNA CUPPA CAWFEE?
YOU COULD EAT OFF MY BATHROOM FLOOR!
THIS IS MY LIFE...
SO YOU REALLY HAVE NO INTEREST IN SEX?
OH NO!
HOW MUCH WEIGHT HAVE YOU LOST?
90 lbs.

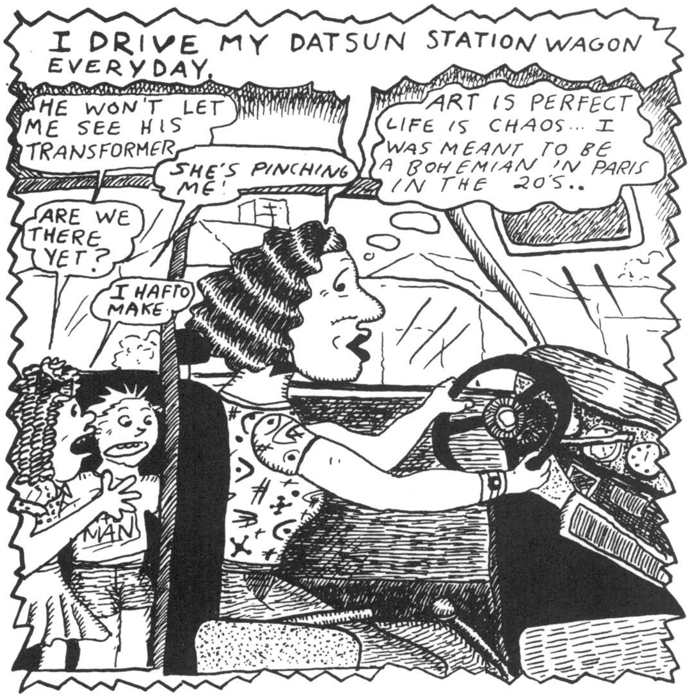

I DRIVE MY DATSUN STATION WAGON EVERYDAY.
HE WON'T LET ME SEE HIS TRANSFORMER
SHE'S PINCHING ME!
ARE WE THERE YET?
I HAFTO MAKE.
ART IS PERFECT LIFE IS CHAOS... I WAS MEANT TO BE A BOHEMIAN IN PARIS IN THE 20'S..
MAN

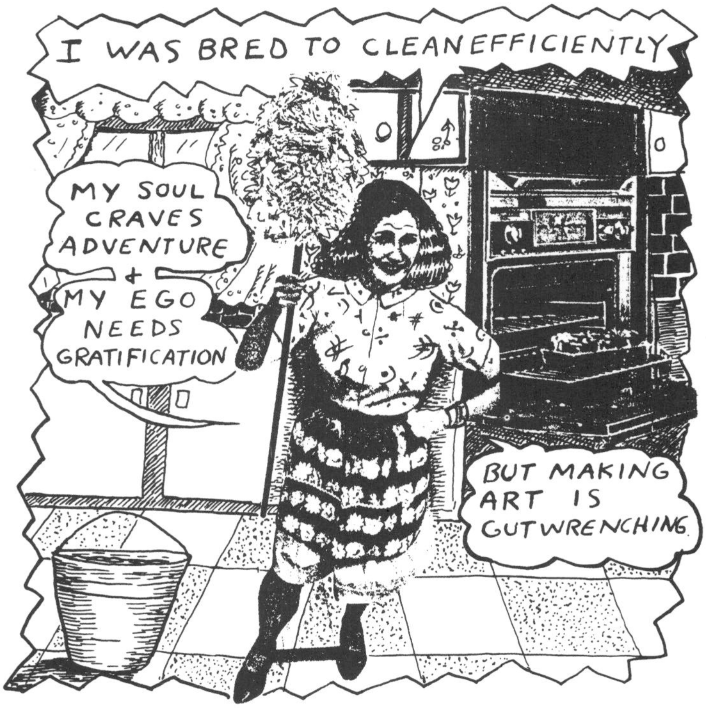

I WAS BRED TO CLEAN EFFICIENTLY
MY SOUL CRAVES ADVENTURE
&
MY EGO NEEDS GRATIFICATION
BUT MAKING ART IS GUTWRENCHING

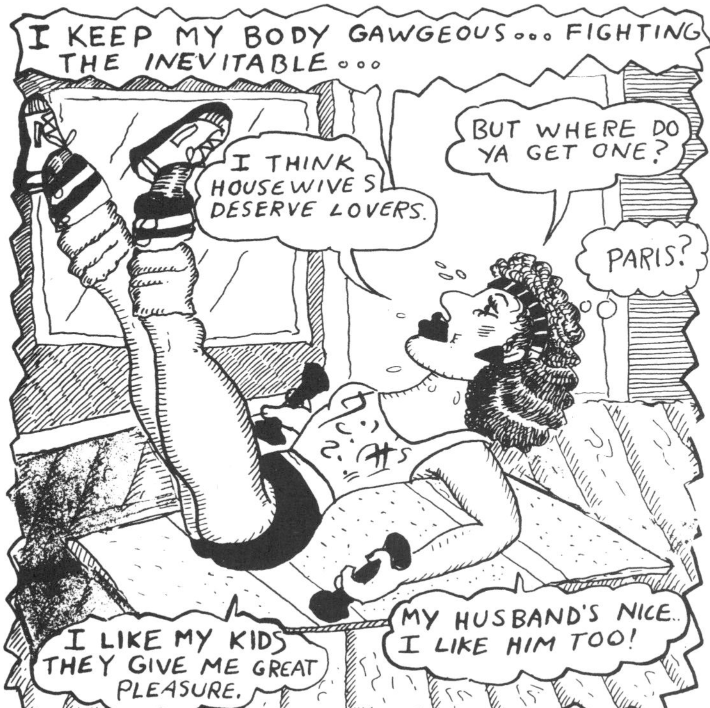

I KEEP MY BODY GAWGEOUS... FIGHTING THE INEVITABLE...
I THINK HOUSEWIVES DESERVE LOVERS.
BUT WHERE DO YA GET ONE?
PARIS?
I LIKE MY KIDS THEY GIVE ME GREAT PLEASURE.
MY HUSBAND'S NICE.. I LIKE HIM TOO!

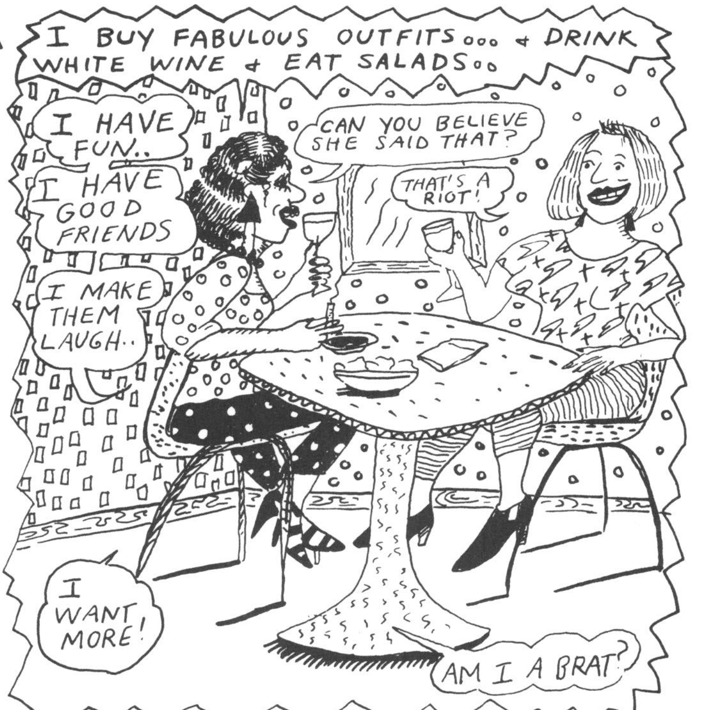

I BUY FABULOUS OUTFITS... & DRINK WHITE WINE & EAT SALADS..
I HAVE FUN..
I HAVE GOOD FRIENDS
I MAKE THEM LAUGH..
CAN YOU BELIEVE SHE SAID THAT?
THAT'S A RIOT!
I WANT MORE!
AM I A BRAT?

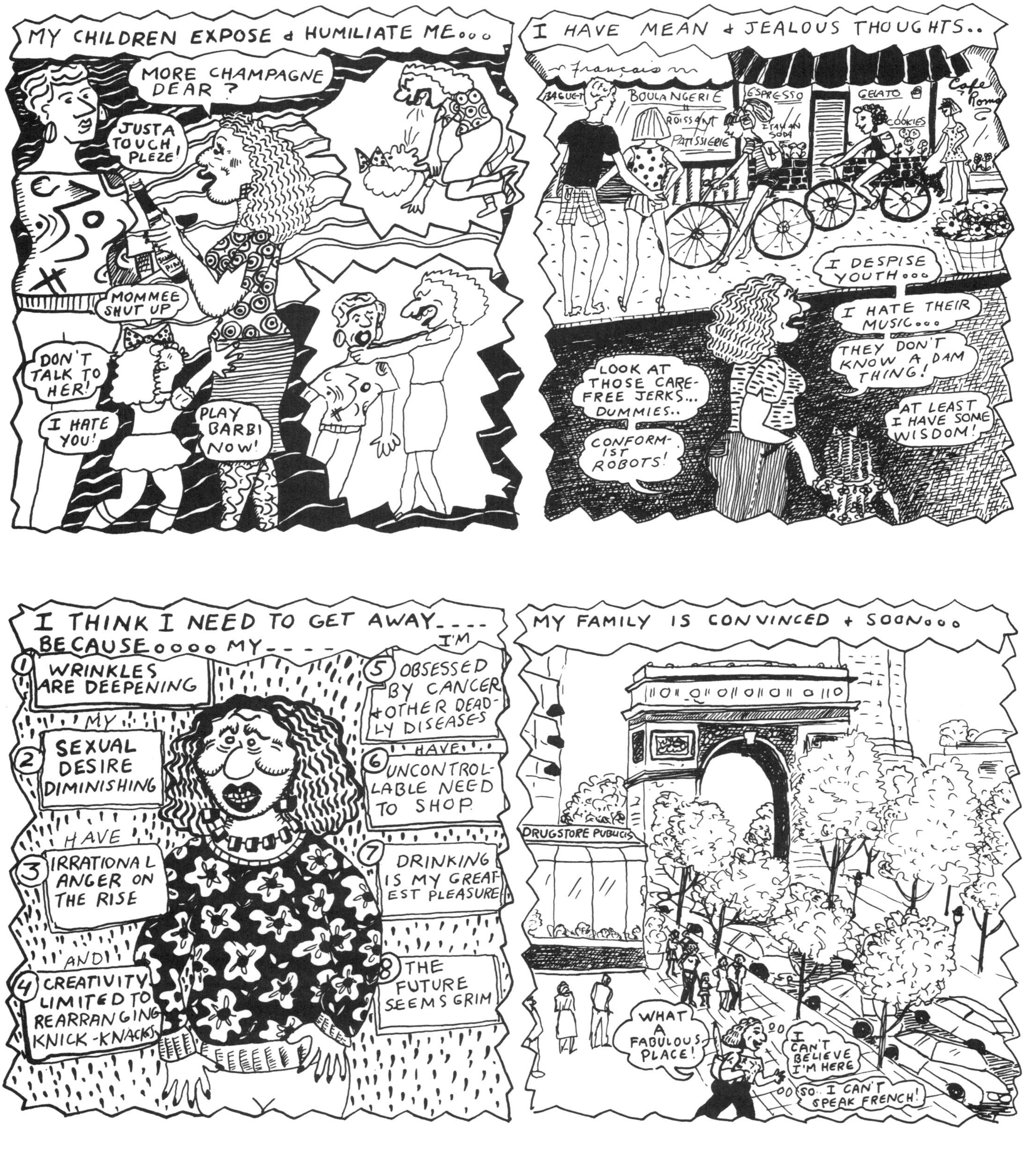

MY CHILDREN EXPOSE & HUMILIATE ME...
MORE CHAMPAGNE DEAR ?
JUSTA TOUCH PLEZE!
MOMMEE SHUT UP
DON'T TALK TO HER!
I HATE YOU!
PLAY BARBI NOW!
I HAVE MEAN & JEALOUS THOUGHTS..
BAGUET
BOULANGERIE
CROISSANT
PATISSERIE
ESPRESSO
ITALIAN SODA
GELATO
COOKIES
Cafe Roma
I DESPISE YOUTH...
I HATE THEIR MUSIC...
THEY DON'T KNOW A DAM THING!
LOOK AT THOSE CARE-FREE JERKS... DUMMIES..
CONFORM-IST ROBOTS!
AT LEAST I HAVE SOME WISDOM!
I THINK I NEED TO GET AWAY.... BECAUSE.... MY....
1 WRINKLES ARE DEEPENING
MY
2 SEXUAL DESIRE DIMINISHING
HAVE
3 IRRATIONAL ANGER ON THE RISE
AND
4 CREATIVITY LIMITED TO REARRANGING KNICK-KNACKS
I'M
5 OBSESSED BY CANCER + OTHER DEADLY DISEASES
HAVE
6 UNCONTROL-LABLE NEED TO SHOP
7 DRINKING IS MY GREAT-EST PLEASURE
8 THE FUTURE SEEMS GRIM
MY FAMILY IS CONVINCED + SOON...
DRUGSTORE PUBLICIS
WHAT A FABULOUS PLACE!
I CAN'T BELIEVE I'M HERE
SO.. I CAN'T SPEAK FRENCH!

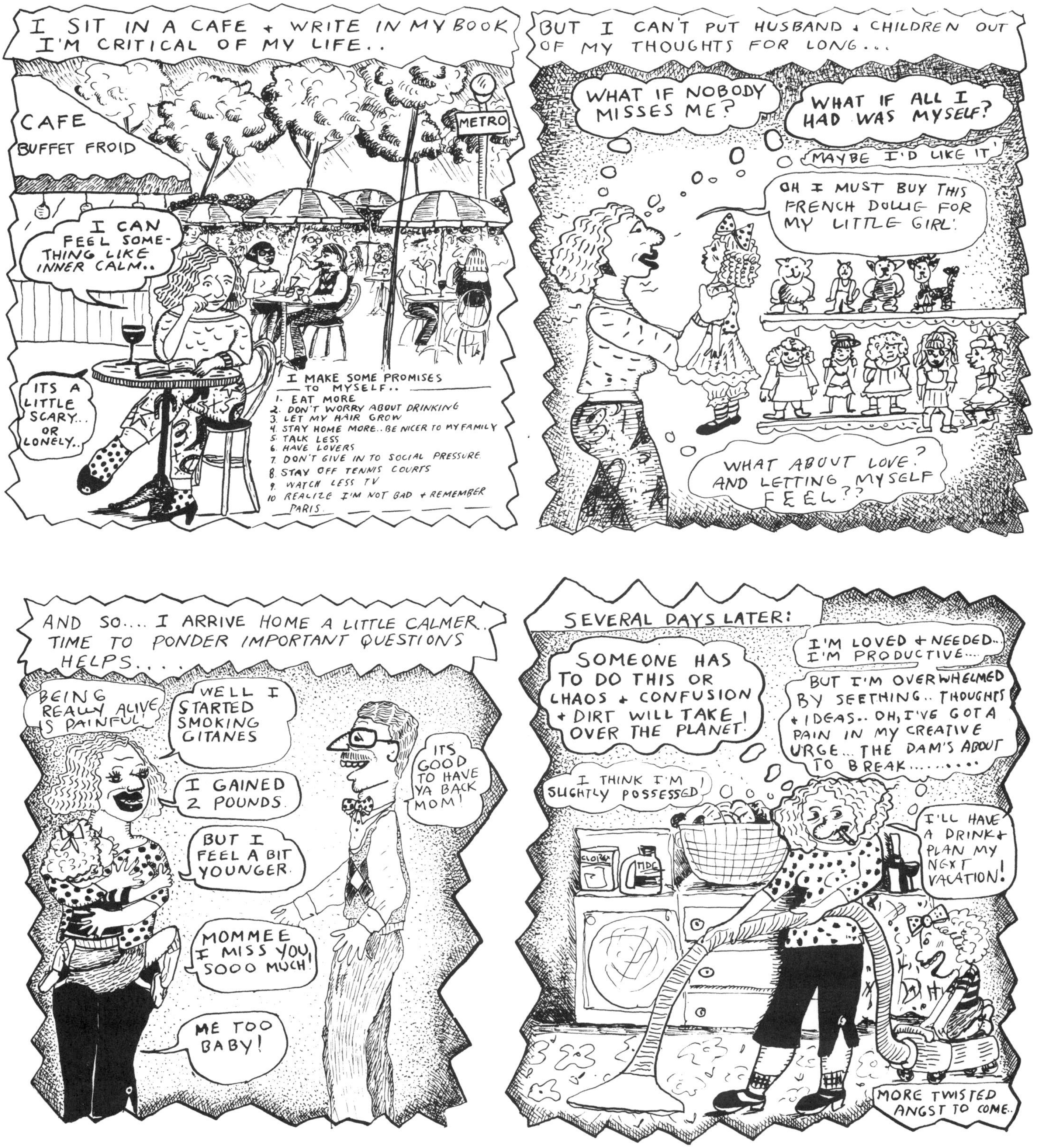
I SIT IN A CAFE + WRITE IN MY BOOK I'M CRITICAL OF MY LIFE..
CAFE
BUFFET FROID
METRO
I CAN FEEL SOMETHING LIKE INNER CALM..
ITS A LITTLE SCARY... OR LONELY..
I MAKE SOME PROMISES TO MYSELF..
1. EAT MORE
2. DON'T WORRY ABOUT DRINKING
3. LET MY HAIR GROW
4. STAY HOME MORE.. BE NICER TO MY FAMILY
5. TALK LESS
6. HAVE LOVERS
7. DON'T GIVE IN TO SOCIAL PRESSURE
8. STAY OFF TENNIS COURTS
9. WATCH LESS TV
10 REALIZE I'M NOT BAD + REMEMBER PARIS
BUT I CAN'T PUT HUSBAND + CHILDREN OUT OF MY THOUGHTS FOR LONG...
WHAT IF NOBODY MISSES ME?
WHAT IF ALL I HAD WAS MYSELF?
MAYBE I'D LIKE IT
OH I MUST BUY THIS FRENCH DOLLIE FOR MY LITTLE GIRL.
WHAT ABOUT LOVE? AND LETTING MYSELF FEEL??
AND SO.... I ARRIVE HOME A LITTLE CALMER. TIME TO PONDER IMPORTANT QUESTIONS HELPS....
BEING REALLY ALIVE IS PAINFUL!
WELL I STARTED SMOKING GITANES
I GAINED 2 POUNDS
BUT I FEEL A BIT YOUNGER
ITS GOOD TO HAVE YA BACK MOM!
MOMMEE I MISS YOU SOOO MUCH!
ME TOO BABY!
SEVERAL DAYS LATER:
SOMEONE HAS TO DO THIS OR CHAOS + CONFUSION + DIRT WILL TAKE OVER THE PLANET!
I'M LOVED + NEEDED.. I'M PRODUCTIVE...
BUT I'M OVERWHELMED BY SEETHING.. THOUGHTS + IDEAS.. OH, I'VE GOT A PAIN IN MY CREATIVE URGE... THE DAM'S ABOUT TO BREAK.........
I THINK I'M SLIGHTLY POSSESSED!
I'LL HAVE A DRINK + PLAN MY NEXT VACATION!
MORE TWISTED ANGST TO COME..

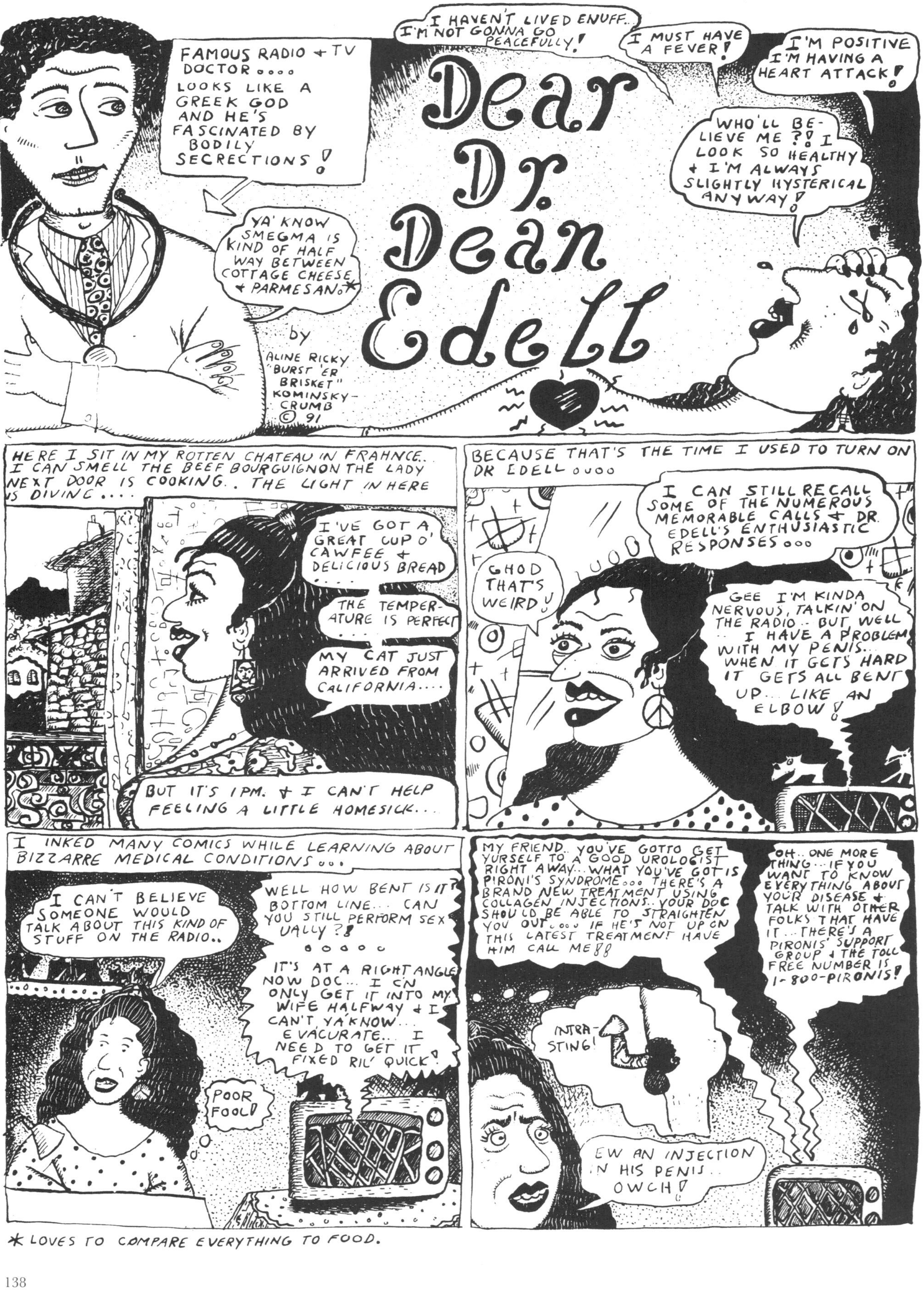
I HAVEN'T LIVED ENUFF.. I'M NOT GONNA GO PEACEFULLY!
I MUST HAVE A FEVER!
I'M POSITIVE I'M HAVING A HEART ATTACK!
FAMOUS RADIO + TV DOCTOR.... LOOKS LIKE A GREEK GOD AND HE'S FASCINATED BY BODILY SECRECTIONS!
Dear Dr. Dean Edell
WHO'LL BELIEVE ME?! I LOOK SO HEALTHY + I'M ALWAYS SLIGHTLY HYSTERICAL ANYWAY!
YA' KNOW SMEGMA IS KIND OF HALF WAY BETWEEN COTTAGE CHEESE + PARMESAN.*
by ALINE RICKY "BURST 'ER BRISKET" KOMINSKY-CRUMB © 91
HERE I SIT IN MY ROTTEN CHATEAU IN FRAHNCE.. I CAN SMELL THE BEEF BOURGUIGNON THE LADY NEXT DOOR IS COOKING.. THE LIGHT IN HERE IS DIVINE....
I'VE GOT A GREAT CUP O' CAWFEE + DELICIOUS BREAD
THE TEMPERATURE IS PERFECT
MY CAT JUST ARRIVED FROM CALIFORNIA....
BUT IT'S 1PM. + I CAN'T HELP FEELING A LITTLE HOMESICK...
BECAUSE THAT'S THE TIME I USED TO TURN ON DR EDELL....
I CAN STILL RECALL SOME OF THE NUMEROUS MEMORABLE CALLS + DR. EDELL'S ENTHUSIASTIC RESPONSES...
GHOD THAT'S WEIRD!
GEE I'M KINDA NERVOUS, TALKIN' ON THE RADIO.. BUT, WELL... I HAVE A PROBLEM WITH MY PENIS.. WHEN IT GETS HARD IT GETS ALL BENT UP.. LIKE AN ELBOW!
I INKED MANY COMICS WHILE LEARNING ABOUT BIZZARRE MEDICAL CONDITIONS...
I CAN'T BELIEVE SOMEONE WOULD TALK ABOUT THIS KIND OF STUFF ON THE RADIO..
WELL HOW BENT IS IT? BOTTOM LINE... CAN YOU STILL PERFORM SEXUALLY?!
IT'S AT A RIGHT ANGLE NOW DOC... I CN ONLY GET IT INTO MY WIFE HALFWAY + I CAN'T, YA'KNOW... EVACURATE... I NEED TO GET IT FIXED RIL' QUICK!
POOR FOOL!
MY FRIEND.. YOU'VE GOTTO GET YOURSELF TO A GOOD UROLOGIST RIGHT AWAY... WHAT YOU'VE GOT IS PIRONI'S SYNDROME... THERE'S A BRAND NEW TREATMENT USING COLLAGEN INJECTIONS.. YOUR DOC SHOULD BE ABLE TO STRAIGHTEN YOU OUT.... IF HE'S NOT UP ON THIS LATEST TREATMENT HAVE HIM CALL ME!!
OH.. ONE MORE THING... IF YOU WANT TO KNOW EVERYTHING ABOUT YOUR DISEASE + TALK WITH OTHER FOLKS THAT HAVE IT... THERE'S A PIRONIS' SUPPORT GROUP + THE TOLL FREE NUMBER IS 1-800-PIRONIS!
INTRA-STING!
EW AN INJECTION IN HIS PENIS.. OWCH!
* LOVES TO COMPARE EVERYTHING TO FOOD.

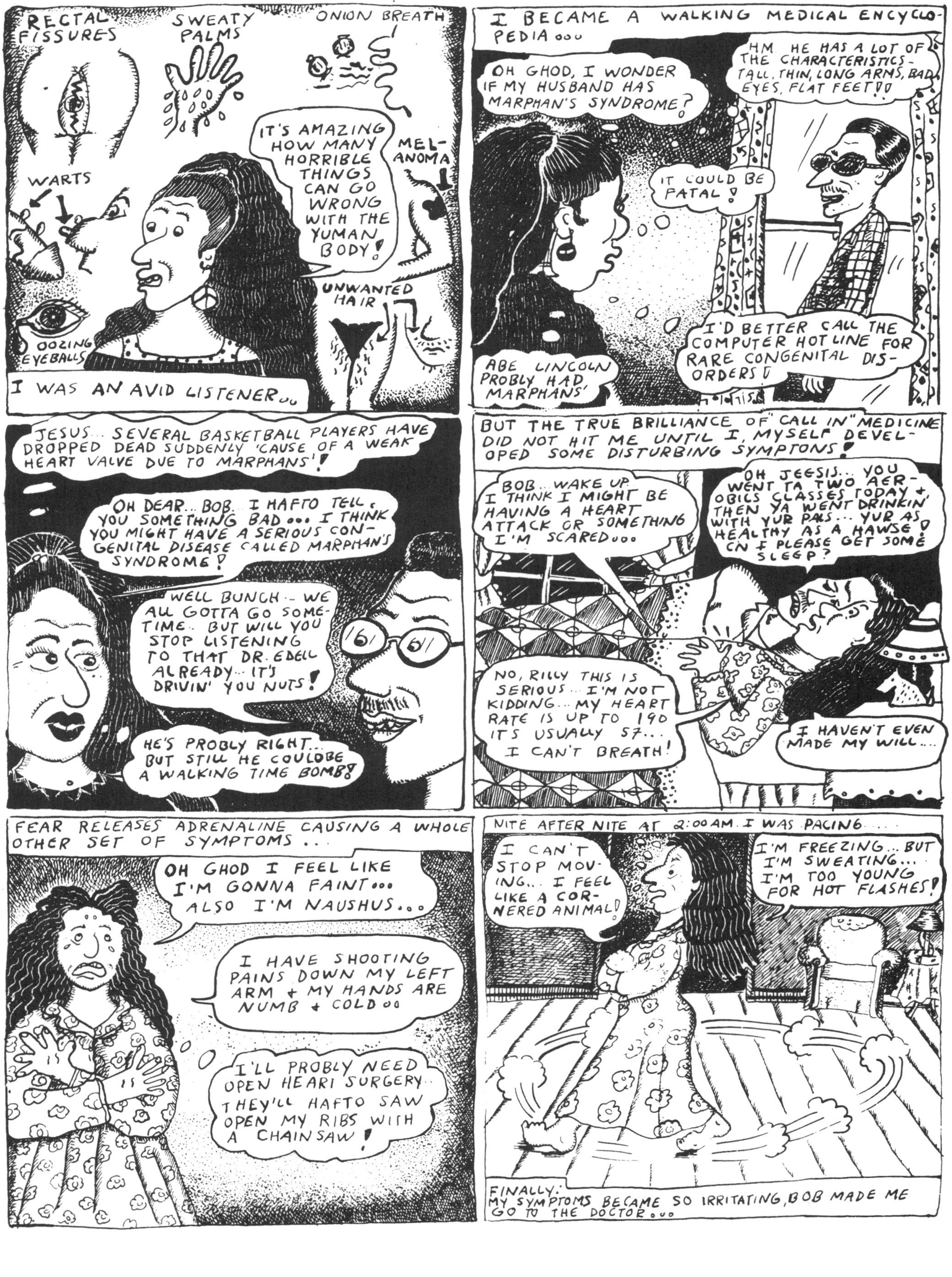

RECTAL FISSURES
SWEATY PALMS
ONION BREATH
WARTS
IT'S AMAZING HOW MANY HORRIBLE THINGS CAN GO WRONG WITH THE YUMAN BODY!
MEL-ANOMA
UNWANTED HAIR
OOZING EYEBALLS
I WAS AN AVID LISTENER...
I BECAME A WALKING MEDICAL ENCYCLO-PEDIA...
OH GHOD, I WONDER IF MY HUSBAND HAS MARPHAN'S SYNDROME?
HM HE HAS A LOT OF THE CHARACTERISTICS - TALL, THIN, LONG ARMS, BAD EYES, FLAT FEET!!
IT COULD BE FATAL!
ABE LINCOLN PROBLY HAD MARPHANS'
I'D BETTER CALL THE COMPUTER HOT LINE FOR RARE CONGENITAL DIS-ORDERS!
JESUS... SEVERAL BASKETBALL PLAYERS HAVE DROPPED DEAD SUDDENLY 'CAUSE OF A WEAK HEART VALVE DUE TO MARPHANS'!
OH DEAR... BOB, I HAFTO TELL YOU SOMETHING BAD... I THINK YOU MIGHT HAVE A SERIOUS CON-GENITAL DISEASE CALLED MARPHAN'S SYNDROME!
WELL BUNCH... WE ALL GOTTA GO SOME-TIME... BUT WILL YOU STOP LISTENING TO THAT DR. EDELL ALREADY... IT'S DRIVIN' YOU NUTS!
HE'S PROBLY RIGHT... BUT STILL HE COULDBE A WALKING TIME BOMB!
BUT THE TRUE BRILLIANCE OF "CALL IN" MEDICINE DID NOT HIT ME UNTIL I, MYSELF DEVEL-OPED SOME DISTURBING SYMPTONS!
BOB... WAKE UP. I THINK I MIGHT BE HAVING A HEART ATTACK OR SOMETHING I'M SCARED...
OH JEESIS... YOU WENT TA TWO AER-OBICS CLASSES TODAY + THEN YA WENT DRINKIN' WITH YUR PALS... YUR AS HEALTHY AS A HAWSE! CN I PLEASE GET SOME SLEEP?
NO, RILLY THIS IS SERIOUS... I'M NOT KIDDING... MY HEART RATE IS UP TO 190 IT'S USUALLY 57... I CAN'T BREATH!
I HAVEN'T EVEN MADE MY WILL...
FEAR RELEASES ADRENALINE CAUSING A WHOLE OTHER SET OF SYMPTOMS...
OH GHOD I FEEL LIKE I'M GONNA FAINT... ALSO I'M NAUSHUS...
I HAVE SHOOTING PAINS DOWN MY LEFT ARM + MY HANDS ARE NUMB + COLD...
I'LL PROBLY NEED OPEN HEART SURGERY... THEY'LL HAFTO SAW OPEN MY RIBS WITH A CHAINSAW!
NITE AFTER NITE AT 2:00 AM I WAS PACING...
I CAN'T STOP MOV-ING... I FEEL LIKE A COR-NERED ANIMAL!
I'M FREEZING... BUT I'M SWEATING... I'M TOO YOUNG FOR HOT FLASHES!
FINALLY. MY SYMPTOMS BECAME SO IRRITATING, BOB MADE ME GO TO THE DOCTOR...

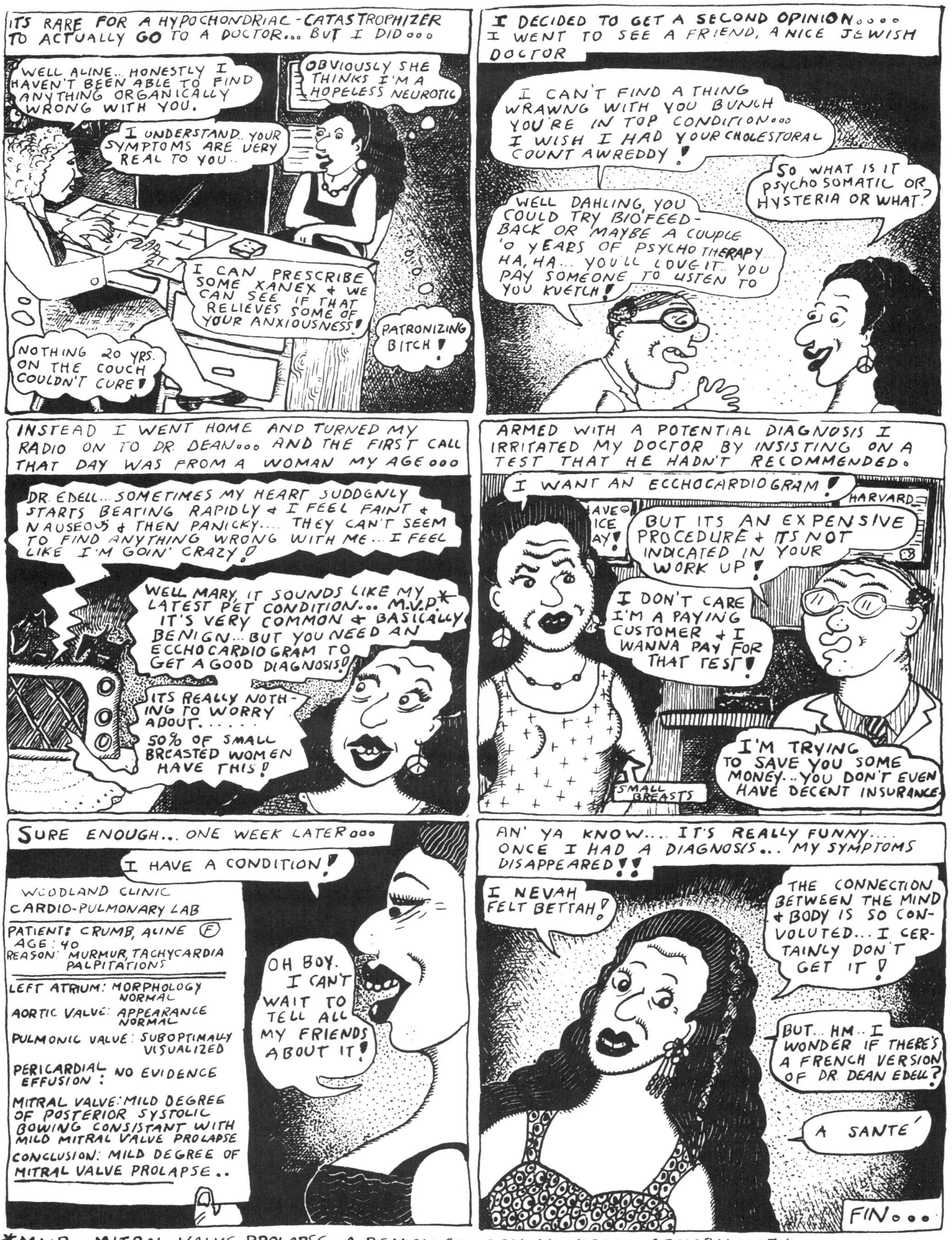
ITS RARE FOR A HYPOCHONDRIAC-CATASTROPHIZER TO ACTUALLY GO TO A DOCTOR... BUT I DID...
WELL ALINE... HONESTLY I HAVEN'T BEEN ABLE TO FIND ANYTHING ORGANICALLY WRONG WITH YOU.
OBVIOUSLY SHE THINKS I'M A HOPELESS NEUROTIC
I UNDERSTAND.. YOUR SYMPTOMS ARE VERY REAL TO YOU..
I CAN PRESCRIBE SOME XANEX & WE CAN SEE IF THAT RELIEVES SOME OF YOUR ANXIOUSNESS!
PATRONIZING BITCH!
NOTHING 20 YRS. ON THE COUCH COULDN'T CURE!
I DECIDED TO GET A SECOND OPINION.... I WENT TO SEE A FRIEND, A NICE JEWISH DOCTOR
I CAN'T FIND A THING WRAWNG WITH YOU BUNCH YOU'RE IN TOP CONDITION... I WISH I HAD YOUR CHOLESTORAL COUNT AWREDDY!
SO WHAT IS IT PSYCHOSOMATIC OR HYSTERIA OR WHAT?
WELL DAHLING, YOU COULD TRY BIOFEED-BACK OR MAYBE A COUPLE 'O YEARS OF PSYCHO THERAPY. HA, HA... YOU'LL LOVE IT.. YOU PAY SOMEONE TO LISTEN TO YOU KVETCH!
INSTEAD I WENT HOME AND TURNED MY RADIO ON TO DR. DEAN... AND THE FIRST CALL THAT DAY WAS FROM A WOMAN MY AGE...
DR. EDELL... SOMETIMES MY HEART SUDDENLY STARTS BEATING RAPIDLY & I FEEL FAINT & NAUSEOUS & THEN PANICKY.... THEY CAN'T SEEM TO FIND ANYTHING WRONG WITH ME... I FEEL LIKE I'M GOIN' CRAZY!
WELL MARY, IT SOUNDS LIKE MY LATEST PET CONDITION... M.V.P.* IT'S VERY COMMON & BASICALLY BENIGN... BUT YOU NEED AN ECCHOCARDIOGRAM TO GET A GOOD DIAGNOSIS!
ITS REALLY NOTHING TO WORRY ABOUT...... 50% OF SMALL BREASTED WOMEN HAVE THIS!
ARMED WITH A POTENTIAL DIAGNOSIS I IRRITATED MY DOCTOR BY INSISTING ON A TEST THAT HE HADN'T RECOMMENDED.
I WANT AN ECCHOCARDIOGRAM!
HARVARD
BUT ITS AN EXPENSIVE PROCEDURE & ITS NOT INDICATED IN YOUR WORK UP!
I DON'T CARE I'M A PAYING CUSTOMER & I WANNA PAY FOR THAT TEST!
I'M TRYING TO SAVE YOU SOME MONEY... YOU DON'T EVEN HAVE DECENT INSURANCE
SMALL BREASTS
SURE ENOUGH... ONE WEEK LATER...
I HAVE A CONDITION!
WOODLAND CLINIC
CARDIO-PULMONARY LAB
PATIENT: CRUMB, ALINE (F)
AGE: 40
REASON: MURMUR, TACHYCARDIA PALPITATIONS
LEFT ATRIUM: MORPHOLOGY NORMAL
AORTIC VALVE: APPEARANCE NORMAL
PULMONIC VALVE: SUBOPTIMALLY VISUALIZED
PERICARDIAL EFFUSION: NO EVIDENCE
MITRAL VALVE: MILD DEGREE OF POSTERIOR SYSTOLIC BOWING CONSISTANT WITH MILD MITRAL VALVE PROLAPSE
CONCLUSION: MILD DEGREE OF MITRAL VALVE PROLAPSE..
OH BOY. I CAN'T WAIT TO TELL ALL MY FRIENDS ABOUT IT!
AN' YA KNOW.... IT'S REALLY FUNNY.... ONCE I HAD A DIAGNOSIS... MY SYMPTOMS DISAPPEARED!!
I NEVAH FELT BETTAH!
THE CONNECTION BETWEEN THE MIND & BODY IS SO CONVOLUTED... I CERTAINLY DON'T GET IT!
BUT.. HM.. I WONDER IF THERE'S A FRENCH VERSION OF DR DEAN EDELL?
A SANTE'
FIN...

*MVP - MITRAL VALVE PROLAPSE - A BENIGN CONGENITAL HEART ABNORMALITY.

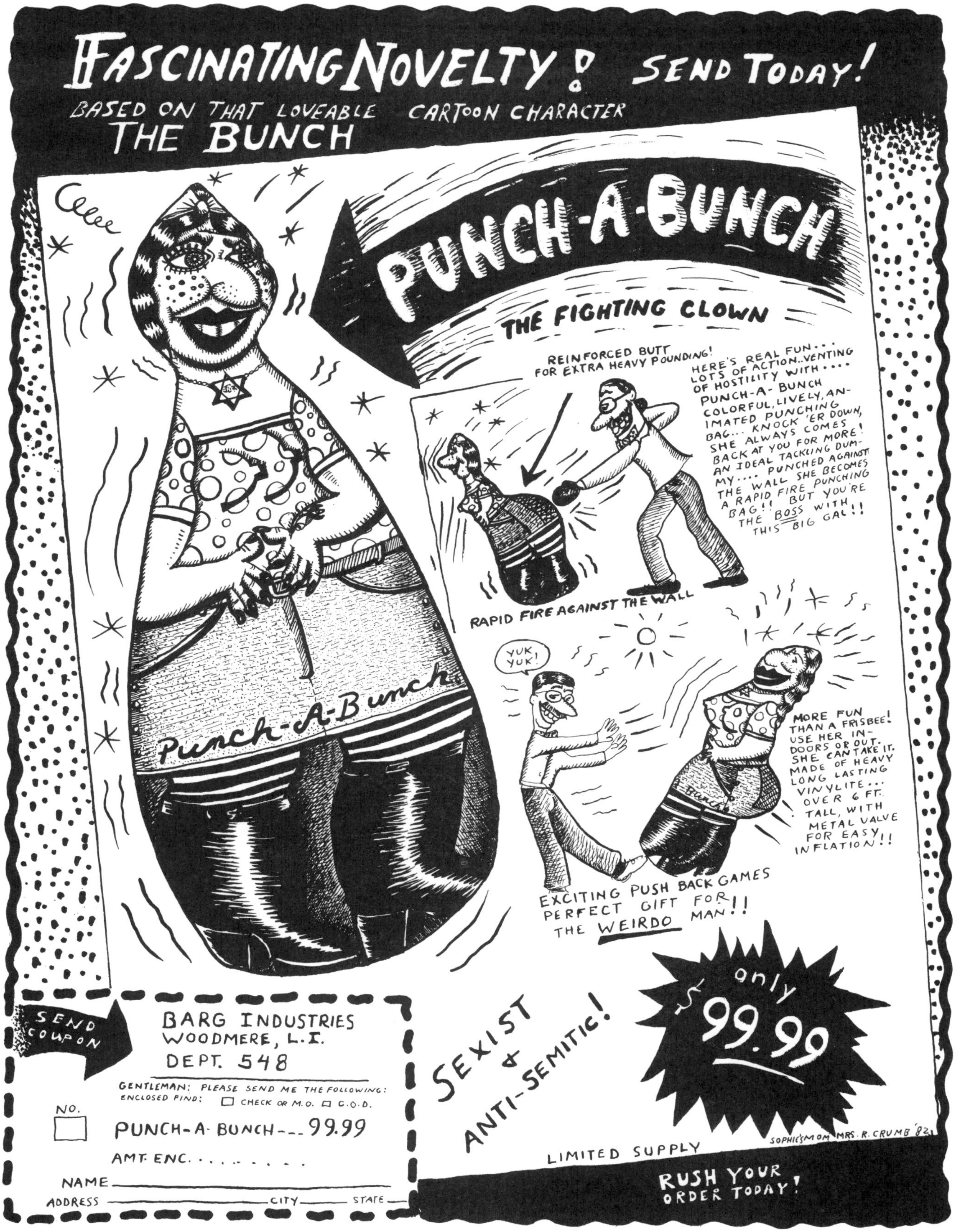

FASCINATING NOVELTY! SEND TODAY!
BASED ON THAT LOVEABLE CARTOON CHARACTER
THE BUNCH
PUNCH-A-BUNCH
THE FIGHTING CLOWN
REINFORCED BUTT FOR EXTRA HEAVY POUNDING!
HERE'S REAL FUN... LOTS OF ACTION.. VENTING OF HOSTILITY WITH.... PUNCH-A-BUNCH COLORFUL, LIVELY, ANIMATED PUNCHING BAG... KNOCK 'ER DOWN, SHE ALWAYS COMES BACK AT YOU FOR MORE! AN IDEAL TACKLING DUMMY.... PUNCHED AGAINST THE WALL SHE BECOMES A RAPID FIRE PUNCHING BAG!! BUT YOU'RE THE BOSS WITH THIS BIG GAL!!
RAPID FIRE AGAINST THE WALL
YUK YUK!
MORE FUN THAN A FRISBEE! USE HER INDOORS OR OUT. SHE CAN TAKE IT. MADE OF HEAVY LONG LASTING VINYLITE... OVER 6 FT. TALL, WITH METAL VALVE FOR EASY INFLATION!!
EXCITING PUSH BACK GAMES
PERFECT GIFT FOR THE WEIRDO MAN!!
Punch-A-Bunch
only $99.99
SEXIST & ANTI-SEMITIC!
SEND COUPON
BARG INDUSTRIES
WOODMERE, L.I.
DEPT. 548
GENTLEMAN: PLEASE SEND ME THE FOLLOWING:
ENCLOSED FIND: CHECK OR M.O. C.O.D.
NO.
PUNCH-A-BUNCH---99.99
AMT. ENC.........
NAME
ADDRESS CITY STATE
LIMITED SUPPLY
SOPHIE'S MOM MRS. R. CRUMB '82
RUSH YOUR ORDER TODAY!

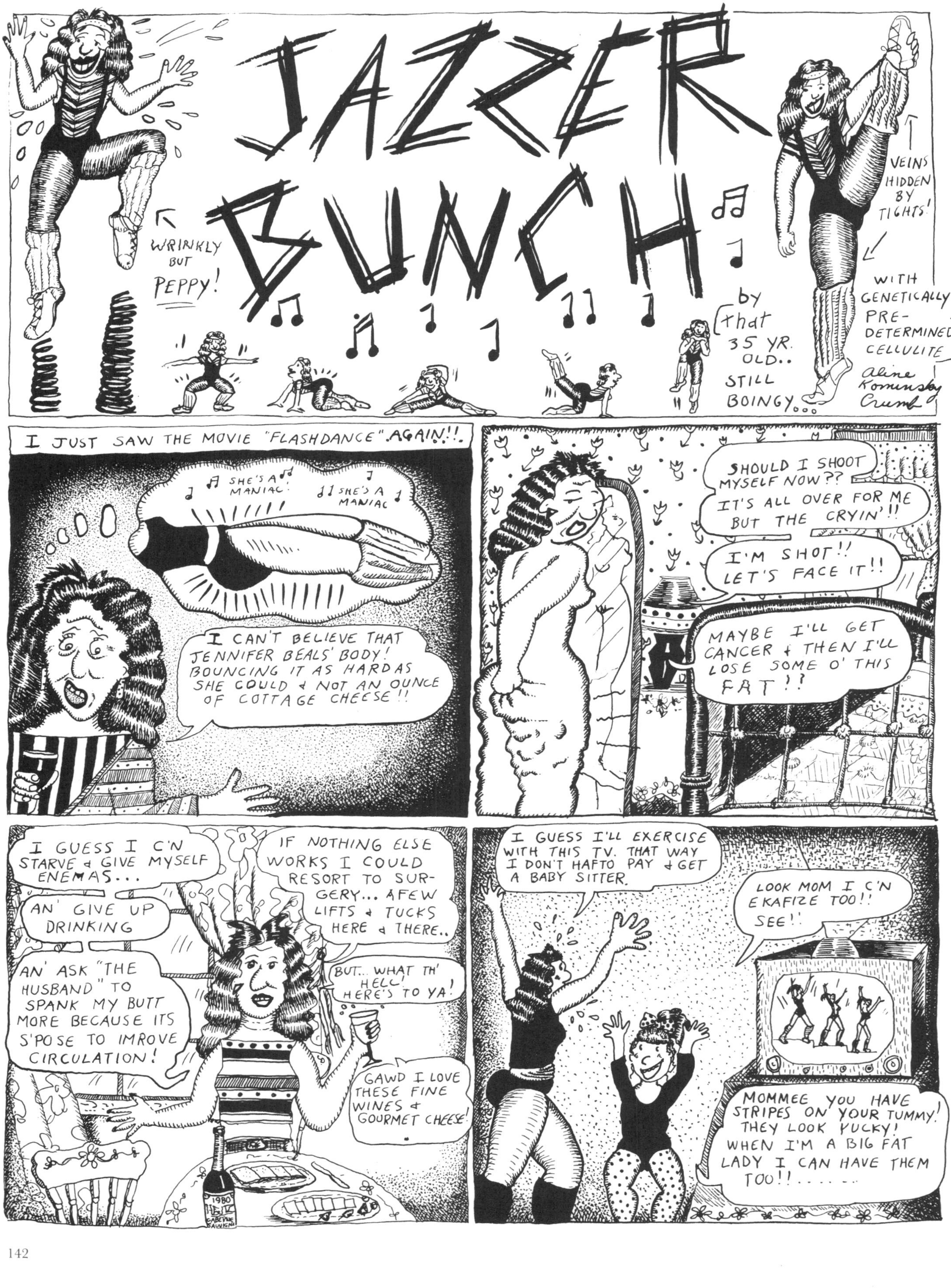

JAZZER BUNCH
WRINKLY BUT PEPPY!
VEINS HIDDEN BY TIGHTS!
WITH GENETICALLY PRE-DETERMINED CELLULITE
by that 35 YR. OLD.. STILL BOINGY...
Aline Kominsky Crumb
I JUST SAW THE MOVIE "FLASHDANCE" AGAIN!!
SHE'S A MANIAC! SHE'S A MANIAC
I CAN'T BELIEVE THAT JENNIFER BEALS' BODY! BOUNCING IT AS HARD AS SHE COULD & NOT AN OUNCE OF COTTAGE CHEESE!!
SHOULD I SHOOT MYSELF NOW??
IT'S ALL OVER FOR ME BUT THE CRYIN'!!
I'M SHOT!! LET'S FACE IT!!
MAYBE I'LL GET CANCER & THEN I'LL LOSE SOME O' THIS FAT!?
I GUESS I C'N STARVE & GIVE MYSELF ENEMAS...
AN' GIVE UP DRINKING
AN' ASK "THE HUSBAND" TO SPANK MY BUTT MORE BECAUSE ITS S'POSE TO IMROVE CIRCULATION!
IF NOTHING ELSE WORKS I COULD RESORT TO SURGERY... A FEW LIFTS & TUCKS HERE & THERE..
BUT... WHAT TH' HELL! HERE'S TO YA!
GAWD I LOVE THESE FINE WINES & GOURMET CHEESE!
I GUESS I'LL EXERCISE WITH THIS TV. THAT WAY I DON'T HAFTO PAY & GET A BABY SITTER.
LOOK MOM I C'N EKAFIZE TOO!! SEE!!
MOMMEE YOU HAVE STRIPES ON YOUR TUMMY! THEY LOOK YUCKY! WHEN I'M A BIG FAT LADY I CAN HAVE THEM TOO!!......

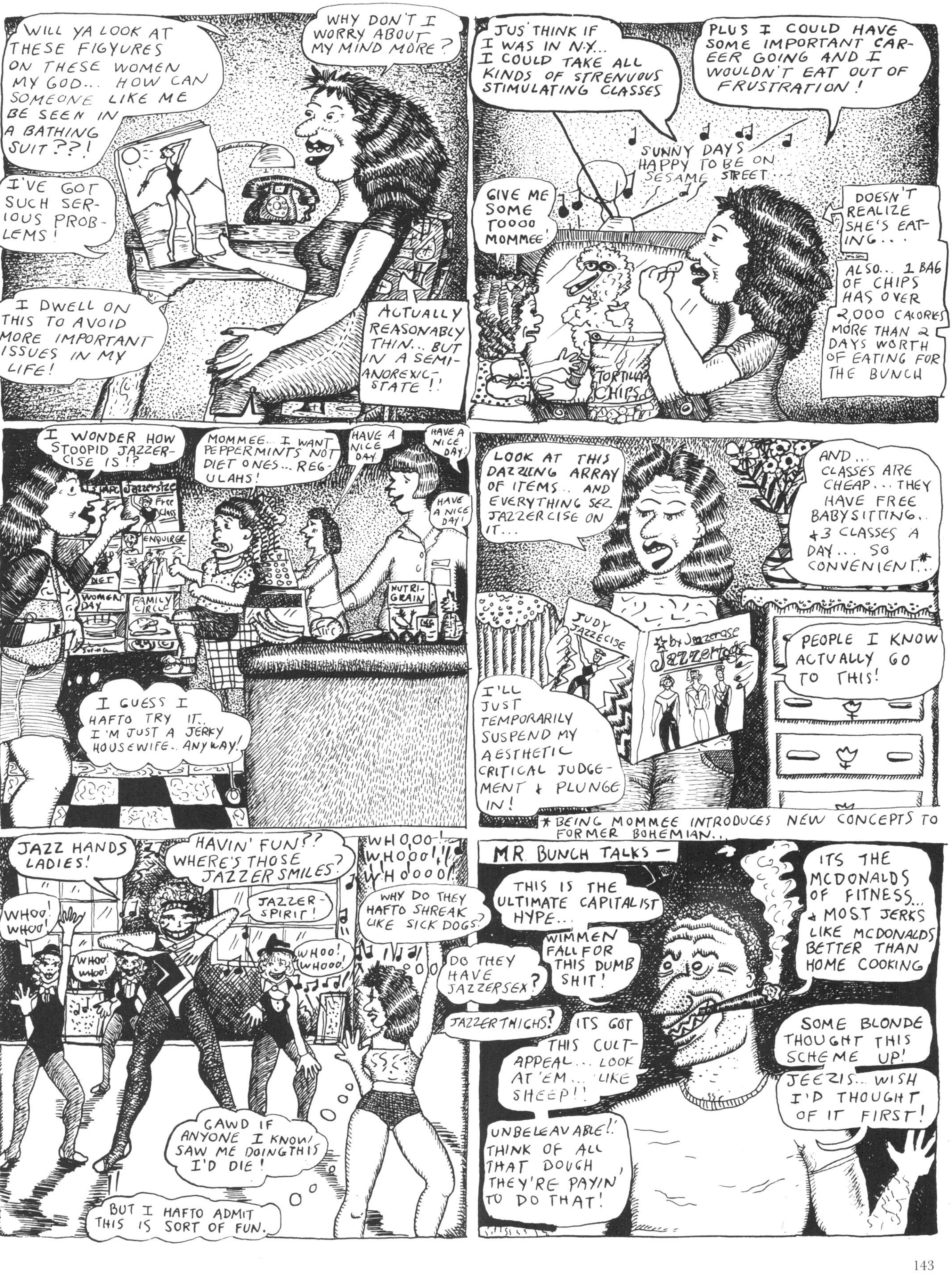

WILL YA LOOK AT THESE FIGYURES ON THESE WOMEN MY GOD... HOW CAN SOMEONE LIKE ME BE SEEN IN A BATHING SUIT??!
WHY DON'T I WORRY ABOUT MY MIND MORE?
I'VE GOT SUCH SERIOUS PROBLEMS!
I DWELL ON THIS TO AVOID MORE IMPORTANT ISSUES IN MY LIFE!
ACTUALLY REASONABLY THIN... BUT IN A SEMI-ANOREXIC STATE!!
JUS' THINK IF I WAS IN N.Y... I COULD TAKE ALL KINDS OF STRENUOUS STIMULATING CLASSES
PLUS I COULD HAVE SOME IMPORTANT CAREER GOING AND I WOULDN'T EAT OUT OF FRUSTRATION!
SUNNY DAYS HAPPY TO BE ON SESAME STREET...
GIVE ME SOME TOOOO MOMMEE!
DOESN'T REALIZE SHE'S EATING...
ALSO... 1 BAG OF CHIPS HAS OVER 2,000 CALORIES MORE THAN 2 DAYS WORTH OF EATING FOR THE BUNCH
TORTILLA CHIPS
I WONDER HOW STOOPID JAZZERCISE IS!?
MOMMEE... I WANT PEPPERMINTS NOT DIET ONES... REGULAHS!
HAVE A NICE DAY.
HAVE A NICE DAY.
HAVE A NICE DAY!
Jazzersize
ENQUIRER
DIET
WOMEN DAY
FAMILY CIRCLE
NUTRI-GRAIN
I GUESS I HAFTO TRY IT.. I'M JUST A JERKY HOUSEWIFE.. ANYWAY!
LOOK AT THIS DAZZLING ARRAY OF ITEMS... AND EVERYTHING SEZ JAZZERCISE ON IT...
AND... CLASSES ARE CHEAP... THEY HAVE FREE BABYSITTING.. +3 CLASSES A DAY... SO CONVENIENT.*
JUDY JAZZECISE
Jazzercise
PEOPLE I KNOW ACTUALLY GO TO THIS!
I'LL JUST TEMPORARILY SUSPEND MY AESTHETIC CRITICAL JUDGEMENT + PLUNGE IN!
* BEING MOMMEE INTRODUCES NEW CONCEPTS TO FORMER BOHEMIAN..
JAZZ HANDS LADIES!
HAVIN' FUN?? WHERE'S THOSE JAZZER SMILES?
WHOOO! WHOOO! WHOOO!
JAZZER-SPIRIT!
WHOO! WHOO!
WHOO! WHOO!
WHOO! WHOOO!
WHY DO THEY HAFTO SHREAK LIKE SICK DOGS?
GAWD IF ANYONE I KNOW SAW ME DOING THIS I'D DIE!
BUT I HAFTO ADMIT THIS IS SORT OF FUN.
MR. BUNCH TALKS —
THIS IS THE ULTIMATE CAPITALIST HYPE...
WIMMEN FALL FOR THIS DUMB SHIT!
ITS THE MCDONALDS OF FITNESS... + MOST JERKS LIKE MCDONALDS BETTER THAN HOME COOKING
DO THEY HAVE JAZZERSEX?
JAZZERTHIGHS?
ITS GOT THIS CULT-APPEAL... LOOK AT 'EM... LIKE SHEEP!!
SOME BLONDE THOUGHT THIS SCHEME UP!
JEEZIS... WISH I'D THOUGHT OF IT FIRST!
UNBELEAVABLE!! THINK OF ALL THAT DOUGH THEY'RE PAYIN' TO DO THAT!

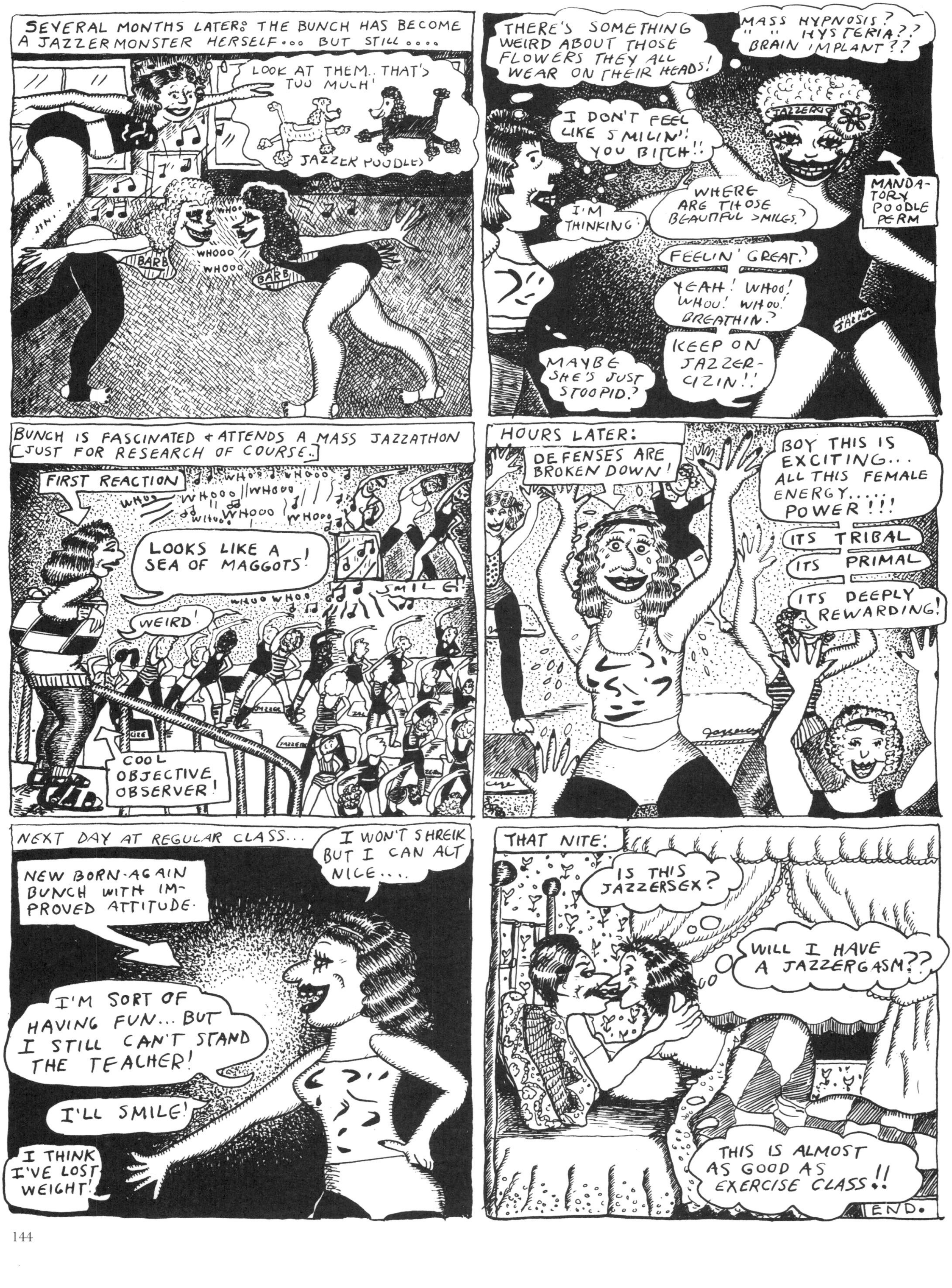

SEVERAL MONTHS LATER: THE BUNCH HAS BECOME A JAZZERMONSTER HERSELF... BUT STILL....
LOOK AT THEM.. THAT'S TOO MUCH!
JAZZER POODLES
BARB
WHOOO
WHOOO
BARB
THERE'S SOMETHING WEIRD ABOUT THOSE FLOWERS THEY ALL WEAR ON THEIR HEADS!
MASS HYPNOSIS? " " HYSTERIA?? BRAIN IMPLANT??
I DON'T FEEL LIKE SMILIN'! YOU BITCH!!
I'M THINKING.
WHERE ARE THOSE BEAUTIFUL SMILES?
MANDATORY POODLE PERM
FEELIN' GREAT!
YEAH! WHOO! WHOO! WHOO! BREATHIN?
KEEP ON JAZZERCIZIN!!
MAYBE SHE'S JUST STOOPID?
BUNCH IS FASCINATED & ATTENDS A MASS JAZZATHON [JUST FOR RESEARCH OF COURSE.]
FIRST REACTION
WHOOO WHOOO WHOOO WHOOO WHOOO
LOOKS LIKE A SEA OF MAGGOTS!
WHOO WHOO
SMILE!
WEIRD!
COOL OBJECTIVE OBSERVER!
HOURS LATER:
DEFENSES ARE BROKEN DOWN!
BOY THIS IS EXCITING... ALL THIS FEMALE ENERGY..... POWER!!!
ITS TRIBAL
ITS PRIMAL
ITS DEEPLY REWARDING!
NEXT DAY AT REGULAR CLASS...
I WON'T SHREIK BUT I CAN ACT NICE...
NEW BORN-AGAIN BUNCH WITH IMPROVED ATTITUDE.
I'M SORT OF HAVING FUN... BUT I STILL CAN'T STAND THE TEACHER!
I'LL SMILE!
I THINK I'VE LOST WEIGHT!
THAT NITE:
IS THIS JAZZERSEX?
WILL I HAVE A JAZZERGASM??
THIS IS ALMOST AS GOOD AS EXERCISE CLASS!!
END.

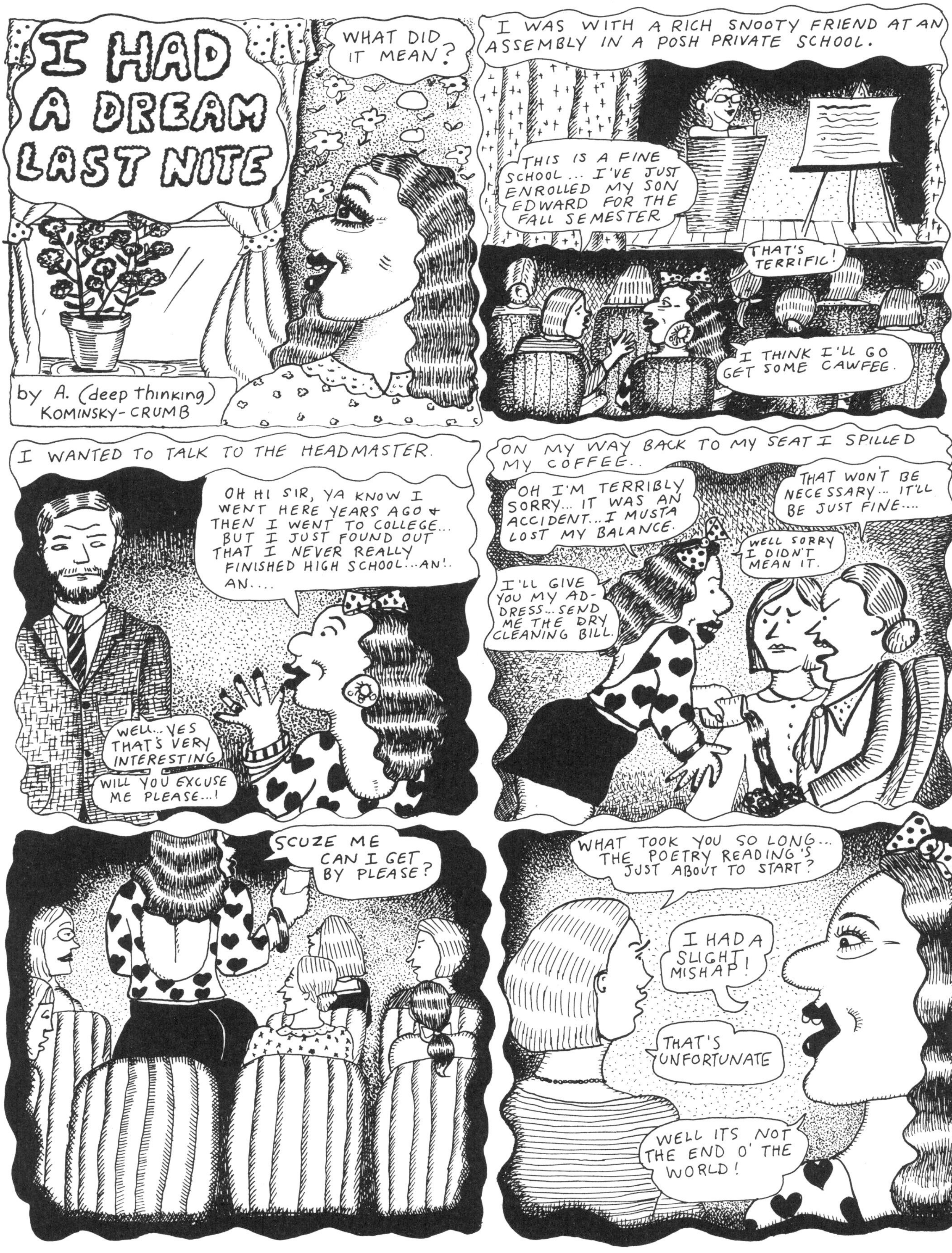
I HAD A DREAM LAST NITE
by A. (deep thinking) KOMINSKY-CRUMB
WHAT DID IT MEAN?
I WAS WITH A RICH SNOOTY FRIEND AT AN ASSEMBLY IN A POSH PRIVATE SCHOOL.
THIS IS A FINE SCHOOL... I'VE JUST ENROLLED MY SON EDWARD FOR THE FALL SEMESTER
THAT'S TERRIFIC!
I THINK I'LL GO GET SOME CAWFEE.
I WANTED TO TALK TO THE HEADMASTER.
OH HI SIR, YA KNOW I WENT HERE YEARS AGO & THEN I WENT TO COLLEGE... BUT I JUST FOUND OUT THAT I NEVER REALLY FINISHED HIGH SCHOOL...AN'. AN....
WELL... YES THAT'S VERY INTERESTING
WILL YOU EXCUSE ME PLEASE...!
ON MY WAY BACK TO MY SEAT I SPILLED MY COFFEE..
OH I'M TERRIBLY SORRY... IT WAS AN ACCIDENT... I MUSTA LOST MY BALANCE.
THAT WON'T BE NECESSARY... IT'LL BE JUST FINE....
WELL SORRY I DIDN'T MEAN IT.
I'LL GIVE YOU MY AD-DRESS... SEND ME THE DRY CLEANING BILL.
SCUZE ME CAN I GET BY PLEASE?
WHAT TOOK YOU SO LONG... THE POETRY READING'S JUST ABOUT TO START?
I HAD A SLIGHT MISHAP!
THAT'S UNFORTUNATE
WELL ITS NOT THE END O' THE WORLD!

PART 2. OF MY DREAM: I WAS AT A PARTY IN MY NEIGHBORHOOD... IT WAS AT A HOUSEWARMING PARTY...

LET'S CHECK THE WEBER

JUST LOVE THE TURRETS!

THE ARCHITECT IS REALLY A GENIUS

I'M EDITING A MAGAZINE CALLED WEIRDO

SEE THESE GAWGEOUS BOOTS!! I GOT THEM IN EXCHANGE FOR SEX!!

CHICKENS DONE!

SUDDENLY I WAS IN THE BACK SEAT OF A CAR WITH TWO COUPLES.

IF YOU EVER DO ANYTHING LIKE SHE DID...I'LL KILL YOU!!

THAT GOES FOR YOU TOO SWEETHEART!

UH OH!

THE WOMEN DIDN'T SAY ANYTHING.

I WAS REALLY SWEATING IT AND THEN MY CLOTHES DISAPPEARED

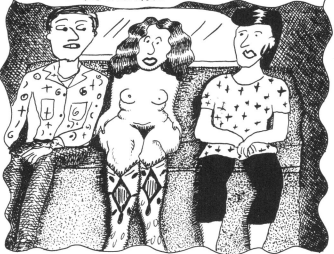

THE CAR STOPPED... I GOT OUT... I WAS NAKED EXCEPT FOR MY BOOTS.

UPTIGHT JERKS!

I JUST STARTED WALKING HOME

BOY, I'M RELIEVED TO BE OUTA THERE!

I FELT ALLRIGHT... CALM....
IT WAS WARM OUT & I DIDN'T CARE...   END.

146

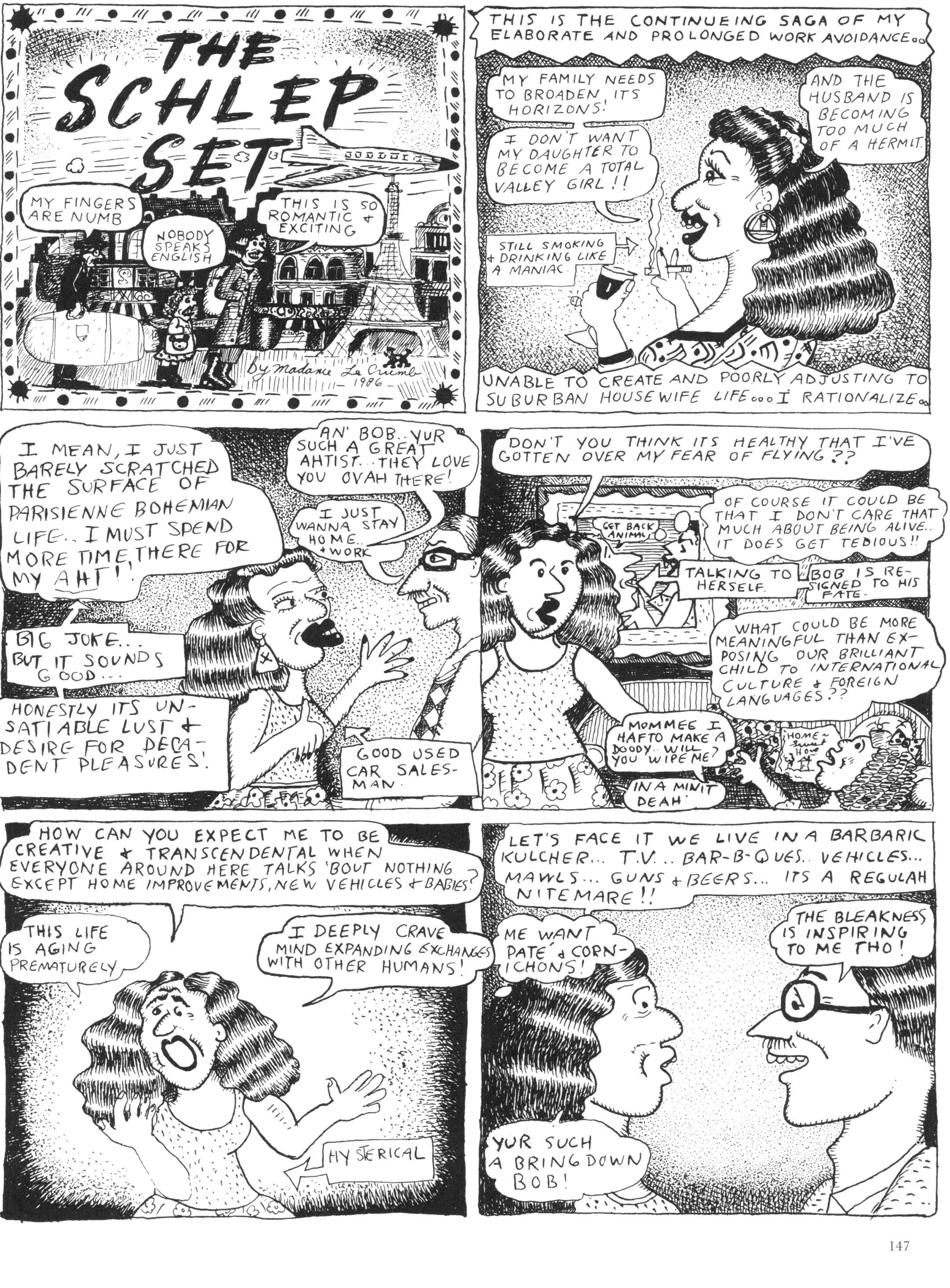
THE SCHLEP SET
MY FINGERS ARE NUMB
NOBODY SPEAKS ENGLISH
THIS IS SO ROMANTIC & EXCITING
by Madame Le Crumb 1986
THIS IS THE CONTINUEING SAGA OF MY ELABORATE AND PROLONGED WORK AVOIDANCE...
MY FAMILY NEEDS TO BROADEN ITS HORIZONS!
I DON'T WANT MY DAUGHTER TO BECOME A TOTAL VALLEY GIRL!!
AND THE HUSBAND IS BECOMING TOO MUCH OF A HERMIT.
STILL SMOKING & DRINKING LIKE A MANIAC.
UNABLE TO CREATE AND POORLY ADJUSTING TO SUBURBAN HOUSEWIFE LIFE... I RATIONALIZE...
I MEAN, I JUST BARELY SCRATCHED THE SURFACE OF PARISIENNE BOHEMIAN LIFE.. I MUST SPEND MORE TIME THERE FOR MY AHT!
AN' BOB.. YUR SUCH A GREAT AHTIST.. THEY LOVE YOU OVAH THERE!
I JUST WANNA STAY HOME.. & WORK
BIG JOKE... BUT IT SOUNDS GOOD...
HONESTLY ITS UNSATIABLE LUST & DESIRE FOR DECADENT PLEASURES!
GOOD USED CAR SALESMAN
DON'T YOU THINK ITS HEALTHY THAT I'VE GOTTEN OVER MY FEAR OF FLYING??
GET BACK ANIMAL
OF COURSE IT COULD BE THAT I DON'T CARE THAT MUCH ABOUT BEING ALIVE.. IT DOES GET TEDIOUS!!
TALKING TO HERSELF.
BOB IS RESIGNED TO HIS FATE.
WHAT COULD BE MORE MEANINGFUL THAN EXPOSING OUR BRILLIANT CHILD TO INTERNATIONAL CULTURE & FOREIGN LANGUAGES??
MOMMEE I HAFTO MAKE A DOODY.. WILL YOU WIPE ME?
IN A MINIT DEAH
HOW CAN YOU EXPECT ME TO BE CREATIVE & TRANSCENDENTAL WHEN EVERYONE AROUND HERE TALKS 'BOUT NOTHING EXCEPT HOME IMPROVEMENTS, NEW VEHICLES & BABIES?
THIS LIFE IS AGING PREMATURELY
I DEEPLY CRAVE MIND EXPANDING EXCHANGES WITH OTHER HUMANS!
HYSTERICAL
LET'S FACE IT WE LIVE IN A BARBARIC KULCHER... T.V... BAR-B-QUES.. VEHICLES... MAWLS... GUNS & BEERS... ITS A REGULAH NITEMARE!!
ME WANT PATÉ & CORNICHONS!
THE BLEAKNESS IS INSPIRING TO ME THO!
YUR SUCH A BRING DOWN BOB!

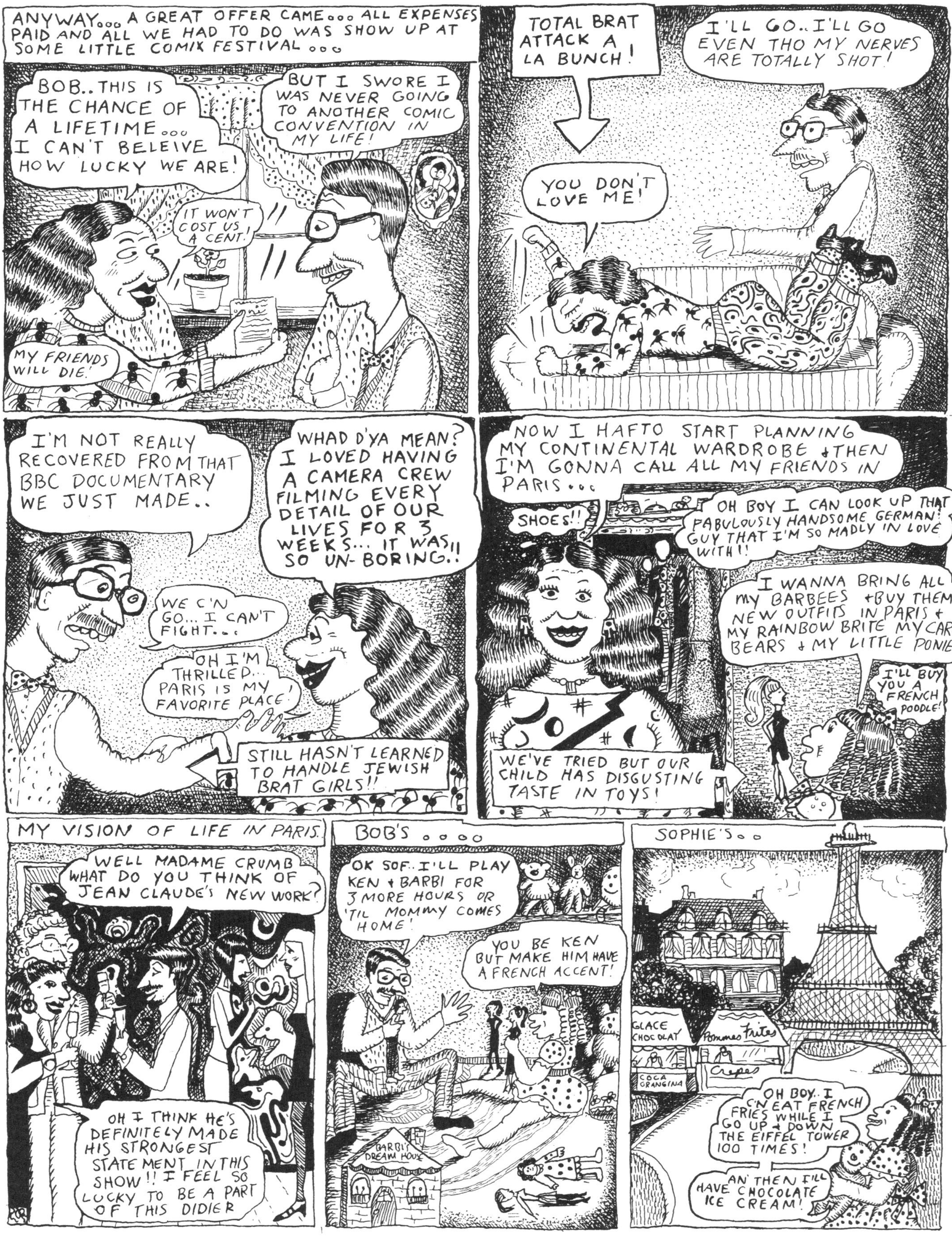

ANYWAY... A GREAT OFFER CAME... ALL EXPENSES PAID AND ALL WE HAD TO DO WAS SHOW UP AT SOME LITTLE COMIX FESTIVAL...
BOB.. THIS IS THE CHANCE OF A LIFETIME... I CAN'T BELEIVE HOW LUCKY WE ARE!
BUT I SWORE I WAS NEVER GOING TO ANOTHER COMIC CONVENTION IN MY LIFE!
IT WON'T COST US A CENT!
MY FRIENDS WILL DIE!
TOTAL BRAT ATTACK A LA BUNCH!
I'LL GO.. I'LL GO EVEN THO MY NERVES ARE TOTALLY SHOT!
YOU DON'T LOVE ME!
I'M NOT REALLY RECOVERED FROM THAT BBC DOCUMENTARY WE JUST MADE..
WHAD D'YA MEAN? I LOVED HAVING A CAMERA CREW FILMING EVERY DETAIL OF OUR LIVES FOR 3 WEEKS... IT WAS SO UN-BORING!!
WE C'N GO... I CAN'T FIGHT...
OH I'M THRILLED.. PARIS IS MY FAVORITE PLACE!
STILL HASN'T LEARNED TO HANDLE JEWISH BRAT GIRLS!!
NOW I HAFTO START PLANNING MY CONTINENTAL WARDROBE & THEN I'M GONNA CALL ALL MY FRIENDS IN PARIS...
SHOES!!
OH BOY I CAN LOOK UP THAT FABULOUSLY HANDSOME GERMAN GUY THAT I'M SO MADLY IN LOVE WITH!!
I WANNA BRING ALL MY BARBEES & BUY THEM NEW OUTFITS IN PARIS & MY RAINBOW BRITE MY CARE-BEARS & MY LITTLE PONIES.
I'LL BUY YOU A FRENCH POODLE!
WE'VE TRIED BUT OUR CHILD HAS DISGUSTING TASTE IN TOYS!
MY VISION OF LIFE IN PARIS.
WELL MADAME CRUMB WHAT DO YOU THINK OF JEAN CLAUDE'S NEW WORK?
OH I THINK HE'S DEFINITELY MADE HIS STRONGEST STATEMENT IN THIS SHOW!! I FEEL SO LUCKY TO BE A PART OF THIS DIDIER
BOB'S....
OK SOF.. I'LL PLAY KEN & BARBI FOR 3 MORE HOURS OR 'TIL MOMMY COMES HOME!
YOU BE KEN BUT MAKE HIM HAVE A FRENCH ACCENT!
BARBI'S DREAM HOUSE
SOPHIE'S..
GLACE CHOCOLAT
Pommes Frites
COCA ORANGINA
Crepes
OH BOY.. I C'N EAT FRENCH FRIES WHILE I GO UP & DOWN THE EIFFEL TOWER 100 TIMES!
AN' THEN I'LL HAVE CHOCOLATE ICE CREAM!

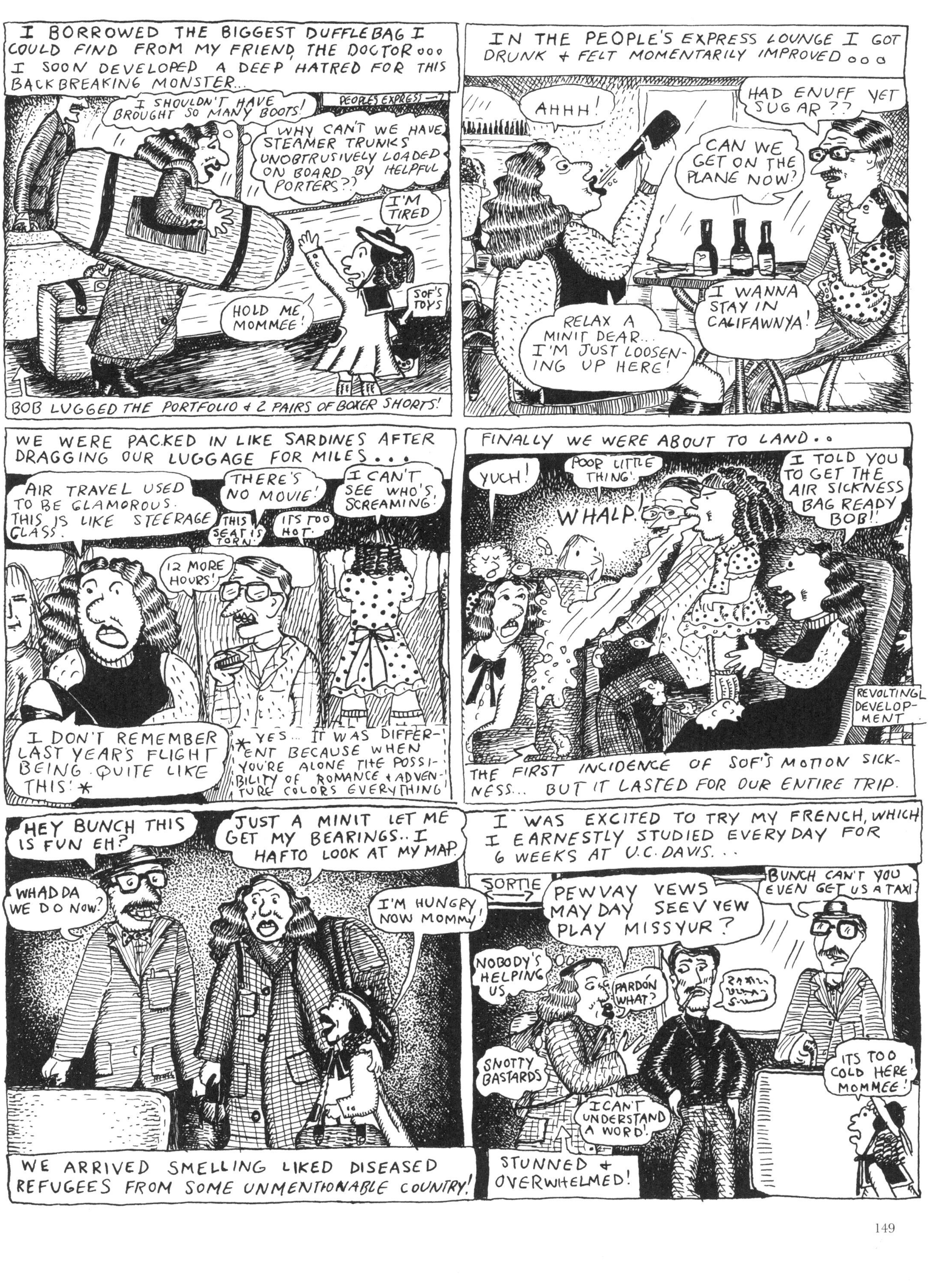

I BORROWED THE BIGGEST DUFFLEBAG I COULD FIND FROM MY FRIEND, THE DOCTOR... I SOON DEVELOPED A DEEP HATRED FOR THIS BACKBREAKING MONSTER..
I SHOULDN'T HAVE BROUGHT SO MANY BOOTS!
PEOPLES EXPRESS
WHY CAN'T WE HAVE STEAMER TRUNKS UNOBTRUSIVELY LOADED ON BOARD BY HELPFUL PORTERS??
I'M TIRED
HOLD ME MOMMEE!
SOF'S TOYS
BOB LUGGED THE PORTFOLIO & 2 PAIRS OF BOXER SHORTS!
IN THE PEOPLE'S EXPRESS LOUNGE I GOT DRUNK & FELT MOMENTARILY IMPROVED...
AHHH!
HAD ENUFF YET SUGAR??
CAN WE GET ON THE PLANE NOW?
I WANNA STAY IN CALIFAWNYA!
RELAX A MINIT DEAR.. I'M JUST LOOSENING UP HERE!
WE WERE PACKED IN LIKE SARDINES AFTER DRAGGING OUR LUGGAGE FOR MILES...
AIR TRAVEL USED TO BE GLAMOROUS. THIS IS LIKE STEERAGE CLASS.
THERE'S NO MOVIE!
I CAN'T SEE WHO'S SCREAMING!
THIS SEAT IS TORN!
ITS TOO HOT.
12 MORE HOURS!
I DON'T REMEMBER LAST YEAR'S FLIGHT BEING QUITE LIKE THIS! *
* YES.. IT WAS DIFFERENT BECAUSE WHEN YOU'RE ALONE THE POSSIBILITY OF ROMANCE & ADVENTURE COLORS EVERYTHING!
FINALLY WE WERE ABOUT TO LAND..
YUCH!
POOR LITTLE THING!
I TOLD YOU TO GET THE AIR SICKNESS BAG READY BOB!!
WHALP!
REVOLTING DEVELOPMENT
THE FIRST INCIDENCE OF SOF'S MOTION SICKNESS... BUT IT LASTED FOR OUR ENTIRE TRIP.
HEY BUNCH THIS IS FUN EH?
JUST A MINIT LET ME GET MY BEARINGS.. I HAFTO LOOK AT MY MAP.
WHADDA WE DO NOW?
I'M HUNGRY NOW MOMMY!
WE ARRIVED SMELLING LIKED DISEASED REFUGEES FROM SOME UNMENTIONABLE COUNTRY!
I WAS EXCITED TO TRY MY FRENCH, WHICH I EARNESTLY STUDIED EVERYDAY FOR 6 WEEKS AT U.C. DAVIS...
SORTIE
PEWVAY VEWS MAY DAY SEEV VEW PLAY MISSYUR?
BUNCH CAN'T YOU EVEN GET US A TAXI
NOBODY'S HELPING US.
PARDÓN WHAT?
SNOTTY BASTARDS
I CAN'T UNDERSTAND A WORD!
ITS TOO COLD HERE MOMMEE!
STUNNED & OVERWHELMED!

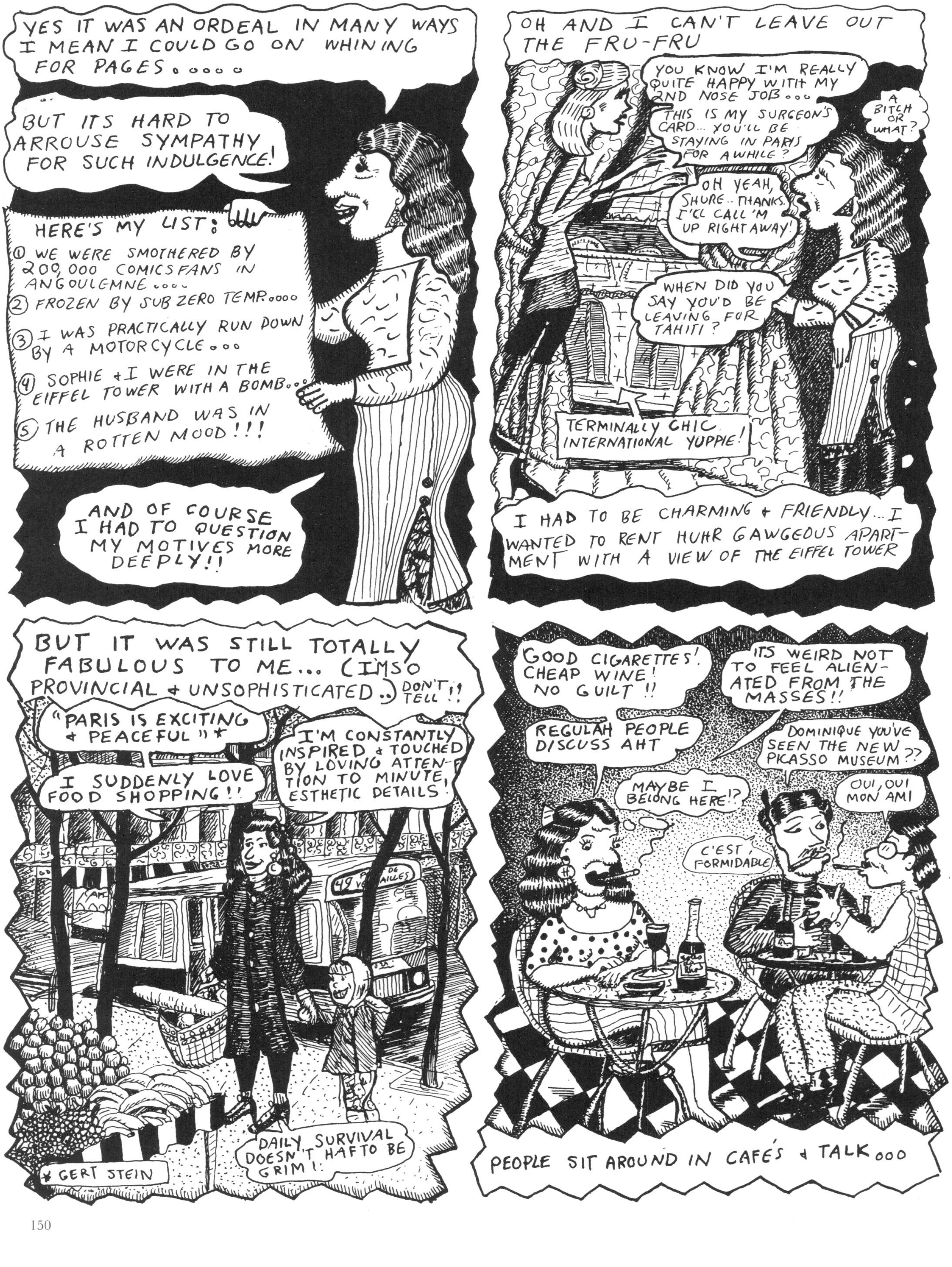
YES IT WAS AN ORDEAL IN MANY WAYS I MEAN I COULD GO ON WHINING FOR PAGES.....
BUT ITS HARD TO ARROUSE SYMPATHY FOR SUCH INDULGENCE!
HERE'S MY LIST:
① WE WERE SMOTHERED BY 200,000 COMICS FANS IN ANGOULEMNE....
② FROZEN BY SUB ZERO TEMP....
③ I WAS PRACTICALLY RUN DOWN BY A MOTORCYCLE...
④ SOPHIE & I WERE IN THE EIFFEL TOWER WITH A BOMB...
⑤ THE HUSBAND WAS IN A ROTTEN MOOD!!!
AND OF COURSE I HAD TO QUESTION MY MOTIVES MORE DEEPLY!!
OH AND I CAN'T LEAVE OUT THE FRU-FRU
YOU KNOW I'M REALLY QUITE HAPPY WITH MY 2ND NOSE JOB...
THIS IS MY SURGEON'S CARD... YOU'LL BE STAYING IN PARIS FOR AWHILE?
A BITCH OR WHAT?
OH YEAH, SHURE.. THANKS. I'LL CALL 'M UP RIGHT AWAY!
WHEN DID YOU SAY YOU'D BE LEAVING FOR TAHITI?
TERMINALLY CHIC INTERNATIONAL YUPPIE!
I HAD TO BE CHARMING & FRIENDLY... I WANTED TO RENT HUHR GAWGEOUS APARTMENT WITH A VIEW OF THE EIFFEL TOWER
BUT IT WAS STILL TOTALLY FABULOUS TO ME... (I'M SO PROVINCIAL & UNSOPHISTICATED..) DON'T TELL!!
"PARIS IS EXCITING & PEACEFUL" *
I'M CONSTANTLY INSPIRED & TOUCHED BY LOVING ATTENTION TO MINUTE, ESTHETIC DETAILS!
I SUDDENLY LOVE FOOD SHOPPING!!
DAILY SURVIVAL DOESN'T HAFTO BE GRIM!
* GERT STEIN
GOOD CIGARETTES! CHEAP WINE! NO GUILT!!
ITS WEIRD NOT TO FEEL ALIENATED FROM THE MASSES!!
REGULAH PEOPLE DISCUSS AHT
DOMINIQUE YOU'VE SEEN THE NEW PICASSO MUSEUM??
MAYBE I BELONG HERE!?
OUI, OUI MON AMI
C'EST FORMIDABLE
PEOPLE SIT AROUND IN CAFÉS & TALK...

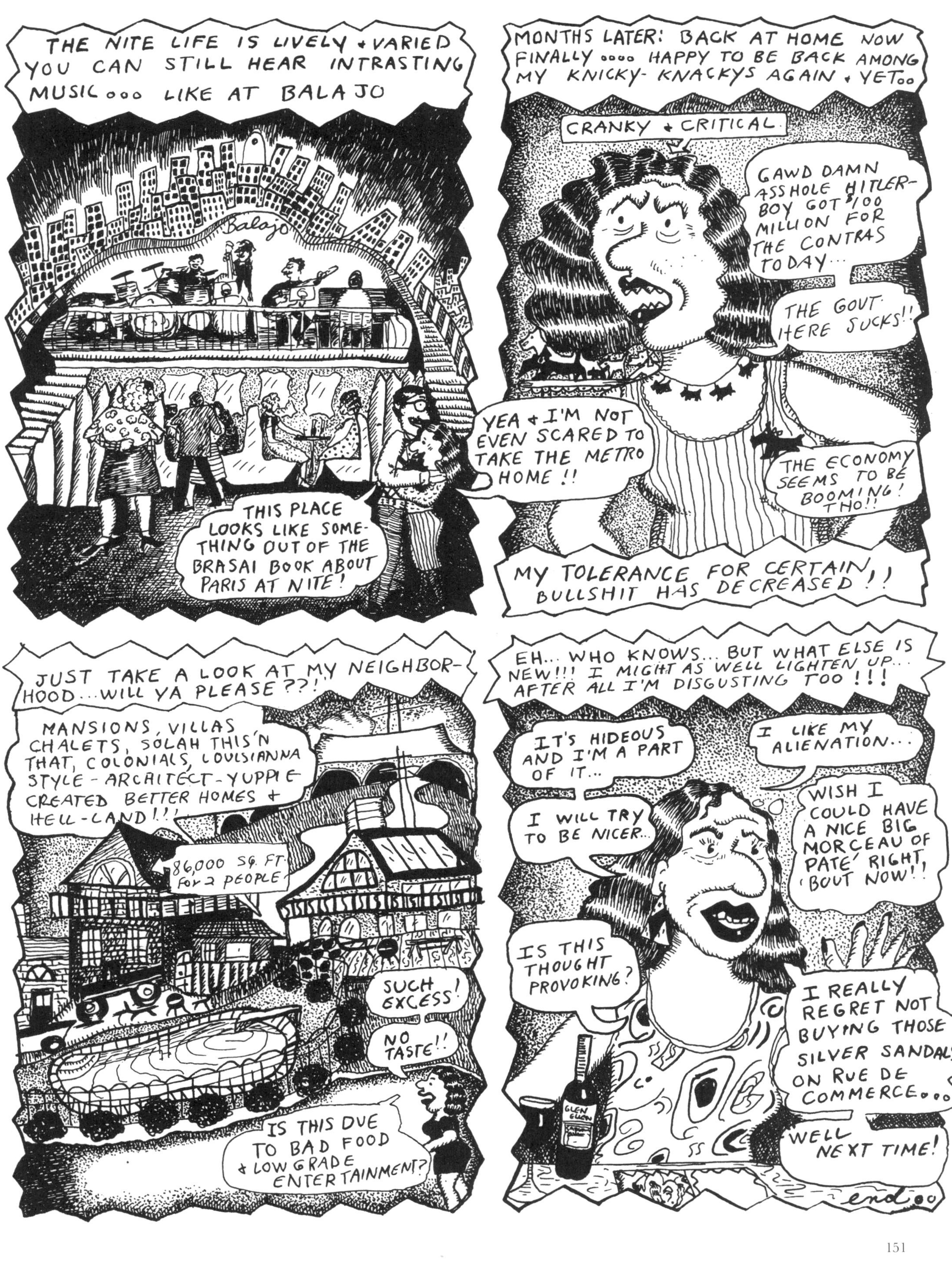
THE NITE LIFE IS LIVELY + VARIED YOU CAN STILL HEAR INTRASTING MUSIC... LIKE AT BALAJO
Balajo
THIS PLACE LOOKS LIKE SOMETHING OUT OF THE BRASAI BOOK ABOUT PARIS AT NITE!
YEA + I'M NOT EVEN SCARED TO TAKE THE METRO HOME!!
MONTHS LATER: BACK AT HOME NOW FINALLY.... HAPPY TO BE BACK AMONG MY KNICKY-KNACKYS AGAIN + YET..
CRANKY + CRITICAL
GAWD DAMN ASSHOLE HITLER-BOY GOT $100 MILLION FOR THE CONTRAS TODAY...
THE GOVT HERE SUCKS!!
THE ECONOMY SEEMS TO BE BOOMING! THO!!
MY TOLERANCE FOR CERTAIN BULLSHIT HAS DECREASED!!
JUST TAKE A LOOK AT MY NEIGHBORHOOD... WILL YA PLEASE??!
MANSIONS, VILLAS CHALETS, SOLAH THIS'N THAT, COLONIALS, LOUISIANNA STYLE-ARCHITECT-YUPPIE CREATED BETTER HOMES + HELL-LAND!!!
86,000 SQ. FT. FOR 2 PEOPLE
SUCH EXCESS!
NO TASTE!!
IS THIS DUE TO BAD FOOD + LOW GRADE ENTERTAINMENT?
EH... WHO KNOWS... BUT WHAT ELSE IS NEW!!! I MIGHT AS WELL LIGHTEN UP... AFTER ALL I'M DISGUSTING TOO!!!
IT'S HIDEOUS AND I'M A PART OF IT...
I LIKE MY ALIENATION...
I WILL TRY TO BE NICER...
WISH I COULD HAVE A NICE BIG MORCEAU OF PATE' RIGHT 'BOUT NOW!!
IS THIS THOUGHT PROVOKING?
I REALLY REGRET NOT BUYING THOSE SILVER SANDALS ON RUE DE COMMERCE...
WELL NEXT TIME!
GLEN ELLEN
end..

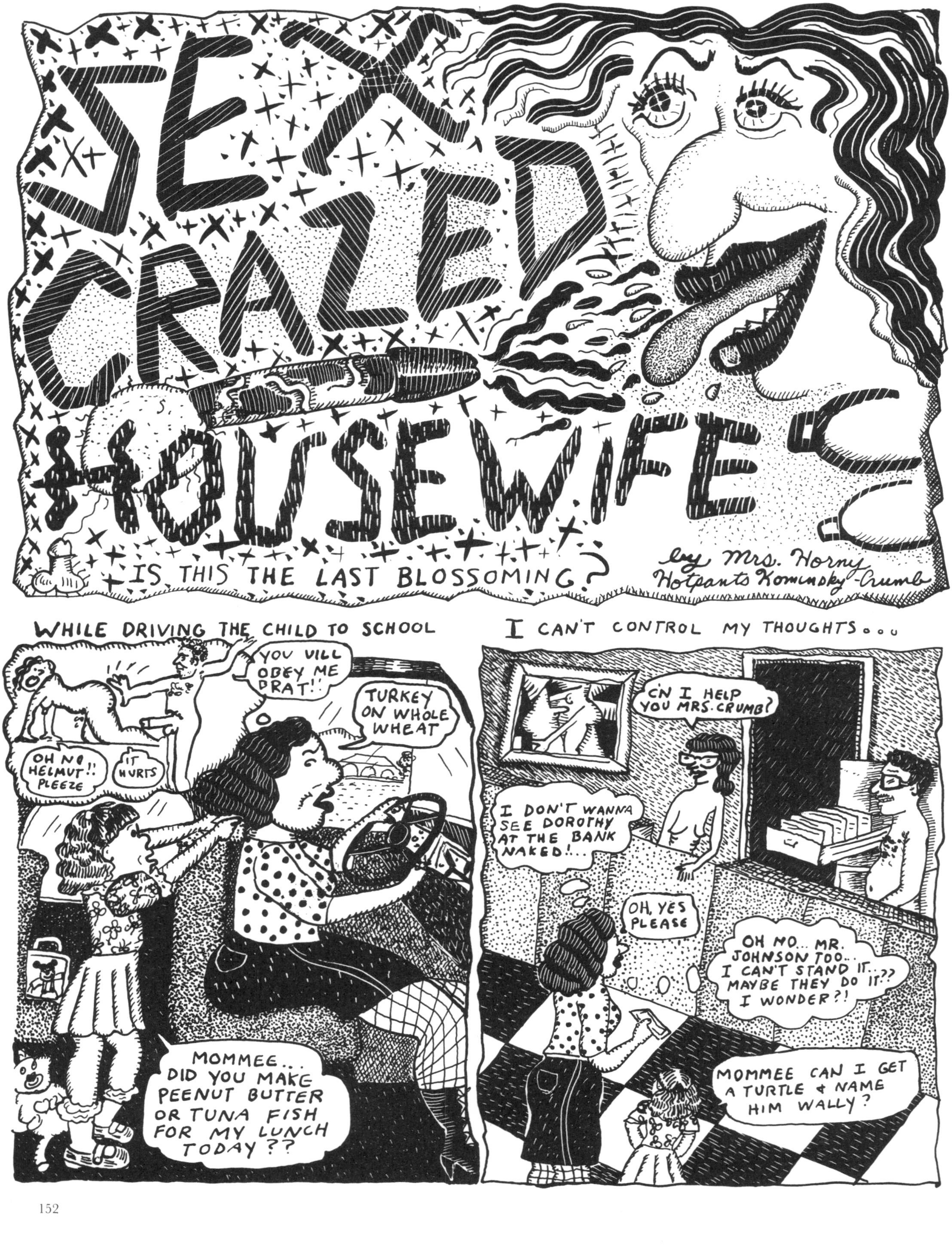
SEX CRAZED HOUSEWIFE
IS THIS THE LAST BLOSSOMING?
by Mrs. Horny Hotpants Kominsky-Crumb
WHILE DRIVING THE CHILD TO SCHOOL
YOU VILL OBEY ME BRAT!!
OH NO HELMUT!! PLEEZE
IT HURTS
TURKEY ON WHOLE WHEAT
MOMMEE.. DID YOU MAKE PEENUT BUTTER OR TUNA FISH FOR MY LUNCH TODAY??
I CAN'T CONTROL MY THOUGHTS...
C'N I HELP YOU MRS. CRUMB?
I DON'T WANNA SEE DOROTHY AT THE BANK NAKED!..
OH, YES PLEASE
OH NO.. MR. JOHNSON TOO.. I CAN'T STAND IT..?? MAYBE THEY DO IT?? I WONDER?!
MOMMEE CAN I GET A TURTLE & NAME HIM WALLY?

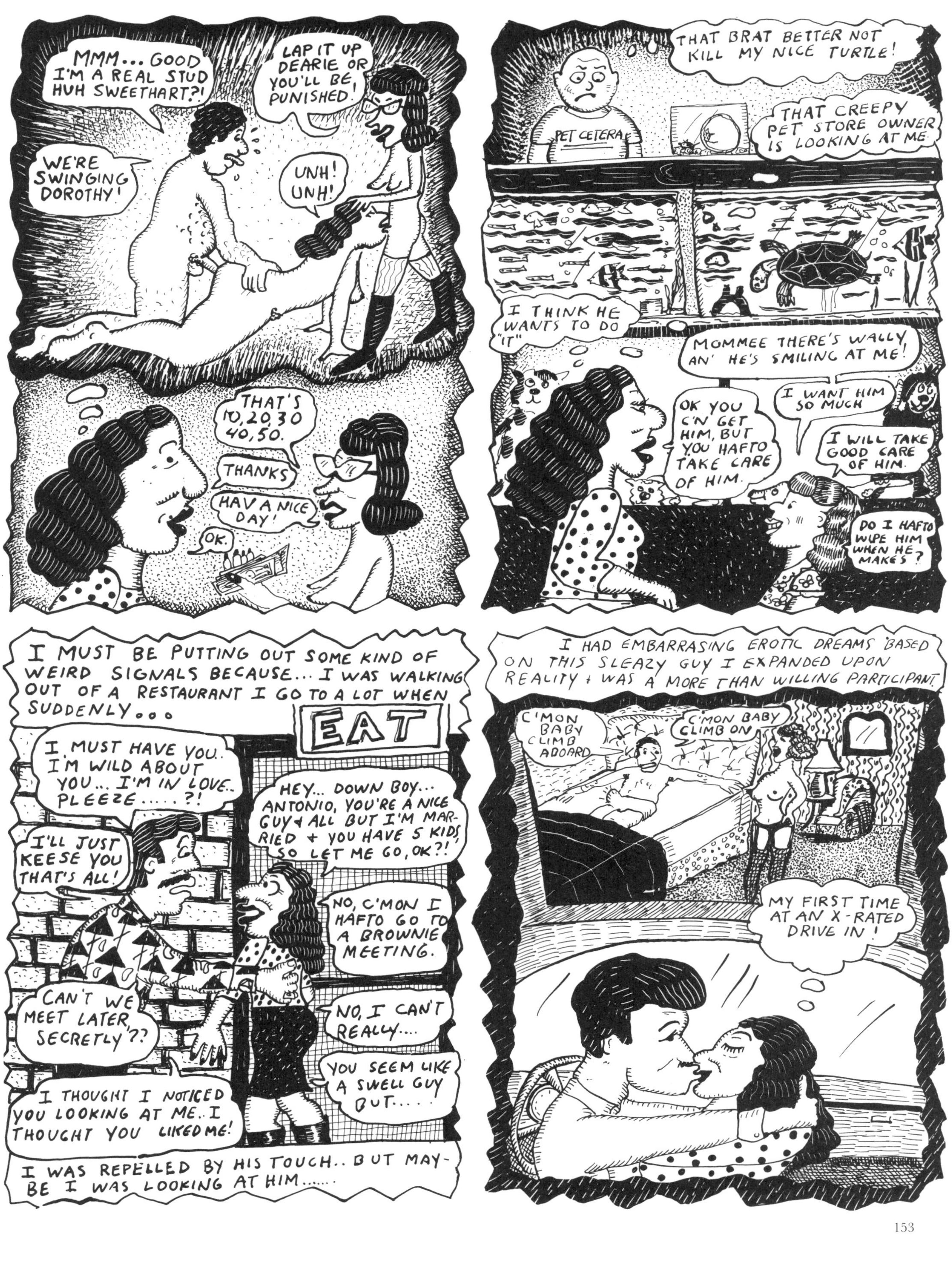
MMM... GOOD I'M A REAL STUD HUH SWEETHART?!
LAP IT UP DEARIE OR YOU'LL BE PUNISHED!
WE'RE SWINGING DOROTHY!
UNH! UNH!
THAT'S 10, 20, 30 40, 50.
THANKS
HAV A NICE DAY!
OK.
THAT BRAT BETTER NOT KILL MY NICE TURTLE!
PET CETERA
THAT CREEPY PET STORE OWNER IS LOOKING AT ME
I THINK HE WANTS TO DO "IT"
MOMMEE THERE'S WALLY, AN' HE'S SMILING AT ME!
OK YOU C'N GET HIM, BUT YOU HAFTO TAKE CARE OF HIM.
I WANT HIM SO MUCH
I WILL TAKE GOOD CARE OF HIM.
DO I HAFTO WIPE HIM WHEN HE MAKES?
I MUST BE PUTTING OUT SOME KIND OF WEIRD SIGNALS BECAUSE... I WAS WALKING OUT OF A RESTAURANT I GO TO A LOT WHEN SUDDENLY...
EAT
I MUST HAVE YOU. I'M WILD ABOUT YOU... I'M IN LOVE.. PLEEZE.....?!
HEY... DOWN BOY... ANTONIO, YOU'RE A NICE GUY & ALL BUT I'M MARRIED & YOU HAVE 5 KIDS, SO LET ME GO, OK?!
I'LL JUST KEESE YOU THAT'S ALL!
NO, C'MON I HAFTO GO TO A BROWNIE MEETING.
CAN'T WE MEET LATER, SECRETLY??
NO, I CAN'T REALLY....
YOU SEEM LIKE A SWELL GUY BUT....
I THOUGHT I NOTICED YOU LOOKING AT ME.. I THOUGHT YOU LIKED ME!
I WAS REPELLED BY HIS TOUCH.. BUT MAYBE I WAS LOOKING AT HIM......
I HAD EMBARRASING EROTIC DREAMS BASED ON THIS SLEAZY GUY I EXPANDED UPON REALITY & WAS A MORE THAN WILLING PARTICIPANT.
C'MON BABY CLIMB ABOARD
C'MON BABY CLIMB ON
MY FIRST TIME AT AN X-RATED DRIVE IN!

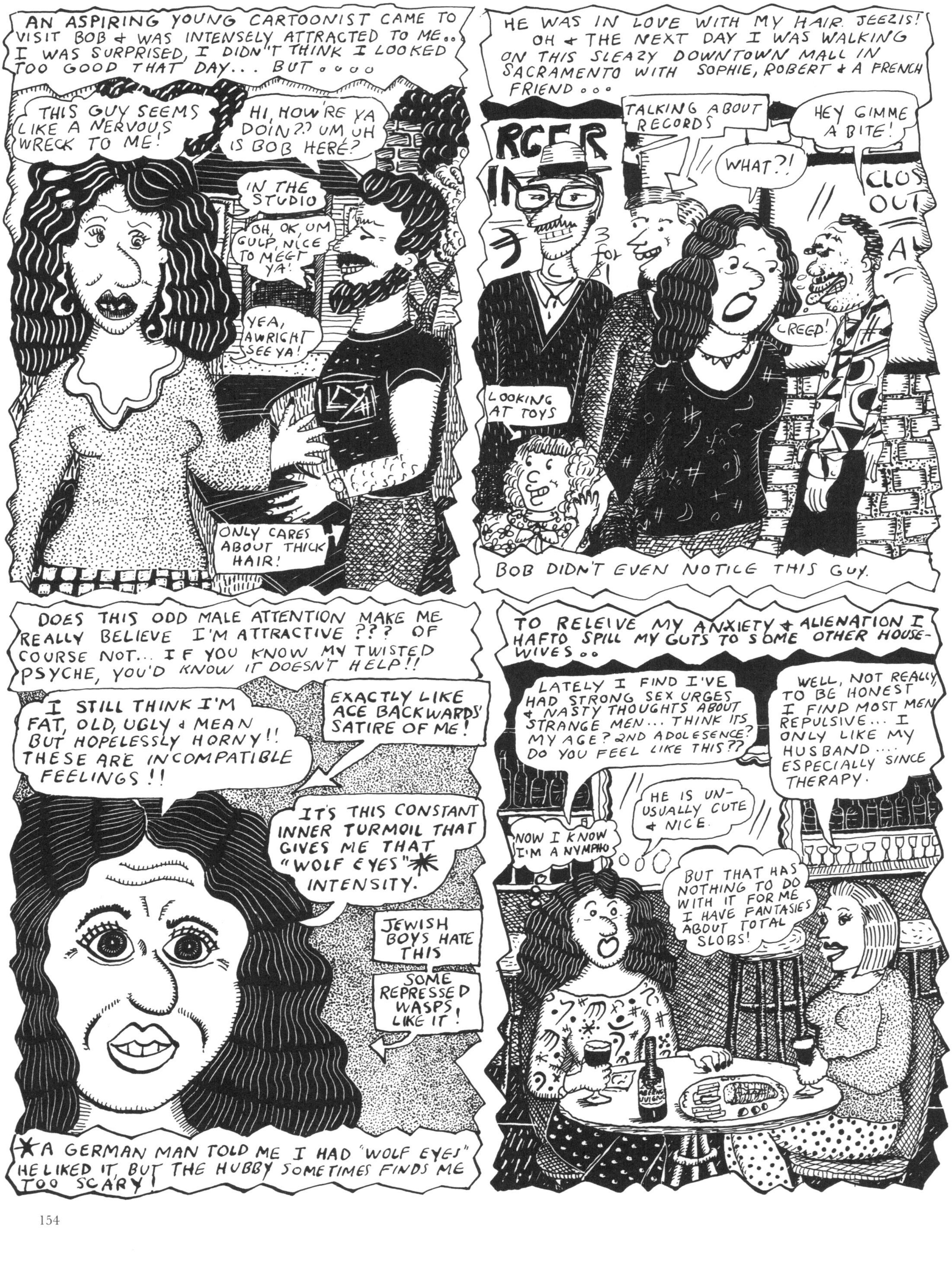
AN ASPIRING YOUNG CARTOONIST CAME TO VISIT BOB & WAS INTENSELY ATTRACTED TO ME... I WAS SURPRISED, I DIDN'T THINK I LOOKED TOO GOOD THAT DAY... BUT....
THIS GUY SEEMS LIKE A NERVOUS WRECK TO ME!
HI, HOW'RE YA DOIN?? UM UH IS BOB HERE?
IN THE STUDIO
OH, OK, UM GULP, NICE TO MEET YA!
YEA, AWRIGHT SEE YA!
ONLY CARES ABOUT THICK HAIR!
HE WAS IN LOVE WITH MY HAIR. JEEZIS! OH & THE NEXT DAY I WAS WALKING ON THIS SLEAZY DOWNTOWN MALL IN SACRAMENTO WITH SOPHIE, ROBERT & A FRENCH FRIEND...
TALKING ABOUT RECORDS
HEY GIMME A BITE!
WHAT?!
CREEP!
LOOKING AT TOYS
BOB DIDN'T EVEN NOTICE THIS GUY.
DOES THIS ODD MALE ATTENTION MAKE ME REALLY BELIEVE I'M ATTRACTIVE??? OF COURSE NOT... IF YOU KNOW MY TWISTED PSYCHE, YOU'D KNOW IT DOESN'T HELP!!
I STILL THINK I'M FAT, OLD, UGLY & MEAN BUT HOPELESSLY HORNY!! THESE ARE INCOMPATIBLE FEELINGS!!
EXACTLY LIKE ACE BACKWARDS' SATIRE OF ME!
IT'S THIS CONSTANT INNER TURMOIL THAT GIVES ME THAT "WOLF EYES"* INTENSITY.
JEWISH BOYS HATE THIS
SOME REPRESSED WASPS LIKE IT!
*A GERMAN MAN TOLD ME I HAD "WOLF EYES" HE LIKED IT, BUT THE HUBBY SOMETIMES FINDS ME TOO SCARY!
TO RELEIVE MY ANXIETY & ALIENATION I HAFTO SPILL MY GUTS TO SOME OTHER HOUSE-WIVES..
LATELY I FIND I'VE HAD STRONG SEX URGES & NASTY THOUGHTS ABOUT STRANGE MEN... THINK ITS MY AGE? 2ND ADOLESENCE? DO YOU FEEL LIKE THIS??
WELL, NOT REALLY TO BE HONEST I FIND MOST MEN REPULSIVE... I ONLY LIKE MY HUSBAND... ESPECIALLY SINCE THERAPY.
HE IS UNUSUALLY CUTE & NICE.
NOW I KNOW I'M A NYMPHO
BUT THAT HAS NOTHING TO DO WITH IT FOR ME I HAVE FANTASIES ABOUT TOTAL SLOBS!

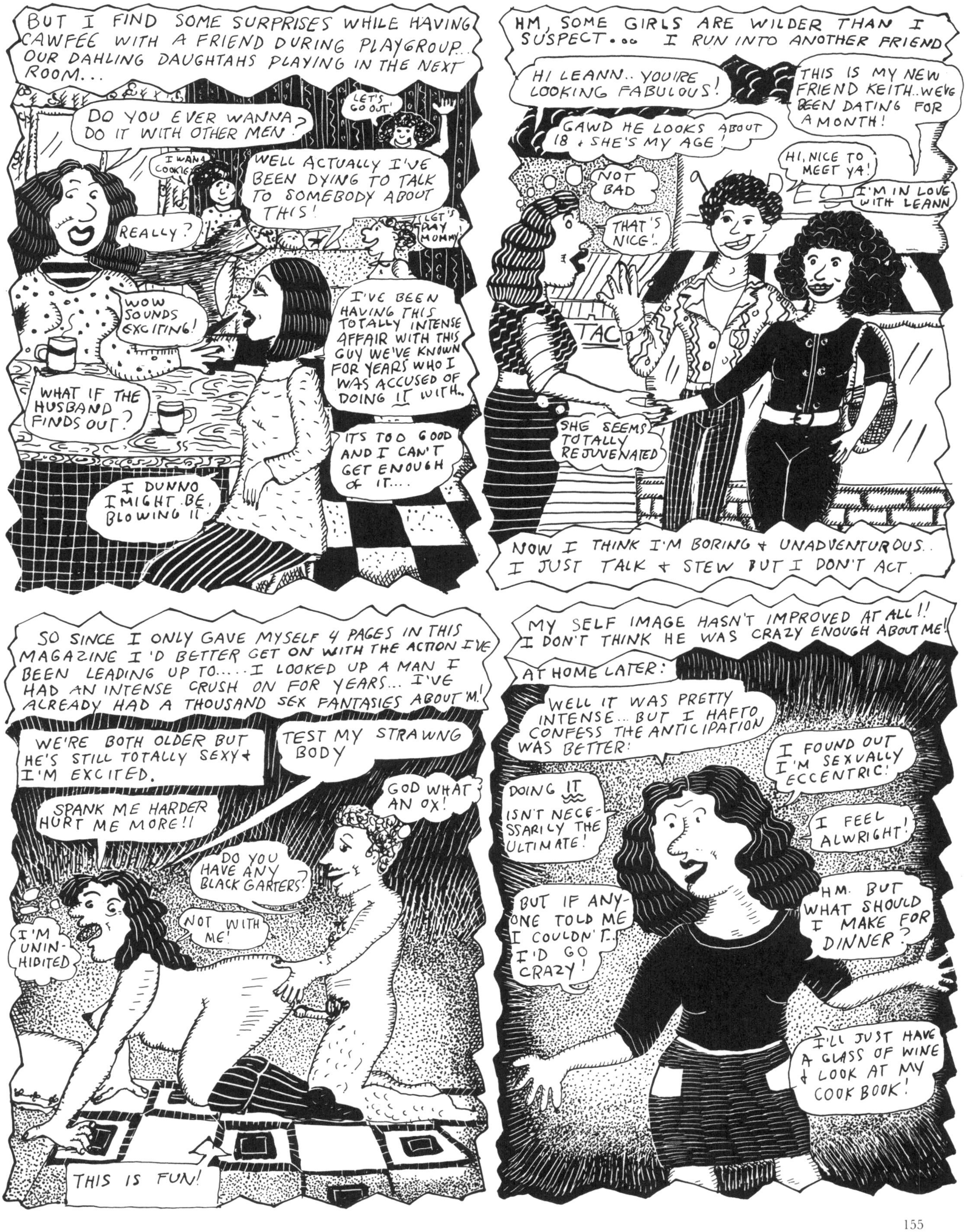
BUT I FIND SOME SURPRISES WHILE HAVING CAWFEE WITH A FRIEND DURING PLAYGROUP.. OUR DAHLING DAUGHTAHS PLAYING IN THE NEXT ROOM...
LET'S GO OUT!
DO YOU EVER WANNA DO IT WITH OTHER MEN?
I WANA COOKIE
WELL ACTUALLY I'VE BEEN DYING TO TALK TO SOMEBODY ABOUT THIS!
LET'S PLAY MOMMY!
REALLY?
WOW SOUNDS EXCITING!
I'VE BEEN HAVING THIS TOTALLY INTENSE AFFAIR WITH THIS GUY WE'VE KNOWN FOR YEARS WHO I WAS ACCUSED OF DOING IT WITH..
WHAT IF THE HUSBAND FINDS OUT?
ITS TOO GOOD AND I CAN'T GET ENOUGH OF IT....
I DUNNO I MIGHT BE BLOWING IT
HM, SOME GIRLS ARE WILDER THAN I SUSPECT... I RUN INTO ANOTHER FRIEND
HI LEANN.. YOU'RE LOOKING FABULOUS!
THIS IS MY NEW FRIEND KEITH..WE'VE BEEN DATING FOR A MONTH!
GAWD HE LOOKS ABOUT 18 + SHE'S MY AGE!
HI, NICE TO MEET YA!
NOT BAD
I'M IN LOVE WITH LEANN
THAT'S NICE!
SHE SEEMS TOTALLY REJUVENATED
NOW I THINK I'M BORING + UNADVENTUROUS.. I JUST TALK + STEW BUT I DON'T ACT.
SO SINCE I ONLY GAVE MYSELF 4 PAGES IN THIS MAGAZINE I'D BETTER GET ON WITH THE ACTION I'VE BEEN LEADING UP TO..... I LOOKED UP A MAN I HAD AN INTENSE CRUSH ON FOR YEARS... I'VE ALREADY HAD A THOUSAND SEX FANTASIES ABOUT 'M!
WE'RE BOTH OLDER BUT HE'S STILL TOTALLY SEXY + I'M EXCITED.
TEST MY STRAWNG BODY
GOD WHAT AN OX!
SPANK ME HARDER HURT ME MORE!!
DO YOU HAVE ANY BLACK GARTERS?
NOT WITH ME!
I'M UNIN-HIDITED
THIS IS FUN!
MY SELF IMAGE HASN'T IMPROVED AT ALL!! I DON'T THINK HE WAS CRAZY ENOUGH ABOUT ME!
AT HOME LATER:
WELL IT WAS PRETTY INTENSE... BUT I HAFTO CONFESS THE ANTICIPATION WAS BETTER.
I FOUND OUT I'M SEXUALLY ECCENTRIC!
DOING IT ISN'T NECE-SSARILY THE ULTIMATE!
I FEEL ALWRIGHT!
BUT IF ANY-ONE TOLD ME I COULDN'T.. I'D GO CRAZY!
HM. BUT WHAT SHOULD I MAKE FOR DINNER?
I'LL JUST HAVE A GLASS OF WINE + LOOK AT MY COOK BOOK!

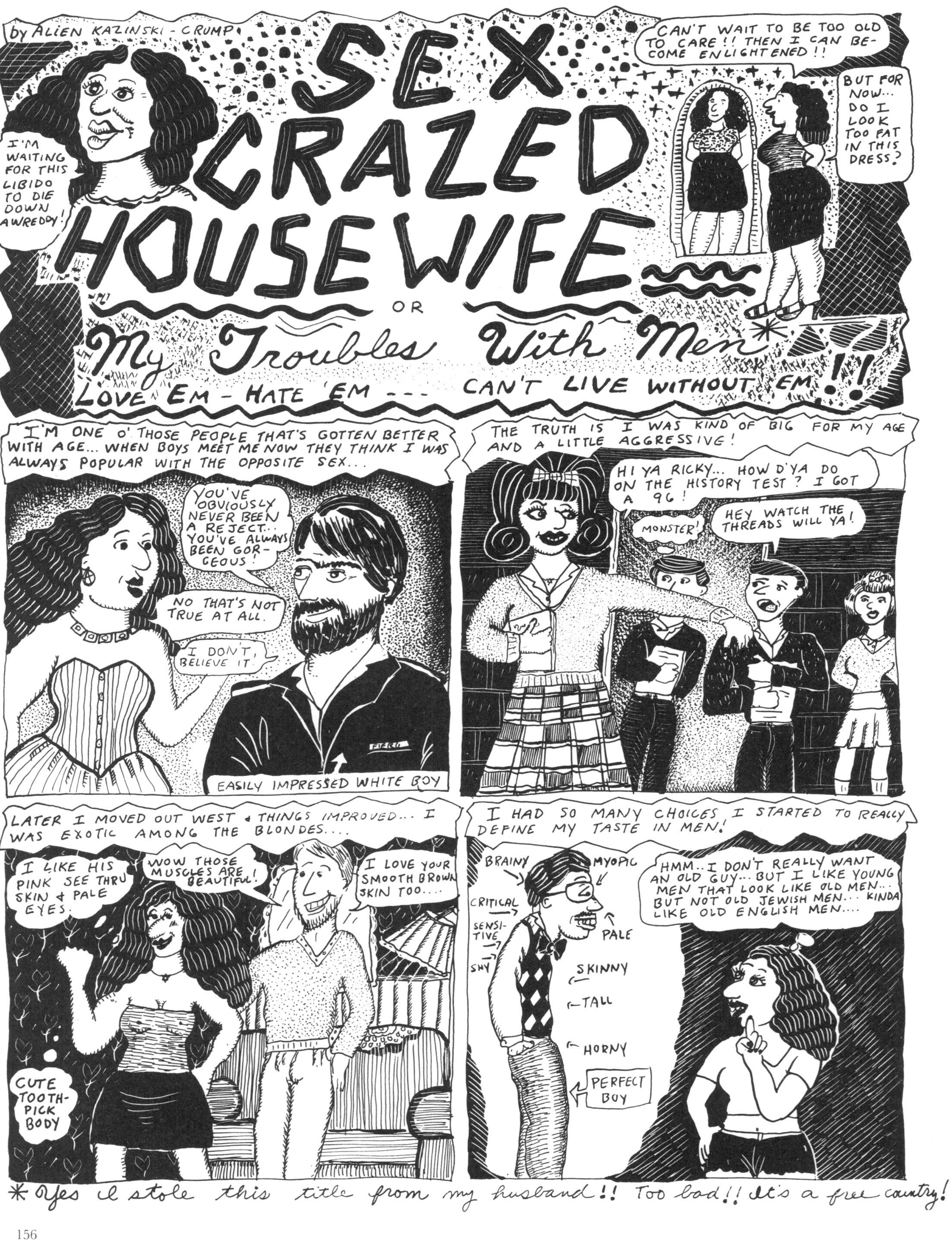
by ALIEN KAZINSKI-CRUMP
SEX CRAZED HOUSEWIFE
OR
My Troubles With Men*
LOVE 'EM - HATE 'EM --- CAN'T LIVE WITHOUT 'EM!!
I'M WAITING FOR THIS LIBIDO TO DIE DOWN AWREDDY!
CAN'T WAIT TO BE TOO OLD TO CARE!! THEN I CAN BECOME ENLIGHTENED!!
BUT FOR NOW... DO I LOOK TOO FAT IN THIS DRESS?
I'M ONE O' THOSE PEOPLE THAT'S GOTTEN BETTER WITH AGE... WHEN BOYS MEET ME NOW THEY THINK I WAS ALWAYS POPULAR WITH THE OPPOSITE SEX...
YOU'VE OBVIOUSLY NEVER BEEN A REJECT.. YOU'VE ALWAYS BEEN GORGEOUS!
NO THAT'S NOT TRUE AT ALL.
I DON'T BELIEVE IT.
EASILY IMPRESSED WHITE BOY
THE TRUTH IS I WAS KIND OF BIG FOR MY AGE AND A LITTLE AGGRESSIVE!
HI YA RICKY... HOW D'YA DO ON THE HISTORY TEST? I GOT A 96!
MONSTER!
HEY WATCH THE THREADS WILL YA!
LATER I MOVED OUT WEST & THINGS IMPROVED... I WAS EXOTIC AMONG THE BLONDES....
I LIKE HIS PINK SEE THRU SKIN & PALE EYES.
WOW THOSE MUSCLES ARE BEAUTIFUL!
I LOVE YOUR SMOOTH BROWN SKIN TOO....
CUTE TOOTH-PICK BODY
I HAD SO MANY CHOICES I STARTED TO REALLY DEFINE MY TASTE IN MEN!
BRAINY
MYOPIC
CRITICAL
SENSITIVE
SHY
PALE
SKINNY
TALL
HORNY
PERFECT BOY
HMM.. I DON'T REALLY WANT AN OLD GUY... BUT I LIKE YOUNG MEN THAT LOOK LIKE OLD MEN... BUT NOT OLD JEWISH MEN... KINDA LIKE OLD ENGLISH MEN....
* Yes I stole this title from my husband!! Too bad!! It's a free country!

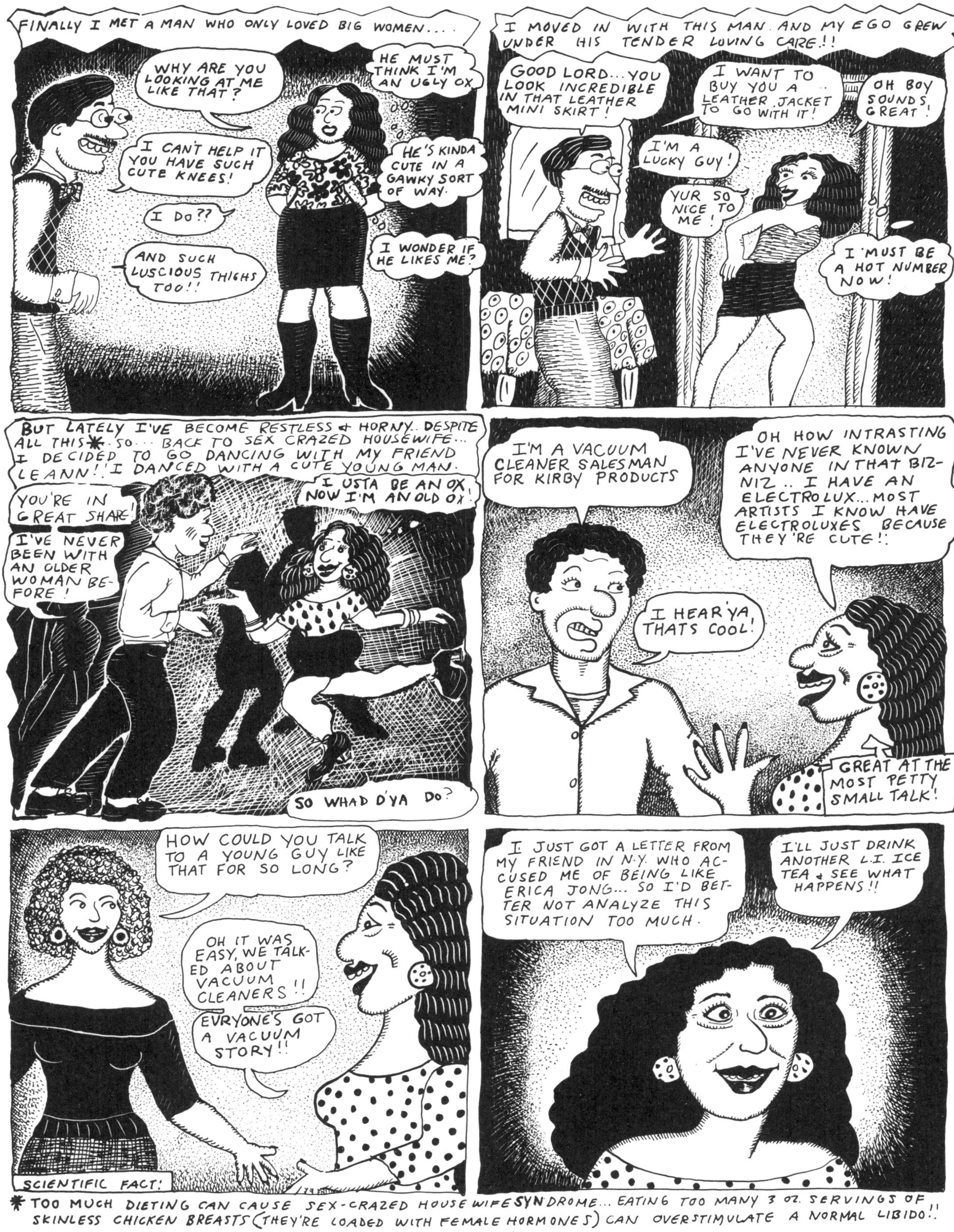
FINALLY I MET A MAN WHO ONLY LOVED BIG WOMEN....
WHY ARE YOU LOOKING AT ME LIKE THAT?
HE MUST THINK I'M AN UGLY OX
I CAN'T HELP IT YOU HAVE SUCH CUTE KNEES!
HE'S KINDA CUTE IN A GAWKY SORT OF WAY.
I DO??
AND SUCH LUSCIOUS THIGHS TOO!!
I WONDER IF HE LIKES ME?
I MOVED IN WITH THIS MAN AND MY EGO GREW UNDER HIS TENDER LOVING CARE!!
GOOD LORD... YOU LOOK INCREDIBLE IN THAT LEATHER MINI SKIRT!
I WANT TO BUY YOU A LEATHER JACKET TO GO WITH IT!
OH BOY SOUNDS GREAT!
I'M A LUCKY GUY!
YUR SO NICE TO ME!
I MUST BE A HOT NUMBER NOW!
BUT LATELY I'VE BECOME RESTLESS & HORNY.. DESPITE ALL THIS* SO... BACK TO SEX CRAZED HOUSEWIFE... I DECIDED TO GO DANCING WITH MY FRIEND LEANN! I DANCED WITH A CUTE YOUNG MAN.
YOU'RE IN GREAT SHAPE!
I USTA BE AN OX NOW I'M AN OLD OX!
I'VE NEVER BEEN WITH AN OLDER WOMAN BEFORE!
SO WHAD D'YA DO?
I'M A VACUUM CLEANER SALESMAN FOR KIRBY PRODUCTS
OH HOW INTRASTING I'VE NEVER KNOWN ANYONE IN THAT BIZNIZ.. I HAVE AN ELECTROLUX...MOST ARTISTS I KNOW HAVE ELECTROLUXES BECAUSE THEY'RE CUTE!
I HEAR 'YA, THATS COOL!
GREAT AT THE MOST PETTY SMALL TALK!
HOW COULD YOU TALK TO A YOUNG GUY LIKE THAT FOR SO LONG?
OH IT WAS EASY, WE TALKED ABOUT VACUUM CLEANERS!!
EVRYONE'S GOT A VACUUM STORY!!
SCIENTIFIC FACT!
I JUST GOT A LETTER FROM MY FRIEND IN N.Y. WHO ACCUSED ME OF BEING LIKE ERICA JONG... SO I'D BETTER NOT ANALYZE THIS SITUATION TOO MUCH.
I'LL JUST DRINK ANOTHER L.I. ICE TEA & SEE WHAT HAPPENS!!

* TOO MUCH DIETING CAN CAUSE SEX-CRAZED HOUSEWIFE SYNDROME... EATING TOO MANY 3 OZ. SERVINGS OF SKINLESS CHICKEN BREASTS (THEY'RE LOADED WITH FEMALE HORMONES) CAN OVERSTIMULATE A NORMAL LIBIDO!!

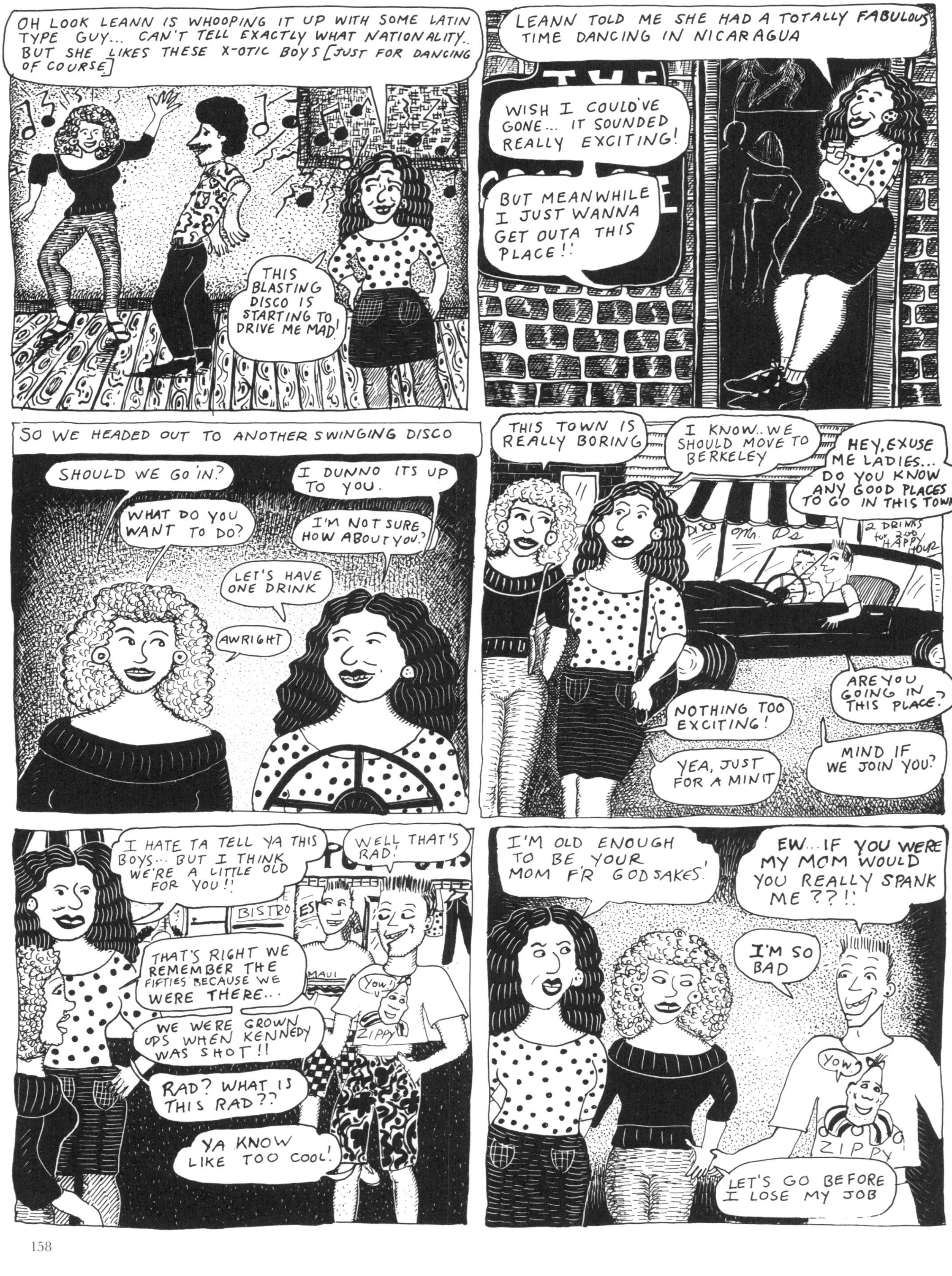
OH LOOK LEANN IS WHOOPING IT UP WITH SOME LATIN TYPE GUY... CAN'T TELL EXACTLY WHAT NATIONALITY.. BUT SHE LIKES THESE X-OTIC BOYS [JUST FOR DANCING OF COURSE]
THIS BLASTING DISCO IS STARTING TO DRIVE ME MAD!
LEANN TOLD ME SHE HAD A TOTALLY FABULOUS TIME DANCING IN NICARAGUA
WISH I COULD'VE GONE... IT SOUNDED REALLY EXCITING!
BUT MEANWHILE I JUST WANNA GET OUTA THIS PLACE!!
SO WE HEADED OUT TO ANOTHER SWINGING DISCO
SHOULD WE GO IN?
I DUNNO ITS UP TO YOU.
WHAT DO YOU WANT TO DO?
I'M NOT SURE HOW ABOUT YOU?
LET'S HAVE ONE DRINK
AWRIGHT
THIS TOWN IS REALLY BORING
I KNOW..WE SHOULD MOVE TO BERKELEY
HEY, EXUSE ME LADIES... DO YOU KNOW ANY GOOD PLACES TO GO IN THIS TOWN?
2 DRINKS for 200 HAPPY HOUR
NOTHING TOO EXCITING!
ARE YOU GOING IN THIS PLACE?
YEA, JUST FOR A MINIT
MIND IF WE JOIN YOU?
I HATE TA TELL YA THIS BOYS... BUT I THINK WE'RE A LITTLE OLD FOR YOU!!
WELL THAT'S RAD!
BISTRO
THAT'S RIGHT WE REMEMBER THE FIFTIES BECAUSE WE WERE THERE...
MAUI
YOW!
WE WERE GROWN UPS WHEN KENNEDY WAS SHOT!!
ZIPPY
RAD? WHAT IS THIS RAD??
YA KNOW LIKE TOO COOL!
I'M OLD ENOUGH TO BE YOUR MOM F'R GODSAKES!
EW...IF YOU WERE MY MOM WOULD YOU REALLY SPANK ME??!!
I'M SO BAD
YOW!
ZIPPY
LET'S GO BEFORE I LOSE MY JOB

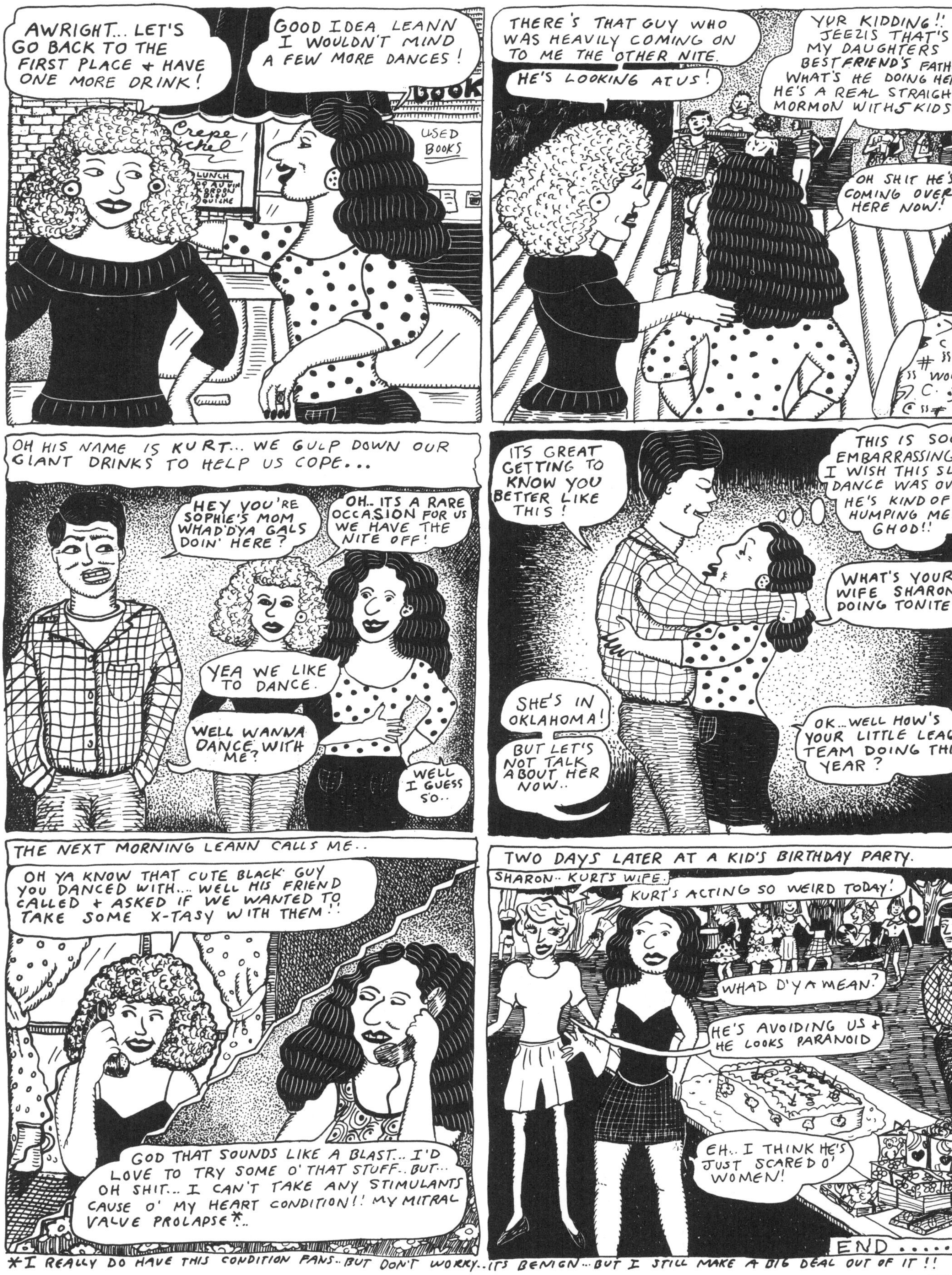
AWRIGHT... LET'S GO BACK TO THE FIRST PLACE + HAVE ONE MORE DRINK!
GOOD IDEA LEANN I WOULDN'T MIND A FEW MORE DANCES!
USED BOOKS
THERE'S THAT GUY WHO WAS HEAVILY COMING ON TO ME THE OTHER NITE.
HE'S LOOKING AT US!
YUR KIDDING!! JEEZIS THAT'S MY DAUGHTERS BEST FRIEND'S FATHER WHAT'S HE DOING HERE? HE'S A REAL STRAIGHT MORMON WITH 5 KIDS!
OH SHIT HE'S COMING OVER HERE NOW!
OH HIS NAME IS KURT... WE GULP DOWN OUR GIANT DRINKS TO HELP US COPE...
HEY YOU'RE SOPHIE'S MOM WHAD'DYA GALS DOIN' HERE?
OH.. ITS A RARE OCCASION FOR US WE HAVE THE NITE OFF!
YEA WE LIKE TO DANCE.
WELL WANNA DANCE WITH ME?
WELL I GUESS SO..
ITS GREAT GETTING TO KNOW YOU BETTER LIKE THIS!
THIS IS SOOO EMBARRASSING... I WISH THIS SLOW DANCE WAS OVER... HE'S KIND OF HUMPING ME... GHOD!!
WHAT'S YOUR WIFE SHARON DOING TONITE?
SHE'S IN OKLAHOMA!
BUT LET'S NOT TALK ABOUT HER NOW..
OK... WELL HOW'S YOUR LITTLE LEAGUE TEAM DOING THIS YEAR?
THE NEXT MORNING LEANN CALLS ME..
OH YA KNOW THAT CUTE BLACK GUY YOU DANCED WITH.... WELL HIS FRIEND CALLED + ASKED IF WE WANTED TO TAKE SOME X-TASY WITH THEM!!
GOD THAT SOUNDS LIKE A BLAST... I'D LOVE TO TRY SOME O' THAT STUFF.. BUT... OH SHIT... I CAN'T TAKE ANY STIMULANTS CAUSE O' MY HEART CONDITION!! MY MITRAL VALVE PROLAPSE*..
TWO DAYS LATER AT A KID'S BIRTHDAY PARTY.
SHARON.. KURT'S WIFE.
KURT'S ACTING SO WEIRD TODAY!
WHAD D'YA MEAN?
HE'S AVOIDING US + HE LOOKS PARANOID
EH.. I THINK HE'S JUST SCARED O' WOMEN!
END.....
*I REALLY DO HAVE THIS CONDITION FANS.. BUT DON'T WORRY.. IT'S BENIGN... BUT I STILL MAKE A BIG DEAL OUT OF IT!!

ANATOMY of the BUNCH BODY

THE BUNCH'S MOUTH IS LIKE A CLIFF SHE SHOVELS FOOD IN AND PUSHES IT TO THE EDGE..... LITTLE OR NO CHEWING NECESSARY.

TEETH ARE SMALL & DON'T HAFTO DO MUCH

THE FOOD BOUNCES OFF THE BACK OF THE THROAT & THEN IS PROPELLED DOWN.

THE BUNCH BODY MERELY HAS A LEDGE WHERE MOST PEOPLE'S STOMACHES ARE LOCATED.

SOME O' THE FOOD WAITS HERE BEFORE FALLING DOWN.

STOCKPILE IN CASE THE BUNCH IS HUNGRY IN BETWEEN MEALS 'N SNACKS.

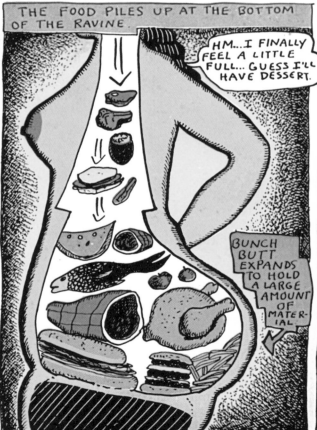

THE FOOD PILES UP AT THE BOTTOM OF THE RAVINE.

HM...I FINALLY FEEL A LITTLE FULL... GUESS I'LL HAVE DESSERT.

BUNCH BUTT EXPANDS TO HOLD A LARGE AMOUNT OF MATERIAL

THIS IS A SATISFIED BUNCH!

BELCH!

GUESS I'LL JOG NOW!

BUNCH TADPOLE HAS A LITTLE ROOM & GETS ITS SHARE OF FOOD!

EXCESS STORAGE

EMERGENCY STORAGE

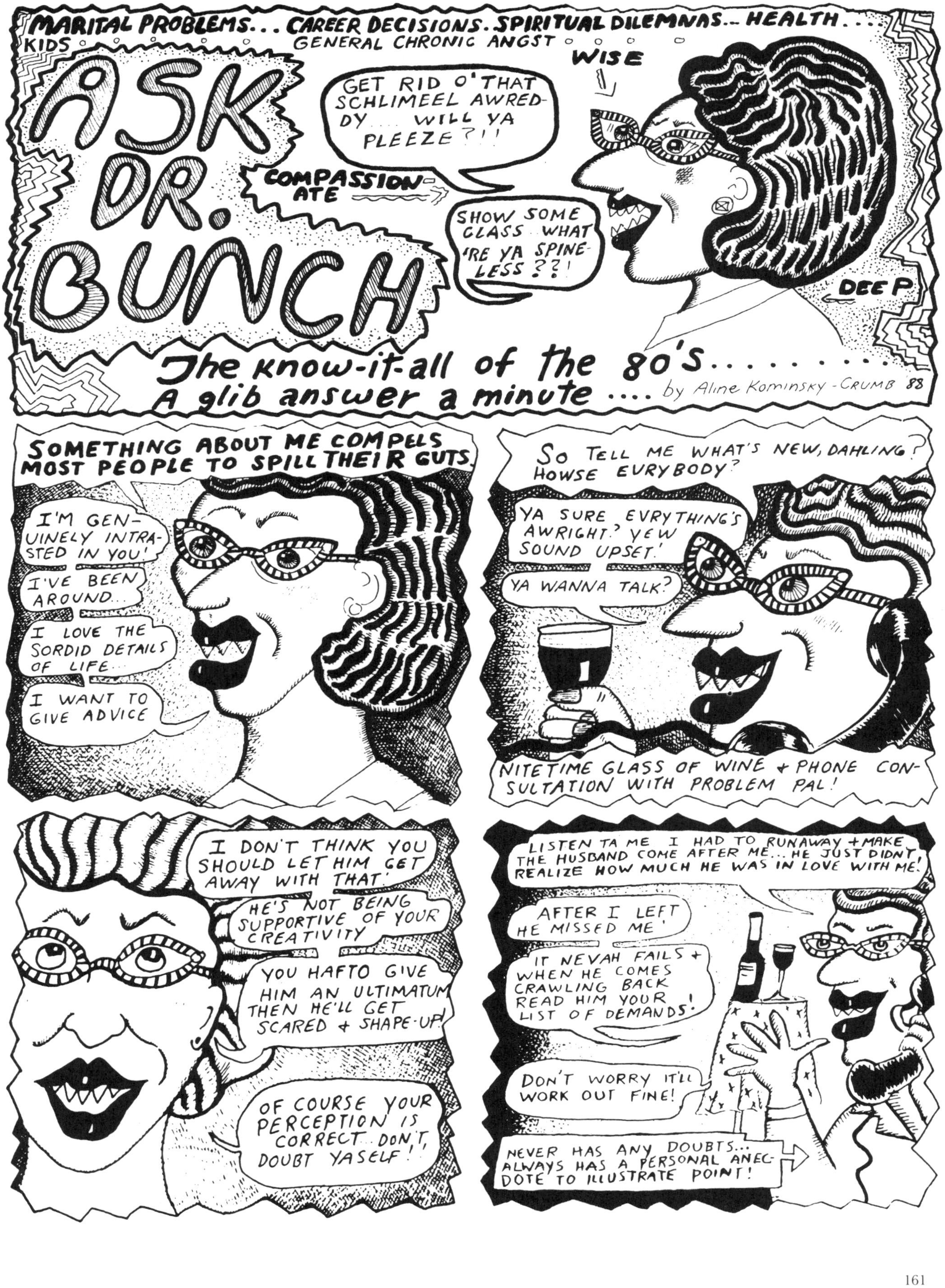

MARITAL PROBLEMS... CAREER DECISIONS. SPIRITUAL DILEMNAS... HEALTH...
KIDS
GENERAL CHRONIC ANGST
ASK DR. BUNCH
GET RID O'THAT SCHLIMEEL AWREDDY... WILL YA PLEEZE?!!
WISE
COMPASSIONATE
SHOW SOME CLASS WHAT 'RE YA SPINELESS??!
DEEP
The know-it-all of the 80's........
A glib answer a minute....
by Aline Kominsky-Crumb 88
SOMETHING ABOUT ME COMPELS MOST PEOPLE TO SPILL THEIR GUTS.
I'M GENUINELY INTRASTED IN YOU!
I'VE BEEN AROUND..
I LOVE THE SORDID DETAILS OF LIFE..
I WANT TO GIVE ADVICE
So TELL ME WHAT'S NEW, DAHLING? HOWSE EVRYBODY?
YA SURE EVRYTHING'S AWRIGHT? YEW SOUND UPSET!
YA WANNA TALK?
NITETIME GLASS OF WINE + PHONE CONSULTATION WITH PROBLEM PAL!
I DON'T THINK YOU SHOULD LET HIM GET AWAY WITH THAT!
HE'S NOT BEING SUPPORTIVE OF YOUR CREATIVITY
YOU HAFTO GIVE HIM AN ULTIMATUM THEN HE'LL GET SCARED + SHAPE-UP!
OF COURSE YOUR PERCEPTION IS CORRECT. DON'T DOUBT YASELF!
LISTEN TA ME I HAD TO RUNAWAY + MAKE THE HUSBAND COME AFTER ME... HE JUST DIDNT REALIZE HOW MUCH HE WAS IN LOVE WITH ME!
AFTER I LEFT HE MISSED ME!
IT NEVAH FAILS + WHEN HE COMES CRAWLING BACK READ HIM YOUR LIST OF DEMANDS!
DON'T WORRY IT'LL WORK OUT FINE!
NEVER HAS ANY DOUBTS... ALWAYS HAS A PERSONAL ANECDOTE TO ILLUSTRATE POINT!

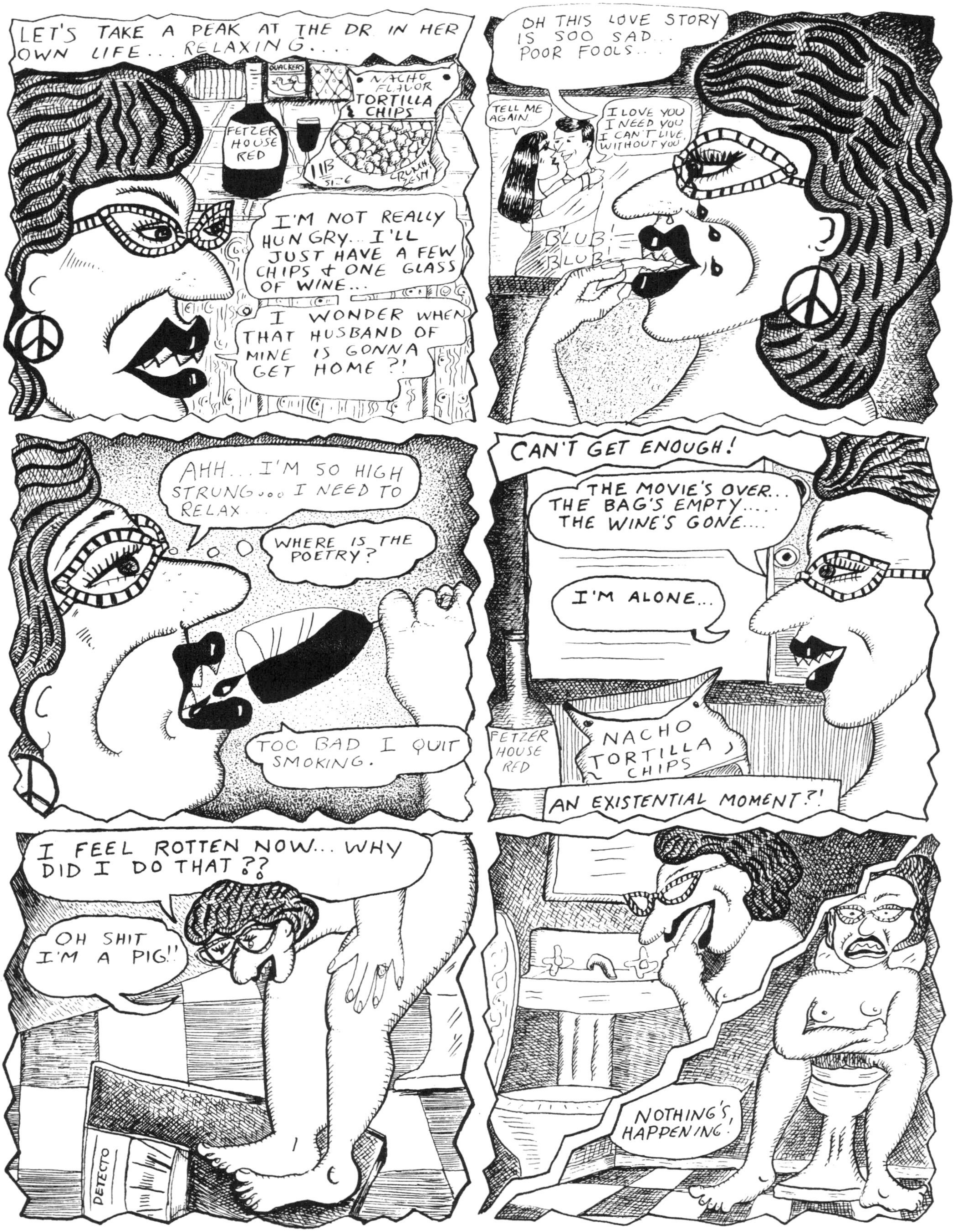

LET'S TAKE A PEAK AT THE DR IN HER OWN LIFE... RELAXING....
QUACKERS
NACHO FLAVOR TORTILLA CHIPS
FETZER HOUSE RED
1 LB SIZE
CRUNCHY
I'M NOT REALLY HUNGRY... I'LL JUST HAVE A FEW CHIPS & ONE GLASS OF WINE...
I WONDER WHEN THAT HUSBAND OF MINE IS GONNA GET HOME?!
OH THIS LOVE STORY IS SOO SAD... POOR FOOLS...
TELL ME AGAIN
I LOVE YOU I NEED YOU I CAN'T LIVE WITHOUT YOU
BLUB! BLUB!
AHH... I'M SO HIGH STRUNG... I NEED TO RELAX...
WHERE IS THE POETRY?
TOO BAD I QUIT SMOKING.
CAN'T GET ENOUGH!
THE MOVIE'S OVER... THE BAG'S EMPTY..... THE WINE'S GONE....
I'M ALONE...
FETZER HOUSE RED
NACHO TORTILLA CHIPS
AN EXISTENTIAL MOMENT?!
I FEEL ROTTEN NOW... WHY DID I DO THAT??
OH SHIT I'M A PIG!!
DETECTO
NOTHING'S HAPPENING!

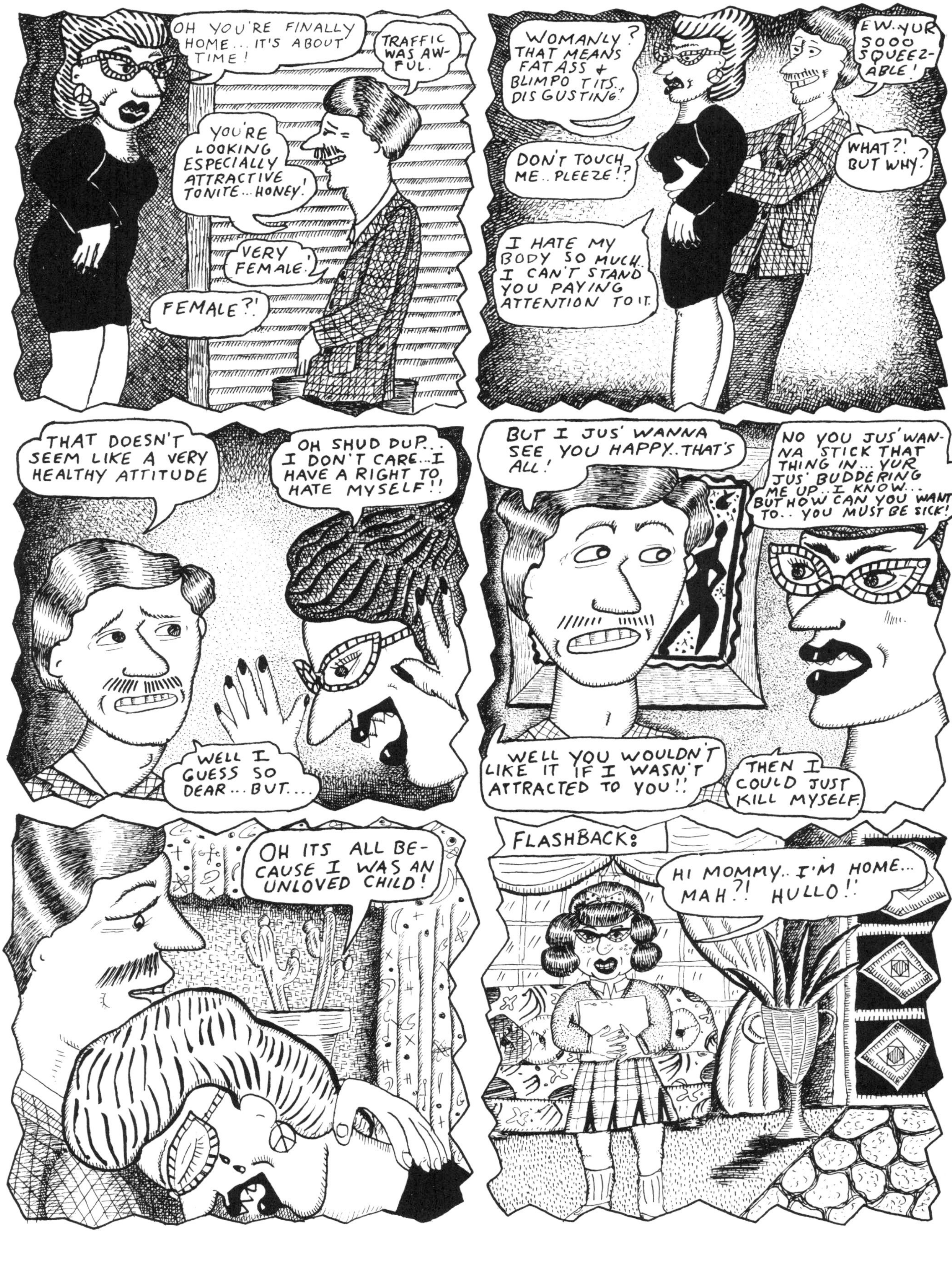

OH YOU'RE FINALLY HOME... IT'S ABOUT TIME!
TRAFFIC WAS AW-FUL.
YOU'RE LOOKING ESPECIALLY ATTRACTIVE TONITE... HONEY!
VERY FEMALE.
FEMALE?!
WOMANLY? THAT MEANS FAT ASS + BLIMPO TITS. DISGUSTING!
EW. YUR SOOO SQUEEZ-ABLE!
DON'T TOUCH ME.. PLEEZE!?
WHAT?! BUT WHY?
I HATE MY BODY SO MUCH.. I CAN'T STAND YOU PAYING ATTENTION TO IT.
THAT DOESN'T SEEM LIKE A VERY HEALTHY ATTITUDE
OH SHUD DUP.. I DON'T CARE... I HAVE A RIGHT TO HATE MYSELF!!
WELL I GUESS SO DEAR... BUT....
BUT I JUS' WANNA SEE YOU HAPPY.. THAT'S ALL!
NO YOU JUS' WAN-NA STICK THAT THING IN... YUR JUS' BUDDERING ME UP.. I KNOW.. BUT HOW CAN YOU WANT TO.. YOU MUST BE SICK!
WELL YOU WOULDN'T LIKE IT IF I WASN'T ATTRACTED TO YOU!!
THEN I COULD JUST KILL MYSELF.
OH ITS ALL BE-CAUSE I WAS AN UNLOVED CHILD!
FLASHBACK:
HI MOMMY.. I'M HOME... MAH?! HULLO!!

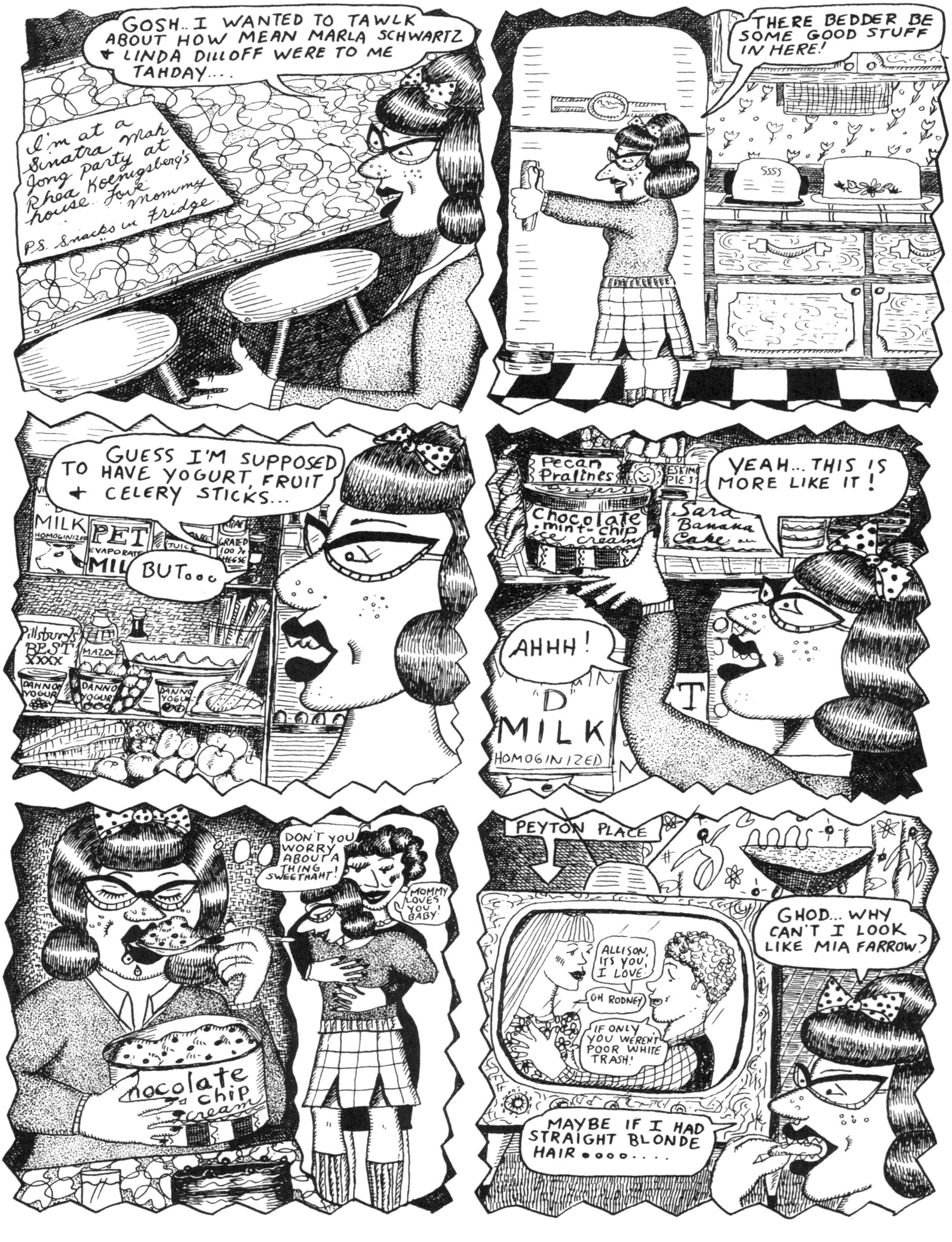

GOSH.. I WANTED TO TAWLK ABOUT HOW MEAN MARLA SCHWARTZ + LINDA DILLOFF WERE TO ME TAHDAY....
I'm at a Sinatra Mah Jong party at Rhea Koenigsberg's house. Love Mommy
P.S. Snacks in Fridge
THERE BEDDER BE SOME GOOD STUFF IN HERE!
GUESS I'M SUPPOSED TO HAVE YOGURT, FRUIT + CELERY STICKS...
BUT...
MILK HOMOGINIZED
PET EVAPORATED MILK
Pillsbury's BEST XXXX
YEAH... THIS IS MORE LIKE IT!
Pecan Pralines
ESKIMO PIES
Chocolate mint-chip ice cream
Sara Banana Cake
AHHH!
"D" MILK HOMOGINIZED
DON'T YOU WORRY ABOUT A THING SWEETHAHT!
MOMMY LOVES YOU, BABY.
hocolate chip cream
PEYTON PLACE
GHOD... WHY CAN'T I LOOK LIKE MIA FARROW?
ALLISON, IT'S YOU I LOVE.
OH RODNEY
IF ONLY YOU WEREN'T POOR WHITE TRASH!
MAYBE IF I HAD STRAIGHT BLONDE HAIR.......

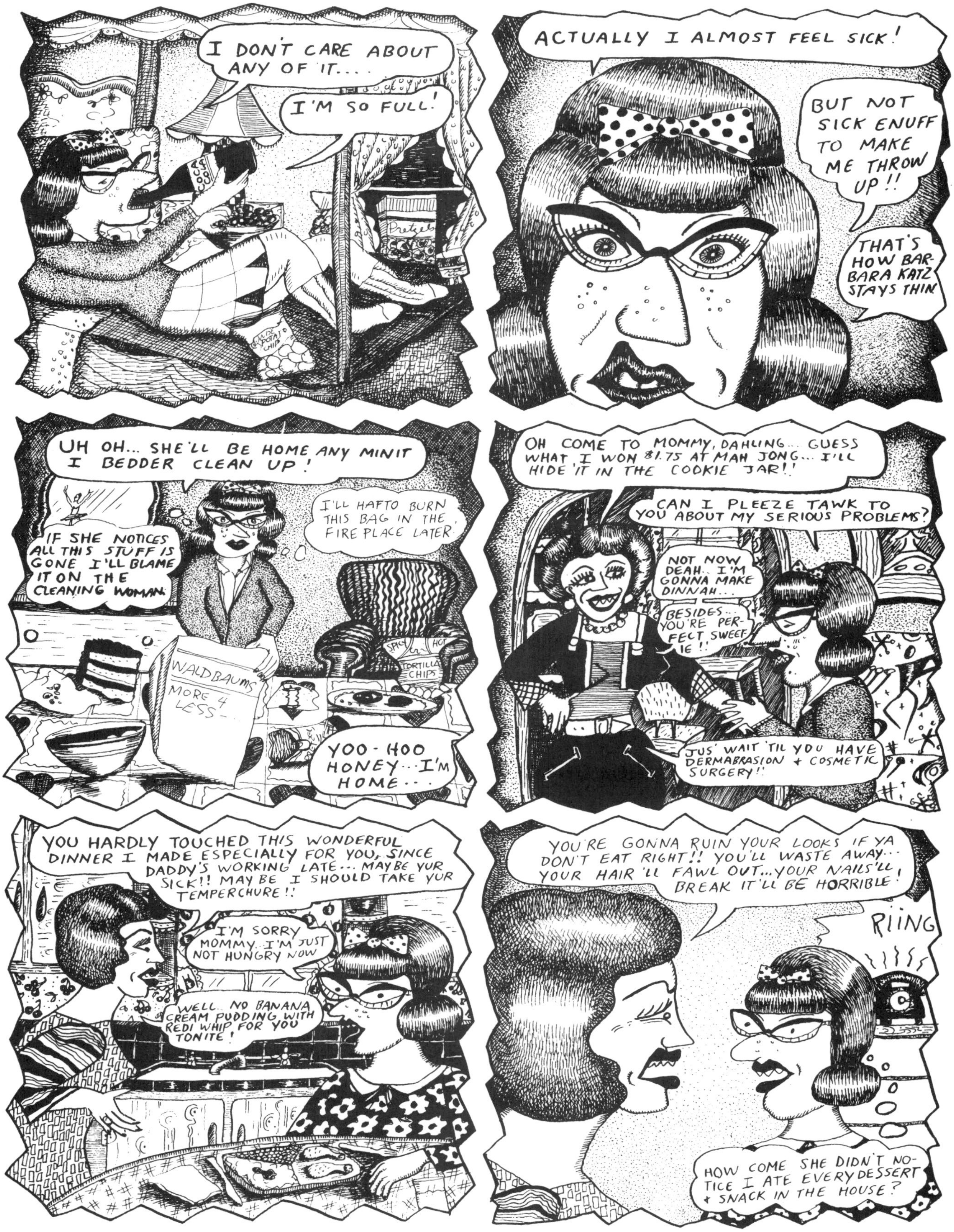

I DON'T CARE ABOUT ANY OF IT....
I'M SO FULL!
COCA COLA
POTATO CHIPS
ACTUALLY I ALMOST FEEL SICK!
BUT NOT SICK ENUFF TO MAKE ME THROW UP!!
THAT'S HOW BARBARA KATZ STAYS THIN
UH OH... SHE'LL BE HOME ANY MINIT I BEDDER CLEAN UP!
IF SHE NOTICES ALL THIS STUFF IS GONE I'LL BLAME IT ON THE CLEANING WOMAN
I'LL HAFTO BURN THIS BAG IN THE FIRE PLACE LATER
WALDBAUMS MORE 4 LESS
SPICY HOT TORTILLA CHIPS
YOO-HOO HONEY... I'M HOME...
OH COME TO MOMMY, DAHLING... GUESS WHAT, I WON $1.75 AT MAH JONG... I'LL HIDE IT IN THE COOKIE JAR!!
CAN I PLEEZE TAWK TO YOU ABOUT MY SERIOUS PROBLEMS?
NOT NOW DEAH... I'M GONNA MAKE DINNAH...
BESIDES... YOU'RE PERFECT SWEETIE!!
JUS' WAIT 'TIL YOU HAVE DERMABRASION + COSMETIC SURGERY!!
YOU HARDLY TOUCHED THIS WONDERFUL DINNER I MADE ESPECIALLY FOR YOU, SINCE DADDY'S WORKING LATE... MAYBE YUR SICK!! MAYBE I SHOULD TAKE YUR TEMPERCHURE!!
I'M SORRY MOMMY... I'M JUST NOT HUNGRY NOW
WELL... NO BANANA CREAM PUDDING WITH REDI WHIP FOR YOU TONITE!
YOU'RE GONNA RUIN YOUR LOOKS IF YA DON'T EAT RIGHT!! YOU'LL WASTE AWAY... YOUR HAIR'LL FAWL OUT... YOUR NAILS'LL BREAK IT'LL BE HORRIBLE!
RIING
HOW COME SHE DIDN'T NOTICE I ATE EVERY DESSERT + SNACK IN THE HOUSE?

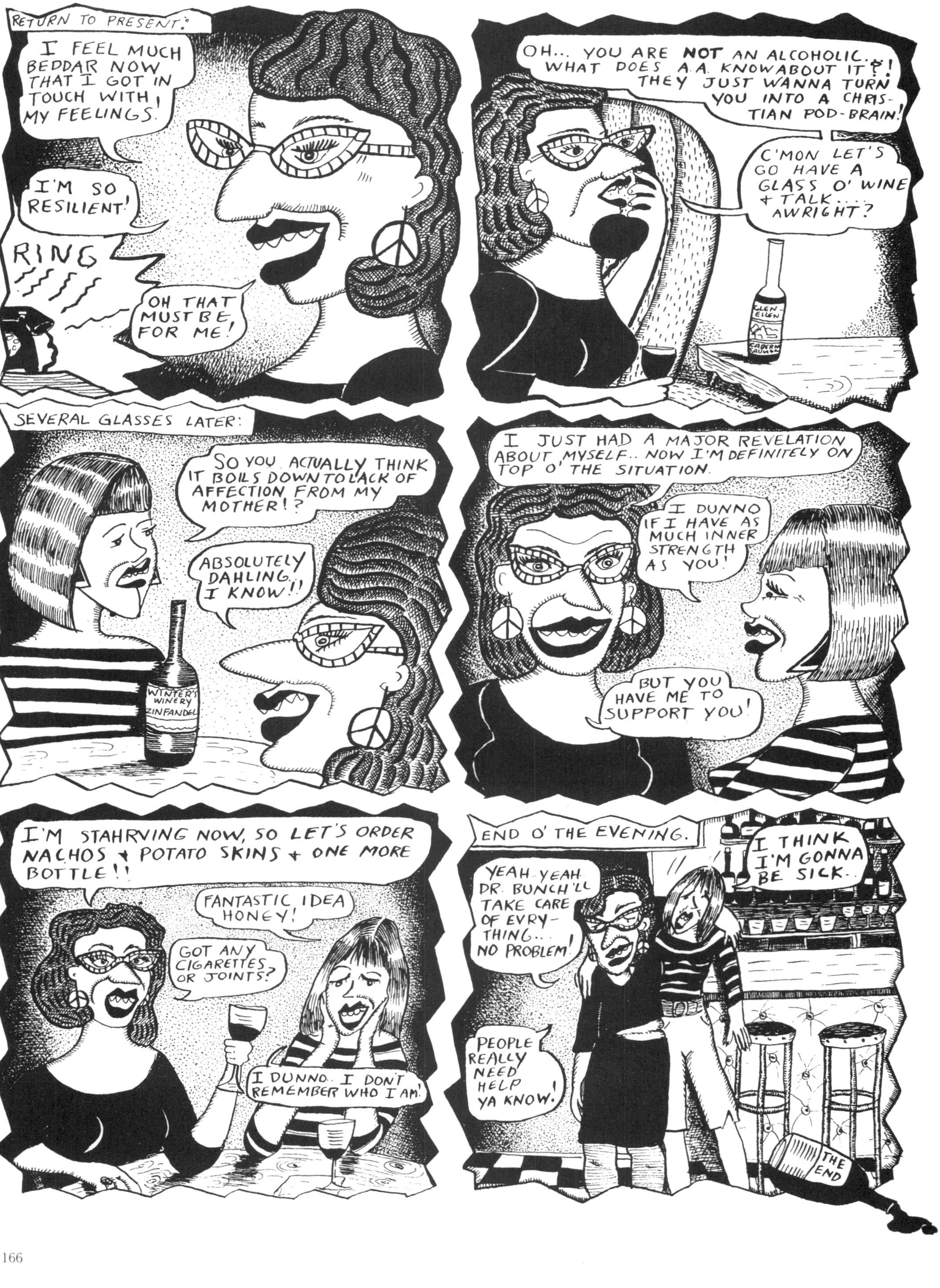
RETURN TO PRESENT:
I FEEL MUCH BEDDAR NOW THAT I GOT IN TOUCH WITH MY FEELINGS!
I'M SO RESILIENT!
RING
OH THAT MUST BE FOR ME!
OH... YOU ARE NOT AN ALCOHOLIC... WHAT DOES A.A. KNOW ABOUT IT?! THEY JUST WANNA TURN YOU INTO A CHRISTIAN POD-BRAIN!
C'MON LET'S GO HAVE A GLASS O' WINE + TALK... AWRIGHT?
GLEN ELLEN CABERNET SAUVIGNON
SEVERAL GLASSES LATER:
SO YOU ACTUALLY THINK IT BOILS DOWN TO LACK OF AFFECTION FROM MY MOTHER!?
ABSOLUTELY DAHLING, I KNOW!!
WINTER'S WINERY ZINFANDEL
I JUST HAD A MAJOR REVELATION ABOUT MYSELF.. NOW I'M DEFINITELY ON TOP O' THE SITUATION.
I DUNNO IF I HAVE AS MUCH INNER STRENGTH AS YOU!
BUT YOU HAVE ME TO SUPPORT YOU!
I'M STAHRVING NOW, SO LET'S ORDER NACHOS + POTATO SKINS + ONE MORE BOTTLE!!
FANTASTIC IDEA HONEY!
GOT ANY CIGARETTES OR JOINTS?
I DUNNO. I DON'T REMEMBER WHO I AM!
END O' THE EVENING.
I THINK I'M GONNA BE SICK..
YEAH. YEAH. DR. BUNCH'LL TAKE CARE OF EVRYTHING.. NO PROBLEM!
PEOPLE REALLY NEED HELP YA KNOW!
THE END

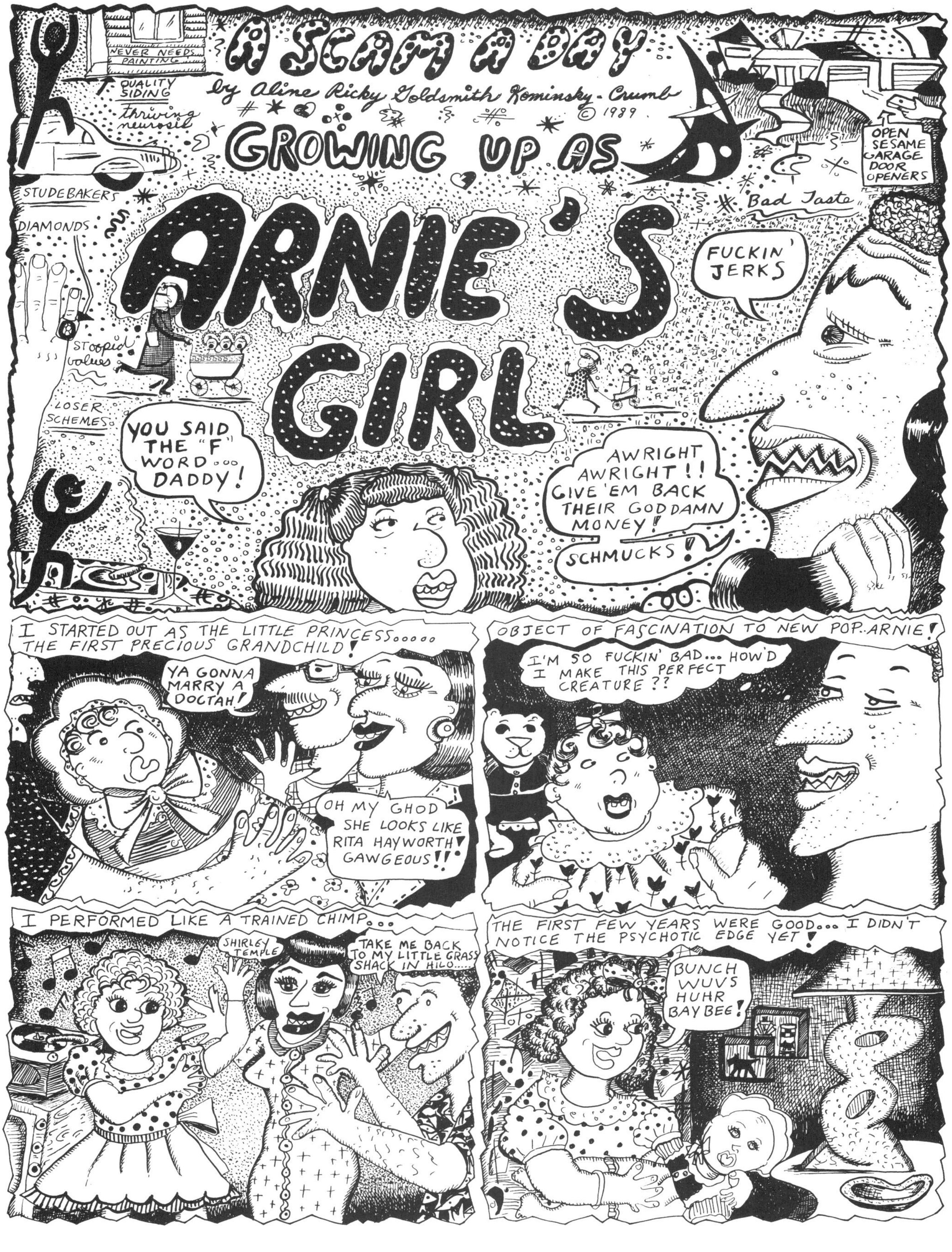
A SCAM A DAY
by Aline Ricky Goldsmith Kominsky-Crumb © 1989
NEVER NEEDS PAINTING
QUALITY SIDING
thriving neurosis
GROWING UP AS
OPEN SESAME GARAGE DOOR OPENERS
STUDEBAKERS
Bad Taste
DIAMONDS
ARNIE'S GIRL
FUCKIN' JERKS
stoopid values
LOSER SCHEMES
YOU SAID THE "F" WORD... DADDY!
AWRIGHT AWRIGHT!! GIVE 'EM BACK THEIR GODDAMN MONEY!
SCHMUCKS!
I STARTED OUT AS THE LITTLE PRINCESS..... THE FIRST PRECIOUS GRANDCHILD!
YA GONNA MARRY A DOCTAH!
OH MY GHOD SHE LOOKS LIKE RITA HAYWORTH! GAWGEOUS!!
OBJECT OF FASCINATION TO NEW POP ARNIE!
I'M SO FUCKIN' BAD... HOW'D I MAKE THIS PERFECT CREATURE??
I PERFORMED LIKE A TRAINED CHIMP...
SHIRLEY TEMPLE
TAKE ME BACK TO MY LITTLE GRASS SHACK IN HILO...
THE FIRST FEW YEARS WERE GOOD... I DIDN'T NOTICE THE PSYCHOTIC EDGE YET!
BUNCH WUVS HUHR BAYBEE!

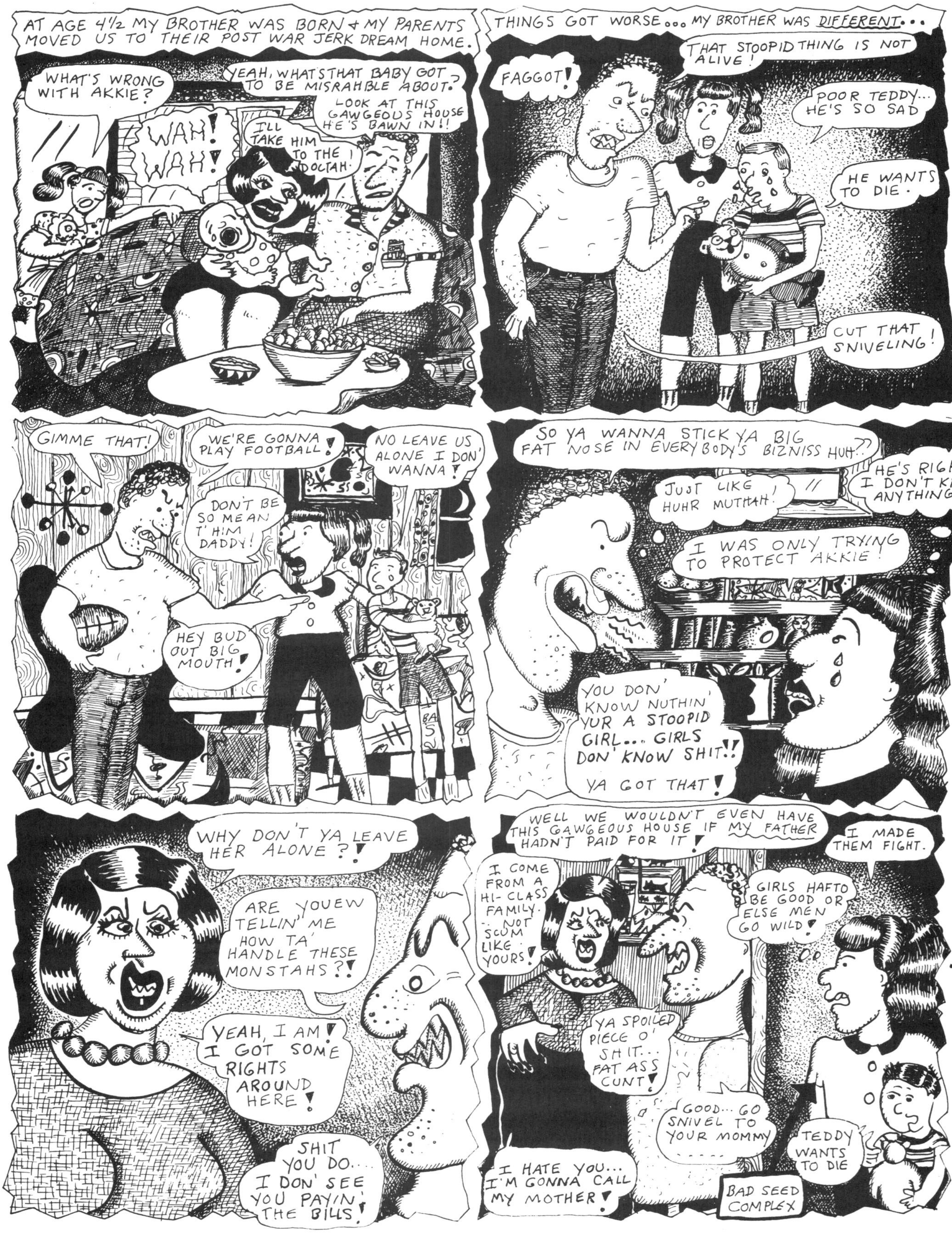
AT AGE 4½ MY BROTHER WAS BORN & MY PARENTS MOVED US TO THEIR POST WAR JERK DREAM HOME.
WHAT'S WRONG WITH AKKIE?
YEAH, WHAT'S THAT BABY GOT TO BE MISRAHBLE ABOUT?
LOOK AT THIS GAWGEOUS HOUSE HE'S BAWN IN!!
WAH! WAH!
I'LL TAKE HIM TO THE DOCTAH!
THINGS GOT WORSE... MY BROTHER WAS DIFFERENT...
FAGGOT!
THAT STOOPID THING IS NOT ALIVE!
POOR TEDDY... HE'S SO SAD
HE WANTS TO DIE.
CUT THAT SNIVELING!
GIMME THAT!
WE'RE GONNA PLAY FOOTBALL!
NO LEAVE US ALONE I DON' WANNA!
DON'T BE SO MEAN T'HIM DADDY!
HEY BUD OUT BIG MOUTH!
SO YA WANNA STICK YA BIG FAT NOSE IN EVERYBODY'S BIZNISS HUH??
JUST LIKE HUHR MUTHAH!
HE'S RIGHT I DON'T KNOW ANYTHING.
I WAS ONLY TRYING TO PROTECT AKKIE!
YOU DON' KNOW NUTHIN' YUR A STOOPID GIRL... GIRLS DON' KNOW SHIT!!
YA GOT THAT!
WHY DON'T YA LEAVE HER ALONE?!
ARE YOUEW TELLIN' ME HOW TA' HANDLE THESE MONSTAHS?!
YEAH, I AM! I GOT SOME RIGHTS AROUND HERE!
SHIT YOU DO... I DON' SEE YOU PAYIN' THE BILLS!
WELL WE WOULDN'T EVEN HAVE THIS GAWGEOUS HOUSE IF MY FATHER HADN'T PAID FOR IT!
I MADE THEM FIGHT.
I COME FROM A HI-CLASS FAMILY... NOT SCUM LIKE YOURS!
GIRLS HAFTO BE GOOD OR ELSE MEN GO WILD!
YA SPOILED PIECE O' SHIT... FAT ASS CUNT!
GOOD... GO SNIVEL TO YOUR MOMMY.....
TEDDY WANTS TO DIE
I HATE YOU... I'M GONNA CALL MY MOTHER!
BAD SEED COMPLEX

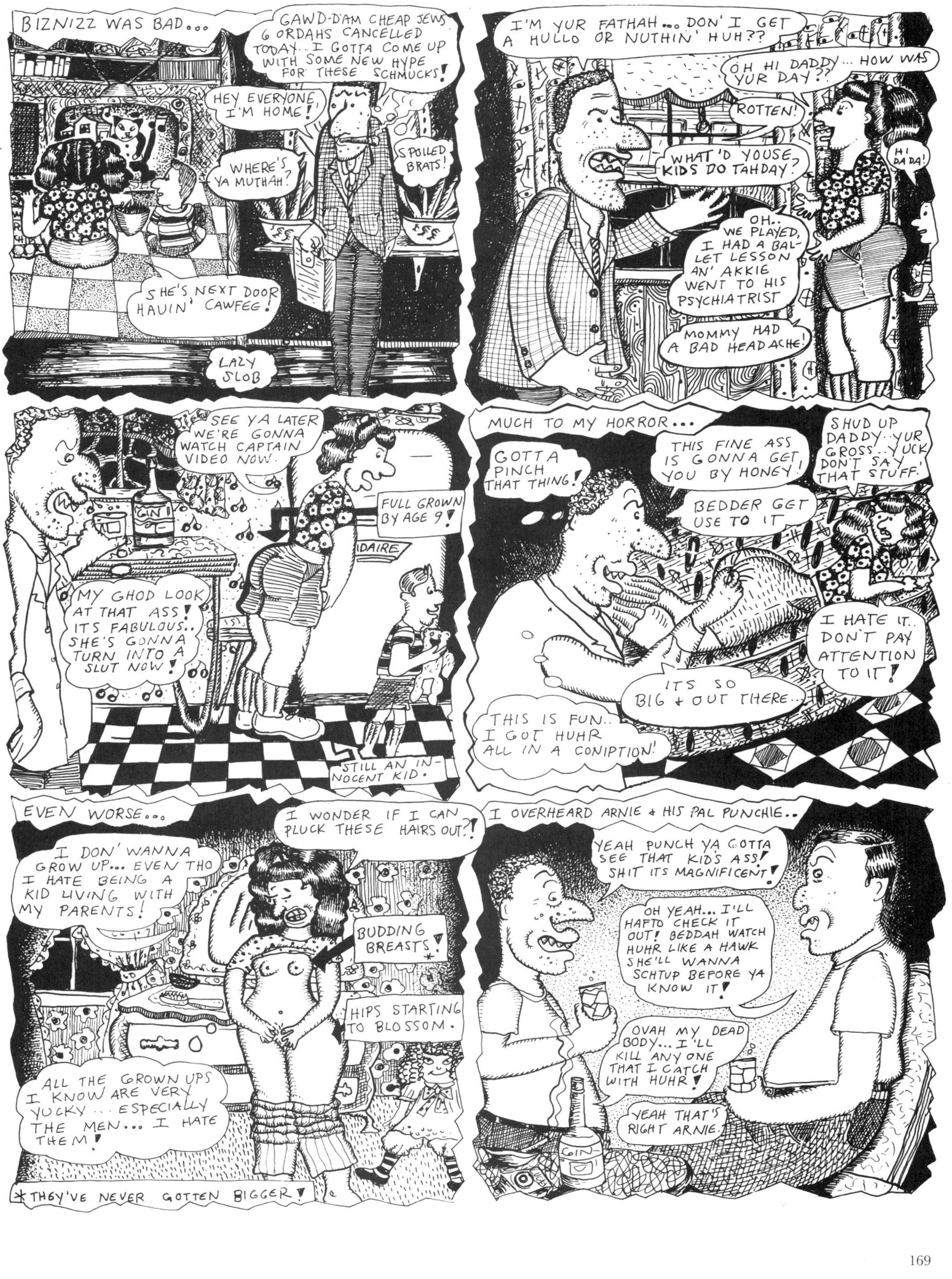
BIZNIZZ WAS BAD...
GAWD-DAM CHEAP JEWS 6 ORDAHS CANCELLED TODAY.. I GOTTA COME UP WITH SOME NEW HYPE FOR THESE SCHMUCKS!
HEY EVERYONE I'M HOME!
WHERE'S YA MUTHAH?
SPOILED BRATS!
SHE'S NEXT DOOR HAVIN' CAWFEE!
LAZY SLOB
I'M YUR FATHAH... DON' I GET A HULLO OR NUTHIN' HUH??
OH HI DADDY... HOW WAS YUR DAY??
ROTTEN!
WHAT'D YOUSE KIDS DO TAHDAY?
HI DA DA!
OH.. WE PLAYED, I HAD A BAL-LET LESSON AN' AKKIE WENT TO HIS PSYCHIATRIST
MOMMY HAD A BAD HEADACHE!
SEE YA LATER WE'RE GONNA WATCH CAPTAIN VIDEO NOW.
GIN
FULL GROWN BY AGE 9!
MY GHOD LOOK AT THAT ASS! ITS FABULOUS.. SHE'S GONNA TURN INTO A SLUT NOW!
STILL AN IN-NOCENT KID.
MUCH TO MY HORROR...
GOTTA PINCH THAT THING!
THIS FINE ASS IS GONNA GET YOU BY HONEY!
SHUD UP DADDY YUR GROSS.. YUCK DON'T SAY THAT STUFF!
BEDDER GET USE TO IT
I HATE IT.. DON'T PAY ATTENTION TO IT!
ITS SO BIG + OUT THERE...
THIS IS FUN.. I GOT HUHR ALL IN A CONIPTION!
EVEN WORSE...
I WONDER IF I CAN PLUCK THESE HAIRS OUT?!
I DON' WANNA GROW UP... EVEN THO I HATE BEING A KID LIVING WITH MY PARENTS!
BUDDING BREASTS!*
HIPS STARTING TO BLOSSOM.
ALL THE GROWN UPS I KNOW ARE VERY YUCKY... ESPECIALLY THE MEN... I HATE THEM!
*THEY'VE NEVER GOTTEN BIGGER!
I OVERHEARD ARNIE + HIS PAL PUNCHIE..
YEAH PUNCH YA GOTTA SEE THAT KID'S ASS! SHIT ITS MAGNIFICENT!
OH YEAH... I'LL HAFTO CHECK IT OUT! BEDDAH WATCH HUHR LIKE A HAWK SHE'LL WANNA SCHTUP BEFORE YA KNOW IT!
OVAH MY DEAD BODY... I'LL KILL ANY ONE THAT I CATCH WITH HUHR!
YEAH THAT'S RIGHT ARNIE.
GIN

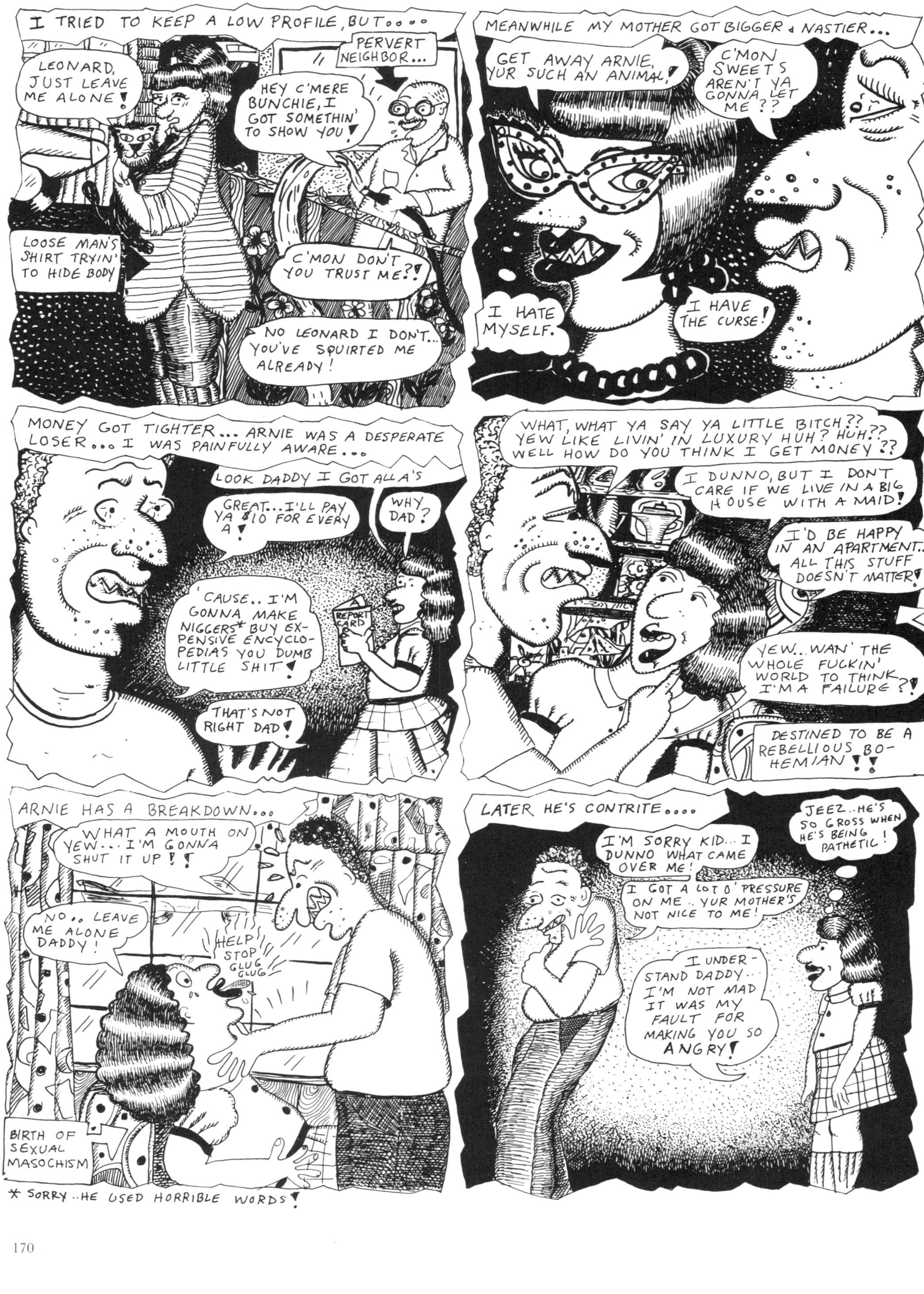
I TRIED TO KEEP A LOW PROFILE, BUT....
LEONARD, JUST LEAVE ME ALONE!
PERVERT NEIGHBOR...
HEY C'MERE BUNCHIE, I GOT SOMETHIN' TO SHOW YOU!
LOOSE MAN'S SHIRT TRYIN' TO HIDE BODY
C'MON DON'T YOU TRUST ME?!
NO LEONARD I DON'T... YOU'VE SQUIRTED ME ALREADY!
MEANWHILE MY MOTHER GOT BIGGER & NASTIER...
GET AWAY ARNIE, YUR SUCH AN ANIMAL!
C'MON SWEETS AREN'T YA GONNA LET ME??
I HATE MYSELF.
I HAVE THE CURSE!
MONEY GOT TIGHTER... ARNIE WAS A DESPERATE LOSER... I WAS PAINFULLY AWARE...
LOOK DADDY I GOT ALL A'S
GREAT...I'LL PAY YA $10 FOR EVERY A!
WHY DAD?
'CAUSE.. I'M GONNA MAKE NIGGERS* BUY EXPENSIVE ENCYCLOPEDIAS YOU DUMB LITTLE SHIT!
REPORT CARD
THAT'S NOT RIGHT DAD!
WHAT, WHAT YA SAY YA LITTLE BITCH?? YEW LIKE LIVIN' IN LUXURY HUH? HUH?? WELL HOW DO YOU THINK I GET MONEY??
I DUNNO, BUT I DON'T CARE IF WE LIVE IN A BIG HOUSE WITH A MAID!
I'D BE HAPPY IN AN APARTMENT... ALL THIS STUFF DOESN'T MATTER!
YEW..WAN' THE WHOLE FUCKIN' WORLD TO THINK I'M A FAILURE?!
DESTINED TO BE A REBELLIOUS BOHEMIAN!!
ARNIE HAS A BREAKDOWN...
WHAT A MOUTH ON YEW... I'M GONNA SHUT IT UP!!
NO.. LEAVE ME ALONE DADDY!
HELP STOP GLUG GLUG
BIRTH OF SEXUAL MASOCHISM
LATER HE'S CONTRITE....
I'M SORRY KID... I DUNNO WHAT CAME OVER ME!
JEEZ..HE'S SO GROSS WHEN HE'S BEING PATHETIC!
I GOT A LOT O' PRESSURE ON ME.. YUR MOTHER'S NOT NICE TO ME!
I UNDERSTAND DADDY.. I'M NOT MAD IT WAS MY FAULT FOR MAKING YOU SO ANGRY!
* SORRY..HE USED HORRIBLE WORDS!

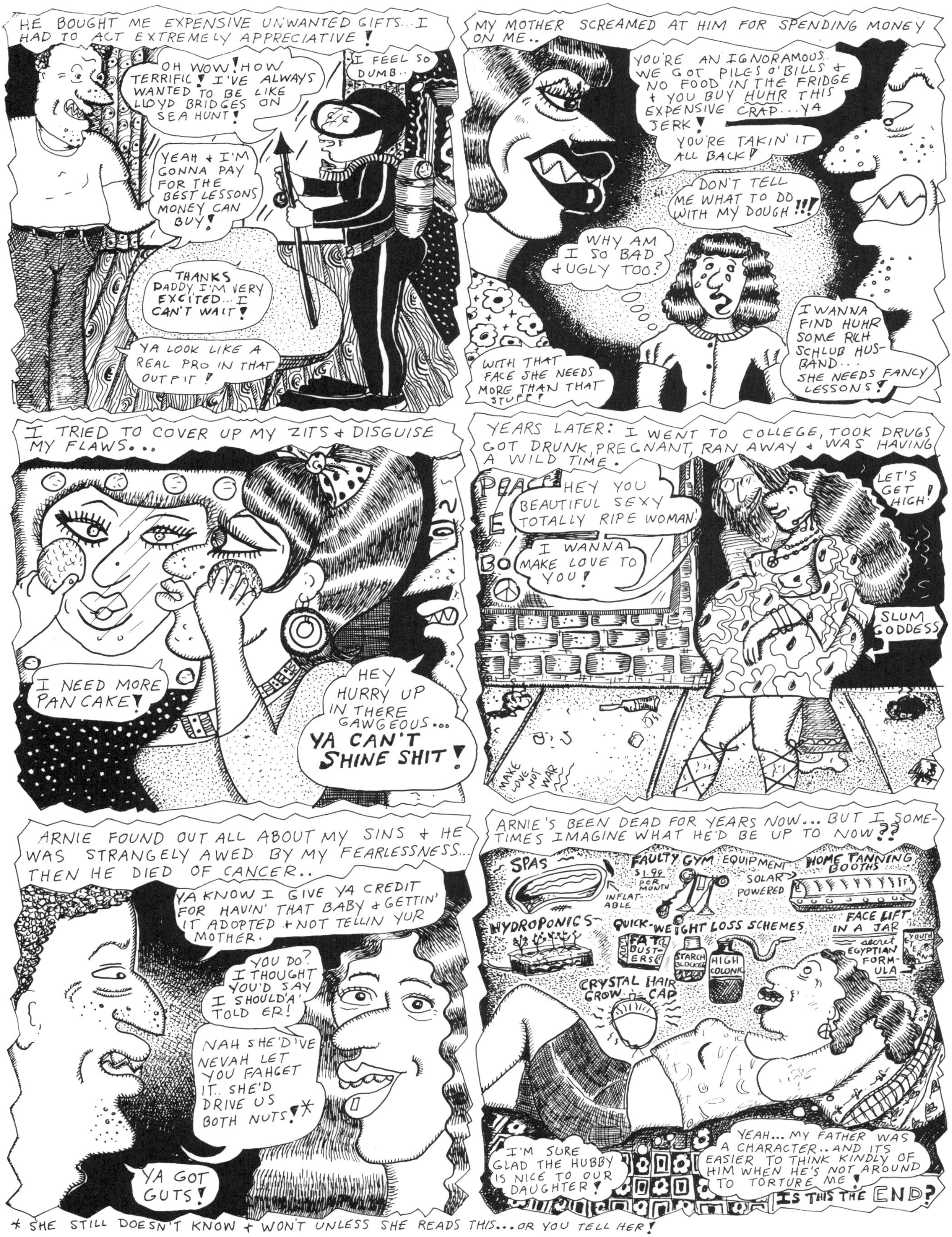
HE BOUGHT ME EXPENSIVE UNWANTED GIFTS... I HAD TO ACT EXTREMELY APPRECIATIVE!
OH WOW! HOW TERRIFIC! I'VE ALWAYS WANTED TO BE LIKE LLOYD BRIDGES ON SEA HUNT!
I FEEL SO DUMB..
YEAH + I'M GONNA PAY FOR THE BEST LESSONS MONEY CAN BUY!
THANKS DADDY I'M VERY EXCITED... I CAN'T WAIT!
YA LOOK LIKE A REAL PRO IN THAT OUTFIT!
MY MOTHER SCREAMED AT HIM FOR SPENDING MONEY ON ME..
YOU'RE AN IGNORAMOUS. WE GOT PILES O' BILLS + NO FOOD IN THE FRIDGE + YOU BUY HUHR THIS EXPENSIVE CRAP... YA JERK!
YOU'RE TAKIN' IT ALL BACK!
DON'T TELL ME WHAT TO DO WITH MY DOUGH!!!
WHY AM I SO BAD + UGLY TOO?
I WANNA FIND HUHR SOME RICH SCHLUB HUSBAND... SHE NEEDS FANCY LESSONS!
WITH THAT FACE SHE NEEDS MORE THAN THAT STUFF!
I TRIED TO COVER UP MY ZITS + DISGUISE MY FLAWS...
I NEED MORE PAN CAKE!
HEY HURRY UP IN THERE GAWGEOUS... YA CAN'T SHINE SHIT!
YEARS LATER: I WENT TO COLLEGE, TOOK DRUGS GOT DRUNK, PREGNANT, RAN AWAY + WAS HAVING A WILD TIME.
HEY YOU BEAUTIFUL SEXY TOTALLY RIPE WOMAN!
I WANNA MAKE LOVE TO YOU!
LET'S GET HIGH!
SLUM GODDESS
MAKE LOVE NOT WAR
ARNIE FOUND OUT ALL ABOUT MY SINS + HE WAS STRANGELY AWED BY MY FEARLESSNESS... THEN HE DIED OF CANCER..
YA KNOW I GIVE YA CREDIT FOR HAVIN' THAT BABY + GETTIN' IT ADOPTED + NOT TELLIN YUR MOTHER.
YOU DO? I THOUGHT YOU'D SAY I SHOULD'A TOLD ER!
NAH SHE'D'VE NEVAH LET YOU FAHGET IT.. SHE'D DRIVE US BOTH NUTS!*
YA GOT GUTS!
ARNIE'S BEEN DEAD FOR YEARS NOW... BUT I SOMETIMES IMAGINE WHAT HE'D BE UP TO NOW??
SPAS
INFLATABLE
FAULTY GYM EQUIPMENT
$1.99 PER MONTH
HOME TANNING BOOTHS
SOLAR POWERED
HYDROPONICS
QUICK-WEIGHT LOSS SCHEMES
FAT BUSTERS
STARCH BLOCKER
HIGH COLONIC
FACE LIFT IN A JAR
secret EGYPTIAN FORMULA
CRYSTAL HAIR GROW CAP
I'M SURE GLAD THE HUBBY IS NICE TO OUR DAUGHTER!
YEAH... MY FATHER WAS A CHARACTER.. AND ITS EASIER TO THINK KINDLY OF HIM WHEN HE'S NOT AROUND TO TORTURE ME!
IS THIS THE END?

* SHE STILL DOESN'T KNOW + WON'T UNLESS SHE READS THIS... OR YOU TELL HER!

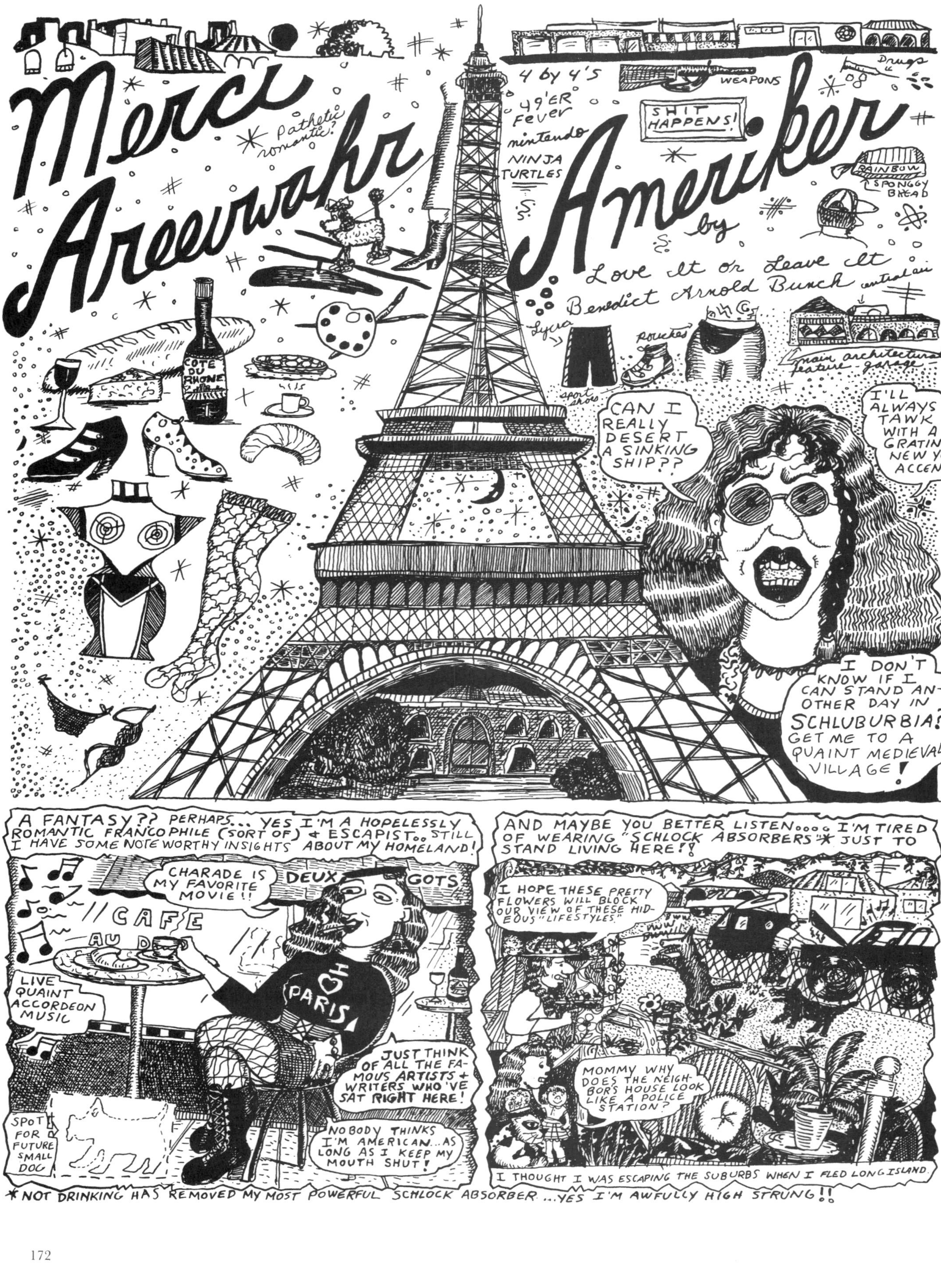
Merci Areevwahr Ameriker
by
Love It or Leave It
Benedict Arnold Bunch
pathetic romantic?
4 by 4'S
49'ER fever
nintendo
NINJA TURTLES
WEAPONS
Drugs
SHIT HAPPENS!
RAINBOW
SPONGGY BREAD
central air
Lycra
Rouckes
sport shoes
main architectural feature - garage
COTE DU RHONE
CAN I REALLY DESERT A SINKING SHIP??
I'LL ALWAYS TAWK WITH A GRATING NEW YORK ACCENT!
I DON'T KNOW IF I CAN STAND ANOTHER DAY IN SCHLUBURBIA? GET ME TO A QUAINT MEDIEVAL VILLAGE!
A FANTASY?? PERHAPS... YES I'M A HOPELESSLY ROMANTIC FRANCOPHILE (SORT OF) & ESCAPIST.. STILL I HAVE SOME NOTEWORTHY INSIGHTS ABOUT MY HOMELAND!
CHARADE IS MY FAVORITE MOVIE!!
DEUX GOTS
CAFE AU D
LIVE QUAINT ACCORDEON MUSIC
OH PARIS
JUST THINK OF ALL THE FAMOUS ARTISTS & WRITERS WHO'VE SAT RIGHT HERE!
SPOT FOR FUTURE SMALL DOG
NOBODY THINKS I'M AMERICAN... AS LONG AS I KEEP MY MOUTH SHUT!
AND MAYBE YOU BETTER LISTEN.... I'M TIRED OF WEARING "SCHLOCK ABSORBERS"* JUST TO STAND LIVING HERE!!
I HOPE THESE PRETTY FLOWERS WILL BLOCK OUR VIEW OF THESE HIDEOUS "LIFESTYLES."
MOMMY WHY DOES THE NEIGHBOR'S HOUSE LOOK LIKE A POLICE STATION?
I THOUGHT I WAS ESCAPING THE SUBURBS WHEN I FLED LONG ISLAND.
* NOT DRINKING HAS REMOVED MY MOST POWERFUL SCHLOCK ABSORBER ... YES I'M AWFULLY HIGH STRUNG!!

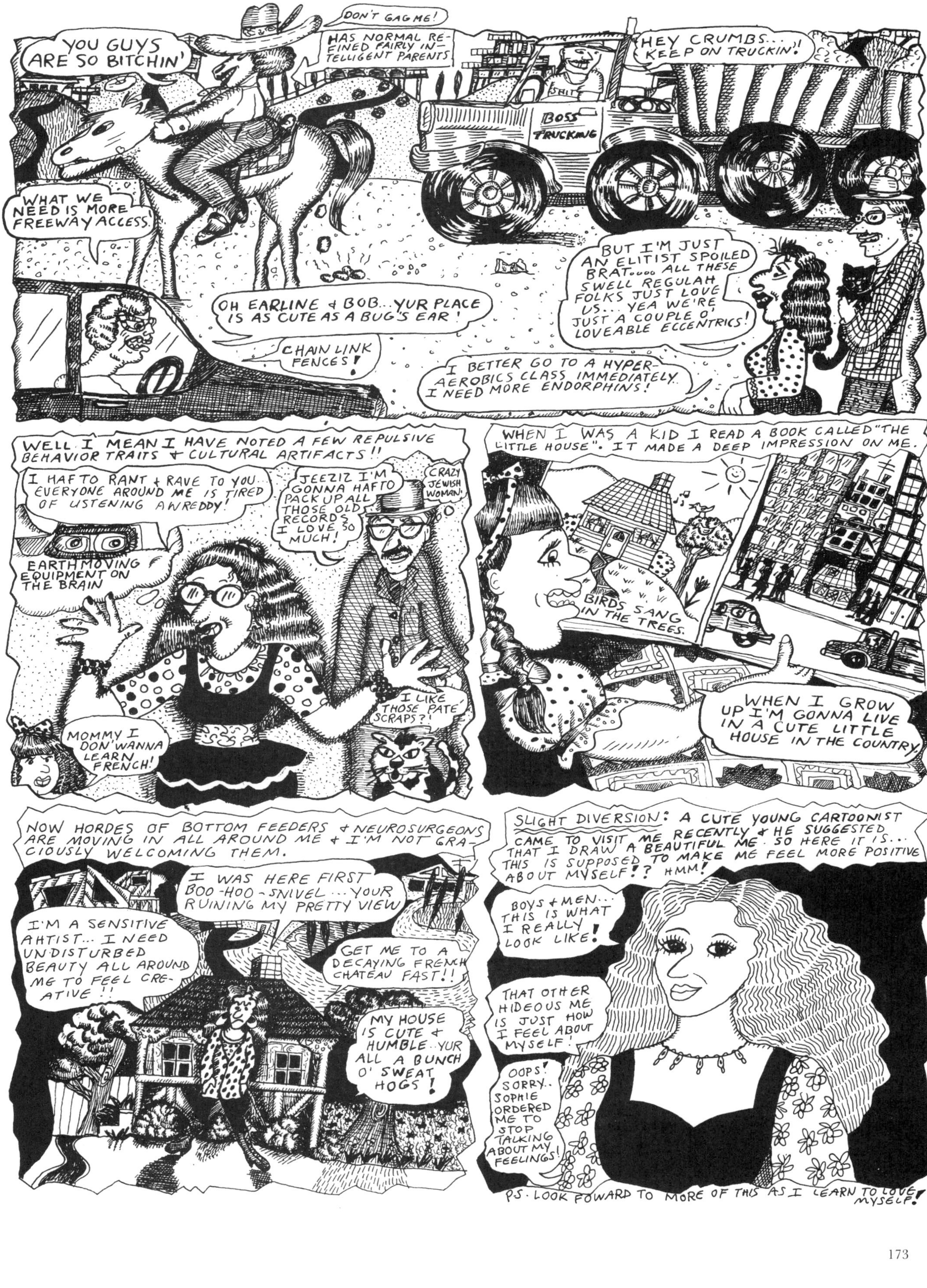
DON'T GAG ME!
YOU GUYS ARE SO BITCHIN'
HAS NORMAL REFINED FAIRLY INTELLIGENT PARENTS
HEY CRUMBS... KEEP ON TRUCKIN'!
BOSS TRUCKING
WHAT WE NEED IS MORE FREEWAY ACCESS!
BUT I'M JUST AN ELITIST SPOILED BRAT.... ALL THESE SWELL REGULAH FOLKS JUST LOVE US.. YEA WE'RE JUST A COUPLE O' LOVEABLE ECCENTRICS!
OH EARLINE & BOB.. YUR PLACE IS AS CUTE AS A BUG'S EAR!
CHAIN LINK FENCES!
I BETTER GO TO A HYPER-AEROBICS CLASS IMMEDIATELY. I NEED MORE ENDORPHINS!
WELL I MEAN I HAVE NOTED A FEW REPULSIVE BEHAVIOR TRAITS & CULTURAL ARTIFACTS!!
I HAFTO RANT & RAVE TO YOU.. EVERYONE AROUND ME IS TIRED OF LISTENING AWREDDY!
JEEZIZ I'M GONNA HAFTO PACK UP ALL THOSE OLD RECORDS I LOVE SO MUCH!
CRAZY JEWISH WOMAN.
EARTHMOVING EQUIPMENT ON THE BRAIN
I LIKE THOSE PATE SCRAPS?!
MOMMY I DON'WANNA LEARN FRENCH!
WHEN I WAS A KID I READ A BOOK CALLED "THE LITTLE HOUSE". IT MADE A DEEP IMPRESSION ON ME.
BIRDS SANG IN THE TREES.
WHEN I GROW UP I'M GONNA LIVE IN A CUTE LITTLE HOUSE IN THE COUNTRY.
NOW HORDES OF BOTTOM FEEDERS & NEUROSURGEONS ARE MOVING IN ALL AROUND ME & I'M NOT GRACIOUSLY WELCOMING THEM.
I WAS HERE FIRST BOO-HOO-SNIVEL... YOUR RUINING MY PRETTY VIEW
I'M A SENSITIVE AHTIST... I NEED UNDISTURBED BEAUTY ALL AROUND ME TO FEEL CREATIVE!!
GET ME TO A DECAYING FRENCH CHATEAU FAST!!
MY HOUSE IS CUTE & HUMBLE.. YUR ALL A BUNCH O' SWEAT HOGS!
SLIGHT DIVERSION: A CUTE YOUNG CARTOONIST CAME TO VISIT ME RECENTLY & HE SUGGESTED THAT I DRAW A BEAUTIFUL ME. SO HERE IT IS... THIS IS SUPPOSED TO MAKE ME FEEL MORE POSITIVE ABOUT MYSELF!? HMM!
BOYS & MEN... THIS IS WHAT I REALLY LOOK LIKE!
THAT OTHER HIDEOUS ME IS JUST HOW I FEEL ABOUT MYSELF!
OOPS! SORRY.. SOPHIE ORDERED ME TO STOP TALKING ABOUT MY FEELINGS!
P.S. LOOK FOWARD TO MORE OF THIS AS I LEARN TO LOVE MYSELF!

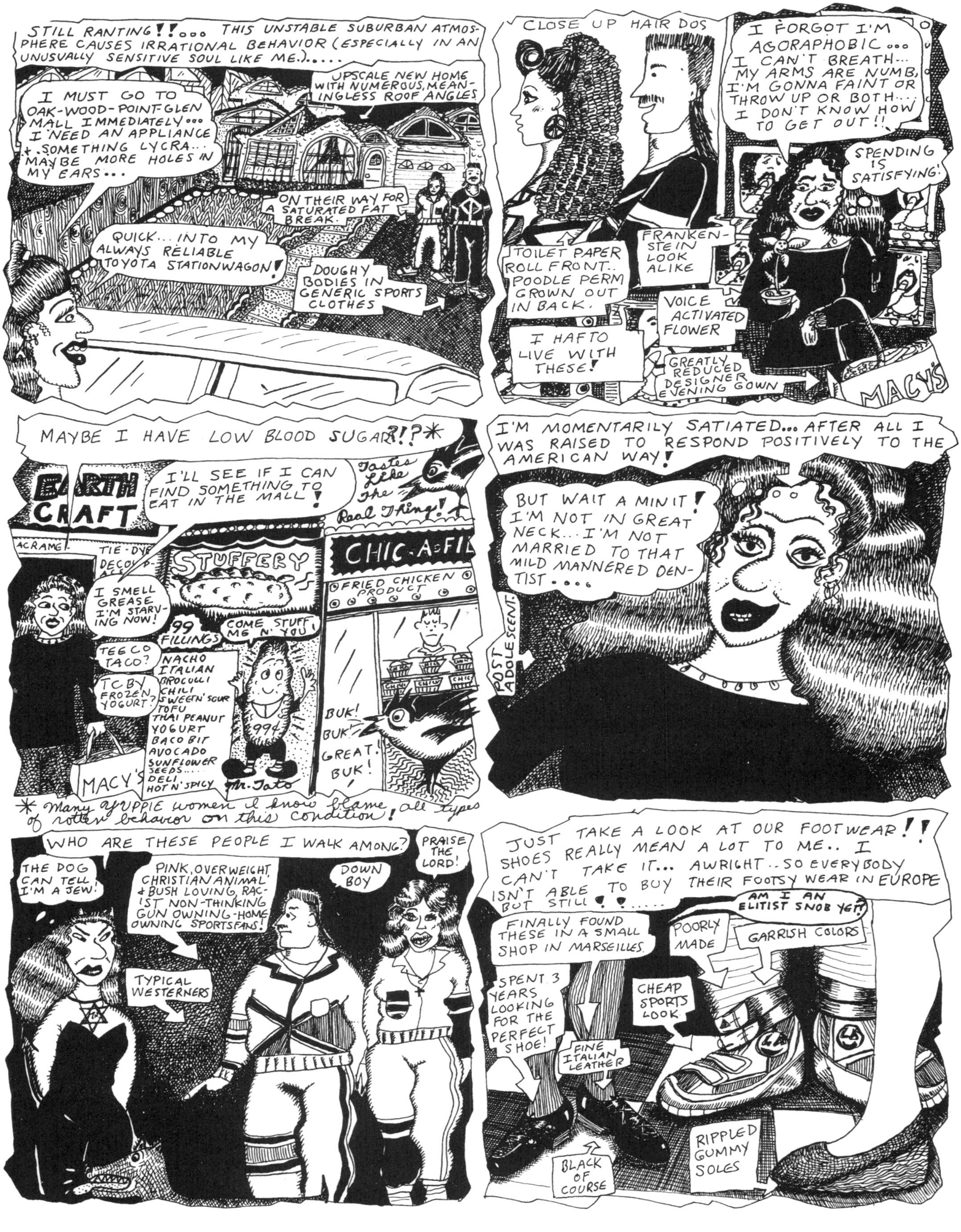

STILL RANTING!!... THIS UNSTABLE SUBURBAN ATMOSPHERE CAUSES IRRATIONAL BEHAVIOR (ESPECIALLY IN AN UNUSUALLY SENSITIVE SOUL LIKE ME.).....
I MUST GO TO OAK-WOOD-POINT-GLEN MALL IMMEDIATELY... I NEED AN APPLIANCE +.SOMETHING LYCRA.. MAYBE MORE HOLES IN MY EARS...
UPSCALE NEW HOME WITH NUMEROUS, MEANINGLESS ROOF ANGLES
ON THEIR WAY FOR A SATURATED FAT BREAK.
QUICK... INTO MY ALWAYS RELIABLE TOYOTA STATIONWAGON!
DOUGHY BODIES IN GENERIC SPORTS CLOTHES
CLOSE UP HAIR DOS
TOILET PAPER ROLL FRONT.. POODLE PERM GROWN OUT IN BACK.
FRANKENSTEIN LOOK ALIKE
I HAFTO LIVE WITH THESE!
I FORGOT I'M AGORAPHOBIC... I CAN'T BREATH... MY ARMS ARE NUMB, I'M GONNA FAINT OR THROW UP OR BOTH... I DON'T KNOW HOW TO GET OUT!!
SPENDING IS SATISFYING!
VOICE ACTIVATED FLOWER
GREATLY REDUCED DESIGNER EVENING GOWN
MACY'S
MAYBE I HAVE LOW BLOOD SUGAR?!?*
EARTH CRAFT
I'LL SEE IF I CAN FIND SOMETHING TO EAT IN THE MALL!
Tastes Like The Real Thing!
ACRAME
TIE-DYE
STUFFERY
CHIC-A-FIL
FRIED CHICKEN PRODUCT
I SMELL GREASE I'M STARVING NOW!
99 FILLINGS
COME STUFF ME N' YOU!
TEECO TACO?
TCBY FROZEN YOGURT?
NACHO ITALIAN BROCCOLI CHILI SWEETN' SOUR TOFU THAI PEANUT YOGURT BACO BIT AVOCADO SUNFLOWER SEEDS..... DELI HOT N' SPICY
99¢
Mr. Tato
BUK! BUK! GREAT! BUK!
MACY'S
* Many yuppie women I know blame all types of rotten behavior on this condition!
I'M MOMENTARILY SATIATED... AFTER ALL I WAS RAISED TO RESPOND POSITIVELY TO THE AMERICAN WAY!
BUT WAIT A MINIT! I'M NOT IN GREAT NECK... I'M NOT MARRIED TO THAT MILD MANNERED DENTIST....
POST ADOLESCENT.
WHO ARE THESE PEOPLE I WALK AMONG?
THE DOG CAN TELL I'M A JEW.
PINK, OVERWEIGHT, CHRISTIAN ANIMAL & BUSH LOVING, RACIST NON-THINKING GUN OWNING-HOME OWNING SPORTSFANS!
DOWN BOY
PRAISE THE LORD!
TYPICAL WESTERNERS
JUST TAKE A LOOK AT OUR FOOTWEAR!! SHOES REALLY MEAN A LOT TO ME.. I CAN'T TAKE IT... AWRIGHT.. SO EVERYBODY ISN'T ABLE TO BUY THEIR FOOTSY WEAR IN EUROPE BUT STILL!!.....
AM I AN ELITIST SNOB YET?
FINALLY FOUND THESE IN A SMALL SHOP IN MARSEILLES.
POORLY MADE
GARRISH COLORS
SPENT 3 YEARS LOOKING FOR THE PERFECT SHOE!
CHEAP SPORTS LOOK
FINE ITALIAN LEATHER
RIPPLED GUMMY SOLES
BLACK OF COURSE

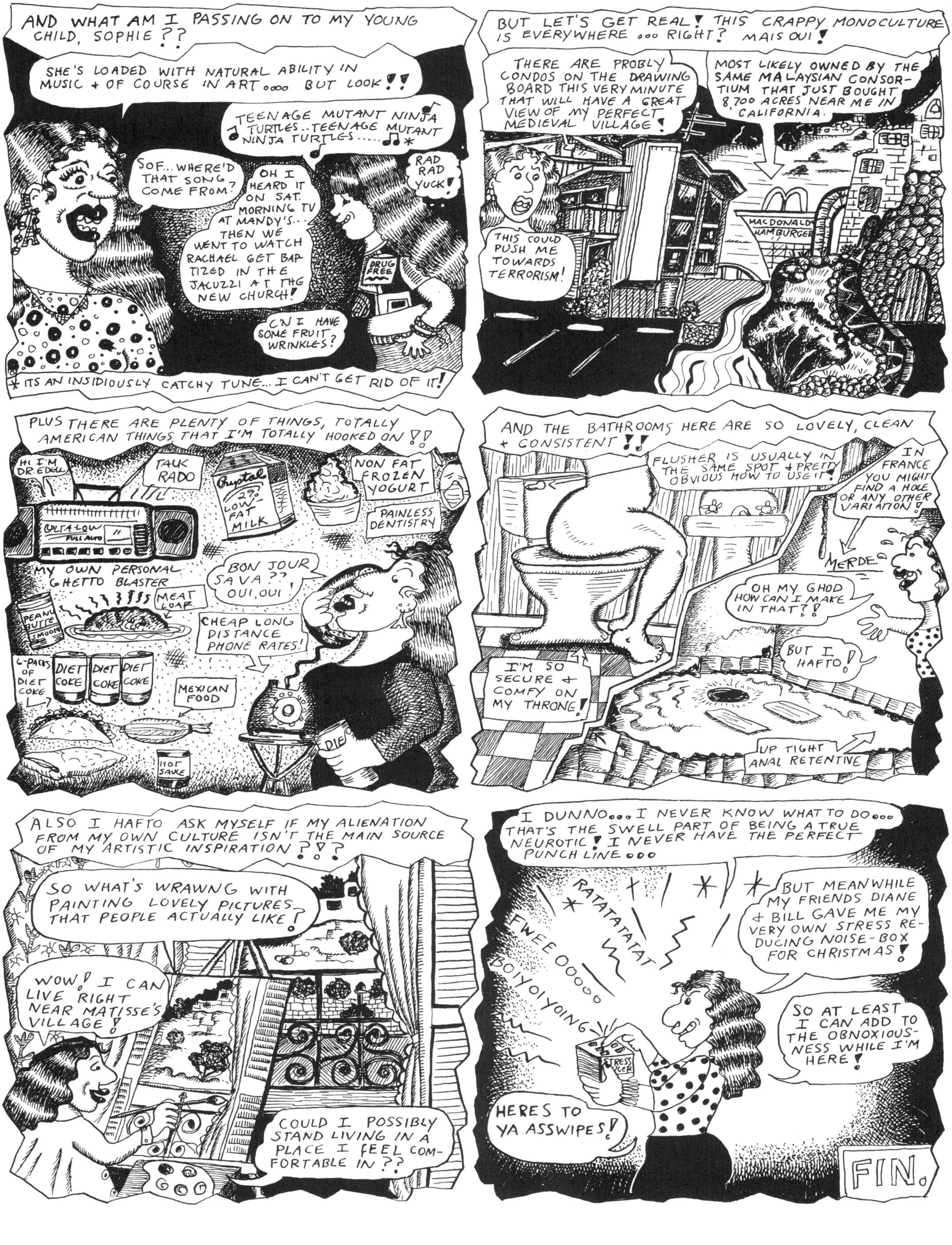
AND WHAT AM I PASSING ON TO MY YOUNG CHILD, SOPHIE??
SHE'S LOADED WITH NATURAL ABILITY IN MUSIC + OF COURSE IN ART... BUT LOOK!!
TEENAGE MUTANT NINJA TURTLES.. TEENAGE MUTANT NINJA TURTLES..... *
SOF... WHERE'D THAT SONG COME FROM?
OH I HEARD IT ON SAT. MORNING TV AT MANDY'S... THEN WE WENT TO WATCH RACHAEL GET BAPTIZED IN THE JACUZZI AT THE NEW CHURCH!
RAD RAD YUCK!
DRUG FREE
C'N I HAVE SOME FRUIT WRINKLES?
* ITS AN INSIDIOUSLY CATCHY TUNE... I CAN'T GET RID OF IT!
BUT LET'S GET REAL! THIS CRAPPY MONOCULTURE IS EVERYWHERE ... RIGHT? MAIS OUI!
THERE ARE PROBLY CONDOS ON THE DRAWING BOARD THIS VERY MINUTE THAT WILL HAVE A GREAT VIEW OF MY PERFECT MEDIEVAL VILLAGE!
MOST LIKELY OWNED BY THE SAME MALAYSIAN CONSORTIUM THAT JUST BOUGHT 8,700 ACRES NEAR ME IN CALIFORNIA.
MACDONALD HAMBURGER
THIS COULD PUSH ME TOWARDS TERRORISM!
PLUS THERE ARE PLENTY OF THINGS, TOTALLY AMERICAN THINGS THAT I'M TOTALLY HOOKED ON!!
HI I'M DR. EDELL
TALK RADO
Crystal 2% LOW-FAT MILK
NON FAT FROZEN YOGURT
PAINLESS DENTISTRY
ULTRA-LOW FULL AUTO
MY OWN PERSONAL GHETTO BLASTER
BON JOUR SAVA?? OUI, OUI!
MEAT LOAF
PEANUT BUTTER
CHEAP LONG DISTANCE PHONE RATES!
6-PACKS OF DIET COKE
DIET COKE
DIET COKE
DIET COKE
MEXICAN FOOD
HOT SAUCE
DIET
AND THE BATHROOMS HERE ARE SO LOVELY, CLEAN + CONSISTENT!!
FLUSHER IS USUALLY IN THE SAME SPOT + PRETTY OBVIOUS HOW TO USE IT!
IN FRANCE YOU MIGHT FIND A HOLE OR ANY OTHER VARIATION!
MERDE
OH MY GHOD HOW CAN I MAKE IN THAT?!
BUT I HAFTO!
I'M SO SECURE + COMFY ON MY THRONE!
UP TIGHT ANAL RETENTIVE
ALSO I HAFTO ASK MYSELF IF MY ALIENATION FROM MY OWN CULTURE ISN'T THE MAIN SOURCE OF MY ARTISTIC INSPIRATION ?!?
SO WHAT'S WRAWNG WITH PAINTING LOVELY PICTURES THAT PEOPLE ACTUALLY LIKE?
WOW! I CAN LIVE RIGHT NEAR MATISSE'S VILLAGE!
COULD I POSSIBLY STAND LIVING IN A PLACE I FEEL COMFORTABLE IN??
I DUNNO... I NEVER KNOW WHAT TO DO... THAT'S THE SWELL PART OF BEING A TRUE NEUROTIC! I NEVER HAVE THE PERFECT PUNCH LINE...
RATATATATAT
FWEEOOOOO
BOIYOIYOING
BUT MEANWHILE MY FRIENDS DIANE + BILL GAVE ME MY VERY OWN STRESS REDUCING NOISE-BOX FOR CHRISTMAS!
STRESS RED.
SO AT LEAST I CAN ADD TO THE OBNOXIOUSNESS WHILE I'M HERE!
HERES TO YA ASSWIPES!
FIN.

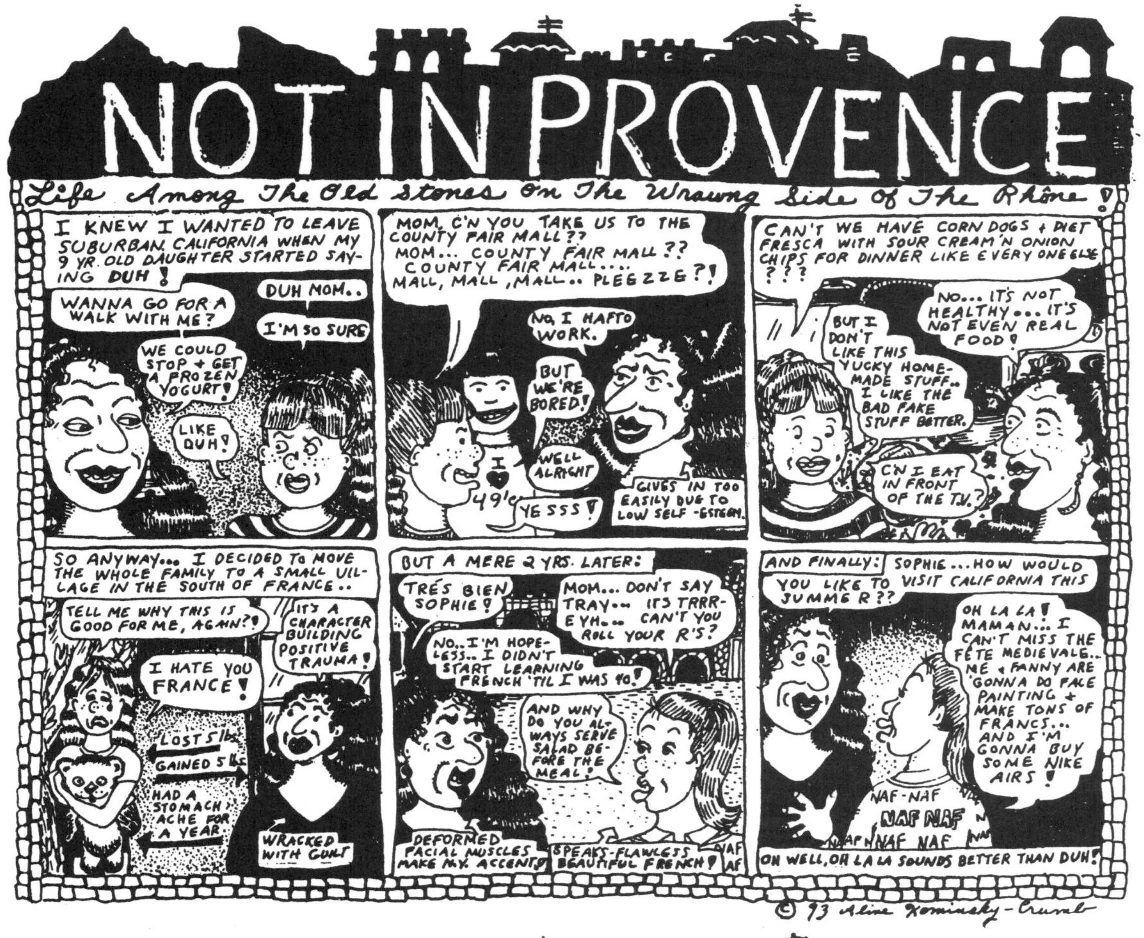
NOT IN PROVENCE
Life Among The Old Stones On The Wrawng Side Of The Rhône!
I KNEW I WANTED TO LEAVE SUBURBAN CALIFORNIA WHEN MY 9 YR. OLD DAUGHTER STARTED SAYING DUH!
WANNA GO FOR A WALK WITH ME?
DUH MOM..
I'M SO SURE
WE COULD STOP + GET A FROZEN YOGURT!
LIKE DUH!
MOM, C'N YOU TAKE US TO THE COUNTY FAIR MALL??
MOM... COUNTY FAIR MALL?? COUNTY FAIR MALL.... MALL, MALL, MALL.. PLEEZZE?!
NO, I HAFTO WORK.
BUT WE'RE BORED!
WELL ALRIGHT
YESSS!
GIVES IN TOO EASILY DUE TO LOW SELF-ESTEEM
CAN'T WE HAVE CORN DOGS + DIET FRESCA WITH SOUR CREAM'N ONION CHIPS FOR DINNER LIKE EVERYONE ELSE???
NO... IT'S NOT HEALTHY... IT'S NOT EVEN REAL FOOD!
BUT I DON'T LIKE THIS YUCKY HOME-MADE STUFF.. I LIKE THE BAD FAKE STUFF BETTER.
C'N I EAT IN FRONT OF THE T.V.?
SO ANYWAY... I DECIDED TO MOVE THE WHOLE FAMILY TO A SMALL VILLAGE IN THE SOUTH OF FRANCE..
TELL ME WHY THIS IS GOOD FOR ME, AGAIN?!
IT'S A CHARACTER BUILDING POSITIVE TRAUMA!
I HATE YOU FRANCE!
LOST 5 lbs
GAINED 5
HAD A STOMACH ACHE FOR A YEAR
WRACKED WITH GUILT
BUT A MERE 2 YRS. LATER:
TRÉS BIEN SOPHIE!
MOM... DON'T SAY TRAY.. IT'S TRRR-EYH.. CAN'T YOU ROLL YOUR R'S?
NO.. I'M HOPELESS.. I DIDN'T START LEARNING FRENCH 'TIL I WAS 40!
AND WHY DO YOU ALWAYS SERVE SALAD BEFORE THE MEAL?
DEFORMED FACIAL MUSCLES MAKE MY ACCENT!
SPEAKS FLAWLESS BEAUTIFUL FRENCH!
AND FINALLY:
SOPHIE... HOW WOULD YOU LIKE TO VISIT CALIFORNIA THIS SUMMER??
OH LA LA! MAMAN... I CAN'T MISS THE FÊTE MEDIEVALE.. ME + FANNY ARE GONNA DO FACE PAINTING + MAKE TONS OF FRANCS... AND I'M GONNA BUY SOME NIKE AIRS!
NAF NAF
OH WELL, OH LA LA SOUNDS BETTER THAN DUH!
© 93 Aline Kominsky-Crumb

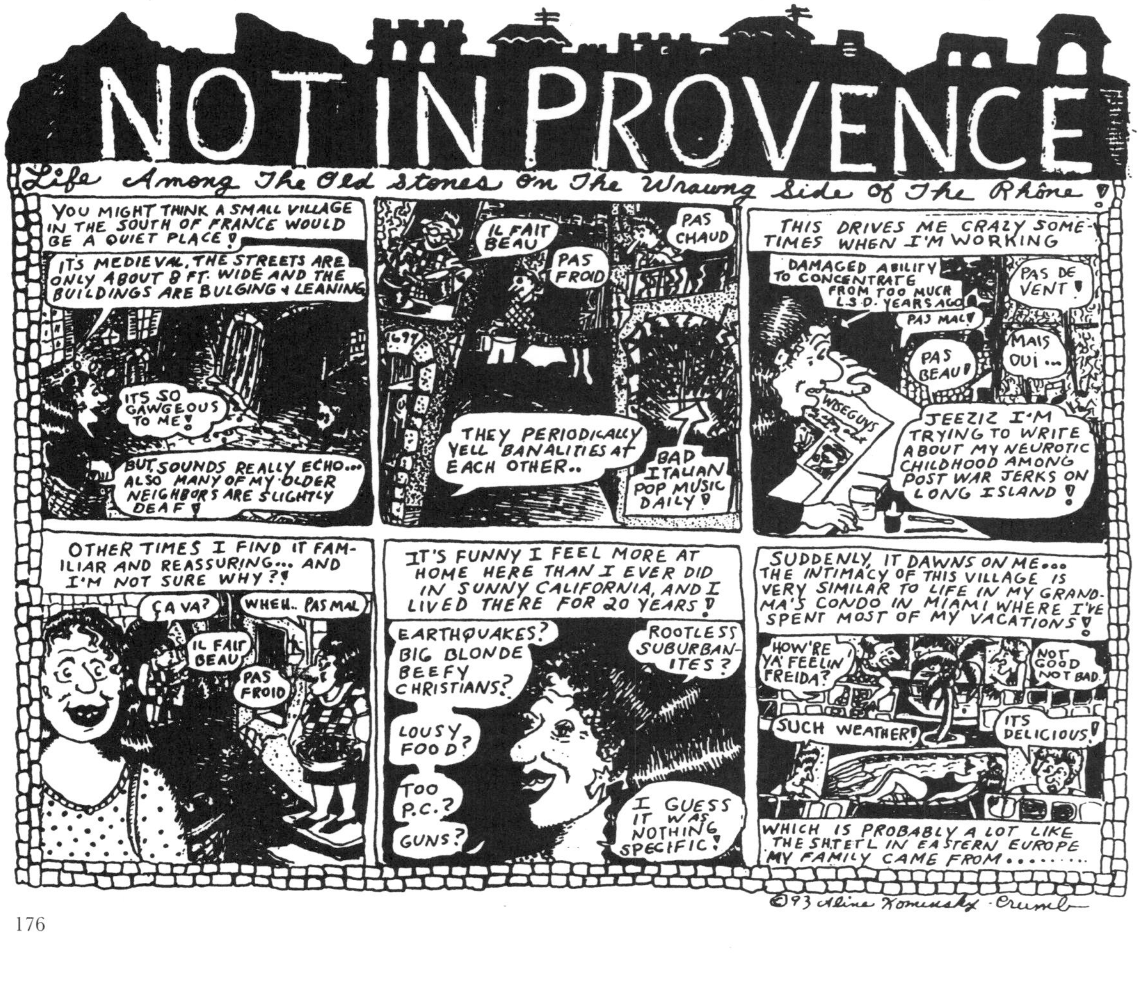
NOT IN PROVENCE
Life Among The Old Stones On The Wrawng Side Of The Rhône!
YOU MIGHT THINK A SMALL VILLAGE IN THE SOUTH OF FRANCE WOULD BE A QUIET PLACE!
ITS MEDIEVAL, THE STREETS ARE ONLY ABOUT 8 FT. WIDE AND THE BUILDINGS ARE BULGING + LEANING
ITS SO GAWGEOUS TO ME!
BUT SOUNDS REALLY ECHO... ALSO MANY OF MY OLDER NEIGHBORS ARE SLIGHTLY DEAF!
IL FAIT BEAU
PAS CHAUD
PAS FROID
THEY PERIODICALLY YELL BANALITIES AT EACH OTHER..
BAD ITALIAN POP MUSIC DAILY!
THIS DRIVES ME CRAZY SOMETIMES WHEN I'M WORKING
DAMAGED ABILITY TO CONCENTRATE FROM TOO MUCH L.S.D. YEARS AGO
PAS DE VENT!
PAS MAL
PAS BEAU!
MAIS OUI...
JEEZIZ I'M TRYING TO WRITE ABOUT MY NEUROTIC CHILDHOOD AMONG POST WAR JERKS ON LONG ISLAND!
OTHER TIMES I FIND IT FAMILIAR AND REASSURING... AND I'M NOT SURE WHY?!
ÇA VA?
WHEH.. PAS MAL
IL FAIT BEAU
PAS FROID
IT'S FUNNY I FEEL MORE AT HOME HERE THAN I EVER DID IN SUNNY CALIFORNIA, AND I LIVED THERE FOR 20 YEARS!
EARTHQUAKES?
BIG BLONDE BEEFY CHRISTIANS?
ROOTLESS SUBURBANITES?
LOUSY FOOD?
TOO P.C.?
GUNS?
I GUESS IT WAS NOTHING SPECIFIC!
SUDDENLY, IT DAWNS ON ME... THE INTIMACY OF THIS VILLAGE IS VERY SIMILAR TO LIFE IN MY GRANDMA'S CONDO IN MIAMI WHERE I'VE SPENT MOST OF MY VACATIONS!
HOW'RE YA FEELIN FREIDA?
NOT GOOD NOT BAD
SUCH WEATHER!
ITS DELICIOUS!
WHICH IS PROBABLY A LOT LIKE THE SHTETL IN EASTERN EUROPE MY FAMILY CAME FROM........
©93 Aline Kominsky-Crumb

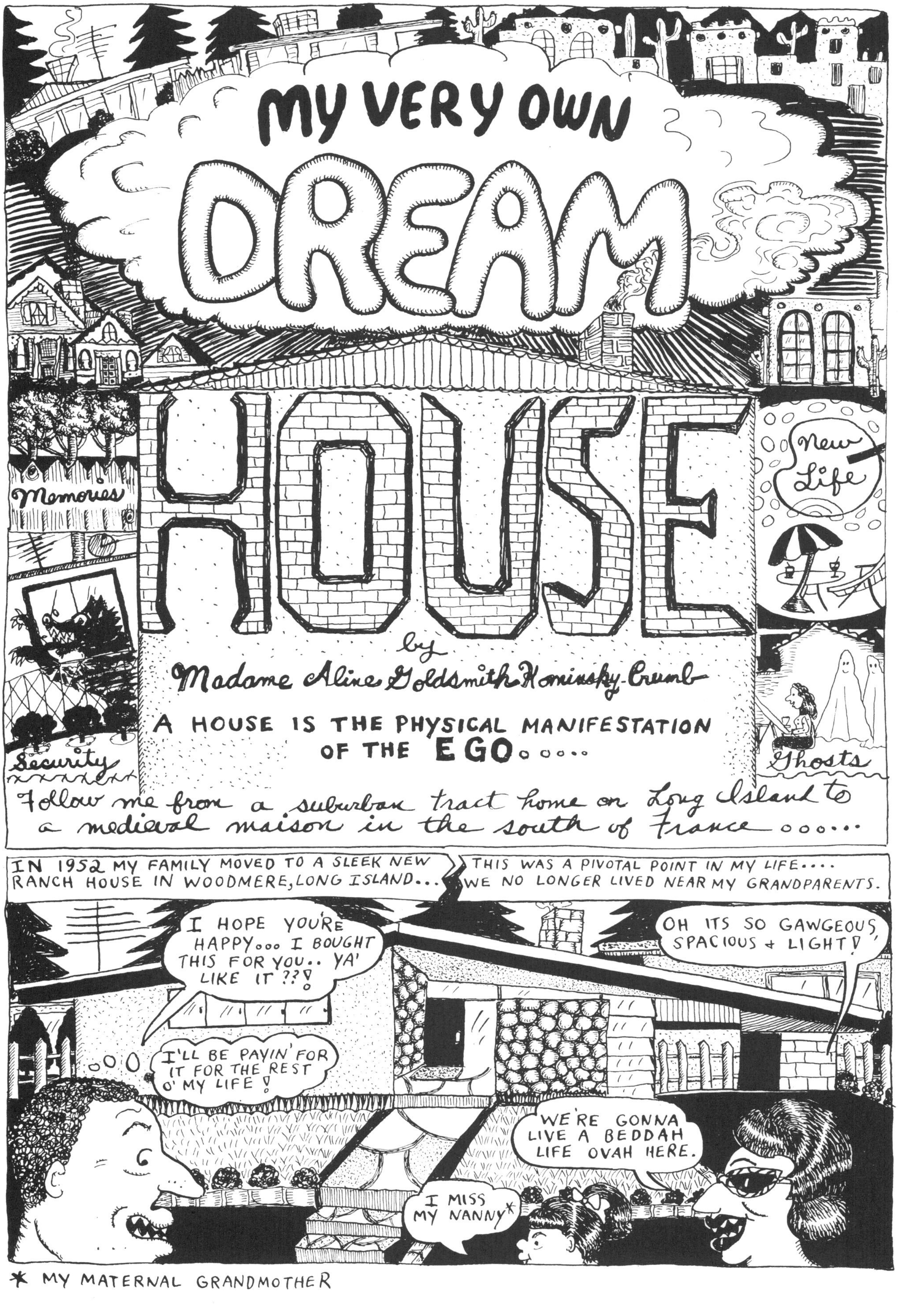
MY VERY OWN
DREAM
HOUSE
by
Madame Aline Goldsmith-Kominsky-Crumb
Memories
New Life
Security
Ghosts
A HOUSE IS THE PHYSICAL MANIFESTATION OF THE EGO.....
Follow me from a suburban tract home on Long Island to a medieval maison in the south of France.....
IN 1952 MY FAMILY MOVED TO A SLEEK NEW RANCH HOUSE IN WOODMERE, LONG ISLAND...
THIS WAS A PIVOTAL POINT IN MY LIFE.... WE NO LONGER LIVED NEAR MY GRANDPARENTS.
I HOPE YOU'RE HAPPY... I BOUGHT THIS FOR YOU.. YA' LIKE IT ??!
I'LL BE PAYIN' FOR IT FOR THE REST O' MY LIFE!
OH ITS SO GAWGEOUS, SPACIOUS + LIGHT!
WE'RE GONNA LIVE A BEDDAH LIFE OVAH HERE.
I MISS MY NANNY*

* MY MATERNAL GRANDMOTHER

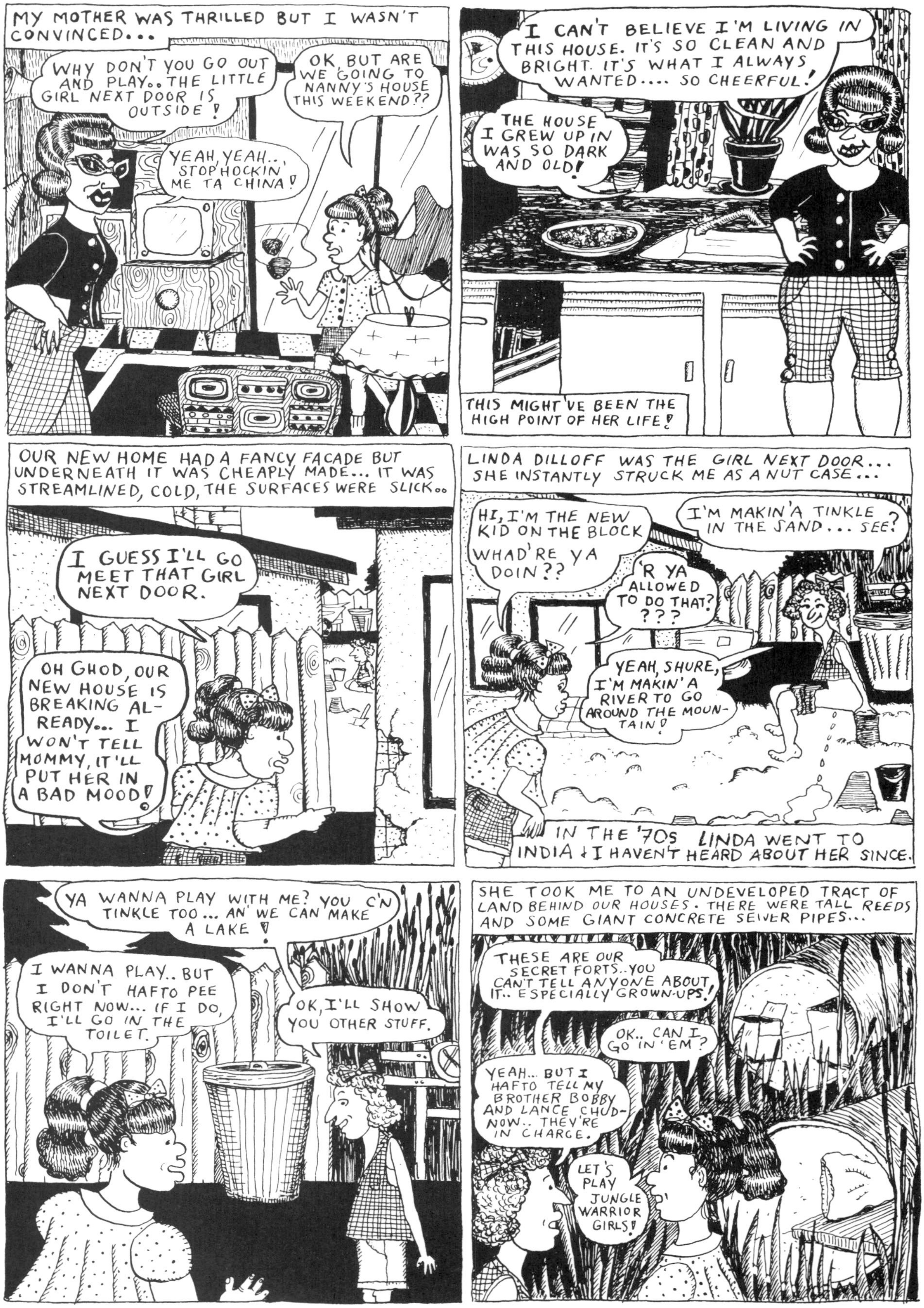

MY MOTHER WAS THRILLED BUT I WASN'T CONVINCED...
WHY DON'T YOU GO OUT AND PLAY.. THE LITTLE GIRL NEXT DOOR IS OUTSIDE!
OK, BUT ARE WE GOING TO NANNY'S HOUSE THIS WEEKEND??
YEAH, YEAH.. STOP HOCKIN' ME TA CHINA!
I CAN'T BELIEVE I'M LIVING IN THIS HOUSE. IT'S SO CLEAN AND BRIGHT. IT'S WHAT I ALWAYS WANTED.... SO CHEERFUL!
THE HOUSE I GREW UP IN WAS SO DARK AND OLD!
THIS MIGHT'VE BEEN THE HIGH POINT OF HER LIFE!
OUR NEW HOME HAD A FANCY FACADE BUT UNDERNEATH IT WAS CHEAPLY MADE... IT WAS STREAMLINED, COLD, THE SURFACES WERE SLICK..
I GUESS I'LL GO MEET THAT GIRL NEXT DOOR.
OH GHOD, OUR NEW HOUSE IS BREAKING AL-READY... I WON'T TELL MOMMY, IT'LL PUT HER IN A BAD MOOD!
LINDA DILLOFF WAS THE GIRL NEXT DOOR... SHE INSTANTLY STRUCK ME AS A NUT CASE...
HI, I'M THE NEW KID ON THE BLOCK WHAD'RE YA DOIN??
I'M MAKIN' A TINKLE IN THE SAND... SEE?
'R YA ALLOWED TO DO THAT???
YEAH, SHURE, I'M MAKIN' A RIVER TO GO AROUND THE MOUN-TAIN!
IN THE '70s LINDA WENT TO INDIA & I HAVEN'T HEARD ABOUT HER SINCE.
YA WANNA PLAY WITH ME? YOU C'N TINKLE TOO... AN' WE CAN MAKE A LAKE!
I WANNA PLAY.. BUT I DON'T HAFTO PEE RIGHT NOW... IF I DO, I'LL GO IN THE TOILET.
OK, I'LL SHOW YOU OTHER STUFF.
SHE TOOK ME TO AN UNDEVELOPED TRACT OF LAND BEHIND OUR HOUSES. THERE WERE TALL REEDS AND SOME GIANT CONCRETE SEWER PIPES...
THESE ARE OUR SECRET FORTS.. YOU CAN'T TELL ANYONE ABOUT IT.. ESPECIALLY GROWN-UPS!
OK.. CAN I GO IN 'EM?
YEAH... BUT I HAFTO TELL MY BROTHER BOBBY AND LANCE CHUD-NOW.. THEY'RE IN CHARGE.
LET'S PLAY JUNGLE WARRIOR GIRLS!

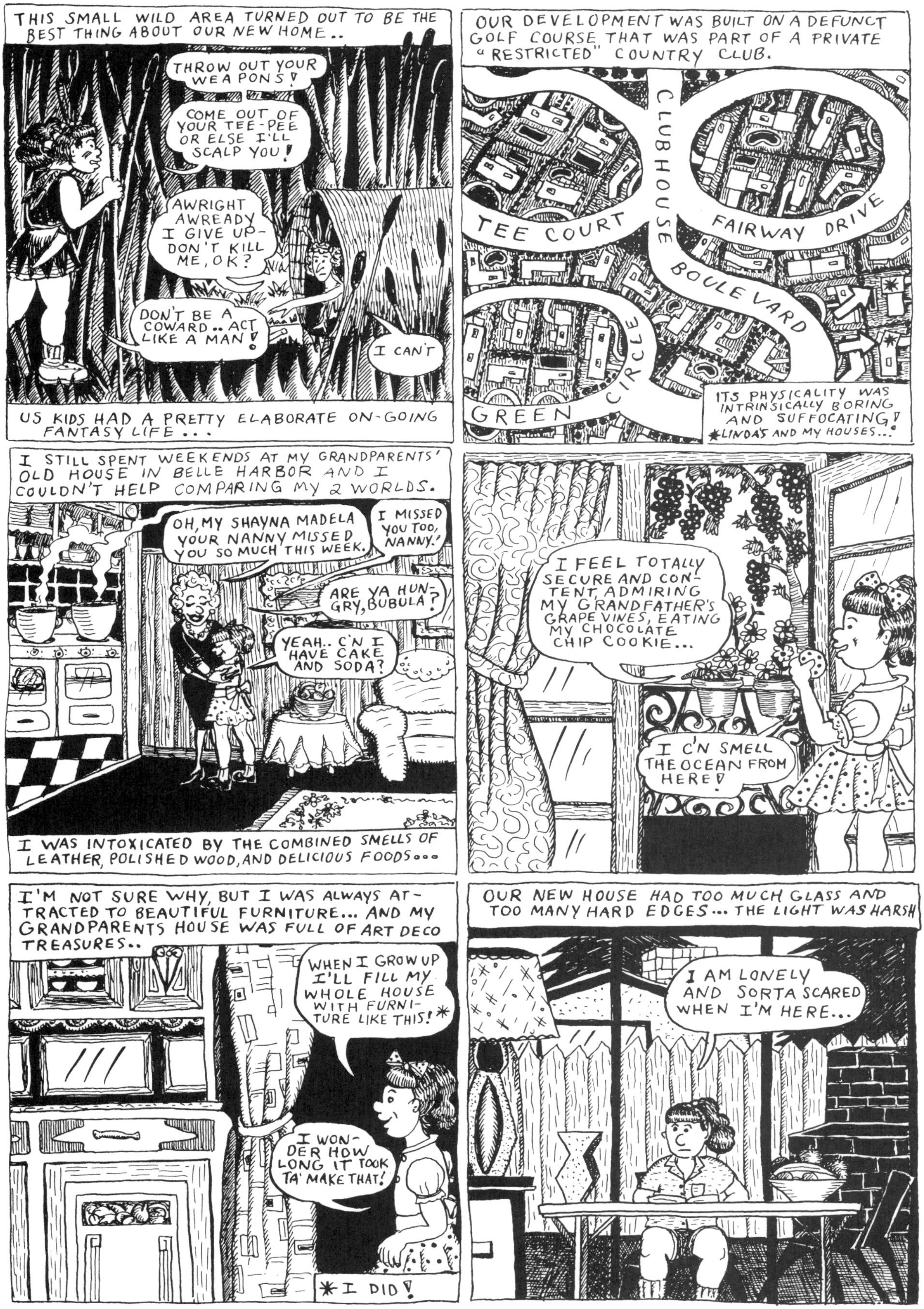

THIS SMALL WILD AREA TURNED OUT TO BE THE BEST THING ABOUT OUR NEW HOME..
THROW OUT YOUR WEAPONS!
COME OUT OF YOUR TEE-PEE OR ELSE I'LL SCALP YOU!
AWRIGHT AWREADY I GIVE UP- DON'T KILL ME, OK?
DON'T BE A COWARD.. ACT LIKE A MAN!
I CAN'T
US KIDS HAD A PRETTY ELABORATE ON-GOING FANTASY LIFE...
OUR DEVELOPMENT WAS BUILT ON A DEFUNCT GOLF COURSE THAT WAS PART OF A PRIVATE "RESTRICTED" COUNTRY CLUB.
CLUBHOUSE
TEE COURT
FAIRWAY DRIVE
BOULEVARD
CIRCLE
GREEN
ITS PHYSICALITY WAS INTRINSICALLY BORING AND SUFFOCATING!
*LINDA'S AND MY HOUSES...
I STILL SPENT WEEKENDS AT MY GRANDPARENTS' OLD HOUSE IN BELLE HARBOR AND I COULDN'T HELP COMPARING MY 2 WORLDS.
OH, MY SHAYNA MADELA YOUR NANNY MISSED YOU SO MUCH THIS WEEK.
I MISSED YOU TOO, NANNY!
ARE YA HUNGRY, BUBULA?
YEAH.. C'N I HAVE CAKE AND SODA?
I WAS INTOXICATED BY THE COMBINED SMELLS OF LEATHER, POLISHED WOOD, AND DELICIOUS FOODS...
I FEEL TOTALLY SECURE AND CONTENT, ADMIRING MY GRANDFATHER'S GRAPE VINES, EATING MY CHOCOLATE CHIP COOKIE...
I C'N SMELL THE OCEAN FROM HERE!
I'M NOT SURE WHY, BUT I WAS ALWAYS ATTRACTED TO BEAUTIFUL FURNITURE... AND MY GRANDPARENTS HOUSE WAS FULL OF ART DECO TREASURES..
WHEN I GROW UP I'LL FILL MY WHOLE HOUSE WITH FURNITURE LIKE THIS! *
I WONDER HOW LONG IT TOOK TA' MAKE THAT!
*I DID!
OUR NEW HOUSE HAD TOO MUCH GLASS AND TOO MANY HARD EDGES... THE LIGHT WAS HARSH
I AM LONELY AND SORTA SCARED WHEN I'M HERE...

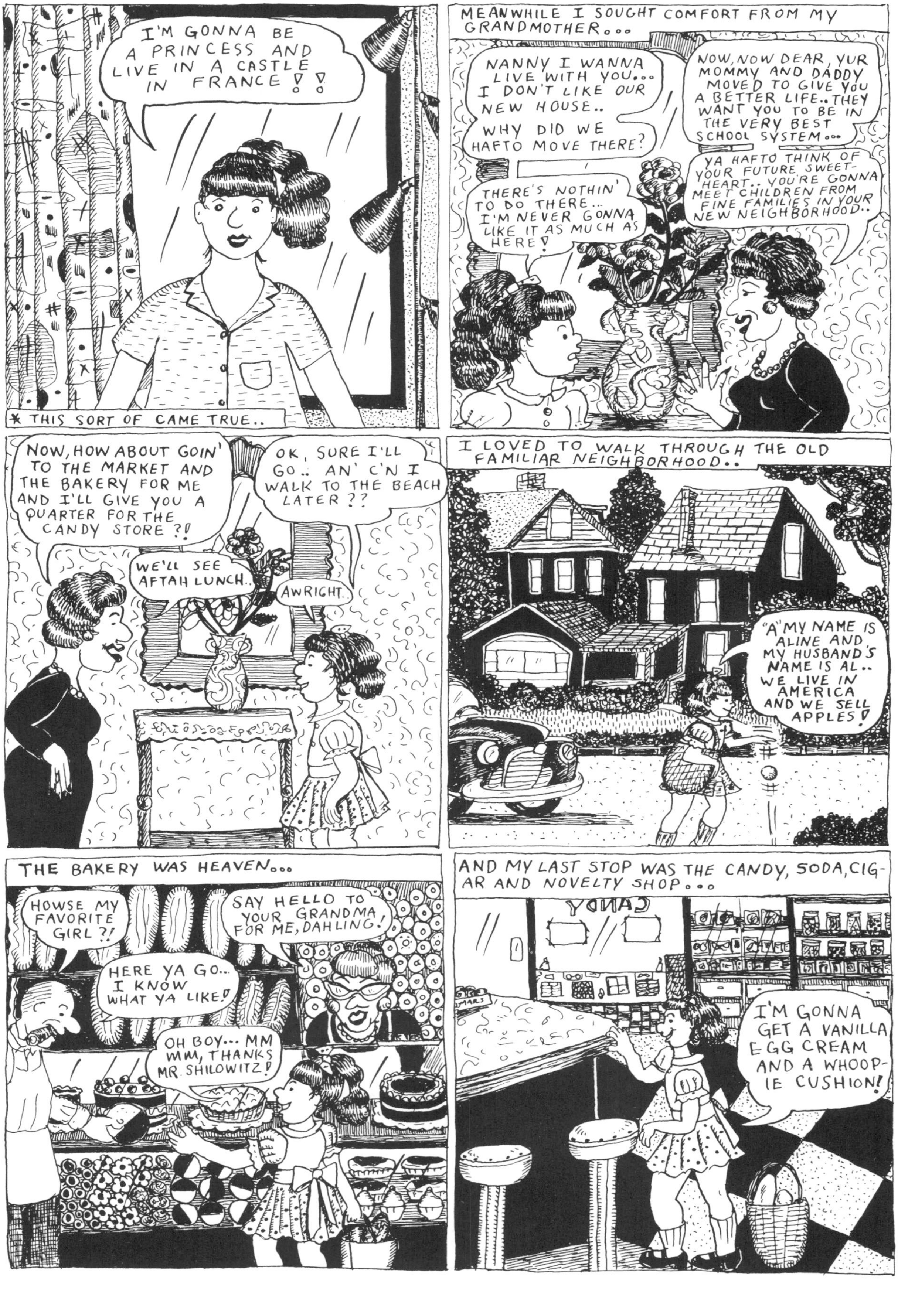

I'M GONNA BE A PRINCESS AND LIVE IN A CASTLE IN FRANCE!!
* THIS SORT OF CAME TRUE..
MEANWHILE I SOUGHT COMFORT FROM MY GRANDMOTHER...
NANNY I WANNA LIVE WITH YOU... I DON'T LIKE OUR NEW HOUSE.. WHY DID WE HAFTO MOVE THERE?
NOW, NOW DEAR, YUR MOMMY AND DADDY MOVED TO GIVE YOU A BETTER LIFE.. THEY WANT YOU TO BE IN THE VERY BEST SCHOOL SYSTEM...
THERE'S NOTHIN' TO DO THERE... I'M NEVER GONNA LIKE IT AS MUCH AS HERE!
YA HAFTO THINK OF YOUR FUTURE SWEET-HEART.. YOU'RE GONNA MEET CHILDREN FROM FINE FAMILIES IN YOUR NEW NEIGHBORHOOD..
NOW, HOW ABOUT GOIN' TO THE MARKET AND THE BAKERY FOR ME AND I'LL GIVE YOU A QUARTER FOR THE CANDY STORE?!
OK, SURE I'LL GO.. AN' C'N I WALK TO THE BEACH LATER??
WE'LL SEE AFTAH LUNCH..
AWRIGHT.
I LOVED TO WALK THROUGH THE OLD FAMILIAR NEIGHBORHOOD..
"A" MY NAME IS ALINE AND MY HUSBAND'S NAME IS AL.. WE LIVE IN AMERICA AND WE SELL APPLES!
THE BAKERY WAS HEAVEN...
HOWSE MY FAVORITE GIRL?!
SAY HELLO TO YOUR GRANDMA FOR ME, DAHLING!
HERE YA GO... I KNOW WHAT YA LIKE!
OH BOY... MM MM, THANKS MR. SHILOWITZ!
AND MY LAST STOP WAS THE CANDY, SODA, CIGAR AND NOVELTY SHOP...
CANDY
I'M GONNA GET A VANILLA EGG CREAM AND A WHOOPIE CUSHION!

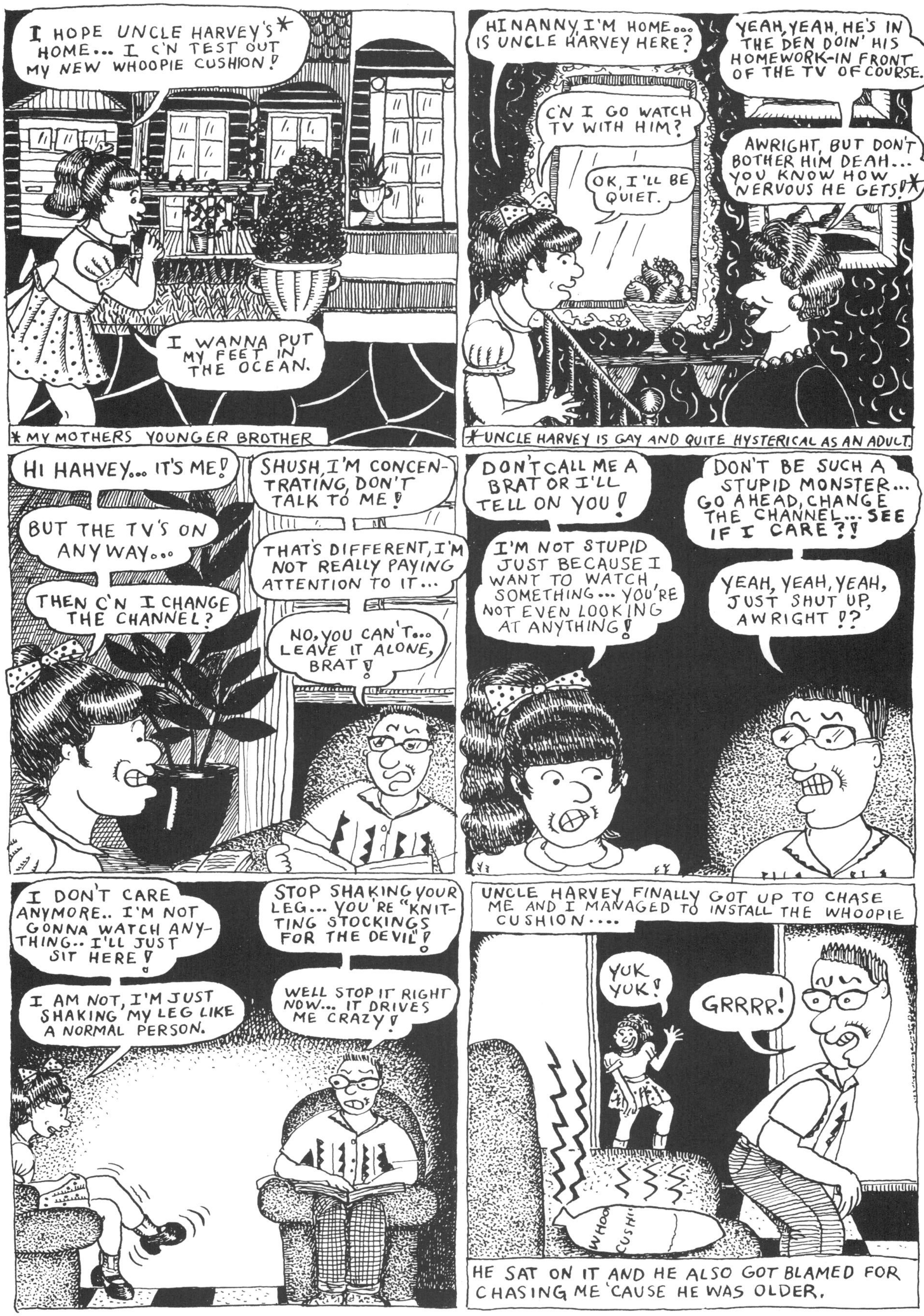

I HOPE UNCLE HARVEY'S* HOME... I C'N TEST OUT MY NEW WHOOPIE CUSHION!
I WANNA PUT MY FEET IN THE OCEAN.
*MY MOTHERS YOUNGER BROTHER
HI NANNY, I'M HOME... IS UNCLE HARVEY HERE?
YEAH, YEAH, HE'S IN THE DEN DOIN' HIS HOMEWORK-IN FRONT OF THE TV OF COURSE.
C'N I GO WATCH TV WITH HIM?
AWRIGHT, BUT DON'T BOTHER HIM DEAH... YOU KNOW HOW NERVOUS HE GETS!*
OK, I'LL BE QUIET.
*UNCLE HARVEY IS GAY AND QUITE HYSTERICAL AS AN ADULT.
HI HAHVEY... IT'S ME!
SHUSH, I'M CONCENTRATING, DON'T TALK TO ME!
BUT THE TV'S ON ANYWAY...
THAT'S DIFFERENT, I'M NOT REALLY PAYING ATTENTION TO IT...
THEN C'N I CHANGE THE CHANNEL?
NO, YOU CAN'T... LEAVE IT ALONE, BRAT!
DON'T CALL ME A BRAT OR I'LL TELL ON YOU!
DON'T BE SUCH A STUPID MONSTER... GO AHEAD, CHANGE THE CHANNEL... SEE IF I CARE?!
I'M NOT STUPID JUST BECAUSE I WANT TO WATCH SOMETHING... YOU'RE NOT EVEN LOOKING AT ANYTHING!
YEAH, YEAH, YEAH, JUST SHUT UP, AWRIGHT!?
I DON'T CARE ANYMORE.. I'M NOT GONNA WATCH ANYTHING.. I'LL JUST SIT HERE!
STOP SHAKING YOUR LEG... YOU'RE "KNITTING STOCKINGS FOR THE DEVIL"!
I AM NOT, I'M JUST SHAKING MY LEG LIKE A NORMAL PERSON.
WELL STOP IT RIGHT NOW... IT DRIVES ME CRAZY!
UNCLE HARVEY FINALLY GOT UP TO CHASE ME AND I MANAGED TO INSTALL THE WHOOPIE CUSHION....
YUK YUK!
GRRRR!
HE SAT ON IT AND HE ALSO GOT BLAMED FOR CHASING ME 'CAUSE HE WAS OLDER.

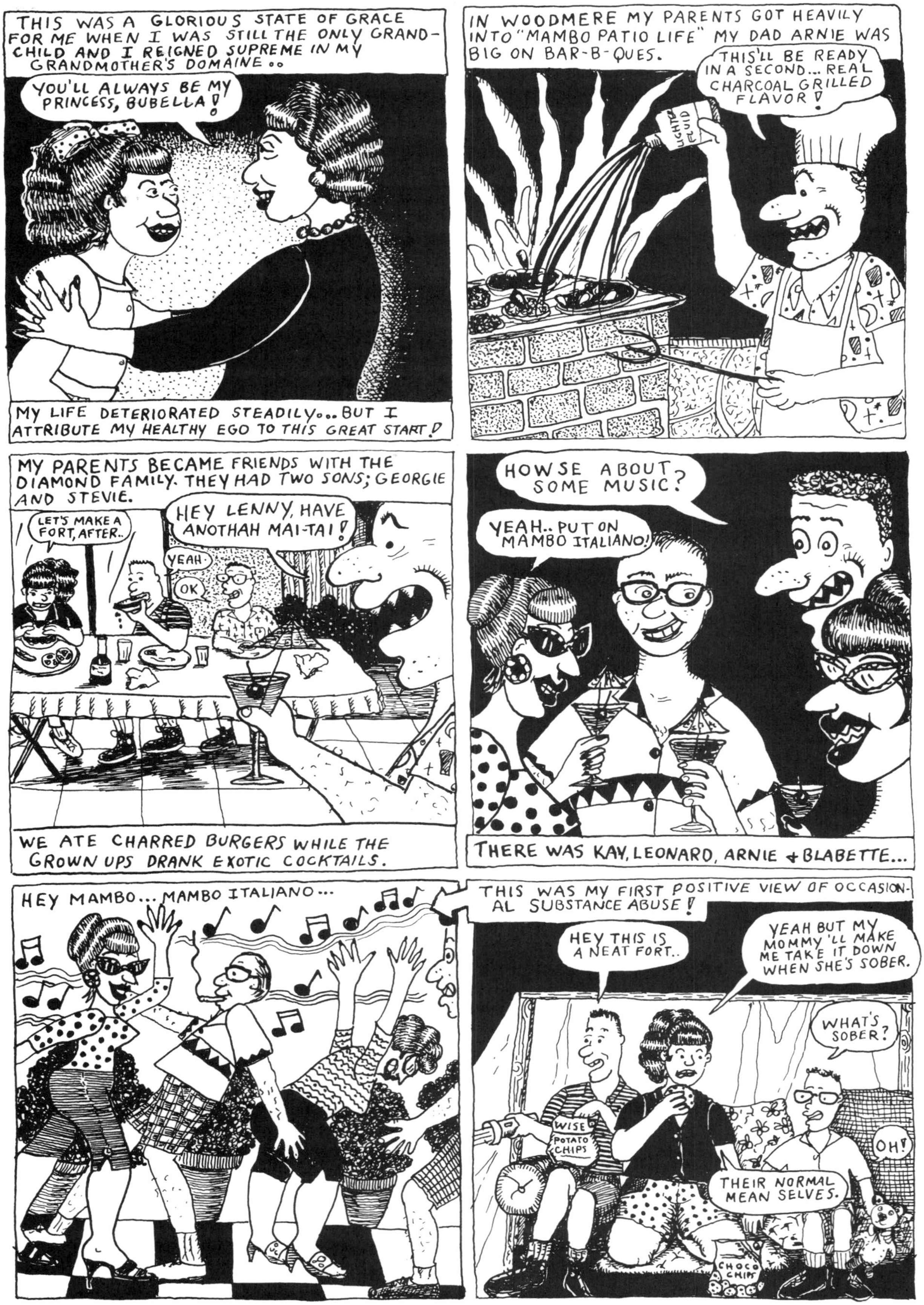
THIS WAS A GLORIOUS STATE OF GRACE FOR ME WHEN I WAS STILL THE ONLY GRAND-CHILD AND I REIGNED SUPREME IN MY GRANDMOTHER'S DOMAINE..
YOU'LL ALWAYS BE MY PRINCESS, BUBELLA!
MY LIFE DETERIORATED STEADILY... BUT I ATTRIBUTE MY HEALTHY EGO TO THIS GREAT START!
IN WOODMERE MY PARENTS GOT HEAVILY INTO "MAMBO PATIO LIFE" MY DAD ARNIE WAS BIG ON BAR-B-QUES.
THIS'LL BE READY IN A SECOND... REAL CHARCOAL GRILLED FLAVOR!
LIGHTER FLUID
MY PARENTS BECAME FRIENDS WITH THE DIAMOND FAMILY. THEY HAD TWO SONS; GEORGIE AND STEVIE.
LET'S MAKE A FORT, AFTER..
HEY LENNY, HAVE ANOTHAH MAI-TAI!
YEAH.
OK
WE ATE CHARRED BURGERS WHILE THE GROWN UPS DRANK EXOTIC COCKTAILS.
HOWSE ABOUT SOME MUSIC?
YEAH.. PUT ON MAMBO ITALIANO!
THERE WAS KAY, LEONARD, ARNIE + BLABETTE...
HEY MAMBO... MAMBO ITALIANO...
THIS WAS MY FIRST POSITIVE VIEW OF OCCASION-AL SUBSTANCE ABUSE!
HEY THIS IS A NEAT FORT..
YEAH BUT MY MOMMY 'LL MAKE ME TAKE IT DOWN WHEN SHE'S SOBER.
WHAT'S SOBER?
OH!
THEIR NORMAL MEAN SELVES.
WISE POTATO CHIPS
CHOCO CHIPS

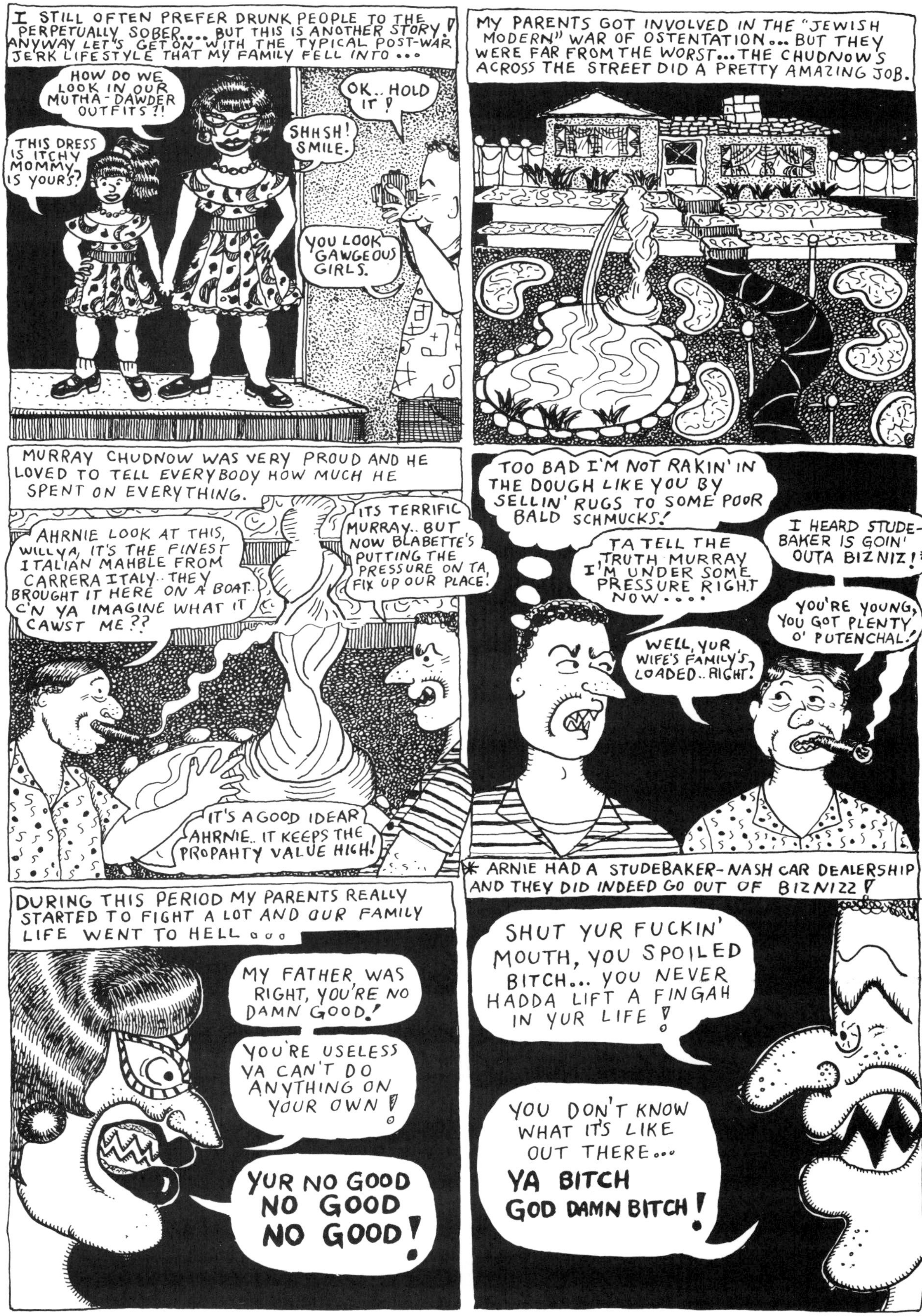

I STILL OFTEN PREFER DRUNK PEOPLE TO THE PERPETUALLY SOBER... BUT THIS IS ANOTHER STORY! ANYWAY LET'S GET ON WITH THE TYPICAL POST-WAR JERK LIFESTYLE THAT MY FAMILY FELL INTO...
HOW DO WE LOOK IN OUR MUTHA-DAWDER OUTFITS?!
THIS DRESS IS ITCHY MOMMY, IS YOURS?
OK.. HOLD IT!
SHHSH! SMILE.
YOU LOOK GAWGEOUS GIRLS.
MY PARENTS GOT INVOLVED IN THE "JEWISH MODERN" WAR OF OSTENTATION... BUT THEY WERE FAR FROM THE WORST... THE CHUDNOW'S ACROSS THE STREET DID A PRETTY AMAZING JOB.
MURRAY CHUDNOW WAS VERY PROUD AND HE LOVED TO TELL EVERYBODY HOW MUCH HE SPENT ON EVERYTHING.
AHRNIE LOOK AT THIS, WILLYA, IT'S THE FINEST ITALIAN MAHBLE FROM CARRERA ITALY.. THEY BROUGHT IT HERE ON A BOAT.. C'N YA IMAGINE WHAT IT CAWST ME??
ITS TERRIFIC MURRAY.. BUT NOW BLABETTE'S PUTTING THE PRESSURE ON TA FIX UP OUR PLACE!
IT'S A GOOD IDEAR AHRNIE.. IT KEEPS THE PROPAHTY VALUE HIGH!
TOO BAD I'M NOT RAKIN' IN THE DOUGH LIKE YOU BY SELLIN' RUGS TO SOME POOR BALD SCHMUCKS!
TA TELL THE TRUTH MURRAY I'M UNDER SOME PRESSURE RIGHT NOW...
I HEARD STUDEBAKER IS GOIN' OUTA BIZNIZ!*
WELL, YUR WIFE'S FAMILY'S LOADED.. RIGHT?
YOU'RE YOUNG, YOU GOT PLENTY O' PUTENCHAL!
* ARNIE HAD A STUDEBAKER-NASH CAR DEALERSHIP AND THEY DID INDEED GO OUT OF BIZNIZZ!
DURING THIS PERIOD MY PARENTS REALLY STARTED TO FIGHT A LOT AND OUR FAMILY LIFE WENT TO HELL...
MY FATHER WAS RIGHT, YOU'RE NO DAMN GOOD!
YOU'RE USELESS YA CAN'T DO ANYTHING ON YOUR OWN!
YUR NO GOOD NO GOOD NO GOOD!
SHUT YUR FUCKIN' MOUTH, YOU SPOILED BITCH... YOU NEVER HADDA LIFT A FINGAH IN YUR LIFE!
YOU DON'T KNOW WHAT IT'S LIKE OUT THERE... YA BITCH GOD DAMN BITCH!

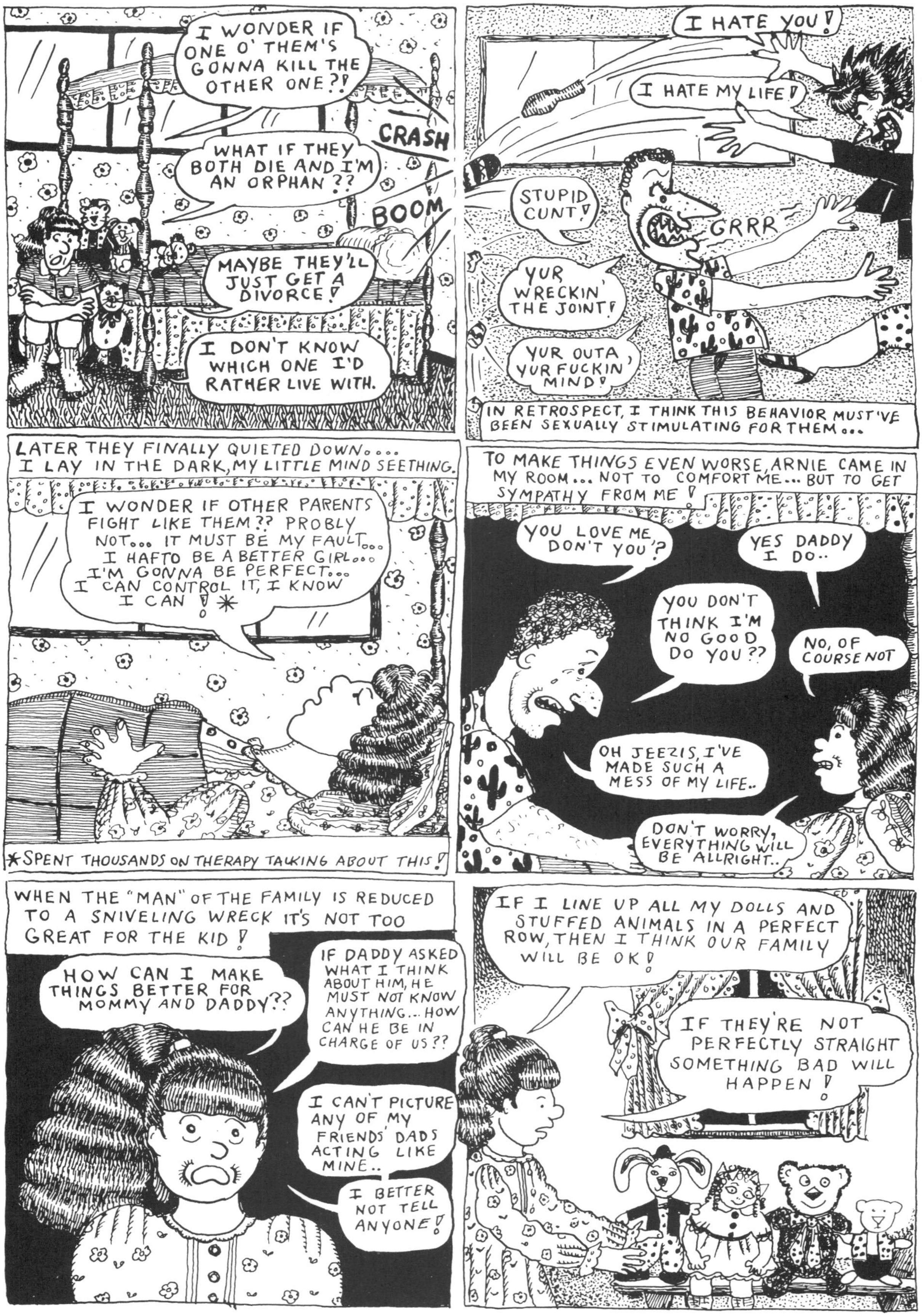
I WONDER IF ONE O' THEM'S GONNA KILL THE OTHER ONE?!
WHAT IF THEY BOTH DIE AND I'M AN ORPHAN??
CRASH
BOOM
MAYBE THEY'LL JUST GET A DIVORCE!
I DON'T KNOW WHICH ONE I'D RATHER LIVE WITH.
I HATE YOU!
I HATE MY LIFE!
STUPID CUNT!
GRRR
YUR WRECKIN' THE JOINT!
YUR OUTA YUR FUCKIN' MIND!
IN RETROSPECT, I THINK THIS BEHAVIOR MUST'VE BEEN SEXUALLY STIMULATING FOR THEM...
LATER THEY FINALLY QUIETED DOWN.... I LAY IN THE DARK, MY LITTLE MIND SEETHING.
I WONDER IF OTHER PARENTS FIGHT LIKE THEM?? PROBLY NOT... IT MUST BE MY FAULT... I HAFTO BE A BETTER GIRL... I'M GONNA BE PERFECT... I CAN CONTROL IT, I KNOW I CAN!*
*SPENT THOUSANDS ON THERAPY TALKING ABOUT THIS!
TO MAKE THINGS EVEN WORSE, ARNIE CAME IN MY ROOM... NOT TO COMFORT ME... BUT TO GET SYMPATHY FROM ME!
YOU LOVE ME, DON'T YOU?
YES DADDY I DO..
YOU DON'T THINK I'M NO GOOD DO YOU??
NO, OF COURSE NOT
OH JEEZIS, I'VE MADE SUCH A MESS OF MY LIFE..
DON'T WORRY, EVERYTHING WILL BE ALLRIGHT..
WHEN THE "MAN" OF THE FAMILY IS REDUCED TO A SNIVELING WRECK IT'S NOT TOO GREAT FOR THE KID!
HOW CAN I MAKE THINGS BETTER FOR MOMMY AND DADDY??
IF DADDY ASKED WHAT I THINK ABOUT HIM, HE MUST NOT KNOW ANYTHING... HOW CAN HE BE IN CHARGE OF US??
I CAN'T PICTURE ANY OF MY FRIENDS' DADS ACTING LIKE MINE..
I BETTER NOT TELL ANYONE!
IF I LINE UP ALL MY DOLLS AND STUFFED ANIMALS IN A PERFECT ROW, THEN I THINK OUR FAMILY WILL BE OK!
IF THEY'RE NOT PERFECTLY STRAIGHT SOMETHING BAD WILL HAPPEN!

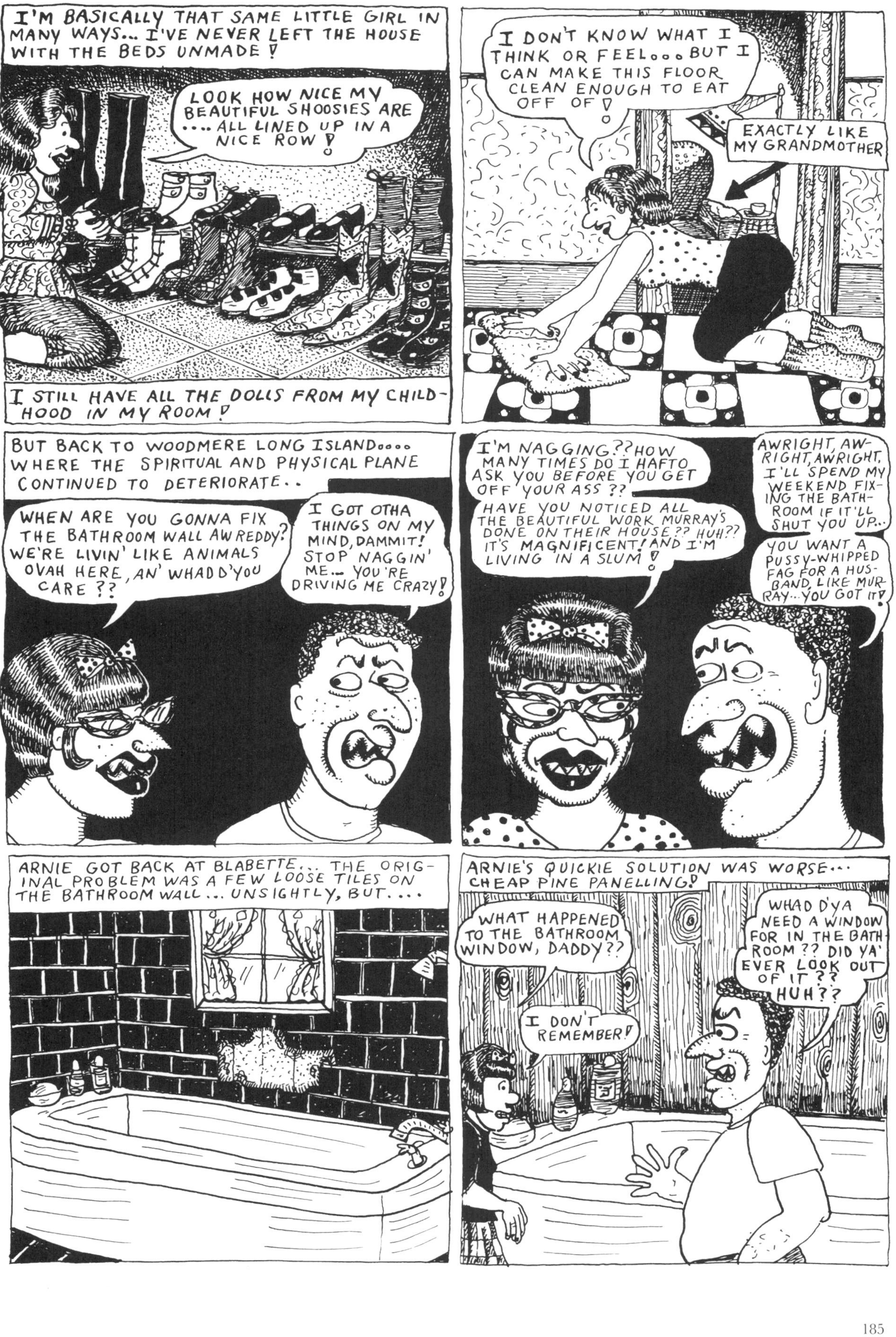

I'M BASICALLY THAT SAME LITTLE GIRL IN MANY WAYS... I'VE NEVER LEFT THE HOUSE WITH THE BEDS UNMADE!
LOOK HOW NICE MY BEAUTIFUL SHOOSIES ARE .... ALL LINED UP IN A NICE ROW!
I STILL HAVE ALL THE DOLLS FROM MY CHILD-HOOD IN MY ROOM!
I DON'T KNOW WHAT I THINK OR FEEL... BUT I CAN MAKE THIS FLOOR CLEAN ENOUGH TO EAT OFF OF!
EXACTLY LIKE MY GRANDMOTHER
BUT BACK TO WOODMERE LONG ISLAND.... WHERE THE SPIRITUAL AND PHYSICAL PLANE CONTINUED TO DETERIORATE..
WHEN ARE YOU GONNA FIX THE BATHROOM WALL AWREDDY? WE'RE LIVIN' LIKE ANIMALS OVAH HERE, AN' WHADD'YOU CARE??
I GOT OTHA THINGS ON MY MIND, DAMMIT! STOP NAGGIN' ME... YOU'RE DRIVING ME CRAZY!
I'M NAGGING?? HOW MANY TIMES DO I HAFTO ASK YOU BEFORE YOU GET OFF YOUR ASS?? HAVE YOU NOTICED ALL THE BEAUTIFUL WORK MURRAY'S DONE ON THEIR HOUSE?? HUH?? IT'S MAGNIFICENT! AND I'M LIVING IN A SLUM!
AWRIGHT, AWRIGHT, AWRIGHT, I'LL SPEND MY WEEKEND FIXING THE BATHROOM IF IT'LL SHUT YOU UP..
YOU WANT A PUSSY-WHIPPED FAG FOR A HUSBAND, LIKE MURRAY.. YOU GOT IT!
ARNIE GOT BACK AT BLABETTE... THE ORIGINAL PROBLEM WAS A FEW LOOSE TILES ON THE BATHROOM WALL... UNSIGHTLY, BUT....
ARNIE'S QUICKIE SOLUTION WAS WORSE... CHEAP PINE PANELLING!
WHAT HAPPENED TO THE BATHROOM WINDOW, DADDY??
WHAD D'YA NEED A WINDOW FOR IN THE BATHROOM?? DID YA' EVER LOOK OUT OF IT?? HUH??
I DON'T REMEMBER!

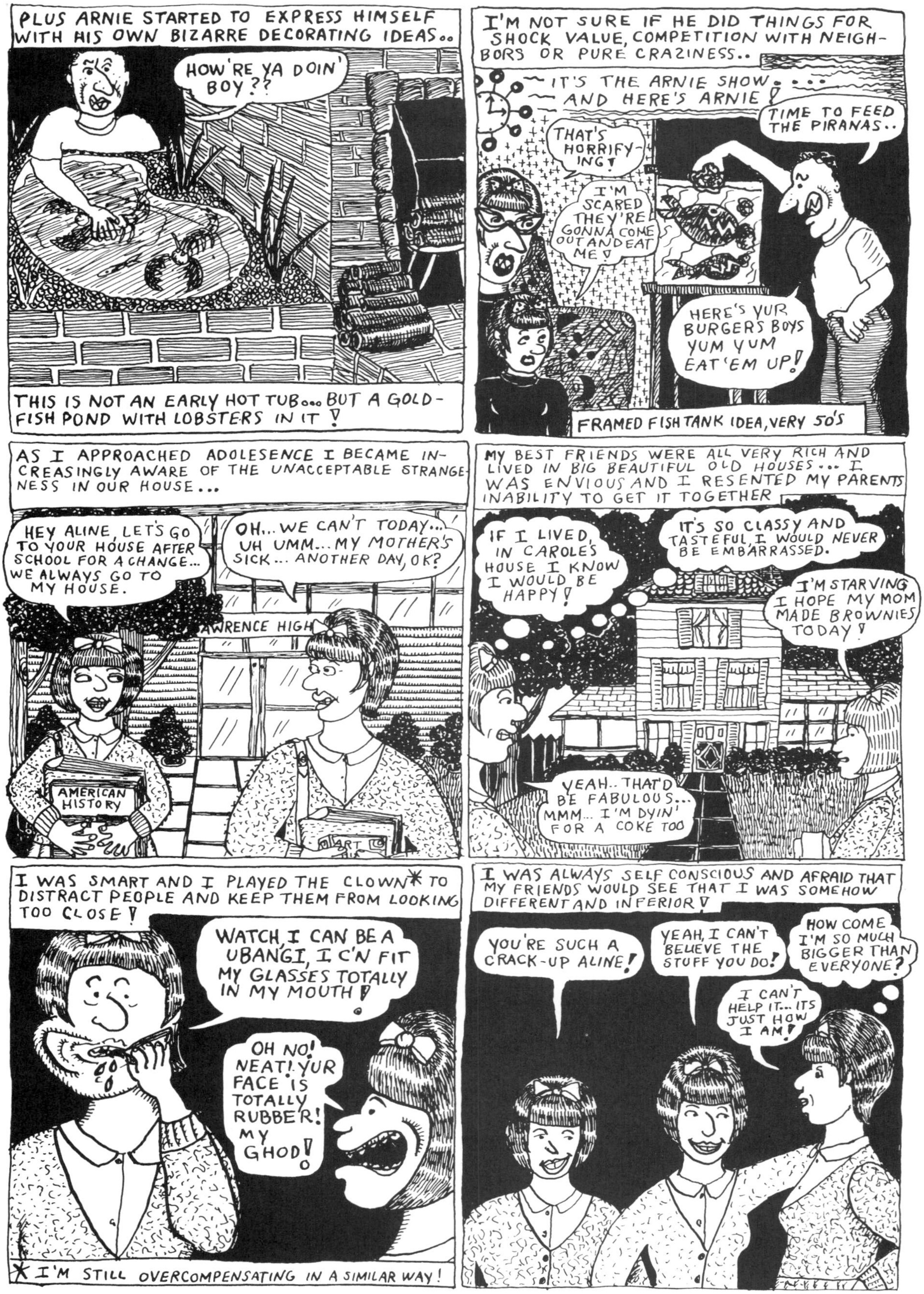
PLUS ARNIE STARTED TO EXPRESS HIMSELF WITH HIS OWN BIZARRE DECORATING IDEAS..
HOW'RE YA DOIN' BOY??
THIS IS NOT AN EARLY HOT TUB... BUT A GOLD-FISH POND WITH LOBSTERS IN IT!
I'M NOT SURE IF HE DID THINGS FOR SHOCK VALUE, COMPETITION WITH NEIGHBORS OR PURE CRAZINESS..
IT'S THE ARNIE SHOW.... AND HERE'S ARNIE!
TIME TO FEED THE PIRANAS..
THAT'S HORRIFYING!
I'M SCARED THEY'RE GONNA COME OUT AND EAT ME!
HERE'S YUR BURGERS BOYS YUM YUM EAT 'EM UP!
FRAMED FISH TANK IDEA, VERY 50'S
AS I APPROACHED ADOLESENCE I BECAME INCREASINGLY AWARE OF THE UNACCEPTABLE STRANGENESS IN OUR HOUSE...
HEY ALINE, LET'S GO TO YOUR HOUSE AFTER SCHOOL FOR A CHANGE... WE ALWAYS GO TO MY HOUSE.
OH... WE CAN'T TODAY... UH UMM... MY MOTHER'S SICK... ANOTHER DAY, OK?
AWRENCE HIGH
AMERICAN HISTORY
ART
MY BEST FRIENDS WERE ALL VERY RICH AND LIVED IN BIG BEAUTIFUL OLD HOUSES... I WAS ENVIOUS AND I RESENTED MY PARENTS INABILITY TO GET IT TOGETHER
IF I LIVED IN CAROLE'S HOUSE I KNOW I WOULD BE HAPPY!
IT'S SO CLASSY AND TASTEFUL, I WOULD NEVER BE EMBARRASSED.
I'M STARVING I HOPE MY MOM MADE BROWNIES TODAY!
YEAH.. THAT'D BE FABULOUS... MMM... I'M DYIN' FOR A COKE TOO
I WAS SMART AND I PLAYED THE CLOWN* TO DISTRACT PEOPLE AND KEEP THEM FROM LOOKING TOO CLOSE!
WATCH, I CAN BE A UBANGI, I C'N FIT MY GLASSES TOTALLY IN MY MOUTH!
OH NO! NEAT! YUR FACE IS TOTALLY RUBBER! MY GHOD!
* I'M STILL OVERCOMPENSATING IN A SIMILAR WAY!
I WAS ALWAYS SELF CONSCIOUS AND AFRAID THAT MY FRIENDS WOULD SEE THAT I WAS SOMEHOW DIFFERENT AND INFERIOR!
YOU'RE SUCH A CRACK-UP ALINE!
YEAH, I CAN'T BELIEVE THE STUFF YOU DO!
HOW COME I'M SO MUCH BIGGER THAN EVERYONE?
I CAN'T HELP IT... ITS JUST HOW I AM!

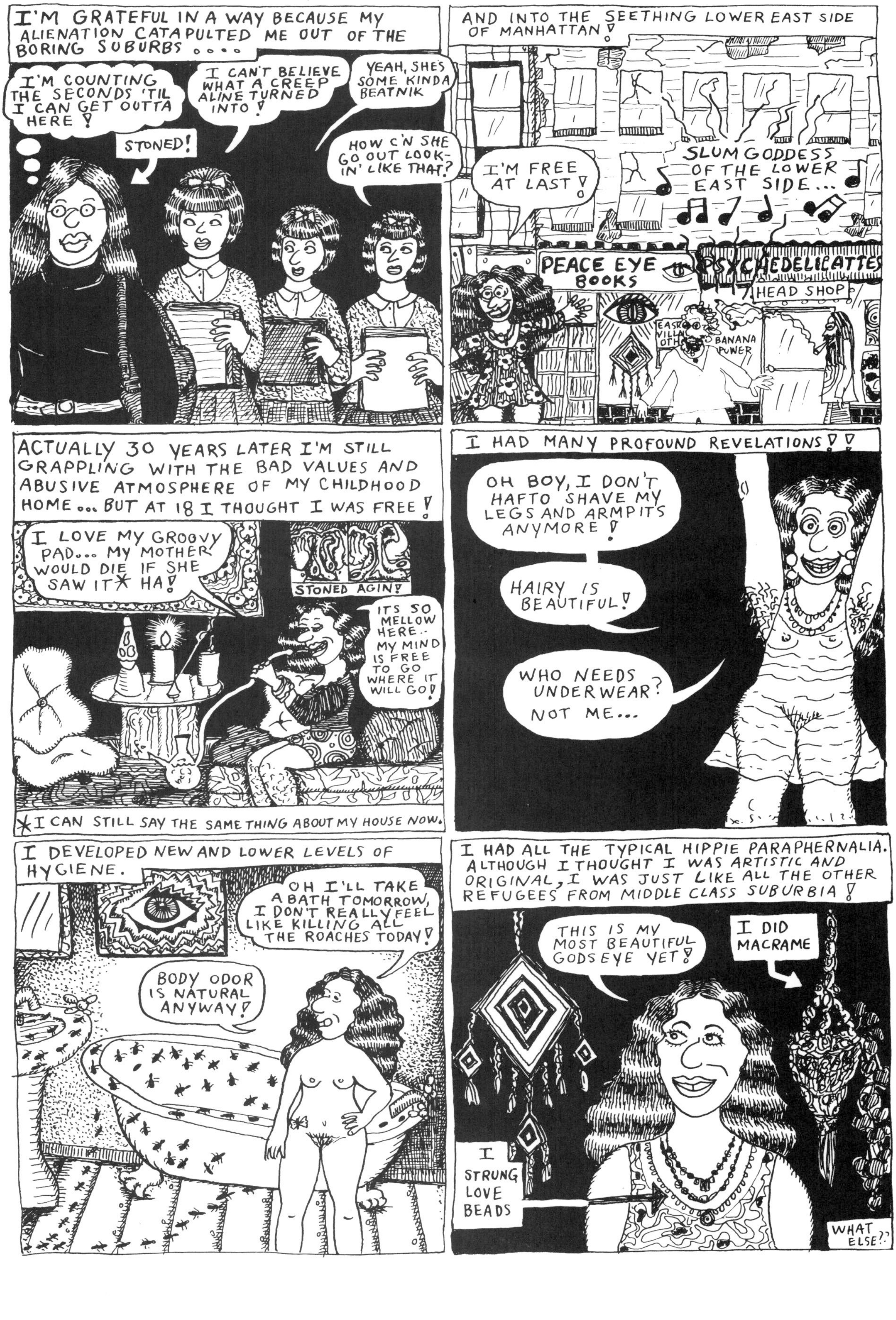
I'M GRATEFUL IN A WAY BECAUSE MY ALIENATION CATAPULTED ME OUT OF THE BORING SUBURBS ....
I'M COUNTING THE SECONDS 'TIL I CAN GET OUTTA HERE!
I CAN'T BELIEVE WHAT A CREEP ALINE TURNED INTO!
YEAH, SHES SOME KINDA BEATNIK
HOW C'N SHE GO OUT LOOK-IN' LIKE THAT?
STONED!
AND INTO THE SEETHING LOWER EAST SIDE OF MANHATTAN!
I'M FREE AT LAST!
SLUM GODDESS OF THE LOWER EAST SIDE...
PEACE EYE BOOKS
PSYCHEDELICATTES
HEAD SHOP
BANANA POWER
ACTUALLY 30 YEARS LATER I'M STILL GRAPPLING WITH THE BAD VALUES AND ABUSIVE ATMOSPHERE OF MY CHILDHOOD HOME... BUT AT 18 I THOUGHT I WAS FREE!
I LOVE MY GROOVY PAD... MY MOTHER WOULD DIE IF SHE SAW IT* HA!
STONED AGIN!
ITS SO MELLOW HERE.. MY MIND IS FREE TO GO WHERE IT WILL GO!
*I CAN STILL SAY THE SAME THING ABOUT MY HOUSE NOW.
I HAD MANY PROFOUND REVELATIONS!!
OH BOY, I DON'T HAFTO SHAVE MY LEGS AND ARMPITS ANYMORE!
HAIRY IS BEAUTIFUL!
WHO NEEDS UNDERWEAR? NOT ME...
I DEVELOPED NEW AND LOWER LEVELS OF HYGIENE.
OH I'LL TAKE A BATH TOMORROW, I DON'T REALLY FEEL LIKE KILLING ALL THE ROACHES TODAY!
BODY ODOR IS NATURAL ANYWAY!
I HAD ALL THE TYPICAL HIPPIE PARAPHERNALIA. ALTHOUGH I THOUGHT I WAS ARTISTIC AND ORIGINAL, I WAS JUST LIKE ALL THE OTHER REFUGEES FROM MIDDLE CLASS SUBURBIA!
THIS IS MY MOST BEAUTIFUL GODSEYE YET!
I DID MACRAME
I STRUNG LOVE BEADS
WHAT ELSE?!

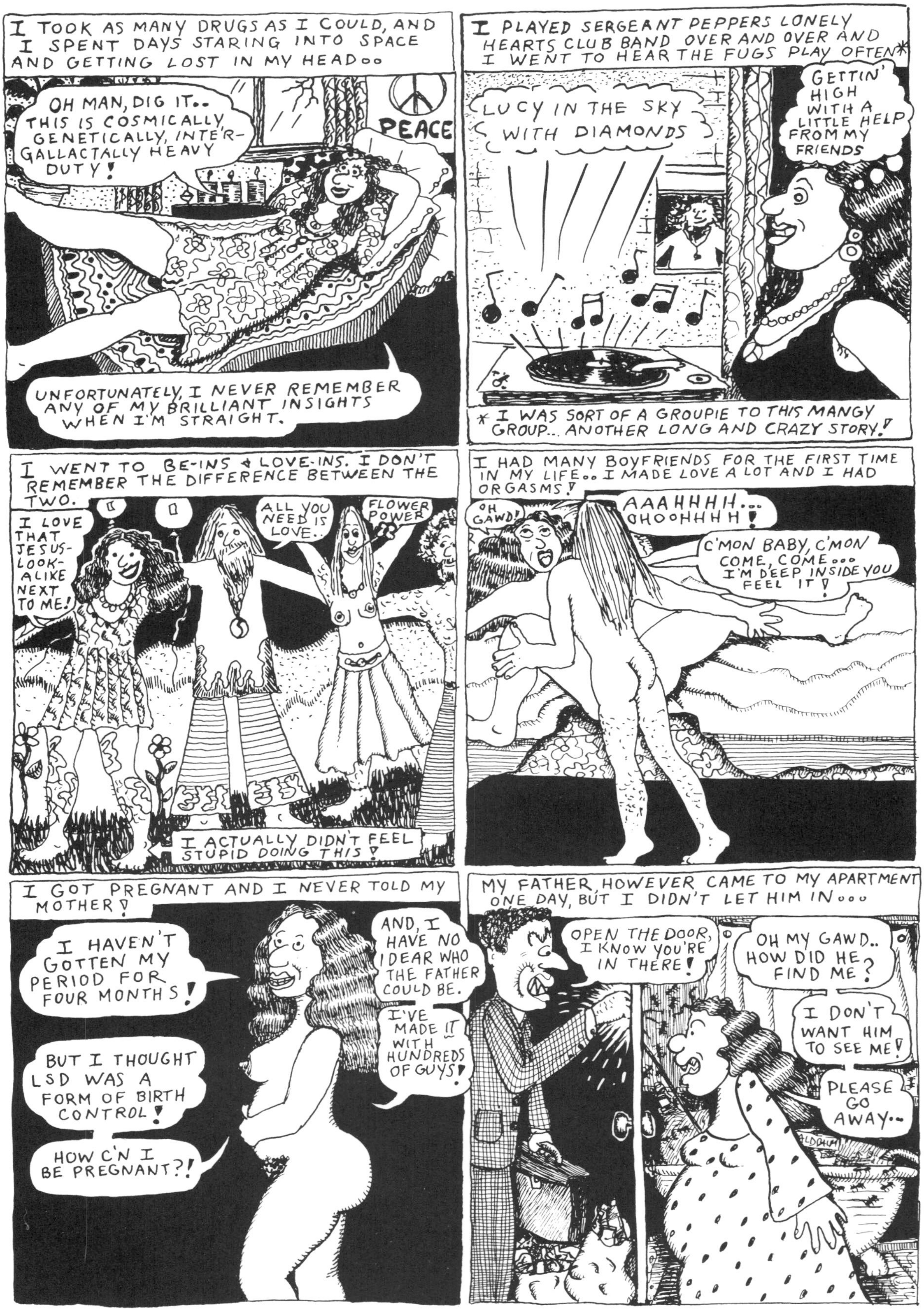

I TOOK AS MANY DRUGS AS I COULD, AND I SPENT DAYS STARING INTO SPACE AND GETTING LOST IN MY HEAD..
OH MAN, DIG IT.. THIS IS COSMICALLY, GENETICALLY, INTER-GALLACTALLY HEAVY DUTY!
PEACE
UNFORTUNATELY, I NEVER REMEMBER ANY OF MY BRILLIANT INSIGHTS WHEN I'M STRAIGHT.
I PLAYED SERGEANT PEPPERS LONELY HEARTS CLUB BAND OVER AND OVER AND I WENT TO HEAR THE FUGS PLAY OFTEN*
LUCY IN THE SKY WITH DIAMONDS
GETTIN' HIGH WITH A LITTLE HELP FROM MY FRIENDS
* I WAS SORT OF A GROUPIE TO THIS MANGY GROUP... ANOTHER LONG AND CRAZY STORY!
I WENT TO BE-INS & LOVE-INS. I DON'T REMEMBER THE DIFFERENCE BETWEEN THE TWO.
I LOVE THAT JESUS-LOOK-ALIKE NEXT TO ME!
ALL YOU NEED IS LOVE.
FLOWER POWER
I ACTUALLY DIDN'T FEEL STUPID DOING THIS!
I HAD MANY BOYFRIENDS FOR THE FIRST TIME IN MY LIFE.. I MADE LOVE A LOT AND I HAD ORGASMS!
OH GAWD!
AAAHHHH... OOOHHHHH!
C'MON BABY, C'MON COME, COME... I'M DEEP INSIDE YOU FEEL IT!
I GOT PREGNANT AND I NEVER TOLD MY MOTHER!
I HAVEN'T GOTTEN MY PERIOD FOR FOUR MONTHS!
AND, I HAVE NO IDEAR WHO THE FATHER COULD BE.
I'VE MADE IT WITH HUNDREDS OF GUYS!
BUT I THOUGHT LSD WAS A FORM OF BIRTH CONTROL!
HOW C'N I BE PREGNANT?!
MY FATHER, HOWEVER CAME TO MY APARTMENT ONE DAY, BUT I DIDN'T LET HIM IN...
OPEN THE DOOR, I KNOW YOU'RE IN THERE!
OH MY GAWD.. HOW DID HE FIND ME?
I DON'T WANT HIM TO SEE ME!
PLEASE GO AWAY..

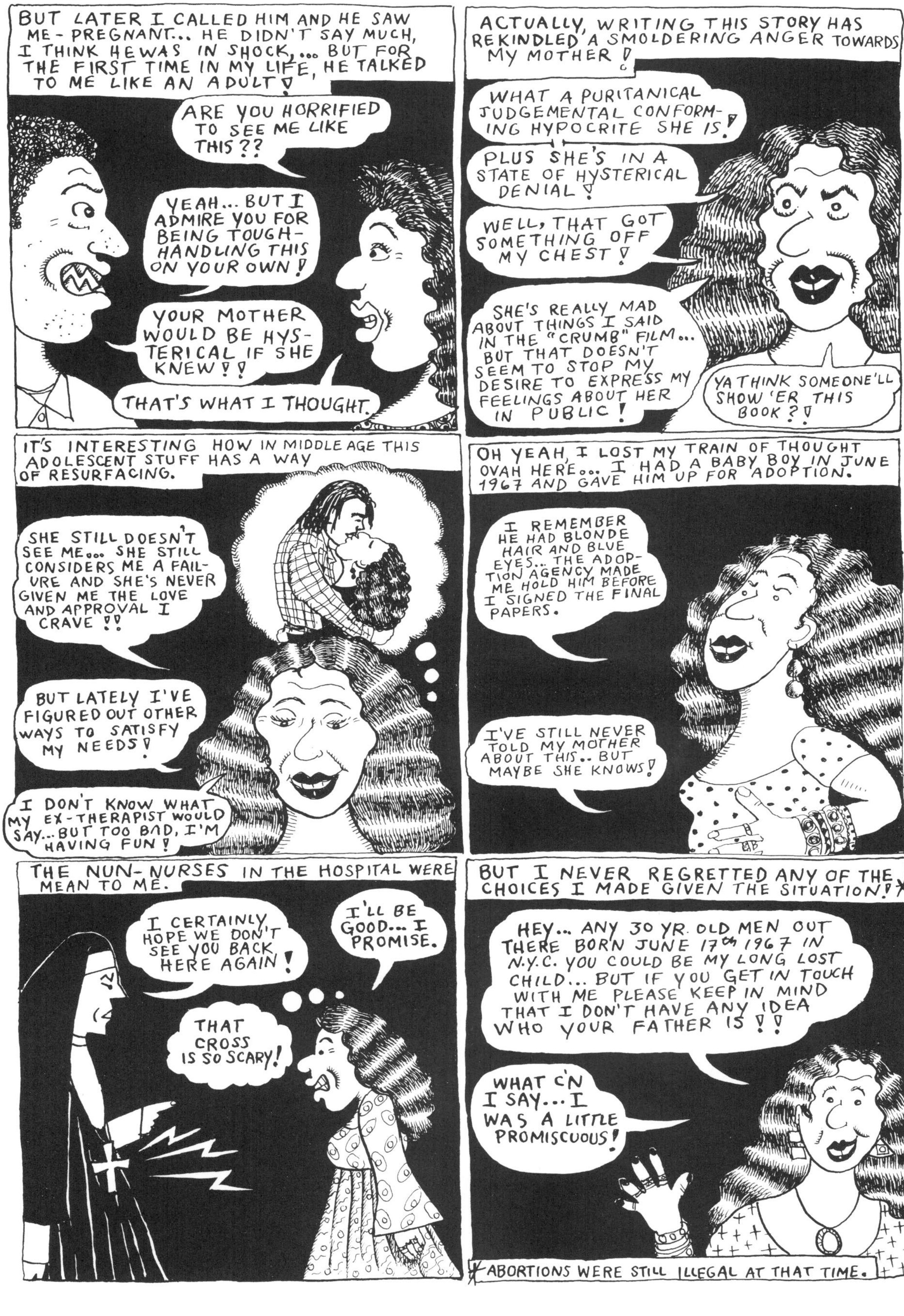
BUT LATER I CALLED HIM AND HE SAW ME - PREGNANT... HE DIDN'T SAY MUCH, I THINK HE WAS IN SHOCK,... BUT FOR THE FIRST TIME IN MY LIFE, HE TALKED TO ME LIKE AN ADULT!
ARE YOU HORRIFIED TO SEE ME LIKE THIS??
YEAH... BUT I ADMIRE YOU FOR BEING TOUGH - HANDLING THIS ON YOUR OWN!
YOUR MOTHER WOULD BE HYSTERICAL IF SHE KNEW!!
THAT'S WHAT I THOUGHT.
ACTUALLY, WRITING THIS STORY HAS REKINDLED A SMOLDERING ANGER TOWARDS MY MOTHER!
WHAT A PURITANICAL JUDGEMENTAL CONFORMING HYPOCRITE SHE IS!
PLUS SHE'S IN A STATE OF HYSTERICAL DENIAL!
WELL, THAT GOT SOMETHING OFF MY CHEST!
SHE'S REALLY MAD ABOUT THINGS I SAID IN THE "CRUMB" FILM... BUT THAT DOESN'T SEEM TO STOP MY DESIRE TO EXPRESS MY FEELINGS ABOUT HER IN PUBLIC!
YA THINK SOMEONE'LL SHOW 'ER THIS BOOK?!
IT'S INTERESTING HOW IN MIDDLE AGE THIS ADOLESCENT STUFF HAS A WAY OF RESURFACING.
SHE STILL DOESN'T SEE ME... SHE STILL CONSIDERS ME A FAILURE AND SHE'S NEVER GIVEN ME THE LOVE AND APPROVAL I CRAVE!!
BUT LATELY I'VE FIGURED OUT OTHER WAYS TO SATISFY MY NEEDS!
I DON'T KNOW WHAT MY EX-THERAPIST WOULD SAY... BUT TOO BAD, I'M HAVING FUN!
OH YEAH, I LOST MY TRAIN OF THOUGHT OVAH HERE... I HAD A BABY BOY IN JUNE 1967 AND GAVE HIM UP FOR ADOPTION.
I REMEMBER HE HAD BLONDE HAIR AND BLUE EYES... THE ADOPTION AGENCY MADE ME HOLD HIM BEFORE I SIGNED THE FINAL PAPERS.
I'VE STILL NEVER TOLD MY MOTHER ABOUT THIS.. BUT MAYBE SHE KNOWS!
THE NUN-NURSES IN THE HOSPITAL WERE MEAN TO ME.
I CERTAINLY HOPE WE DON'T SEE YOU BACK HERE AGAIN!
I'LL BE GOOD... I PROMISE.
THAT CROSS IS SO SCARY!
BUT I NEVER REGRETTED ANY OF THE CHOICES I MADE GIVEN THE SITUATION!*
HEY... ANY 30 YR. OLD MEN OUT THERE BORN JUNE 17th 1967 IN N.Y.C. YOU COULD BE MY LONG LOST CHILD... BUT IF YOU GET IN TOUCH WITH ME PLEASE KEEP IN MIND THAT I DON'T HAVE ANY IDEA WHO YOUR FATHER IS!!
WHAT C'N I SAY... I WAS A LITTLE PROMISCUOUS!
*ABORTIONS WERE STILL ILLEGAL AT THAT TIME.

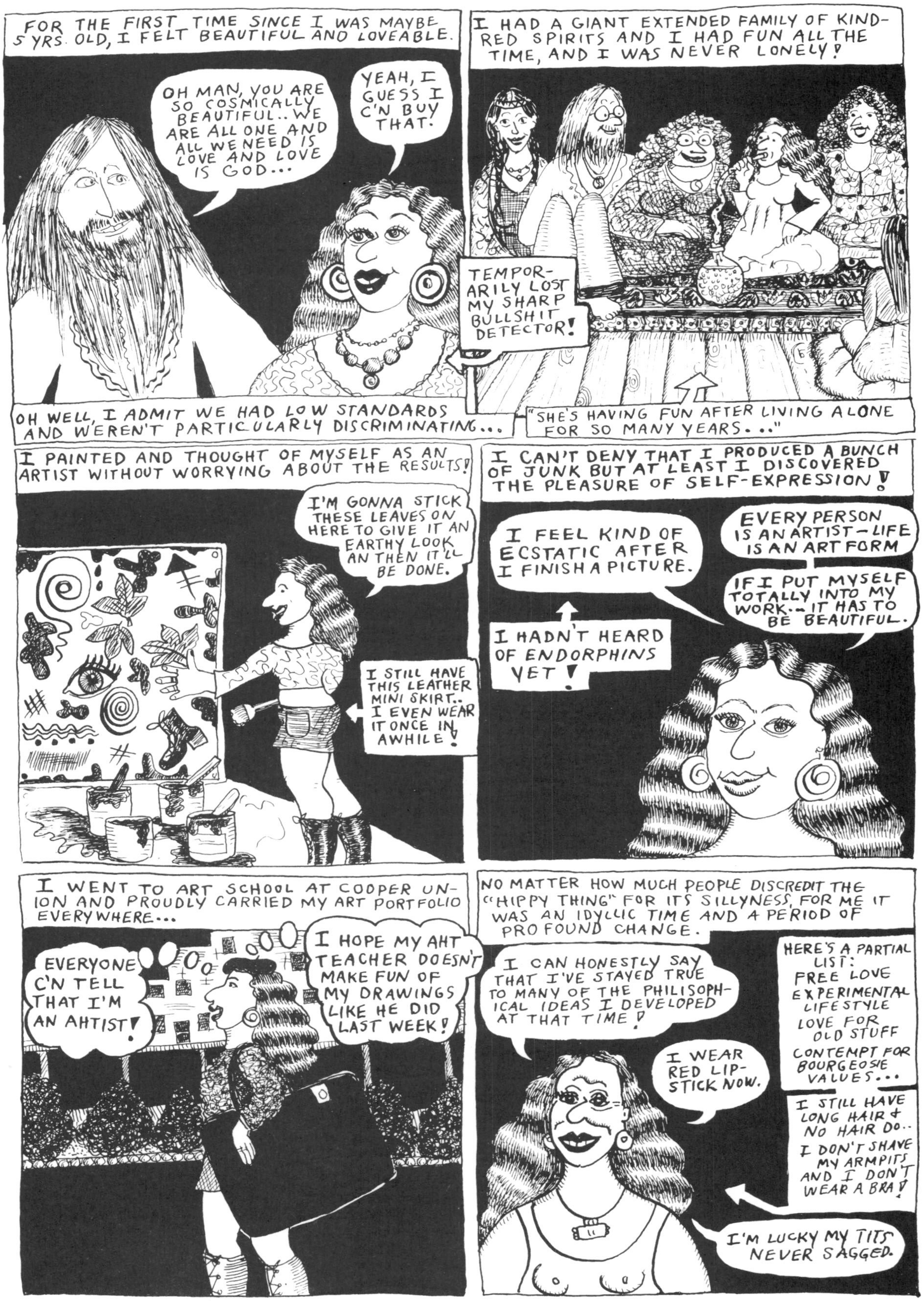

FOR THE FIRST TIME SINCE I WAS MAYBE 5 YRS. OLD, I FELT BEAUTIFUL AND LOVEABLE.
OH MAN, YOU ARE SO COSMICALLY BEAUTIFUL.. WE ARE ALL ONE AND ALL WE NEED IS LOVE AND LOVE IS GOD...
YEAH, I GUESS I C'N BUY THAT.
TEMPOR-ARILY LOST MY SHARP BULLSHIT DETECTOR!
OH WELL, I ADMIT WE HAD LOW STANDARDS AND WEREN'T PARTICULARLY DISCRIMINATING...
I HAD A GIANT EXTENDED FAMILY OF KIND-RED SPIRITS AND I HAD FUN ALL THE TIME, AND I WAS NEVER LONELY!
"SHE'S HAVING FUN AFTER LIVING ALONE FOR SO MANY YEARS..."
I PAINTED AND THOUGHT OF MYSELF AS AN ARTIST WITHOUT WORRYING ABOUT THE RESULTS!
I'M GONNA STICK THESE LEAVES ON HERE TO GIVE IT AN EARTHY LOOK AN THEN IT'LL BE DONE.
I STILL HAVE THIS LEATHER MINI SKIRT.. I EVEN WEAR IT ONCE IN AWHILE!
I CAN'T DENY THAT I PRODUCED A BUNCH OF JUNK BUT AT LEAST I DISCOVERED THE PLEASURE OF SELF-EXPRESSION!
I FEEL KIND OF ECSTATIC AFTER I FINISH A PICTURE.
I HADN'T HEARD OF ENDORPHINS YET!
EVERY PERSON IS AN ARTIST - LIFE IS AN ART FORM
IF I PUT MYSELF TOTALLY INTO MY WORK.- IT HAS TO BE BEAUTIFUL.
I WENT TO ART SCHOOL AT COOPER UN-ION AND PROUDLY CARRIED MY ART PORTFOLIO EVERYWHERE...
EVERYONE C'N TELL THAT I'M AN AHTIST!
I HOPE MY AHT TEACHER DOESN'T MAKE FUN OF MY DRAWINGS LIKE HE DID LAST WEEK!
NO MATTER HOW MUCH PEOPLE DISCREDIT THE "HIPPY THING" FOR ITS SILLYNESS, FOR ME IT WAS AN IDYLLIC TIME AND A PERIOD OF PROFOUND CHANGE.
I CAN HONESTLY SAY THAT I'VE STAYED TRUE TO MANY OF THE PHILISOPH-ICAL IDEAS I DEVELOPED AT THAT TIME!
HERE'S A PARTIAL LIST: FREE LOVE EXPERIMENTAL LIFESTYLE LOVE FOR OLD STUFF CONTEMPT FOR BOURGEOSIE VALUES...
I WEAR RED LIP-STICK NOW.
I STILL HAVE LONG HAIR & NO HAIR DO.. I DON'T SHAVE MY ARMPITS AND I DON'T WEAR A BRA!
I'M LUCKY MY TITS NEVER SAGGED.

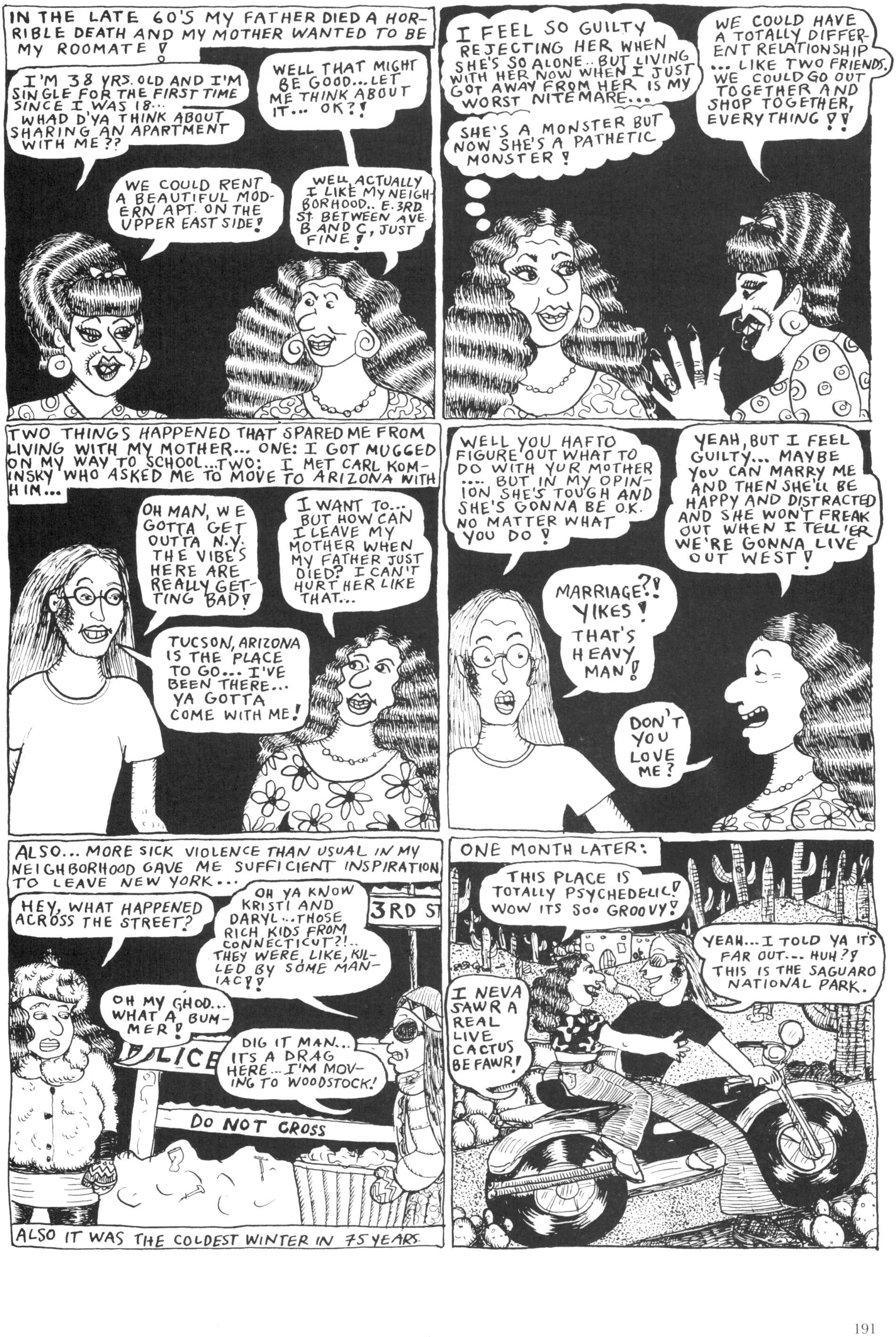

IN THE LATE 60'S MY FATHER DIED A HORRIBLE DEATH AND MY MOTHER WANTED TO BE MY ROOMATE!
I'M 38 YRS. OLD AND I'M SINGLE FOR THE FIRST TIME SINCE I WAS 18... WHAD D'YA THINK ABOUT SHARING AN APARTMENT WITH ME??
WELL THAT MIGHT BE GOOD... LET ME THINK ABOUT IT... OK?!
WE COULD RENT A BEAUTIFUL MODERN APT. ON THE UPPER EAST SIDE!
WELL ACTUALLY I LIKE MY NEIGHBORHOOD.. E. 3RD ST. BETWEEN AVE. B AND C, JUST FINE!
I FEEL SO GUILTY REJECTING HER WHEN SHE'S SO ALONE.. BUT LIVING WITH HER NOW WHEN I JUST GOT AWAY FROM HER IS MY WORST NITEMARE...
SHE'S A MONSTER BUT NOW SHE'S A PATHETIC MONSTER!
WE COULD HAVE A TOTALLY DIFFERENT RELATIONSHIP ... LIKE TWO FRIENDS. WE COULD GO OUT TOGETHER AND SHOP TOGETHER, EVERYTHING!!
TWO THINGS HAPPENED THAT SPARED ME FROM LIVING WITH MY MOTHER... ONE: I GOT MUGGED ON MY WAY TO SCHOOL...TWO: I MET CARL KOMINSKY WHO ASKED ME TO MOVE TO ARIZONA WITH HIM...
OH MAN, WE GOTTA GET OUTTA N.Y. THE VIBE'S HERE ARE REALLY GETTING BAD!
I WANT TO... BUT HOW CAN I LEAVE MY MOTHER WHEN MY FATHER JUST DIED? I CAN'T HURT HER LIKE THAT...
TUCSON, ARIZONA IS THE PLACE TO GO... I'VE BEEN THERE... YA GOTTA COME WITH ME!
WELL YOU HAFTO FIGURE OUT WHAT TO DO WITH YUR MOTHER .... BUT IN MY OPINION SHE'S TOUGH AND SHE'S GONNA BE O.K. NO MATTER WHAT YOU DO!
YEAH, BUT I FEEL GUILTY... MAYBE YOU CAN MARRY ME AND THEN SHE'LL BE HAPPY AND DISTRACTED AND SHE WON'T FREAK OUT WHEN I TELL 'ER WE'RE GONNA LIVE OUT WEST!
MARRIAGE?! YIKES! THAT'S HEAVY, MAN!
DON'T YOU LOVE ME?
ALSO... MORE SICK VIOLENCE THAN USUAL IN MY NEIGHBORHOOD GAVE ME SUFFICIENT INSPIRATION TO LEAVE NEW YORK...
HEY, WHAT HAPPENED ACROSS THE STREET?
3RD ST
OH YA KNOW KRISTI AND DARYL...THOSE RICH KIDS FROM CONNECTICUT?!.. THEY WERE, LIKE, KILLED BY SOME MANIAC!!
OH MY GHOD... WHAT A BUMMER!
DIG IT MAN... ITS A DRAG HERE... I'M MOVING TO WOODSTOCK!
DO NOT CROSS
ALSO IT WAS THE COLDEST WINTER IN 75 YEARS.
ONE MONTH LATER:
THIS PLACE IS TOTALLY PSYCHEDELIC! WOW ITS SOO GROOVY!
YEAH... I TOLD YA IT'S FAR OUT... HUH?! THIS IS THE SAGUARO NATIONAL PARK.
I NEVA SAWR A REAL LIVE CACTUS BEFAWR!

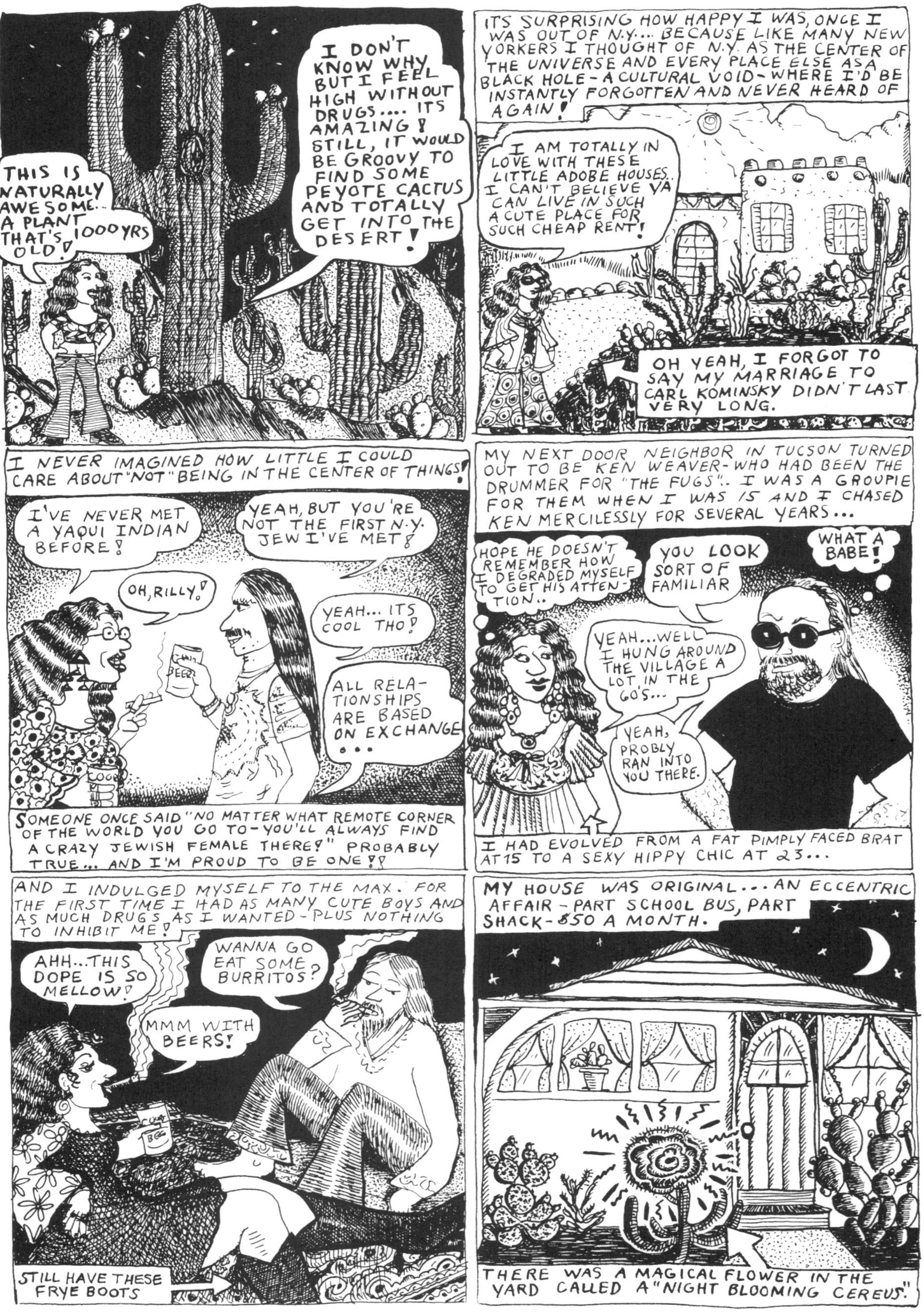
THIS IS NATURALLY AWESOME.. A PLANT THAT'S 1000 YRS OLD!
I DON'T KNOW WHY BUT I FEEL HIGH WITHOUT DRUGS.... ITS AMAZING! STILL, IT WOULD BE GROOVY TO FIND SOME PEYOTE CACTUS AND TOTALLY GET INTO THE DESERT!
ITS SURPRISING HOW HAPPY I WAS, ONCE I WAS OUT OF N.Y... BECAUSE LIKE MANY NEW YORKERS I THOUGHT OF N.Y. AS THE CENTER OF THE UNIVERSE AND EVERY PLACE ELSE AS A BLACK HOLE - A CULTURAL VOID - WHERE I'D BE INSTANTLY FORGOTTEN AND NEVER HEARD OF AGAIN!
I AM TOTALLY IN LOVE WITH THESE LITTLE ADOBE HOUSES.. I CAN'T BELIEVE YA CAN LIVE IN SUCH A CUTE PLACE FOR SUCH CHEAP RENT!
OH YEAH, I FORGOT TO SAY MY MARRIAGE TO CARL KOMINSKY DIDN'T LAST VERY LONG.
I NEVER IMAGINED HOW LITTLE I COULD CARE ABOUT "NOT" BEING IN THE CENTER OF THINGS!
I'VE NEVER MET A YAQUI INDIAN BEFORE!
YEAH, BUT YOU'RE NOT THE FIRST N.Y. JEW I'VE MET!
OH, RILLY!
YEAH... ITS COOL THO!
ALL RELATIONSHIPS ARE BASED ON EXCHANGE...
BEER
SOMEONE ONCE SAID "NO MATTER WHAT REMOTE CORNER OF THE WORLD YOU GO TO - YOU'LL ALWAYS FIND A CRAZY JEWISH FEMALE THERE!" PROBABLY TRUE... AND I'M PROUD TO BE ONE!!
MY NEXT DOOR NEIGHBOR IN TUCSON TURNED OUT TO BE KEN WEAVER - WHO HAD BEEN THE DRUMMER FOR "THE FUGS". I WAS A GROUPIE FOR THEM WHEN I WAS 15 AND I CHASED KEN MERCILESSLY FOR SEVERAL YEARS...
HOPE HE DOESN'T REMEMBER HOW I DEGRADED MYSELF TO GET HIS ATTENTION..
YOU LOOK SORT OF FAMILIAR
WHAT A BABE!
YEAH...WELL I HUNG AROUND THE VILLAGE A LOT IN THE 60'S...
YEAH, PROBLY RAN INTO YOU THERE.
I HAD EVOLVED FROM A FAT PIMPLY FACED BRAT AT 15 TO A SEXY HIPPY CHIC AT 23...
AND I INDULGED MYSELF TO THE MAX. FOR THE FIRST TIME I HAD AS MANY CUTE BOYS AND AS MUCH DRUGS AS I WANTED - PLUS NOTHING TO INHIBIT ME!
AHH...THIS DOPE IS SO MELLOW!
WANNA GO EAT SOME BURRITOS?
MMM WITH BEERS!
BEER
STILL HAVE THESE FRYE BOOTS
MY HOUSE WAS ORIGINAL... AN ECCENTRIC AFFAIR - PART SCHOOL BUS, PART SHACK - $50 A MONTH.
THERE WAS A MAGICAL FLOWER IN THE YARD CALLED A "NIGHT BLOOMING CEREUS".

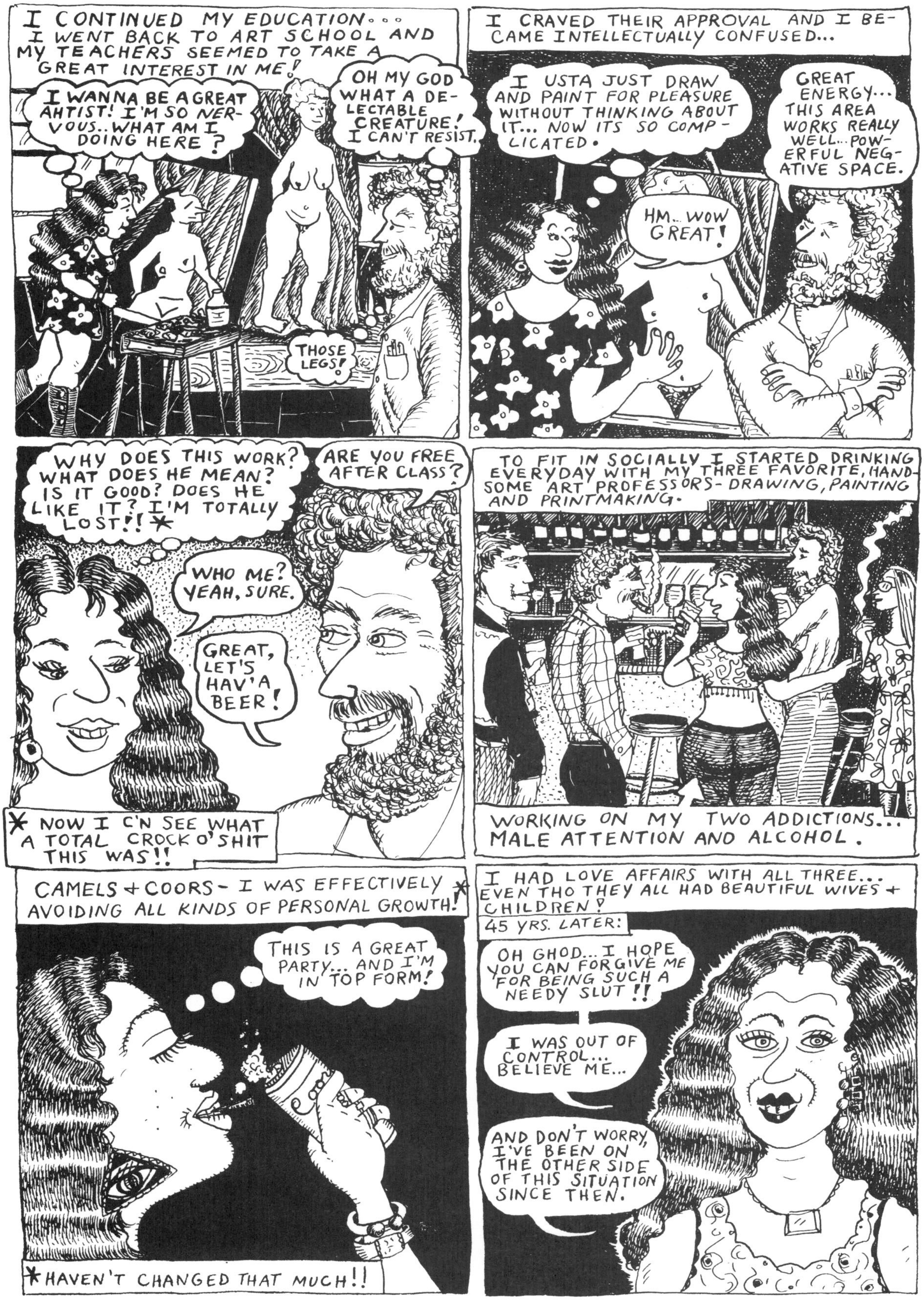
I CONTINUED MY EDUCATION...
I WENT BACK TO ART SCHOOL AND MY TEACHERS SEEMED TO TAKE A GREAT INTEREST IN ME!
I WANNA BE A GREAT AHTIST! I'M SO NERVOUS.. WHAT AM I DOING HERE?
OH MY GOD WHAT A DELECTABLE CREATURE! I CAN'T RESIST.
THOSE LEGS!
I CRAVED THEIR APPROVAL AND I BECAME INTELLECTUALLY CONFUSED...
I USTA JUST DRAW AND PAINT FOR PLEASURE WITHOUT THINKING ABOUT IT... NOW ITS SO COMPLICATED.
GREAT ENERGY... THIS AREA WORKS REALLY WELL... POWERFUL NEGATIVE SPACE.
HM... WOW GREAT!
WHY DOES THIS WORK? WHAT DOES HE MEAN? IS IT GOOD? DOES HE LIKE IT? I'M TOTALLY LOST!! *
ARE YOU FREE AFTER CLASS?
WHO ME? YEAH, SURE.
GREAT, LET'S HAV'A BEER!
* NOW I C'N SEE WHAT A TOTAL CROCK O'SHIT THIS WAS!!
TO FIT IN SOCIALLY I STARTED DRINKING EVERYDAY WITH MY THREE FAVORITE, HANDSOME ART PROFESSORS - DRAWING, PAINTING AND PRINTMAKING.
WORKING ON MY TWO ADDICTIONS... MALE ATTENTION AND ALCOHOL.
CAMELS + COORS - I WAS EFFECTIVELY AVOIDING ALL KINDS OF PERSONAL GROWTH! *
THIS IS A GREAT PARTY... AND I'M IN TOP FORM!
* HAVEN'T CHANGED THAT MUCH!!
I HAD LOVE AFFAIRS WITH ALL THREE... EVEN THO THEY ALL HAD BEAUTIFUL WIVES + CHILDREN!
45 YRS. LATER:
OH GHOD... I HOPE YOU CAN FORGIVE ME FOR BEING SUCH A NEEDY SLUT!!
I WAS OUT OF CONTROL... BELIEVE ME...
AND DON'T WORRY, I'VE BEEN ON THE OTHER SIDE OF THIS SITUATION SINCE THEN.

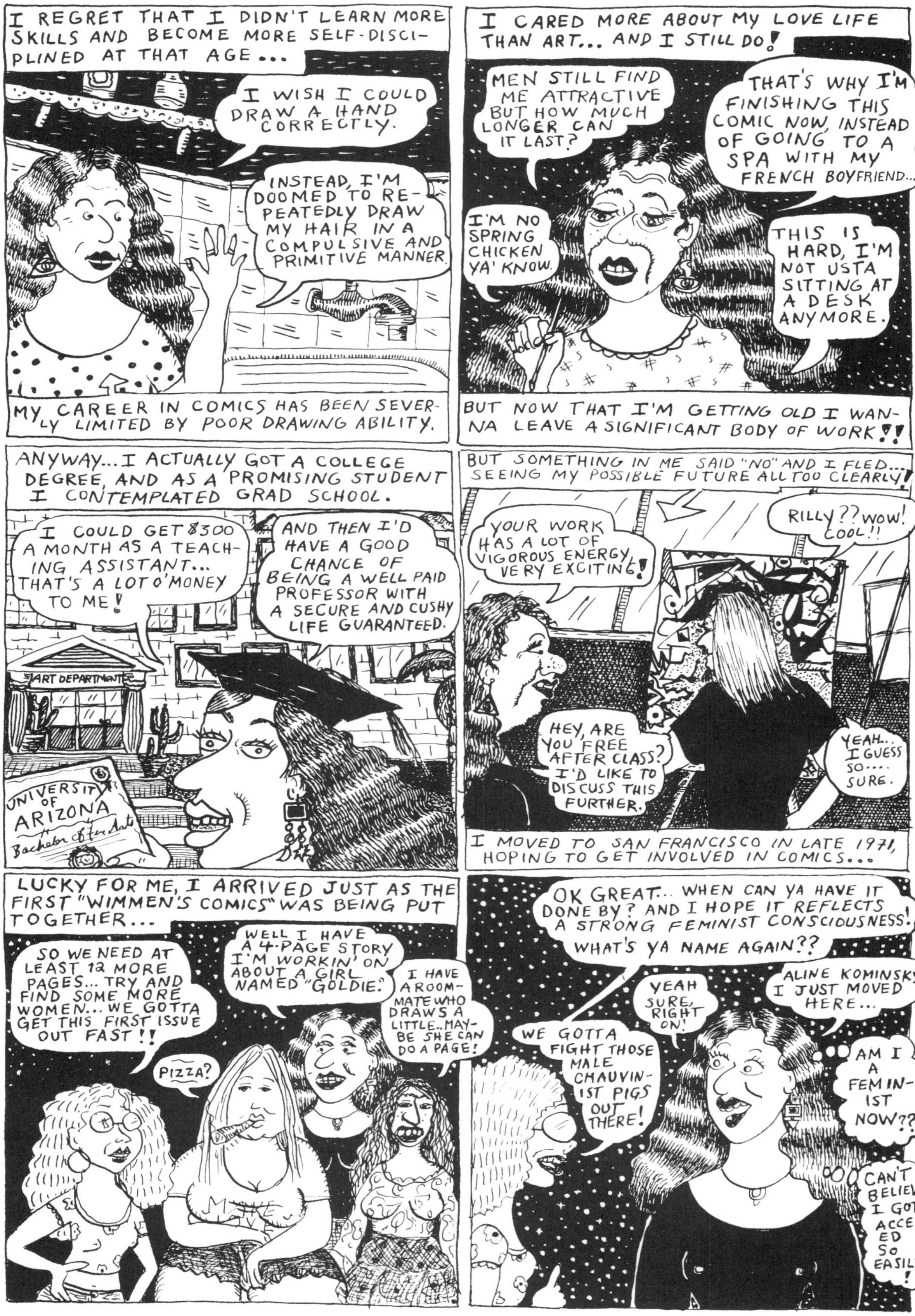

I REGRET THAT I DIDN'T LEARN MORE SKILLS AND BECOME MORE SELF-DISCIPLINED AT THAT AGE...
I WISH I COULD DRAW A HAND CORRECTLY.
INSTEAD, I'M DOOMED TO REPEATEDLY DRAW MY HAIR IN A COMPULSIVE AND PRIMITIVE MANNER.
MY CAREER IN COMICS HAS BEEN SEVERLY LIMITED BY POOR DRAWING ABILITY.
I CARED MORE ABOUT MY LOVE LIFE THAN ART... AND I STILL DO!
MEN STILL FIND ME ATTRACTIVE BUT HOW MUCH LONGER CAN IT LAST?
THAT'S WHY I'M FINISHING THIS COMIC NOW, INSTEAD OF GOING TO A SPA WITH MY FRENCH BOYFRIEND...
I'M NO SPRING CHICKEN YA' KNOW.
THIS IS HARD, I'M NOT USTA SITTING AT A DESK ANYMORE.
BUT NOW THAT I'M GETTING OLD I WANNA LEAVE A SIGNIFICANT BODY OF WORK!!
ANYWAY... I ACTUALLY GOT A COLLEGE DEGREE, AND AS A PROMISING STUDENT I CONTEMPLATED GRAD SCHOOL.
I COULD GET $300 A MONTH AS A TEACHING ASSISTANT... THAT'S A LOT O'MONEY TO ME!
AND THEN I'D HAVE A GOOD CHANCE OF BEING A WELL PAID PROFESSOR WITH A SECURE AND CUSHY LIFE GUARANTEED.
ART DEPARTMENT
UNIVERSITY OF ARIZONA
Bachelor of Fine Arts
BUT SOMETHING IN ME SAID "NO" AND I FLED... SEEING MY POSSIBLE FUTURE ALL TOO CLEARLY!
YOUR WORK HAS A LOT OF VIGOROUS ENERGY, VERY EXCITING!
RILLY?? WOW! COOL!!
HEY, ARE YOU FREE AFTER CLASS? I'D LIKE TO DISCUSS THIS FURTHER.
YEAH.. I GUESS SO.... SURE.
I MOVED TO SAN FRANCISCO IN LATE 1971, HOPING TO GET INVOLVED IN COMICS...
LUCKY FOR ME, I ARRIVED JUST AS THE FIRST "WIMMEN'S COMICS" WAS BEING PUT TOGETHER...
SO WE NEED AT LEAST 12 MORE PAGES... TRY AND FIND SOME MORE WOMEN... WE GOTTA GET THIS FIRST ISSUE OUT FAST!!
WELL I HAVE A 4-PAGE STORY I'M WORKIN' ON ABOUT A GIRL NAMED "GOLDIE."
I HAVE A ROOMMATE WHO DRAWS A LITTLE.. MAYBE SHE CAN DO A PAGE!
PIZZA?
OK GREAT.. WHEN CAN YA HAVE IT DONE BY? AND I HOPE IT REFLECTS A STRONG FEMINIST CONSCIOUSNESS! WHAT'S YA NAME AGAIN??
ALINE KOMINSKY. I JUST MOVED HERE...
YEAH SURE, RIGHT ON!
WE GOTTA FIGHT THOSE MALE CHAUVINIST PIGS OUT THERE!
AM I A FEMINIST NOW??
CAN'T BELIEVE I GOT ACCEPTED SO EASILY!

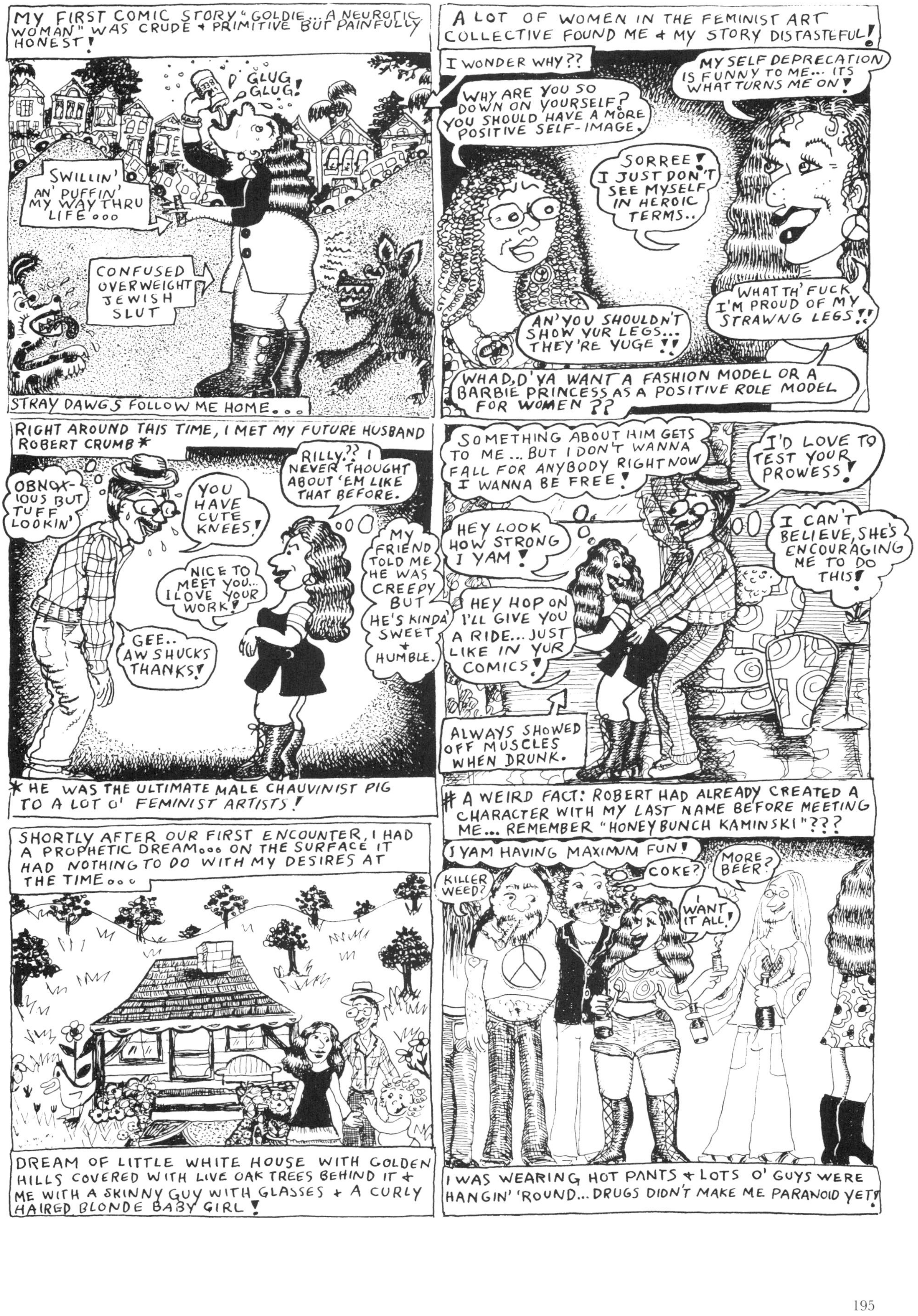

MY FIRST COMIC STORY "GOLDIE... A NEUROTIC WOMAN" WAS CRUDE + PRIMITIVE BUT PAINFULLY HONEST!
GLUG GLUG!
SWILLIN' AN' PUFFIN' MY WAY THRU LIFE...
CONFUSED OVERWEIGHT JEWISH SLUT
STRAY DAWGS FOLLOW ME HOME...
A LOT OF WOMEN IN THE FEMINIST ART COLLECTIVE FOUND ME + MY STORY DISTASTEFUL!
I WONDER WHY??
WHY ARE YOU SO DOWN ON YOURSELF? YOU SHOULD HAVE A MORE POSITIVE SELF-IMAGE.
MY SELF DEPRECATION IS FUNNY TO ME... ITS WHAT TURNS ME ON!
SORREE! I JUST DON'T SEE MYSELF IN HEROIC TERMS..
AN' YOU SHOULDN'T SHOW YUR LEGS... THEY'RE YUGE!!
WHAT TH' FUCK I'M PROUD OF MY STRAWNG LEGS!!
WHAD,D'YA WANT A FASHION MODEL OR A BARBIE PRINCESS AS A POSITIVE ROLE MODEL FOR WOMEN??
RIGHT AROUND THIS TIME, I MET MY FUTURE HUSBAND ROBERT CRUMB*
OBNOXIOUS BUT TUFF LOOKIN'
YOU HAVE CUTE KNEES!
RILLY?? I NEVER THOUGHT ABOUT 'EM LIKE THAT BEFORE.
NICE TO MEET YOU... I LOVE YOUR WORK!
MY FRIEND TOLD ME HE WAS CREEPY BUT HE'S KINDA' SWEET + HUMBLE.
GEE.. AW SHUCKS THANKS!
* HE WAS THE ULTIMATE MALE CHAUVINIST PIG TO A LOT O' FEMINIST ARTISTS!
SOMETHING ABOUT HIM GETS TO ME... BUT I DON'T WANNA FALL FOR ANYBODY RIGHT NOW I WANNA BE FREE!
I'D LOVE TO TEST YOUR PROWESS!
HEY LOOK HOW STRONG I YAM!
I CAN'T BELIEVE, SHE'S ENCOURAGING ME TO DO THIS!
HEY HOP ON I'LL GIVE YOU A RIDE... JUST LIKE IN YUR COMICS!
ALWAYS SHOWED OFF MUSCLES WHEN DRUNK.
A WEIRD FACT: ROBERT HAD ALREADY CREATED A CHARACTER WITH MY LAST NAME BEFORE MEETING ME... REMEMBER "HONEYBUNCH KAMINSKI"???
SHORTLY AFTER OUR FIRST ENCOUNTER, I HAD A PROPHETIC DREAM... ON THE SURFACE IT HAD NOTHING TO DO WITH MY DESIRES AT THE TIME...
DREAM OF LITTLE WHITE HOUSE WITH GOLDEN HILLS COVERED WITH LIVE OAK TREES BEHIND IT + ME WITH A SKINNY GUY WITH GLASSES + A CURLY HAIRED BLONDE BABY GIRL!
I YAM HAVING MAXIMUM FUN!
KILLER WEED?
COKE?
MORE BEER?
I WANT IT ALL!
I WAS WEARING HOT PANTS + LOTS O' GUYS WERE HANGIN' 'ROUND... DRUGS DIDN'T MAKE ME PARANOID YET!

CONFUSED BY LUST, AND WANTING TO AVOID MESSY COMPLICATIONS... I SET OUT ON A ROAD TRIP WITH MY PAL, ANGEL TREAD...

SHE DROVE, I NAVIGATED + KEPT THE DOPE PIPE FULL!

OH BOY, CAN'T WAIT TO SEE SOME CUTE COWBOYS BACK IN THE SADDLE AGIN!

ARIZON

CAN'T DRAW CARS...THIS WAS AN OL' RED MERCEDES

WE WERE BOTH ESCAPING FOR DIFFERENT REASONS... ANGEL WAS SOON TO MEET HER FUTURE HUSBAND ON A CRUISE WITH HER MOTHER ...I WAS SHOCKED WHEN ROBERT SHOWED UP IN BOULDER, COLORADO WHERE I WAS STAYING WITH FRIENDS AND PLANNING A BIZNIZ VENTURE. (I STILL CAN'T FIGURE OUT HOW HE MANAGED TO BUY PLANE TICKET BY HIM-SELF!)

I'LL LEAVE RIGHT AWAY IF YA' DON'T WANNA SEE ME.

NO... ITS JUST THAT I'M RILLY SURPRISED TA SEE YOU HERE!

YEW LOOK SO TUFF + HEALTHY!

YEA, I'VE HAD A LOT O'ADVEN-TURES... A WILD DAWG STOLE MY SHOE IN NEW MEXICO, SO I HADDA GET CUTE NEW BOOTS!

AFTER A ROMANTIC REUNION AT THE BOULDERADO HOTEL, WE TRADED SOME ARTWORK FOR A 1937 CHEVY + I DROVE US BACK TO CALIFORNIA.

NOBODY PLAYS WITH ME LIKE YOU DO...

OH, I MISSED MY CUTE LITTLE HORSIE...

WE DECIDED TO SORT OF TRY LIVING TOGETHER, SO I BORROWED $1000 FROM MY MOTHER, BOUGHT A 1950'S TRAILER + MOVED IT NEXT TO ROBERT'S CABIN IN MENDOCINO COUNTY, CA.

PROUD FIRST TIME HOME OWNER..

WE DISCOVERED THAT OUR COLLECTIONS WERE COMPLEMENTARY + WE BOTH CRAVED ORDER... I HAD DOLLS, HE HAD CARS + SOLDIERS.

WEL HOME

ROBERT WAS IMPRESSED THAT MY LITTLE HOME WAS NEAT + COZY... THIS WAS PROB-ABLY MY STRONGEST SELLING POINT...

ROBERT'S GIRLFRIEND KATHY + HIS EX-WIFE DANA WERE SUCH SLOBS, THAT THEY MADE ME LOOK GOOD!

ROBBIT.. I CAN'T FIND MY FAVORITE JEANS... THAT'S WHY IT'S TAKING ME SO LONG...

PIZZA

$$$ RING RING $$$

KATHY WAS CUTE + SEXY...BUT...

PICKLE

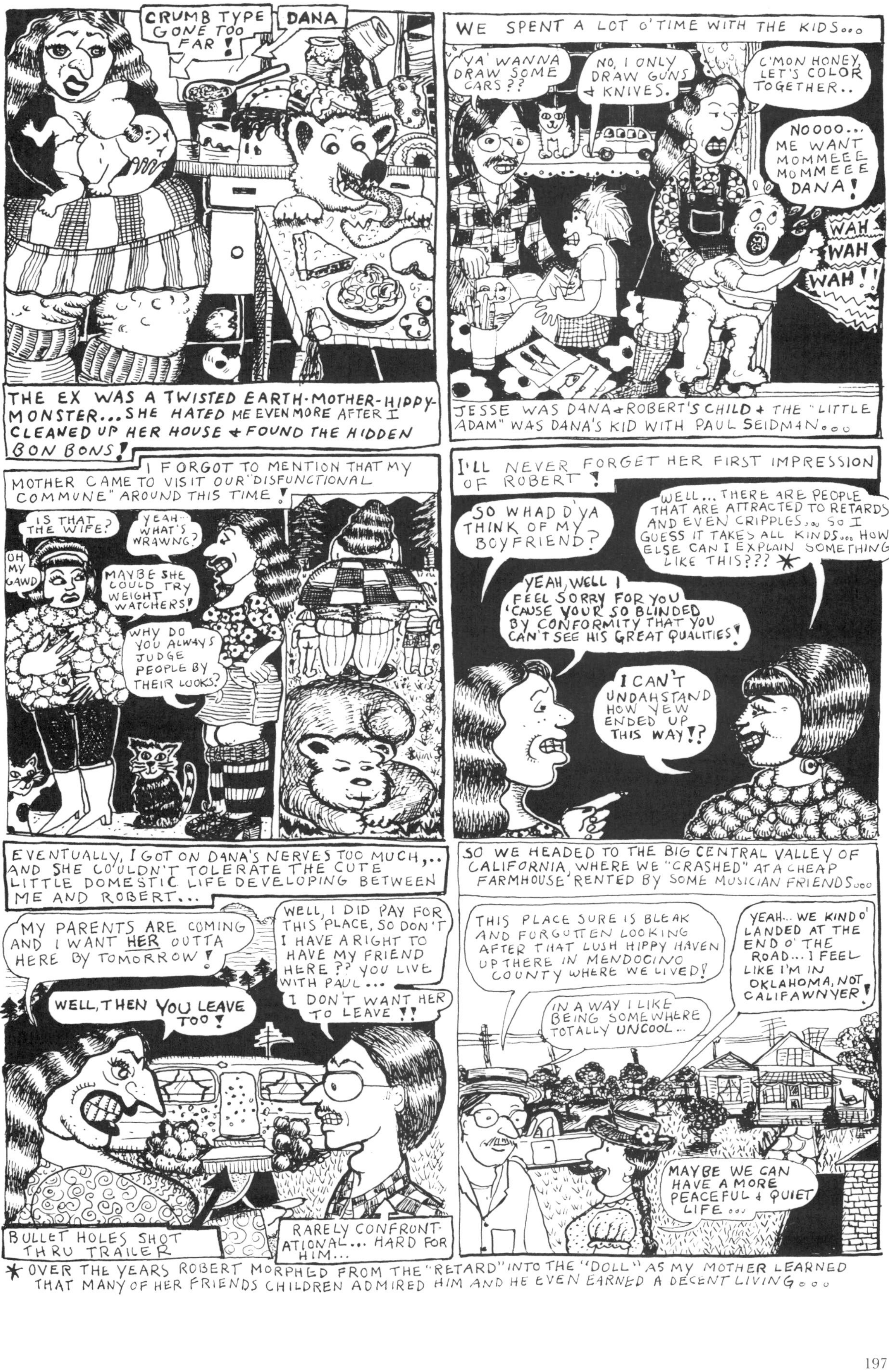
CRUMB TYPE GONE TOO FAR!
DANA
THE EX WAS A TWISTED EARTH-MOTHER-HIPPY-MONSTER... SHE HATED ME EVEN MORE AFTER I CLEANED UP HER HOUSE & FOUND THE HIDDEN BON BONS!
WE SPENT A LOT O'TIME WITH THE KIDS...
YA' WANNA DRAW SOME CARS??
NO, I ONLY DRAW GUNS & KNIVES.
C'MON HONEY, LET'S COLOR TOGETHER..
NOOOO... ME WANT MOMMEEE MOMMEEE DANA!
WAH WAH WAH!!
JESSE WAS DANA & ROBERT'S CHILD & THE "LITTLE ADAM" WAS DANA'S KID WITH PAUL SEIDMAN...
I FORGOT TO MENTION THAT MY MOTHER CAME TO VISIT OUR "DISFUNCTIONAL COMMUNE" AROUND THIS TIME!
IS THAT THE WIFE?
YEAH... WHAT'S WRAWNG?
OH MY GAWD
MAYBE SHE COULD TRY WEIGHT WATCHERS!
WHY DO YOU ALWAYS JUDGE PEOPLE BY THEIR LOOKS?
I'LL NEVER FORGET HER FIRST IMPRESSION OF ROBERT!
SO WHAD D'YA THINK OF MY BOYFRIEND?
WELL... THERE ARE PEOPLE THAT ARE ATTRACTED TO RETARDS AND EVEN CRIPPLES... SO I GUESS IT TAKES ALL KINDS... HOW ELSE CAN I EXPLAIN SOMETHING LIKE THIS??? *
YEAH, WELL I FEEL SORRY FOR YOU 'CAUSE YOUR SO BLINDED BY CONFORMITY THAT YOU CAN'T SEE HIS GREAT QUALITIES!
I CAN'T UNDAHSTAND HOW YEW ENDED UP THIS WAY!?
EVENTUALLY, I GOT ON DANA'S NERVES TOO MUCH,.. AND SHE COULDN'T TOLERATE THE CUTE LITTLE DOMESTIC LIFE DEVELOPING BETWEEN ME AND ROBERT...
MY PARENTS ARE COMING AND I WANT HER OUTTA HERE BY TOMORROW!
WELL, I DID PAY FOR THIS PLACE, SO DON'T I HAVE A RIGHT TO HAVE MY FRIEND HERE?? YOU LIVE WITH PAUL...
WELL, THEN YOU LEAVE TOO!
I DON'T WANT HER TO LEAVE!!
BULLET HOLES SHOT THRU TRAILER
RARELY CONFRONTATIONAL... HARD FOR HIM...
SO WE HEADED TO THE BIG CENTRAL VALLEY OF CALIFORNIA, WHERE WE "CRASHED" AT A CHEAP FARMHOUSE RENTED BY SOME MUSICIAN FRIENDS...
THIS PLACE SURE IS BLEAK AND FORGOTTEN LOOKING AFTER THAT LUSH HIPPY HAVEN UP THERE IN MENDOCINO COUNTY WHERE WE LIVED!
YEAH... WE KIND O' LANDED AT THE END O' THE ROAD... I FEEL LIKE I'M IN OKLAHOMA, NOT CALIFAWNYER!
IN A WAY I LIKE BEING SOMEWHERE TOTALLY UNCOOL...
MAYBE WE CAN HAVE A MORE PEACEFUL & QUIET LIFE...

* OVER THE YEARS ROBERT MORPHED FROM THE "RETARD" INTO THE "DOLL" AS MY MOTHER LEARNED THAT MANY OF HER FRIENDS CHILDREN ADMIRED HIM AND HE EVEN EARNED A DECENT LIVING...

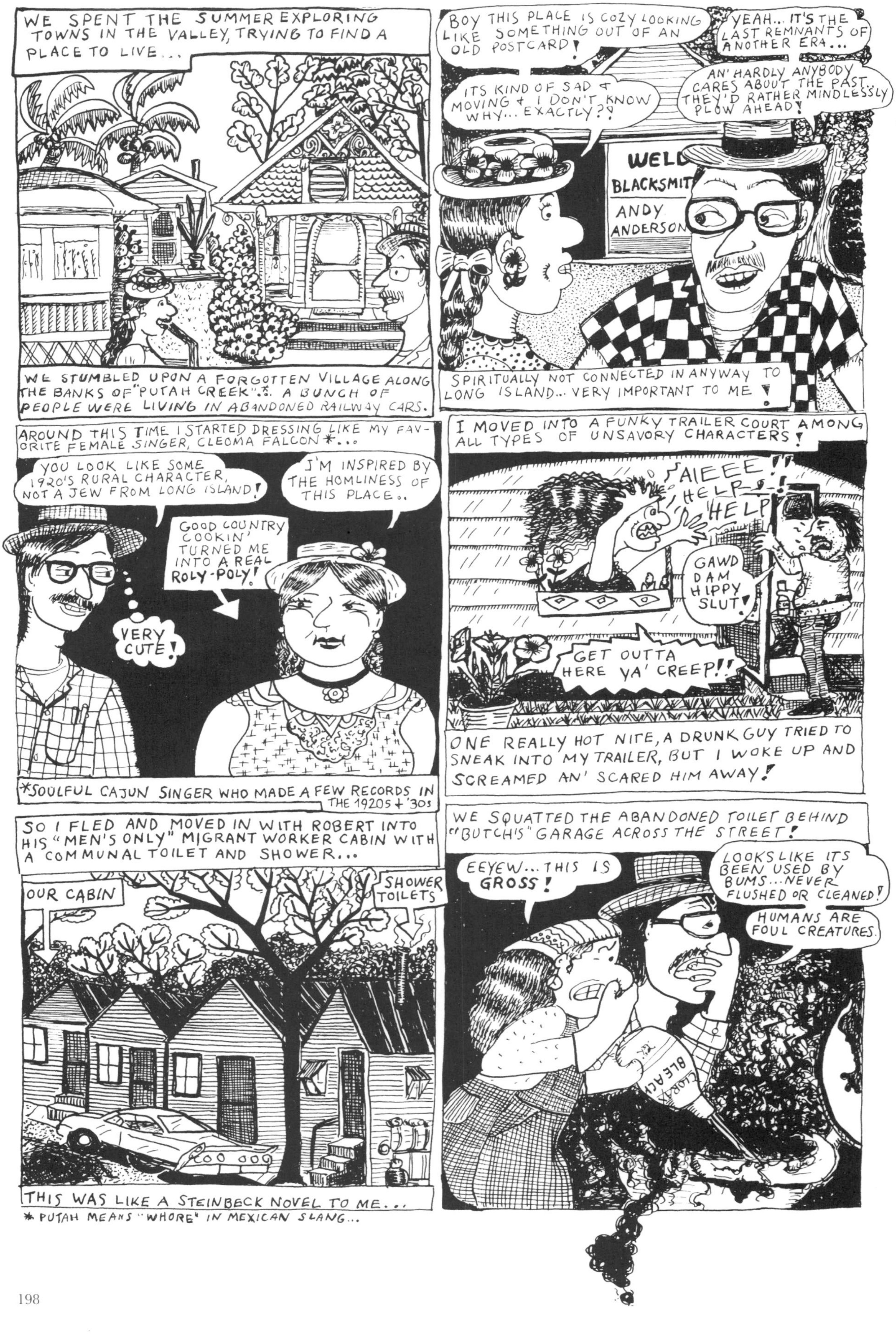

WE SPENT THE SUMMER EXPLORING TOWNS IN THE VALLEY, TRYING TO FIND A PLACE TO LIVE...
WE STUMBLED UPON A FORGOTTEN VILLAGE ALONG THE BANKS OF "PUTAH CREEK"*. A BUNCH OF PEOPLE WERE LIVING IN ABANDONED RAILWAY CARS.
BOY THIS PLACE IS COZY LOOKING LIKE SOMETHING OUT OF AN OLD POSTCARD!
YEAH... IT'S THE LAST REMNANTS OF ANOTHER ERA...
ITS KIND OF SAD & MOVING & I DON'T KNOW WHY... EXACTLY??
AN' HARDLY ANYBODY CARES ABOUT THE PAST... THEY'D RATHER MINDLESSLY PLOW AHEAD!
WELD
BLACKSMIT
ANDY ANDERSON
SPIRITUALLY NOT CONNECTED IN ANYWAY TO LONG ISLAND... VERY IMPORTANT TO ME!
AROUND THIS TIME I STARTED DRESSING LIKE MY FAVORITE FEMALE SINGER, CLEOMA FALCON*...
YOU LOOK LIKE SOME 1920'S RURAL CHARACTER, NOT A JEW FROM LONG ISLAND!
I'M INSPIRED BY THE HOMLINESS OF THIS PLACE..
GOOD COUNTRY COOKIN' TURNED ME INTO A REAL ROLY-POLY!
VERY CUTE!
*SOULFUL CAJUN SINGER WHO MADE A FEW RECORDS IN THE 1920S + '30S
I MOVED INTO A FUNKY TRAILER COURT AMONG ALL TYPES OF UNSAVORY CHARACTERS!
AIEEE!! HELP! HELP
GAWD DAM HIPPY SLUT!
GET OUTTA HERE YA' CREEP!!
ONE REALLY HOT NITE, A DRUNK GUY TRIED TO SNEAK INTO MY TRAILER, BUT I WOKE UP AND SCREAMED AN' SCARED HIM AWAY!
SO I FLED AND MOVED IN WITH ROBERT INTO HIS "MEN'S ONLY" MIGRANT WORKER CABIN WITH A COMMUNAL TOILET AND SHOWER...
OUR CABIN
SHOWER TOILETS
THIS WAS LIKE A STEINBECK NOVEL TO ME...
* PUTAH MEANS "WHORE" IN MEXICAN SLANG...
WE SQUATTED THE ABANDONED TOILET BEHIND "BUTCH'S" GARAGE ACROSS THE STREET!
EEYEW... THIS IS GROSS!
LOOKS LIKE ITS BEEN USED BY BUMS... NEVER FLUSHED OR CLEANED!
HUMANS ARE FOUL CREATURES.

WE IMPROVISED A BATHTUB WITH THE HELP OF ANDY ANDERSON, THE BLACKSMITH...

GOOD THING YUR SO SKINNY...OR ELSE WE WOULN'T FIT IN HERE...

I FEEL LIKE I'M TAKIN'A BATH WITH A SMALL BEAR

WHEN WE WERE DONE WE DUMPED THE WATER OUT THE FRONT DOOR...

AND ALTHOUGH ROBERT WAS PROFOUNDLY SAD ABOUT LEAVING HIS SON, JESSE, WE PASSED A QUIET, ROMANTIC FEW MONTHS EXPLORING OUR NEW TOWN AND MAKING DAILY MEALS TOGETHER...

WINTERS OPERA HO

CALIFOR MARKE

CHER

ENWOODS TMENT ORE

I LOOK BACK AT THOSE FEW MONTHS WITH FONDNESS + NOSTALGIA WHEN I THINK ABOUT THE DEEP BOND THAT DEVELOPED BETWEEN ROBERT + ME...

KISSY-KISSY
SLURP-SLURP!!

WE SPENT HOURS TAWKING AND WE NEVER SEEMED TO BORE EACH OTHER..MIRACULOUS!

WE EVENTUALLY GOT SOME MONEY TOGETHER AND BOUGHT A LITTLE WOODEN HOUSE °°°

IT'S JUST BAKING IN THE SUN WE'LL HAFTO PLANT A LOT OF TREES...

SO STRANGE THIS IS THE VERY HOUSE I DREAMED OF WHEN I FIRST MET ROBERT!

OI VEH...THERE WAS A LITTLE BLONDE CURLY HAIRED CHILD IN THAT DREAM TOO!?

WE BECAME OBSESSED WITH SHADE AND WE HAD TO LEARN HOW TO PLANT TREES°°°

THE SHIMMERING HEAT REMINDED ME OF CAMUS' DESCRIPTION OF ALEXANDRIA, EGYPT...

BOB, TAKE A BREAK AND DRINK SOME WATAH... IT'S BOILING OUT HERE!

YEAH..INNA MINIT.. I JUST GOTTA FINISH PLANTING THIS EUCALYPTUS TREE.

Coca Cola

OUR DECORATING MANIA TOOK ON NEW DIMENSIONS. YARD SALES IN THE BACKWATERS OF THE CENTRAL VALLEY WERE LIKE ARCH LOGICAL DIGS!

A TRUE MIRACLE!

CN YOU BELIEVE THIS DELICATE ART DECO COFFEE POT BURIED IN 50 YRS. OF PETRIFIED CAT LITTER??

YEAH! AN HOW 'BOUT THIS ANTIQUE BUG SPRAYER MAGNIFICENT

PERFECT LEVEL OF TECHNOLOGY

Home Sweet Home

* 30 YRS. LATER, AFTER MOVING TO FRANCE, WE VISITED + FOUND OUR OLD HOUSE HIDDEN IN A LUSH, SHADY FOREST!

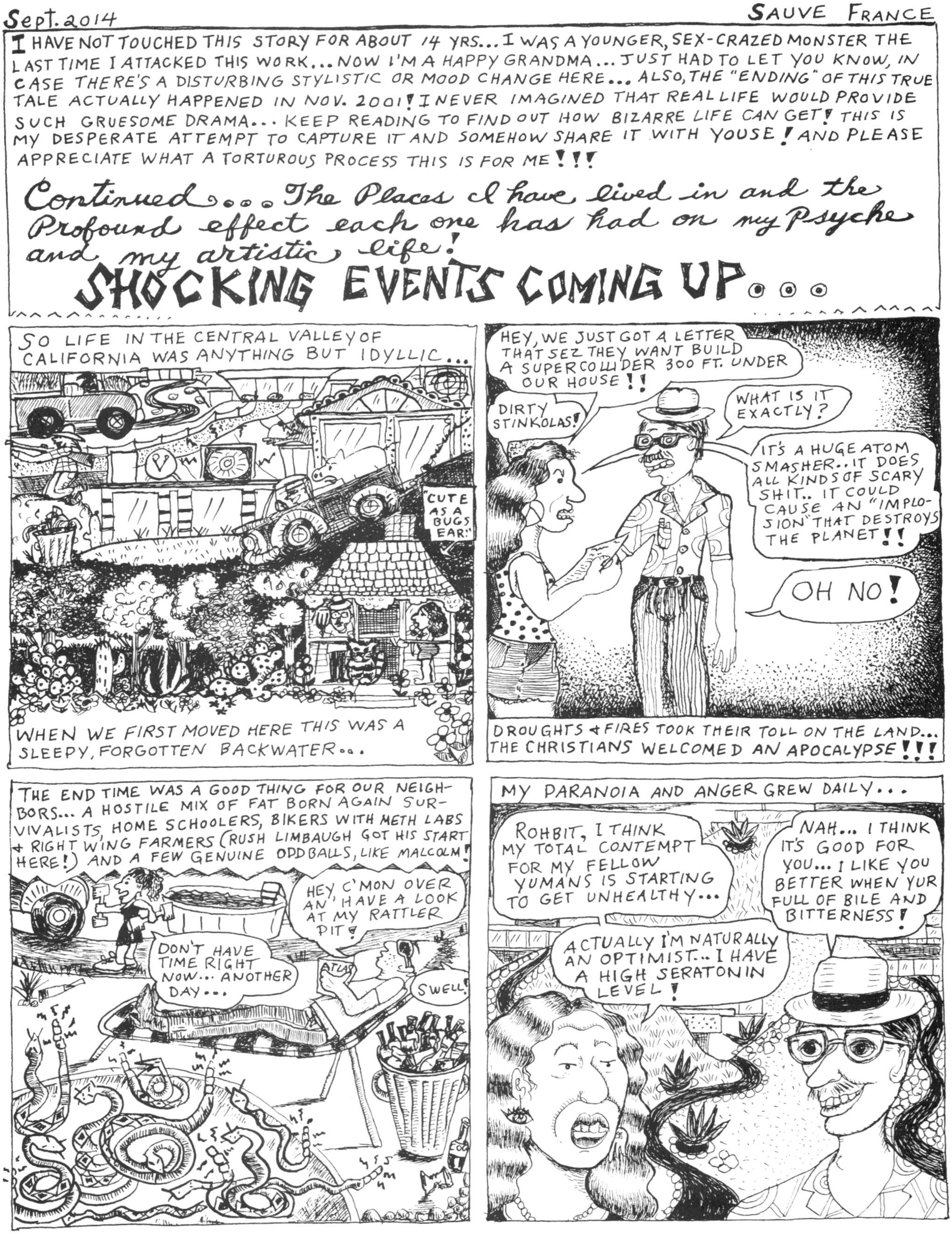
Sept. 2014
SAUVE FRANCE
I HAVE NOT TOUCHED THIS STORY FOR ABOUT 14 YRS... I WAS A YOUNGER, SEX-CRAZED MONSTER THE LAST TIME I ATTACKED THIS WORK... NOW I'M A HAPPY GRANDMA... JUST HAD TO LET YOU KNOW, IN CASE THERE'S A DISTURBING STYLISTIC OR MOOD CHANGE HERE... ALSO, THE "ENDING" OF THIS TRUE TALE ACTUALLY HAPPENED IN NOV. 2001! I NEVER IMAGINED THAT REAL LIFE WOULD PROVIDE SUCH GRUESOME DRAMA... KEEP READING TO FIND OUT HOW BIZARRE LIFE CAN GET! THIS IS MY DESPERATE ATTEMPT TO CAPTURE IT AND SOMEHOW SHARE IT WITH YOUSE! AND PLEASE APPRECIATE WHAT A TORTUROUS PROCESS THIS IS FOR ME!!!
Continued... The Places I have lived in and the Profound effect each one has had on my Psyche and my artistic life!
SHOCKING EVENTS COMING UP...
SO LIFE IN THE CENTRAL VALLEY OF CALIFORNIA WAS ANYTHING BUT IDYLLIC...
"CUTE AS A BUGS EAR."
WHEN WE FIRST MOVED HERE THIS WAS A SLEEPY, FORGOTTEN BACKWATER...
HEY, WE JUST GOT A LETTER THAT SEZ THEY WANT BUILD A SUPERCOLLIDER 300 FT. UNDER OUR HOUSE!!
DIRTY STINKOLAS!
WHAT IS IT EXACTLY?
IT'S A HUGE ATOM SMASHER.. IT DOES ALL KINDS OF SCARY SHIT.. IT COULD CAUSE AN "IMPLOSION" THAT DESTROYS THE PLANET!!
OH NO!
DROUGHTS & FIRES TOOK THEIR TOLL ON THE LAND... THE CHRISTIANS WELCOMED AN APOCALYPSE!!!
THE END TIME WAS A GOOD THING FOR OUR NEIGHBORS... A HOSTILE MIX OF FAT BORN AGAIN SURVIVALISTS, HOME SCHOOLERS, BIKERS WITH METH LABS & RIGHT WING FARMERS (RUSH LIMBAUGH GOT HIS START HERE!) AND A FEW GENUINE ODDBALLS, LIKE MALCOLM!
HEY, C'MON OVER AN' HAVE A LOOK AT MY RATTLER PIT!
DON'T HAVE TIME RIGHT NOW... ANOTHER DAY...
ATLAS
SWELL!
MY PARANOIA AND ANGER GREW DAILY...
ROHBIT, I THINK MY TOTAL CONTEMPT FOR MY FELLOW YUMANS IS STARTING TO GET UNHEALTHY...
NAH... I THINK IT'S GOOD FOR YOU... I LIKE YOU BETTER WHEN YUR FULL OF BILE AND BITTERNESS!
ACTUALLY I'M NATURALLY AN OPTIMIST.. I HAVE A HIGH SERATONIN LEVEL!

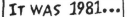

IT WAS 1981...

WHILE ALL AROUND US THEY WERE BUSY BULLDOZING TOWARD THE APOCALYPSE! X X X X X X X

Our beautiful curly haired little girl was born....

WE LOVED HER SOOO MUCH THAT IT HURT.... FOR ME, IT FELT LIKE MY HEART WAS NOW OUTSIDE MY BODY!..

TELL 'EM HOW NICE THAT SOPHIE LOOKS!

WOBBLE WOBBLE

GOO

CUTEST LITTLE THING THAT EVER LIVED!

JEALOUS

KILL

R. CRUMB '81

WE TRIED TO MAKE AN IDYLLIC LIFE FOR HER... DESPITE OUR DISGUST FOR THE MODERN WORLD!

MOMMEE LOOK AT ME... LOOK NOW!

ONE MINUTE! I HAF TO FINISH MILKING DAISY!

NO! RIGHT NOW!!

WHA... AHHH!

ROBERT OBSESSIVELY BABIED OUR PATHETIC LITTLE TREES... IN A DESPERATE ATTEMPT TO BLOCK THE SCORCHING SUN AND THE HIDEOUS "OTHERS".

SURE HOPE THESE TREES MAKE IT!

IT'S SO FUCKIN' HOT HERE IN THIS PARCHED HELL VALLEY!

TO KEEP THE DEER FROM EATING BARK...

I MADE EVERY OCCASION LOOK LIKE MY FANTASY OF THE 1920'S *

MOMMY... THIS DRESS IS ITCHY AND YUCKY!

I WANNA TAKE IT OFF...

THIS HAT'S DUMB

ITS SO PRETTY DEAH...

YOU LOOK GREAT SOF!

THERE'S NO FOOD I LIKE HERE.

CAB BAGE PAT

IT'S PERFECTLY COMFORTABLE... IT'S JUST A LITTLE OLD FASHIONED... IT'S NOT A JOGGING SUIT!

WHY CAN'T WE GO TO... CHUCKIE CHEESE?

* OBVIOUSLY I WANT EVERYTHING TO LOOK LIKE MY GRANDMA'S HOUSE 'CAUSE I WAS HAPPY THERE! ♥♥

I HATE WEARING THIS, DADDY... I WANNA BE NAKED!!!

GET ME OUTTA THIS DRESS... I HATE IT!

DADDY HELP!

C'MERE, I'LL TAKE IT OFF...

I JUST WANT EVERY-THING TO LOOK NICE... SORRY!

OUR CHILD IS POWERFUL, CHALLENGING AND TALENTED! *

WE BOTH NEED TO BE LIKED TOO MUCH... THAT'S OUR PROBLEM... WE CAN'T BE TOUGH!

OUR NEUROSIS DAMPENED THE CUTENESS FACTOR!

YUP!

* STILL IS!

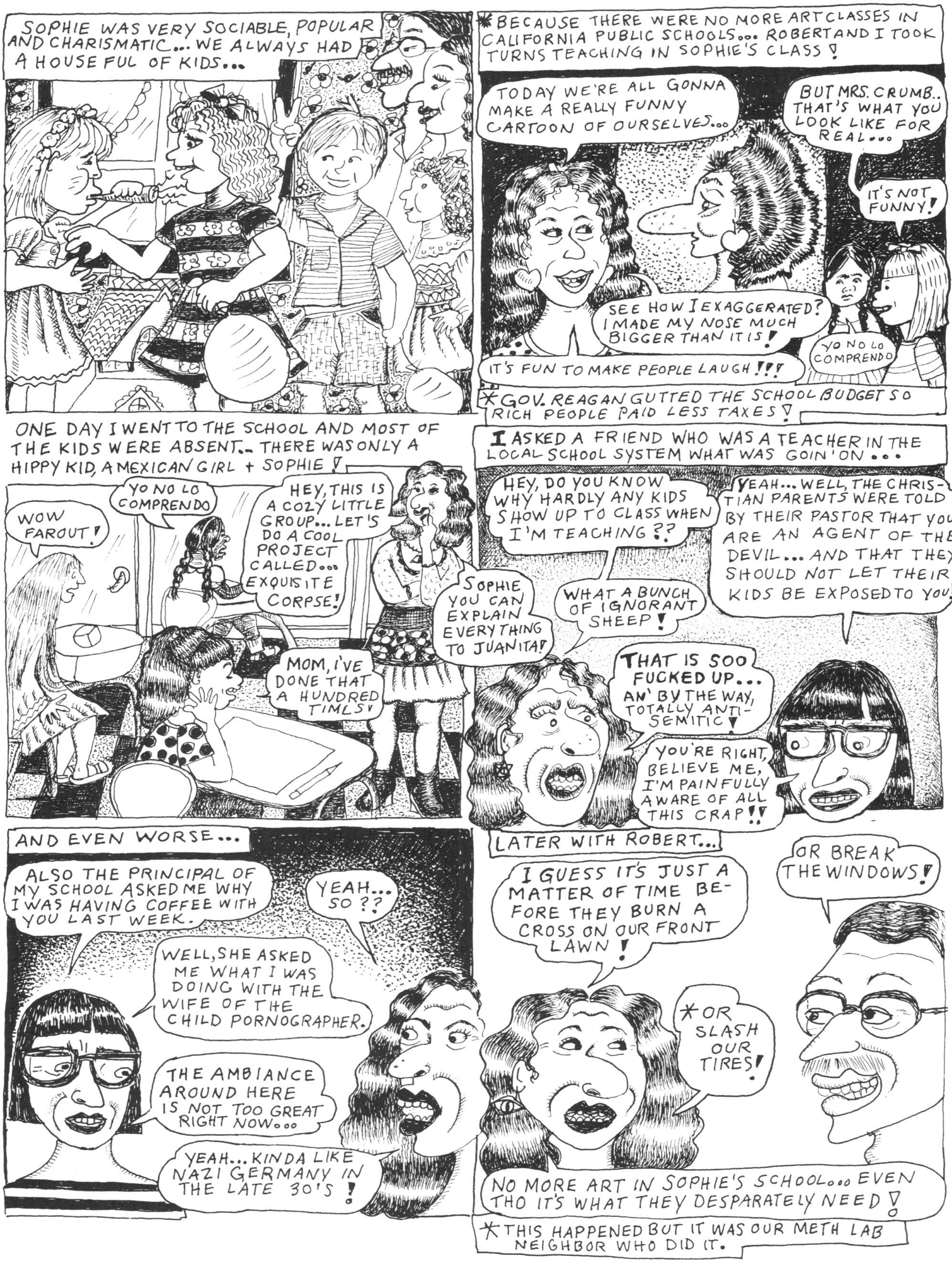
SOPHIE WAS VERY SOCIABLE, POPULAR AND CHARISMATIC... WE ALWAYS HAD A HOUSEFUL OF KIDS...
*BECAUSE THERE WERE NO MORE ART CLASSES IN CALIFORNIA PUBLIC SCHOOLS... ROBERT AND I TOOK TURNS TEACHING IN SOPHIE'S CLASS!
TODAY WE'RE ALL GONNA MAKE A REALLY FUNNY CARTOON OF OURSELVES...
BUT MRS. CRUMB.. THAT'S WHAT YOU LOOK LIKE FOR REAL...
IT'S NOT FUNNY!
SEE HOW I EXAGGERATED? I MADE MY NOSE MUCH BIGGER THAN IT IS!
IT'S FUN TO MAKE PEOPLE LAUGH!!!
YO NO LO COMPRENDO
*GOV. REAGAN GUTTED THE SCHOOL BUDGET SO RICH PEOPLE PAID LESS TAXES!
ONE DAY I WENT TO THE SCHOOL AND MOST OF THE KIDS WERE ABSENT.. THERE WAS ONLY A HIPPY KID, A MEXICAN GIRL + SOPHIE!
WOW FAROUT!
YO NO LO COMPRENDO
HEY, THIS IS A COZY LITTLE GROUP... LET'S DO A COOL PROJECT CALLED... EXQUISITE CORPSE!
SOPHIE YOU CAN EXPLAIN EVERYTHING TO JUANITA!
MOM, I'VE DONE THAT A HUNDRED TIMES!
I ASKED A FRIEND WHO WAS A TEACHER IN THE LOCAL SCHOOL SYSTEM WHAT WAS GOIN' ON...
HEY, DO YOU KNOW WHY HARDLY ANY KIDS SHOW UP TO CLASS WHEN I'M TEACHING??
YEAH... WELL, THE CHRISTIAN PARENTS WERE TOLD BY THEIR PASTOR THAT YOU ARE AN AGENT OF THE DEVIL... AND THAT THEY SHOULD NOT LET THEIR KIDS BE EXPOSED TO YOU!
WHAT A BUNCH OF IGNORANT SHEEP!
THAT IS SOO FUCKED UP... AN' BY THE WAY, TOTALLY ANTI-SEMITIC!
YOU'RE RIGHT, BELIEVE ME, I'M PAINFULLY AWARE OF ALL THIS CRAP!!
AND EVEN WORSE...
ALSO THE PRINCIPAL OF MY SCHOOL ASKED ME WHY I WAS HAVING COFFEE WITH YOU LAST WEEK.
YEAH... SO??
WELL, SHE ASKED ME WHAT I WAS DOING WITH THE WIFE OF THE CHILD PORNOGRAPHER.
THE AMBIANCE AROUND HERE IS NOT TOO GREAT RIGHT NOW...
YEAH... KINDA LIKE NAZI GERMANY IN THE LATE 30'S!
LATER WITH ROBERT...
I GUESS IT'S JUST A MATTER OF TIME BEFORE THEY BURN A CROSS ON OUR FRONT LAWN!
OR BREAK THE WINDOWS!
*OR SLASH OUR TIRES!
NO MORE ART IN SOPHIE'S SCHOOL... EVEN THO IT'S WHAT THEY DESPARATELY NEED!
*THIS HAPPENED BUT IT WAS OUR METH LAB NEIGHBOR WHO DID IT.

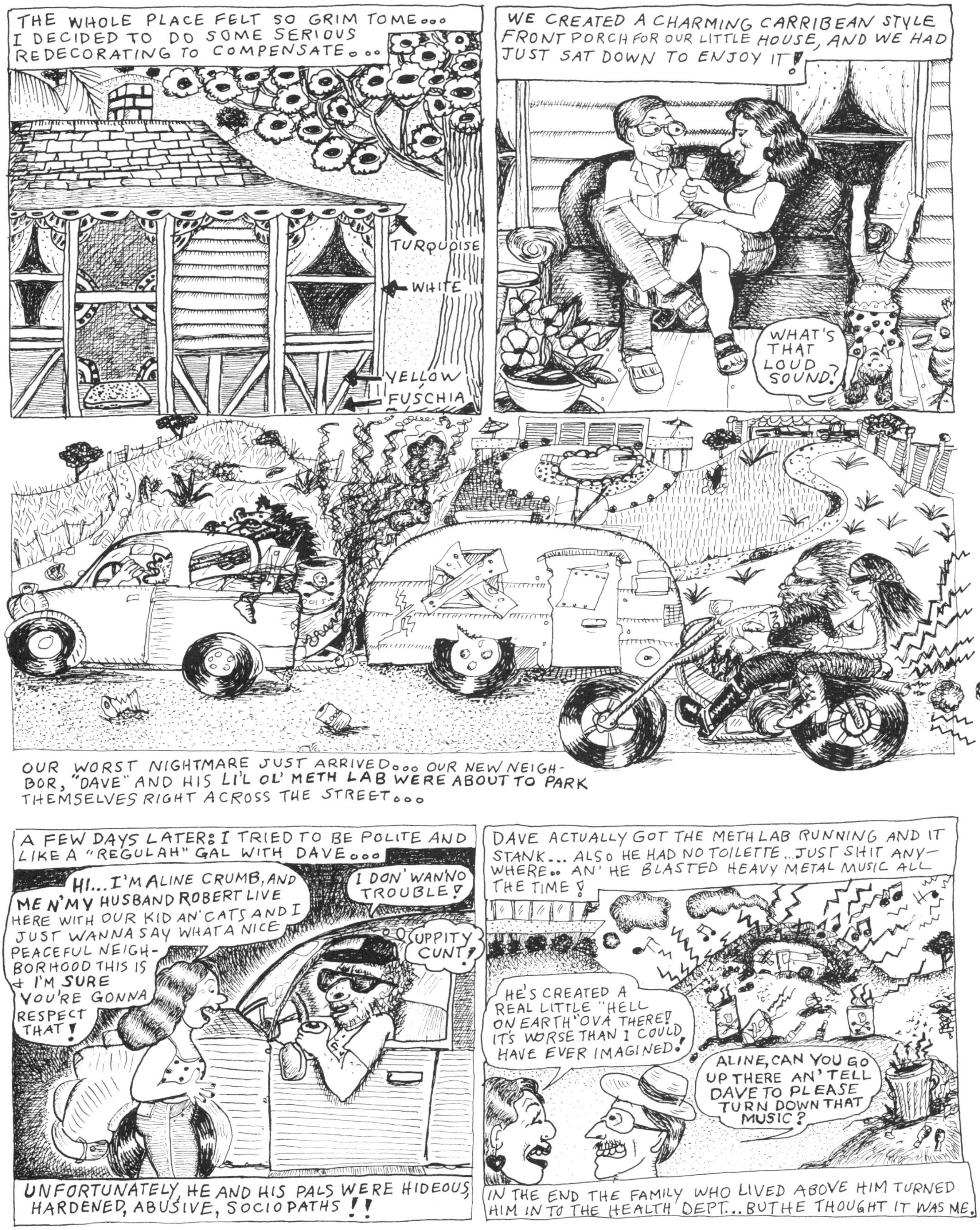
THE WHOLE PLACE FELT SO GRIM TO ME... I DECIDED TO DO SOME SERIOUS REDECORATING TO COMPENSATE...
TURQUOISE
WHITE
YELLOW
FUSCHIA
WE CREATED A CHARMING CARRIBEAN STYLE FRONT PORCH FOR OUR LITTLE HOUSE, AND WE HAD JUST SAT DOWN TO ENJOY IT!
WHAT'S THAT LOUD SOUND?
OUR WORST NIGHTMARE JUST ARRIVED... OUR NEW NEIGHBOR, "DAVE" AND HIS LI'L OL' METH LAB WERE ABOUT TO PARK THEMSELVES RIGHT ACROSS THE STREET...
A FEW DAYS LATER: I TRIED TO BE POLITE AND LIKE A "REGULAH" GAL WITH DAVE...
HI... I'M ALINE CRUMB, AND ME N' MY HUSBAND ROBERT LIVE HERE WITH OUR KID AN' CATS AND I JUST WANNA SAY WHAT A NICE PEACEFUL NEIGHBORHOOD THIS IS & I'M SURE YOU'RE GONNA RESPECT THAT!
I DON' WAN'NO TROUBLE!
UPPITY CUNT!
UNFORTUNATELY, HE AND HIS PALS WERE HIDEOUS, HARDENED, ABUSIVE, SOCIOPATHS!!
DAVE ACTUALLY GOT THE METH LAB RUNNING AND IT STANK... ALSO HE HAD NO TOILETTE... JUST SHIT ANYWHERE.. AN' HE BLASTED HEAVY METAL MUSIC ALL THE TIME!
HE'S CREATED A REAL LITTLE "HELL ON EARTH" OVA THERE! IT'S WORSE THAN I COULD HAVE EVER IMAGINED!
ALINE, CAN YOU GO UP THERE AN' TELL DAVE TO PLEASE TURN DOWN THAT MUSIC?
IN THE END THE FAMILY WHO LIVED ABOVE HIM TURNED HIM IN TO THE HEALTH DEPT... BUT HE THOUGHT IT WAS ME.

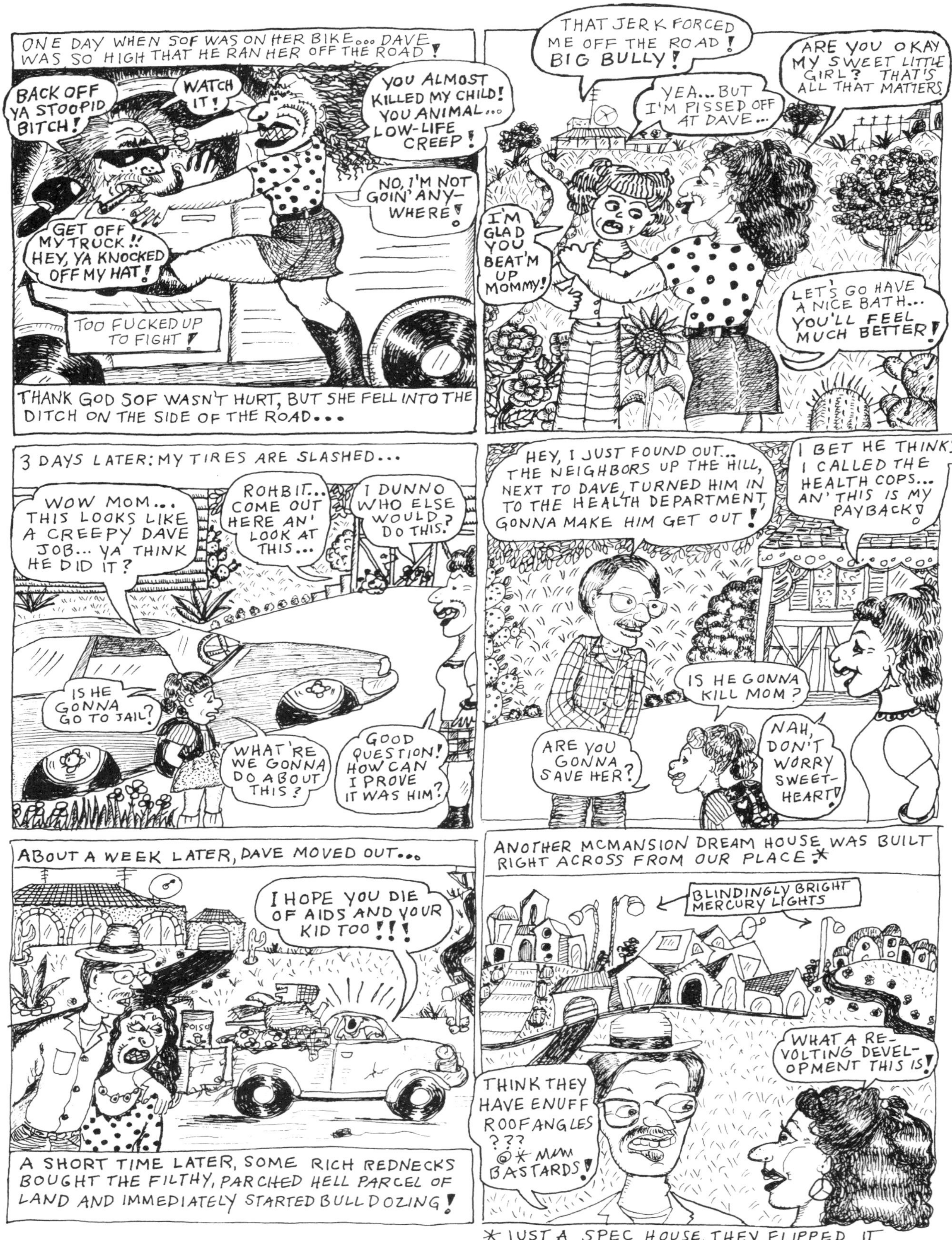
ONE DAY WHEN SOF WAS ON HER BIKE... DAVE WAS SO HIGH THAT HE RAN HER OFF THE ROAD!
BACK OFF YA STOOPID BITCH!
WATCH IT!
YOU ALMOST KILLED MY CHILD! YOU ANIMAL... LOW-LIFE CREEP!
NO, I'M NOT GOIN' ANYWHERE!
GET OFF MY TRUCK!! HEY, YA KNOCKED OFF MY HAT!
TOO FUCKED UP TO FIGHT!
THANK GOD SOF WASN'T HURT, BUT SHE FELL INTO THE DITCH ON THE SIDE OF THE ROAD...
THAT JERK FORCED ME OFF THE ROAD! BIG BULLY!
YEA... BUT I'M PISSED OFF AT DAVE...
ARE YOU OKAY MY SWEET LITTLE GIRL? THAT'S ALL THAT MATTERS
I'M GLAD YOU BEAT'M UP MOMMY!
LET'S GO HAVE A NICE BATH... YOU'LL FEEL MUCH BETTER!
3 DAYS LATER: MY TIRES ARE SLASHED...
WOW MOM... THIS LOOKS LIKE A CREEPY DAVE JOB... YA THINK HE DID IT?
ROHBIT... COME OUT HERE AN' LOOK AT THIS...
I DUNNO WHO ELSE WOULD DO THIS.
IS HE GONNA GO TO JAIL?
WHAT'RE WE GONNA DO ABOUT THIS?
GOOD QUESTION! HOW CAN I PROVE IT WAS HIM?
HEY, I JUST FOUND OUT... THE NEIGHBORS UP THE HILL, NEXT TO DAVE, TURNED HIM IN TO THE HEALTH DEPARTMENT, GONNA MAKE HIM GET OUT!
I BET HE THINKS I CALLED THE HEALTH COPS... AN' THIS IS MY PAYBACK!
IS HE GONNA KILL MOM?
ARE YOU GONNA SAVE HER?
NAH, DON'T WORRY SWEETHEART!
ABOUT A WEEK LATER, DAVE MOVED OUT...
I HOPE YOU DIE OF AIDS AND YOUR KID TOO!!!
A SHORT TIME LATER, SOME RICH REDNECKS BOUGHT THE FILTHY, PARCHED HELL PARCEL OF LAND AND IMMEDIATELY STARTED BULLDOZING!
ANOTHER MCMANSION DREAM HOUSE WAS BUILT RIGHT ACROSS FROM OUR PLACE.*
BLINDINGLY BRIGHT MERCURY LIGHTS
WHAT A REVOLTING DEVELOPMENT THIS IS!
THINK THEY HAVE ENUFF ROOF ANGLES??? @*MM BASTARDS!

*JUST A SPEC HOUSE, THEY FLIPPED IT 6 MONTHS LATER.

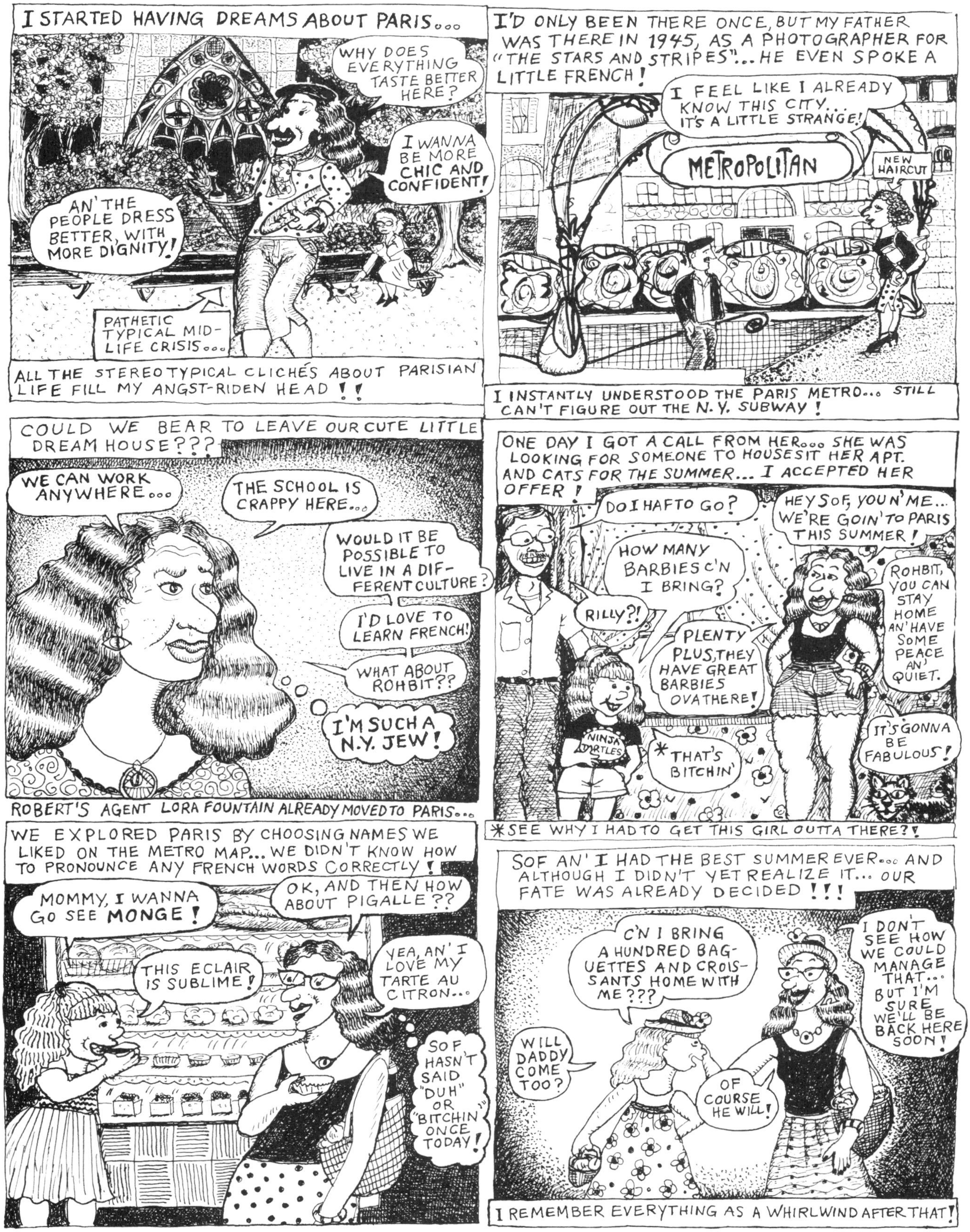

I STARTED HAVING DREAMS ABOUT PARIS...
WHY DOES EVERYTHING TASTE BETTER HERE?
I WANNA BE MORE CHIC AND CONFIDENT!
AN' THE PEOPLE DRESS BETTER, WITH MORE DIGNITY!
PATHETIC TYPICAL MID-LIFE CRISIS...
ALL THE STEREOTYPICAL CLICHÉS ABOUT PARISIAN LIFE FILL MY ANGST-RIDEN HEAD!!
I'D ONLY BEEN THERE ONCE, BUT MY FATHER WAS THERE IN 1945, AS A PHOTOGRAPHER FOR "THE STARS AND STRIPES"... HE EVEN SPOKE A LITTLE FRENCH!
I FEEL LIKE I ALREADY KNOW THIS CITY... IT'S A LITTLE STRANGE!
METROPOLITAN
NEW HAIRCUT
I INSTANTLY UNDERSTOOD THE PARIS METRO... STILL CAN'T FIGURE OUT THE N.Y. SUBWAY!
COULD WE BEAR TO LEAVE OUR CUTE LITTLE DREAM HOUSE???
WE CAN WORK ANYWHERE...
THE SCHOOL IS CRAPPY HERE...
WOULD IT BE POSSIBLE TO LIVE IN A DIFFERENT CULTURE?
I'D LOVE TO LEARN FRENCH!
WHAT ABOUT ROHBIT??
I'M SUCH A N.Y. JEW!
ROBERT'S AGENT LORA FOUNTAIN ALREADY MOVED TO PARIS...
ONE DAY I GOT A CALL FROM HER... SHE WAS LOOKING FOR SOMEONE TO HOUSESIT HER APT. AND CATS FOR THE SUMMER... I ACCEPTED HER OFFER!
DO I HAFTO GO?
HEY SOF, YOU N' ME... WE'RE GOIN' TO PARIS THIS SUMMER!
HOW MANY BARBIES C'N I BRING?
ROHBIT, YOU CAN STAY HOME AN' HAVE SOME PEACE AN' QUIET.
RILLY?!
PLENTY PLUS, THEY HAVE GREAT BARBIES OVA THERE!
NINJA TURTLES
*THAT'S BITCHIN'
IT'S GONNA BE FABULOUS!
*SEE WHY I HAD TO GET THIS GIRL OUTTA THERE?!
WE EXPLORED PARIS BY CHOOSING NAMES WE LIKED ON THE METRO MAP... WE DIDN'T KNOW HOW TO PRONOUNCE ANY FRENCH WORDS CORRECTLY!
MOMMY, I WANNA GO SEE MONGE!
OK, AND THEN HOW ABOUT PIGALLE??
THIS ECLAIR IS SUBLIME!
YEA, AN' I LOVE MY TARTE AU CITRON...
SOF HASN'T SAID "DUH" OR "BITCHIN" ONCE TODAY!
SOF AN' I HAD THE BEST SUMMER EVER... AND ALTHOUGH I DIDN'T YET REALIZE IT... OUR FATE WAS ALREADY DECIDED!!!
C'N I BRING A HUNDRED BAGUETTES AND CROISSANTS HOME WITH ME???
I DON'T SEE HOW WE COULD MANAGE THAT... BUT I'M SURE WE'LL BE BACK HERE SOON!
WILL DADDY COME TOO?
OF COURSE HE WILL!
I REMEMBER EVERYTHING AS A WHIRLWIND AFTER THAT!

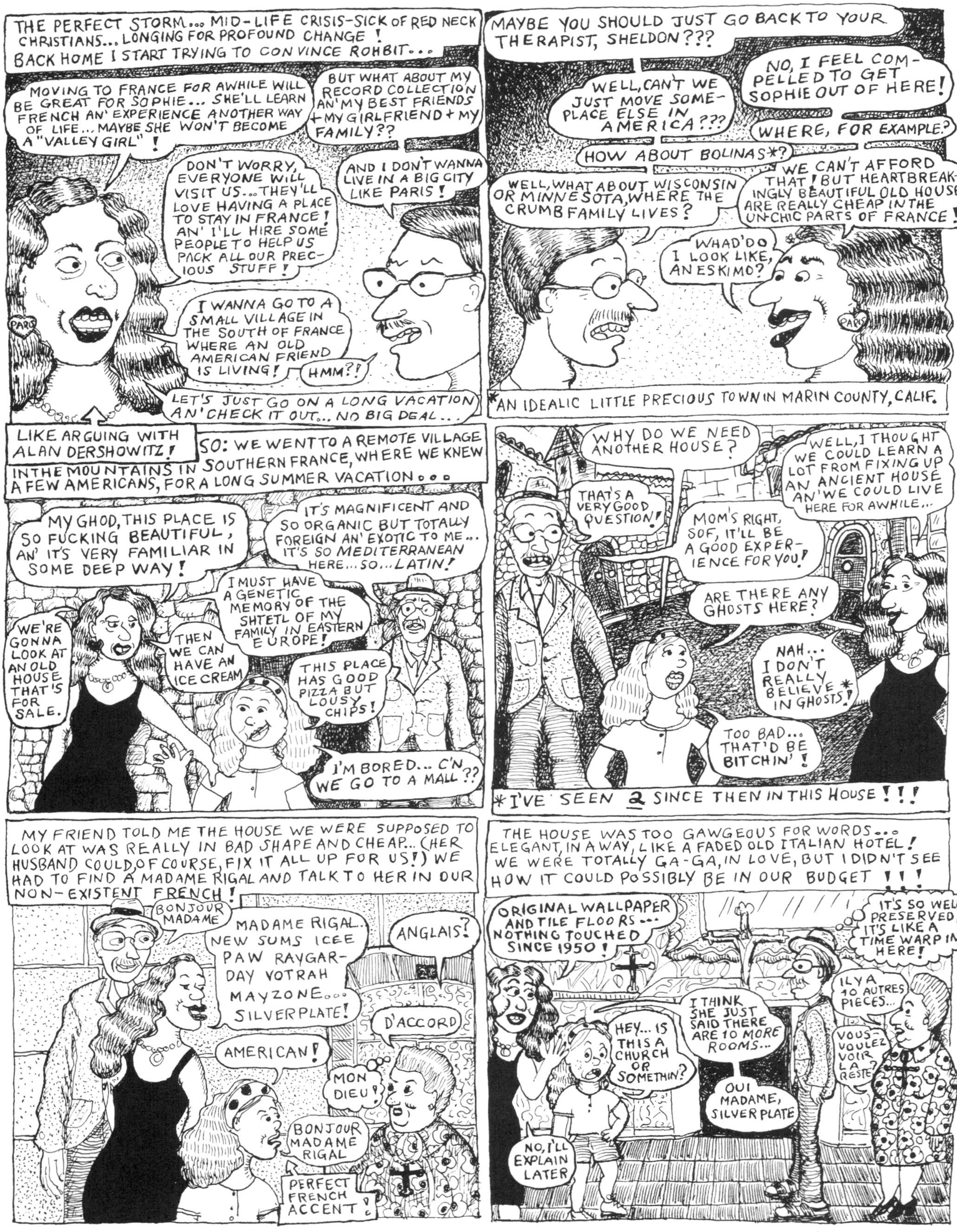
THE PERFECT STORM... MID-LIFE CRISIS-SICK OF RED NECK CHRISTIANS... LONGING FOR PROFOUND CHANGE! BACK HOME I START TRYING TO CONVINCE ROHBIT...
MOVING TO FRANCE FOR AWHILE WILL BE GREAT FOR SOPHIE... SHE'LL LEARN FRENCH AN' EXPERIENCE ANOTHER WAY OF LIFE... MAYBE SHE WON'T BECOME A "VALLEY GIRL"!
BUT WHAT ABOUT MY RECORD COLLECTION AN' MY BEST FRIENDS + MY GIRLFRIEND + MY FAMILY??
DON'T WORRY, EVERYONE WILL VISIT US... THEY'LL LOVE HAVING A PLACE TO STAY IN FRANCE! AN' I'LL HIRE SOME PEOPLE TO HELP US PACK ALL OUR PRECIOUS STUFF!
AND I DON'T WANNA LIVE IN A BIG CITY LIKE PARIS!
I WANNA GO TO A SMALL VILLAGE IN THE SOUTH OF FRANCE WHERE AN OLD AMERICAN FRIEND IS LIVING!
HMM?!
LET'S JUST GO ON A LONG VACATION AN' CHECK IT OUT... NO BIG DEAL...
PARIS
MAYBE YOU SHOULD JUST GO BACK TO YOUR THERAPIST, SHELDON???
WELL, CAN'T WE JUST MOVE SOMEPLACE ELSE IN AMERICA???
NO, I FEEL COMPELLED TO GET SOPHIE OUT OF HERE!
WHERE, FOR EXAMPLE?
HOW ABOUT BOLINAS*?
WELL, WHAT ABOUT WISCONSIN OR MINNESOTA, WHERE THE CRUMB FAMILY LIVES?
WE CAN'T AFFORD THAT! BUT HEARTBREAKINGLY BEAUTIFUL OLD HOUSES ARE REALLY CHEAP IN THE UN-CHIC PARTS OF FRANCE!
WHAD'DO I LOOK LIKE, AN ESKIMO?
PARIS
*AN IDEALIC LITTLE PRECIOUS TOWN IN MARIN COUNTY, CALIF.
LIKE ARGUING WITH ALAN DERSHOWITZ!
SO: WE WENT TO A REMOTE VILLAGE IN THE MOUNTAINS IN SOUTHERN FRANCE, WHERE WE KNEW A FEW AMERICANS, FOR A LONG SUMMER VACATION...
MY GHOD, THIS PLACE IS SO FUCKING BEAUTIFUL, AN' IT'S VERY FAMILIAR IN SOME DEEP WAY!
IT'S MAGNIFICENT AND SO ORGANIC BUT TOTALLY FOREIGN AN' EXOTIC TO ME... IT'S SO MEDITERRANEAN HERE... SO... LATIN!
I MUST HAVE A GENETIC MEMORY OF THE SHTETL OF MY FAMILY IN EASTERN EUROPE!
WE'RE GONNA LOOK AT AN OLD HOUSE THAT'S FOR SALE.
THEN WE CAN HAVE AN ICE CREAM
THIS PLACE HAS GOOD PIZZA BUT LOUSY CHIPS!
I'M BORED... C'N WE GO TO A MALL??
WHY DO WE NEED ANOTHER HOUSE?
THAT'S A VERY GOOD QUESTION!
WELL, I THOUGHT WE COULD LEARN A LOT FROM FIXING UP AN ANCIENT HOUSE AN' WE COULD LIVE HERE FOR AWHILE...
MOM'S RIGHT, SOF, IT'LL BE A GOOD EXPERIENCE FOR YOU!
ARE THERE ANY GHOSTS HERE?
NAH... I DON'T REALLY BELIEVE* IN GHOSTS!
TOO BAD... THAT'D BE BITCHIN'!
*I'VE SEEN 2 SINCE THEN IN THIS HOUSE!!!
MY FRIEND TOLD ME THE HOUSE WE WERE SUPPOSED TO LOOK AT WAS REALLY IN BAD SHAPE AND CHEAP... (HER HUSBAND COULD, OF COURSE, FIX IT ALL UP FOR US!) WE HAD TO FIND A MADAME RIGAL AND TALK TO HER IN OUR NON-EXISTENT FRENCH!
BONJOUR MADAME
MADAME RIGAL... NEW SUMS ICEE PAW RAYGAR-DAY VOTRAH MAYZONE... SILVERPLATE!
ANGLAIS?
D'ACCORD
AMERICAN!
MON DIEU!
BONJOUR MADAME RIGAL
PERFECT FRENCH ACCENT!
THE HOUSE WAS TOO GAWGEOUS FOR WORDS... ELEGANT, IN A WAY, LIKE A FADED OLD ITALIAN HOTEL! WE WERE TOTALLY GA-GA, IN LOVE, BUT I DIDN'T SEE HOW IT COULD POSSIBLY BE IN OUR BUDGET!!!
ORIGINAL WALLPAPER AND TILE FLOORS... NOTHING TOUCHED SINCE 1950!
IT'S SO WELL PRESERVED, IT'S LIKE A TIME WARP IN HERE!
IL Y A 10 AUTRES PIECES...
I THINK SHE JUST SAID THERE ARE 10 MORE ROOMS...
HEY... IS THIS A CHURCH OR SOMETHIN'?
VOUS VOULEZ VOIR LA RESTE?
OUI MADAME, SILVER PLATE
NO, I'LL EXPLAIN LATER

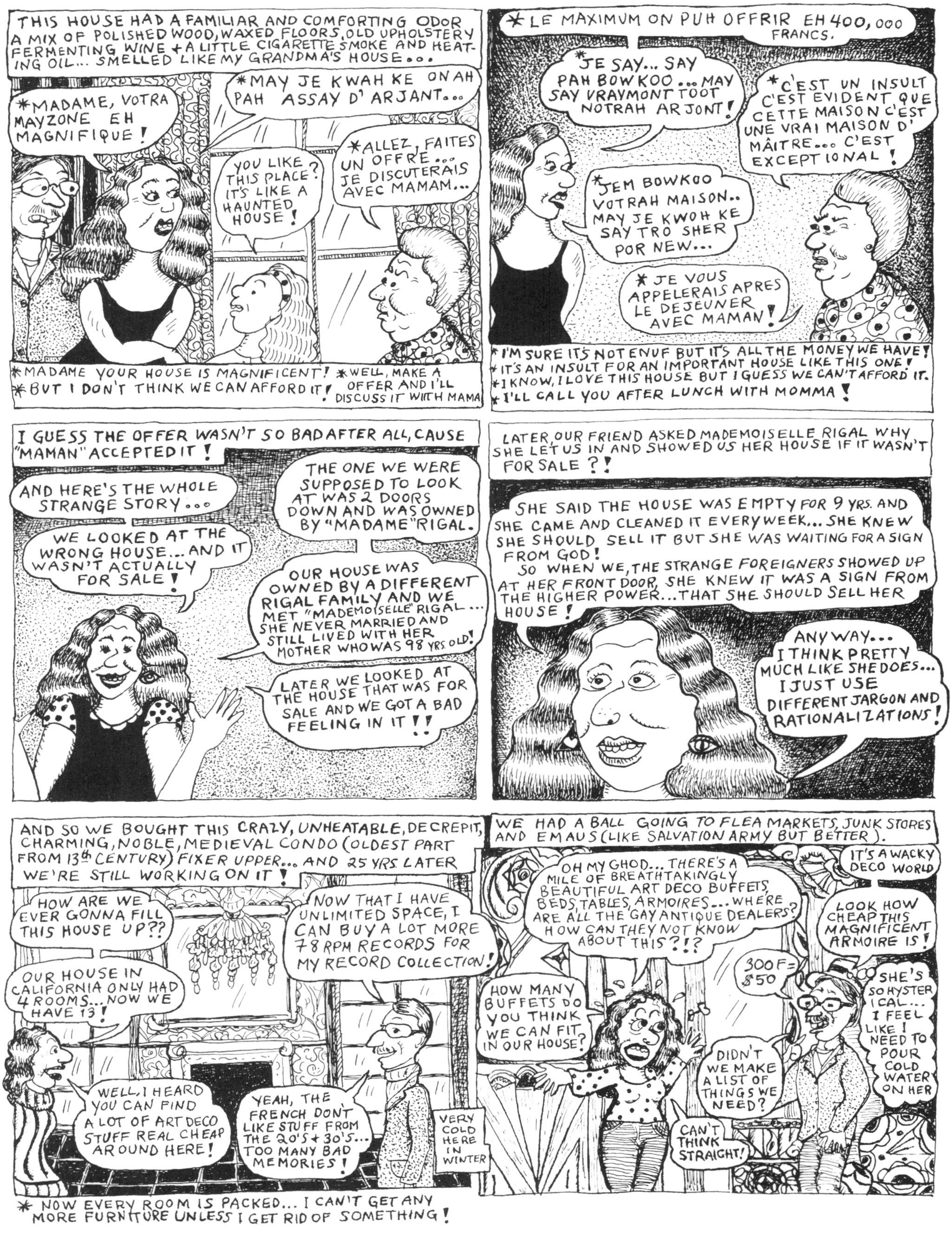

THIS HOUSE HAD A FAMILIAR AND COMFORTING ODOR A MIX OF POLISHED WOOD, WAXED FLOORS, OLD UPHOLSTERY FERMENTING WINE + A LITTLE CIGARETTE SMOKE AND HEATING OIL... SMELLED LIKE MY GRANDMA'S HOUSE...
*MADAME, VOTRA MAYZONE EH MAGNIFIQUE!
*MAY JE KWAH KE ON AH PAH ASSAY D' ARJANT...
YOU LIKE THIS PLACE? IT'S LIKE A HAUNTED HOUSE!
*ALLEZ, FAITES UN OFFRE... JE DISCUTERAIS AVEC MAMAM...
*MADAME YOUR HOUSE IS MAGNIFICENT!
*BUT I DON'T THINK WE CAN AFFORD IT!
*WELL, MAKE A OFFER AND I'LL DISCUSS IT WITH MAMA
*LE MAXIMUM ON PUH OFFRIR EH 400,000 FRANCS.
*JE SAY... SAY PAH BOWKOO... MAY SAY VRAYMONT TOOT NOTRAH ARJONT!
*C'EST UN INSULT C'EST EVIDENT QUE CETTE MAISON C'EST UNE VRAI MAISON D' MÂITRE... C'EST EXCEPTIONAL!
*JEM BOWKOO VOTRAH MAISON.. MAY JE KWOH KE SAY TRO SHER POR NEW...
*JE VOUS APPELERAIS APRES LE DEJEUNER AVEC MAMAN!
*I'M SURE IT'S NOT ENUF BUT IT'S ALL THE MONEY WE HAVE!
*IT'S AN INSULT FOR AN IMPORTANT HOUSE LIKE THIS ONE!
*I KNOW, I LOVE THIS HOUSE BUT I GUESS WE CAN'T AFFORD IT.
*I'LL CALL YOU AFTER LUNCH WITH MOMMA!
I GUESS THE OFFER WASN'T SO BAD AFTER ALL, CAUSE "MAMAN" ACCEPTED IT!
AND HERE'S THE WHOLE STRANGE STORY...
THE ONE WE WERE SUPPOSED TO LOOK AT WAS 2 DOORS DOWN AND WAS OWNED BY "MADAME" RIGAL.
WE LOOKED AT THE WRONG HOUSE... AND IT WASN'T ACTUALLY FOR SALE!
OUR HOUSE WAS OWNED BY A DIFFERENT RIGAL FAMILY AND WE MET "MADEMOISELLE" RIGAL... SHE NEVER MARRIED AND STILL LIVED WITH HER MOTHER WHO WAS 98 YRS. OLD!
LATER WE LOOKED AT THE HOUSE THAT WAS FOR SALE AND WE GOT A BAD FEELING IN IT!!
LATER, OUR FRIEND ASKED MADEMOISELLE RIGAL WHY SHE LET US IN AND SHOWED US HER HOUSE IF IT WASN'T FOR SALE?!
SHE SAID THE HOUSE WAS EMPTY FOR 9 YRS. AND SHE CAME AND CLEANED IT EVERY WEEK... SHE KNEW SHE SHOULD SELL IT BUT SHE WAS WAITING FOR A SIGN FROM GOD! SO WHEN WE, THE STRANGE FOREIGNERS SHOWED UP AT HER FRONT DOOR, SHE KNEW IT WAS A SIGN FROM THE HIGHER POWER... THAT SHE SHOULD SELL HER HOUSE!
ANY WAY... I THINK PRETTY MUCH LIKE SHE DOES... I JUST USE DIFFERENT JARGON AND RATIONALIZATIONS!
AND SO WE BOUGHT THIS CRAZY, UNHEATABLE, DECREPIT, CHARMING, NOBLE, MEDIEVAL CONDO (OLDEST PART FROM 13th CENTURY) FIXER UPPER... AND 25 YRS. LATER WE'RE STILL WORKING ON IT!
HOW ARE WE EVER GONNA FILL THIS HOUSE UP??
NOW THAT I HAVE UNLIMITED SPACE, I CAN BUY A LOT MORE 78 RPM RECORDS FOR MY RECORD COLLECTION!
OUR HOUSE IN CALIFORNIA ONLY HAD 4 ROOMS... NOW WE HAVE 13!
WELL, I HEARD YOU CAN FIND A LOT OF ART DECO STUFF REAL CHEAP AROUND HERE!
YEAH, THE FRENCH DON'T LIKE STUFF FROM THE 20'S + 30'S... TOO MANY BAD MEMORIES!
VERY COLD HERE IN WINTER
* NOW EVERY ROOM IS PACKED... I CAN'T GET ANY MORE FURNITURE UNLESS I GET RID OF SOMETHING!
WE HAD A BALL GOING TO FLEA MARKETS, JUNK STORES AND EMAUS (LIKE SALVATION ARMY BUT BETTER).
OH MY GHOD... THERE'S A MILE OF BREATHTAKINGLY BEAUTIFUL ART DECO BUFFETS, BEDS, TABLES, ARMOIRES... WHERE ARE ALL THE GAY ANTIQUE DEALERS? HOW CAN THEY NOT KNOW ABOUT THIS?!?
IT'S A WACKY DECO WORLD
LOOK HOW CHEAP THIS MAGNIFICENT ARMOIRE IS!
300 F= $50
HOW MANY BUFFETS DO YOU THINK WE CAN FIT IN OUR HOUSE?
SHE'S SO HYSTERICAL... I FEEL LIKE I NEED TO POUR COLD WATER ON HER
DIDN'T WE MAKE A LIST OF THINGS WE NEED?
CAN'T THINK STRAIGHT!

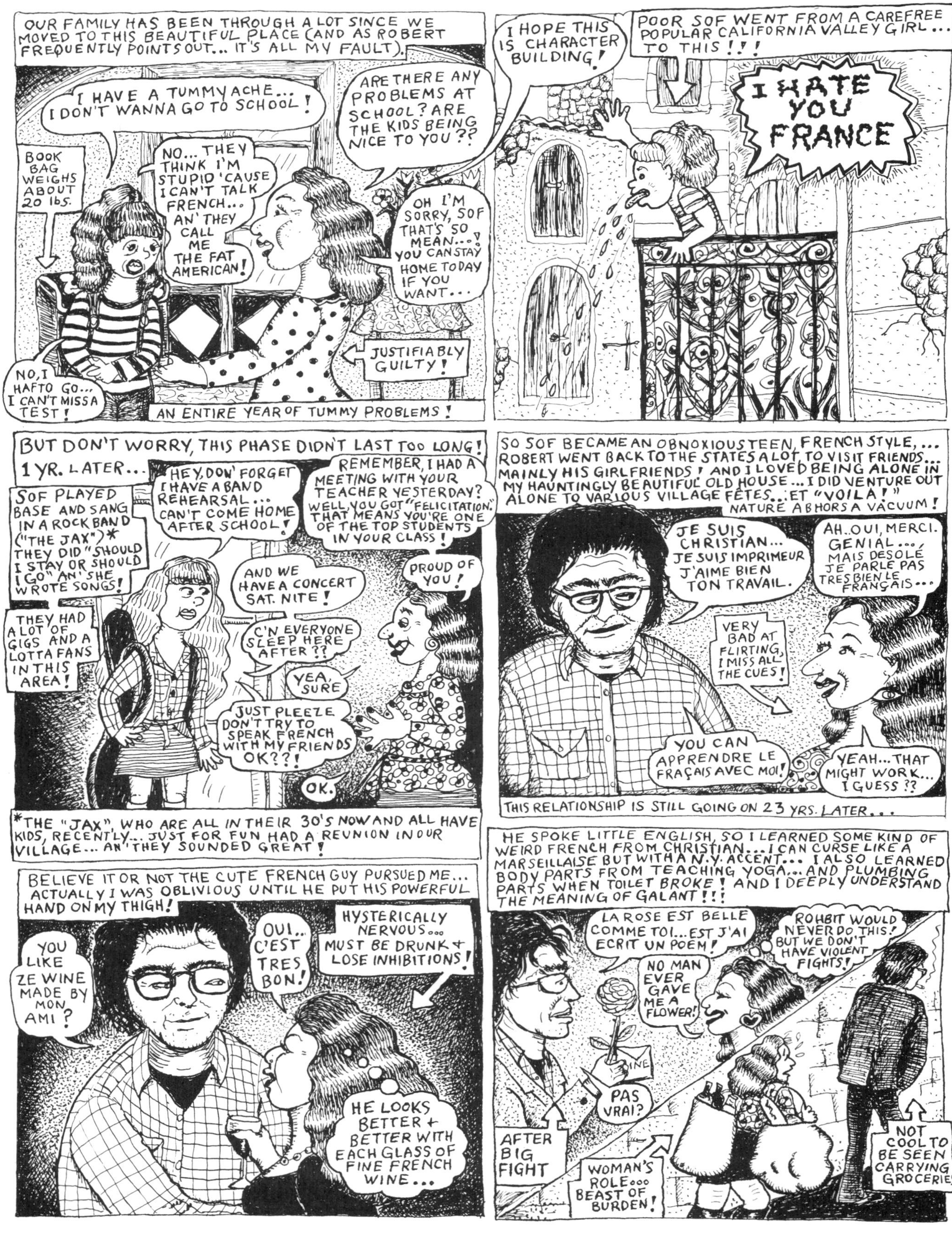

OUR FAMILY HAS BEEN THROUGH A LOT SINCE WE MOVED TO THIS BEAUTIFUL PLACE (AND AS ROBERT FREQUENTLY POINTS OUT... IT'S ALL MY FAULT).
I HAVE A TUMMY ACHE... I DON'T WANNA GO TO SCHOOL!
ARE THERE ANY PROBLEMS AT SCHOOL? ARE THE KIDS BEING NICE TO YOU??
BOOK BAG WEIGHS ABOUT 20 lbs.
NO... THEY THINK I'M STUPID 'CAUSE I CAN'T TALK FRENCH... AN' THEY CALL ME THE FAT AMERICAN!
OH I'M SORRY, SOF THAT'S SO MEAN...! YOU CAN STAY HOME TODAY IF YOU WANT...
JUSTIFIABLY GUILTY!
NO, I HAFTO GO... I CAN'T MISS A TEST!
AN ENTIRE YEAR OF TUMMY PROBLEMS!
I HOPE THIS IS CHARACTER BUILDING!
POOR SOF WENT FROM A CAREFREE POPULAR CALIFORNIA VALLEY GIRL... TO THIS!!!
I HATE YOU FRANCE
BUT DON'T WORRY, THIS PHASE DIDN'T LAST TOO LONG!
1 YR. LATER...
HEY, DON' FORGET I HAVE A BAND REHEARSAL... CAN'T COME HOME AFTER SCHOOL!
REMEMBER, I HAD A MEETING WITH YOUR TEACHER YESTERDAY? WELL, YOU GOT "FELICITATION." THAT MEANS YOU'RE ONE OF THE TOP STUDENTS IN YOUR CLASS!
SOF PLAYED BASE AND SANG IN A ROCK BAND ("THE JAX")* THEY DID "SHOULD I STAY OR SHOULD I GO" AN' SHE WROTE SONGS!
AND WE HAVE A CONCERT SAT. NITE!
PROUD OF YOU!
THEY HAD A LOT OF GIGS AND A LOTTA FANS IN THIS AREA!
C'N EVERYONE SLEEP HERE AFTER??
YEA, SURE
JUST PLEEZE DON'T TRY TO SPEAK FRENCH WITH MY FRIENDS OK??!
OK.
*THE "JAX", WHO ARE ALL IN THEIR 30'S NOW AND ALL HAVE KIDS, RECENTLY... JUST FOR FUN HAD A REUNION IN OUR VILLAGE... AN' THEY SOUNDED GREAT!
SO SOF BECAME AN OBNOXIOUS TEEN, FRENCH STYLE,... ROBERT WENT BACK TO THE STATES A LOT, TO VISIT FRIENDS... MAINLY HIS GIRLFRIENDS! AND I LOVED BEING ALONE IN MY HAUNTINGLY BEAUTIFUL OLD HOUSE... I DID VENTURE OUT ALONE TO VARIOUS VILLAGE FÊTES... ET "VOILA!"
NATURE ABHORS A VACUUM!
JE SUIS CHRISTIAN... JE SUIS IMPRIMEUR J'AIME BIEN TON TRAVAIL.
AH.. OUI, MERCI. GENIAL..., MAIS DESOLÉ JE PARLE PAS TRES BIEN LE FRANÇAIS...
VERY BAD AT FLIRTING, I MISS ALL THE CUES!
YOU CAN APPRENDRE LE FRANÇAIS AVEC MOI!
YEAH... THAT MIGHT WORK... I GUESS??
THIS RELATIONSHIP IS STILL GOING ON 23 YRS. LATER...
BELIEVE IT OR NOT THE CUTE FRENCH GUY PURSUED ME... ACTUALLY I WAS OBLIVIOUS UNTIL HE PUT HIS POWERFUL HAND ON MY THIGH!
YOU LIKE ZE WINE MADE BY MON AMI?
OUI.. C'EST TRES BON!
HYSTERICALLY NERVOUS... MUST BE DRUNK + LOSE INHIBITIONS!
HE LOOKS BETTER + BETTER WITH EACH GLASS OF FINE FRENCH WINE...
HE SPOKE LITTLE ENGLISH, SO I LEARNED SOME KIND OF WEIRD FRENCH FROM CHRISTIAN... I CAN CURSE LIKE A MARSEILLAISE BUT WITH A N.Y. ACCENT... I ALSO LEARNED BODY PARTS FROM TEACHING YOGA... AND PLUMBING PARTS WHEN TOILET BROKE! AND I DEEPLY UNDERSTAND THE MEANING OF GALANT!!!
LA ROSE EST BELLE COMME TOI... EST J'AI ECRIT UN POEM!
NO MAN EVER GAVE ME A FLOWER!
ROHBIT WOULD NEVER DO THIS! BUT WE DON'T HAVE VIOLENT FIGHTS!
PAS VRAI?
AFTER BIG FIGHT
WOMAN'S ROLE... BEAST OF BURDEN!
NOT COOL TO BE SEEN CARRYING GROCERIES

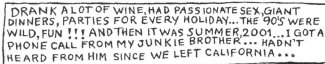
DRANK A LOT OF WINE, HAD PASSIONATE SEX, GIANT DINNERS, PARTIES FOR EVERY HOLIDAY... THE 90'S WERE WILD, FUN !!! AND THEN IT WAS SUMMER, 2001... I GOT A PHONE CALL FROM MY JUNKIE BROTHER... HADN'T HEARD FROM HIM SINCE WE LEFT CALIFORNIA...

5:00 AM

OH MY GHOD! I HOPE NO ONE DIED... HULLO?

YEAH... HI ALEX... IT'S 5 AM HERE... YEAH, YEAH... OY! SOUNDS AWFUL... I DUNNO WHAT TO SAY... CAN YOU CALL ME BACK IN A FEW WEEKS? I HAFTO TALK ABOUT THIS WITH ROHBIT... HAFTO THINK ABOUT IT. I DUNNO ???

OH JEEZ, IT'S ALEX... CAN'T BE GOOD NEWS!

MY BROTHER IS LIVING IN HIS CAR IN NEW JERSEY... HE SEZ HE'S DYING, WON'T LIVE MUCH LONGER.★ HE WANTS US TO TAKE HIM IN!

IT'S HIS OWN FAULT THAT HE'S A TOTAL DISASTER. HE CREATES CHAOS + PAIN WHENEVER HE'S AROUND... REMEMBER WHEN HE SHOWED UP IN CALIFORNIA? HE STOLE MY GRANDMA'S SILVER + BROUGHT CRIMINALS TO OUR HOUSE... HE'LL NEVER CHANGE!

WELL, WE DO HAVE THAT EMPTY APT. DOWNSTAIRS... I GUESS HE COULD STAY THERE. I KNOW HE'S A WRECK, AS USUAL... BUT WHAT IF HE DIES? CAN YOU HANDLE THE GUILT?? IT'S REALLY UP TO YOU... I'LL GO ALONG WITH YOUR DECISION!

YUR SO KIND! I'M A LUCKY WOMAN!

★ 2016, HE'S STILL HERE, ALIVE + SORT OF HEALTHY...

SEPTEMBER 11, 2001, A BEAUTIFUL, SUNNY DAY... MY BROTHER CALLED AGAIN.

ALINE, I'M BY THE RIVER IN NEW JERSEY ... AND I'M NOT BULLSHITTING... A FUCKING PLANE JUST CRASHED INTO ONE OF THE WORLD TRADE CENTER TOWERS... IT'S LIKE ON FIRE, SMOKE IS POURING OUT OF IT!

OH MY GHOD, WHAT A HORRIBLE ACCIDENT (EVEN IF IT IS AN ARCHITECTURAL NIGHTMARE)!

OH NO! I JUST LOST THE CONNECTION!

OH SHIT! ANOTHER PLANE JUST CRASHED INTO THE 2ND TOWER! WHAT THE FUCK?!

CAN'T BE AN ACCIDENT NOW... WHAT IS IT ???

BIRTH OF TERRORISM AWARENESS!

SOON ALL THE AMERICANS AROUND HERE WERE AT OUR HOUSE WATCHING CNN WITH US...

MY SISTER LIVES IN TRIBEKA!

WE'RE AT WAR!

...SAME IMAGES OVER AND OVER... WE WERE MESMER-IZED BY THE BEAUTY AND HORROR OF DESTRUCTION!

SONY

HOPE THE SPIEGELMANS ARE OK!!

I FEEL LIKE I'VE ALREADY SEEN THIS HORROR FILM!

DICK CHENEY IS PROBABLY INVOLVED IN THIS!

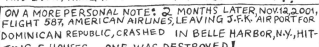
AND EVERYTHING IS SO MUCH SCARIER SINCE THEN!!

ON A MORE PERSONAL NOTE: 2 MONTHS LATER, NOV. 12, 2001, FLIGHT 587, AMERICAN AIRLINES, LEAVING J.F.K. AIRPORT FOR DOMINICAN REPUBLIC, CRASHED IN BELLE HARBOR, N.Y., HIT-TING 5 HOUSES... ONE WAS DESTROYED!

WE'LL GET TO THE BOTTOM OF THIS... BUT AS OF NOW, THERE ARE NO INDICATIONS THAT THIS WAS AN ACT OF TERRORISM!

B.131 ST. NEWPORT AVE.

THE N.Y.C. FIRE DEPT. HAS DONE AN INCREDIBLE JOB TODAY, GETTING THIS SITUATION UNDER CONTROL!

TWO PEOPLE DIED TODAY IN THE FIRST HOUSE HIT BY THIS PLANE... OTHER HOUSES HAD SOME DAMAGE... NO OTHER CASUALTIES ON THE GROUND!

ON THE NEWS THAT NIGHT I RECOGNIZED THE CORNER WHERE MAYOR GIULIANI WAS STANDING... IT WAS ACROSS THE STREET FROM MY GRAN'PARENTS' HOUSE...

AND SO MY STORY ENDS: MY GRANPARENTS' HOUSE WAS DESTROYED... MY FIRST AND HAPPIEST HOME WAS HIT BY THIS PLANE... AND IT WAS AN ACCIDENT!

I CALLED MY MOTHER AND SHE CONFIRMED THAT THE COUPLE WHO BOUGHT THE HOUSE FROM US WERE KILLED!

6 MONTHS EARLIER MY UNCLE HAD TRIED TO BUY THE HOUSE BACK WITH A VERY GENEROUS OFFER.

THE PEOPLE WERE CONSIDERING IT!

THE PROPERTY IS WORTH A FORTUNE, I'M SURE THERE'S A GIANT, UGLY MODERN MONSTER BUILT THERE BY NOW!

I'VE BEEN BACK TO N.Y. MANY TIMES SINCE THEN BUT I HAVEN'T HAD THE NERVE TO GO AND SEE WHAT'S THERE.

THE HOUSE STAYS THE SAME FOREVER IN MY MEMORIES AND IN MY DREAMS.......... The End ....

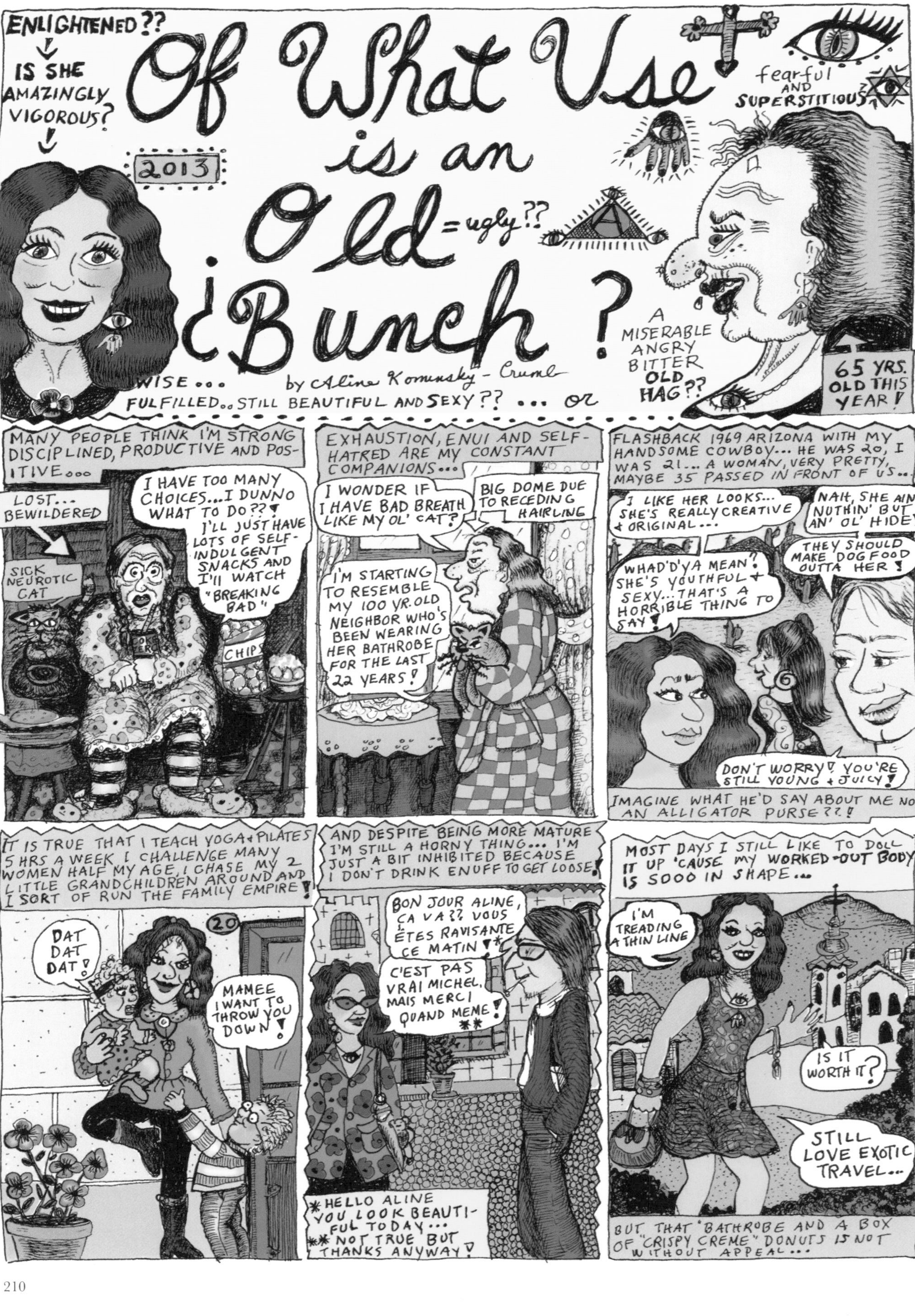

ENLIGHTENED?? IS SHE AMAZINGLY VIGOROUS?
Of What Use is an Old = ugly?? ¿Bunch?
2013
fearful AND SUPERSTITIOUS
WISE... FULFILLED.. STILL BEAUTIFUL AND SEXY?? ... or
by Aline Kominsky-Crumb
A MISERABLE ANGRY BITTER OLD HAG??
65 YRS. OLD THIS YEAR!
MANY PEOPLE THINK I'M STRONG DISCIPLINED, PRODUCTIVE AND POSITIVE...
LOST... BEWILDERED
SICK NEUROTIC CAT
I HAVE TOO MANY CHOICES...I DUNNO WHAT TO DO??! I'LL JUST HAVE LOTS OF SELF-INDULGENT SNACKS AND I'LL WATCH "BREAKING BAD"
CHIPS
EXHAUSTION, ENUI AND SELF-HATRED ARE MY CONSTANT COMPANIONS...
I WONDER IF I HAVE BAD BREATH LIKE MY OL' CAT?
BIG DOME DUE TO RECEDING HAIRLINE
I'M STARTING TO RESEMBLE MY 100 YR. OLD NEIGHBOR WHO'S BEEN WEARING HER BATHROBE FOR THE LAST 22 YEARS!
FLASHBACK 1969 ARIZONA WITH MY HANDSOME COWBOY... HE WAS 20, I WAS 21... A WOMAN, VERY PRETTY, MAYBE 35 PASSED IN FRONT OF US...
I LIKE HER LOOKS... SHE'S REALLY CREATIVE + ORIGINAL...
NAH, SHE AIN'T NUTHIN' BUT AN' OL' HIDE!
THEY SHOULD MAKE DOG FOOD OUTTA HER!
WHAD'D'YA MEAN? SHE'S YOUTHFUL + SEXY... THAT'S A HORRIBLE THING TO SAY!
DON'T WORRY! YOU'RE STILL YOUNG + JUICY!
IMAGINE WHAT HE'D SAY ABOUT ME NOW! AN ALLIGATOR PURSE??!
IT IS TRUE THAT I TEACH YOGA + PILATES 5 HRS A WEEK I CHALLENGE MANY WOMEN HALF MY AGE, I CHASE MY 2 LITTLE GRANDCHILDREN AROUND AND I SORT OF RUN THE FAMILY EMPIRE!
DAT DAT DAT!
20
MAMEE I WANT TO THROW YOU DOWN!
AND DESPITE BEING MORE MATURE I'M STILL A HORNY THING... I'M JUST A BIT INHIBITED BECAUSE I DON'T DRINK ENUFF TO GET LOOSE!
BON JOUR ALINE, CA VA?? VOUS ÊTES RAVISANTE CE MATIN!*
C'EST PAS VRAI MICHEL, MAIS MERCI QUAND MEME!**
*HELLO ALINE YOU LOOK BEAUTIFUL TODAY... **NOT TRUE BUT THANKS ANYWAY!
MOST DAYS I STILL LIKE TO DOLL IT UP 'CAUSE MY WORKED-OUT BODY IS SOOO IN SHAPE...
I'M TREADING A THIN LINE
IS IT WORTH IT?
STILL LOVE EXOTIC TRAVEL...
BUT THAT "BATHROBE AND A BOX OF "CRISPY CREME" DONUTS IS NOT WITHOUT APPEAL...

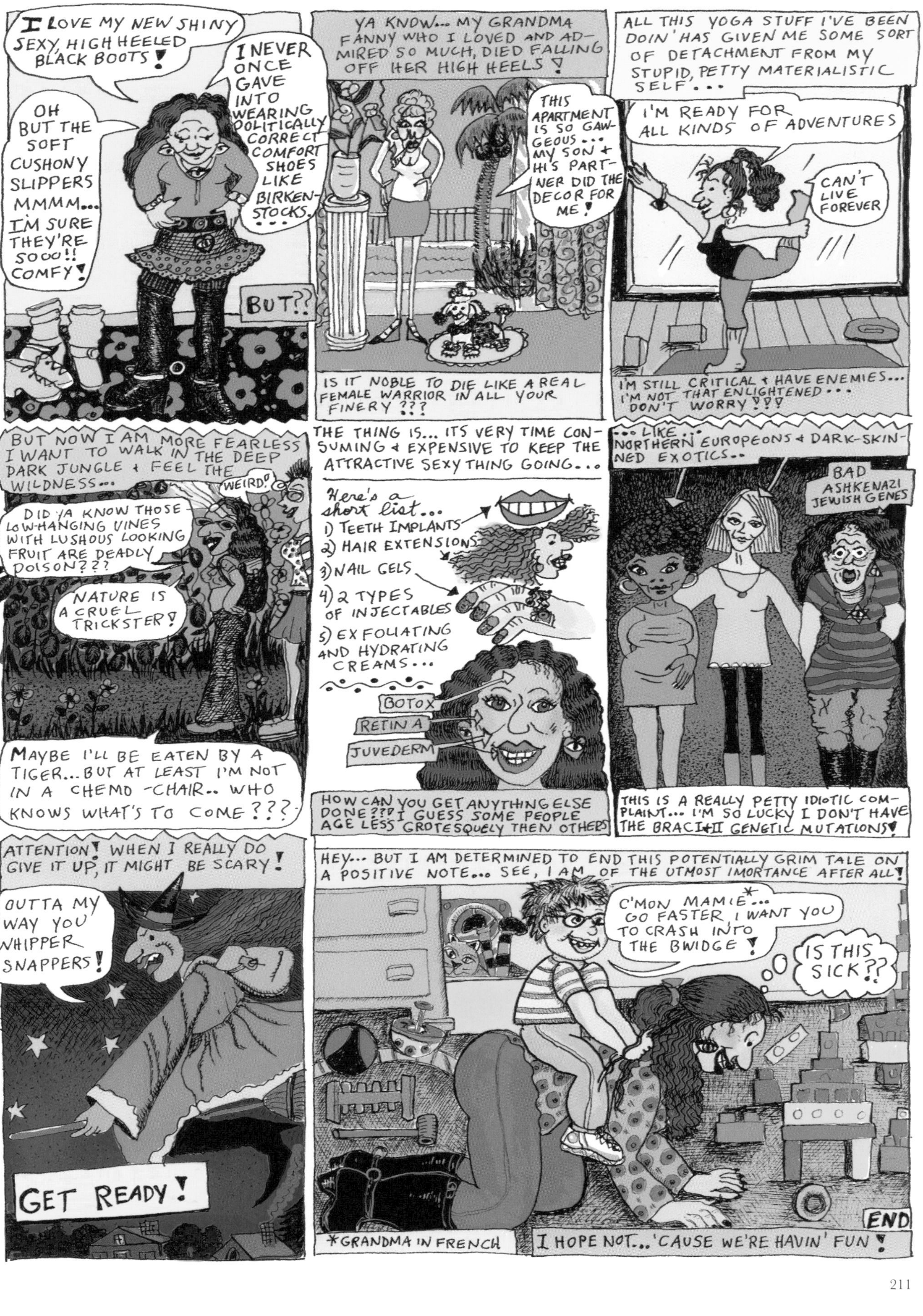
I LOVE MY NEW SHINY SEXY, HIGH HEELED BLACK BOOTS!
OH BUT THE SOFT CUSHONY SLIPPERS MMMM... I'M SURE THEY'RE SOOO!! COMFY!
I NEVER ONCE GAVE INTO WEARING POLITICALLY CORRECT COMFORT SHOES LIKE BIRKENSTOCKS...
BUT??
YA KNOW... MY GRANDMA FANNY WHO I LOVED AND ADMIRED SO MUCH, DIED FALLING OFF HER HIGH HEELS!
THIS APARTMENT IS SO GAWGEOUS... MY SON + HIS PARTNER DID THE DECOR FOR ME!
IS IT NOBLE TO DIE LIKE A REAL FEMALE WARRIOR IN ALL YOUR FINERY???
ALL THIS YOGA STUFF I'VE BEEN DOIN' HAS GIVEN ME SOME SORT OF DETACHMENT FROM MY STUPID, PETTY MATERIALISTIC SELF...
I'M READY FOR ALL KINDS OF ADVENTURES
CAN'T LIVE FOREVER
I'M STILL CRITICAL + HAVE ENEMIES... I'M NOT THAT ENLIGHTENED... DON'T WORRY???
BUT NOW I AM MORE FEARLESS I WANT TO WALK IN THE DEEP DARK JUNGLE + FEEL THE WILDNESS...
WEIRD!
DID YA KNOW THOSE LOW-HANGING VINES WITH LUSHOUS LOOKING FRUIT ARE DEADLY POISON???
NATURE IS A CRUEL TRICKSTER!
MAYBE I'LL BE EATEN BY A TIGER... BUT AT LEAST I'M NOT IN A CHEMO-CHAIR.. WHO KNOWS WHAT'S TO COME???
THE THING IS... ITS VERY TIME CONSUMING + EXPENSIVE TO KEEP THE ATTRACTIVE SEXY THING GOING...
Here's a short list...
1) TEETH IMPLANTS
2) HAIR EXTENSIONS
3) NAIL GELS
4) 2 TYPES OF INJECTABLES
5) EXFOLIATING AND HYDRATING CREAMS...
BOTOX
RETIN A
JUVEDERM
HOW CAN YOU GET ANYTHING ELSE DONE??? I GUESS SOME PEOPLE AGE LESS GROTESQUELY THEN OTHERS
...LIKE... NORTHERN EUROPEONS + DARK-SKINNED EXOTICS..
BAD ASHKENAZI JEWISH GENES
THIS IS A REALLY PETTY IDIOTIC COMPLAINT... I'M SO LUCKY I DON'T HAVE THE BRACI+II GENETIC MUTATIONS!
ATTENTION! WHEN I REALLY DO GIVE IT UP, IT MIGHT BE SCARY!
OUTTA MY WAY YOU WHIPPER SNAPPERS!
GET READY!
HEY... BUT I AM DETERMINED TO END THIS POTENTIALLY GRIM TALE ON A POSITIVE NOTE... SEE, I AM OF THE UTMOST IMORTANCE AFTER ALL!
C'MON MAMIE*... GO FASTER, I WANT YOU TO CRASH INTO THE BWIDGE!
IS THIS SICK??
END
*GRANDMA IN FRENCH
I HOPE NOT... 'CAUSE WE'RE HAVIN' FUN!

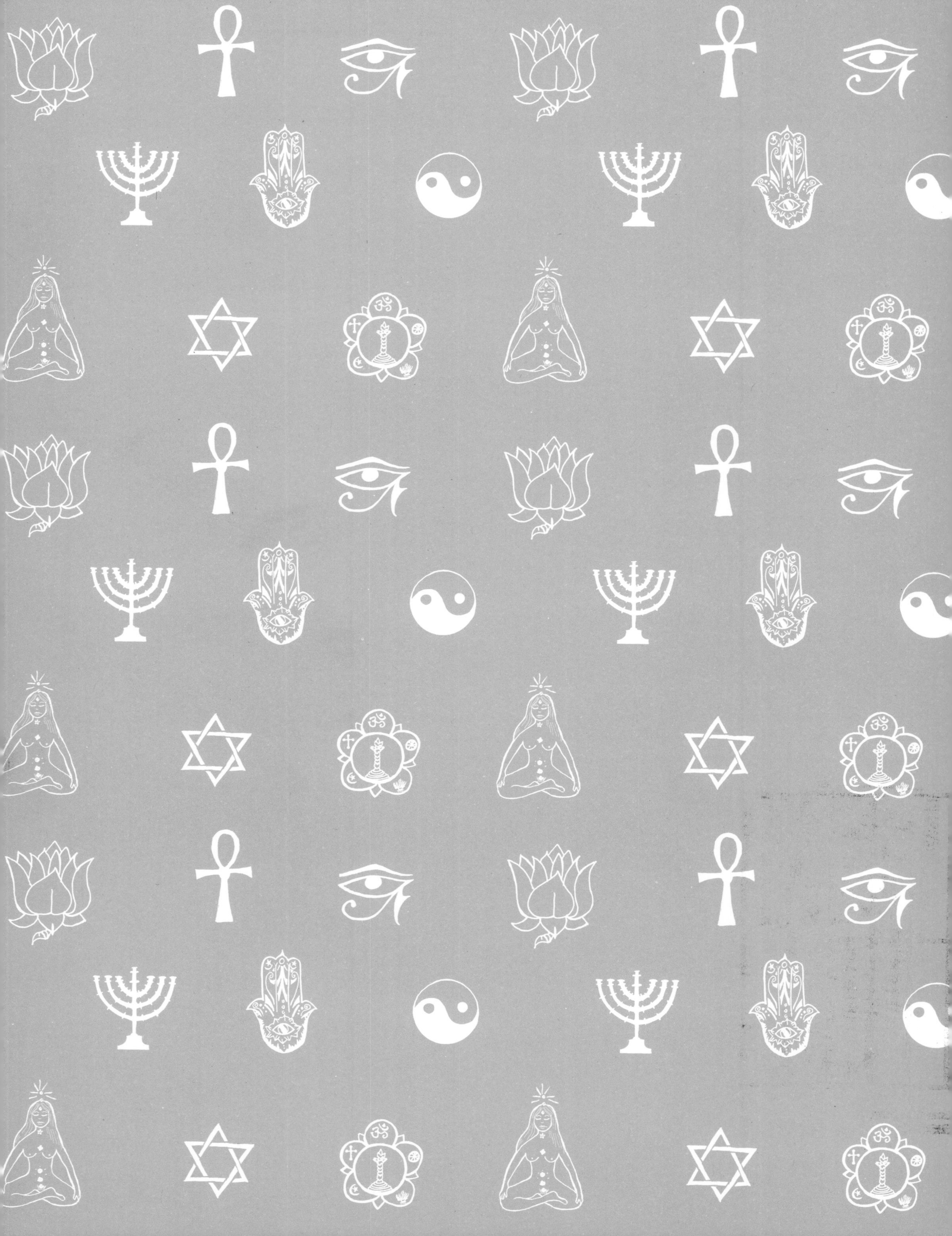